GONE
WITH THE
WORLD WARS

GONE
WITH THE
WORLD WARS
God's Love Heals All Wounds

Hildegard Bonacker Bruni

XULON PRESS

Xulon Press
2301 Lucien Way #415
Maitland, FL 32751
407.339.4217
www.xulonpress.com

Paperback ISBN-13: 978-1-6628-4709-7
Hard Cover ISBN-13: 978-1-6628-4710-3
eBook ISBN-13: 978-1-6628-4711-0

Table of Contents

Acknowledgments

I WOULD LIKE TO express much gratitude to my mother and father for raising my brothers, sisters, and me with Christian and high moral values. I am grateful to my brothers and sisters and their spouses for helping me recall how we lived at home before and during World War II. I am also thankful to all the people who sheltered us and gave us food during our escape from East Prussia and the soldiers who helped and protected us.

I thank my late husband, Dr. Aldo R. Bruni, MD, who loved me dearly and offered me an exciting lifestyle beyond my dreams. I treasure my family's love and encouragement and am grateful for the many friends I met.

I take pleasure in acknowledging the help and kindness of my friends Kathryn Teitzel and David Long. They took the time to read and edit my book's manuscript, and their love and friendship have blessed me in many ways.

I thank Joachim Vonhoff, a radio operator for the Merchant Marine. He resided in Berlin after World War II. He also contributed to my story. So did my girlfriend, Ilse Stritzke, who lived in East Prussia after the Russians claimed part of it. She told me how the Russian soldiers mistreated her family.

Mostly, I am grateful to God who spared my life many times and allowed me to tell my story. I give all the glory and honor to Him for having protected and guided me all my life.

Where my memory fell short, imagination took over to complete the facts with fiction.

Introduction

MY PARENTS GUSTAV and Emilie (Schlikat) Bonacker were born in East Prussia, as were their four daughters, Emma, Marta, Meta, Hildegard, and four sons Georg, Edmund, Richard, and Horst.

My father's ancestors lived in France before the Huguenot's persecution during the 16th and 17th centuries. King Luis XIV and the Catholic Church considered the Protestants a threat to their country. Some fled to Salzburg, Austria. Later, my father's ancestors resettled in East Prussia.

My mother's ancestors date back to the original Prussian tribe who lived in a commune by the Baltic Sea. My Prussian ancestors tilled the rich soil, hunted in the forests, and fished in the many lakes. Each tribe spoke a different language, but all practiced pagan mythology.

During the 13th century, the German Teutonic knights assisted Polish Duke Conrad of Mazovia in a crusade against these pagan Prussians. After a forty-year-long battle, the crusaders won the war. The Polish duke rewarded the crusaders who wanted to stay in Prussia with land called Rittergut (Estate of the Knight). Later the crusaders intermarried with the conquered Prussians and developed a Christian German State of liberty, justice, and deep love for their country and God.

My maternal grandparents Jan August and Ana Schlikat, and my parents grew up during World War I, and their eight children during World War II. They endured the tragedies of both world wars. In July 1944, my father was drafted into the Army.

The Russian front rapidly approached the East Prussian border and our hometown of Wizajny. On August 3, 1944, the mayor of our town sent messengers to all the residents, urging them to escape to avoid being massacred by the Russian Red Army. All persons were to meet at the village square the next morning at 9:00 a.m. Mother had no time or means to notify our sister Marta, who worked for a teacher's family in the nearby village Hellrau. Mother began an eight-month-long journey on a horse-drawn wagon with her seven children. Horst, the youngest son, was only one year and nine months old. I was seven years old when we began our journey westward without a known destination. We endured ten weeks of a bitterly cold winter, at times being bombarded. Often, we went hungry or got sick while on the road. We slept in barns, abandoned houses, or in the wagon in forests or on the roadside. We landed in Sophienhof, a huge ranch in Schleswig Holstein, on March 26, 1945. Even there, the British dropped bombs at night, and the Americans bombed us during the day. We lived in constant fear of being killed. One month before the war ended, a group of German soldiers with Polish prisoners stayed in Sophienhof. The German soldiers helped the civilians wherever they could.

After the German generals surrendered on May 7, 1945, World War II ended. Unfortunately, according to the Potsdam Treaty, the allies agreed and gave the northern region of East Prussia to Russia and the southern part to Poland. After 700 years, the beautiful fertile land along the Baltic Sea with a rich German heritage no longer belonged to Germany. Thus, East Prussia was gone with World War II forever.

My parents lived under four different governments. They were born during the Monarchy of Kaiser Wilhelm II, lasting until the end of WWI in 1918. They respected the Kaiser and lived peacefully and well. Kaiser Wilhelm II joined Austria who started WWI fighting Serbia. The allies declared Kaiser Wilhelm II guilty of war crimes and forced him to abdicate and flee to the Netherland. After WWI, the Weimar Republic existed from 1918 until 1933. The Versailles Treaty required Germany to pay heavy restitution to the allies, resulting in chaos, high unemployment, and hyperinflation. Adolf Hitler came to power and established the Third Reich, ruling from 1933 to 1945. For six years, Hitler was at war, and the German people suffered humiliations, the ravages of war, and territorial losses. Other countries lost many soldiers, civilians, and the destruction of many cities but no territories or land.

For four years, from May 8, 1945, to May 24, 1949, the four allies, the United States, England, France, and Russia, divided Germany into four sections and governed the zones they occupied according to the laws of their countries.

I, Hildegard Bonacker, was born, January 2, 1937, in the Third Reich. I lived throughout World War II, during the time Germany had no government of its own and also in the German Republic. The German Republic (Deutsche Bundesrepublik) began on May 24, 1949. Dr. Theodor Heuss became the first president of the German Republic, and Conrad Adenauer the first chancellor. Growing up in a post-war–destroyed Germany presented my family and me with many hardships and challenges. Getting an education and obtaining a profession was difficult because of a shortage of teachers and school facilities. But God, to whom I entrusted my life in 1949, has helped me overcome all the obstacles I faced while growing up and throughout my entire life.

After I graduated from medical school as a commercial and practical doctor's assistant, I worked in a medical clinic for one year in Germany. In December 1956, I immigrated to the United States. After staying with Dr. and Mrs. Jefferies's family for six months in Des Moines, Iowa, I joined my brother Edmund and my sister Emma's family in Chicago, Illinois. My knowledge of medical terms in English was insufficient to work in a doctor's office, so I started working as a laboratory technician at Bethesda Hospital in Chicago. While there, I met Dr. Aldo Bruni, who was on the hospital staff. We collided on a staircase while I carried a tray of patient's blood samples to the laboratory.

Once Dr. Bruni and I got married, I managed his two clinics. We began an exciting, adventurous, and at times a challenging life together. We not only enjoyed working together but going to opera performances, traveling, sailing, and exploring nature's beauty. We made friends with doctors, professionals, and opera singers who gave lavish parties and entertained us. At one of the musical get-togethers, I had the pleasure of meeting American General Healy. We talked about World War II. I mentioned a recording on a tape given to me by my brother-in-law, Gustav, who worked for the Science and Industry Museum in Chicago. On the tape, the German soldiers and people were described as barbarians and warmongers. I told him that we lived with German soldiers on a big farm for one month before the war ended. The soldiers helped in the fields, entertained the people, and were always kind and respectful toward us.

General Healy responded, "Well, Hildegard, it was like this; we had propaganda written against England, France, Russia, and Germany. We would have to make them look bad to justify our entry into the war, depending on whom we would fight. However, if the propaganda is repeated often enough, it is believed; the damage is done to the country and the people, and only a few find out the truth."

General Healy's comment prompted me to start searching for the truth about both world wars and the historical events during the turbulent years before and after the wars. The information about both wars is endless; so is the multiplicity of reasons and guilt of World War I and World War II. I merely scratch the surface in my book as a background for me and my family's story. It takes time and dedication to learn to separate the truth from lies and facts from fiction. The truth is still the truth, even if nobody believes it. A lie is still a lie, even if everyone believes it. Only God knows all the truth. He is the ultimate judge of the people and the world.

I thank God and my Savior Jesus Christ who protected my family so that we survived the dangers of war and life's hardships. I was privileged to go through a full spectrum of positive and negative physical, emotional, intellectual, and spiritual experiences. I tasted the agony and ecstasy of life during my dangerous and difficult, yet peaceful and exciting journey. In His mercy, God taught me to understand, love, comfort, and help others who go through trying circumstances. To my Creator, I give the glory for teaching me how to use all challenges, suffering, and obstacles along life's journey as steppingstones to get closer to Him. Now I am on my last journey here on earth to my heavenly home, not knowing when it will end. I believe it will end in heaven. God took me through all the storms of life triumphantly, and I trust Him to continue doing the same until I reach heaven, the final destination of my journey.

Chapter 1
Brief History of Prussia and Germany

BEFORE I START my family's journey, I like to go back in time and briefly describe the history of Prussia, the country where my grandparents and parents were born.[1] My mother's ancestors belonged to the old Prussian tribe, one of the ten ethnic tribes who lived at the turn of the century on the Baltic Sea, east of the Weichsel (Vistula) river. They formed communes to protect themselves from human and nature's enemies. Each tribe spoke a different language and practiced pagan mythology. They tilled the rich soil, hunted in the many forests, fished in the numerous lakes, and lived off the land.

Map of East Prussia

During the 13th century, the German Teutonic knights, a German military order under Herman Salza, agreed to assist Polish Duke Conrad of Mazovia in the war against the pagan Prussians. Even though the crusaders had to overcome the resistance through many bloody battles with the tenacious and hardy Prussians, they conquered them. The duke promised that the crusaders could remain in Prussia to keep the peace, govern, and oversee the development of the newly conquered domain. Duke Conrad granted the crusaders, who stayed behind, titles of nobility, and large parcels of land — the estate was called Rittergut (Knighthood Estate).

Under Bohemian King Ottokar II's rule, the Prussians inter-married with the crusaders and the settlers. They developed a German Christian state of liberty, justice, patriotism, and a deep love of God. The king built the well-known Prussian city,

Konigsberg (Hill of the King), named after him, and 1,400 villages and ninety-three towns.

Settlers came from different parts of Germany and other European countries, built cities, cultivated the land, and converted the heathens to Christianity. In due time, the settlers, together with the native Prussians, transformed the country and practiced good modern government, religious freedom, and tolerance. Thus, Prussia became a refuge for persecuted religious as well as political persons.[2]

During the Reformation, 200,000 to 300,000 French Protestants (known as Huguenots), who were considered a threat to the throne of King Louis XIV and the Catholic Church, were persecuted and evicted from France. A lot of the Protestants fled to Austria.

When the Austrian Archbishop, Leopold of Firmian, issued a decree on October 31, 1731, all the Protestants and Lutherans who did not reconvert to Catholicism would be exiled. Many took their Bibles, and religious books, left Austria, and settled in Prussia. Among the settlers in Prussia were some French bankers, doctors, lawyers, artisans, fabric workers, and farmers who enriched their host country.

Prussia began to emerge in the fine arts and science. In 1544, King Leopold II founded the first university in Koenigsberg, where science, philosophy, and higher learning were taught. The world-renowned German philosopher Emanuel Kant (1714–1804) was born in Koenigsberg (where he first studied philosophy) and later taught at the university. "Critique of Practical Reason" (Kritik der Praktischen Vernunft) and "Toward Eternal Peace" (Zum Ewigen Frieden) are two of the many well-known books he wrote and published. He fostered German idealism, and even today, his works inspire and influence European and World philosophy.

Prussia flourished under the forty-six-year reign of Frederick II who was born January 24, 1712, in the Hohenzollern's royal family. Later, Frederick II was called Frederick the Great. He considered himself an absolute ruler, a servant of the State and God. He traveled to all parts of the kingdom to see the people's needs and ensure workers and the poor were treated justly. He raised the working standard, but he also expected every man to do his duty, use common sense, and obey the country's laws. He stripped all pomp from his court, worked daily himself, and practiced sound financial management. He considered himself a defender of the poor. The people held him in high esteem.

In Potsdam, near Berlin, he led a disciplined life at his castle, "San Souci," and took daily walks in the castle's magnificent gardens. He loved art, science, religion, and philosophy and granted his court and subjects the freedom to choose their faith, contrary to other rulers who forced their religion onto their subjects.

The Austrian ruler Maria Theresa threatened to attack the Prussian kingdom. Frederick the Great defended his country and engaged in a seven-year war (1756-1763). With his elite soldiers (the Prussian Junkers) and Tzar Peter II of Russia's aid, he won the final battle and the war itself. After the war ended and his kingdom was secure, he built churches, schools, theaters, and villages, and developed industries.

Historians claim that the king's greatness was not winning battles, for he also suffered defeats. Frederic the Great had the ability and determination to find resources to turn challenges to his advantage. His Christian faith and tolerance toward the religion of his people contributed to his greatness. He ruled his monarchy according to Christian principles. He felt responsible toward God for all the decisions he made and the actions he took.

A year before his death on September 10, 1785, he made a treaty with the United States of America and founded the government's constitution on Christian principles. The two young nations, Prussia and the United States of America, signed a friendship and trade contract which lasted 132 years until America entered World War I in 1917.

Almost one hundred years later, Wilhelm I, seventh king of Prussia (1871-1888), aided by his able statesman and chancellor, Otto von Bismarck, unified the various kingdoms of Germany. He also became the emperor (Kaiser) of unified Germany. During his reign, Germany prospered and became the strongest, best-managed country in Europe and the envy of Britain and France. Germany and the prosperous European countries acquired several colonies in Africa and other parts of the world.

My mother and father grew up during the reign of Wilhelm II, the ninth king of Prussia, who became the third kaiser of Germany on June 15, 1988. He took over his father's throne, Kaiser Friedrich III, who died from larynx cancer after being the emperor of Germany for only ninety-nine days.

KAISER WILHELM II, LAST EMPEROR OF GERMANY

Kaiser Wilhelm II was born on January 27, 1859, in Berlin. His mother, Victoria, was the daughter of Queen Victoria of England.

She had a difficult time giving birth to her first son, and she called him Wilhelm. Her joy waned when she discovered later that his left arm was defective. Doctors used cruel treatments and methods to stimulate the normal development of the arm, with negative results. He later tried to overcome his handicap, but his demanding mother's resentment left a strained relationship between him and his mother. However, he was very fond of his grandmother, Queen Victoria of England.

The strict Calvinistic educator of Kaiser Wilhelm II instilled in him to believe in God and love for peace, justice, beauty, and art. He also studied political science and law in Bonn, Germany. He received his military training under the watchful eye of Commander in Chief and Chancellor Otto von Bismarck.

In 1881, while still king of Prussia, he married Princess Augusta Victoria of Schleswig-Holstein. Together they had six sons and one daughter.

Kaiser Wilhelm II enjoyed hunting in the Rominter Heide, a beautiful territory of heather and forests, well stocked with deer and wildlife. Even though he himself could not hunt due to his handicap, he enjoyed hunting rituals and celebrations. He frequently stayed in Rominten in his favorite hunting castle, built of lumber in the Norwegian architectural style. Next to the royal lodge, he had a church constructed. Rominten was only ten miles from Wizajny, our birthplace and home. The forests of Rominten extended close to our town. The villagers and relatives enjoyed picking mushrooms, hazelnuts, and berries in the Rominter Heide and our ranch's surrounding woods. The German people revered their king and kaiser, whom they believed to be just and caring for the people's good. They lived well under his reign.

Kaiser Wilhelm I and Kaiser Wilhelm II had a competent chancellor and commander in chief, Otto von Bismarck. He was born Prussian Prince Otto Eduard Leopold von Bismarck in

Schoenhausen. Kaiser Wilhelm I and Otto von Bismarck united the German states and kingdoms to form the German Empire, and he managed responsibly and justly the national and international affairs. He possessed extraordinary, cunning political and diplomatic skills, meriting the reputation of being the "Iron Chancellor".

During his monarchy, Germany changed at a faster pace from an agricultural society to an industrial nation. The number of workers increased rapidly; they formed a political party in 1875 and called themselves social democrats (In German: Sozialistischte Arbeiterpartei Deutschland's, (SPD abbreviated). As their numbers increased, so did their power and demands. Chancellor von Bismarck initiated social programs like health insurance, workman's compensation, and pension plans for the elderly and invalids to pacify the laborers.

During this time, Germany prospered and established colonies in Southwest Africa (now called Namibia), Cameroon, New Guinea, Bismarck-Archipelagos, and the Marshall Islands. England, France, and Italy also colonized parts of Africa and Asia. Kaiser Wilhelm II expanded his navy fleet considerably under highly competent Admiral Alfred Tirpitz's direction to protect the colonies from aggressors. Great Britain sought supremacy at sea and looked with disdain at the advances in the German fleet.

Chapter 2
World War I

CERTAIN EVENTS LED to the beginning of World War I.[3] Kaiser Wilhelm II was jealous of the fame of Otto von Bismarck, and conflicts between them developed. The Kaiser forced Otto von Bismarck to retire in 1890. The Kaiser himself became commander in chief of the military, and he implemented his plans. He appointed Leo von Caprivi to be his new chancellor. The Kaiser spent much time with the military and navy officials. When he needed to make significant military or political decisions, he first requested advice from his generals and admirals and later presented the facts to his chancellor. The Kaiser had contempt for civilian opinion. During his thirty-year reign, he sought power and left a mark of his influence on Germany and the world. Germany became the dominant industrial power in Europe, the sole rival of England. However, Kaiser Wilhelm II neglected to renew the treaty with Russia that Bismarck had made under Kaiser Wilhelm I. France filled the vacuum quickly by signing a treaty with Russia. Now the three allies, Russia, France, and England, called the Entente, encircled Germany.

Then, an unfortunate event happened in Austria-Hungary. Archduke Franz Ferdinand, the future heir to Austria-Hungary's throne, was killed June 28, 1914, by a student, Gavrilo Princip, who belonged to the Black Hand, A Serbian secret society. Duke Berchtold of Austria-Hungary issued an ultimatum to Serbia that the assassin be brought to justice and Serbia's sovereignty be nullified. Serbia accepted all the terms of the request, except it refused to give up its independence. Austria-Hungary ceased its diplomatic relationships with Serbia. Austria-Hungary first ordered a partial mobilization to crush Serbia's nationalistic movement and cement their political influence in Bulgaria and Rom.

If war broke out, Kaiser Wilhelm II promised aid and gave Austria-Hungary a blank check (Blankovollmacht), which the other European Nations misinterpreted and accused Germany of wanting action. The Kaiser considered the conflict between Austria-Hungary and Serbia a personal one and was hoping to avoid entering the war. However, having Germany's blank check encouraged Austria-Hungary to declare war on Serbia on July 28, 1914. Russia, bound by a treaty to Serbia, announced mobilization to defend Serbia. Czar Nikolaus II realized his aid to Serbia meant an indirect war against Austria-Hungary and Germany. He tried to recall the mobilization, but his generals disagreed with him. Russian Commander Sergei Dobrorolski later conveyed to the czar that the generals decided to go to war on July 25, 1914. Three days before, even Austria-Hungary declared war on Serbia. The Russian generals knew that their mobilization would provoke Germany to enter the war, which Russia wanted to accomplish. Germany tried to halt the conflict by sending them an ultimatum to stop the preparation for war immediately, but Russia did not comply. Germany viewed this an act of war, and Kaiser Wilhelm II declared war on Russia on August 1, 1914.

Now, France, bound by a treaty with Russia, declared war against Germany and began mobilization. At war on the eastern and western fronts, Germany hoped to secure victory over France through the Schlieffen Plan: marching through Belgium, beating France's army quickly, and then concentrating on fighting Russia.

When the German army marched through neutral Belgium, the Belgium people fought back. Being an ally of France, England was provoked and declared war against Germany on August 4, 1914.

After England declared war against Germany, Kaiser Wilhelm II appealed to the German people in a speech on August 6, 1914:

> *"Since the establishment of the German monarchy, it has been the desire of my ancestors and mine as well to keep peace and peacefully reach our goals. However, our opponents are jealous of our success. So far, we have tolerated East and West's open and secret animosity and from across the sea. Now they want to humiliate us. They expect us to tolerate the invasion of our Austrian-Hungarian ally, who is struggling for recognition as a superpower. By permitting this humiliation, our strength and honor are also lost. So, let the world decide! During peacetime, the enemy attacks us. Therefore, take up your weapons and fight. Every hesitation and uncertainty would be treason to our fatherland. It is a matter of our Reich's existence or non-existence, our forefathers established, and a matter of being and non-being of the German power and the German culture. We shall defend ourselves to the last breath with infantry and cavalry. We will overcome this battle against a world of enemies. Never was Germany besieged when it stood united. Forward with God, who will be with us, as he was with our forefathers.[4]*

The German army began to march through Belgium, breaking their neutrality agreement, and the Belgian civilians attacked the German soldiers. Both countries suffered heavy losses of soldiers and civilians. Many buildings were also destroyed.

When Great Britain's commander, Sir John French, learned about Germany disregarding Belgium's neutrality, he dispatched to Mons, Belgium, 100,000 soldiers from his infantry corps. General Horace Smith-Dorrien tried to stop the German army from advancing. The British Fusiliers blew up the bridge over the Mons-Conde Canal.

On August 23, 1914, Alexander von Kluck attacked the British front. Even though the German soldiers suffered heavy losses from the British rifle fire, the commander-in-chief, Sir John French and his army retreated to France's Marne River. When the German army, now under General Falkenhayn's command, advanced to Antwerp and Brugge, the allied forces offered strong resistance at Yepern. By September 4, 1914, even though the German army broke through the front and crossed the Marne River, it retreated due to heavy casualties and abandoned the Schlieffen plan to advance to Paris through Belgium. A stationary war, or trench war, broke out.

The French introduced the use of chemical weapons: tear gas and xylol bromide. However, both proved to be ineffective because they dissipated in the air before reaching their target. April 22, 1915, the Germans used chloropicrin gas successfully in the battle at Yepern, which killed 5,000 enemies. The newly invented gas masks prevented many fatalities. Later, a chemist developed the deadly mustard gas, also called the yellow gas. April 22, 1915, is considered the beginning of chemical warfare.

On the Eastern Front, the Russians outnumbered the German army. At first, the German army suffered setbacks and heavy casualties when the Russians invaded East Prussia. The German army lost twenty thousand soldiers. Then, General Erich Ludendorff and Paul von Hindenburg replaced the previous general, Maximillian von Prittwitz. They met the Russian general Alexander Samsonov and his artillery at Tannenberg, East Prussia, with reinforced troops. After six days of intense fighting, Russia suffered heavy casualties. General Alexander Samsonov tried without success to retreat, but most of his soldiers were slaughtered or captured. Of

150,000 Russian soldiers, 92,000 were arrested, 10,000 escaped, and the rest were killed. Such a defeat was too much to take for the Russian general, and he committed suicide.

At the beginning of World War I, all superpowers' weakly constructed planes were mainly used for surveillance on the Western front. The pilots reported the accurate location and advances of the front and how attacks could be planned more precisely. Later, by installing machine guns in the planes, air battles took place. The German pilots could outmaneuver the French, British, and Belgian planes. In fact, in the air battle called "Bloody April," the Allied Air Corp lost 912 pilots.

Manfred Albrecht Freiherr von Richthofen, known as the Red Baron, became the Ace of Aces and the German pilots' idol. He alone shot down eighty airplanes. However, Captain Douglas Connell and Albert Woodbridge inflicted a bullet wound into his head after which he suffered from severe headaches and could not fly for a while. When he took to the air again on April 21, 1918, he went too far into the British territory, flew too low, was shot down, and crashed to the ground. His body was later recovered and flown to Wiesbaden, Germany, where he was buried with full military honors.

Toward the end of World War I, manufacturers equipped airplanes to carry and drop bombs. The bombers aimed to destroy military sites and industrial establishments. Unfortunately, hoping to lower the enemy's morale, the bombers also killed many civilians along the way.

Even though President Woodrow Wilson promised absolute neutrality of the United States, he was drawn into the war by Winston Churchill, who was the Lord of the Admiralty at that time. The United States entered the war and brought many planes and well-trained pilots to Europe. Unable to get quick aircraft replacements, the outnumbered German squadron realized that the victory would be decided at sea or on the ground and not in the air.

The British and American fleets introduced a prototype of an aircraft carrier. Hydroplanes took off from a ship's platform but had to land on the water and be hauled up to the aircraft carrier's deck by a crane.

The German U-boat war, initiated in 1915, came to a halt after the British passenger ship Lusitania was sunk on May 7, 1915, by the German U-boat 20 at the southern shore of Ireland. One thousand, one hundred, ninety-two passengers died. Among them were 128 Americans.

When Mr. Colin Simpson, a correspondent of the *Sunday Times* of London, who also studied history at Oxford University, read conflicting reports about this tragedy, he began a six-year-long search for the truth about the Lusitania incident, which he describes in his book The Lusitania.[5] Mr. Simpson discovered the inventory list of the last cargo loaded in New York on April 30, 1915, of the Cunard line, varied from the original copy which United States President Woodrow Wilson had in his possession.

The British government informed the president of the Cunard Lines, Mr. Alfred Booth, to build a faster passenger ship than the German ship named Kaiser Wilhelm II which cruised at 23.5 knots per hour—the fastest at that time. Mr. Booth promised to build two ships, Lusitania, and Mauretania, which would reach 25 knots per hour. At that time, Mr. Winston Churchill, the Marine minister paid a visit to Mr. Booth and gave him specific instructions and specifications to install the necessary equipment to be transformed quickly into a battleship. The government would pay him a certain sum and a yearly operating cost of 75,000.00 pounds as compensation.

On May 12, 1913, the Lusitania was put in a dry dock under the pretense to install the newest turbine engines but keeping secret the actual changes made. Winston Churchill urged the wharf master to install the equipment rapidly because a war with Germany was inevitable. The Lusitania resumed her cruise passages to New York on July 21, 1913. The admiral ordered to equip fourteen more merchant ships with weapons.

When England declared war on Germany on August 4, 1914, England was well prepared. The Lusitania had the weapons installed and was registered on September 17, 1914, as one of the armed battleships of the home fleet of the British Admiralty.

Winston Churchill planned to pass through the German patrol by flying flags of neutral countries, especially the United States. Ships of neutral countries could not be attacked. Winston Churchill also ordered to treat the German captains, if captured, like criminals and not provide them with prisoner status. For Winston Churchill, it was more convenient to shoot them than to take them captive. The English Admiralty denied these practices. However, when the German U-boat U-21 searched the Ben Cruachan ship, they discovered the English Admiralty's orders to fly an American flag and ram any U-boat, which was against the law. The German captain saved the British crew and then sank the Ben Cruachan.

Such practices horrified the German government and the submarine officers. They demanded removing the blockade, upholding the sea rules, and permitting the German Marine to attack any merchant ship without warning. Germany also declared the waters surrounding England and Ireland, including the English Channel, a war zone. The English only declared the North Sea a war zone.

The German government sent a dispatch of this unfair practice and a copy of the British Admiralty orders, documenting their statement to the American Secretary of State William Bryan. In his absence, Mr. Robert Lansing accepted the dispatch. He drafted his response and willfully omitted to mention that he had a copy of the British Admiralty order and issued a warning to the American passengers not to book cruises on the English cruise ships.

When Mr. William Bryan returned and learned about such omissions, he was upset. Nevertheless, the draft and opinion of Mr. Robert Lansing prevailed.

To save the American neutrality's face, the United States warned England, prohibiting the English ships from flying American flags. Germany received notice that if they attacked another neutral ship, Germany would be brought to justice. The consequences of such action would make the United States enter the war.

The British foreign minister answered with a slick diplomatic lie. He asserted that neither the British government nor the Admiralty had given any such orders. The warning startled the Germans but delighted the English, especially Winston Churchill. His tactics to lure the Germans into conflict with neutral countries paid off. He believed to be one step closer to drawing the United States into the war.

In the Falaha incident, the English Admiralty again failed to report 13 tons of gunpowder cargo. It left out the report that the German captain warned to clear all passengers from the ship before sinking it. Instead, the media portrayed the German captain and his officers as cold-blooded murderers.

Many Germans living in the United States despised such false reports. A group of prominent German Americans met in New York. George Viereck, a publisher of the pro-German newspaper, The Fatherland, led the meeting. He said, should any cruise ship with American passengers be sunk, the devil will be released. A person present said the Lusitania is anchored in New York Harbor and was supposed to sail for Liverpool, England, on May 1, 1915. Mr. Viereck received unanimous approval to run an article in fifty different newspapers warning the American passengers, who were booked on the Lusitania, to cancel their reservations and book their cruises with an American cruise ship. The Lusitania was carrying ammunition to England and might be attacked or sunk by German U-boats.

The warnings, sealed in fifty envelopes with enclosed checks, left the office on April 23, 1915, and took a week to reach the passengers. Due to red tape and bureaucracy, only one newspaper. The Register of Des Moines, Iowa, printed the warning. After a long wait, Mr. Viereck even went to the foreign minister and spoke to him personally. Mr. Viereck pointed out to Mr. Bryan that the Lusitania was carrying ammunition to England and had done so on all but one trip.

In New York, the customs officer collaborated with Mr. Ryan by accepting only a partial shipping list of the common goods. He received the list of the Lusitania's actual war material four or five days after it had left New York. Mr. Ryan promised to inform President Wilson to warn the American people to cancel their cruise reservations on the Lusitania because it transported war materials. President Wilson did nothing. However, he must have known about the actual cargo and the danger the passengers might encounter. When President Wilson heard that the Lusitania was attacked by a German U-boat and sank, he admitted knowing the ship's ill fate. It caused him to spend many sleepless nights.

Meanwhile, Winston Churchill and Admiral Fisher met. They looked at the chart where every German battleship and U-boat location was marked and paid particular attention to U-20, which directed its course toward Fastnet Rock, Ireland. Cruise ships received superior protection from battleships before entering a harbor. The battleship Juno was on the way to meet the Lusitania. Winston Churchill used the excuse that Juno could not withstand an attack from a U-boat; he ordered Juno to return to Queenstown. Winston Churchill mentioned this to Admiral Fisher and requested a destroyer from Milford to protect the Lusitania. Still, he did not inform her captain, William Turner, of this fact and that a German U-boat was in the surrounding waters. Captain Turner also received an admiralty order to change course and enter Queenstown's harbor, rather than Liverpool, the Lusitania's original destination. The new course directed the Lusitania toward U-boat 20. This decision led to the catastrophic sinking of the Lusitania on May 7, 1915. To this day, it remains unknown who gave the orders to the English ships. However, Winston Churchill and Admiral Fisher supposedly set up this unfortunate plot. After Captain Hunter finally received the U-boat warning, he could not change course without an admiralty order. Captain Hunter only reduced the speed to 15 knots. When the Lusitania was within 700 m from U-20, Captain Schwieger of U-Boat 20 fired only one torpedo to the starboard's vessel. In his logbook, he wrote that a second explosion ripped the bridge to pieces and caused the ship to sink with the bow first. Captain Hunter gave orders to abandon the ship immediately. Due to the ship's awkward position, only six of the forty-eight lifeboats could safely be put in the water.

Many passengers jumped off the boat and swam among the debris, hoping to be saved by another ship. However, 1,198 passengers sank with the vessel. Among them were 128 Americans and the millionaire Alfred Vanderbilt. When Admiral Fisher heard that the boat Juno almost reached the survivors, he ordered the Juno's captain to change course and return to the harbor. The survivors endured two hours of fear and panic before other boats came and fished them out of the water and removed them from the lifeboats.

When President Wilson received news of this sea catastrophe, he procured the list of the Lusitania's complete shipment from the customs office. It revealed that almost the entire cargo was contraband war material and explosives. President Wilson and Mr. Lansing, afraid of being discovered for withholding the truth from the United States people, tainted the truth and issued a warning to

Germany, stating the German government and Kaiser Wilhelm II were misinformed. Mr. Bryan, who knew the truth, refused to sign the warning. Winston Churchill, Admiral Fisher, and the English people were disappointed that President Wilson did not declare war immediately against Germany. However, Germany stopped using the U-boats in sea battles. Winston Churchill and Admiral Fisher put all the guilt on Lusitania's Captain Hunter to shield their involvement in this plot from being discovered.

Three years after this incident, the New York Customs Office head delivered President Wilson the Lusitania's original shipping list. He sealed it in a big envelope and wrote on it, only to be opened by the United States president, and then handed it over to the Treasury Department's archives. It remained untouched until 1940, when Britain and the United States found themselves in a similar position in May 1945. At that time, President Franklin D. Roosevelt, who was also Marine's undersecretary, knew about this document, opened it, and made it part of his private Marine Memoir collection.

In this incident, he showed us how the people's fate is in the government's hands, who will plot intrigues and sacrifice human lives if it serves their purpose.

Winston Churchill felt that he was one step closer to getting the United States involved in World War I. Another incident that the British Marine Secret Service used was decoding the Zimmermann Dispatch and sending it to President Wilson, who published it in American newspapers. In this telegram of January 16, 1917, Kaiser Wilhelm II asked Mexican President Venustiano Carranza to join Germany as their ally to start a war against the United States. In turn, the German government offered to win back for Mexico the states of Arizona, Texas, and New Mexico. The Mexican generals assessed the feasibility of such an alliance and refused this offer.

The American people were devastated by such news, and Congress gave President Wilson the approval to enter the war against Germany. On April 6, 1917, President Woodrow Wilson officially declared war against Germany.

My grandparents and the German people, but mostly the military personnel, were alarmed by this news and feared the worst scenario could happen. Germany would have no chance to win the war if American troops would invade Germany.

In desperation, the Kaiser initiated the U-boat war again as a last resource to bring a favorable change for Germany. However, it caused other European countries to become involved. At first, Italy avoided the war but later joined the conflict, broke her allegiance to Austria-Hungary and Germany, and joined their opposing Triple Entente.

Greece, who had stayed neutral up to now, felt the British and French government's pressure when they had put a blockade around the Greek shores. To have the embargo removed, they joined the allies on June 27, 1917. Earlier, French Commander Jonnart gave King Constantin of Greece an ultimatum to abdicate, which he did. President Venizelos's new Greek government cooperated with the Triple Entente and declared war against Austria-Hungary and Germany.

Meanwhile, Lenin, who had been in Finland, returned to Russia. He and the Bolsheviks took over the provisional government formed during the October revolution. On November 8, 1917, Lenin issued a decree to end the war, which Kaiser Wilhelm II and Austrian King and Commander-in-Chief Charles I welcomed. An armistice took place on December 15, 1917, but the peace proposal brought no success at first. Finally, after torturous negotiations, Germany reached a peace agreement on February 9, 1918, first with Romania and later, on March 3, 1918, with Russia, which Lenin signed in Brest-Litovsk. Russia sacrificed twenty-five percent of its European territory to end fighting in the war.

Now, the German armies, relieved from the Eastern front, could reinforce the western battles. On March 21, 1918, the German generals planned a successful spring offensive, and the German army broke through the French front and advanced to the Marne River in France.

Soon, American troops joined the French forces and stopped the German advance. American General Hunter Liggett ordered 300 tanks, and General William Mitchell flew in 500 aircrafts for a counterattack in the Amiens battle on August 8, 1918. The German soldiers suffered heavy losses from the allied forces. The battle was called "The Black Day" by the German army, which had to retreat.

In desperation, the Kaiser drafted seventeen-year-old boys. My father escaped the draft, but his older brothers Matthew and Georg were drafted into the Army earlier. Thank God, they sustained only minor injuries and returned safely at the end of the war.

Early in September, the Allied forces also penetrated Bulgaria and conquered Macedonia. The German commanders in chief von Hindenburg and Ludendorff realized that a victory against the allies, reinforced continuously by fresh American troops and war equipment, became hopeless. On September 29, 1918, the German generals suggested that Kaiser Wilhelm II and the German empire work out an Armistice (Waffenstillstand) agreement. President Woodrow Wilson requested that the German army retreat from all occupied territories immediately. He promised to send a representative to negotiate the terms of the agreement.

On November 7, 1918, the negotiations began in a train wagon in Compiegne's Forest, where France, the United States, and Germany agreed. They made eighteen demands from Kaiser Wilhelm II and the German Empire.

1. "Effective six hours after signing. 2. Immediate clearing of Belgium, France, Alsace- Lorraine to be concluded in fourteen days. Any troops remaining in these areas were to be interned or taken prisoners of war. 3. Surrender 5000 Cannons and 30 000 machine guns, 3000 trench mortars, 2000 planes, 4. Evacuation of the left bank of the Rhine River. Mayence, Coblence, Cologne to occupied by the enemy to a radius of 30 km. 10. Renunciation of the Treaties of Brest-Litovsk and Bucharest, to name only a few demands by the allies." (Armistice Demands published in the Kreuz-Zeitung November 11, 1918).

All representatives signed the document on November 11, 1918, at 5:00 a.m.[6] The truce began at 11:00 a.m. on the same day. *The New York Times* headlines read:

With the American Army in France, November 11— They stopped fighting at 11:00 o'clock this morning. In the twinkling of an eye, four years of killing and massacre stopped as if God had swept His omnipotent finger across the scene of the world's carnage and cried, enough.

Each year in the United States, Veterans Day is celebrated on November 11, commemorating the soldiers who lost their lives in World War I and all wars. A soldier is not dead until he is forgotten. Every country's soldier gave something of himself in the wars, but some sacrificed their most precious possession—life itself. Soldiers from all countries deserve respect, honor, and gratitude from their patriots.

Grandpa Heinrich and Grandma Marta welcomed the good news that the war had ended and that their two older sons, Matthew and Georg, returned from the battlefield with only minor wounds. However, they and most German people felt sad that Kaiser Wilhelm II was forced to abdicate. He fled from his head-quarters in Spa to the Netherlands on November 10, 1918. Later he bought a home in Doorn in the Province of Utrecht, where he set up a modest household with his wife Augustine Victoria and his family. And thus, after 300 years, the reign of the Hohenzollern royal family ended after World War I.

The Entente demanded the kaiser's release to try him as a war criminal, but Queen Wilhelmina of the Netherlands did not yield to the Entente's demands and threats. The kaiser remained in Doorn. After his first wife, Augusta Victoria, died, he remarried Princess von Schoenach, Hermine von Reuss. He wrote and published his war memoirs, absolving himself from the guilt of World War I. He kept abreast of Germany's political activities and still hoped to be recalled as Kaiser again, but his hopes remained only hopes. He died on June 4, 1941, during World War II. Doorn honored the Kaiser with an elaborate state funeral. Later, the German govern-ment brought the remains of Kaiser Wilhelm II back to Berlin.

After the monarchy ended, my grandparents worried about how the new government, called the Weimar Republic, would affect them and Germany's people. They had watched how the alli-ance with Austria-Hungary and the alliance among other nations, hoping to ward off war, triggered a domino effect and engulfed one country after the other into World War I. Thirty-two nations participated in that war, called the first global war, claiming 10 million lives, wounding 20 million soldiers, and 8 million became prisoners of war.

The German Empire, the Prussian kingdom, and many European monarchies were gone after World War I ended. Gone was the epoch of the elegant court life of the royal families. With a different political regime, a new society of the masses arose. The African and Asian colonies sought their independence, and the United States became a superpower.

Chapter 3
Versailles Treaty

JANUARY 18, 1919, began the infamous peace conference of the League of Nations drafting the Versaille Treaty.[7] One representative from each of the following countries took part in this assembly: the United States of America, Belgium, Bolivia, Brazil, Great Britain, Canada, Australia, South Africa, New Zealand, India, China, Cuba, Ecuador, France, Greece, Guatemala, Haiti, Hedjaz, Honduras, Italy, Japan, Liberia, Nicaragua, Panama, Peru, Poland, Rumania, Serb Croat-Slovene State, Siam, Czechoslovakia, and Uruguay. Russia chose not to send a representative. Germany, whose fate and future depended on this conference's outcome, was prohibited from participating in the negotiations for fear the German representative might play nation against nation for Germany's advantage. The Germans could only respond in writing, which mostly brought no results.

The French primier, George Clemenceau, presided over the assembly; his revenge made unreasonable demands from Germany. He was called the tiger, ready to tear apart his prey. President Woodrow Wilson of the United States, Britain's Prime Minister Lloyd George, and the Italian Minister of Foreign Affairs, Victor Emanuele Orlando, were also present. President Woodrow Wilson suggested keeping the Treaty simple and combining the demands in fourteen points, but he gave way to other representatives during the negotiations. In six months, they drafted four-hundred and forty articles with many annexes.

*In Annex II, Paragraph 12, CI—3 reads: Germany
is obligated to pay for repairing, reconstructing, and
rebuilding the property in the invaded countries. The
cost shall be calculated at the time when work is done.*

Annex III:
*1. Germany recognizes the Allied Associated Powers'
right to the replacement, ton for ton and class for
class, merchant ships, fishing boats lost or damaged
during the war.*

*2. Germany turn over to the Allied Forces and
Associate Governments the property in all German
merchant ships, over 1600 tons, one-half of the ships
between 1000 to 1600 tons, and one quarter of all
other fishing boats. All ships are to be delivered within
two months of coming into force of this Treaty."[8]*

Germany could have only an army of 100,000 soldiers. The
construction of tanks, submarines, and airplanes was strictly forbidden. Germany was not allowed to ever ally with Austria.

The League of Nations ordered Germany to give up all her colonies and place them under their mandate. Part of West Prussia,
including Poznan and the Polish Corridor, and part of Silesia, was
awarded to Poland. Danzig remained a free German city. Belgium
took over Eupen and Malmedy, Denmark got part of Schleswig-
Holstein. France reclaimed Alsace-Lorrain and administrated
the Saarland for fifteen years. Germany lost one-eighth of the
German Reich.

The Allies presented the 440 articles, annexes, and sub-para-
graphs of the Versailles Treaty to the German government on
May 7, 1919, and the deadline of June 28, 1919, was set to read,

absorb, and respond to the demands. The allies did not lower the requested modifications of the high reparation costs and restrictions Germany requested. Neither did they remove Article 231, in which Germany recognizes guilt for the war.

The Allied Forces threatened to occupy Germany and resume the war if they would not sign the document as presented. With heavy hearts and deep-seated resentment toward the Versailles Treaty's drafters, the German representatives signed the document under protest on June 28, 1919.

My grandparents and the German people felt tormented, humiliated, and resentful that the war's responsibility was solely ascribed to Germany and not partly to Austria-Hungary that started World War I. The German people also thought the assessed reparation payments, their industries' dismantling, reducing their military forces, delivering livestock, other goods, and suffering territorial loss were unjust and too fierce.

President Woodrow Wilson did not find the Versailles Treaty acceptable, nor did the United States Senate ratify it. Twice the Senate opposed the ratification. Some senators favored isolationism, others opposed the League of Nations, and others lamented the excessive reparations. Marshall Ferdinand Foch, representing the United States, signed a separate agreement on August 25, 1921.

On September 10, 1919, the European Allies signed a Peace Treaty, and Austria had to grant independence to Yugoslavia, Czechoslovakia, Hungary, and Poland. The Allies prohibited Austria from joining Germany. Other peace treaties between Bulgaria, Hungary, and Turkey followed. Forming the League of Nations, President Woodrow Wilson wanted to make the world safe by discussing problems without inflicting war. British Prime Minister David Lloyd George, who aimed to control the seas and expand trade, asked not to be too harsh with Germany. He told the leaders that it might cause another costlier war in the future if we are too severe in our demands. Germany paid a prohibitive price unjustly for aiding Austria during their conflict with Serbia.

Chapter 4
Germany's Weimar Republic

THE MONARCHY OF Kaiser Wilhelm II ended in 1919. The first president, Friedrich Ebert, drafted a new constitution for the Weimar Republic,[9] named after the City of Weimar, where the officials wrote the new constitution. Friedrich Ebert was the first, and Paul von Hindenburg, the second elected president of the new Weimar Republic.

The Weimar Republic tried to rebuild its fatherland, but the enormous restitution demands broke its economy and industry. The government started to print much more money than its collateral's worth to meet their financial obligations, which caused a hyperinflation of a magnitude never before seen in history. Imagine in 1923 one US dollar was worth 4.21 billion German marks. In 1923, the reichsmark replaced the paper mark at an exchange rate of 1:1,000,000.000.00 (one Reichsmark to one billion paper Marks). In 1923, one egg costs 320 billion paper Marks. Families needed a wheel barrel full of money to buy groceries. After the new Reichsmark became the German currency, the economy improved and stabilized for a short period. The Weimar Republic was divided into three phases: the crisis years, the years of stabilization, and decline and dissolutions. When the reichsmark was devaluated in 1923, the economic condition improved and stabilized somewhat until 1928. According to the Versailles Treaty, Germany's high payments to France and Belgium could not be met; France and Belgium invaded the industrial area of the Ruhr and took whatever they wanted to stifle the German production of goods and reduce jobs in the coal mines. This condition led to severe depression and put a tremendous burden and hardship on my and all German families.

Chapter 5
Beginning of My Family

My grandparents lived during the reign of Wilhelm II, the last Kaiser of Germany. They respected the Kaiser and lived well with his just rules for his subjects. The whole family prospered.

My paternal grandparents, Heinrich and Marta Bonacker, lived in a small town in Wirballen, East Prussia; later, they moved to Wizajny. They had two daughters named Minna and Marta and five sons, Matheus, Georg, Gustav, Otto, and August. Grandfather was an excellent carpenter and saw to it that each of his sons learned a trade. My father, Gustav, became a mason. During that time, the daughters did not need to acquire a profession; they married and raised their families. Grandpa Bonacker was grateful that the three young sons Gustav, Otto, and August were too young to be drafted into the World War I army. Matheus and Heinrich returned with minor injuries from having served as soldiers in that war.

My maternal grandparents, Jan August and Anna Schlikat, had three daughters: Marie, Lene, and my mother, Emilie, born March 11, 1898. Unfortunately, the Russian government agents forcefully took my mother's parents to a labor camp, leaving the three young daughters behind to fend for themselves. To survive, the three sisters had to find shelter and food by working in households. They neither heard what happened to their parents nor learned of their whereabouts.

AUNT KATARINA & HUSBAND

At the age of twenty, my father, Gustav Bonacker, moved to Wizajny to the farm owned by his aunt Katarina. When Aunt Katerina's husband, Georg Klaus, suddenly died and her only son, Martin, had immigrated to America, she asked her nephew, Gustav, to help her manage the farm. Being a farmer at heart, Gustav worked diligently, tilling the soil and raising animals for personal consumption and selling. After World War I ended, life during the Weimar Republic was tough. The government restricted the farmers as to how many animals they could raise for personal consumption and the livestock to be delivered to the government. The severe restrictions put an enormous burden on the farmers. Due to the high monetary demand for restitution, inflation was rampant.

As time passed, Aunt Katarina grew older and weaker. She considered getting help with her domestic chores. Every Friday, villagers and ranchers went to the market square of Wizajny to sell and buy goods. The merchants of the town set up booths to sell their merchandise and produce. The farmers brought in their wagons pigs, sheep, various fouls, and whatever they wanted to sell or trade, including the fruits of their land. Many other activities transpired at the village square. Workers who needed work advertised their skills and waited to find an employer. One day, Aunt Katarina went with Gustav to the market to look for a household helper. After walking around and looking for a while, her eyes stopped at a young lady, an attractive brunette. Aunt Katarina approached her and asked what her name was and if she would be willing to work at her farm. Emilie Schlikat introduced herself and agreed to go with Aunt Katarina to the farm to work for her.

While driving through a patchwork of green meadows and wheat fields, Aunt Katarina asked Emilie where her parents lived and why she had left home. The very thought of being reminded of the horrible scene when her parents, at gunpoint, were threatened to have their daughters killed if they would not go with the Russian agent brought a lump to her throat. The scene flashed before her eyes when, in desperation to save their daughter's lives, her parents, emotionally agonized, had to leave them behind and follow the Russian agent. Tears flowed from her parent's and their daughter's cheeks, and many remained unshed in their aching hearts when begging for mercy was to no avail, and they tore their parents away from their daughters. Emilie explained the horrible destiny of her parents very briefly. Emilie, reliving the traumatic experience, began to cry. Aunt Katarina showed much compassion for Emilie. She welcomed her and bid her to forget about the tragic past. She encouraged Emilie to look forward to a better life on her ranch out in the country. However, neither Emilie nor Aunt Katarina could forget about her family's tragedy and the war's horrible events, consequences, and the hard times afterward.

Emilie fulfilled all the household tasks to Aunt Katarina's satisfaction. As time passed, Gustav grew fond of Emilie and asked her to become his wife. On March 28, 1923, spring had just arrived according to the calendar, but snow still covered the ground; Gustav and Emilie exchanged marriage vows in the Lutheran Church in Wizajny. A family celebration followed at home for the newlyweds.

Wizajny School and Catholic Church

Aunt Katarina got attached to Gustav and Emilie, treated them like her own children, and made them heirs of her estate. They believed in God and lived in harmony with each other, the neighbors, and nature.

Almost a year passed, and winter winds blew across the fields, piling up drifts around the buildings and trees. Gustav prepared the sleigh and rushed to town to bring the midwife to the house. Emilie was to give birth to their first child. A neighbor came over and kept a pot of water boiling on the stove. Next to Emilie's bed stood a cradle Gustav had built for the new family member. Aunt Katarina and Gustav were relieved when the midwife delivered a baby girl on February 20, 1924. Gustav would have preferred a son as his firstborn, but he consoled himself quickly, knowing mother and daughter were well. He looked at his tiny daughter in the cradle and felt proud to be a father. They named their first-born daughter Emma.

MOTHER, SISTERS MARIE, LENE AND DAUGHTER EMMA

A year and eight months later, on October 3, 1925, Emilie was expecting her second child. Gustav whistled as he drove through the fallow fields and watched the Canadian geese gathering for their migration south, on his way to the midwife. This time he expected a son who would help him in the fields and at home. Gustav was greatly disappointed when Emilie presented him with another daughter. Emma, however, welcomed her baby sister. She walked over to the cradle and took a good look at her baby sister, who was later named Marta. Gustav soon overcame his disappointment and accepted his second daughter as his new family member. Aunt Katarina adored her two grandnieces, Emma and Marta. She treated them as if they were her grandchildren. Emilie was relieved to know her daughters were in loving hands. Now she gladly accompanied her husband to the fields to help him harvest wheat, rye, or potatoes.

In October, the potato plants laid dry on the raised furrows. All summer long, tiny potatoes grew under the green plants. When they reached a specific size, they stopped growing, and the plant above the ground died. That was the indication to remove them from the field before they would freeze and rot. Father guided the plow through each raised bed to turn over the ground and expose the potatoes. Emilie and some neighbors or relatives would follow behind, loosen the potatoes from the dried plant and the soil, placing them first in baskets, then emptying them in sacks. Gustav loaded the full sacks on the wagon and drove them home. He put enough into the cellar for the winter consumption, and the rest he buried below the frost line in the sandy ground not too far away from the house. Gustav raked the dried potato plants, put them in large piles, and burnt each heap.

Gustav and Emilie accepted the fruits of the fertile fields with gratitude and thanked God for an abundant crop. Each season brought a certain natural rhythm, marking the end of one routine and the beginning of another.

Two years passed quickly. Soon Emilie was to give birth to a third child. This time, Father's hopes grew high to have a son. However, he was deeply disappointed when January 8, 1928, Meta was born and not a son, as he expected.

At last, two years later, on December 15, 1930, his long-awaited son was born on a cold winter day. He named him Georg after his brother. Georg was the pride and joy of his father. For his baptism, he invited all his family to celebrate this special event with him. He could hardly wait to see him grown up and working with him. Emma and Marta watched their little brother and played with him frequently. After Georg was able to walk, Marta took him down to the pond. Father had placed a long board across the pond's narrow part, so their mother could wash the clothes there. Marta found the board tempting and ran from one side to the other. Little

35

Georg followed her, slipped, and fell into the water. Marta's heart stood still when she could not see him coming up right away. She was afraid he had drowned. Finally, after what seemed a long time, Georg came to the surface. Marta grabbed him and pulled him quickly out of the water. He lay on the grass lifeless, then started coughing up water and began to breathe again. Marta was relieved to see him alive. She ran to her mother with him and told her what had happened. Mother scolded her and forbade her to take Georg to the pond.

Georg did not have to wait too long to have a baby brother named Edmund, born on November 14, 1932. Father was delighted to have two sons, who, when grown up, would help him in the fields and in caring for the horses and cows. Mother was content to have three daughters to share her domestic chores and watch the younger brothers.

After a year passed and Edmund still could not walk, his mother became concerned when she saw no muscles developing on his thin legs. She feared that he had polio and would become crippled for the rest of his life. At that time, there was no cure for polio. After two years passed and he still could not stand on his feet or make a few steps, his mother was sure he had polio. Her heart broke when she watched him crawling to his brother or sisters. Grandma Katarina, that's what the children called her, would pick up Edmund, sit him next to her, massage his leg muscles, and move them back and forth. Emma, Marta, and Meta helped with the exercises. Finally, at the age of three, and with his sisters' aid, Edmund took his first steps and was able to stand on his feet by himself. Gradually, he improved and soon could walk and run normally. Mother considered it a miracle and thanked God for healing her son and that no atrophy remained in either leg.

As the family grew, the house became crowded. In 1933, Father decided to build a new one. While the fields and forests still laid under a dense cover of snow and winter winds wailed their polar song, Father hitched the horses to the sleigh and drove to the woods. He selected young, straight trees, just the right thickness, to serve as wall-supporting beams for the house. Father would trim all the branches and put the clean tree trunks on piles. When he had enough tree trunks, Father would call a neighbor to help him haul them to the ranch—the lumber for the windows, door frames, roof, and floors he bought in town. Father collected the best straw to cover the rooftop.

By the end of March, the first snowbells peeked through the moist soil and announced spring's arrival. Father built temporary living quarters in the barn when the weather was pleasant before tearing down the old house. The children enjoyed sleeping in the barn, but Aunt Katarina, Mother, and Father found it uncomfortable. Knowing that this was only a temporary accommodation, they bore the inconveniences and discomfort patiently.

Father's brothers, Matheus, Georg, Otto, and August helped dig the foundation and drive the corner posts into the ground. Neighbors also came to pitch in and help. Father also had to till the soil and sow wheat, rye, oats, and plant potatoes during the construction of the house.

Slowly, the walls emerged, and with the rafters of the roof put in place, it gave the structure the appearance of a house. When Father and his helpers fastened the last beams to the roof, Emilie made a wreath of flowers, and Gustav secured the wreath with colored ribbons to the roof's top rafter. This old German custom called "Richtfest" is celebrated to ask God to bless the house and to express gratitude to all the workers. Uncles, aunts, cousins, and neighbors joined in the celebration. Uncle August played the piano accordion, and everyone sang along until late hours. Mother served an array of her homemade sausages, freshly baked bread, and cake. Father offered his self-brewed beer and schnapps, that he had saved for this special occasion. Juice made from the berries of the garden delighted the taste buds of the children.

Now began the race to harvest the fields and complete the house before the winter arrived. When the winds shifted from the southwest to northwest in late September and temperatures began to drop, Father finished putting on the thatched roof on the rafters. Neighbors helped to insulate the outside and inside walls. Father used a mixture of clay, gypsum, and finely cut straw instead of cement to cover the inside and outside walls. The Canadian geese gathering in the wheat fields to migrate South indicated the arrival of fall. Father hurried to install the windows and doors to keep the cold out. Father applied several coats of white paint on the inside and outside walls, and the family moved in. What a happy day that was for Father and Mother. They thanked God that nobody got hurt during construction and that the house was completed before the winter began. November arrived with a whirlwind of snow whipping around the house in wild profusion, covering all the fields and meadows with a thick, fluffy blanket.

Now the house needed to be furnished. Grandpa Heinrich Bonacker was a fine cabinetmaker. He offered to build tables, bed frames, benches, and whatever was necessary to make it a comfortable home. A week before Christmas, Father went by sleigh to the forest, brought a tall pine tree home, and set it up in the living room. Father heated the green tile oven so Emilie and the girls could decorate the tree in comfort. Mother opened box after box and handed the shining, colored bulbs, paper stars, tinsel, and many other ornaments, which Emma, Marta, and Meta hung on the tree. As a final touch, they placed many candles in candleholders and clipped them on various branches.

Christmas Eve, after darkness descended over the snow-covered land, Mother lit candle by candle, which illuminated the room, and the flickering flames reflected in the colored bulbs. The family entered, and the children stood in awe before this magically transformed tree. Mother told the Christmas story about celebrating the remembrance of the birth of Christ on Christmas Eve. The family gathered around the Christmas tree and sang: "Oh Tannenbaum, Oh Tannenbaum" (Oh Christmas Tree, Oh Christmas Tree), and "Stille Nacht, Heilige Nacht," (Silent Night, Holy Night), and several other Christmas songs. Mother gave each child a gift, hand-knitted gloves, or socks, then served a small dinner before Father hitched the horses to the sleigh and drove his family to church to celebrate the birth of Christ with the parishioners in Wizajny. As the horses trotted through the snow, sleigh bells rang, and the dark dome of the sky filled with myriads of stars. The children, snuggled in furs, watched in awe the magic winter scenery passing by. After Father arrived at the church plaza, he unhitched the horses from the sleigh, fastened them to a beam, and tied a small sack of oats on their harness. While devouring their oats, they would keep themselves occupied and calm during the church service.

Mother and the children would enter the church first, then Father followed. The celebration of the Christmas service began with the organist playing a composition by Johann Sebastian Bach. Then the church members sang a Christmas song, followed by the sermon about the birth of Christ in Bethlehem. At the end of the sermon, two boys lit all the candles on both tall Christmas trees right and left of the altar and turned off all other lights. The church choir sang "Silent Night, Holy Night," creating a festive atmosphere to highlight the celebration. After the benediction, the altar boys put out all the candles with a small bell-shaped cup at the end of a long stick. Accompanied by organ music, the parishioners exited the church. The men went to hitch the horses to the sleighs, lit the lanterns on each side, and began their journey home. Moonlight glistened like diamonds in the snow-covered meadows and fields under the star-studded sky.

The next day, each child found a plate filled with cookies, candies, and apples on the table. We called it "Bunte Teller" in German. Santa Claus brought the goodies during the night. The children happily devoured the treats immediately. In the afternoon, relatives came to celebrate Christmas. Father proudly showed off his newly constructed home to his family. Mother prepared several roasted geese, red cabbage, and potato dumplings. For dessert, she served a homemade stollen, filled with marzipan, she made herself. On the second day of Christmas, neighbors came to celebrate with the family. The magical Christmas in the new house passed rapidly, and so did the year 1933. On New Year's Eve Mother and Father took the family to Grandpa Heinrich's home; together with other family members, they rang in 1934.

During the winter months, our father built an oven in the kitchen so that our mother could bake her bread and cakes at home. He also constructed a rectangular brick bench about four feet high, six feet deep, and eight feet long with open channels running under the bench connected to the kitchen stove. When the fire was burning in the kitchen hearth, the smoke went directly through the chimney outside in the summertime. In the wintertime, father opened the trap leading to the bench in the living room. The smoke and hot air would go through the channels, warming up the stone bench and the room without dealing with wood and ashes in the living room. In winter, it was the favorite gathering place. Grandma Katarina fascinated the children by telling them fairytales or stories of her past. Mother would knit socks, gloves, or scarves; so did her daughters.

Father shaped a square structure out of loam and straw in the attic that narrowed at the top and connected to the hearth's chimney. It served as a smokehouse. With a shutter, the amount of smoke could be regulated or shut off completely. Metal rods crossing from one side to the other served to hang sausages or meat from a butchered pig for smoking. Being a mason, Father enjoyed working on different projects around the house when the fields did not need attention.

The first winter in the new house passed only too quickly, and spring arrived. Emma, Marta, and Meta helped their mother prepare a vegetable garden and arranged flower beds around the house. The flowers were in full bloom by July and August and filled the air with a delightful fragrance. By mid-August 1934, their mother announced the arrival of her sixth child. On August 15, the midwife delivered another baby boy, later named Richard. Richard was a very delicate baby, had big blue eyes, and the family welcomed him with curiosity and joy. Father and Mother were grateful all went well, and they thought having three daughters, and three sons would complete their family.

Emma, Marta, and Meta helped raise Richard, and after a year passed, he was able to walk and say a few words. Edmund and Richard would sit on the floor and play. Sometimes, their mother would put a blanket in the garden so that they got some fresh air and sunshine.

At the beginning of August 1935, the sky grew dark and gloomy, and the pregnant clouds gathered in the sky. Thunder rolled, roared, and shook the whole house. Lightning zigzagged through the atmosphere as the warm and cold air masses collided. Suddenly, our father watched the sky remain illuminated by fire. He saw the neighbor's house going up in flames. Father thought lightning must have struck the home. Quickly, he hitched the horses to the wagon and rushed to the neighbor family Reinke. By the time father arrived, the flames had consumed most of the house and all their possessions. Mr. and Mrs. Reinke saved only some documents, a few furniture pieces, and some personal belongings. Thank God, none of the family members were struck by lightning and hurt. Suddenly, the heavens opened, and a downpour of rain flooded the burning house and slowly put out the fire. The family, Father, and other neighbors sought shelter in the barn. Sadness filled the heart of Mrs. Reinke, and tears flowed down her cheeks when she realized the fire reduced her house and the treasured contents to a black pile of charred rubble.

Father felt sorry for the neighbors and asked Mr. and Mrs. Reinke to come and stay at our house until they had made other provisions to rebuild their home. They waited until the rain eased. Then Father asked Alfred, Ophelia, and their three sons Erwin, Oswald, and Helmut to get in the wagon and come with him. Mother welcomed the neighbors, and the boys were happy to have temporary playmates.

The following day, Father drove with Mr. and Mrs. Reinke to their ranch to see if they could salvage anything from the charred debris of the house and feed the livestock. They told our father to return, and they would join him in the evening in their wagon. Alfred and Ophelia made plans to rebuild their house immediately. They were grateful to have a place to stay until they set up a provisional kitchen and quarters in their barn. The neighbors worked on their house during the day and only came to spend the night with us. Their relatives and other neighbors pitched in to help with the construction of the house. They completed the structure to make it livable before winter.

Soon a new person would move in. Mother's sister, Marie, worked in a wealthy family household in Sudauen and suffered from bone tuberculosis. The severe pain and festering wounds prevented her from continuing her job. She had no other place to go and asked her sister Emilie and brother-in-law Gustav if she could live with their family. They agreed, and Father drove to Sudauen to pick up Aunt Marie. It took her some time to adjust to being surrounded by six children all the time. Even though Aunt Marie was an intelligent and beautiful woman, she never had gotten married.

Soon she grew fond of her nieces and nephews and was grateful for the love they expressed in many acts of kindness toward her. Emma and Meta helped her out of bed each day, and Marta took over cleaning and dressing her wounds. She was grateful and never complained. Her nieces' and nephews' love and faith in God gave her the strength to endure her incurable disease. The children would gather around her bed in the evening, and she would tell fairytales and stories, which the children enjoyed.

Meanwhile, Aunt Katarina, our adopted grandma, became frail, and her health worsened. She needed help to get out of bed and into the chair. The girls helped her wherever they could, and whenever they were in school, Mother took care of both Aunt Katarina and her sister Marie. Aunt Katarina regained some strength during the summer, but she took her last breath on September 9, 1936, and went to be with her heavenly Father, whom she had served and worshipped all her life. Before she died, she gave Emma her golden wedding ring as a keepsake, which Emma treasured all her life. Grandma Katrina left a great void for Emma, Marta, and Meta. Many relatives and neighbors came for the three-day wake at home. Four days later, the hearse drove the closed coffin to church. The pastor spoke a farewell sermon to all the mourners before the pallbearers carried the coffin to the nearby cemetery, where her body was laid to rest.

One life passes and a new one arrives. Emilie announced to her husband that soon the stork would bring a new baby. Christmas passed, so did1936! The year 1937 came, so did the midwife on New Year's Day. Three hours past midnight, January 2, 1937, a baby girl cried out to be accepted into the family and world while parting from her mother's womb. Everyone greeted her with joy, and Emma chose the name Hildegard for her. As one light faded, another began to shine. The perpetual cycle of life and death continues -—they belong together like day and night.

According to my sister Emma, I, Hildegard, was a happy child and brought joy to my parents, brothers, and sisters, who cared for me and played with me. Unfortunately, I never knew my grand aunt Katarina, whom everyone loved and called grandma. Neither did I remember Aunt Marie. The infection of tuberculosis slowly deteriorated her bones. She withered like a beautiful flower in full bloom on Maundy Thursday, April 4, 1938, at age thirty-eight. Emilie, her sister Lena, the nephews, and the older nieces treasured Aunt Marie's most fond memories. I only remember seeing her in a photo taken while working for a noble family in Sudauen. She looked lovely, with curly hair and a beautiful smile.

Chapter 6

The Third Reich

The Weimar Republic lasted fifteen years, from 1918 to 1933. The government tried to rebuild its fatherland, but the enormous restitution demands of the Versailles Treaty broke its economy and industry. Adolf Hitler appeared and formed a new government, called the Third Reich.

How did Adolf Hitler, born in Braunau, Austria, become a German citizen and chancellor of the Weimar Republic?

Adolf Hitler was born on April 20, 1889, in Braunau, Austria. His father, Alois, was an illegitimate child of Maria Ana Schickelgrube and Leopold Frankenberger. His mother, born Klara Poelzl, was his cousin. Ashamed of his inbred ancestors, he hid or destroyed all documents and even graves of his Austrian ancestors. Neighbors called him a Jewish boy while he was a child. In an article on history, Jeannie Cohen states that Jean-Paul Mulders and Marc Vermeeren, a Belgian historian, studied Hitler's roots extensively. They collected saliva from thirty-nine different distant relatives of Hitler. Their study concluded that Hitler's ancestors may have included African Jewish blood.

When he was supposed to be drafted into the Austrian army, he fled to Munich. On November 8 and 9, 1923, he tried to overthrow the German government. This ill-fated insurrection is known as the Beer Hall Putsch. Hitler was found guilty of high treason and sentenced to five years in prison. Before he was released nine months later, he wrote the book *Mein Kampf* (My Battle).[10] In it, Hitler expresses hate for the Jews. He gave eloquent speeches about Germany's challenging condition during the trial that he even impressed the judges, and they released him after nine months. He obtained German citizenship and formed the National Socialistic Worker's Party (that everyone calls the Nazi Party).

During this chaotic time, the Germans were demoralized and humiliated. By 1933, Adolf Hitler became the chancellor of the Reichstag, and in 1934, he was elected president of the Weimar Republic; combining both titles, he called himself Fuehrer (Leader). He renamed the Weimar Republic the Third Reich.[11] On March 12, 1938, Adolf Hitler annexed Austria to Germany. The killing on November 7, 1938, of the German diplomat Ernst Rath by the Jewish Herschel Grynszpan triggered the beginning of the persecution of Jews on Crystal night (Kristallnacht). He first gave the Jewish citizens a choice to leave Germany before eliminating them from Germany and later from Europe. Adolf Hitler had the idea of creating a pure Arian race. It was exclusively his idea and not the desire of the German government or people. He also wanted to expand the territory of the Third Reich. His eloquent speeches had played on the emotions of the struggling workers, and he slowly gained power. Adolf Hitler demanded absolute obedience and to be saluted by everyone "Heil Hitler" (Hail Hitler).

Hitler ignored the Versailles Treaty, restored the Germans' national pride, and rebuilt Germany's infrastructure, schools, and industries. At the beginning of the Third Reich, he appeared to be Germany's right leader. He trained soldiers and built ships, airplanes, and destructive weapons, also rockets in underground factories.

Adolf Hitler created Hitler Youth for the fourteen- to eighteen-year-old boys. Their leaders indoctrinated them with Hitler's political ideology and subjected them to vigorous physical training to prepare them to be good warriors. Unfortunately, some Hitler

Youth members were drafted into the army before World War II ended, and many never returned.

He formed the League of German Maidens (BDM) for the young girls at the same age. They received instructions to be competent homemakers, good wives, and mothers. They also did physical exercises and sports to develop healthy bodies. Before the end of the war, they assisted doctors and nurses in caring for the wounded soldiers in the hospitals.

Unfortunately, after reaching his power's pinnacle, he became a ruthless dictator. Everyone opposing him, his ideas, and his regime was put in prison or punished with death.

He began military conquests to reclaim German territories lost during World War I. On September 1, 1939, Hitler invaded Poland and started World War II[12]. England and France, allies of Poland, declared war against Germany on September 3, 1939. Even the army of the Soviet Union entered Warsaw after it was bombed and surrendered. Then Hitler concentrated on conquering the Western European countries. Hitler reached the pinnacle of his popularity when he took over Paris and occupied France.

Italy and Japan joined Germany September 27, 1940, and formed an allegiance called the axis.

On August 13, 1940, Hitler began an aerial attack on England. After the heavy losses of the German Luftwaffe, Hitler felt defeated and stopped bombarding London and other English cities. Prime Minister Winston Churchill sought the help of President Roosevelt, but it was not until after the Japanese attack on Pearl Harbor on December 7, 1941, that President Roosevelt declared war on Japan just four days later. Adolf Hitler learned that America, while still neutral, attacked German U-boats, and Adolf Hitler declared war on December 11, 1941, against the United States. The German people, generals, and most Americans disapproved of Adolf Hitler's decision and questioned his sanity. Adolf Hitler committed his unsurmountable atrocity when he began persecuting Jews. He filled the concentration camps, not only with Jews, but with anyone who opposed him and his regime. The prisoners were forced to do hard labor, and some died of malnutrition and diseases. So much has been written about the mass killing by Zyklon B gas; some are facts and some fiction.

British and American troops invaded Sicily in 1943 and ended fascism in Italy by removing Bonito Mussolini from power. The new Italian prime minister Badoglio signed an unconditional armistice with General Dwight Eisenhower in July 1943.

General Dwight Eisenhower, the commander of the Allied Forces, invaded Normandy on June 6, 1944 (D-Day), bringing thousands of new airplanes and ships, and landing with over a million soldiers on the beach of France. The troops advanced to Paris on August 26, 1944, and General Charles de Gaulle and the citizens of France welcomed the American liberators with great jubilation.

Meanwhile, three million Russians of the red army advanced toward Berlin and met the American troops on April 25, 1945, surrounding Berlin. After many German soldiers died in combat, Hitler drafted older men, my father included, and teenagers to replace them. After a horrific battle, Berlin capitulated on May 2, 1945.

When Hitler felt defeated and he saw no way out of being captured, he and Eva Brown hid in the Berlin bunker and committed suicide on April 30. 1945. Hitler first took a cyanide capsule and then shot himself in the head. The German generals agreed to stop fighting and surrender, and General Alfred Jodl signed the declaration of surrender in Reims, France. The allies demanded the surrender of all fighting forces, and General Wilhelm Keitel signed the unconditional surrender document in Berlin on May 8, 1945, ending World War II in Germany. However, the war in the Pacific continued with Japan until the United States, with the consent of Britain, dropped an atomic bomb over Hiroshima, August 6, 1945, and three days later, another over Nagasaki. It instantly killed over 200,000 civilians. For months, many people died from burns, radiation, sicknesses, malnutrition, and severe injuries. Six days later, the emperor of Japan, Hirohito, surrendered. On September 2, 1945, on the USS Missouri, Japan's Foreign Minister Mamoru Shigemitsu and General Yoshijiro Umezu signed their names on the surrender document, which became part of the Potsdam Treaty.[13] General Douglas MacArthur was also present at this somber ceremony when World War II ended officially. The allies allowed Emperor Hirohito to remain on the throne but restricted his political power in a newly established Japanese government.

The Allies forced Germany again to pay heavy reparation and permanently give up certain territories of Germany and other regions that Hitler had conquered at the beginning of the war. As demanded by the Potsdam Peace Treaty of World War II, Russia claimed the northern part of East Prussia, and Poland claimed the southern part of East Prussia, Pomerania, and Silesia. Denmark claimed a part of North Schleswig and France part of Alsace Lorraine.

Gone with both world wars was a total of one-third of the territory of Germany. Fourteen million persons had to leave their homes and property behind and flee to the West. Millions of ethnic Germans who lived in Russia, Poland, Czechoslovakia, Hungary, and the Eastern European countries were expelled from their homes, often subjected to violence and terror, including murder, torture, and rape. Hundreds of thousands of Germans ended up in internment camps, which before were concentration camps.

Many German inhabitants, including my own family, escaped in 1944 before Russian armies invaded and surrounded East Prussia. But those who remained were stripped of their property, treated brutally, and transported like cattle in crowded cargo trains to West

Germany. East Prussia became a Russian enclave. The Russian populace, who settled in East Prussia, destroyed all the historic landmarks, and rebuilt the war-torn towns and villages.

The Polish government treated the German inhabitants in East Prussia badly. They, too, confiscated their properties and ordered the Germans out; however, they permitted some to stay behind. Poland annexed the area where I was born to their country.

Gone with World War II were the Third Reich and my beloved homeland (Heimat), East Prussia. The four Allies divided Germany into military zones. Northern Germany was occupied by England, the South by France, central Germany was occupied by the United States, and the East by Russia. For four years, Germany had no government. Each ally ruled their occupied region according to their country's laws.

On May 23, 1949, a new government, the Federal Republic of Germany (BRD), took shape under President Theodor Heuss and Chancellor Conrad Adenauer. With the American Marshall Plan aid and hard work, Germany's war-torn western sections slowly grew into a prosperous nation. Three years after the war's end, the reichsmark was replaced by the Deutsche Mark or D.M. due to high inflation.

However, under the Russian occupation of East Germany, called the German Democratic Republic (DDR), the eastern part regressed. The Russian government built a wall (Iron Curtain) and a five-kilometer-wide demilitarized zone to prevent people from leaving East Germany. Anyone trying to escape from East Germany over the border illegally would be put in prison or shot on the spot.

Gone with World War II were East and West Prussia and the seven-hundred-year-old Prussian culture. Almost seven decades passed since my family fled from East Prussia, I still mourn the loss of my beloved native country and culture. The fact that I will never see my birthplace again, that East Prussia might never be returned to Germany, welled up profound sadness in my heart and tears in my eyes.

The country that once offered asylum to many religiously and politically persecuted persons now ordered its inhabitants to leave to prevent them from being massacred by brutal armies. They escaped, seeking refuge in other German regions or foreign countries.

How strange life can be; I found a new home in North America, which once signed a friendship and trade agreement with the Prussian king, Frederick the Great, over two hundred years ago. I love my newly adopted country and am a naturalized citizen. However, I will always cherish my native East Prussia's memory, mourn her loss, and never forget my roots.

Mother's strong faith helped me and all of my siblings through the tragedy of war and life's hardships. She found comfort in God, who promised that we only sojourn temporarily on earth, but our permanent home is in heaven, where we will be reunited with our loved ones and live forever with God and our Savior, Jesus Christ.

After a glimpse into Prussia's and Germany's historical background, I will go back to my place of birth, the small village Wizajny, East Prussia, and recall memories of my childhood and the story of my family.

Chapter 7
Life at Home

FATHER FELT CONTENT, living on the ranch with his large family. On November 19, 1942, another son, called Horst, was added to his seven children. He enjoyed life, dancing, singing, and had a good sense of humor. He was a craftsman in masonry. He was tall, blond, and had blue eyes. Mother was a brunette, had brown eyes, was taciturn, and very religious. Both worked diligently to till the soil, raise crops and animals to feed their large family, and sell the surplus to buy necessary goods for the house and children.

The seasons created a rhythmic pattern for our lives, and nature prompted us to follow her order. Life began to stir underneath the snow when the winter shadows grew shorter, and the days grew longer. Soon the first spring flowers pierced their delicate leaves through the snow and blossomed. The snowdrops' fragile white bells rang in the beginning of spring.

Some hens showed signs of change in their behavior in springtime. They stopped laying eggs, lost the feathers on their tummy, and made a strange crackling noise. My mother knew when a hen was ready to incubate eggs. Emma, Marta, and Meta prepared nests in wooden boxes and baskets, filled them with straw, and lined them with goose feathers. They placed them in the big entrance to the kitchen because the hen house was not heated, and the cold nights might hinder the incubation of the eggs. Before my mother put a dozen or so eggs in a nest, she held each egg against the sunlight to check if it was fertile or not. Then she set a hen (Glucke, in German) on top of each batch. The girls sectioned parts in the stable, setting up nests for ducks, geese, and turkeys.

Warmer winds blew each day and melted the snow around the house and the ice on the pond. Close to the shore of the pond, water lily leaves appeared and other flowers and grasses. The trees and bushes around the house unfurled their delicate leaves and lovely blossoms. The meadows grew lush green grass and multi-colored wildflowers, and the fallow fields exposed their rich dark soil.

Father became anxious to toil the soil. First, he drove in special wagon loads of cow manure to the fields and spread it with a pitchfork all over the ground. The next day, my father took a plow to the field, hitched it behind one horse, and began to turn over one row after another to cover the natural fertilizer and loosen the topsoil. He whistled or hummed a happy tune while pushing the blade into the ground at the beginning of a row, keeping it at a certain depth, and lifting it at the end of each row. He went back and forth until the earth of the entire field lay exposed to the sun and fresh air. Crows followed behind to pick a fat exposed worm. A skylark twittered a happy song while ascending to the blue celestial dome. Father waited a few days for the topsoil to dry before raking the field to break up the clumps and prepare the ground for sowing.

The next day, Georg helped him after he came home from school. Father swung a sack full of wheat on the wagon and fastened the rake to the wagon. Once they arrived at the field, Georg raked the field first. Then father filled with wheat grains half a sack with a strap attached to each end and swung the strap over his head and shoulder. He walked from one end of the field to the other, spreading handful after handful of seeds in a sweeping motion over the topsoil. Georg raked again the portion where my father had thrown the seeds. Georg went back and forth several times to cover the seeds loosely with dirt. Now, Father hoped for gentle spring rain to speed up the germinating process.

When evening cloaked the farm and fields in darkness, my mother lit the oil lamp and put it on the table. In the country, electrical power was nonexistent. After dinner, for two or three hours, Edmund and Georg would do their homework. Richard and I played board games (Muehle, or Mensch Aerger Dich Nicht), while Mother and Emma would spin wool or sew clothes for the younger siblings.

Mother, Emma, and Meta prepared the vegetable garden, which Father had plowed in the fall the year before. Mother would draw, the beds for the various vegetables with the end of the rake. Emma and Meta dug out a path between each parcel, which Emma raked. Now and then, she turned the rake over and gave a whack to a clump of clay to break it up. Once the dirt was smooth, Mother drew shallow, narrow furrows on the vegetable beds. She placed seeds, which she had saved from the previous crop, of carrots, radishes, cucumbers, horseradish, red beets, beans, sugar peas, various types of lettuces, and cabbages, in them. She covered the seeds loosely with soil. Turnips, sugar beets, and white beets served as pig food were planted in a larger parcel away from the house. I could hardly wait until the seedlings sprouted and poked their first two leaflets through the ground.

Shortly after the arrival of spring, the migratory birds returned. I welcomed with great enthusiasm the two storks, who had a nest on top of our barn. I enjoyed listening to the clatter of their beaks. I would run out of the house to talk to them in East Prussian dialect: "Storch, Storch, goder, bring mi e kleenem Broder. Storch, Storch bester, bring mi e kleene Schwester." Translation: Stork, stork, be good and bring me a little brother. Stork, stork, be the best and get me a little sister.

The honking of wild geese flying north, the call of the cuckoo, and the sweet song of the nightingale announced the official arrival of spring, and with it came Easter. We all looked forward to Easter when our sister Marta came home to visit us. After Marta graduated from grammar school, at the age of fourteen, she found a position in a nearby village Hellrau with a teacher's family to help with their three children. She gathered enough experience at home, helped my mother raise her younger siblings, and now enjoyed caring for the teacher's children. However, the special holidays, like Easter, Pentecost, and Christmas, Mr. Kessler, the teacher's name, allowed her to take off a few days to spend them with her own family.

Each day, during the week before Easter, I kept a lookout for Marta. Finally, I saw her walking along the hill to the house, carrying packages in both hands. I ran to greet her. She put her bags down, embraced me, and lifted me to swing me around in a circle: "My, have you grown," she observed, "How good to see you and be home again." "What is in those bags?" I ask.

"You will have to wait until Easter. I cannot tell you yet. It is a surprise."

I jumped and skipped next to her, holding on to one bag, wondering if there was a doll in it. Everyone embraced her at home and welcomed her with many questions:

"How do you like working for the teacher?"

"Are they treating you well?"

"How many children do they have?"

"Are the children as obedient as we are?"

The questions went on until my mother interceded: "Stop asking so many questions; Marta is tired from the long walk. Let her rest a while!"

The next day, we celebrated Good Friday. Mother told us the story of Christ's crucifixion, and out of respect for the suffering of Christ, we were not allowed to carry on any unnecessary conversations. Mother and Father, Emma, Marta, Meta, and Georg fasted because they would partake in the Holy Communion in church.

Mother insisted that everyone asked forgiveness for unkind words said or any wrongdoings. Mother and Father embraced, and so did the sisters and Georg, who asked their parents first to be forgiven and then each other. Sometimes, tears expressed how sorry they were for telling a little lie or disobeying their mother or father. Everyone felt relieved when Father hitched the coach (Kutsche) and drove us to church. I cuddled up in Marta's lap. She put her arms around me, but we did not dare say a word or break the silence.

Father and Georg unhitched the horses from the coach at the church square and tied them to the long beam where the other villagers' horses already stood. We all entered the vast church. Richard and I joined the other children in the front rows while our parents and the adults sat behind us. Three crosses stood to the right of the altar. A black veil draped the center cross.

After the parishioners sat, the organist played a prelude, followed by a community song. The pastor read the crucifixion story of Christ from the Bible. The sermon followed the theme: Christ died and suffered for our salvation, and we should also carry our cross and that of others. Then the pastor invited the parishioners to partake in the Holy Communion. They went to the altar, knelt, received the host first, and then the wine. One more song followed after the pastor served the last communion participant; then, the pastor dismissed the congregation with a benediction. Everyone departed solemnly from the church.

According to an old tradition, we ate only fish on Good Friday. After lunch, Emma, Marta, and Meta prepared the ingredients for coloring Easter Eggs. They cooked red beets, onion peels, moss, and eggs in separate pots. Marta pealed the red beets and cut them in slices, so the rich purple color oozed into the hot water, then she strained the beet juice into a small pot and gently dropped, with a spoon, eggs into the pot. After a few minutes, Marta lifted each egg out of the pot and put it in a dish. Emma dyed eggs yellow or amber in the onion peel juice and Meta, greenish brown in the moss liquid. Soon, eggs of various colors filled the container. I ran out to the meadow, picked buttercups, forget-me-nots, and larkspur, and handed them to Marta. Marta cut the stems shorter and pleasingly arranged them on a deep plate next to the colorful eggs on the dining room table.

The next morning, my mother prepared the dough for wheat and rye bread in two separate large wooden bowls and set it aside to rise. Emma heated the oven with firewood. When the oven was ready, my mother patted the wheat dough into elongated shapes and the rye dough in round loaves, flattened some wheat dough on a baking pan, and set them on the table to let them rise once more. When the dough rose enough, my mother placed each loaf on a wooden utensil (Schieber in German) and pushed them into the oven. Emma mixed flour, butter, and sugar and sprinkled the mixture over the dough on the cookie sheet, which our mother placed into the oven later. A delightful aroma filled the kitchen after Mother opened the oven and took out one loaf after the other. We could hardly wait until my mother would serve it.

Saturday, each one of us had to polish our shoes and put out the clothes for Sunday. I asked my sister Marta: "Can you pick a dress for me?"

"Come here, Hildke (that's what she used to call me); I have something for you." She went to the bedroom and came back, holding one hand behind her back. "Close your eyes, Hildke," I squeezed my eyelids down quickly and up again when Marta announced, "You can open your eyes now, look what I made for you." I glanced at a red sleeveless dress with embroidery around the neckline.

"It is beautiful; you made this for me? Thank you, thank you, Marta," I uttered while embracing her and kissing her on the cheek.

"You might need to wear a blouse under the dress tomorrow. The air is still brisk," Marta added. I admired the beautiful embroidery and could hardly wait to wear it to church.

Saturday was bathing time. Mother boiled a large pot of water, poured it into an oval tub, and added enough cold water until the temperature was right. Marta led me by the hand, helped me undress, and I stepped into the tub, situated in the middle of the kitchen. She took a bar of soap and washed my hair first and then the rest of my body while I splashed happily in the water. Marta dried me in a big towel, helped me put on my nightgown, then took me to the bedroom. First, she knelt with me to say a prayer before she tucked me under the featherbed and kissed me good night. My sisters Emma, Marta, and Meta took their bath next. Each added more hot water before stepping into the tub. Then, my brothers, Georg, Edmund, and Richard, took their turns. When finished, they dumped the bathwater in the garden. Mother poured new hot and cold water into the tub for her husband and herself.

When dawn tiptoed over the land and drenched the countryside in color, Emma rose to fetch water from the running creek the following day. We called it Easter water. It was supposed to have healing power. Everyone washed their faces with this blessed water and hoped it would work some magic.

Marta hid all the colored eggs in various places around the house and told us, "The Easter bunny took the eggs and hid them outside for you. Go and look for them." My three brothers and I ran outside and began hunting for Easter eggs. "I found some," I shouted when I saw a nest under a bush.

"Look where I discovered eggs!" Edmund hollered, pointing to the wagon in the barn. Georg found a nest in a box in front of the house. Richard discovered Easter eggs in a basket by the barn. We dashed inside to show our mother, father, and sisters, our found treasures. Even though each one could keep the found eggs, we always shared them with every family member.

"Now, children, it is time to get ready for church; we leave in ten minutes." Mother reminded us. Quickly, we changed into our Sunday clothes. When our father brought the coach in front of the house, we all jumped into the coach. My mother sat in front next to my father. Off to church drove Father with his whole family over the unpaved country road. Now and then, he cracked the whip to make the horses trot faster. I snuggled on Marta's lap and enjoyed watching the green fields passing right and left of us and listening to the skylark twitter a happy tune while she was ascending into the blue sky.

Today, on Easter Sunday, everyone joined in, celebrating the resurrection of Christ joyfully. Emma sang with the church choir before the sermon began. At the end of the sermon, the pastor exclaimed: "Christ is risen!" The parishioners responded joyfully, "He is risen indeed!" After the sermon about the resurrection of Christ and the benediction, everyone left the church. People stopped at the church square to visit neighbors and friends. Georg and Father hitched the horses to the carriage and drove swiftly home.

Easter Sunday, relatives came to visit us. Mother and my sisters prepared duck with a special potato dish (Kugel in German) and red cabbage for lunch. Since my father could not afford to buy real coffee, hickory coffee and cake followed for dessert. We especially welcomed Aunt Minna Schloesser, the sister of my father, and her five children. My sisters played board games with our cousins Greta, Wilma, and Emma, while the boys and cousin Erich amused themselves with outdoor fun. Herta, the youngest cousin, and I entertained ourselves with the Easter eggs. We each rolled an egg down the knoll on the lawn to see whose egg would go furthest. We also played with my doll, which my sister Marta had made for me the previous year. Unfortunately, Uncle Schloesser could not join us because he served as a soldier in World War II, and so did Uncles Otto, August, and Georg. The day passed only too fast before my aunt and cousins returned to the village, and we went content to sleep.

The next few days passed happily, following my sister Marta around the house and outside. One day, when we walked by the hen incubating eggs, we heard a chirp. Gently Marta moved the hen over, and we saw a petite chick breaking the shell of an egg. I ran to Mother, took her hand, and told her: "Mother, Mother, come quickly; a chick is peeking from an egg!" Mother followed me, and I showed her the baby chick in the broken eggshell.

"It is still too early to take it from the nest, but we will watch the eggs very closely from now on," Mother replied. She went to get a box and put it next to the nest. Later my mother and Marta retrieved one little chick after the other, placed them gently in a box by the stove, and threw away the broken eggshells. After two or three days, all eggs had hatched, and the hen left the nest to be with her baby chicks in a small pen surrounded by chicken wire. Unfortunately, it was also time for Marta to go, which made us all sad.

"Do you have to leave?" I questioned her, "Why can't you stay with us all the time?"

"I need to help Mrs. Kessler with her three children." Marta answered, "Come, let us go and say goodbye to everyone before I leave." I did not let her hand go and walked with her until the end of the hill. "You better run home now." Marta insisted.

"When are you coming back?" I inquired while Marta bent down to embrace me.

"Pretty soon, go now, go." I turned and dashed home quickly.

A few more days passed, and the ducklings hatched, and four weeks later, the baby geese and turkeys arrived. After Edmund came home from school, he watched the little ducklings, the baby geese, and warded off crows and hawks from snatching them away. I helped Richard with the chicks. Every morning Mother counted each baby fowl and did the same in the evening before putting them in the hen house for the night. One day, Richard and I played with an old bicycle and drove too far away from the hen with the chicks. A crow dove down, snatched a baby chick, and flew off with it. We yelled at the craw, hoping she would drop her prey, but to no avail. The rest of the afternoon we spent in fear of awaited punishment. We hoped my mother would forget to count the chicks that day, but she did not—instead, she scolded us and gave us a spanking with Father's leather belt. From then on, we always stayed close to the hen with the chicks. I enjoyed watching the ducklings, and the baby geese waddling down to the pond, jumping into the water, and taking their first swim, following the mother duck and goose very closely. While my brother Edmund herded the baby ducks and geese by the pond, he fished with his homemade fishing pole and hook. He tied a cork on the line as a bobber. When the cork disappeared in the water, he knew he had caught a fish, and he raised the stick quickly and brought the fish to the shore. Sometimes, he became more absorbed in fishing than carrying out his chore. A punishment awaited him at the end of the day when my mother discovered a missing duckling.

A week or so after Easter, my father prepared the field for planting potatoes. Mother and Emma cut each potato in half and put them in big baskets. Then they placed each half with the cut side on the bottom, about a foot apart in shallow furrows. Father covered the potatoes with a plow from each side, forming grooves and rows of knolls.

Pentecost followed in the middle of June when nature put on the most festive and colorful attire. Emma and Meta went to the nearby grove and cut birch branches. I ran along and picked flowers I found along the way. We placed a bouquet of wildflowers on the dining room table. We wove a garland from tender green twigs and fastened it on the frame of the entrance door. All the young girls wore white dresses. We celebrated Pentecost at home, or we went to visit uncles, aunts, and cousins. The entire family went to church. To all our delight, Marta came again to celebrate this memorable holiday with us. Little did we know that this was the last Pentecost we all would celebrate together as a family.

In July, the grass in the meadows stood high, and many wildflowers, clover, and other leafy plants spread a thick carpet over the fields. When we heard the musical tinkle of the whetstone and Father sharpening his scythe, we knew it was time to cut the grass in the meadows. Mother and I would take lunch to Father, so he would not waste time coming home. Mother spread a small tablecloth on the freshly cut hay and unwrapped sandwiches with homemade sausage. "Sit down, Gustav, it is time to take a break and eat. You got quite a bit mowed already; you think you will be able to finish by tonight?" Mother asked while handing a sandwich to Father along with a bottle of raspberry juice.

"I should finish before sunset," Father replied, then took one bite after the other until he consumed two sandwiches. Mother and I ate one each while we sat in the grass and inhaled the delightful aroma of the fresh-cut hay and many flowers that lay in long-faded rows. I ran into the field and picked some wildflowers before my father mowed them down. Happily, my mother and I headed home.

For several days, the hay lay in the sun to dry. Then, Emma, Meta, and Georg went to the meadow to turn the hay with a rake and form rows. After the sun dried the grass completely, Father Emma, Meta, and Georg brought the hay wagon to the meadow. Georg held the horses. Emma stayed on top of the wagon while Father and Meta lifted the hay with a pitchfork. Emma stacked the hay up in front of the wagon first and then moved back until she reached the end of the wagon. Meta raked the hay. Father left behind. Sometimes, Edmund, Richard, and I fetched a ride home in the soft hay on the wagon. Once home, Father and Georg unloaded the hay and stacked it up in the barn.

The wheat swayed gently in the breeze and undulated in waves across the field. Father knew by the end of August that it was harvesting time. He called the young men and women from our neighborhood to help us. In turn, Father, Emma, and Meta would help the neighbors when ready for their harvest. The men cut row after row with their scythes. A woman followed behind each man, quickly taking two handfuls of wheat stalks, making a knot at the end to form a rope. They gathered an armful of wheat stalks and promptly tied the rope around to create a sheaf, which they dropped to the ground.

Mother remained home to prepare a hefty lunch, which she took to the field. I ran along and helped her carrying a bundle of plates. Everyone welcomed a break at noon to rest and eat and engage in lively conversations. The men discussed the recent political affairs, while women and girls chatted about family events. The men helped the women and girls to put up the sheaves into stacks. Before the sun painted the western sky golden, the men put their scythes over the shoulder and marched home. Women and girls followed them. Everyone rushed to the pond to wash off the dust from their faces, arms, and legs. The women and girls wore no socks, and their legs and feet bled from the stubble's cuts.

While everyone cleaned up and chatted happily, I stood on the shore and watched the cheerful bathers. Emma approached me with a stone in her hand: "Here, Hildke, take this stone and throw it into the water to splash the neighbor." I took the stone and flung it into the water. Unfortunately, it hit our neighbor Gustav Both's leg instead of dropping straight into the water. He screamed: "Who was the scoundrel? Wait until I get you." He limped out of the water, looking at the bleeding wound on his leg. When he saw me running away, he knew it was I who tossed the stone.

I dashed uphill and hid in the outhouse, hoping he would not find me there. I did not want to face Mother either; she would have punished me also. I quickly secured the door with the hook, stood behind the door, and peeked through the heart-shaped hole to ensure nobody followed me. Nobody did. One after the other came up from the pond and entered the house. I listened to the chatting inside during supper while I shivered in the outhouse, and my stomach growled. I was hungry, very hungry. I watched and waited, watched and waited. Darkness enveloped the farm; only the lights of the house illuminated the courtyard dimly. I guess nobody even noticed my absence. Time seemed to stand still. I was cold and hoped to see the neighbors leave, but they stayed and stayed. It seemed like midnight when I finally saw the neighbors and Father come out of the house and say good night to each other. I waited a little longer before I dared to go into the house.

"It was your fault, Emma," I scolded her. "You should not have asked me to throw the stone in the water."

"I am very sorry; I ask your forgiveness," Emma responded while she embraced me. "Where were you all this time?"

"I hid in the outhouse until I saw the neighbors leave,"

"All this time, you waited in the outhouse, you poor thing. You must be cold and hungry. Sit down and eat something before I put you to bed."

"Let me have a glass of milk and a sandwich," I replied, looking at mother, wondering if she would reprimand me. I felt relieved when my mother said nothing, and I jumped on the bed and quickly crawled under the warm feather cover. It took three more days to mow the wheat fields. But from that time on, I always hid someplace when our neighbor Gustav Both came to visit us. I still felt remorse and was afraid of his punishment.

Father waited until the stalks with the grain dried in the field before he brought them home. They unloaded the sheaves in the barn. After the last wagon came home, Emma made a harvest crown. With a string, she attached short stalks of grain to a crown-shaped form made of wire. She hung it on the kitchen ceiling. It was a yearly tradition to show gratitude to the Creator for a bountiful harvest. Neighbors, relatives, and family celebrated with good food and drinks, the rich yield of the fields.

After all the neighbors finished bringing in the crops, they helped each other with the wheat, oats, and rye thrashing. We had neither electric nor gasoline machinery; Father built a special contraption (called Rosswerk in German) to move the thrashing machine's wheels. Father attached two or more horses to the end of a long beam. Someone led one horse or rode on it to keep it moving at a steady pace. When the horses moved around and around, they put the wheels and the belt in motion. In turn, the belt moved the mechanism in the thrashing machine that separated the grain from the chaff. A person pushed down only a few stalks at a time so it would not jam and stop. It took several days before the threshing process ended at our farm. Then my father went to neighbors or relatives to help them with their threshing.

Cutting Turf and Harvesting Flax

When wildflowers spread their blossoms across the meadows and the marshes during the summer, Father prepared a part of the swamp for cutting turf. Father staked out a square of about fifteen feet. He dug a narrow trench around the area. Then he cut the turf piece by piece with a spade and threw it up to the adjacent marsh. After he removed two or three layers of peat, water filled up the hole. He dug a ditch to drain the water into a lower meadow. When the heap reached a specific size, Father handed buckets of water to Emma and Meta, who threw the water over the turf. Father climbed out of the pit, harnessed the two horses, and trampled barefoot behind the horse until the turf pieces were broken up and formed a thick semi-solid black sludge. Father drove a sled-like box of sludge further away to the meadow. Emma and Meta filled a form sectioned off in brick-sized compartments with the sludge, lifted it, leaving the brick-like turf on the ground. They repeated the process until they finished all the black turf mud. After a few days, my mother and older sisters turned the turf bricks to let them dry completely on both sides. Father took them to the ranch and stored them in the shed. Since turf burnt slower than wood, my mother used it in addition to firewood for cooking on the wood range and heating the tiled oven (Kachelofen) in the wintertime.

Making Turf

The flax harvest began when the delicate blue blossoms turned to seeds. Father, Mother, and Emma walked through the field and collected the seeds first. The entire family then pulled the plants by the handful out of the ground and tied them into sheaves. Father loaded the flax sheaves into a wagon and drove them home. Father dug a hole, built a square wooden structure of thin posts around it, and stacked the flax sheaves against it. He lit a fire inside the hole to quickly dry the flax stalks. Father and Mother untied bundle after bundle, placed them on the floor in the barn, and beat them with a wooden flail until the husks broke up into small pieces and, when shaken, fell out of the shell. Mother washed the fibers in another water bath, and when semi-dry, she pulled one handful at a time through a fine metal comb made from many rows of thin nails to remove the refined husks and divide the fiber into delicate threads. Once more, the threads needed to dry before my mother tied them into small bundles.

In winter, the fields lay fallow, and work began at home. Mother, Emma, and Meta took turns to spin the flax threads into fine yarn. Later they wove linen cloth and sewed bed sheets, shirts, and underwear from the woven material. The home-woven fabric was at first rough to the touch, but it softened somewhat after repeated washings. During the summer, my mother spread the linens on the lawn and let the sunlight bleach them. Sometimes the geese or ducks waddled across the sheets and left green spots behind, which made it necessary to rewash them.

First Day of School

In 1943, World War II ravaged all around us, but we still felt safe at home. I turned six years in January and became eligible to enroll in grammar school. On the first day, my father made it a point to drive me with my brothers to the big schoolhouse in Wizajny. I slowed down to look around as my father walked me to the classroom, which the teacher assigned. First, the teacher introduced herself: "My name is Miss (Fraeulein) Brandt." Miss Brandt called each student by name and asked them to stand up so the classmates could remember their names. Then the teacher handed each pupil a slate board (Schiefertafel) surrounded by a wooden frame and a pen (Griffel in German) made of light gray slate. A foot-long string tied to a hole in the frame with two small sponges dangled on the strings.

The sponges served to erase the writing. On one side of the slate board, small squares were engraved for writing numbers and on the other side lines for writing words. The first day Miss Brandt wrote the numbers from l to 10 on the big blackboard. She asked us to copy each number in a little square as she made us repeat each number after her. Then she wrote the A B C letters on the blackboard and told us to write them on the lines on the other side. When we completely covered our slate board with numbers and letters, we went to the front and showed it to the teacher. She told us where we needed to improve our writing. We dipped one sponge in water, erased the letters and numbers, and dried the board with the other. Then we started to write all over again.

My brother, Georg, who attended the same school, waited until my class was over and walked home with me. Father had too much work to do on the ranch to pick me up at school. I ran to my mother and showed her the first letters and numbers I had learned to write.

"Look, Mother, I can write," I exclaimed while pointing to the letters on the slate board. After lunch, I sat down and practiced and practiced until the letters flowed more easily and looked neater.

The following day, with my slate board under my arm, I walked to school with Georg, Edmund, and Richard. We took a shortcut across the big pasture that saved us a lot of time. I enjoyed learning new things each day and getting acquainted with my classmates. After Fraeulein Brandt worked with the students for several months, she separated the quick and slow learners. To my delight, she placed me in the rapid learner group. She taught all students together first; then, she gave the slow learners projects while teaching the fast learners more advanced subjects and vice versa. I satisfied my curiosity by learning new things each day. I also did not mind walking to school by myself once I knew the shortcut to Wizajny. I had no classes on Saturday and Sunday.

As time flew by, the storks also flew away and left the empty nest on the barn roof. When Horst was born, I thanked the storks the following spring for bringing us another baby brother. I enjoyed playing with him after I got home from school. In October flocks of wild geese settled on the nearby fields to feed. They honked, then raised their wings to take flight. They assembled in V formations and migrated south to spend the winter in a warmer climate. Many other migratory birds departed, and November marked the end of fall.

Father and Georg hurried to the nearby forest to cut firewood for the winter. Yes, winter came quickly and transformed the scenery, covering our path to school with snow. It took us much longer to plod through the deep snow across the pastures to school. Once I got caught in a blizzard. I could not see any reference points and got lost. I just kept going while the wind propelled the snowflakes into my face and eyes and blinded me. When I began climbing the hill, the only one in our area, I knew I was close to our house, and my mother would welcome me home shortly. After that episode, my father or a neighbor drove us to and from school by sleigh whenever a blizzard blustered through our area.

Our hand-knitted wool socks, mittens, and sweaters kept our bones from clattering. Coats made from home-woven woolen material kept the wind and cold from our bodies. Before entering the classroom, we had to take off our coats, caps, and shoes and put on slippers made from straw. During intermission, the school provided fresh raw carrots, turnips, or sauerkraut for nourishment.

Due to the war, supplies were scarce; only the school owned books, which the students could use in class. We were not allowed to take any books home. We formed sentences with the different words we had learned. We also copied sentences on our slate board and read them repeatedly until we knew the sentences by heart. However, we made do with the little we had. After we learned the numbers, the teacher showed us how to solve simple mathematical addition and subtraction problems.

Before Christmas, our teacher took us tobogganing. We pulled our sleds up a small hill, then two students sat together, and with a push of our feet, we started downhill. Faster and faster, we raced downhill onto the frozen lake. The toboggans kept going for some time on the ice before they came to a complete stop. Quickly, we went up the hill to take yet another and another downhill run until the teacher asked us to go home. How invigorating! When I arrived home, I was exhausted and crawled under the warm down cover shortly after supper.

Edmund and Richard each took two curved boards from a big barrel, put some leather straps on top to fasten their shoes to the boards, and skied down the nearby hill. Sometimes, they stumbled and rolled over several times and slid for a while before they could stand up on their homemade skis and complete the downhill run. Edmund made ice skates for my brother Richard and me by nailing two thick wires on each sole of our wooden shoes. We skated back and forth on the frozen pond, seeing who could go fastest. Mostly, Richard won the races.

The winter and the year 1943 came to an end, and 1944 brought many changes. Almost five years passed since Germany began World War II. During spring, German soldiers dug trenches close to our village and prepared the terrain to fight against the Russian red army that slowly approached East Prussia's border. By midsummer, many civilians, young boys who belonged to the Hitler Youth, and young girls were ordered to dig deep, wide trenches along the eastern border to prevent the Russian tanks from advancing into East Prussia.

In the middle of July 1944, my father was drafted into the army. Broken-hearted, he left my mother and his eight children behind. Tears rolled down his cheeks while he embraced each of his children to say goodbye. I had never seen Father crying before. I was wondering what happened? My mother explained to us later that my father was drafted into the army. He did not have to fight as a combat soldier but was ordered to prepare the battlefield, digging trenches, building structures, or destroying bridges.

Only for a short time were the German soldiers able to prevent the Russian army from reaching the border and invading East Prussia. Hitler and his local commander, Erich Koch, made no provision for the civilians in a Russian offensive. Their command was to hold the Prussian front under any circumstances and not permit the people to leave. He wanted to keep the highways and roads free for the soldiers to fight the Russians if they invaded East Prussia. However, many mayors took it upon themselves to order their citizens to abandon their homes and go to the West.

Chapter 8
Escape from East Prussia

IT HAPPENED ON August 3, 1944, a messenger from Wizajny came by bicycle. He knocked on the door at midnight. Mother woke up and rushed to the door, thinking perhaps a neighbor needed help. Instead, when she opened the door, she was stunned to see a stranger standing before her. He announced, "The Russians are coming! Hurry, hurry, you must leave! Be at the village square at 9:00 a.m. this morning." Before my mother had a chance to ask any questions, the stranger mounted his bicycle and hurried away.

Mother, stunned by such grim news, rushed into the bedroom, shouting, "Children get up quickly; we have to leave in a few hours; the Russians are coming." We jumped out of bed and followed Mother's orders: "Georg, you get the wagon ready, feed the horses, and take plenty of oats along. Also, give enough hay for the cows. Emma, you gather all the sausages and ham from the smokehouse. Pack the canned goods from the cellar and take a sack of flour from the attic. Meta, you pack clothes for everyone. Also, take winter coats, bulky sweaters, woolen socks, and gloves along. Edmund, Richard, you feed the turkeys, geese, ducks, and hens. Hilda, you wash and dress Horst." From midnight to dawn, we rushed back and forth to get ready as rapidly as possible. Mother discovered only two loaves of bread in the pantry. Immediately, she lit a fire in the oven and prepared bread dough. While the dough was rising, she gathered all her good china, silverware, and other valuable household articles in a wooden box. Mother asked Georg and Edmund to dig a deep hole in the garden to bury the box, hoping to find her things when returning home. Mother managed to have five extra loaves of bread ready before dawn. Still warm, she put them in a clean sack to cool off and then placed them on the wagon. We rushed nonstop by lantern light until dawn, packing all the things and items we could think of we would need.

The sun rose and spread her golden rays around our house and over the fields like any other day. Quickly, Mother gathered her family around the dining table, and after saying grace, served them a soup made from flour dumplings boiled in milk; we called it Klunkersuppe in East Prussian dialect. She also fried some pancakes, made mainly from eggs with a bit of flour. Emma stacked them on a metal plate, tied them in a clean cloth, and put them on the wagon with all the other foodstuffs.

"Meta, fill a milk can with water and tie it to the wagon," Mother demanded.

I grabbed my dollhouse, ran to my mother: "Can I take my dollhouse along, too?" "No, Hildke, we don't have enough room on the wagon; just take the doll with you." Even though I was sad to leave behind my beautiful dollhouse, I obeyed my mother's request.

We all gathered outside by the wagon. Mother went once more from room to room and took a last look at all the things she cherished. Sadness stretched her heart and welled up tears in her eyes as she said goodbye to her beloved home, where all of her eight children were born, and where she found her husband and happiness raising her family. She did not know if or when she would ever see her homestead again.

She was also concerned about Marta. My mother could not send a message to her. We all worried about what would happen to her. Would she be able to flee with the teacher's family on time? These thoughts grieved Mother. She folded her hands, lifted her eyes to heaven, and commended her safety into the hands of God. She called Emma and Meta and asked them: "Gather all the feather beds and put them on top of the wagon, too." Mother walked rapidly into the stable and gave a last glance at her cows, calves, and pigs. She opened the door to the hen house and let out the hens, geese, ducks, and turkeys. She spread sufficient food outside to last for several days.

Emma ran over to our German Shepherd Senta, hugged her, and released her from the chain. "Hildke, and Richard, you get on the wagon." Mother also climbed with Horst on the front seat next to Emma, who took the reins. Emma cracked the whip, and our two horses Kastan and Kobel, began pulling our loaded wagon toward our town, Wizajny. Meta, Georg, and Edmund walked uphill alongside the wagon until we reached the top. Emma stopped the horses and let everybody climb on the wagon. Mother turned around once more to look at her beloved home. The thought of not knowing when or if she might see her homestead again filled her heart with profound sadness. She was concerned about Marta's fate. She also worried about her husband's whereabouts.

When Emma saw Senta, our faithful dog, following us, she climbed down from the wagon. She took her head, looked into her eyes, and tearfully demanded: "Senta, you must go back and watch the farm. You can't come with us; go, go back, Senta." Senta understood; obediently, she made a turn and slowly trotted homeward. Emma hopped on the wagon, and off we drove. We passed through golden wheat and rye fields ready to be harvested in two to three weeks. We drove by green pastures filled with grazing cattle. Shortly before 9:00 a.m., we reached Wizajny.

Wagon after wagon filled the town square. Women, children, and older adults sat on top of the gathered household goods, loaded quickly on the wagons.

"Form a line and let's go," the mayor shouted, pointing to the next wagon to enter the line, and a long procession began to move.

Our journey to an unknown destination started on August 4. 1944, and nobody knew how long it would last or where it would end.

The August sun spread her warm rays over the somber trek of people sitting on their laden wagons. Children chattered and asked many questions, but adults found no words, for their hearts overflowed with grief and melancholy for having to leave their homes so suddenly.

The horses trotted over the dusty country road for several hours before they came to a halt in the Rominter Heide forest. We paused to feed the horses and give them water, and the folks ate sandwiches or whatever they had brought along. Mother gave us her homemade pancakes and a cup of water to drink. Georg packed oats into the small feeding sack and fastened it to each horse's bridle so they could eat without wasting any fodder. After he removed the fodder bags, he gave them a bucket of water. Now Georg took the reins, and Mother and Horst sat beside him; I sat right behind Horst while Emma, Meta, Edmund, and Richard walked alongside the wagon.

The wagons rolled on until dusk draped the landscape slowly; it was time to stop and look for shelter in the forest. The wagons moved over to the right as far as possible to leave enough room for passing trucks. While Mother and Emma made sandwiches, Edmund, Richard, and I explored the forest. "Stay close to the wagons," Mother warned. "We will," Edmund replied. Off we went. How good it felt to be able to run around after sitting in the wagon all day long.

"It is getting dark; we better return to the wagon," Edmund signaled us to follow him, which we did. During twilight, we consumed our sandwiches and settled down to sleep on the open wagon among the feather beds. Four of us lined up in front and four in the wagon's rear end—all legs facing toward the inside. The mothers comforted their crying children while putting them to sleep. My eyes stared at the fading light in the sky and watched one star after the other, filling the dark emptiness. Soon, the full moon rose behind the forest, spread a pale veil over the landscape and weary travelers, and wiped away so many stars. Now and then, a cry of a child, a groaning older person, or the howling of wolves broke the silence. Finally, after I said my evening prayer, I fell asleep.

As soon as the sun broke the darkness of the night and kissed creation to life, we rose. Birds twittered happily in the forest, while sad, soundless melodies resonated in the hearts of the mothers and elderly. After we ate and the horses devoured their oats, Georg hitched the horses to the wagon and joined the trek in motion. The clang of horses' hoofs created a rhythmic sound while they pulled their precious cargo of people, food, and household goods hour after hour until sunset. The golden rays swept lavishly over the fields and meadows as we approached the town of Goldap.

We entered the town square, surrounded by a beautiful church and other significant buildings. Soldiers assigned the wagons to various streets and different houses for the night. Some residents had already escaped, leaving their empty houses behind. Others still waited at home, hoping the German army could stop the Russians from advancing into East Prussia. We found shelter with two other families in a beautiful empty farmhouse on the outskirts of Goldap. Georg unhitched the wagon and went to look for some fodder for the horses. The mothers went in first to check where each family would sleep. Since we were the largest family of eight, they decided to occupy one bedroom for Mother, Horst, me, and the rest could sleep in the living room.

Both other Kirstein families would each settle in the more over-sized bedrooms. The mothers gathered in the kitchen. They looked around and found some canned fruit in the pantry and potatoes in the cellar. They decided to cook potato soup and serve the canned fruit as dessert.

The children went to explore the other buildings on the farm. We climbed on top of the haystack and discovered a big bull surrounded by walls of hay. The owner wanted to make sure he could survive on his own for a long time on such an ample hay supply. We were intrigued by his size and mean looks and tried to tease him by throwing hay in his face. He shook it off and started scratching the ground with his right foot. The more fodder we threw at his head, the faster he scratched, giving us vicious looks that sent a chill up my spine.

"We better go back to the house before someone falls into the bull's pit," I begged my brothers. We climbed down and went back to the house, where dinner awaited us. We carried our feather beds into the house and settled down for the night.

The next morning, when the sun's golden glow illuminated the horizon, we began our journey toward Angerburg. By now, soldiers accompanied the trek. They set up outdoor kitchens in strategic locations to offer a sandwich or a vegetable soup with a small amount of meat to the travelers. Today the air felt heavy. In the west, dark clouds raced toward us. We saw flashes of lightning traversing the sky. The thunder rolled closer and closer. Mother busied herself, pulling out a large piece of the canvas she had packed underneath the featherbed. With the help of Emma, she spread it over the feather beds.

"Children, you better climb on the wagon and crawl underneath the canvas before the rain starts."

"Can I walk?" Emma asked, "I love to feel the warm rain running down my face and arms."

"You better come up; you do not know when you can change your wet clothes," Mother insisted.

No sooner had everyone sought shelter under the canvas and the rains came pouring down in sheets. Emma sat down on Georg's right side, Mother in the middle with Horst, and Meta to the left.

Emma and Meta held the canvas over our heads and their own. Georg held the reins tight to steady the horses. Emma and Meta had tied the two back corners of the canvas to the wagon to prevent the wind from blowing it away.

I inched my way to the back, lifted the cover, and stuck my hands outside. The warm raindrops caressed my hands. I turned both palms up, formed a cup, and let it fill with water until it ran down and created a small waterfall. However, when I saw a lightning flash and heard the rolling thunder nearby, I pulled my hands in quickly. I feared the lightning might strike them. The small water pools filled up. When the raindrops hit the surface of the puddles, they created tiny fountains. My feet just itched to get down and dash through the water puddles. The rain ran down the horse's backs and dripped from their mane. Now and then, they would shake their heads to release the water quickly. Their skin looked shiny and clean as they trod over the muddy road. The rain poured down for what seemed to be a long time. Fields and forests welcomed the rain having the dust washed off their foliage.

Slowly the thunder sounded more and more distant, the lighting dimmed and became smaller, and soon the rain stopped completely. A beautiful rainbow spanned across the sky as the sun appeared. Emma and Meta pulled the canvas back, and my mother helped shake off the water that had collected on the cover. "Mother, Mother, can I get down now?" I asked excitedly. "You can get down, but stay on the right side, close to the wagon."

Before she could finish her sentence, I jumped down. Edmund and Richard followed me. We left our shoes on the wagon. How exhilarating to dash through the warm water of the puddles. Richard lifted his right foot out of the water and sent a splash toward me. I quickly returned one to him. Edmund joined us. We played tag for a while. It felt so good to run after sitting still on the wagon for what seemed a long time. We saw another big puddle.

Richard and Edmund began a splashing contest. Richard lifted his right foot, swung it way back, and with the sole sent a water sprout up in the air, "See if you can go further than me," Richard challenged Edmund.

"Of course, I can," Edmund responded. He lifted his foot high and swung backward. He lost his balance and fell back in the water, creating a big splash. I broke out in laughter, which embarrassed him and made him angry.

"Don't laugh at me, you little Biskraet (Ugly toad, in dialect). I'll get you," he shouted at me. I darted forward before he got up. I feared he would punish me for making fun of him. I felt guilty and apologized to him. Cautiously, I hid behind Richard's back while waiting for his response. When he stopped chasing me, I knew he had accepted my apology. I tapped Richard on the shoulder, "Let's play catch," and ran away from him. Richard dashed over to touch Edmund and engage him in the game too.

Emma and Meta stepped down from the wagon to stretch and enjoy a brisk walk, as did many other travelers. Horst fell asleep on his mother's lap. She took one of the square pillows, shaped it like a cradle, and put Horst into it to continue his nap.

At noon, we reached the village of Budden. Everyone hoped to stop there for a short rest. However, the leader sent a message from wagon to wagon to continue in order to reach the next town before nightfall.

Mother called us to come up to the wagon. She prepared a sandwich with homemade sausage for each one of us. It tasted so good outdoors. Tired from playing, I laid down and fell asleep.

By the time I woke up, I could see in the distance the town of Angerburg. The church's spire, the tower, and the castle, which stood on a hill, formed a pleasing silhouette. We drove along the river Angerapp for a short time before we reached the town's market square.

The inhabitants of the town met the wagons and offered the trekkers their homes for spending the night. When our turn came, the official designating places asked, "Who has room for a mother with seven children?" An elderly gentleman stepped forward, "I will take them." As he approached our wagon, he introduced himself as Mr. Lemke and invited us to come to his place. Georg asked him to mount the wagon. He greeted the whole family, and my mother thanked him for taking us to his home. Mr. Lemke and my mother talked along the way. He asked my mother where she came from and where she thought she was going?

"I would like to stay as close to Wizajny as possible, so when the war is over, I can return home again," mother answered.

"I listened to the radio this morning; the Russian army advanced 1000 kilometers within the last six weeks and is not too far away from the East Prussian border. Up to now, East Prussia was an oasis of peace, but now I am afraid the red army might invade our area. I do not know how long the German soldiers will be able to hold back the advancing Russians. At this point, I do not care whether we win or lose the war. I just want it to end before East Prussia falls into the hands of the Russians. I fear for my wife; she has crippling arthritis and is bedridden. In her condition, she cannot travel. So, I have no choice but to remain here. Just the thought of her being tortured or killed by the Russian soldiers makes me tremble," Mr. Lemke expressed his concern to my mother.

"I would be terrified to see my daughters being brutalized by the Russian soldiers also. I heard they rape any woman regardless of age. God forbid they would harm or kill my daughters," Mother uttered while her expression turned sinister, and she shrugged her shoulders.

"Let's hope that will never happen," Mr. Lemke responded. He then pointed to the farm ahead, "This is my house. Children, you can get down and run ahead. But be quiet, my wife is sick, and she might be asleep."

Edmund, Richard, and I jumped from the wagon and ran to the house. Quietly, we looked around until the wagon arrived in the courtyard. "Wait, children, first I want my wife to meet you all." With those words, he waited until everyone was assembled at the front door, then asked us to come in. Mr. Lemke knocked on the bedroom door first, "I brought a mother with seven children to stay with us for a while. Darling (Liebchen), is it alright to come in?" When he heard her saying, "Yes, come in," he opened the bedroom door. Mrs. Lemke wore a pink knitted bed jacket and rested in bed. She greeted us with a smile when Mr. Lemke introduced her to us, "This is my wife, Erna Lemke," then pointing to mother, "this is Mrs. Bonacker and her seven children. I'll let Mrs. Bonacker introduce her children to you." Mother named my oldest sisters first, then the three boys, then me, and at last Horst, whom she held in her arms. The girls smiled and made a curtsy, and the boys bowed their heads and smiled when my mother introduced them.

Mrs. Lemke welcomed us. Then Mr. Lemke showed us the living room, where we were supposed to sleep. He also took my mother to the kitchen. "This is our kitchen. We will have to take turns in cooking. Now you can use the kitchen. We already ate before I went to town. Your children must be hungry. Go ahead and get settled."

Mother stretched out her hand and, with a handshake, responded, "Thank you so much for sharing your lovely home with us." Then my mother turned to us: "Go and bring all the feather beds and linens in the house. Emma and Meta, you prepare supper." Emma and Meta took the food supplies to the kitchen and prepared sausage sandwiches for us.

After supper, Richard and I went outside to check out the farm. We found Mr. Lemke milking the cow. We investigated the vegetable garden next to the barn. We did not dare to pick a cucumber or pull a carrot out of the ground. The red apples and ripe pears peeking at us from the trees tempted us even more. Mother had strictly forbidden us to take anything that did not belong to us. So, we just passed by, longing for the taste of a juicy apple or a sweet pear. As we ran by the hen house, the hens jumped up and croaked loudly. Georg and Edmund had tied up our horses next to Mr. Lemke's and put a hay heap in front of them. Soon, my mother called us to come into the house. It was bedtime.

The second day, Mr. Lemke permitted me to visit Mrs. Lemke. I entered a beautifully decorated bedroom and greeted Mrs. Lemke with a curtsy and a "Good Morning, Mrs. Lemke."

"Come here, little girl," she invited me to come close to her. She took my hand and asked me what my name was.

"Hildegard," I replied.

"Where did you come from?"

"From Wizajny," I responded.

"Where are you going?"

"I do not know," I replied, shrugging my shoulders.

Mrs. Lemke asked no further questions; instead, she invited me to sit down on the bed next to her: "I will tell you a story. Do you know the fairytale of Hansel and Gretel?"

"No!"

"Then I will tell it to you,"

She began, "Hansel and Gretel lived in the forest. One day while picking berries, they got lost. They came to a gingerbread house where a wicked witch lived, who wanted to kill and eat them. But Hansel was courageous; he pushed the wicked witch into the burning furnace. They found their way back home again. Their parents welcomed their children with great joy when they returned unharmed from the woods."

"You see, Hildegard, never walk away from home alone; otherwise, a witch might get you, too," she warned me.

"No, no, I will never walk away from Mother," I reassured her while thinking of the wicked witch. She released my hand and let me go.

"You can come back tomorrow if you like to."

"Thank you; I will. Can I bring my brother Richard, too?" I asked.

"Sure."

I ran back to my mother and reported to her the kind lady told me a fairytale. She invited Richard and me to come back tomorrow for another story.

"That is good; you can go again," Mother informed me. I was so glad that my mother approved. I looked forward to my next visit with Mrs. Lemke.

After lunch, Edmund invited Richard and me to go to town. We walked along the lake and reached the town square where the red brick church of St. Peter and Paul stood. The church was built in a simple Roman architectural style. The colossal clock on the tower chimed one. Edmund wanted to see the inside of the church. He pushed against the heavy door. To his dismay, he found it locked. We walked through part of town and discovered the old castle. We explored the courtyard and checked for open doors, but we had no luck peeking inside. Then we strolled along the lake before we headed back to the farm.

When Georg saw Edmund, he asked him if he could help him cleaning the cow stall. Richard and I looked around to see if we could find a chip of a porcelain plate to play "School." When he found none, he picked up two small flat stones and gave me one, "This will do."

He picked up a stick and drew a big rectangle on the ground. Then he divided it into six equal squares of approximately one and a half feet wide. He drew a semi-circle on the rectangle's end, which was named heaven (Himmel).

Richard offered me to start the game we called class (Klasse). I took my stone and threw it backward. If it landed outside the lines or on a line, I lost my turn. When it landed inside a square or in heaven, I would start pushing the stone in the following box with the right foot while lifting the left foot off the ground. My stone landed in the second square, so I pushed it into the third. We could only give it one push each turn.

Richard threw his stone backward right into heaven and then pushed it directly into the 4th class. The objective was to get through all the squares (classes) flawlessly as fast as possible to win the game. You could also push your opponent out of the class or on a line with your stone. Then he had to start from the beginning again. We played four games. Richard won three games and I only one.

When we saw Mr. Lemke, we asked him, "Could we visit Mrs. Lemke now?" When he said yes, we went inside the house and knocked on the bedroom door. "Come in," Mrs. Lemke answered. We opened the door and walked over to her. After I curtsied, I introduced my brother Richard; she bade us sit down on the floor next to her bed.

"Which fairy tale do you want to hear today, Rumpelstilzchen or Little Red Riding Hood?"

Before Richard had a chance to speak, I quickly responded, "Little Red Riding Hood, please." We sat there quietly as she narrated how little Red Riding Hood took a basket full of food to her grandmother who lived in the forest. Little Red Riding Hood found that the big, bad wolf ate her grandmother and slept in her grandmother's bed to her horror. She ran to the tailor. He came, opened the belly of the wolf, and removed the grandmother, who was still alive. The tailor filled the stomach with stones and sewed it back together. When the wolf woke from his sleep, he was thirsty. He hobbled to the river to drink, keeled over, and drowned. Little Red Riding Hood and Grandmother lived happily ever after.

"That is all for today; you can come back tomorrow." Richard and I got up. We both shook hands.

I expressed our gratitude with the following words, "Thank you, thank you so much for telling us stories; we shall see you tomorrow."

We ran back to the kitchen, where my mother and dinner awaited us. Mr. Lemke brought a metal pitcher filled with warm milk, some sausage, and freshly baked bread. He pointed to the kitchen cabinets, "You can use the porcelain plates and cups, which are in there."

After my mother thanked Mr. Lemke, Emma and Meta set the table with the colorful porcelain plates. The table looked festive. However, a bouquet of fresh flowers would have enhanced it. After all of us children sat down and folded our hands, Mother bowed her head and thanked God for her children's safety, the generous landlord, and his gifts. As soon as she said, "Amen," all hands reached for a piece of bread and some sausage. It tasted so good with a glass of fresh milk.

The warm August air, filled with the scent of flowers, entered through the open window. The sun began to descend and painted the horizon orange and gold. A gentle breeze carried a melodious song of a nightingale through the window. The night gently spread her soft dark cloak over the land and put nature and people to sleep. However, I could not fall asleep for some time, thinking about the big, bad wolf and hoping he would not come to devour one of us.

The following day, while we ate breakfast, we heard a male voice shouting, "Attention, this is an order." We all ran out of the kitchen and saw a messenger on horseback. When he saw us, he continued announcing through the megaphone, "The pasture is full of cows that need milking. Come and bring as many containers with you as you can. Go to the town square, and someone will take you to the pasture."

The messenger lowered the megaphone and rode off to deliver his message to the next ranch.

"Mother, Mother, can Richard and I go along," I begged mother.

"Only if you promise to stay close to Emma and Meta and help them," Mother responded.

I replied, "I will; I will, I promise," jumping up and down in excitement. Richard and I ran to Emma and Meta, who gathered and washed buckets and milk cans. Off we went. Emma and Meta carried the milk can and a bucket; so did Georg and Edmund. Richard and I followed them while Mother and Horst stayed home.

We came to the marketplace where people passed through to the designated pastures. Shortly after we left the town, we heard the mooing of the cows in the distance. The closer we got to the field, the louder it grew.

"Wow, look at all these cows," Georg exclaimed, astounded.

Edmund added in astonishment as he glimpsed over the vast number of cows in two separate pastures, "I never saw so many cows before. Where did they all come from?"

The cows which needed milking were gathered in one pasture, and the ones already milked filled the adjacent field.

Many women milked already, and more and more came to fill their containers with fresh milk. Emma and Meta each found a cow. They patted the cow first on her head and then on the belly before sitting down on the buckets and starting to milk. We heard the loud stream hitting the metal bottom of the bucket, mixed with the cows' mooing. Some cows not milked for several days had extended udders and experienced pain when touched. They first kicked and mooed in agony but calmed down after the pressure of their udder was relieved, and the last drop of milk streamed into the pail.

Emma always asked us to stay close to her. Emma and Meta filled one pail after another, then poured it into the milk can. When the milk can was half full, Emma asked Georg and Edmund to take it back to the farm and have my mother empty it.

"Make sure you come back as soon as possible," she insisted.

"We will," Georg assured her.

When Georg and Edmund brought the milk, my mother poured it into a portable metal washtub. She washed the milk can and sent the boys back to the pasture with six sandwiches placed on a metal plate wrapped in a clean dishcloth. She gave the bundle to Georg, warning him, "Make sure you do not eat them along the way."

The clock of the church steeple struck twelve times when Edmund and Georg passed through the town. They knew it was lunchtime and hurried to the pasture. It took a while to find Emma, Meta, Richard, and me among the crowd. We were all delighted to fill our hungry stomachs with a salami sandwich, washed down with warm milk.

After the brief pause for lunch, Emma and Meta continued to milk until they filled up both milk cans and their pails. Then we all went back to the farm with our fresh milk.

"I am glad the day is over. My hands are aching," Emma remarked.

Meta added, "Mine are sore, too. I never milked so many cows in one day. Some cows must not have been milked for some time. Their udders were extended to the point of bursting."

"Yes, the poor cows suffer if nobody milks them frequently."

"You see, how lucky the bulls are; they do not need to be milked," Georg interposed and giggled.

Emma and Meta began to chuckle also, "Yes, they sure are lucky; they do not bear calves either."

By the time we reached the farm, the sun stood low and tinged our brows with a golden glow. Mother welcomed us with dinner. Utilizing the fresh milk, she made a soup with flour dumplings in it. She took the filled buckets from us and poured them into the metal tub. They placed the two milk cans in the pantry, which had no windows and was cooler than the other rooms. Shortly after dinner, Emma and Meta went to bed. We all sat around the table and talked for a while before joining them, and sleep came quickly, and we closed our eyes.

When the faint blush of dawn entered through the window, we arose and began another busy day. Mother asked Emma and Meta to help with the milking and give the milk to someone else. We had enough for the moment. So, they went to the pasture with their empty pails, and my brothers and I followed them.

Mother waited until enough cream settled on the top of the milk. She removed it and poured it into a barrel for making butter. My mother then sat down next to the barrel, putting the stem with the round wooden disk into it. She closed the barrel with a wooden cover and began to push the inner disk vigorously up and down to move the cream quickly around. After some time, the fat clumps formed. My mother removed the butter clumps and placed them in a pot of cold water. She moved them around to get the milk washed out. She repeated the procedure until the water was clear. Then she squeezed all the small clusters together and formed a big ball of butter. She placed it in a pot and took it down to the cold cellar. She also saved the buttermilk in the basement to keep it from turning rancid. Mother also gave Mr. and Mrs. Lemke a big chunk of butter to express gratitude for providing shelter to her large family and all utensils needed. The milking and churning butter went on for a short time before a messenger came and told us to be ready to leave town in two days.

Mother, Emma, and Meta washed all the bed linens and clothes and baked bread for the journey. Georg and Edmund groomed the horses and asked Mr. Lemke for some oats to take along for the horses. Richard and I asked permission to visit Mrs. Lemke once more and to listen perhaps to another fairytale. Mrs. Lemke enjoyed telling stories to children and welcomed the opportunity to entertain us. She told us some pranks of Max and Moritz from Wilhelm Busch's book to cheer us up. In the end, Mrs. Lemke warned us not to repeat their mischievous tricks. Even though sadness wreathed her kind face because she knew she would never see us again, she still wanted us to be happy during these brief hours shared with her.

After breakfast, we all carried our belongings and featherbeds to the wagon.

"Can I run over to Mrs. Lemke and say goodbye to her?" I begged mother.

"Make it quick; we have to leave and meet the other wagons in a few minutes."

"I will; I will," I promised and ran to Mrs. Lemke. "I came to say goodbye."

I reached for her hand, and she took mine. She held my hand in hers for some time before she uttered with tears in her eyes, "Goodbye, little girl, God protect you from all harm."

"Goodbye, Mrs. Lemke," I replied while I kissed her on the forehead. I dashed out when I heard my mother calling me. Mother entered the bedroom to thank Mrs. Lemke and said goodbye on behalf of the whole family. Then we all thanked Mr. Lemke for letting us stay with him and for the food he gave us to take along.

Off we went. We joined the other refugees at the town square and began our journey. We drove along the east shore of Mauer Lake, then continued going westward. We only made a short stop for lunch and continued until dusk. When we reached a large estate already vacated, we decided to spend the night there, and six wagons joined us.

Several children got off the wagons and got acquainted with each other. Mrs. Marta Kirstein, a war widow, had a nine-month-old baby girl named Renate, besides a son Waldemar. Ernst

Hein was only a toddler like my brother Horst, and Ewald Heisel was five. Mrs. Heisel's husband died in combat during the war. We also met the eighty-year-old father of Mrs. Helene Hein; we called him Mr. Balschat. Fritz Kirstein, a wounded soldier on leave, joined his family.

My sisters engaged in conversations with Grete Kirstein, Wanda and Greta Liedke, and Erna Ambrosat while the mothers attended to their young children's needs. The women gathered in the kitchen. They checked the pantry, hoping to come across some food. Unfortunately, they only saw empty shelves.

"Perhaps, there is a cellar under the house. Why don't we look around and see if we can find the entrance to the cellar, I am sure they must have one somewhere," Emma pondered.

"I will go outside and look around the house to see if I can find the entrance," Meta offered to investigate. She went outside and walked around the house. She stumbled upon, what looked like a window well, but it had a metal door instead of a window. She ran back to the kitchen, announcing: "I think I found the entrance to the cellar, but I need help to go down the well." My sister Emma and Greta Liedke followed Meta to the location.

"We would need a ladder to climb down into the well. Where can we find a ladder?" Emma verbalized.

"I tell you what, Meta, you go backward, hold on to the rim and Grete and I will hold your hands and lower you down."

So, they did. Meta pried the door open and saw a big, semi-dark room. Luckily, there stood a ladder leading into the cellar.

Meta, not afraid, stepped on the ladder and climbed down. Slowly, her eyes adjusted to the semi-darkness, and she saw some barrels on the lower wide shelves. She lifted one cover and smelled sauerkraut. Then she went to the next one, and she discovered pickled pork bellies. "I found food," Meta shouted, "Go and get some containers. Meta looked around some more and stumbled into a heap of potatoes. She took potato after potato and began to throw them up into the well, and some landed on the ground.

Meanwhile, Emma and Greta came back with some big pots. "Stop throwing potatoes at us; come up and get the pots," Emma shouted. Meta came up and took one pot down, then the next and filled one with meat, the other with sauerkraut.

"Greta, you take the meat to the kitchen and bring a container for the potatoes."

Then she began picking up the loose potatoes and putting them on a pile. "Do you have enough potatoes?" Meta inquired.

"Throw some more; we will get out of the way." When Emma thought it was enough, she shouted, "Come up; we have enough."

"OK," Meta called back, "I am coming up." After Meta threw enough potatoes from the cellar up to the ground, she climbed up the ladder from the well, closed the cellar door, and Emma and Greta pulled her up.

Mothers and their older daughters gathered in the kitchen, peeled potatoes, and prepared a big pot of sauerkraut, pickled pork belly, and potatoes. Everyone devoured the foods with gusto. After dinner, the men fed hay to the horses. The adults gathered in the living room and engaged in conversations while the children played outside. We came in when the night embraced the land and dropped a dark cloak over the farm.

Mothers and the more minor children slept in the house while the boys spent the night in the barn on the hayloft. I cuddled up next to my mother and my little brother. I said my prayers and fell asleep.

When night gave birth to a new day, and the sun rays pierced through the broken clouds and threw long shadows over the land, we began our journey. Birds twittered, and the song of the skylark, ascending to heaven, accompanied us. Clouds drifted into oblivion, and the sun glistened over the golden wheat fields ready to be harvested. We crossed the Angerapp River flowing into Mauer Lake. The river murmured its ancient song, unaware of the long wagon train passing over the bridge. Now and then, we caught a glimpse of Mauer Lake before we entered the dense forest of Goerlitz. Mother pointed out that Hitler built a bunker for himself and his staff in this dense forest to hide from the battles of the war.

We passed by the famous bunker, Wolfschanze, that Hitler built in 1941 in Goerlitz's forest between Angerburg and Rastenburg. Up to 1944, East Prussia had not come under direct fire, and Hitler and his staff found a haven in this region. The bunker consisted of buildings for the Fuehrer himself and his generals, commanders, high government officials, and close associates. It housed hotels and a casino for the entertainment of his staff and guests. The different buildings included a gas station accessible by paved roads. A daily train from Angerburg passed through and stopped at the bunker railroad station before arriving in Berlin. Hitler had one of the oldest Prussian regiments, dating back to Frederic the Great, protecting his bunker. After a failed assassination on Hitler's life on July 20, 1944, by General and Duke von Stauffenberg, Hitler became more sinister and brutal and ordered all East Prussians to stay in their places, even if it meant death for them.

I looked around, hoping to catch a glimpse of a soldier guarding the bunker; however, I saw none. Instead, the stomping of the horse's hoofs, the squeaking, and the rattling of the wagon wheels pierced the stillness of the dense forest.

We passed through the town of Rastenburg, which the crusaders founded in the 14th century by building a castle to rest and protect themselves from the Prussian warriors.

After a few days of traversing ripe wheat and potato fields, meadows, and forests, we reached the town of Allenstein. We entered through the arch of the high castle tower, leading into the old part of town. We saw the mighty St. Jacob's Church dominating the skyline. A statue of the German-Polish astronomer Nicolaus Copernicus guarded the castle entrance.

We made a brief stop in the town square and waited for instructions. The mayor of the town told us to stay in Allenstein until further notice. Then he directed each family to a different farm or residence.

We ended up on a beautiful estate managed by three sisters. Their husbands, drafted in World War II, were still soldiers in active combat. They greeted us warmly and assigned rooms to us, with an enclosed porch facing a garden. My mother thanked the ladies and asked Emma and Meta to bring our bedding and clothes inside the house. Georg unhitched the horses, took them to the stable, and gave them hay and water. Edmund and Richard started to explore the surroundings of the farm. I joined them later. The apple and pear trees were laden with ripe fruit. We gazed at the pears and longed to have one so badly. One of the sisters must have seen us ogling at the fruit; she remarked: "Don't pick any fruit from the tree; you can eat only the fruit which has fallen to the ground." "Yes," we all responded in unison. Every day we checked under the pear tree to see if we could find a pear on the ground. When I spotted the first one in the grass, I shouted for joy while picking it up. Each brother got a bite, too. We would always wait for strong winds or for overripe pears to fall from the tree. If we found several pears on a stormy day, we would take one to Mother and my sisters too.

After a few days, we adjusted to the routine of the three sisters. Emma and Meta went with the sisters to milk cows in the nearby pasture each morning and evening. Edmund, Richard, and I ran along and rounded up the cows into a small fenced-in area. Georg took care of the horses and cleaned the stables and pig pens. I never learned the three sisters' names; we addressed them each with Liebe Frau (dear lady).

Mother stayed home, watched Horst, and prepared breakfast, lunch, and dinner.

The mayor of Allenstein sent a messenger on horseback to all the refugees, informing them that the Eastern front had not advanced and that we could stay until further notice. We welcomed the good news. Emma asked my mother if she could go with her girlfriend Martha to our home in Wizajny and see what they could do to save the crop on our farm. Mother did not think it safe for two young ladies to travel alone. But Emma insisted they would return right away if they encountered danger. Reluctantly, Mother relented and let her go.

The next day, my mother prepared sandwiches for her trip. With tears in her eyes, Mother embraced Emma, and with these words: "God protect you, my child, and bring you safely back." Emma took the bundle with the sandwiches and a bottle of juice and quickly met her girlfriend, Martha.

Emma and Martha walked toward Allenstein. Within an hour, they reached the train station. After they waited a while, they got on a train to Rastenburg, where they changed the train for Goldap. They arrived late in the evening. No trains ran from Goldap to Wizajny. They decided to spend the night at the train station in Goldap to get some rest. Early the next day, when the full moon still pierced through the forest, they began their long walk home. Soon the sun slithered through the trees and gave birth to a new day. Emma and Martha covered the next forty kilometers (twenty-five miles) by foot, passing through Rominten, where they stopped for a short time.

"Do you know that Kaiser Wilhelm II had his hunting castle in Rominten?" Emma asked Martha.

"Yes, I remember my mother telling me about the frequent hunting trips the Kaiser made to this area."

Emma responded: "Even though the Kaiser could not hunt himself, he enjoyed the outdoors and the hunting ritual with his friends."

"Emma, wouldn't it be exciting to see the castle?"

"Yes, Martha, but we do not have the time; let's go."

They ceased talking when they entered the forest and looked around carefully for any soldiers hiding behind trees. The call of a cuckoo, the crackling of craws, and the droning of airplanes broke the silence. Exhausted, tired, and hungry, they reached Wizajny before sunset. One hour later, they parted at Martha's house, and a few minutes later, Emma entered the courtyard of our farm. Emma was surprised to hear voices when she approached the entrance to the house. Her heart was pounding at the thought that Russian soldiers might be in the house. Emma stood in front of the door and listened carefully, trying to make out the language the persons inside were speaking.

When the door opened, a German soldier, with a look of surprise and disbelief, greeted her, "Fraeulein, what are you doing here? Where did you come from?"

"My name is Emma; I am the daughter of the owner of this farm. I wanted to check and see if I could preserve the garden's vegetables for the winter and harvest some wheat to have food if we should return home soon. The soldier bowed his head slightly, saying, "My name is Hans; please, come in and join my other comrades." She entered the kitchen and went to the dining room, where she saw three more soldiers sitting at the table, consuming their dinner. They looked at her with great surprise as if she was a phantom appearing from heaven. Pointing at each soldier, Hans introduced his three comrades, Erich, Dieter, and Peter.

"Where did you come from?" Erich asked.

"I came from Allenstein, where my family is temporarily staying."

"How did you get here?" Dieter inquired.

"My neighbor Martha and I rode the train to Goldap and then walked the rest of the way," Emma responded, then looked at the food and felt suddenly very hungry.

"You must be hungry, come and share our meal," Peter made a gesture for Emma to sit down, then went to bring a plate and silverware to her and filled her plate with pork and vegetable stew.

"Thank you," she uttered and ate with gusto, for she had not had anything to eat all day long. The soldiers waited before they barraged her with questions and warnings:

"What made you come back?" "Don't you know that it is dangerous for you to be here?" The Russian front is only twenty kilometers away from here. Some Russian soldiers already roam in this area You better stay in the house and don't venture out into the fields."

Emma listened and then responded: "I shall remain inside." Then she began to clear the table and helped wash the dishes.

"You must be tired. You can take my bed for tonight, and I sleep with my comrades in the living room," Hans assured her.

They sat around the table for a while, conversing before saying "Good night" to each other.

Tired from the long walk, Emma sank into the bed without undressing and fell sound asleep.

Emma got up when the sun appeared on the eastern horizon and painted the clouds in many pink, orange, and golden shades. She took a towel and went down to the pond to wash her face, then combed her fingers through her hair to put them in order before she went back to the house. The soldiers busied themselves, preparing breakfast, and greeted her friendly: "Did you sleep well?"

"Oh, yes, very well. Can I help you in the kitchen?" Emma responded when she saw Hans standing by the wooden stove, putting more logs on the glowing ember.

"You can fry the eggs if you like; we will warm up some milk and cut bread. Erich, Dieter, and Peter also came into the kitchen to greet Emma and to consume breakfast.

"Emma, I do not think you should stay here; you should get back to your family as soon as possible," Erich emphasized. "It looks bleak for our fatherland. Hitler fled to his bunker in Berlin. Even Hitler fears that Germany will suffer defeat." Dieter added.

"The Russian front is advancing each day to the west and is encircling East Prussia. I do not know how long our army will be able to hold them back. Russian soldiers already broke through the German front and hid in the forest during the day. At night they vandalized, shot the Germans, and raped the women," warned Dieter. "You should leave tomorrow. There is nothing you can do here anyway," Peter added.

Emma listened intently and responded, "Let me rest a day or two and help wherever I can before I head back to my family." They all agreed that the longest she should stay would be for two days. "If you insist, I shall leave the day after tomorrow," Emma responded. "Can I be of any help to you while I am here?" she asked.

"Perhaps you can help with the cooking," Peter answered.

"Let me look around and see what I can do," With these words, she got up from the table, cleared the dishes, and washed them.

The soldiers got up and went to the stable to feed and groom the horses.

Emma walked over to the carpet in the dining room, moved it over, and lifted the loose boards covering the cellar's entrance. Slowly she stepped down the ladder while her eyes adjusted to the darkness. Emma was surprised to find a barrel half full of sauerkraut and another with pickled pork that her mother left behind. She thought we would be back soon and would find something to eat. A small heap of old, wrinkled sprouting potatoes lay on the cellar floor. The soldiers had not discovered the secret entrance to the cellar.

Emma went upstairs to get containers and took a dish full of sauerkraut, a slab of ribs, and some potatoes to the kitchen. She did not like the looks of the potatoes. Emma remembered that her mother always planted a patch of potatoes in the vegetable garden in early spring. Emma went to the garden and removed the soil around one of the potato plants to check if she could find some new potatoes big enough to be eaten. She was delighted to see, here and there, some big ones among bunches of smaller ones. She rushed to the barn to find a hoe. Then she dug into the ground and removed the soil carefully on the side of several potato plants. Not disturbing the plant's growth, she picked only the bigger potatoes from each plant and placed them in a basket until it was packed. She pulled out a handful of onions and went down to the pond to wash the produce. She put a slab of ribs and the sauerkraut into a pot in the kitchen and added some water. She placed more logs and turf into the hearth to cook the food. Later she added the peeled potatoes and the chopped onions and let them simmer.

Then she went outside to check how many cows were in the nearby pasture? She counted only five and wondered what had happened to the other six? All the geese and ducks were gone, just a few hens remained in the hen house, and one pig lay on a patch of straw in the pigpen. Hans saw Emma walking out of the pigpen and approached her: "You wonder what happened to the other pigs and cows, don't you?"

"Yes, I do," she answered.

"We sold them to your neighbor, who decided to stay here, even if the Russians invade the area.

"I wish I could tell you that the war will be over soon, and you can come back to your home, but the conditions look very grim for our fatherland. After American General Dwight Eisenhower, with his allies' participation, invaded Normandy on June 6, 1944, our defenses weakened. The German generals Erwin Rommel and Gerd von Rundstedt hold their positions, even though they have less than a fourth of the human resources and fewer planes than their opponents to defend their troops. Thousands of Americans, their allies, and German soldiers have already lost their lives fighting the war," he sadly stated,

"We do not know how long the German military will be able to hold their positions." Hans paused for a moment and looked at Emma's somber expression. Then he continued, "I wish I could give you hope instead of doubt about the future of your home."

Emma looked up to him and, holding back the tears, and uttered: "I did not know that the fate of our country was that hopeless."

Waves of peril passed through her mind while thinking of losing her beloved homestead.

"Come, come, young lady, don't be so sad. Let us go and see what my comrades are doing," Hans tried in vain to cheer her up.

"You go ahead; I have a pot on the stove. I better return to the kitchen and check the food," Emma replied. On the way to the kitchen, tears welled up her eyes and ran down her cheeks. She went outside and picked a bunch of asters and put them on the table. The flowers brightened her somber mood and added some beauty to the room.

She stirred the food and put some more wood in the hearth before she set the table. Then she walked from room to room and recalled memories of her childhood and youth. She looked at the cradle her father had made and saw her mother rocking her eight babies. Being the oldest of eight, Emma remembered rocking her younger siblings to sleep while singing a lullaby to them. Now it stood empty and abandoned in the living room.

She walked over to the spinning wheel in the corner and turned the wheel with her hand. She thought of how much fine thread she had spun from wool for knitting socks, gloves, and sweaters for her younger brothers and sisters. Melancholy and nostalgia filled her heart as her thoughts were dwelling in the past. On the window-sill stood the myrtle plant she had grown for many years to weave a headband for her wedding veil one day. She did not dare think about what would happen if the Russians would invade her home.

The voices of the soldiers brought her thoughts back to the present. She left the living room and went to the kitchen to greet them.

She announced lunch would be ready in an hour. "We shall go on horseback and survey the area," Peter recommended.

"It is dangerous for Emma to be alone here; one person should stay with her," Erich suggested.

"You go ahead, I will remain here," Hans replied.

"Perhaps you could ride to my neighbor's farm and let my girl-friend, Martha, know that she should be ready to leave tomorrow. I shall show you where she lives."

"We can do that," Peter confirmed before he and his two com-rades went to the stable and mounted their horses. Emma followed them and pointed to her girlfriend's family farm. They said, "Auf Wiedersehen (Goodbye)," and rode away.

Once they arrived at the neighbor's ranch, they dismounted from their horses, secured them on a tree, and knocked on the door: "Hello, we bring you a word from your girlfriend Emma," Peter yelled to make sure the sound penetrated the door. The knock on the door startled Martha. She rushed to the door, and before she opened, asked:

"Who is it?"

"We bring you a message from your girlfriend, Emma!"

Peter repeated. When she heard the name Emma, she opened the door: "Good day, soldiers, what about Emma?"

"Good day, Fraeulein; your girlfriend Emma lets you know that you should be ready to leave tomorrow early in the morning. It is too dangerous for both of you to stay here!" Peter assured her.

"The Russian front is only 20 kilometers (twelve and a half miles) east of Wizajny, and I do not know how long our soldiers will be able to hold the Russians back," Erich added.

"Can we do anything for you while we are here?" Dieter inquired.

"Thank you for offering your help, but I am fine," Martha responded.

"Why don't you come over to your girlfriend's house today and spend the night there so that you can leave together early in the morning. It is not safe for you to be here by yourself. We have seen Russian soldiers in the area," Dieter warned.

The thought that Russian soldiers could appear during the night put fear in Martha's mind, and she replied: "I will take care of a few things, close up the house, and then come over. Thank you so much for your concern and for bringing me the message from Emma. Goodbye. I'll see you later." The soldiers returned to their horses and rode away.

"It is still early; why don't we ride into the village?" Peter suggested.

"Yes, we can do that," Erich agreed. They took a shortcut and passed through the meadows, galloped next to the cemetery, and reached the village of Wizajny.

Usually, vendors trying to sell their homemade goods, livestock, and produce crowded the market square on Saturdays and Sundays. Today only a small number of Polish farmers offered their goods to a few prospective buyers. Most of the German residents had already left.

Peter and Erich met three other soldiers on horseback with whom they engaged in a conversation. They inquired about any changes in the orders of the commander and if the Russian frontier had advanced. One of the soldiers replied: "Every day, the Russian front line moves a kilometer or so forward. Our defenses are just too weak to push them back. We can only try to slow down the Russian invasion, so our people can get out safely."

"Yes, it looks bleak for us. There is no longer hope to win the war. All we can do now is hold the Russians back as long as possible to prevent them from slaughtering our civilians," added the other soldier. Erich shuddered at the thought of his citizens falling into the hands of the brutal Russian soldiers, and he uttered, "Heaven help all the victims and us of this futile war." Erich and Peter said goodbye with a military salute and started to move to the horses' cadence.

When they reached the top of the hill, called Fuchsenberg (Fox Hill), they paused. The sun stood at her zenith and cast a golden veil over the rolling countryside carpeted with fields of ripe wheat and green pastures.

"What a beautiful countryside! How sad the owners who cultivated and tilled the soil all their lives long had to leave." Peter expressed.

Erich added, "I have a lot of compassion for Emma as well as all the residents who had to abandon their homestead. Who knows if they will ever be able to return? I hate what the Fuehrer has done to our country and our people. His grandiose idea of being the supreme ruler of Europe has shed so much blood, sacrificed many human lives, and brought so much devastation not only to our own country but to the world. And still, he will not give up the fight, even though winning the war is out of the question."

"No, he will not surrender; his motto is: 'Victory or death.' He did not listen to his generals when they suggested surrender to save human lives and prevent more destruction of our beloved fatherland." Peter quoted with disdain, "Yes, for what are we soldiers fighting?"

"I gave up fighting for the Fuehrer a long time ago; I fight for my countrymen and to protect their lives from war's brutality. I hope we all come out of this combat alive," Erich agreed.

When they thought of the upcoming Russian invasion and the fate of their beloved country, silence gripped their hearts like the talons of an eagle gripping the throat of its prey. A silence that rose above tears, proclaiming the upcoming peril. Then they pulled on the harness to set the horses in motion. When they arrived at the farm, Emma set the table and bade them sit down to have lunch.

"Where did you find sauerkraut and pork? I have not had it since I left home. It tastes so good." Erich commented after he ate several morsels.

"Mother left some in the cellar. There is more. I will show you where the opening to the cellar is."

"We suggested that Martha should come over to spend the night with you here. It is too dangerous for her to stay by herself. She agreed and will come over in the afternoon." Peter informed Emma.

"I am glad she is coming; she will be safer here," Emma responded.

They ate with gusto and thanked Emma for having prepared such a tasty lunch. Then excused themselves with these words: "We shall survey the area."

"I think I would rather stay here with Emma to protect her," Hans informed his comrades and began to help Emma clearing the table while his comrades mounted their horses and rode to survey the area.

When they finished the dishes, Emma told Hans that she would like to see what vegetables she could find in the garden for dinner. She took a basket from the kitchen and walked over to the shed for a hoe. "Can I accompany you?" Hans asked. "Of course,"

Emma responded. Emma pulled a bundle of carrots, shook off the soil, and placed them on the ground.

"I also want to dig more potatoes for tonight.

"Let me dig, and you gather the potatoes." Emma handed the hoe to Hans, and he began to remove the dirt from several plants. Hans asked a lot of questions about the family. He admired Emma's courage by leaving the family and coming back home to look after the farm. He took a liking to Emma. Not only did she have a good, strong character, but she was attractive, had blond hair, blue eyes, and a good figure, too. He looked affectionately at Emma and said: "You are not only beautiful but courageous and good-hearted. I like you."

Emma was caught entirely off guard and blushed. When Hans saw her blushing, he looked to the ground and started to dig again. They filled the basket with potatoes in no time. Emma also pulled out some turnips and onions.

"Let us go and wash our produce in the pond. It saves us time fetching water from the well and carrying it to the house. Hans carried the basket of potatoes while Emma brought a bunch of carrots, onions, and turnips to the board that spanned the pond's corner.

"Let me have the potatoes; I shall wash them," she told Hans.

Hans handed her the basket. She dipped it up and down in the water to remove the dirt from the potatoes. To clean the carrots, turnips, and onions, she swung the bundles back and forth.

"Why don't you leave everything here and let us go for a walk? The day is too beautiful to stay indoors?" Emma agreed. They walked along the pond then passed the golden fields of ripe wheat, ready for harvesting.

"I wished I could do something to prevent this beautiful crop from going to waste," Emma remarked sadly.

"Yes, it is heartbreaking. You had to abandon your beautiful homestead. Who knows what will happen to our country and all the people? If we come out of this war alive, perhaps I can come and help you recultivate your farm," With these words, he moved closer to Emma, took her hand, stopped, and looked into her eyes, expecting an expression of acceptance. Emma blushed again and could not utter a word. She only nodded her head as a positive response. They started to walk again. Both were silent for some time; they thought of the future and a possible reunion after the war. Finally, Hans broke the silence, "You do not have to answer now; I will give you my home address, and you can contact me if you like after the war is over."

"I hope we can return to our home again after the end of the war. I love my birthplace where I have spent all my life," Emma continued.

"I was born in Palmnicken by the Baltic Sea. I, too, love East Prussia. My father is a fisherman and my mother, a high school teacher. I have not seen my parents for some time. I sure hope they also escaped and won't fall into the hands of the Russian army." Hans added.

Hans spotted a bunch of bachelor buttons in the wheat field. He bent down and picked them. Then, he handed them to Emma with the words: "Beautiful flowers for a lovely Fraeulein." Emma accepted them with a smile and a "Thank you." Hans lifted his hand to his ear and whispered, "Listen, listen, the skylark sings a sweet serenade for you."

Emma looked up and saw just a small dark dot in the sky and joyfully proclaimed: "What a melodious song; I am so glad I heard the skylark sing once more before I have to leave tomorrow."

"The joyful song of the skylark expresses my affection for you," Hans uttered while he moved closer to Emma and tried to embrace her.

Even though Emma's heart expressed affection for him, too, she stepped back and added, "Tomorrow I have to leave you, who knows, if we will survive this war, let us not make departing more difficult for each other." Hans respected her wishes and released her hand.

"Let us go back to the house; it is time to think about preparing supper," Emma suggested. They hardly spoke for the rest of the way. Each one was absorbed in their thoughts about the hopeless outcome of the war, their fate, and their country's fate and future.

As soon as they arrived, Emma first put the bachelor buttons in a cup, placed them on the table, and prepared dinner. She wanted to surprise the soldiers and make something special for them, potato pancakes. After Emma peeled enough potatoes, she grated them. Meanwhile, Dieter and Peter also came home. When they saw Emma working so hard, Dieter offered to help. Emma accepted his help. She looked around the kitchen for some lard or oil but could not find any. "What can I use for frying the pancakes?" she pondered.

"Oh yes, I can sauté the pork bellies and use the grease for frying the potato pancakes. That is good; we still have some more in the cellar,"

"Come, I show you where the entrance to the cellar is, so you can use the rest of the supplies that remain there."

When they got to the dining room, she folded over the rug and removed the three boards that formed the door. "Let me go down and get what you want and familiarize myself with things that are there." Dieter offered.

"Please, get me a slab of pork belly," Emma requested.

"All right, I shall bring one," Dieter responded. He climbed down the ladder, waited a moment until his eyes adjusted to the semi-darkness before he walked over to the two barrels. Dieter lifted one cover and saw sauerkraut at the bottom of the barrel. When he opened the second barrel, he took a slab of salted pork belly. She thanked Dieter before he stepped from the ladder to the floor. Then they placed the loose boards over the beams and pulled the rug over the area again to hide the cellar entrance.

"It is good to know that we still have some extra food provision in case we don't get enough supplies from the army," Dieter remarked before he went back to the kitchen to finish grating the rest of the potatoes.

Emma washed off the salt from the meat, dried it, cut the whole slab into strips, and fried them. She removed the fried bacon strips and poured the grease into a pot until she had enough fat. Emma walked over to Dieter and thanked him for his help. She took the bowl with the grated potatoes, added eggs, and several pinches of salt to it. She stirred the mixture and let it sit for a while.

Meanwhile, Martha arrived, and greeted Emma with an embrace. She remarked: "What are you cooking? It smells so good."

"I am frying bacon and will use the grease for potato pancakes," Emma responded. Martha offered to help. "You can set the table, Martha, and then help me frying the pancakes," Emma requested.

Martha set the table and helped Emma fry batches of potato pancakes. Then Emma put new turf pieces in the hearth, warmed up sauerkraut and pork leftovers from lunch, and waited for the soldiers.

It was almost 6:00 p.m. when Peter and Dieter returned from their surveillance ride. "I am starved," Peter called out.

"So am I. It smells so good. What did you ladies prepare?" Dieter asked.

Before Emma had a chance to respond, Peter looked at the stove, announcing gleefully: "Potato pancakes, my favorite dish. I do not remember when I ate some last. It is so long ago."

A few minutes later, Hans and Erich walked in, and all sat down to enjoy their home-cooked dinner.

"Thank you, Emma, for spoiling our pallets tonight. You are quite a cook," Hans complimented Emma.

"Thank you, Hans, it gives me great pleasure to do something for you and your comrades," Emma replied, "You give your life to defend our beloved Fatherland, and preparing your favorite dish is the least I can do for you under these circumstances," Emma replied.

Everyone enjoyed dinner. However, Peter became somber when he announced: "The Eastern Russian front advances daily; it is less than fifteen kilometers away. Unfortunately, our limited defenses will not be able to hold the Russian army back. They could overrun us at any time."

Not only that, but the Russian air force sent 1,400 airplanes twenty-five miles northeast from here. Who knows how long our 28th Infantry Division will be able to hold back the Russians? Young ladies, you risked your lives by returning to your homes. I sure hope you get back safely to your families."

After everyone finished dinner, the soldiers excused themselves from the table:

"Why don't you join us in the garden? It is such a beautiful evening," Hans suggested.

"We will after we clear the table and wash the dishes," Martha agreed.

The soldiers walked around the house to check if no intruders prowled around the neighborhood before sitting down in the garden under the apple tree. Emma and Martha joined them later. The aroma of the reseda flowers filled the air and added to the beauty of the mid-summer evening. On the pond, the frogs began their croaking concert enhanced by the melodious song of the nightingale. All absorbed a momentary peaceful interlude of nature before their dreams shattered, and they faced the brutal reality of the war.

Hans broke the silence and began woefully to air the compassion for his people and his country: "How different would be the fate of Germany now, had the plot to kill Hitler at the Bunker Wolfschanze, in Rastenburg, East Prussia, been successful. Claus

Schenk Graf von Stauffenberg placed a bomb in the bunker during a conference held on July 20, 1944. Unfortunately, it did not kill Hitler; it only singed his pants, killed three of his staff members, and injured others present. Heavily guarded, Hitler fled from the bunker in Rastenburg to the one in Berlin."

Dieter disclosed, "You know what will happen to all the generals and thousands of civilians participating in the resistance movement? They will be hunted down and executed by Hitler. Many generals and their families committed suicide rather than being hung or shot by Hitler's Gestapo or SS Soldiers. Who knows, how many more innocent people will have to sacrifice their lives due to the brutal actions of the Fuehrer and the lack of cooperation of the Allies?"

"As early as 1938, 1939, and throughout the war, the German generals, leading the Wehrmacht (civilian army), attempted to negotiate with the British and American government to overthrow Hitler's Nazi regime. However, neither Prime Minister Churchill nor President Roosevelt cooperated with the resistance movement and their generals," Erich disclosed. "They feared a new military government in Germany would regain power. Their goal was not only to eradicate Hitler and his Nazi regime but to destroy Germany. The Allies released propaganda that all Germans were cruel Nazis. They painted their chosen enemy, the German army, and the German people as vicious and bad to justify their entry into the war against Germany."

"Carl Friedrich Goerdeler, one of the many emissaries of the resistance, tried to convince the Allies that most Germans thought differently, were decent people, and hated Hitler's Nazi regime, and he implored the cooperation of the Allies to kill or imprison Hitler. The resistance planned to replace Hitler's brutal dictatorship with a peaceful government. The resistance had already secretly set up a list of names for the new president and the other heads of State of a new German government. Unfortunately, all diplomatic negotiations and attempts failed," Peter disclosed.

Meanwhile, Emma and Martha walked into the garden. Peter and Erich stood up and offered them their seats. "Please, sit down and keep us company."

"Thank you, we will. What a serene evening," Emma remarked.

"I sure hope the war will end soon, and my family can come back home."

Peter went to the stable and got two big buckets. They placed them in front of the bench and sat on them. For a while, everyone remained silent, enchanted by the serenity and beauty of the evening.

Hans broke the silence, "Young ladies, what time would you like to leave tomorrow morning?"

"Perhaps at 7:00 a.m.," Martha responded.

"I think you should start earlier, so you can make it to Goldap before it gets dark. There you can catch the train to Angerburg. You will be safer in the train station at night than on the road," Hans instructed them. "Perhaps 5:00 or 6:00 a.m. would be more advantageous."

"Do you have enough money for a train ticket?" Erich asked.

"I have 10.00 RM," Emma responded. "I have 15.00 RM," added Martha.

The soldiers thought it would not be sufficient for the long way back to Allenstein. Each comrade reached in their pocket and gave them some of their money.

With the words, "Thank you so much," Emma and Martha expressed their gratitude simultaneously and added: "How generous of you, but will you have enough for yourself?"

"We do have sufficient for our needs," Dieter responded.

Nobody spoke for a while; everyone thought of home, their families, and the deep affection for their country with such beautiful scenery. They pondered what might happen yet before the war ends and after it's over. This momentary silence proclaimed the forthcoming tempest brewing in the East.

Foreseeing the Russian invasion and the tragedy of his people and country, Hans wanted to savor these few peaceful moments with his comrades and the young ladies. He pulled a small mouth harmonica from his pocket and began to play the East Prussian folk song "Land of the Dark Forests and Crystal Lakes." His comrades first hummed, then sang verse after verse, joined by Emma and Martha. By the time they reached the fourth verse, tears had welled up in Emma's and Martha's eyes, and instead of singing the words, they sobbed. They thought of the Russians destroying their beautiful homes and beloved East Prussia.

Hans understood their feelings and waited for a while until Emma and Martha regained their composure. He began playing happier tunes to cheer them up. They sang familiar folk songs and conversed until the night embellished heaven's garment with stars and a half-moon, which ascended above the fields.

Hans got up with the words, "Ladies, you had better get some sleep," he walked over to Emma and Martha, shook hands with both, and wished them a good night.

With the response, "Good night," both ladies excused themselves and walked into the house.

"I think I am just going to lay down dressed as I am, just in case we have to get out of the house in a hurry," Emma suggested.

"I will do the same," Martha responded. Both settled down in the same bed, closed their eyes, and waited to fall asleep.

Outside, the soldiers decided Peter would keep guard during the night, and the others would try to get some sleep, too. For a while, a barn owl broke the silence with her anguished sound.

Suddenly, past midnight, awakened by a loud barrage of shots, Emma and Martha jumped out of bed and ran out of the house. Frightened, they asked Peter, who stood at the entrance, "What is happening?" Get back in the house immediately," Peter shouted while he stepped in front of them, adding, "Polish partisans are attacking us." Hans, Erich, and Dieter stormed out of the house and joined Peter. All of them opened fire. Emma and Martha, once inside the living room, dropped on the floor. Emma looked up to heaven and asked God to protect the soldiers and themselves from harm. As bullets darted through the air, they listened intensely. The soldiers took cover in the shed to divert the shooting at the house.

After a while, the firing stopped. The soldiers waited outside until they thought it safe to come into the house. However, Peter and Erich offered to stay out if the partisans hid nearby and decided to attack again. Fortunately, no bullets hit the soldiers. Hans and Dieter walked into the living room announcing, "The danger seems to be over, at least for the moment," Hans announced,

"Try to get some sleep now."

"Did anyone get wounded?" Emma inquired.

"No, we escaped the bullets," Hans reassured them.

"Thank God, the bullets missed you and us."

"I heard one of the partisans howling. One of our bullets must have hit the intruder," Hans added.

Hans and Dieter wished them good night and went to their room to rest while Emma and Martha returned to the bedroom. Both turned and tossed for some time, thinking about the recent confrontation with the partisans and the dangers the ladies might encounter on their way back to their families. Finally, after they prayed and asked for God's protection, they fell asleep for a few hours. Dim light slithered through the window when Emma and Martha woke up. They got up, washed, and prepared pancakes and eggs for the soldiers before starting their journey back. Hans offered to accompany them, which Emma and Martha appreciated very much.

Meanwhile, the sun had ascended above the barn and threw a bright glow over the golden fields.

"What sadness fills my heart to see the wheat in the fields going to waste when so many people do not have enough to eat," Hans remarked.

"I wished I could have stayed and asked neighbors to help me harvest the wheat," Emma replied in a distressed tone of voice.

"It is impossible for you to stay! We just do not know how long we can hold the Russian front at bay. Since America entered the war, Stalin received tanks, planes, and other military supplies from President Roosevelt and Prime Minister Churchill as well." Hans vented his fear of defeat.

"Our soldiers are far outnumbered, and war supplies diminished. There is no way we can fight for long and winning is out of the question. My main concern now is to see that you two get back to your families the fastest possible way."

"We both are so grateful for your help. I hope you will not suffer any consequences for taking time off from your duty." Martha remarked.

"My comrades and I oversee the digging of the trenches nearby; nobody will know if I am not there for a few hours," Hans replied. Rather than walking on the road, they took a shortcut and swiftly crossed the large pasture to reach the village faster. Usually, the village square teamed with life; today, no people came; most residents already fled. Only some tanks and army transport trucks stood next to the village hall.

Hans, Emma, and Martha walked to one of the trucks. Hans asked the driver if anyone was driving to Goldap and could take the two ladies along.

"I do not know if someone else is going, but I have no assignment yet; I could drive them to Goldap," the driver responded. He introduced himself as Heinrich Schulz.

Hans responded while he shook the driver's hand. My name is Hans Gudat, and this is Emma Bonacker and Martha Thomas.

"Thank you for offering your help, so the ladies can get back to their families faster," Then he turned to Emma and Martha: "This driver will take you to Goldap, where you can catch the train," Hans informed the ladies. Then he turned to Emma, embraced her, kissed her on the forehead, and told her: "May God protect you and let you get safely to your destination. I do care for you. Farewell, my dear." Emma looked at Hans. Their eyes met, and they expressed their affection for each other. She embraced him and parted with these words,

"Goodbye, Hans. Thank you for protecting us. God willing, we shall see each other after the war is over. God watch over you."

He handed her a piece of paper, "Here is my home address; you can write to me after you reach your destination, and God willing, we might see each other again."

Then Hans turned to Martha and shook her hand: "Goodbye, Martha, and have a safe journey. I hope you reunite with your family in Allenstein safely."

"Thank you so much for your help. May God protect you from danger and death." Hans waved goodbye, then began to walk swiftly back to the farm.

Heinrich stepped out of the driver's seat, walked around, and opened the truck door for Emma and Martha. They entered the truck and sat down next to the driver. Heinrich put the stick shift in gear and drove off. After a while, they entered the principal road to Rominten; they passed along the refugee trek line. Heinrich asked the ladies a lot of questions, such as why they came back home, where the families were, how long ago the family left, and so on. While they talked, suddenly, a plane flew over them. What seemed like seconds later, they heard a barrage of bullets pierce the air and hit a horse and wagon a short distance ahead. Heinrich stopped the truck abruptly, jumped out, and helped Emma and Martha get down.

"Run into the woods quickly; another plane is approaching," Heinrich yelled. He shut off the engine and followed the ladies. Finally, all the traffic stopped, and the people ran for cover into the forest. They dropped to the ground and waited for the dive bomber to pass.

"My God, I hope they don't bomb the railroad station in Goldap or the railroad tracks to Rastenburg. I sure hope you can make it back to your families unharmed," Heinrich remarked.

Emma sighed, "I pray to God; we will make it."

A third plane approached the truck. Luckily the aircraft passed without opening fire. Everyone waited and waited until they heard no sounds of roaring airplane engines.

Heinrich broke the silence, "I think it is safe now; let us go."

He got up and helped Emma and Martha to stand up, too. They walked back to the truck and entered the cabin. Heinrich started the engine, put the stick shift in gear, and began to drive.

"Thank God, my truck was not hit. It still runs."

Heinrich drove off in a hurry to the train station, where Emma and Martha hoped to catch the next train.

"You both stay here with the truck; I will inquire when the next train to Rastenburg departs," Heinrich addressed the Fraeuleins and went to the ticket counter to look at the train schedule.

He returned quickly, "The next train leaves at 11:30 a.m. to Rastenburg." Looking at his watch, he continued, "You have an hour and a half before the train leaves. Do you have enough money to buy the tickets?"

Before Emma or Martha responded, Heinrich reached into his pocket and pulled out twenty Reichsmarks, and handed it to Emma, who did not want to accept it,

"Thank you; I think we do have enough for tickets," Emma replied.

"Just take it; you might need to buy some food."

Heinrich insisted. Reluctantly, Emma accepted his gift.

"I have to leave you now and return to my post. I hope you get back safely to your families and live to see the end of the war." With these words, Heinrich said goodbye to his passengers.

Emma and Martha shook his hand and expressed their deep gratitude for his help: "Thank you so very much for taking us here. May God watch over you and your comrades, protect you from being wounded, and bring you home safely after the war is over."

Heinrich returned to his truck and drove to his post to report for active duty.

A long line formed at the ticket booth, mothers with children of all ages and older men, and women who had no means of transportation of their own were trying to get on the train. Some carried backpacks; others pulled small carts loaded with suitcases, sacks, blankets, personal belongings, and food items. Some persons pushed baby buggies stuffed with things and carried the babies in their arms. Some walked from the surrounding villages for hours. Though exhausted from pulling their load, they waited with great anticipation for the train and a chance to escape from falling into the hands of the brutal Russian soldiers who were only a short distance away from the East Prussian border.

Emma and Martha felt lucky that the train was still in service and that they got tickets for the 11:30 a.m. departure. The Russian dive bombers blew up many railroad stations and tracks to halt soldiers' and civilians' transports.

People lined up along the railroad track, waiting patiently for the train's arrival. Finally, smoke from the locomotive appeared on the horizon. The locomotive engine's rhythmic puffing and the sound of the wheels turning became louder and louder as the train approached the railroad station. Soon, the train came to a screeching halt. The doors opened, but strangely, no passengers got off.

The rush to step into the train began. Mothers with small children and older adults occupied most seats, which compelled Emma and Martha to stand up during the whole trip.

Shortly before the train reached the next destination, a conductor pressed through the crowd, checked the passengers' tickets, and announced Angerburg to be the next stop.

Many people lined up along the tracks, but only a tiny number could get on. The rest, disappointed, had to wait and hope to get on the next train.

The locomotive puffed and slowed down, carrying a long train and an overload of people with baggage. It took much longer to reach the next town of Allenstein, where Emma and Martha got off.

"Thank God, we made it so far. I am starving," Emma announced.

"So am I," responded Martha. "Let us wait until we get out of the city before we eat. I feel guilty about eating in front of hungry children and adults."

"That is a good idea." Emma agreed.

Thinking of food and their families hastened their pace and made them oblivious to all the town's architectural beauty.

After walking alongside many wagons outside the city perimeter, they turned on a small path, found a stone as a bench, and sat down. Emma pulled out a link of sausage and a piece of bread, broke it in half, and handed it to Martha.

"Here, Martha, I am sure you are hungry, too."

"Thank you, Emma, I sure am. It feels good to sit down after standing for hours on the train," Martha replied.

They devoured their food, got up, and started their last stretch of the road to the farm where she had left her mother and her six siblings.

They came to a crossroad where they parted with an embrace. "Let's hope we still will find our families here."

"I sure hope they have not left yet. Goodbye!" "Goodbye!" Emma responded. She hastened her steps, anxious to reunite with her family.

As Emma approached the farm, she saw Hilde and Horst playing outside. She felt relieved.

As soon as Horst and I spotted Emma, we ran toward her. Emma bent down and embraced us.

"How glad I am to find you still here," Emma sighed, relieved.

When Emma entered the kitchen, where Mother and Meta cleared the dinner table, my mother almost dropped the plates she carried in her hands. She put them in the sink quickly and embraced Emma.

"Thank God, you are back." She could not utter any more words; tears of joy expressed more than words could have done. Meta, Georg, Edmund, and Richard all rushed to her and gave her a big hug. Even Emma's eyes filled with tears of gratitude to reunite with her family. Mother looked up and sent a prayer, without words, to her heavenly Father, thanking Him for the safe return of her oldest daughter.

"You must be starving; Meta warm up the borscht soup and bring it to Emma," Mother told Meta. Mother turned to Emma again and continued, "After you finish eating and rest a while, you have to tell us all about your trip and how you found things at home."

Emma nodded.

"Yes, Mother, I will." After she enjoyed the hot soup she excused herself and went to bed. Emma thanked her Heavenly Father for bringing her and her friend back safely to their families. Then, exhausted from the long trip, she fell into a deep slumber.

The following day, the family gathered around the table and listened to Emma's answering question after question about home. Mother expressed her gratitude that the house still stood undamaged and had not been bombed or burned down. Mother worried when Emma told her the Russian front is advancing rapidly. Now it was only 20 kilometers (twelve and a half miles) away from our homestead. The German soldiers built trenches near our house to halt the Russian tanks. The German soldiers did not know how long they could hold back the Russian invasion. The soldiers urged us to get out of East Prussia as soon as possible, for the Russian soldiers treat the German women and people brutally. Mother listened intently, then asked Emma to go to Mr. Kirstein, who became the group leader, and inform him about the grim situation at home.

After helping to milk the cows in the stable, Emma walked quickly through the open fields to the house where the Kirstein family had found refuge. She spotted Mr. Kirstein on the porch, smoking his pipe. She greeted him courteously and told him about the situation at home and the soldiers' message to leave East Prussia as soon as possible. Mr. Kirstein thanked Emma for the news but gave her no definite answer of what he intended or could do.

Then Emma knocked on the door, entered, and greeted the rest of the family. After a short conversation, she excused herself and said, "Auf Wiedersehen (goodbye)" to the Kirstein family and rushed back to her own family.

Being concerned about the rapidly approaching Russian front, Mr. Kirstein sent out his three sons, Fritz, Edmund, and Georg, to notify our group members to get ready we need to leave quickly. Mr. Kirstein was grateful to have his three sons with him. Fritz, the oldest, was a wounded soldier on furlough at the time the family left home. Edmund and Georg were too young to be drafted. However, Gustav, the second-oldest son, was still in active combat. For some time, Mr. Kirstein had not heard from his son, Gustav, and hoped he was still alive. Now he and all the other families thought only of preparing for a quick departure.

However, nobody could leave without the permission of the government official (Gauleiter).

The month of August came to an end, and September began. With fall approaching, the weather could suddenly turn cold. Mr. Kirstein thought it wise to install covers on the wagons. He notified all the capable men in our group to help each family cover the wagons.

One day the group came to our farm. They brought heavy branches from willow or other trees. The men tied the poles, long enough to be arched over the wagon, on each side of the wagon.

Mother and Emma looked around for material to stretch over the arches. They did not find enough wool blankets. Mother asked the oldest sister of the ranch if she had some canvas or more blankets to spare.

"Let me look." With these words, she excused herself. After a while, she returned, carrying an armful of canvas and blankets.

"Take whatever you need."

"Thank you very much; I think this is more than enough."

When Emma returned, she urged her mother to prepare the wagon for departure. Alongside the wagon, Mother, Emma, and Meta spread the canvas and blankets on the floor, overlapping a few inches. Emma picked up one of the poles still on the ground and used it as a ruler to measure the width and length of the cover. They allowed extra material for each side and sufficient to cover the opening in front and the back.

Mother, Emma, and Meta stitched them together with strong thread, which the three sisters gave them. The men tied a rope on each corner and pulled the canvas over the arches. Once in the proper place, they fastened the canvas with cords to the wagon's right and left side. They used a thin narrow board to nail the canvas to the ladder on each side of the wagon. In a few hours, they finished their job and went on to help the next family.

The following day, Mother found me crying in bed.

"What is the matter, Hildke?" Mother asked.

"I have pain in the groins and behind the knees."

"Let me take a look."

I lifted my sheet and showed my mother where it hurt. She noticed redness and swelling in the groins.

"It looks like you are developing abscesses. You better stay in bed. I will put on hot compresses to soothe the pain."

"Can I get up for breakfast, Mother?"

"I guess you can, but then you go back to bed again."

"Yes, Mother, I will."

When I made the first step, the pain increased. However, I managed to have breakfast and then went back to bed again and tried to sleep, but I could not because the throbbing increased.

Emma came and put hot towels over the area. The warmth relieved the pain somewhat, and I fell asleep for a while.

For a few days, Emma continued with the hot compresses. On the second day, I heard the wind howling, and I asked Emma to take me to the enclosed porch, where I could look outside. The pear tree swayed back and forth. I watched closely if not by chance; a pear would fall. Suddenly I let out a shriek of joy, "Yippy, one pear fell to the ground."

I thought about running outside to retrieve it before my brothers would see it. I tried to get up and made a few steps, but I had to return to my seat quickly. The pain was too severe.

I called Richard. He did not come. Then I called Edmund; he was not around the house either. When Emma came back to change the compresses, I pointed to the spot where the pear had fallen. I asked her to get it for me. Emma went outside and looked around. Finally, she found not only one but two pears and brought them to me. I was delighted to bite into a ripe, juicy pear. Temporarily, I forgot my pain while I munched on the delicious fruit.

The wind brought rain and cooler temperatures. But my temperature rose. When mother came and touched my forehead, she remarked alarmingly, "You have a fever." My mother went to the three sisters and asked if they had any aspirins?

They did not.

"Is there an elderberry bush nearby?"

"Yes, by the pasture."

"Good. Thank you."

My mother called Emma immediately and gave her instructions to pick some elderberries.

Emma took a bucket along and rushed to the pasture, where she found the elderberry bush laden with ripe berries. She picked cluster after cluster, filled the bucket half full, and walked quickly back to the farm.

My mother put a pot of water on the hearth. She and Emma removed the berries from the stems, washed them, and dumped them in the boiling water. She waited a while, then squashed them to get all the juice out of each berry. She strained the berries through a cloth, filled a cup with the juice, put some sugar in it, and brought it to me.

"Drink this. It will help to bring down your fever!"

I emptied the whole cup. It tasted good. I tried to sleep again but felt hot first and then cold. My body trembled from the chills. I called my mother and asked her to stay with me.

When my mother looked at the abscesses, she decided to lance them. My mother instructed Emma to sterilize a sharp, pointed knife in boiling water and get a clean bed sheet. Mother snipped the sheet then tore off several strips and rectangular pieces.

"Emma, bring the knife. Put some salt in the pot, then dip this cloth into the water. Wait until it cools off, then bring it to me."

Emma followed my mother's instructions. Mother pulled the cover back and asked me to turn over on my stomach. She cleansed each abscess behind my knee with the moist cloth dipped in warm saltwater. Then she took the knife and quickly lanced the head of each abscess and squeezed the puss out of the opening. My body jerked, and tears flowed onto the pillow when I felt the pain of each incision.

Emma folded the square cloth then put it on the openings of the abscesses. She used the strips as bandages and wrapped them around the knees to hold the fabric in place.

"You can turn on your back now and rest a moment."

I felt the throbbing pain behind my knees and could not find a comfortable position. Soon, Mother and Emma returned and put me through the same torturous procedure on the groin's abscesses. My body burned with fever, and I shivered. I was exhausted and finally found some relief in a restless stupor and sleep.

My mother instructed Emma to burn the rags soiled with puss and blood so no one else would get infected. The next day, the fever was still high. However, each day the temperature dropped, and the throbbing pain slowly diminished. From time to time, Emma carried me to the porch and made me comfortable in a chair. I enjoyed watching the birds and listening to their chirping and songs. Now and then, a squirrel amused me while it jumped from branch to branch and nibbled on a pear.

After a week, the abscesses stopped festering and started to close. The fever went away, too. Finally, I could go outdoors. It felt so good to be able to walk and run again.

Meanwhile, August passed, and so did part of September, and no order came from the evacuation commander, Erich Koch, for the refugees to move on. However, the Russian front advanced daily, from the East toward Koenigsberg and the West toward Osterode and Allenstein, where we stayed.[14] The Russians already overran my hometown, Wizajny, and the northeastern part of East Prussia as the army marched toward Koenigsberg. The Russian objective was to encircle East Prussia entirely and cut it off from the rest of Germany.

On a still-warm late September afternoon, Mr. and Mrs. Kirstein sat on the enclosed porch. Mrs. Kirstein knitted a sweater, and Mr. Kirstein enjoyed smoking his pipe while absorbed in thought. Now and then, he would look out of the window up and down the road. In the distance, Mr. Kirstein noticed a bicycle rider coming closer and closer toward the house. He tried to see the face and if he could recognize the person.

"Could it be my son Gustav?" he thought for a second, "No, it could not; how would he know where we are?" He corrected his thoughts momentarily, but then he took a closer look as the bicyclist slowed down in front of the house. "Yes, he looks like Gustav. Yes, it is Gustav." He pulled his wife on the arm.

"Look, look, that is Gustav; he is coming to us," he shouted for joy. At first, she thought her husband was fantasizing. When she took a closer look and recognized her son, she threw down her knitting, pulled up her husband from the chair, and both ran to greet him on the road.

Mr. and Mrs. Kirstein shouted, "Gustav, Gustav, thank God you are alive and found us here." Tears of joy filled their eyes as they embraced Gustav and welcomed him.

"Come, come; you must be tired and hungry. I will fix you something to eat, and then you can tell us how you found us here.

"You even brought your accordion with you," Mrs. Kirstein remarked as she saw the case of the accordion fastened to the back of the bicycle.

"How happy I am to have found you!" Gustav expressed his joy in reuniting with his family, so did his mother, sister Greta and his brothers Fritz, Edmund, and Georg.

Everyone barraged him with questions.

"Children, children, let Gustav rest first. Tomorrow he can answer all your questions."

After the family consumed their eggs and pancakes for breakfast the following day, they remained seated around the table, waiting anxiously to hear Gustav's story.

"I still cannot believe that I was able to find you here alive and well. Now I will tell you where I served in the army. I joined the Air Force. I suffered from severe frostbite on my hands and feet, which disqualified me. Since I knew carpentry, the military officials sent me nine months to Czechoslovakia to train as an army engineer. Our job was to build bridges where the German tanks and armies could cross and destroy them once they served their purpose, so the enemies could not use them.

The Czech citizens and the Polish and Russian citizens formed resistance groups and called themselves partisans. These untrained civilians fought for their countries. They would hide in forests, on top of trees, in ditches, abandoned buildings, or wherever they could. They shot and killed any soldier in sight. When the German soldiers asked them to surrender, they did not. They captured them and threw them in bunkers. Then they would put fire in the bunker. Some with burning clothes came running out, and with raised arms, surrendered, crying for mercy only to be machine-gunned to death. It was a horrible sight; I will never forget.

The Russian army tried to surround East Prussia. As they moved south, and west, I got involved in a battle against the Russians. Fortunately, the German soldiers could hold their position and not let the Russian army advance, saving the German citizens from massacre.

I was wounded and sent to a military hospital, where I was treated and released and sent on leave in this battle. I went home by train, military trucks, or on foot, slept wherever I thought it would be safe. I made it home only to be disappointed to find out that you had already left. I had to report to the Gestapo in Wizajny. I took some homemade sausage and some home-brewed schnapps (alcohol) that I still found at home and gave them to the commander in charge. Rather than sending me to another battlefield, he told me to wait for further orders.

I went to the mayor's office and inquired when the villagers had left, and where they had gone. I packed a few clothes, food, and my accordion on the bicycle and began looking for you. Sometimes I was lucky to find a train stopped in a railroad station that I jumped on. Sometimes I found a transport truck loaded with soldiers who took me along for a stretch of the way. Once, when I rode in a train, the locomotive disengaged from the car and remained in the forest. When I realized that the locomotive and the rest of the train moved ahead without the car I was in, I took my bike and peddled on.

I slept in barns, abandoned houses, forests, or fields, with danger lurking around me. I always had to be on the lookout. I ducked when a hand grenade or a bullet flew over my head or next to me. I often had to hide in the forest when Russian dive bombers passed over me and dropped bombs on anyone and anything that moved. Russian and Polish partisans, who had penetrated East Prussia, opened fire on me. I often thought a bullet or a bomb would kill me, but thank God; I escaped unharmed.

Sometimes I thought I would die of hunger. I scavenged for food and killed a piglet, a rabbit, or whatever I could find alive."

Mr. and Mrs. Kirstein, who were listening intently, interrupted briefly, looking up to heaven, "Thank God for saving our son and bringing him to us unharmed."

Then Gustav continued, "Once, while I was recovering from my injuries in a hospital, I met a soldier who fought in the battle of Stalingrad and sustained injuries.

He told me the Wehrmacht, soldiers who did not belong to the Nazis (National Socialistic Party), disliked Hitler and his SS soldiers, as did the Wehrmacht generals. A conflict and disharmony existed between both groups of soldiers. The SS soldiers stayed in the background and let the Wehrmacht engage in active combat.

General Paulus, who commanded the German army in Stalingrad, surrendered voluntarily to the Russians and did not lose the battle because of food supply and ammunition shortage, as broadcasted to the public on radio and newspapers. General Paulus preferred to become a prisoner of war rather than a servant under the ruthless dictator Hitler who commended his generals and soldiers for fighting to the end and never giving up. 'Victory or death' was his slogan.

After the Russians won the battle in Stalingrad, the army advanced rapidly. They are attempting to encircle East Prussia on their march toward Berlin. If we want to stay alive, we had better head southwest, where there is still an opening toward the Polish Corridor. I think I should go to all the other families and notify them to be ready to leave in two days."

"Yes, my son, that is a good idea," his father responded.

"I will go with you; I know where all the families live." His oldest brother Fritz offered to accompany Gustav.

They went from family to family until they informed all six of them. The news of a sudden departure alarmed my mother, but the fear her daughters could be raped and tortured by Russian soldiers was more painful than leaving. So, our stay at the farm came to an end. Fall and frost arrived and tinged the trees with brilliant colors, and forests fringed the golden meadows. Days grew shorter, and the shadows longer.

Unfortunately, while nature prepared for her long winter sleep, we were forced to end our stay and start our journey again. So many tears flowed as we said goodbye to the three sisters on the day of departure.

We could not thank them enough for giving us food, shelter, and so much kindness while staying with them. The sisters offered us to take along a cow to have milk for Horst and the family. Mother accepted this generous living gift. Georg tied the cow with a rope to the wagon, and off we drove. All our eyes focused on the farm until the distance swallowed the contours of the buildings and trees.

We reached the town square of Allenstein, filled with many horses and wagons, and looked for our village's families. We lined up behind each other and began a new segment of our journey. The mayor of the town told us to go southwest, where the Russians had not yet closed the circle around East Prussia and where there still stood a bridge for crossing the river Weichsel.

Onward rolled the wagons by day and stopped at sunset so the weary travelers could get some nourishment and hopefully some rest. Horses, also tired from pulling the heavy load all day long, needed a well-deserved break and fresh fodder to go on, as did our cow. Each day we stayed in a different place, on a farm or camped outdoors in the forests. Sometimes we slept in abandoned houses, stables, barns, or wherever we could find a vacant building.

Once, we found an abandoned schoolhouse. One big room had straw on the floor along both opposite walls. We took our sheets and pillows and settled in for the night. As soon as we put our heads on the pillows, we heard a rustling in the straw. I woke up several times and felt something crawling over my body. I started scratching. The strange noise in the straw woke up my mother as well as my brothers and sisters.

The following day, we saw lice crawling all over us. We realized lice infested the straw on which we slept. Later, someone told us Russian prisoners had slept there, and nobody bothered to change the straw after they moved out.

Mother gathered all the linens and shook them in the hopes of removing the lice. She also made us change our clothes. She tied all the infested clothes in a bedsheet to hope that any remaining lice would not crawl out and settle in the rest of the wagon. However, our effort to rid ourselves of all the lice failed. Some lice took up residence on our heads and became our unwelcome new traveling companions. The lice attached their eggs to our hair to assure the continuance of their species. Their itching and crawling on our heads annoyed us to no end.

As soon as we found an abandoned house with running water, mother and Emma boiled all the infested linens and our clothes, thus killing many of the lice, but still, our heads remained their favorite dwelling place and nursery for new crops.

We only advanced slowly. Sometimes a wagon broke down, or army transporting trucks halted the traffic.

Once, we stayed on a beautiful estate, where the owners must have moved out recently. Fritz and Mr. Kirstein forced the entrance door open and found everything inside still intact and very orderly. They decided to spend the night there and announced, "We will spend the night here."

After all the wagons lined up in the courtyard, everyone stepped down. The women went directly to the kitchen, where everything was still in order and beautifully arranged. When they entered the pantry, they were delighted to find the shelves well-stocked with canned goods. Then they explored all the other rooms and decided where each family would set up sleeping quarters for the night. Marta Kirstein settled with her baby daughter, Renate, and son, Waldemar, in one bedroom, and Mrs. Heisel with her three children, Helmut, Edna, and Gustav, in the other bedroom. With her aged father, young son, Ernst, daughter, Elfriede, and Oswald, Mrs. Hein took another bedroom. My mother and her seven children settled down in a big bedroom. The Kirstein family of six set up their sleeping quarters in the living room and the Liedke family of five in the library. Mrs. Ambrosat and her daughter, Greta, used the benches in the dining room as bunks for the night.

While men unhitched the horses from the wagons and looked for fodder, they found a male pig in one of the pig pens. They decided to butcher it so that everyone could have some fresh meat for dinner.

Elfriede, Edna, and I ran up a staircase and discovered a small room in the attic where two chests stood. We opened them and found one filled with dolls and the other with games and toys for boys. I took a doll with a beautiful porcelain face and long braids dressed in a lovely green striped dress with red and white flowers.

"I will take this one," I announced to Elfriede and Etna, "there are more in the chest for you."

"OK, you can keep her. I will take this one," showing another pretty doll to me.

Etna picked yet another fine-looking doll. We also took a more petite doll to Renate. We told the boys about the games in the attic. They dashed upstairs, picked a checker and chess game out of the box, and brought a little stuffed horse to my brother Horst and another animal to Ernst. Playing with these toys made us children so happy. We forgot about all the hardships of the war that evening.

After the mothers cooked some fresh pig meat, potatoes, and sauerkraut, they fed the children before all the adults consumed their dinner. We three girls took our dolls into the living room and played with them until we went to bed. Suddenly screams of male voices awakened me. I got up and peeked through the door. I saw Fritz with a knife in his hand chasing his brother Gustav while shouting obscene words. I closed the door quickly, crawled back into bed, and pulled the cover over my head while shaking for fear he might come into the room and harm me or someone else. I waited for what seemed like a long time for my mother to come. As soon as I heard her step into the room, my fear lessened, and I asked her, "What happened to the Kirstein brothers?"

Mother responded: "They got drunk and started to fight with each other. You can go back to sleep. Fritz and Gustav stopped quarreling and made peace."

Even though my mother sounded reassuring, it took me some time to fall asleep.

After breakfast, we loaded all our belongings on the wagons the following morning, joined our group of seven, and began our journey in a southwestern direction. We hoped we could pass safely through an opening in the Russian front.

By the beginning of October 1944, the Russian armies broke through the Prussian border at the Memel region for the first time. Airplanes bombarded the city of Memel. Tanks opened fire at the escaping people, rolled over them and their horse-drawn wagons, and the chains squeaked while squashing and massacring everyone and everything in their path. The German army was weakened and could no longer force back the Russian front; they retreated and helped the escaping Prussian civilians as much as possible. After the Russians broke through the northeastern border of the Memel region, they began to encircle East Prussia completely. Goldap, the city close to us, fell into the Russian hands by the end of October.

Chills ran through the people's minds when the news spread that the Russians invaded East Prussia, which until now was considered a peaceful haven for the political leaders, relatives, and civilians alike.

Even winning the war seemed hopeless; Hitler mobilized every male between the ages of sixteen and sixty-five and sent them to the battlefield. This inexperienced, untrained group of men, called "Volksturm," did not help the cause. Contrarily, it left children, women, and older adults to fend for themselves while fleeing from the Russians and abandoning their beloved homesteads. All that generations had worked for and cultivated for many years had to be left behind. It brought more suffering, hardship, and chaos to the families.

The trek of refugees advanced each day very slowly. Transport trucks loaded with soldiers and the newly drafted Volksturm rushing to the eastern battlefields slowed down the trek. Some days we only traveled five miles or less. However, our seven families were fortunate to have two soldiers, Fritz and Gustav, with us, even though their father and Mr. Liedke, already past sixty-five, were physically still capable of helping and protecting our group. Mother thanked God that Georg, her oldest son, now fourteen years old, did not have to enroll in the Volksturm. Georg took over the responsibility of caring for the horses and the wagon. However, Fritz and Gustav, skilled artisans in carpentry and farming equipment, repaired broken wagon wheels, harnesses, or whatever needed repair. They also looked out for food supplies and our safety. They replaced horseshoes and fixed damaged or worn-out gear.

In November, the sky turned gray, and fog settled on the ground. Some days the rain soaked the covers of the wagon, and water dripped on us inside. It created mud puddles on the unpaved country road. Pedestrians and horses trotted through them, splashing the dirty water to the side—no time to pause. We must press forward.

November ended, and we covered only small distances each day. December was ushered in with subzero temperatures and snow. The days grew shorter and the nights longer and more and more chilly. Frost spread a crystal blanket over the fields, bushes, and trees. They glistened in the morning when the sun rays shed their golden rays upon them. Some days, snow blizzards blew furiously against the pathetic-looking trek and slowed down the horses and wagons. The wind pelted against the coverings of the wagons that swayed back and forth as if they were ready to tear off and fly away. The forceful blasts found even the tiniest opening in the cover, and we felt the chill inside. Mother tugged the four youngest children between the feather beds to keep them from freezing. She joined Georg, who oversaw driving the wagon. To lighten the load for the horses, Emma and Meta walked next to the wagon. As the snow piled up, it became more difficult for the horses to pull the wagon. The horses huffed and puffed with each move forward, and so did Emma and Meta.

Only when darkness set in, we tried to find shelter to give travelers and horses rest. We hoped to get a warm meal for the families and fodder for horses. We slept in abandoned houses, in barns, in hay lofts, or whatever standing structure we could find to escape the bitter cold. Once, to get out of a blizzard, we spent a night with cows in a stable. While our mothers prepared the sleeping area by piling sufficient hay on the concrete floor where no cows stood, Emma, Meta, and the other young ladies milked some cows to get fresh warm milk for the young, hungry children. After we drank warm milk, which tasted so good, my mother brought the bedsheets and the feather beds from the wagon and tucked us in for the night. I could not fall asleep. The stench from the cow droppings was nauseating. I closed my nose. It did not help much either. I turned and tossed for quite some time before pulling the cover over my head to keep the stench out and finally fell asleep. At dawn, the mooing of the cows woke us up. We gathered our gear and continued our journey.

When no village or farm was in sight, we had to move ahead or perish in the cold. It was a continuous stop and go, and the trek struggled to get even a few kilometers ahead to stay alive. Meanwhile, the middle of December approached, and so did Christmas. The men in charge decided to find a place to stay for a while and spend Christmas in a house.

We found a Polish widow, Mrs. Grabowski, willing to take us in and share part of her house with us. After searching at the adjacent farms, the other six families also found willing ranchers to accommodate them.

The farm lady, where we stayed, helped us settle in a small room with a stove and assigned the big living room for sleeping quarters.

She also shared some of her food supplies with us. We were so grateful to be in a warm place and get warm food again. Before bedtime, Mother boiled water and prepared a bath in a big half barrel for us. First, she washed Horst. Then it was my turn. How good it felt to plunge into warm water and be scrubbed clean from tip to toe. Mother kept a pot of boiling water on the stove. When each bather was done, she added more hot water to the tub. After everyone finished bathing and had gone to bed, she cleaned herself. Before she went to bed, she thanked God for having her family sheltered and well.

The following day, we learned that the lady had a son named Janek and a daughter named Stella. We did not meet Janek until after dark. He was over eighteen and was eligible to be drafted by the Polish Army. His mother hid him in the hay barn to prevent him from going to war. He stayed in a big cubicle where a bale of hay, serving as a door, could be pushed out when the sister took food to him or when he wanted to come to the house after it was dark. The poor mother lived in constant fear that a government agent would show up to take her only son away.

Emma and Meta helped milk the cows and whatever the lady asked them to do in the house. Georg and Edmund fed the horses and cows. Richard, Horst, and I stayed with my mother in the kitchen, helped her peel potatoes, or did other small kitchen chores.

Christmas approached quickly. Emma and Meta decided to put up a Christmas tree. They asked Georg and Edmund to go to the forest to look for a medium-sized pine tree. The boys took a sled and went to the nearby woods. After finding a well-formed, symmetrical spruce, they cut it down, fastened it to the sled, and pulled it back to the farm. Emma was delighted with the shape and size. She helped her brothers make a stand from some old boards that they found in the barn. They carried it into the living room and placed it in the corner.

"What about ornaments?" Meta asked.

"We will make some," Emma responded, "Come, let us go to the barn and get some straw. We will make stars from straw; I will show you how to assemble them."

They went to the barn and picked a handful of thick, long straws. They cut off the thin parts and the knots and soaked them overnight in a dish of water to make the straws pliable and prevent them from breaking. After they finished their chores the next day, they took the straws out of the water and dried them with a cloth. Then they split the straws in the middle and flattened them with a knife.

"Look, Meta, now you fold the straw, so the bright side stays outside and the dull inside. Make one end about one inch longer, like this," Emma showed Meta how to do it.

"Do the same to all four straws. Then you interweave them like this to form a square. Now fold over the longer straws, so you have eight straws, two on each side, and interlock them like this." Emma waited until Meta completed her instructions.

"Now you cut all straws to the same length, then make a loop and secure each end to the center, like this. You see, and there you have a nice-looking ornament." After they finished several of the same ornaments, Emma showed Meta other variations of straw creations. I sat quietly next to them and observed each move they made. After a while, I asked Emma if I could make a star, too.

"Here, let me start one for you, and you can finish it."

Emma folded the four straws and interlocked them into a square before handing it to me with the following instructions.

"You see, next, you bring each straw over, so you have eight straws, two on each side."

She waited until I finished bending over one straw at a time.

"Now, you cut them all to the same length, about this long." She cut the first ones, and I did the rest.

"Is this okay?" I asked.

"Yes, now you take each straw and secure it to the center square, like this," she instructed while bending over and securing the first straw.

"Okay, I will try," I replied. Then I bent each straw over until I finished all of them.

"Look, Emma, I made my first ornament. Can I make more by myself now?" I told Emma while proudly presenting my first handiwork.

"Sure, you can," Emma replied.

I felt so grown up to contribute my help to such a fine craft. The first ornaments were somewhat loose and the bows uneven, but they looked better and better with little practice. I could hardly wait to hang them on the tree. Each day after lunch and dinner, we sat around the table and made straw ornaments. One day, Emma announced she had obtained some paper from the lady of the house. I will show you how to make paper stars from it. She cut even, wide paper strips and folded them until they looked like stars. For me, it was more challenging to work with paper strips than with straw. However, after several trials and errors, I finally got the hang of it and could make paper stars.

"Do you have any candles?" Meta inquired.

"I shall ask Mrs. Grabowski; perhaps she can spare a few of her own," Emma replied.

The next day, Emma gleefully announced, while holding up a handful of candles to me, "Look what Mrs. Grabowski gave me. Isn't it wonderful, now we have real candles to put on the tree?"

"That is wonderful; I can hardly wait; when are we going to put them on the tree?"

"First, we have to put threads on all the ornaments. We will do that today. Perhaps, tomorrow we can start to hang them on the tree."

Emma asked my mother for some yarn. Mother brought us white thread on a spool with two needles. She brought them with her, knowing she would always need to mend some children's clothes.

"Here is the white spool, but do not use too much," Mother cautioned.

Emma cut a bunch of threads about four inches long and handed them to me. Then she took one strand and showed me how to pull it through the bow and make a knot. I watched carefully and then followed her instructions. Emma and Meta threaded a needle, pulled the yarn through the corner of each paper star, and then made a knot. We worked all evening long to finish.

After dinner, Emma instructed Georg and Edmund to go to all the six families tomorrow and invite them for a Christmas Eve celebration.

"Georg, ask Gustav Kirstein to bring his accordion with him."

After feeding the horses and cows the next day, Georg and Edmund trampled through the deep snow from farm to farm, where the other refugees stayed, and invited them to get together for a Christmas Eve celebration at 5:00 p.m.

Exhausted, freezing, and hungry, they returned late in the afternoon before the sun cast her last rays on the white snow and vanished into the darkness of the night.

Christmas approached quickly. Our anticipation grew with the passing of each day. Finally, a few days before Christmas, Emma said, "We will decorate the tree this afternoon. First, we must heat the room. Go and ask Georg and Edmund to bring some kindling wood and logs to the house."

I rushed out to the barn, where both gathered hay to take to the cows and horses.

"Emma would like you to take some wood inside. She wants to heat the room where the Christmas tree will stand. Hurry up so we can start right away," I added.

They stopped their chores and fulfilled Emma's request promptly.

I carried a few kindling sticks myself into the house to speed up the process. Emma placed the thin, wooden pieces on the bottom, then stacked the logs in a pyramid shape in the oven (Kachelofen). She took a long, thin splinter of wood, went to the kitchen, and lit the twig in the hearth. Then she shielded the tiny flame with her hand while she carried it into the living room. Soon the fire crackled in the oven and consumed the logs simultaneously while radiating warmth through the openings in the oven. We waited until the place was warm enough before we hung our handmade stars on the tree.

"Now, let us put the candles on. Here, you hold them for me, and I will tie them to the branches," Emma instructed me.

Soon we finished decorating.

"It looks beautiful," I expressed my joy while stepping back to get a good look at the decorated tree. I ran into the kitchen, grabbed my mother by the hand, and shouted, "Mother, mother, come see our lovely, decorated tree." She followed me into the living room.

"Yes, it is nice, but it would be much prettier if we had the colorful ornaments from home", Mother commented.

I felt saddened that my mother did not share my enthusiasm and remarked, "But mother, we made all the ornaments ourselves, and to me, they are beautiful on the tree."

"I guess we can be grateful to have a Christmas tree and to be in a warm place and not on the road in the cold," Mother replied while returning to the kitchen to prepare dinner.

Outside, winter lashed out in its fury. The blustering north winds roared and rattled the windowpanes. Big snowflakes danced to the fast rhythm of the whistling wind before they fell exhausted to the ground. At dawn, when the sun burned the last remnant of the night, it revealed the magic transformation into a winter wonderland. The pure white blanket of snow-covered roofs, erased all footsteps, grooves, and furrows. The ground appeared almost sacred as the snowflakes sparkled in the sunlight. As soon as my brothers discovered the newly fallen snow, they dressed up, ran out, and started a snowball fight. I rushed outside to join them. Most of my snowballs missed my brothers, but theirs did not.

"Let's build a snowman," I suggested after I was covered all over with snow. They agreed, and we began rolling the snow into balls. I offered to do the head, which was the smallest. Soon they put one big ball on the bottom, a medium one in the center, and the smallest on top, representing the head. I ran into the house and asked my mother if I could have a carrot, which I would need for the nose.

She replied, "I do not have any carrots, but you can use a short stick from the kindling wood." I took it to Edmund,

"Here is a stick for the nose," I said as I handed him the stick.

"What about a hat?"

"I'll carve one from the turf," Edmund replied and went to the barn to get a few squares of turf and some sticks. He stuck first fine sticks through two pieces of turf to form a perfect square. Then Edmund cut another rectangular piece in half and put both pieces on top of the square. Then he broke off the corners of the square and shaped it round. Edmund removed some snow from the top of the head with Georg and Richard's help and fastened the hat to the snowman's head with more sticks. He took turf segments, shaped them into small round balls, and pressed two on the head as eyes. He made a curved groove underneath the nose. Georg made a line of round holes on both lower balls and stuck turf in them, serving as black buttons. We had placed the snowman next to the entrance, so everyone who visited us could see it.

"What a nice snowman," I shouted for joy. "But now I am going into the house; my hands are getting cold."

I invited everyone to go outside and see our snowman. Mother stepped outside, smiled at our creation, then asked the boys to dig out pathways to the barn and the stable. They worked hard to shovel two walkways from the barn entrance and the stable before they began their daily chores of cleaning the stable and feeding the animals.

Two days before Christmas Eve, Emma and Meta cleaned the living room and prepared for the celebration with our fellow travelers. The mayor of the city had sent each refugee family a half a brick—sized piece of butter, and the lady of the house gave my mother some flour, sugar, and eggs to bake some cookies for her children and the guests. When I heard this good news, I stayed in the kitchen with my mother and offered to help her. First, my mother put the flour on the table, made an indentation in the center, and placed a piece of butter, some sugar, and two eggs in it. Then she mixed the flour slowly with the ingredients into a dough and kneaded it before rolling it out into a sheet on the table. Next, Mother took a glass, covered the rim with flour, and then pressed it into the dough sheet. She moved the glass back and forth a few times until it cut a perfectly round-shaped cookie. Finally, she lifted it out of the circle and placed it on the cookie sheet.

"Mother, Mother, can I cut the cookies?" I asked.

"Yes, you can, but be careful not to press too hard. The glass may break. Here try," Mother instructed me while handing me the glass she had dipped into flour.

"Thank you, Mother, I will be very gentle," I replied and got busy pressing out round cookies. At first, I did not entirely cut through the dough, and the cookies did not separate from the dough very well. However, after a few more tries, they came out nice and round. After my mother placed the cookies on the sheet, she put them in the preheated oven. Soon the aroma of the baked cookies filled the kitchen. I could hardly wait to taste one.

"Mother, can I have one cookie?" I begged.

"Wait until they cool off, then you can have one." So, I waited for what seemed such a long time. Finally, my mother picked up a cookie and handed it to me. I rapidly took a bite, "Um," how good it tasted. I had not eaten a cookie for such a long time.

Mother placed a cookie for each of us on the table and then put away the rest of them for Christmas Eve and Day. I could hardly wait for Christmas Eve and Day to come. Finally, it was here, and so was the new snow that had fallen the day before and transformed the landscape into a winter wonderland. The day passed slowly, and my anticipation of celebrating the evening in the company of our fellow travelers grew by the minute. I did not take my eyes off the window all day long.

Suddenly, at dusk, I heard sleigh bells ringing. I ran outside as the Kirstein and Liedke families arrived. Shortly after, Hein and Heisel's sleigh pulled in, too. I was delighted to see Gustav bring his accordion with him to add music to this special celebration. After everyone arrived, Emma and Meta lit the candles on the Christmas tree. We gathered around the glimmering tree and sang first, "Oh Tannenbaum, oh Tannenbaum wie gruen sind deine Blaetter" (Oh Christmas tree, Oh Christmas tree, how green are your branches) accompanied by Gustav on the accordion. Each Christmas song lifted the festive mood and cast a sparkle in the eyes of the celebrants.

As we sang "Silent Night, Holy Night, all is calm, all is bright," we did not think about the horrors of the raging war around us. Instead, we thought of the peaceful scenery in Bethlehem where Jesus, the Savior and the Prince of peace, was born. We all longed for the end of the war and to be back home and living in peace and harmony. After we finished singing Christmas songs, Emma and Meta extinguished the tree's candles and lit the oil lamps. Mother passed around a plate of her homemade cookies. Everyone still stayed for a while, engaging in vivid conversations. Now and then,

Gustav played familiar folk songs and invited everyone to sing along. At midnight, the festivity ended, the visitors said, "Good night," stepped into their sleighs, and glided back into the starry night accompanied by the sound of the sleigh bells. The magic of the evening remained vivid in my thoughts after I went to bed and kept me awake for some time. Finally, sleep closed my eyes, and I dreamed of Santa Claus, wondering if he would bring anything to us this Christmas? We missed our sister Marta and wondered where she celebrated Christmas and if she was safe.

Christmas Day, when we entered the kitchen, we found seven plates on the table with three cookies in each one.

"Mother, Mother, Santa Claus did not forget us; he even found us here," I shouted for joy when I saw the plates with the cookies. My mother did not want to disappoint us; she wanted us to believe that Santa Claus found us here, too. She put the seven plates (Bunte Teller) on the table during the night. She had nothing else except cookies to offer. Even though we could not go to church to celebrate the birth of the Christ child, we dressed in our best clothes to His honor. Mother, Emma, and Meta spent most of the morning in the kitchen, preparing a traditional Christmas dinner of goose, red cabbage, and potatoes, a gift of the lady of the house. The aroma of the roasting goose and warmth filled the kitchen, where we all gathered, waiting for these specialties to be cooked and served.

Finally, Emma brought the roasted goose to the table and Meta the vegetables. Mother cut and dished out a piece of goose on each plate, and Meta added the vegetables. Mother said grace and thanked God for the food and our Savior's birth and that we were all together in a warm house. What a feast! How wonderful it tasted! We all enjoyed this extraordinary meal. After Emma cleared the table, she read the story of baby Jesus's birth in a stable in Bethlehem. We sang some Christmas songs and thanked God we were inside, protected from the chills of winter raging outside.

Our thoughts however took us back to the last Christmas at home, wondering when and if we would celebrate Christmas home again.

The next day, my mother, Emma, and Meta sat by the kitchen stove and knitted scarves, mittens, and socks for their young siblings. The kind lady of the house collected all her wool remnants and gave them to our mother. Mother was very grateful for her generosity because she did not bring sufficient warm clothes for the winter. The week between Christmas and New Year passed rather slowly, as we rang in the year 1945 quietly at our temporary home. Mother, Emma, and Meta prepared the traditional donuts, but this time without marmalade inside. However, they rolled them in sugar to serve us something sweet. The rest of Christmas we spent quietly in the warm kitchen. Mother was concerned about the future of her family and prayed to God for His protection.

On new year, Mr. Kirstein sent his sons Fritz and Gustav to our group to update us on the Russian front. Our village and region were overrun and plundered in October 1944. In January 1945, they invaded the Rominter Heide and Goldap and marched toward Gumbinnen and Tilsit rapidly. Each time, the Kirstein brothers warned us to be ready to leave at a moment's notice. Georg made sure the local blacksmith put the right winter horseshoes on our horses. He checked the wagon and canvas and reinforced the arches where necessary. Mother, Emma, and Meta mended socks and stockings. They washed clothes more frequently, so we would always be ready to leave at a moment's notice.

On Sunday, January 7, Gustav came and announced the red army planned a significant attack shortly. We need to leave on Friday, January 12. 1945. You should be at the ranch where we are staying at 8:00 a.m. He rode away quickly and disappeared in the winter storm to bring the urgent message to the next family. My mother immediately went to Mrs. Grabowski and informed her that we had to leave by Friday. Mother asked, "Could you spare some flour and other food for us to take along? Some blankets and warm clothes would help, too."

"Yes," she answered, "I will check and give you whatever I can spare." My mother thanked Mrs. Grabowski and returned to the kitchen. "Emma and Meta, gather all the dirty clothes and start washing them. Georg and Edmund, you check that the horses' harnesses and the wagon are in good repair."

On Tuesday afternoon, Gustav and his brother, Fritz, came over. They bought special winter horseshoes from a local blacksmith and offered to put them on our horses. They also brought all the tools along and in no time had removed the old horseshoes and put the new ones on. Then they left and went helping to shoe the horses of the other families.

In the next few days, we all pitched in to get ready for departing. By Thursday night, the thermometer dropped to -21°C (-6°F). Mother got us all up very early, prepared breakfast for us, and by 7:00 a.m., we went to say "goodbye to Mrs. Grabowski. My mother embraced her first and thanked her for sharing her home and food with us for several weeks. Tears of gratitude welled up in Mothers' eyes first and then in Mrs. Grabowski's. She looked at each one of us with great compassion as we shook her hand, saying goodbye, wondering how we would survive the winter and what our fate would be. Georg hitched the horses to the wagon. Mother put Horst, Richard, and me in the wagon and covered us with a feather bed to keep us warm. Mother got up on the right side of the wagon seat and Georg on the left to take the reins. Emma, Meta, and Edmund decided to walk to reduce the load for the horses. Georg cracked the whip to make the horses move. The dry snow crackled as the horses stepped forward to pull the wagon through the hardened snow. Frigid winds pelted against the cover, and cold blasts blew through the openings. The force of the wind slowed down the steps of Emma, Meta, and Edmund. They wrapped scarves around their heads in order not to inhale the frigid air. The moisture of their breath turned to ice crystals the minute they exhaled. They bent forward to overcome the wind resistance.

By 8:00 a.m., all seven wagons gathered at the farm where the Kirstein family stayed. Mr. Kirstein, the head of our group, set his wagon in motion, and all six wagons followed him. Our most demanding, roughest, and longest stretch of our journey began without knowing when and where it would end.

The recent snowfall, chilling temperatures, and strong wind slowed us down considerably. We had only covered a short distance by sunset before Mr. Kirstein decided to spend the night in an abandoned farmhouse. The mothers put together some of their food supplies and made hot soup for the children and the adults. They brought their feather beds into the house and bedded down for the night. The next day, we started early, for Mr. Kirstein wanted to reach Plock's town, where he hoped to cross the Weichsel River. Before noon, we met and joined a long line of wagons with the same intentions, only to be informed that the bridges over the Weichsel were blasted to keep the enemy's tanks from crossing. What to do now was an urgent question. The mayor of the town sent messengers to redirect the traffic northeast along the right riverbank. After passing through the town and stopping in a wooded area, the messenger pointed to a narrow, steep road leading diagonally down the river. The last week's frigid temperature covered the river with a thick sheet of ice, strong enough to permit wagons to drive over it. Now we embraced the winter as our friend who spanned an ice bridge across the river for us to cross. We stopped on top of the riverbank. Many wagons who tried to get down the steep icy road never made it across the river. Some horses slipped and fell, sliding down the frozen riverbank with the wagons still attached. Some were severely injured or killed by the wagons that landed on top of them. Dead horses, broken wagons, and household articles scattered all over the river embankment, and the frozen river created a catastrophic scene. I was horrified by this sight when I thought the same thing could happen to our horses and wagon.

Mr. Kirstein and his two older sons, Fritz and Gustav, assessed the dangerous situation and planned to minimize the risk of getting the wagons down the steep icy road.

"We need two thick poles about twice the length of the width of the wagon. We can put them through the wheels' rear spokes to prevent the wagon from picking up speed going downhill. Go and cut down two trees thick and strong enough for that job."

" Yes, Father, we will find the right size of the tree to serve our purpose."

They took an ax and a saw and went into the wooded area to select two trees of the right thickness. They opted to have one spare post just in case one should break. Meanwhile, Mr. Kirstein and his younger son Edmund went from wagon to wagon and instructed the folks how their sons would help them down the hill and that all, even young children and older adults, had to step off the wagon and cross the river on foot.

Soon Fritz and Gustav returned with two long, slender tree trunks. They pushed one of them through the back wheels, cut off the thinner part to the desired length, and then cut the second to the same size. They prepared Mr. Kirstein's wagon first by pushing the post between the spokes through the rear wheels. Fritz and Mr. Liedke grabbed the beam on one side of the wagon, and Gustav and Edmund went on the other side while Mr. Kirstein held the horses' reins tightly. When everyone was ready, Mr. Kirstein commanded the horses to move, pulling the wagon behind them. The front wheels turned, but the rear ones slid over the ice. The men had to pull back forcefully, so the wagon would not pick up speed, slam into the horses, and knock them over. A safe distance had to be kept between the wagon and the horses to keep them steady. The further down they drove, the steeper the road and the harder they held back the wagon.

Except for the very young children and the eighty-year-old Mr. Maschat, who stayed in the wagon, all other persons got out of their wagons and watched how each wagon made its way down the riverbank onto the ice. At first, the horses skidded somewhat when stepping on the ice but moved steady and pulled the wagon over the river's ice surface. We all held our breath until the wagon reached the other side of the river. Even though the west bank was lower, there was no diagonal road leading uphill. It was an arduous ordeal for the horses to pull the wagon up over the icy riverbank. Mrs. Kirstein, her daughter Greta, and youngest son Georg had shuffled slowly down the road unto the frozen river. When their wagon reached the other side of the river, they joined hands, formed a line crossing the river, and climbed up on the other side. We all were grateful the men had helped the wagon to get downhill safely.

The next wagon to come downhill was Mr. Liedke's family and ours, with Georg in charge of the horses and wagon. Mother anxiously watched how Georg maneuvered the wagon with Gustav and Fritz's help down the hill unto the ice. Then the men removed the beam from the wheels and carried it uphill to help the next wagon down. Gustav directed us to go downhill and to follow the wagon at a distance. Emma brought Horst downhill, and we followed her. When we all gathered on the icy surface of the river, Emma, with Horst in her arms, took the lead; Mother, holding my hand, was next. I held Richard' hand, then my older brother Edmund and Meta followed at the end.

I pushed one foot after the other forward and listened for a noise of cracking ice. We reached the other side of the river and climbed up the riverbank. Our horses struggled and skidded back time after time while pulling the wagon up the high icy riverbank. Kastan and Kobel broke out in a sweat, and foam oozed from their jaws. Mr. Kirstein and Mr. Liedke came to our aid and gave a push to the wagon from the rear when the horses pulled uphill. After many attempts, they finally succeeded. When our family, the horses, and the wagon stood safely on top of the other side of the riverbank, my mother thanked God. We all hoped the rest of our group and all the wagons would safely cross the frozen river. We watched how one wagon after the other came safely down the steep icy road while we waited. When all persons and their wagons reached and stood on the west bank, the sun spread her last rays over the snow-covered landscape. Darkness and frigid air embraced us and made us shiver. Hunger gnawed in our stomachs.

Fritz and Gustav had brought a few bricks and some logs just in case we would not be able to find a place to stay overnight. Fritz and Gustav started a fire. They handed a big pot to Edmund and Rudolf and asked them to fill it with fresh snow, which they let melt over the fire. Edmund and Rudolf took a bucket, kept bringing snow, and dumped it into the pot until three-quarters full. The mothers and older daughters took some water from the pot before it got hot and mixed flour and water to form small dumplings (Klunker in East Prussian dialect). The flour dumplings were added to the boiling water and stirred so the dumplings would not stick together. Fritz and Gustav cut up half a slab of pork belly. They tossed the small pieces as well as some salt into the pot. We all gathered around the fire. Even though the warm air did not caress us, we felt warmer by watching the dancing flames. After the soup was ready, Mr. Kirstein asked everyone to come and get hot soup. We ran to the wagon and lined up and waited until Fritz and Gustav poured a ladle full of soup into our bowls. Even though the pork skin was tough like leather, we were grateful to have something warm to put into our empty stomachs. Emma and Meta collected our dirty dishes and wiped them with snow to remove the food remnants.

Mother asked us to take our shoes off but leave our clothes on before crawling under the cold feather beds for the night. Edmund, Richard, sister Meta and I laid down with our heads in the back of the wagon. Mother, Horst, and Emma settled down for the night in the front part of the wagon. Georg joined us after feeding the horses. He threw a blanket on their backs to keep them warm and unhitched them from the wagon. He tied them to a nearby tree. We cuddled up under the cover not only to warm up the feather bed but to benefit from our body's warmth. I exhaled the warm air under the raised blanket to warm up quicker. I rapidly put it down when I inhaled.

No sooner did I close my eyes as the droning of approaching airplanes became louder and louder. Each time they threw a bomb, the explosion caused a loud bang that I quickly put my head under the cover and my hands over my ears to reduce the noise level. Bombs caused not only destruction but also fires. Flames danced in the darkness of the night, and their light penetrated even the cover of our wagon. The German flak followed a barrage of cannon shots on the river's east bank, hoping to shoot down or scare the Russian planes to retreat. None of us could fall asleep. Mother tried to comfort us and prayed God would save our lives by preventing a bomb from landing on us. Well past midnight, the airplanes' droning stopped as the Russian fighter planes returned to their base, and the cannon fire of the defending German flak ceased. However, the dreadful night seemed endless.

At last, the golden globe of the sun appeared on the eastern horizon and illuminated our wagons. Fritz and Gustav were the first ones to get up to start a fire. They filled a big pot with snow, put it on the fire to melt then bring it to a boil so that everyone could have a hot drink to fill up the empty stomachs. Some had coffee brewed from hickory; my mother made a big pot of peppermint tea for us. Then she prepared a sandwich with homemade sausage for each of us.

Georg put fodder, consisting of oats mixed with chopped-up straw, for the horses in two bags and hung them on the harness. He also gave them a bucket of water. After the families and horses were ready, the six wagons lined up behind Mr. Kirstein, and the horses began to pull the wagons through the snow-covered secondary road. Mothers with the younger children stayed tucked in the wagons' feather beds while the adults trampled through the snow next to the wagons. Other covered and open wagons joined the tragic-looking trek. The wind whistled and shook the cover while the horses strained and stomped through the snow to pull the loaded wagons slowly forward. The squeaking of the wheels mixed with the blasting of distant cannon shots created a woeful, chilling tune. Even though the sun rose above the horizon, the temperatures stayed below zero centigrade.

On we went. Before dusk, we reached a farm. Mr. Kirstein decided to stop and give the horses and all the persons who walked a rest. He approached the farmer and asked if the wagons could find shelter for the night at his farm. First, the farmer grumbled but permitted Mr. Kirstein to stay. All the mothers with their children rushed into the house to escape the cold and warm up their freezing bodies. Meanwhile, the farmer allowed us to put the horses in the barn. He also gave them water and hay.

The compassionate farmer's wife prepared soup and dished out steaming hot soup to the hungry travelers. Everyone relished each spoonful of soup and was thankful to have something warm in their stomach. After the house's lady designated a spot for each family, Mother asked Emma and Meta to bring in the four featherbeds and put them in the heated living room. Meta put first a sheet down, put two featherbeds on the floor to serve as a mattress, and two on top for covering. Mrs. Hein did the same for her family next to ours. After a while, we all crawled under the covers. My mother, Horst, Richard, and I cuddled up toward the wall, and Emma, Meta, Georg, and Edmund were on the opposite side. Even though many persons filled the room, just being warm felt so good.

Fritz, Gustav, and Edmund Kirstein took turns watching the horses and the house and woke us up before dawn to get ready and start early. The temperatures dropped to below zero, building up ice under the packed snow, making it difficult for the horses to pull the wagons. They had to forcefully stomp down through the snow until the unique studs would lodge in the ice and keep them from slipping. Their breath turned immediately to ice crystals as soon as it hit the chilly air; so did the breath of the persons who walked or sat on the front of the wagon. Emma, Meta, and Edmund walked next to the wagon. They crossed their arms quickly and continuously over their chests to keep their hands and fingers from freezing. They wiggled their toes inside their shoes to keep the circulation flowing. Around their face, they wrapped wool scarves to keep the blustering wind from hitting their skin.

The pathetic trek moved on by day and looked for shelter at night. If luck was with us, we found an abandoned house or some farms where the people, who had not yet fled, gave us refuge and food for a night. The mayors of some villages we passed through provided places to stay prepared and served hot meals and food for the weary travelers. Some days, we had only a sandwich; several days, we went hungry. Then hunger clasped its claws into the stomach and slowly drained and weakened its weary victims. The bones stretched the thin skin, and the air blew up the empty gut. Driven by fear of death, we had to move on or perish.

Even Mother and Horst moved into the covered wagon and sought warmth underneath the featherbeds. Emma and Meta took the reign of the horses now and then to give Georg a break. Mother thanked God each day that her children were still alive.

Dead, frozen horses, and some human corpses lay beside the road. The families who lost loved ones could not dig a grave in the frozen ground to bury their dead.

The Russian airplanes had distributed leaflets for the red army to add to the people's and refugees' misery. Some of them fell in the hands of the German soldiers and civilians, too, which read:

"Rotarmist: Du stehst jetzt auf Deutschem Boden. Die Stunde der Rache hat geschlagen. (Soldier of the red army, you stand on German soil. The hour of revenge is here.
Wir vernichten den Feind. (We destroy the enemy)
Wir werden alle totschlagen. (We will beat all of them to death)
Die Deutschen sind keine Menschen. (The Germans are not human beings).
Wir werden nicht sprechen. (We will not speak.)
Wir werden uns nicht aufregen. (We will not aggravate ourselves).
Wir werden töten. (We will kill.)
Brenne verfluchtes Deutschland. (Burn, damn Germany.)

Joseph Stalin, who was a radical dictator, fired up the Russian generals and the Russian soldiers to rape the German women, destroy their villages, and kill, kill, kill. Ilya Ehrenburg, a Russian Jewish journalist, and Joseph Stalin's propaganda minister, expressed his hatred in many Russian newspapers. He indoctrinated the Russian soldiers, "Kill the Germans -— this requests your aged mother kill the Germans—this request your children to kill the Germans, so calls your motherland. Do not neglect your duty—kill, kill, kill. After you killed one German, kill a second one for us. There is nothing more amusing than to see German corpses.

Bombing of Berlin WWII

Knowing what was awaiting the German civilians, the German soldiers on the East Prussian border fought relentlessly, even giving their lives to hold back the Russian red army. Now, they no longer thought of victory for their Fuehrer or saving their country. Their only thoughts were to save as many lives of their people as possible, often sacrificing their own lives. They helped wherever they could to evacuate the people. Russian soldiers would treat the Germans, especially the German women, out of revenge for killing Russians and destroying some of their cities during the last years of fighting in Russia.

The wagons rolled on through snow and ice. Some days, the trek of pitiful travelers only advanced a few kilometers; other days, a little further. Some days, we got food; other days, we starved. The weather was brutal during the remainder of January 1945, and the temperatures rarely rose above zero during the day and plunged well below zero during the night. The cold twisted the lips over the grinding gritting teeth, and eyes looked pitifully into space.

Horses and humans alike endured hardship. Faith in God and fear of being run over by Russian tanks or being killed by bombs forced us to press forward and bear the ordeals and danger that each day brought with it.

At the beginning of February, the temperature rose. It was still too cold to open the canvas of the front and rear of the wagon or to be sitting outside in front of the wagon. As the days grew longer and the sun warmer, we saw the light filter through the cover. We even felt the warmth of the sun when we put our hands above the down covers. The snow started melting, and the wagons' wheels rolled over solid ground and paved streets again.

We passed smaller towns along the way. However, the most exciting city we passed through until now was Stettin, the capital of Pomerania. Fortunately, some bridges were still standing, and we were able to cross the Oder River, which flows through Dammscher Lake (Dammscher See) and later empties into the Baltic Sea. Driving over the bridge and watching the towers on both riverbanks and seeing the churches' spires and other essential buildings was an exhilarating experience. We also passed through sections where the bombs destroyed most of the buildings. Only partial, ragged walls with the window holes stood among the piles of rubble—what a bleak picture of the once-beautiful city we encountered. Every time we passed a beautiful structure that was still intact, I pointed it out to ensure my brothers did not miss seeing them.

After we passed Stettin and went as far as possible away from the center of the city, Mr. Kirstein decided to find shelter before darkness set in, just in case the Royal Airforce should choose to drop some more bombs over Stettin during the night. When Mr. Kirstein saw a house still intact in Stettin's outskirts, he decided to try staying there. All six wagons followed him. Luckily, an elderly couple lived there. They were kind enough to allow us to spend the night in their home. They did not have enough food, so all families shared whatever they still possessed.

February passed. March arrived, and so did warmer temperatures. The wagons rolled on a little faster now. Georg pulled back the front and the rear canvases in the afternoon, and the mild, fresh air invigorated somewhat our weakened, skinny bodies.

The snow had melted, and the meadows began to turn green. Even the trees and bushes showed signs of spring and started to bud. The skylark rose high and thrilled everyone with her sweet melodic songs, which were not affected by the destruction on the ground. The storks had also returned. Many found their nests on the rooftops destroyed and had to find a new location to rebuild their nests. They stalked through the meadows to pick up a morsel here and there. After the children lay and sat for two months in the covered wagons, they longed to move their skinny legs. They wanted to run across the meadows and play with the sun rays and chase the storks. The children could only dream of playing; they had to remain on the wagons and continue the journey. Nobody knew neither how much longer the trek had to travel nor where its destination would be.

We journeyed through the beautiful province of Mecklenburg and reached the outskirts of the City of Schwerin. Fortunately, the city endured only four air attacks and few damaged structures because it had no essential industries. The romantic palace stood unchanged in one of the seven lakes surrounding the old part of Schwerin.

Since the trek remained on the town's periphery, the travelers could only see a distant silhouette of the skyline and the palace. However, the children got excited each time they saw a castle, a fancy tower, or a church turret still intact.

The trek continued to travel through Mecklenburg's lovely pastoral scenery, then passed through Ratzenburg towards Luebeck.

The city suffered horrible air raids during March 1942, when Arthur Harris of the Royal Airforce of Britain attacked civilian areas and created a firestorm. It destroyed three of the significant churches and did massive damage to the historic part of the old town of Luebeck. Luckily, the famous Holsten Tower remained intact. The children got excited when passing through the ancient, gothic, red brick structure.

"Look, look," I called the attention of my brothers while pointing to the two massive towers before passing through the gate. At the Gate, officials told the trek leaders what their destination was going to be. They told Mr. Kirstein, his group's destination was Pratjau. Then Mr. Kirstein asked his son Gustav to go to each wagon and tell them we would go via Eutin to Pratjau. Everyone breathed a sigh of relief that the journey would soon end after having been on the road in a covered wagon for almost ten weeks straight.

We passed the Trave River before getting into the old section of the town.

"How sad, bombs damaged some of the medieval buildings," Edmund remarked.

"Yes, it sure is a pity, the ancient buildings stood for hundreds of years, and one air raid destroyed so many structures in minutes," I remarked.

"I sure hope the war and the destruction will end soon, and we can go home," Richard added. Edmund answered, "I surely wish so, also. Unfortunately, nobody knows when the war will end."

However, we knew that our arduous journey would soon end.

It was still daylight while we passed Luebeck. Mr. Kirstein decided to drive as far away from the city center as possible to avoid a possible air raid. When he saw a farm, he stopped and went to ask the owner if he and the other families could spend the night on his farm. The farmer's wife also came out of the house and bade the families settle down for the night.

"Come on in, and I will show you where you can stay; mothers and the children can sleep in the house, and the bigger boys and men can sleep in the hay barn. You can also use some hay for the horses. I will cook some soup for all of you, so you get something warm in your stomachs."

Mr. Kirstein thanked the farmers and told the travelers to remain here for the night and that our destination would be Pratjau, which we should reach within a few days. Everyone got off the wagons and was glad to hear the good news that the journey is almost over.

The mothers and their older daughters carried the featherbeds into the house where the farmer's wife designated them to sleep. The men and older boys unhitched the horses, gave fodder and water. The children gathered in the courtyard and played catch until my mother called us for supper and to get ready for bed.

The next morning the lady cooked some oatmeal with fresh milk for all the children and served bread and marmalade for the adults with hickory brewed coffee. The mothers thanked the farmer's wife for her generosity and kindness, and Mr. Kirstein thanked the farmer for letting us stay overnight and providing fodder for the horses.

Georg, and my mother, with Horst on her lap, sat in front of the wagon. Edmund Richard and I moved to the wagon's back; we dangled our feet through the ladder's spokes, holding on to the upper beam. We wanted to make sure not to miss anything. Emma and Meta chose to walk for a while next to the wagon.

Spring had arrived, not only according to the calendar, but also in nature! Finally, the temperatures rose enough to wear lighter clothes and not stay under the featherbeds all day long. We passed through pastoral green meadows embellished by spring flowers. Delicate green leaves adorned bushes and trees along the way. The migratory birds returned. The storks stalked through the fields, hoping to catch a frog.

"You think the storks also returned to their nest on top of our barn?" I asked.

"I sure hope so. How I wished to be home and watch the swallows build their nests under the roofs," Edmund replied.

"What a thrill to listen to the skylark sing and hear the call of the cuckoo," Richard remarked.

"You think we will find the same birds where we are going that we had at home?" I asked.

"We will have to wait and see what we will find in Pratjau," Edmund responded.

The children looked right and left and did not want to miss anything. Being absorbed with the lovely scenery made the time pass so much faster for the children. Now and then, Emma and Meta climbed up on the wagon and took the rein to give Georg a break and a chance to walk, to loosen up his legs.

Mr. Kirstein stopped around noon at another big farm to ask for some fodder for the horses, give them a rest, and ask for some food, mainly for the children.

In the late afternoon, the silhouette of Eutin appeared on the horizon with the majestic Eutin castle and the two church steeples standing out above the rest of the town. As we approached the city, the red-brick structures came closer and closer. Soon the lake became visible.

"How nice the red buildings look among the delicate green of the budded trees," I exclaimed.

"Yes, it sure is nice to see a town not destroyed by bombs," Edmund remarked.

"I wonder what the place will look like where we are going to stay?" Richard questioned.

"I hope we have a lot of space for playing and running."

"I do, too. I am so tired of sitting all the time."

"Yes, I will be so glad to sleep in a real bed again instead of squeezed in on the wagon or sleep on the floor."

"We will wait and see where we land."

Mr. Kirstein decided to pass through the town during the day just in case the British pilots decided to throw bombs during the night.

When Mr. Kirstein saw a narrow road leading to a sizeable farm, he directed his group there. Fortunately, the farmer pitied us, the pathetic-looking voyagers.

"You can stay here for the night," the farmer's wife said, "I will have my cook prepare a meal for you."

The farmer's wife called her lady cook and instructed her to prepare food for the families. The farm employed many workers who stayed and ate during the week on the farm. On the weekends, the workers went home to their own families. The dining room and their sleeping quarters were vacant on Saturday and Sunday. The lady of the house asked the cook to show the workers' quarters where we could sleep tonight.

"Set the tables in the dining room for the folks."

While the food cooked, mothers took their families to the building where they would sleep. Even though two persons had to share a bed, there were enough for all thirty-five travelers. Once the children knew where they would sleep and eat, they ran outside to check what they could discover. A short distance from the barn, the children saw a pond.

"Let's see who can get there first," Richard said. "Get in line, here."

Frieda, Etna, Helmut, and I formed a line next to Richard. When Richard said, "One, two, three, go," everyone dashed forward. Richard raised his hands and announced that he was the winner. The children got close to the pond and put their hands into the water to see if it was warm enough to take off their shoes and walk into the pond.

"It is way too cold for me, and I do not want to go in the water," Frieda informed her companions. They decided to walk around the pond to check if they could see some frogs or fish but did not see any.

"Let's run around the pond a few times."

"Look, there are some violets in the grass," I called to Frieda and Etna.

"Frieda, I'd like to pick some; you want to stay with me?"

"Sure, let the boys run and play while we remain behind."

"I'll stay with you also," said Etna.

The three of us tracked through the meadow and were delighted each time we found a cluster of violets. When we had a handful of violets, we decided to go back to the house. Frieda, Etna, and I ran to our mothers to present them with our treasured gifts.

"How beautiful the flowers are; where did you find them?"

"I found them by the pond. Can we put the violets on the dining room table for all to enjoy?"

"Of course, my dear. Go and ask the lady of the house if it is okay with her and if she can give you a container to put them in."

I ran to the house, knocked on the door, and waited for the lady to come out.

"Good afternoon," holding up the bouquet of violets, I said, "Look, what I found by the pond. Is it all right to put them on the dining room table, and could you give me a vase?"

"Of course, wait, I will bring one for you,"

"Take this one," she said as she handed me a glass vase.

I thanked the lady and ran to the dining room to show it to my friends.

"Here, Frieda and Etna, we can put all our flowers together." Etna and I gave Frieda the violets. She arranged them and put them on one of the dining room tables in the big hall.

Even though the bouquet looked small on the large table, it added a touch of beauty and reminded the weary travelers of spring's arrival.

The cook called the people to the table and asked the older girls to serve the food. The men indeed were happy to sit down at the table, be served, and not have to stand in line for a long time.

After everyone had eaten, Mr. Kirstein got up. He addressed his group of fellow travelers, "This will probably be the last time we will all be together before each family goes to a different place. I know we endured a lot of hardship, hunger, cold, and danger, but we all have a reason to be grateful to God that no member of our families was injured, killed, or died of starvation or other sicknesses. I want to thank everyone for doing their part and working together to survive the last and most arduous journey. Let us express our gratitude to God, who guided and protected us, without whose help we could have never made it. Let us rise and sing together,

"Now, thank we all our God."

After everyone stood up, Mr. Kirstein began to sing, and everyone joined in:

Now thank we all our God, with hearts and hands and voices,
Who wondrous things has done, in whom this world rejoices.
Who from our mother's arms has blessed us on our way?
With countless gifts of love, and still is ours today.

Emma, both Gretas, and Wanda knew the words of all three verses by heart. The rest hummed the melody. After we finished singing, Mr. Kirstein bade everyone good night and mentioned that we should get an early start tomorrow morning to reach our destination in daylight. The farmer's wife asked the cook to prepare a hot oatmeal breakfast for the children and make bread, butter, and honey sandwiches for the adults.

When the cock crowed early in the morning, my mother woke us up and told us to get ready for the trip.

"Thank God, this will be our last two days on the road; I wonder where we will be staying next,"Mother remarked to Emma. "Go and help Georg feed the horses."

"Meta, you take all the featherbeds to the wagon, then let's have breakfast and be on the road."

The farmer's wife and her husband came out at 6:00 a.m. to say goodbye to us. Mr. Kirstein and all the mothers thanked them for allowing us to spend the night at the farm and providing us with food. We spent one more night in a small village schoolhouse before arriving in the late afternoon in Pratjau.

When we entered the village, Mr. Kirstein pulled into a place with a big courtyard, and all six wagons followed him. The first building was empty, but a family lived next door. Mr. Kirstein knocked on the door, and a friendly person came out.

"Good afternoon, I am Mr. Kirstein; my group of refugees and I were instructed to settle in Pratjau. Can you tell me where the mayor lives, so he can show us where each family should go?"

"Good afternoon, I am Mr. Sabrow, the grammar school-teacher. Wait here; I'll call my maid," She can show you where the mayor lives."

"This is Olga; she will take you to the mayor"

"Good day, Mr. Kirstein."

"We can all go together with the wagons. There is enough space in the village square for all of you," Olga replied.

"Good, then get on my wagon. We will drive there together. A short distance from the school, the wagons stopped in the village square. Olga pointed to the house where the mayor lived.

Mr. Kirstein went there, knocked on the door, and a middle-aged man came out.

Mr. Kirstein introduced himself and his purpose to contact him. The mayor returned his greetings and said he would send his son to the designated family with each wagon.

"However, three of the families will have to go to Sophienhof. It is only one mile away from here."

Mr. Kirstein thanked Olga and dismissed her. He turned to the Hein, Marta Kirstein, and Bonacker families and told them to go to Sophienhof, a huge ranch. Gratefully three families parted from the other travelers and drove to their assigned destination of Sophienhof.

Chapter 9
Life at Sophienhof

THE ESTATE MANAGER, Mr. Otzen, met the three families and showed them where they would live. Eight of us shared a one-bedroom apartment with five of the Hein family, thirteen total. The Hein family occupied the bedroom, and our family, the living room. We all used the kitchen. Mrs. Martha Kirstein and her two children shared a one-bedroom apartment with four other persons next door. The owner of the estate had the two red brick triplexes built for the workers and their families.

"I'll show you where you can put the horses and the wagons," Mr. Otzen pointed to the stable. Before you unload the wagons, you can leave them outside, across from the stable for the moment.," Mr. Otzen informed the families, "go to the dining hall next to the manor house. The cook and her helper have prepared a meal for you."

Georg got off the wagon first, then helped Mother and Horst to come down. All the children followed my mother to the dining hall, and so did the family Hein and Marta Kirstein, with her two children. The cook had prepared a split pea soup with pork belly bits in it. Each could also have a piece of bread. The four small children received a glass of milk.

My mother and Mrs. Hein went into the house first. A small hallway led to three rooms, a kitchen to the left, a small chamber to the right, and the living room straight ahead.

"My God, fourteen persons have to live in these two rooms? How will that work?" questioned Mrs. Hein.

"It sure is a tight squeeze, but we will have to make the best of it," my mother responded. "It beats living on the wagon; I also think we will be safer here," my Mother added while entering the living room.

"I sure hope so," Mrs. Hein responded. They looked at the contents of the rooms.

Three primitive wooden frames, each with a big, straw-filled sack, stood along the walls serving as beds. One big table and a few chairs were placed in the center of the room. An oven, covered with green glazed ceramic tiles, was built in the corner next to the living room entrance. It reached from the floor to the ceiling. When lit, it provided enough heat to warm up the living room and the bedroom.

The kitchen furniture consisted of a big table with a long bench on each side. Buckets filled with water utilized a smaller bench against the wall. There was no running water in the house. We had to carry water from a well or a nearby creek into the house. Against one wall stood the wood hearth for cooking. The entrance and the kitchen floors were concrete, and wooden boards covered the living and bedroom floors.

Mr. Anderson, the estate's assistant manager, lived with his family next door to where we moved in. Mrs. Anderson came out to greet the families.

"I know the apartment is too small for two families, but nothing else is vacant."

"We'll make the best of it. I am so glad to stop living on the wagon and being in a different place each day," Mother responded. "I want you to meet my two older daughters, Emma and Meta."

After Mrs. Anderson shook hands with them, she excused herself and let my mother and her daughters continue unpacking the featherbeds first, then the clothes, and other few belongings they carried into the house until the wagon was empty. Then Georg brought the horses, hitched them to the wagon, and pulled it to the designated area. Afterward, he led the horses to the stable, took off all the harnesses, and tied them with a leather collar and strap to a post next to the feeding place. Then Georg got a bucket of water from the well and hay from the barn for the horses.

Edmund, Richard, and I made rounds, familiarizing ourselves with the surroundings and hoping to meet children our age. A boy and a girl from the house next door came out to look us over.

"Who are you? What are you doing here?" the boy asked us, strangers.

"My name is Edmund; this is my brother Richard and my sister Hilde. We are refugees and are supposed to live here. What are your names"?

"My name is Hans, and this is my sister Lisa," the boy responded. We all shook hands.

"You want me to show you around?" Hans asked.

"Oh, yes! Let me see if Frieda wants to join us."

I went inside and called Frieda, "You want to come with us and see the farm?"

"Not now, I have to help my mother unpack," she responded.

"Okay, then we will go alone."

Hans and Lisa went ahead to the manor' house first. Edmund, Richard, and I followed them.

Pointing to the house, "This is where Mr. Jessen, the estate owner, lives. He is very strict and does not want any children playing inside the barn or other buildings."

"The inside must be gorgeous, judging from lacy curtains on the tall windows," I remarked.

"Yes, the furniture is also exquisite, but Mrs. Jessen seldom comes out of the house, and Mr. Jessen limps. Look behind the house at the marvelous garden. In the summer, the trees are laden with fruits. Their apples and pears are sweet and tasty."

Then they went across the street, "This is where Mr. Diercks and his family live. Mr. Diercks is the manager of the livestock. He can be mean if he sees you doing something he does not like. Mrs. Diercks distributes each day's milk for the families' children. She also receives and distributes mail once each week."

We passed the stall of the cows. In front of the stable stood an enormous cement tank. The workers collected and dumped the cow manure in an open cement pit during the winter and spread it as fertilizer over the fields in spring. Next, they passed the barn and the pigpen and got to Mr. Otzen and his family's house with a beautiful garden next to it.

"You have to watch out for Mr. Otzen. He reports any wrongdoing to Mr. Jessen and can cause you trouble. However, their children, Heike and Willie, are very nice."

"Now, I take you to the pond behind the cow stall. You cannot swim in the pond. The water from washing the stable gets dirty and drains into the pond. You get sick if you get water in your mouth while swimming. However, in winter, we ice skate on it."

"What a shame; I like swimming," Edmund remarked. "I do, too," Richard added.

"When we want to swim, we go to the Selenter Lake. It is only a short distance from here. We go there frequently during the summer. You can come with us if you like."

"We better get back to Mother. She will be wondering where we are," I remarked while turning to the house where we were going to stay.

"Goodbye, Hans and Lisa. Thank you for showing us around. Can we see you tomorrow?" Richard remarked before they went to their apartment.

Meanwhile, the sun began to set, and the mothers were concerned about getting dinner for the children. Mrs. Anderson felt sorry for the children and sent a loaf of bread, a small chunk of butter, and a homemade sausage to Mrs. Hein and my mother. Since the kitchen was too small to feed all fourteen people at one time, Mrs. Hein agreed to let my mother and her family cook and eat first.

Emma started a fire in the hearth to heat a pot of water for tea and wash her brothers' and young sisters' hands and faces. Before getting ready for bed, I asked, "Mother, where is the washroom?"

"It is in the pig stall across from the house," Mother replied.

"In the pig stall?"

"That sounds awful! In case I need to go at night, I have to walk outside in the dark to the pigpen?"

"You will get used to it," Mother replied.

I thought I would never get used to it but did not dare say it to my mother.

I went across to the stall to check out the toilet. I was not too fond of the location nor of the smell. I certainly will not get used to using it, either.

The rest of the evening passed in disarray. My mother assigned the sleeping arrangements for the three beds standing against the wall.

"Emma, Meta, and Hilde, you sleep in this bed in the corner. George, Edmund, and Richard, you sleep in the bed next to your sisters. Horst and I will take the first bed."

Even though we children did not like the idea of three persons sleeping in one narrow bed, we obeyed our mother.

The first night was uncomfortable for me. Every time Emma or Meta turned, they woke me up by kicking me in the side or chin. Getting dressed in my brothers' presence and not knowing when a member of the Hein family would pass through was embarrassing for me. I am sure it was for my sisters too.

When I told Emma and Meta about my discomfort, they found a solution by holding up the featherbed toward the wall, so nobody could see me getting dressed or at bedtime undressed. I did the same for them too.

It took a few days to get used to the new quarters and living arrangements. Soon, Emma set up a bed in the small chamber, and Georg moved to the pantry, so only two siblings slept in one bed. Mother and Mrs. Hein set up the usage of the kitchen. We were to cook and eat breakfast, lunch, and dinner first, and Mrs. Hein and her family afterward. Each family was allocated one day for bathing in a big tub in the kitchen—our family on Friday and Mrs. Hein's family on Saturday. Somehow, we developed a tolerable routine and slowly got acquainted with all the estate's neighbors and families.

Mr. and Mrs. Anderson, our neighbors to the left, got Georg a job taking care of horses and working in the fields when necessary. Mr. Diercks asked Emma and Meta to milk cows, which already grazed in the pastures. The pay was minimal, but in return, the family would receive fresh milk each day, some grain, and other food. A plot for a garden was also assigned, which we shared with family Hein.

In a few days, April 1, 1945, we would celebrate the first Easter away from home. Mother was concerned about going to church and what to feed her family on this memorable holiday.

She asked Mrs. Anderson where the nearest church was.

"We usually go to the next village, Fargau, to church. On special occasions, church service is held in the the castle of Salzau, but not this Easter.

"Are you going to church? Since we do not know where Fargau is, can we follow you"?

"Of course, Mr. and Mrs. Jessen and other families will also be going. The service starts at 9:00 a.m. Be ready at 8:30 a.m. It is only a few miles from here. But we like to be early, so we can find a good spot to secure the horses."

"Thank you; I will let Georg know. My family will be ready at 8:30 a.m."

"By the way, do you have some special food for Easter? If not, I will have my husband butcher some extra chickens for your family."

"Thank you; it is so kind of you to offer me fresh chicken. My family will be very grateful and happy to get meat."

"I will also send over some potatoes and turnips with the chicken."

"Thank you so very, very much."

"We also have an Easter custom here to get water from the creek. It is supposed to heal different diseases after you wash with it. But the person who fetches the water can neither look to the right nor the left nor talk; otherwise, the water loses the healing power. Wait, I'll give you a dozen eggs. Your daughters can color them for the children."

"They sure will appreciate a colored egg for Easter."

Mrs. Anderson handed my mother a bowl full of eggs. My mother thanked her again and took the eggs into the house.

"Look what we got here," showing the bowl of eggs to the family.

Mrs. Anderson gave them to me. She will also butcher some chicken for us. Mrs. Anderson told me that there would be a church service in Fargau on Easter Sunday. Georg, we will drive to Fargau to church. Have the horses and wagon ready by 8:30 a.m.

"Here, Emma, you can boil the eggs and color them for us."

"What shall I use? We have no color?"

"Go to the nearby woods; you might find some flowers. You can also use moss or old bark. Put each item in an individual container, then boil water and pour the hot water over them. Let it steep for a while or overnight before you remove the blossoms, moss, and bark, and you will have some colored solutions for painting the eggs."

"That is a clever idea. I will go right away to the nearby woods and see what I can find there."

"Can I come with you, Emma?" I asked.

"Yes, you can come with me; let's get a bucket first."

Off we went. I gleefully hopped until we got to the woods.

"Look at all those beautiful yellow cowslips," I said as I began to pick one handful after another while Emma gathered some moss and picked up pulverized bark, she found next to a rotten tree stump. We walked carefully through the forest so as not to step on the cowslips and the anemones that covered the floor like a magic carpet.

"Can I also pick some other flowers for the table?"

"Of course, that would be nice to have fresh flowers on the table."

I picked some white anemone spring flowers and wild forget-me-nots that I found on the edge of a small pond and mixed them with the cowslips.

"Is it alright if I run ahead? I want to surprise Mother?"

"Yes, you run along. I'll follow you."

I ran to the house to present the bouquet to my mother.

"Look, Mother, what I found for you, aren't they beautiful?" I remarked while handing the flowers to mother.

"Thank you, they sure are lovely. Let me see where I can find a container for the flowers."

Mother walked into the kitchen and found a cup with a broken handle. She gave it to me.

"Here, use this. Put the flowers in the living room for now, and on Easter Sunday, we can place them on the kitchen table with our meal."

"Very good. I will do so."

Meanwhile, Emma came back with her filled bucket. She went to the kitchen and put a pot of water on the hearth. Then Emma put the moss, the bark, and the florets into individual cups and poured the boiling water into each cup. She let it steep overnight.

After our family had breakfast the next morning, I immediately offered to help Emma color the eggs.

"We have to wait until the Hein family has their breakfast first before we can use the kitchen. Go and play outside; I will call you when I am ready."

I ran outside. I saw two girls playing with their dolls on the steps of the neighboring house. I slowly approached them.

"My name is Hildegard. Everybody calls me Hilde. My family and I got here four days ago. Mother told us; we will be staying here for a while." After the two girls looked me over, they introduced themselves as Katie and Brigitte.

"Come, sit down, and tell us where you came from," Katie invited me.

I answered all the questions the girls asked. Brigitte and Katie were surprised to hear that my family and I came from East Prussia by horse and buggy and even traveled during the winter.

"Mother hopes the war will be over soon, so we all can go home to our farm in East Prussia," I added.

"Yes, our parents and we hope the same. Lately, the school is closed because of the air raids."

"Where do you go to school?"

"We go to Pratjau; it is only a short walk from here," Katie added.

"I sure hope they will be able to start school soon. I like to go to school," I remarked.

"I hope we get a new teacher. I'm not too fond of the current one. He is too strict and punishes us severely if we do something wrong," Brigitte commented.

"It was nice to meet you. Can I come later to play with you? I have to help my sister color Easter eggs." When I heard my sister Emma calling me, I excused myself.

Emma had removed the blossoms, moss, and bark chips from the cups. She waited a little while until the sediment had settled on the bottom of the cups. She put the first egg in the green liquid.

"Let me put the next egg in the yellow-colored liquid," I said.

"Sure, go ahead! You can do the next eggs, too."

I carefully dropped one egg in the yellow, the other egg in the brown solution. Then we waited and watched the eggs taking on the different colors. With a spoon, Emma took out the first egg from the brown liquid and wiped it dry.

"It is dark enough; you can put in another one."

When all eggs were colored, we put them on a plate, carried them into the living room, and placed them next to the flowers. It was a symbol, reminding us of Easter at home.

Emma offered the colored solutions to Frau Hein, but she was not interested in coloring Easter eggs.

Friday was bathing day. After both families had dinner, Emma put a big pot of water on the hearth. Meta and Georg carried buckets of water from the well to the kitchen. Georg had asked the farm manager if he could borrow one of the metal containers, which held water for the cows while they were out in the pasture. The manager gave him one, and he brought it home as a bathtub for our family.

Emma poured first a pot full of hot water in the tub, then enough cold water to make it comfortably warm to the touch. Then she called Horst, undressed him, and sat him in the tub. He was so happy, hit the water with both hands splashing the water all over. But when it came to washing his head with homemade soap, he did not like it and started to cry. When Emma finished with Horst, it was my turn. Emma added more hot water to the tub.

"It feels so good to take a bath; just wash my hair, Emma; the rest I can wash."

"As you wish but make it quick; the rest of your siblings and Mother need to take a bath, too."

"All right, I will hurry up."

I stepped out of the tub, rubbed my hair dry first, and then the rest of my body before putting on my underwear and shirt. I ran to the living room, jumped into bed, and slipped under the cover. I would be very embarrassed if someone saw me in my underwear. I asked my mother for a comb. I wrapped the feather bed around me while combing my wet hair. Then I knelt in bed and said my evening prayer before I fell asleep.

After the boys took their baths, Emma changed the water for our mother, Meta, and herself. The Hein family went through the same ritual on Saturday.

On Saturday night, I woke up several times for fear of sleeping past the sunrise; I wanted to make sure I was the first person to be at the creek. It was still dark when I quietly got up, put on my dress, slipped in the shoes, took the bucket, and went to the creek. Everyone was still sleeping. That was good, I thought. When I reached the stream, I submerged the bucket's opening into the running water until three-quarters full. I picked it up and started going back to the house. Just then, I saw the neighbor, Lisa, coming out of the door. I rushed behind the other side of the house and entered before Lisa could see me. I was glad and carried the magic water into the living room, so nobody but our family could use it. Then I removed my dress, slipped unnoticed under the cover, and waited until my mother would wake up everyone.

Mother's wake-up call made everyone get out of bed.

"Mother, look, I brought for us Easter water from the creek," pointing to the bucket in the corner of the room.

"Good, my child, it is enough for each one of us to wash our faces." Mother had put out for each child the best clothes she could gather from the bundle tied in a bedsheet and gave it to me, Richard, Edmund, and Georg. Emma and Meta picked their own. The dresses, not pressed, looked wrinkled and shabby, but they had to make do for the moment.

At 8:30 a.m. punctually, Georg had the horses in their harness and hitched to the wagon; so did all the other families that wanted to go to church. Today, even the owners, Mr. and Mrs. Jessen, had their elegant stagecoach readied to go to church on Easter Sunday. All wagons followed the stagecoach.

It was a beautiful spring day. The skylark climbed so high one could hardly see her, but one heard her cheerful song. The first spring flowers appeared among the fresh green meadows; what a delight to watch. We arrived on time to unhitch the horses from the wagons and tie them to a beam. The coachman of Mr. Jessen stayed with his horses to watch them and the stagecoach. Mrs. Jessen looked elegant in a bright suit and matching hat, walking next to her limping husband. Everyone followed them. When we entered the church, the local people looked us over from tip to toe as if to say, "Where did these gypsies come from?" We felt uneasy that ours, as well as the other refugees', clothes, looked so pathetic.

As soon as the organ began playing and we sang the first Easter song, we forgot about our appearance and just sang along with the congregation. The pastor delivered an uplifting sermon about the crucifixion and resurrection of Christ and reminded his parishioners that they are serving a living God and Lord. He closed with the word`: "Have courage; God will help us through this senseless war and the difficulties the country is facing." After the benediction, the pastor dismissed the worshippers.

I dashed to the wagon to escape the curious, degrading looks of the people. My family followed and waited until Mr. and Mrs. Jessen led the wagon train back to Sophienhof.

Mother, Emma, and Meta started to prepare chicken, potatoes, and cabbage. I helped to set the table. I put the colored eggs around the bouquet as a centerpiece. Edmund and Richard went with Georg to put the horses in the stable and give them some water and hay.

When everything was ready, my mother sent me to call the boys to the dining table. Everyone sat down on the two benches; mother folded her hands, and so did all the children. Mother thanked God for the food and for having her children brought safely through the last treacherous ten-week-long journey. She also prayed for protecting her husband and daughter, Marta, not knowing where they were or whether they were still alive.

Family Photo

The whole family relished the food. Emma let everyone pick a colored egg. The youngest children each got an extra one, and Emma asked them to save them for tomorrow. In the afternoon, the children went out to check out the different buildings and areas. They also met the children from the adjacent house, Uwe, Brigitte, and Hans. They chatted, played catch, and enjoyed running and moving around after sitting or lying in the wagon for so long.

The second day after Easter was still considered a holiday, and nobody worked except the servants who took care of the animals and the people who had to milk the cows.

The next day April 3, 1945, while the mothers and daughters washed clothes and got settled, suddenly, the sirens pierced the air in the late afternoon. The children from outside ran into the house.

"Mother, Mother, what is happening?"

"It sounds like a warning of an air raid. Let me run over to the neighbor and ask what we are supposed to do. You stay inside."

Mother walked over to Mrs. Anderson and asked why the sirens sounded and what she and the family should do.

"It sounds like an air attack over Kiel; we have no bunker. We run into the woods and wait until it is over. Sometimes, we just stay in the house and wait for the danger to pass. You never know when and where they might drop their bombs."

"Should we run into the woods now?"

"I think the day bombing will not last too long. Just stay inside the house until the alarm sounds again, announcing the end of the attack. However, tell the children to watch out for the dive bombers during the day. They attack persons, trains, cars, or anything at random. At night, make sure you cover the windows with a heavy blanket when you turn on the light, so the pilots cannot see where people live. When the alarm sounds for a long time or at night, we all run to the forest for cover."

"Thank you for your information. I never thought that bombs could kill us after we survived the long strenuous trip," Mother uttered.

Mother returned to her family and warned them of the danger and to look out for the dive bombers who shoot and kill individuals whenever they see them in the open.

Mrs. Hein came into the room and asked my mother why the sirens sounded. Our mother passed on the information that she received from Mrs. Anderson. We all waited quietly and listened intensely. We could hear the distant droning of the airplanes. At one time, the sound of approaching planes became thunderous. We all ran over to our mother, thinking a bomb would fall right on us. Thank God, they only flew over us. The siren sounded again a few hours later, letting us know that the bombing attack was over for now.

We all breathed a sigh of relief that the airplanes dropped no bombs on us, and we could go outside again.

The next day Georg overheard Mr. Otzen mention to Mr. Anderson how badly Kiel's wharves, including battleships, were destroyed, and many persons lost their lives.

Georg passed on the bad news to all of us at lunchtime. We lived in constant danger. The sound of a squadron or a single airplane made us cringe for fear, and we ran either into the house or the barn, whichever was the closest to us.

April 9, 1945, Kiel suffered a big attack when hundreds of airplanes dropped their bombs on the harbors, industrial areas and the residential sections.

The alarm sounded a long time while we already slept. Mother knew the danger and awoke all of us.

"Dress quickly; we have to run into the woods." All other families got ready to go for cover into the woods also. We only reached the pond on the edge of the forest when one bomb pierced the air with a high-pitched shriek sound before it exploded with a thunderous bang. The ground shook from the impact, while the bomb blew up among the trees a short distance beyond the pond. The explosion's ear-splitting noise made us cover our ears and tremble for fear we might be the next target. Mother told us to stay right here at the pond and lay down and cover ourselves with blankets. The chilly April night made us shiver from the cold and tremble from fright of bombs. It was past midnight after we heard no more airplanes flying over us. All families picked up their belongings, and we staggered back to the houses.

"Thank God for watching over us and protecting us from harm," Mother uttered. "Had we gone into the forest as planned, we all would have been killed."

Even though we went to bed again, I held tightly on to Meta, fearing more bombers would return.

The next afternoon, we heard a lot of commotion in the courtyard of the farm. A group of soldiers came in army trucks. They stopped! The driver of one truck stepped down and went to the house of the owner. After he came back, he ordered the soldiers to get off.

"We will set up temporary quarters here until we get further orders," he told the soldiers. Then all got off. One group of soldiers looked kind of raggedy in khaki brown and olive-green uniforms. We found out later that they were Polish and Russian prisoners of war.

More children gathered to watch what was happening. Nobody dared to address the soldiers, but they chatted among each other for a while and aired their curiosity. Then they left.

Edmund went into the forest behind the pond the following day to check the damage the bomb had caused. He saw a deep, wide hole and a lot of shrapnel scattered around the opening. As he started to go back, Edmund noticed a bomb that had not exploded yet. It lodged halfway in the ground. He went really close to inspect the bomb without touching it. He looked around to see if he could spot some more. Edmund went straight back home when he could not find any more and told our mother about the bomb he found. Mother warned him to neither touch nor pick it up. It might explode and kill you.

Meanwhile, German soldiers and a group of prisoners set up a temporary camp at the estate. Some soldiers were lucky enough to get a room, and others erected tents in the forest. Some even slept in the barn. After cleaning and washing down the cow stable, the Polish and Russian prisoners used it as their sleeping quarters; They covered the floor with straw as mattresses.

Soldiers set up a mobile kitchen next to the woodshed, not too far away from our house. The kitchen and surroundings became one of my favorite playgrounds. I was delighted to smell the wonderful aroma coming from the kitchen during the preparation of meals for the soldiers and prisoners.

Soon I met the two daughters of the Diercks family, Katie, the older, Elisabeth, the younger, who was my age.

By Saturday, we saw some soldiers building a table in the meadow. We were curious about what the soldiers were going to do with it. We both walked over to the soldiers, and Elisabeth asked why they were putting up a table in the middle of the meadow.

"Tomorrow is Sunday. We are trying to build a small altar. We like to have a church service for the soldiers and all the residents of the estate. Tell your parents and all the other residents about the service. We will start at 9:00 a.m. Ask them to bring their chairs. We will put together some benches from boards for the soldiers."

"Can we help also?" I asked.

"Ask your parents if they can spare a white tablecloth for the day. Some candles and flowers would look appropriate too."

"I'll ask my mother if I can bring you one of her tablecloths," Elisabeth responded.

"When will you need it?"

"Not until 8:00 a.m. tomorrow, but come back today and let me know what you can bring."

"Will do."

"I'll go and pick some wildflowers," I added.

"I will ask my mother if I can pick some from our garden," Elisabeth said.

"Good, let us go. I'll see you later,"

I ran into the woods, picked a big bouquet of anemones and cowslips, and hurried to the soldiers, still putting together benches.

"Look what I found; can you use these?" I handed the flowers to the soldier.

"Very nice; now we need a container to put them in."

"I will run home and get one."

I hurried back with a metal cup full of water. I put the bouquet into a cup and placed it on the table. Elisabeth arrived with the good news that her mother would lend one of her tablecloths for tomorrow and two candlesticks with candles.

"Tell your mother, I appreciate her kindness. I hope she will come to the service also."

"I think she will. Our whole family will come. See you tomorrow at 8:00 a.m.

I rushed home to tell my mother and my siblings about the Sunday service the soldiers would hold in the meadow. They already built an altar and set up a row of benches in front of the altar.

"Are we all going to go to the service tomorrow?"

"Of course, we are going."

"What time will it be?"

"At 9:00 a.m., but I will go one hour earlier to help to decorate the altar."

"Very good. Make sure you all put your clothes out for tomorrow so that we won't be late."

The next morning, I left at 8:00 a.m. to help Elisabeth put the white tablecloth, candles, and flowers on the altar. After rushing through breakfast, my mother took Horst by the hand and asked all six children to follow her to the service in the open field.

"Georg, take a chair for Mother," Emma said. "We can all sit on the grass."

The soldiers and residents gathered in front of a symbolic altar in the open field with great anticipation. A beautiful big lacy tablecloth that reached the ground covered the table. A soldier had made a cross out of two sticks on a stand, held together by a thin rope. Two candleholders stood to the right and the left of the cross, then two bouquets of various colors of lilac, and at the end, my small yellow and white bouquets. Even though it was simple, it reminded everyone of an actual church altar, symbolizing a place of worship.

A soldier dressed in uniform stepped behind the altar, welcomed all the attendees, and asked them to sing "Nearer my God to Thee."

Another soldier dressed in a marine uniform sat next to the altar and played the melody on a piano accordion.

When singing the second verse:

"Though like a wanderer, the sun has gone down,
Darkness be over me, my rest a stone,
Yet in my dreams, I'd be nearer, my God, to Thee.

Yes, we all felt the darkness, the danger, and the suffering of the war and longed for peace.

Then he read Psalm 25, beginning:

"Unto Thee, I lift my soul. Oh my God, I trust in Thee; let me not be ashamed. Let not my enemies triumph over me."

He finished with the last two verses:

"Let integrity and uprightness preserve me,
for I wait on Thee. Redeem Israel,
O God, out of all this trouble."

And the pastor added, as God has delivered Israel out of her trouble, we pray that God will deliver us from the war and all the hardship it has caused us. After he spoke of King David's trouble and his trust in the Lord, he addressed his people's current problems and encouraged them to trust in God, be patient, and in due time God will deliver us from this evil war and bring us peace.

"Let us close our service with the hymn: "*Befiehl du deine Wege,*" translated in English: "*Commit thy ways unto the Lord.*"

The piano accordion player began with the song, and all the people who remembered the words by heart joined singing:

"*Commit whatever grieves you*
At heart, and all thy ways
To Him who never leaves thee,
On whom creation stays.
Who freely makes courses
For clouds, and air, and wind,
And care whoever taketh
A path for thee to find."

Few persons knew the words to the last verse. They were fitting, and the accordion player sang it so prayerfully:

"*O Lord, no longer lengthen*
Our time of misery,
Our hands and feet now strengthen,
And until death may we
By Thee be watched and cared for,
In faithfulness and love,
We come, Thou hast prepared
For us, a blessed abode."[15]

Unshed tears that had gathered in Mother's heart welled up in her eyes as she listened to the comforting words of the song. Other

183

mothers also cried as a plea for peace. The officiating pastor closed with a prayer, and the benediction before the worshipers, moved by the uplifting sermon, slowly left the open field.

After the service, Elisabeth and I went to the altar to pick up the tablecloth, the candles, and the flowers. I asked if we would have another church service next Sunday.

"God willing, that is our plan."

"Good, then I'll bring more fresh flowers."

"And I will bring the tablecloth and the candles again," added Elisabeth.

"Here, you can also take one bouquet of lilacs, for they would whither quickly in the sun. I took the lilacs and the two small containers with the wildflowers. I placed the lilacs in the living room and the two small ones on the kitchen table.

The residents looked forward to another church service. The soldiers planned more events for the community and even a special one for the children. The children followed the soldiers around to see where they could help. The soldiers asked Mr. Jessen if they could put on a show in the hay barn, where ample vacant space could serve as a stage. The children helped to prepare the seating of hay bales for the adults. The children could climb up to the loft and look down at the provisional stage where the soldiers would perform. Much excitement filled the air as we watched the preparation for the big event. On Friday, the children went from house to house to announce the show on Saturday at 3:00 p.m. Someone also went to the mayor of Pratjau a few days before to inform the villagers of the upcoming event.

Saturday finally came. Most local people from the estate and village filled up the barn seats. And the children climbed up to the loft.

On April 21, at 3:00 p.m., the accordion player began the show with the song: Freut Euch des Lebens so lange das Laempchen glueht (Enjoy life as long as the lamp still glows). He played a piece of joyful music, trying to bring cheerfulness to the war-weary people. Then he announced the first act, a juggler, using eggs. When he added more and more eggs, went faster and faster, we were holding our breath, thinking he might drop one or two eggs. But he was pretty skilled and did not drop any. Then he used bottles without dropping any. He finished his juggling act with three lit torches. The audience applauded with enthusiasm. Various acrobatic stunts on a bicycle and the ground followed. The soldiers even put up a tight rope, and a performer walked across without a net underneath. The children especially enjoyed the clown, Bobby, with a big red nose and an enormous mouth. He wore a multi-colored, shabby suit. Besides doing some funny stunts, he swallowed a watch and even a knife and made them disappear. When he opened his mouth, it was empty. The children were fascinated by the clown and his acts.

In the end, the accordion player played and sang some German folk songs and asked the audience to sing along. The manager of the estate thanked the soldiers for their performance. They brought delight to the people during a time the war was still raging in Germany.

The tranquility did not last long; two days later, we had another brief bombing attack during the night. We did not even have time to leave the house before it ended. The following day we heard that several bombs fell in the Selenter See (Lake of Selent) and outside the village. Fortunately, the bombs killed no one.

As crowded as living quarters were, we developed a specific routine. With each apartment came a vegetable garden. We shared the garden with the Hein family. Emma and Meta enjoyed gardening.

"Where do you think we can get some vegetable seeds?"

"Perhaps, the gardener of the owner could spare some."

"That is a good idea. I will ask the gardener when I see him."

The next day Emma saw the gardener working in the garden. Before she entered, she asked permission to come in.

"Good morning, my name is Emma. I am the daughter of Mrs. Bonacker, the new refugee family who moved here recently."

He extended his hand to Emma, "My name is Mr. Schroeder; what can I do for you?"

"We would like to plant something in the garden but have no seeds. Could you give us some vegetable seeds you can spare?"

"Come back tomorrow. I will check and see what I can find for you."

Emma shook Mr. Schroeder's hand as she said, "Thank you so much, Mr. Schroeder. I will see you tomorrow."

The next day the gardener gave Emma some seeds. She went into the house and told Meta the wonderful news about the vegetable seeds she received.

Emma and Meta immediately hurried into the garden and began to turn over the soil spade by spade and broke up all the clumps. They then divided a garden section into beds and raked them until the soil was loose and soft. Emma drew a line with a slight indentation with the rake handle in which Meta carefully put small amounts of seeds. Then Emma covered each small hole gently with some soil. Emma marked each row with the name carrots, radishes, lettuce, red beets, written on a piece of paper put on a stick at the end of the row.

"Mother, we planted all the vegetable seeds today. Isn't it fabulous? We will have fresh produce from our garden?" Meta announced as she returned from planting.

"That is very nice. Are you able to get from someone potatoes for planting?"

"I will ask Mrs. Anderson if she can spare some."

A little later, Meta returned with a small basket full of wrinkled potatoes, which had already sprouted.

"Good, give me a potato. You see, if you cut each potato in four parts and put them cut side down and the sprouts up, you will be able to get four times the number of plants."

"I will do that. I will let Emma know; we got potatoes. We will get busy preparing the ground."

Meta took the good news about the potatoes to Emma.

"Let me see if I can borrow a spade from a neighbor, and I will help you turning the ground."

"We will do that tomorrow, we did enough for today."

The next day while Emma and Meta started to turn the soil over spade by spade, a soldier approached them, and introduced himself, "My name is Albert. May I help?"

Before Emma had a chance to answer, he said, "Let me have the spade; this is too hard for you." He stretched out his hand and took the spade.

"Thank you. By the way, my name is Emma, and this is my sister Meta." Emma handed him the spade and took the rake. Meta, you use the hoe and break the clumps of the soil before I rake it. They worked and talked, and soon they had a big patch prepared.

After Albert learned that Emma and her family were refugees from East Prussia, he asked many questions about her background. He told her he was from Stettin, Pomerania. They had vivid conversations that always ended with the same note of hope that the war would be over soon, and everyone could return home again.

Other soldiers helped to work in the fields or wherever they saw things needing repairs. The Polish and Russian prisoners were exempt from work.

My brothers and I got acquainted with the children of the neighbors. They enjoyed seeing all the activities of the soldiers. We learned that the soldiers got permission from Mr. Jessen, the owner, to have a dance in the woodshed on April 21, 1945. We spread the word and invited the young people from Pratjau also.

Edmund, Richard, and I ran to Lill's small grocery store in Pratjau. We announced the upcoming dance and asked Mrs. Lill to invite her customers to the event. We also went to the Kirstein, Liedke, and Heisel families to inform them of the forthcoming dance.

The soldiers prepared the seating in the shed; they took uncut logs, stood them upright a few feet apart, and placed boards on the blocks. At the end stood a few chairs.

The much-anticipated Saturday evening finally came, and so did many young people and all the soldiers. I asked my mother if I could stay up later and go with my brothers to the dance. First, she hesitated to say yes, but then Georg, Edmund, and Richard promised to go with me. Besides, both sisters would be there also.

The lilac's scent filled the air, and so did the sound of the music. The piano accordion player began with a waltz. Soldiers looked around the room to spot a young lady without a companion and rushed to ask her for a dance. I watched my sisters Emma and Meta, wondering with whom they would dance. I recognized the kind soldier, Albert, asking Emma for a dance. Another soldier danced with Meta practically the whole evening. The accordion player began to sing: "Oh, dear Augustine." The attending soldiers joined first and then the dancers, too. Everyone sang, danced, and enjoyed a brief hiatus from the war. Even though I was only eight, I dreamed of learning how to dance when grown up. The magic of the evening vanished just too soon, and everyone returned to the harsh reality of life.

Mother and the other refugees received food stamps for each family member and a small amount of money for life's mere necessities. Georg worked in the fields and took care of horses. Emma and Meta helped milk cows for a meager monetary compensation and half a liter of milk for each child per day; at least, we did not starve. We had little living space and no privacy, but at least we had a roof over our heads. Now and then, the owner of a grocery store from the next bigger village, Bendfeld, would come with a small truck and sell some of his goods. When we ran out of an item, we would go to his store in Bendfeld. Usually, Emma volunteered to go in the morning, and I always accompanied her.

Emma and I started early on Tuesday morning with empty bags in our hands and passed through mustard plants' beautiful yellow fields and green meadows. All of a sudden, an airplane came diving down at us.

"Hilde, run behind the hedge, and lay down." Emma followed quickly and laid down next to me. A few minutes later, we heard a barrage of machine gunshots where we would have been if we had not rushed behind the hedge. I trembled for fear.

"Do you still want to go to Bendfeld? Don't you think we should go back? What if the airplane comes back and shoots at us again?"

"I do not think he will come back this way." Emma tried to console me. She took my hand, helped me up, and we continued the hour-long walk toward Bendfeld. Both Emma and I kept our eyes not only on the road but looked up into the sky for possible airplanes. We arrived at the grocery store and were greeted warmly by Mr. Puck and Mrs. Puck, who stood behind the counter, helping other customers.

Emma waited for her turn, then told Mrs. Puck what she needed to buy. Before she handed Emma the items, she checked the card to see if she had sufficient food rationing stamps to cover them. We got new food-rationing stamps for butter, sugar, flour, bread, meat, and other items every other month. Since it was already the latter part of April, she told Mrs. Puck to give her all the still-available things before the stamps would expire. Every time Mrs. Puck put an article on the counter, she cut off the corresponding stamp until all were gone. Emma paid for the items before placing the sugar, butter, flour, sausage, and bread in the basket and bag. Before we left the store, Mrs. Puck gave me candy. I thanked Mrs. Puck, and then Emma shook hands with Mrs. Puck and said goodbye.

The goods we carried slowed down our pace. Suddenly, I stopped, "Listen, Emma, a skylark is singing. Isn't it just beautiful?" Emma stopped also. She put her basket down for a moment and looked up to the sky to see if she could spot the skylark. When she saw a black dot, she pointed it out to me, "Look, look, there is the lark." I looked up with delight.

"Yes, I can see it now, too." We stood still and listened to the song of the skylark for a little while. It struck a chord in Emma's heart, and she began to sing a spring song. I did not know the words, so I hummed along.

We were happy to see and hear the lark rather than airplanes flying over us. We got back just in time for lunch.

Each morning and afternoon, Emma and Meta volunteered to help milk the cows out in the pasture. A horse-drawn, flat-bed wagon with the empty milk cans in the center picked up all the people who would milk the cows and brought them back again with the full milk cans. Naturally, I looked out for the wagon to return to the ranch. When I saw the wagon with the milk cans, I ran to my mother and picked up the container to get our daily milk allocation. One milk can, which was not filled, was put in front of Mr. and Mrs. Diercks's house under a covered roof between the residence and the milk storage room. Mrs. Diercks or her older daughter Katie would ladle the milk into each person's container. Katie's half-liter measures were always more generous. Children under six years received one liter, and the older children up to fourteen half a liter per day. The workers stored the rest of the milk in a particular room opposite the house. The next morning, a truck came and picked up the full milk cans and took them to a dairy-processing plant in Schoenberg, the closest town to Sophienhof.

The adults and the children would get to know the residents who lived on the ranch. One day Liselotte, her sister, and Brigitte asked me if I would like to make candy.

"Of course," I answered. Candy was hard to come by.

"You will have to bring two tablespoons full of sugar and come tomorrow right after my mother and father go milking," Liselotte told me.

"Let me see if I can get some sugar," I responded and left, thinking how to get sugar without my mother noticing it missing. I knew my mother would never give me any for making candies. The following afternoon, I watched my mother's every step and looked for an opportunity to quickly sneak into the pantry and take some sugar out of the sugar bowl.

Emma and Meta had already left, too. I watched my mother take Horst and go to the garden.

Now was the opportunity to quickly get the sugar and run over to the neighbor's house before my mother would return. I knocked on the neighbor's door; Liselotte asked me to enter.

"I thought you were not coming, so we already started to melt our sugar," Liselotte informed me.

"Here is the sugar I took without my mother noticing it."

"Let me add it to the one in the pan and melt it," Liselotte told me.

I watched the sugar dissolving and slowly turning brown while inhaling the sweet aroma. Finally, all the sugar melted and turned into a sticky, light brown glob. Liselotte took the pan from the fire and spread the substance into a square baking dish to cool off. We sat around the pan, watching and drooling. At last, Liselotte picked up the hardened sugar sheet, broke it into four pieces, and handed a pierce to each one of us.

"Now, you better eat it all here and do not tell anybody about our candy-making; otherwise, we will get into trouble."

"Oh no, we won't," everyone promised while taking one bite after the other of the sweet, crunchy candy until we consumed it all. Liselotte washed the pan and roasted some wheat to eliminate the melted sugar's odor, so her mother would not question her.

Liselotte informed Brigitte and me, she would let them know when they would make candy again. I thanked Liselotte and left. After making candy three more times, Liselotte's mother got sick while milking cows in the pasture. She came home early and discovered our secret. She strictly prohibited us from using her sugar to make candy and threatened to punish us. I feared that Liselotte's mother would tell my mother of our secret activity, so I thought I better tell my mother about taking the sugar without her consent. I waited for the right opportunity when I was alone with my mother in the kitchen.

"Mother, I did something wrong; I took some sugar without asking your permission first. We made candy with Liselotte and her sister in their house. I am so sorry; I did it."

"It is a good thing you realized that you did wrong and asked forgiveness. I forgive you. But if I ever hear or catch you doing anything behind my back again, you will get your deserved punishment."

I ran to my mother and grabbed her hand.

"Thank you for forgiving me and for not being angry with me."

I was relieved of my guilt and happily continued helping my mother peeling potatoes for lunch.

Since the soldiers arrived at the farm, it became alive with different activities. Whether the soldiers worked in the fields, helped milk cows, or split wood, they would get together and sing in the evening. A handsome soldier, dressed in the blue and white marine uniform, played the accordion to accompany the singers. We opened the windows and listened to beautiful music.

On Sunday, Jubilate, at the end of the outdoor church service, the officiating pastor announced that Saturday, April 28, 1945, the soldiers would give a musical performance at 3:00 p.m. He asked the children to invite their families and also the people from Pratjau. How exciting to have a musical performance right here on the farm, I thought. I could hardly wait for the day to come.

"Edmund and Richard, do you want to go to Pratjau this afternoon to tell the storekeeper about the concert so that she can spread the word to her customers?"

"Let's ask our mother if it is all right with her," Edmund responded.

While we ate lunch, Edmund asked his mother's permission for the three of us to go to Pratjau to inform Mrs. Lill about the concert.

"Can we also visit the Heisel family while we are in Pratjau?"

"You can go, but make sure you are home before 5:00 p.m.," our mother responded.

"Thank you, Mother; we will be back before supper," I replied.

"Come on, Edmund and Richard, let's go!"

We walked quickly to Lill's and announced the date and time of the upcoming concert.

"Please, spread the news to your customers and friends," I requested before visiting the Kirstein family, who lived on the mayor's premises. Edmund asked if Mr. Kirstein could talk to the mayor and have his messenger announce the upcoming event to all the village residents. After Mr. Kirstein promised to do so, we went to visit the Heisel family. I told Etna, who was my age, about the concert, and Richard informed Helmut and his brother Gustav.

Edmund talked to Mrs. Heisel while Helmut, Richard, Etna and I played a game of aggravation before returning to Sophienhof.

All week long, we watched every activity on the farm. Three days before the concert, the soldiers started to assemble a stage. They placed a flat-bed wagon in front of the woodshed. Then they put together a frame of wood the length of the wagon and seven feet high above the platform. They nailed the frame to the wagon.

Several children came and asked if they could help. Bobby, the clown, was also among the workers. He entertained the children by making funny facial expressions to see them laugh. Some children were afraid of Bobby and cried when they saw him. Bobby asked the children to get their parent's permission to bring some bedsheets to use as a backdrop for the stage, saying,

"We will need them by Friday ; we would like you to bring cut flowers to decorate the front of the stage on Tuesday." Bobby and three other soldiers took some boards from the woodshed and built three square flower boxes, the length of the front and the sides of the platform and nailed them on the improvised stage. Friday afternoon, several children brought enough bedsheets to cover the square frame in the back.

Saturday after lunch, I ran out to the flower garden to see what I could use for decorating the stage. The lilac bush finished blooming, but we could use the foliage as a filler. The peonies bloomed. After asking my mother's permission, I picked a bouquet of peonies and some lilac branches and took them to the soldiers. Other children came with spring flowers and handed them over to the soldiers, who added the finishing touches to the improvised stage.

"We need some containers with water to keep the flowers fresh," one of the soldiers told the children. Quickly, the children ran home and came back with cups, vases, cans, or whatever they could get. Bobby got a bucket and filled all the containers with water before arranging the flowers in the boxes. It looked attractive.

By 2:30 p.m., the village's first people came; by 3:00 p.m., many persons filled all the benches. Some even brought their chairs to be more comfortable. I saved seats for my family close to the stage. They did not want to miss any part of the performance.

The anxiously awaited moment came. An accordion player entered the stage. He welcomed the audience and announced the first arias are excerpts from the operetta *The Gypsy Baron* (Der

Zigeuner Baron) by Johann Strauss, Jr. He began by playing the overture to The Gypsy Baron. What enchanting waltz music. Many followed the rhythm by tapping with their feet. Others moved their upper bodies to the right and left in the rhythm of the music. Next, a soldier in decorated uniform, representing a nobleman, came on the stage singing:

"As a lively spirit and ended: he is all that, and I know more." (Als flotter Geist... Ja, das alles ist er, das kann ich und noch mehr).

Next, a singer came dressed as a gypsy. He wore a white unbuttoned shirt and a long, red belt tied around the waist and white baggy pants raised below the knees. He sang the aria: Writing and reading was never my strong point (Das Schreiben und das Lesen ist nie mein Fach gewesen). The aria ended with the refrain: "My ideal purpose in life is raising pigs and curing ham" (Mein idealer Lebenszweck, ist Borstenvieh und Schweinespeck).

In the third aria, "Who married us" (Wer uns getraut), the same soldier representing the nobleman sang. The accordion player closed the first part playing the Radetzky March. He invited the audience to clap along to the tune of the music. The cheerful music made people forget momentarily that the war still raged in Germany, and they were delighted to listen to beautiful music in such an unusual setting.

The accordion player announced three arias by Franz Lehar from the Operetta: The Zarewitch, The Volga song. He first played the introduction to the song, then the soldier with the baritone voice began singing: "Alone, again alone, lonesome as ever" (Allein, wieder allein, einsam wie immer). The song's melancholy yet haunting melody made some parents whose sons were still fighting in the war sad.

A tenor sang the following aria: "Why does each spring have only one May" (Warum hat jeder Fruehling ach nur einen Mai). This melodious song changed the gloomy mood of the audience into a more cheerful one. The third aria: "Yours is my heart alone" (Dein ist mein Herz allein) was from the Operetta: *Land of Smiles* (Das Land des Laechelns) by Franz Lehar. In this aria, a lover promises his heart to his sweetheart. After the enthusiastic applause faded and the tenor left the stage, the accordion player announced that there would be a short intermission.

Fifteen minutes later, the accordion player returned with a group of soldiers on the stage and announced that we would commemorate the fallen soldiers by singing, "I had a comrade" (Ich hatte einen Kameraden). Let us all stand to pay tribute to our brave soldiers who lost their lives fighting for our fatherland. After everyone stood, the accordion player started with the soldiers, and whoever knew the song joined in. Many who had lost a family member or relative shed tears; I saw my mother also wiping tears from her eyes, thinking of father and wondering if he was still alive. It was almost a year that we had no news from him. I also thought of my missing father and was hoping he was still alive and would come home soon.

After finishing this emotional song, everyone sat down.

"Now our soldiers will sing German folk songs, and you can sing along with them. We will begin with the song: "Once I return to my home again" (Kehr ich eins zur Heimat wieder). For the next hour, the soldiers and the audience sang several popular folk songs. When the singing stopped, the soldier, who officiated as a pastor, stepped forward. He addressed the soldiers first,

"Thank you all, my comrades, for your talented performance and for brightening the lives of these people. I am sure they are also very grateful to you."

After the long applause faded, he continued, "Regrettably, we are still at war; let us pray to our heavenly Father that the war will be over quickly, and our soldiers can come home. We commit our lives into the hands of God and ask him to watch over us. Let us pray together 'Our Father who art in heaven." The performance ended with the song: "Take Thou my hand and lead me" (So nimm den meine Haende). The heart-warming musical presentation overwhelmed everyone. Quietly, the people got up and went home.

After dinner, Edmund, Richard, myself, and many other children went to the stage and helped dismantling the bedsheets and the flower boxes. The girls who brought bedsheets and flowers took the same home. Before I left, I told a soldier, "What a marvelous musical performance," then asked, "You think you will give another performance before leaving?"

"My dear little girl, we do not know how long we will be staying here or where we will be sent," he answered with a sadness in his voice and left; so did I and the other children.

On May 1, 1945, all the soldiers were in an uproar; they received the news that the Fuehrer had committed suicide on April 30, 1945, in his bunker in Berlin, one day before the Russian Army reached Berlin. Eva Braun, whom he had married one day before his death, died with him.

The soldiers also informed the civilians that on April 30, 1945, Hitler died by taking cyanide and then shooting first Eva Braun and then himself. The soldiers knew that the war would be over soon but feared how the Allies would penalize Germany for starting the war.

The bombing and fighting continued for another week before the German generals signed unconditional surrender documents, May 7, 1945, in the Eisenhower headquarters in Reims, France. President Truman declared May 8 the official end of World War II. All over the world, except in Japan and Germany, people celebrated the victory over Germany in jubilation. The German people, who had suffered the most, saw their country destroyed. They mourned the loss of millions of soldiers and civilians killed or who had died of starvation or diseases. The American and British Air Forces bombed the major big cities, and they looked like hell on earth. The German people, who slowly emerged from the cities' rubble, struggled to stay alive, eating whatever they could find. Some walked for miles out of the towns to beg for food from farmers. They lived in cellars or among the ruins until they could build temporary shelters from the broken bricks and rubble. Now they feared again how their country would be punished for war crimes, while the victors, even though some also committed many war crimes, would be celebrated as heroes, and rewarded through treaties.

My mother was grateful that our family had shelter, even though very inadequate, and had sufficient food to feed her growing children. The children and all the farm residents felt very sad when they heard that the soldiers would leave. Most of the soldiers from our farm departed on May 9. We all were grateful to the soldiers. They were so supportive, kind, and helpful to us. Some, who lived in the eastern states, which the Russians had occupied, did not want to become Russian prisoners. They decided to stay at the farm.

Albert, who had grown fond of my sister Emma, left reluctantly. He had to go back to his family to see if they survived but promised to return if circumstances would allow him to do so. Emma liked Albert, and sadness filled her heart when they said goodbye to each other while working in the garden the day before he left. I enjoyed staying close to them and always found a reason, like helping with the garden work, so I could listen to their conversations and watch their happy expressions when they looked into each other's eyes.

"Emma, you are still fortunate to be on a farm, where you have food. Think of the millions of people in the big cities whose homes were destroyed, and they have to beg and bargain with surrounding stores and farmers for food to survive."

"Yes, I thank God not only for food but also that he saved my family from being killed by bombs or dying of starvation or sicknesses. I guess we will have to stay here until we are allowed to return to East Prussia."

"Do not set your hopes too high; we do not know which part of our country the allies will give away. East Prussia is a rich and fertile part of Germany. Russia and Poland might claim part or all of it."

"I sure hope this will not happen. I love my home and hope to return soon to the place where I was born."

"I certainly wish you and all of us that it will remain a part of our fatherland."

After Albert finished weeding, he gave Emma his hand, and lifted her up. Then he embraced her, kissed her on the forehead, and said, "Goodbye, dear Emma, and perhaps, God willing, we will see each other again."

"Goodbye, Albert. May God watch over you."

They sadly parted from each other. The next morning, May 10, Albert left with the other soldiers and the prisoners. Many people came, not only to say goodbye but also to thank them for their service and help while stationed here. We stood quietly and waved goodbye, saddened by their departure, but the memories of their kindness toward us will remain.

A few days later, two British tanks rolled in and stopped next to Mr. Diercks's house. A bunch of children and I ran to the tanks. We had never seen a tank. We looked in amazement at such a strangely constructed vehicle. We, the children, moved to the side for fear the tanks would run over us. Two black soldiers emerged from one tank and two white soldiers from the second.

I could not keep my eyes off the black soldiers. I had never seen a black person before. I was wondering how they turned black and where they came from.

They waved to the children, then stepped down from the tank and offered chewing gum to them. The children feared to take anything from strangers and stepped away when the colored persons approached them. Then one unwrapped a piece of chewing gum, put it in his mouth, and chewed it.

"Here, take one; it is sweet," the soldier said while offering the chewing gum again to the children.

Knowing it was something to eat, one child after the other accepted a piece of chewing gum. They had never tasted chewing gum before. Then the soldier took his chewing gum out of his mouth and threw it away. He wanted to demonstrate to the children; they should not swallow it but spit it out. I chewed and liked the sweet peppermint flavor. When I tried to throw it away, the soldier motioned to keep chewing longer. So, the children chewed and laughed at each other, and so did the soldiers.

After a while, the two tanks left with the chains making a strange crackling sound. However, instead of driving on the road, they passed through the wheat field, leaving two wide paths of crushed plants behind them. I could never understand why the soldiers had to destroy plants when they could have driven on the road.

I ran home quickly, exclaiming, "Mother, mother, I saw a black person. Why are some people black?"

"My child, God made them so. They are all God's children, regardless of the color of their skin."

"Yes, Mother. I guess I have much to learn; by the way, do you know when school will start?"

"My neighbor told me not until fall. They are looking for a new teacher. The teacher from Pratjau left."

"I sure hope the village will find a teacher soon. I enjoy going to school and learning new things."

May passed, and summer arrived. Edmund and Richard got acquainted with the boys of the farm and I with the girls. The boys played soccer or other ball games, while the girls played with their dolls, jumped rope, or played some board games, like Aggravation and Mill (Muehle).

One afternoon, a big truck arrived at the farm. The pickup truck belonged to a circus, and the driver came to get hay for the animals. He asked the owner for a load of hay and offered, as a partial payment, free tickets for the farm children. When the children heard this news, they immediately asked their parents' permission to see the circus. Mother allowed Georg, Edmund, Richard, and me to go. She gave Georg strict orders to keep a close eye on me, so I would not get lost in the crowd.

The loading seemed to take a long time while we stood around the truck. Finally, the pickup was packed; the driver signaled the children to climb up and settle down in the hay. Everyone rushed toward the center so they would not fall off. We sat down close to each other so we would all fit. The truck rolled over the bumpy, unpaved country road for half an hour until it reached the circus in Schoenberg. The driver let the children off at the tent and told them to wait inside while driving the hay to the animal cages to feed the horses before the show.

With great anticipation, we waited and waited. Two hours seemed long. The people began to crowd the tent, a sign the performance would soon start. When all benches were occupied, the music started to play. The ringmaster came out and announced the first act. Four horseback riders entered the tent. While the horses galloped quickly around the arena, the riders jumped down, performed some tricks, and then jumped up again on their horse's back. Everyone applauded when one rider stood on two horses and rode at a fast pace around the circle. More equestrian dressage performances by beautiful white horses followed. When workers constructed a cage rapidly, and a lion entered with the lion tamer, we held our breath. Many times, the lion growled and showed his teeth when the trainer cracked the whip. Fortunately, the lion finished all his tricks without attacking the trainer, which was a big consolation for the audience. Three clowns twirled into the arena and played all kinds of tricks to make everyone laugh. Then again, the trapeze flyer and catcher held everyone in suspense until they jumped into the net and climbed to the floor, accompanied by explosive applause. Acrobatic acts on bicycles also received much applause, so did the tightrope walker and the elephant act. We felt sad when the show ended. We could have watched it on and on for a long time. Our group of children stayed together outside the tent until the driver came to pick us up. He had left a small amount of hay on the bottom of the truck, so we did not have to sit on the hard floor.

"What an exciting show, don't you think so?" I asked Frieda.

"It certainly was; I liked the trapeze flyer the best."

"The lion tamer made me hold my breath every time he growled at his trainer. But I enjoyed all the acts."

Meanwhile, the sun retracted her golden rays and covered the land with a dark, soft cloak. I laid down on the hay and soon entered the world of dreams. Georg woke me up when the truck arrived at the farm. Mother awaited us and was glad we all came home safely. The children were so fascinated with the circus's different acts. The next day, they imitated the performers and tried to make a summersault while jumping from the hayloft onto a wagon still loaded with hay, not realizing the danger.

During the rest of spring and summer, we cultivated the garden and anxiously waited to harvest the first radishes and lettuce. When the carrot leaves grew tall enough, we would check, by moving the soil away from the plant, to see if we could find a carrot big enough to pull out and eat. Of course, we would clean it first with the leaves. How good it tasted fresh from the garden. Along the garden ran a creek. We would walk down the short path to fetch water for the plants. I thought it would be a perfect spot to build a small place to spend time in solitude. To get away from the crowded apartment would be a treat. First, I dug out an area on the creek's garden side and piled the dirt on the bottom for a base. I looked for some stones and placed them around the square foundation. I cut branches of a nearby willow tree and stuck them on two sides in front of the stones. I left the leaves on the upper part to form a wall.

The next day, I looked around to find a narrow board and wooden blocks and made a bench. Then I put a wider board on two wooden poles as a table and secured the board with two nails. I told no one about my secret place. Each day, when I had no chores to do, I would go to my secret site, sit there, listen to the rippling of the creek, the songs of the birds, and daydream. I was amazed that the leaves on the willow sticks were still green after a week or so. I had a living wall now. I picked some wildflowers, put them in an old cup, and placed them on the table. I felt so happy in my secret hideout. I shared it only with my doll. Even my mother did not know where my hideout was. When I forgot the time and stayed longer than I should have, I told her I was in the garden. All went well for some time. One day, we had a severe thunderstorm with a heavy downpour that lasted into the night. The next morning, I went to check my secret place. I encountered a disaster; the creek rose, and washed out the bottom and the walls of my hideout. I felt so sad about losing my secret place, but life went on.

Chapter 10
Important Events

A PLEASANT EVENT CAME to pass. Uncle August, my father's youngest brother, came to us from Norway where he had been stationed as a soldier until the war ended. He had found us through the Red Cross where our family stayed. Uncle August hoped to find his brother, our father, with us. He was disappointed that his brother Gustav was still detained somewhere. Uncle August used to play the accordion and sing at all our family celebrations. Unfortunately, he had to leave his accordion at home when he joined the army. Uncle August also liked drawing. Each time he wrote a letter to us, he drew beautiful flowers with colored pencils on the letterhead. My brothers and sisters and I admired and loved Uncle August and all uncles and aunts from my father's side. They had a great sense of humor and zest of life, they loved music and dancing. Their cheerful dispositions made everyone around them happy. They also knew how to tell serious and funny stories. Unfortunately, Uncle Otto, the youngest of the five brothers, already died as a World War II soldier. Uncle August brought a small bucket of pickled herring from Norway. What a treat it was for us to bite into the juicy, salty herring. Uncle August stayed with us for about two weeks. He helped to hoe the garden or whatever needed to be done, like splitting wood logs for the hearth.

Emma shared the bed with Meta and me so that Uncle August could have some privacy and the bed in the small chamber. We gladly shared all the fresh produce from the garden. Yet we were sad to see him go. The month of May slipped away with all the beautiful wildflowers in the meadows and forests. I enjoyed running through the pastures and picking whatever I found blooming. My favorite wildflower was forget-me-nots, which grew on the side of the creek and lasted a long time in a vase. However, we were not allowed to pick the yellow rape flower that covered big fields, nor were we allowed to step in the wheat fields to pick bachelor buttons or poppies.

By the end of June or the beginning of July, the yellow rape flower turned to black seeds in a small round pod. It was time to harvest the seeds and mow down the plants. My sister Emma, Elfriede, and I would walk behind the mowing machine and pick up any dry plant left behind. Quickly we crushed the pods and put the seeds in our pouch, tied around our waist. The dried plant we threw away. We probably collected perhaps one or two pounds of seeds in a day. Walking among the freshly cut stalks, we cut our legs to the point of bleeding and burning. After a good night's rest, we were out on the fields gleaning each day until all the fields were mowed. Then Georg would take rape seeds to the mill, where the owner put the black seeds into a press to release the oil. If we got about two liters of rape oil from a harvest, we were grateful. Mother used it in salad dressings or for frying pancakes and other foods.

Next came the wheat harvest. The mowing machine cut down the wheat. Other women who lived on the farm, Emma and Meta included, would gather an armful of wheat, tie it together with twisted wheat stalks, and put them on the ground. Men would gather the sheaves and stand them up against each other forming teepee-like piles. Elfriede and I went gleaning for wheat kernels. We would pick up each cut stalk left behind, rub the head between our hands quickly to remove the grain from the stem, and put them into our sacks. When we had more than half a sack full, we would take it home to our mothers. We returned to the field until the workers finished mowing the wheat.

The sheaves remained standing in the fields for two weeks or so until the stalks turned white, and the ears of the wheat were dry. One empty wagon after another came to the field and returned to the farm loaded with the sheaves. On the last day of bringing in the sheaves, women wove stalks of wheat around a metal crown-shaped frame, tied colored ribbon on the bottom of the circle, and took it back to the farm. Temporarily, it hung in the barn. The following weekend, the owner gave a big dinner dance for all the workers at Lill's Gasthaus in Pratjau. One employee fastened the crown on the ceiling in the center of the hall. The estate manager thanked God for a good harvest and all the workers bringing in the crops, then they served dinner.

The music began to play after the servers cleared the tables. The manager and his wife started the first waltz, and everyone joined them. The children were neither allowed on the tables nor in the hall. But Elfriede, other children from the village, and I crawled up a loft adjacent to the dance hall, sat down quietly, and listened to the music of the accordion player. How I wished I could dance, I thought. Quickly I realized nobody would dance with a child my age. Maybe with my girlfriend Elfriede, who was three years older than me. Quietly, I was listening to the music and watching the rhythmic movements of the feet and hoped one day I could dance like that. The celebration went on until midnight, but I had to be home by 9:00 p.m.

In August, we received the good news that school would start soon. All children from six years to fourteen years should go and register for classes. The teacher, whose name was Mr. Sabrow, greeted all students in the one-room schoolhouse. He asked each child in which class they were last. Then he put the students of each class together in a section. Since my brothers Edmund, Richard, and I had no report cards because we had to escape before they were issued, the teacher gave us tests. Mr. Sabrow placed Edmund into fifth grade, Richard into fourth grade, and me into second grade. Instructing all the students in one room was quite a challenge for the teacher. He gave assignments in writing to the students he did not teach in person. He instructed each class for about forty-five minutes. All students started at 8:00 a.m., had half an hour lunch break, and went home at 1:00 p.m.. Notebooks and paper were in short supply. We had slate tablets and slate pencils to write on, which we easily erased with a moist sponge.

A one-room school presents a fascinating opportunity to listen to advanced subjects taught to the upper classes and gain knowledge quicker. I enjoyed listening in on the geography and history presentations to the upper levels. Since my brothers Edmund and Richard attended the same school, I also could learn from them. It felt so good to be back in school and study so many new things. Mr. Sabrow was very strict with us. If a student did not do his homework or bothered another classmate, the teacher punished the guilty student accordingly. They received a slap on the fingers with a ruler or several strikes with a stick on the bottom. We all put on our best behavior to avoid any punishment.

After one year, Mr. Sabrow moved to Schoenberg to teach in high school. Mr. Reimers and his family replaced him.

GRAMMAR SCHOOL CLASS

August passed only too quickly, and September brought us many unexpected pleasures. My sister Emma and my brother Edmund enjoyed going mushroom hunting in the nearby forest. Finding a mushroom got us excited, and we ran each time to Emma to find out if it was edible or poisonous. Emma could tell the difference between the edible and the poisonous mushrooms. Soon we learned to tell them apart and picked only the good ones. We also picked blackberries on the edge of the forest and wild raspberries in a patch located in the nearby woods. Edmund went into the bushes to look for raspberries then came running out, screaming while slapping his hands on his head and body. We ran to check what happened. When he stepped into a wasp nest, the wasps attacked and stung him. We took him home quickly. Emma looked for stingers, removed a few, then put vinegar over the swollen areas to lessen the pain.

Frieda, Brigitte, and I enjoyed picking hazelnuts. We also gathered the nuts from the beech trees, which grew in the forest nearby. They dropped their pods in the fall. Usually, three or four nuts are in one pod. Only beech trees, which were more than forty years old, bore numerous nuts every seven years. We went several times to gather them. They covered the ground after a windstorm, and it did not take long to fill a gunnysack with beechnuts. Georg would take them to a mill to press the oil out of them, which Mother used for cooking.

The potato harvest began in October. Since the small patch of potatoes our mother grew in the garden did not feed her big family during the entire winter, Emma and Meta went to the harvested potato field to glean potatoes. In the afternoon, Frieda and I also went digging for potatoes after we got out of school. We turned a lot of soil before we found a potato or two, but we managed to fill a basket in one afternoon. Tired from the digging but grateful for the find, we went home to present our mother with the gleaned goods.

Mother, Emma, and Meta preserved as many things from our garden as they could. They would fill a barrel with white cabbage, add the necessary ingredients to start the fermenting process, and turn it into sauerkraut. My Mother stored potatoes, carrots, and beets in the cold cellar for the winter; she made marmalade from various berries. We picked the apples, placed them in boxes, covered them with straw, and put them in the attic for the winter. After the busy fall and gloomy month of November came the anticipated winter and Christmas time. We welcomed the first snowflakes with joy and anticipation of tobogganing and skating. In school, we learned several Christmas songs and sang them happily on the way home. At home, Mother, Emma, and Meta busied themselves knitting socks and mittens for the boys. They taught me how to knit also. I would knit the straight part of the socks, and Emma would do the heel and finish closing the sock's tip. I enjoyed knitting.

Since we had no decorations for a Christmas tree, we made stars from straw and paper strips. Our neighbor gave us a few candles with the holders to light up the tree on Christmas Eve. A week before Christmas, Georg and Edmund went to the nearby forest and cut down a medium-sized pine tree. Edmund looked for a few small boards and made a stand for the tree. Emma, Meta, and I hung all our handmade decorations on the tree and clipped the few holders with the white candles on the branches. It looked very elementary, but it was the symbol of Christmas. My mother looked somber. I knew she missed father and Marta who were not with us. We all missed them too.

On Christmas Eve, we all put on our best clothes and gathered around the Christmas tree. Emma told the story about the birth of Christ, which we commemorated that day. Then we all sang our favorite Christmas song, "Silent Night, Holy Night," and several other songs before Emma and Meta handed to Mother and each of their brothers and me a pair of hand-knitted socks and gloves and took the same for themselves. We did not have any paper to wrap the gifts, but they were made with love and would keep us warm in the upcoming cold winter season.

On Christmas Day, Georg and Edmund hitched the horses to the wagon, and the whole family drove to Castle Salzau to attend the church service. It snowed enough to transform the scenery into a winter wonderland but not enough stayed on the road to use a sled. A big, beautifully decorated tree stood next to the pulpit in the spacious hall designated for the church services. The service began with the song. "*Oh Thou Joyful, Oh Thou wonderful Grace revealing Christmas Time.*" After the benediction, we left the hall and spoke with most of the refugees we traveled with during our escape from East Prussia. We conversed for some time, then wished each other a Merry Christmas and drove back to Sophienhof.

We celebrated the second Christmas away from home. We all missed father and Marta, who always played Santa Claus and brought a handmade gift for each of us. Nevertheless, we were glad that the war was over, and we had food, a bed to sleep in, and a roof over our heads, the three basic needs. All other things would be considered luxuries at this time.

Baked chickens replaced the traditionally roasted goose for dinner this Christmas with red cabbage and potatoes. Each one received a cookie and an apple for dessert. We thanked God and were content.

The cattle stayed in the stable during the winter, and Meta and Emma no longer had to go to the pasture to milk the cows. It gave them more time to help our mother with domestic chores. Edmund, Richard, and I tried the strength of the ice on the pond. When it did not crackle anymore by stomping on it really hard, we knew the ice was thick enough, and it was safe to go ice skating. Of course, we did not have fancy ice skates. Edmund would put two wires on our shoes' wooden soles, which made us slide over the ice smoothly. If we hit a rough spot, we would fall, but we got up and continued skating. The neighbor's children would join the fun until dark or until they called us to come home. Of course, we could only ice-skate after eating lunch together and doing our homework and domestic chores first.

All of us children stayed home with our mother on New Year's Eve. She had baked the traditional donuts filled with marmalade and gave one to each of us after dinner. Georg went to visit his friend Hugo. Emma befriended Gustav Kirstein and Meta, Ernst Seidel, and they went together to a dance held at Lill's Gasthaus in Pratjau. They came home after they rang in the new year 1946. I lay awake a long time, thinking about home and the sleigh ride under the clear starlit sky, going to my grandparents and playing with my cousins, who visited them also. I wondered who lives in our house now and if we would ever be able to return to our home in East Prussia.

Two days later, I celebrated my 9th birthday. Mother managed to get enough ingredients to bake a simple cake, which we all shared in the afternoon. My mother and all my siblings congratulated me, but there were no candles nor did they sing "Happy Birthday" to me. Emma gave me a pair of knitted mittens, which I needed. My brothers and I joined the neighborhood children on the pond, ice skating until dark.

The winter passed slowly. Keeping the room and kitchen warm was quite a chore for Emma and Meta. I helped mother with the laundry for the whole family. I brought in bucket after bucket of water from the well. Clothes soaked overnight in a big pot of water and soap. The next day we boiled the clothes for some time. We waited for the water to cool. My mother or Emma washed each item by hand and rinsed them in fresh water. Then they hung the clothes outside on a line. When the temperature was below zero and Emma pinned the clothes on the line, they froze immediately and became stiff. They would watch for the sun to come out and thaw the clothes and dry them somewhat. On a cloudy winter day, Emma and Meta put several lines of clothes around the oven (Kachelofen) and waited until each item dried. They only ironed the dresses, pants, and shirts for Sunday. Live ambers, placed inside the iron, heated it. The temperature of the iron always varied. When Emma or Meta put fresh embers in the iron, it would be scorching; she always had a wet cloth next to the iron to check the temperature and avoid burning a hole in a shirt or dress.

Winter was the time for butchering one of the pigs we raised in the small pig pen across from the house. The adults worked hard cutting up the pig, making sausages and pickled ham. They placed pork bellies in big barrels, salted them, and saved them in the cellar. We marked each sausage link with a strip of cloth, counted them, and then took them to the butcher in the nearest village to have them smoked. The butcher would send a messenger when the customer could pick up the smoked sausages. To compensate the butcher for his service, people would give him either sausages or pay him the requested amount. We could hardly wait until Georg drove us to the butcher to pick up the smoked goods. It was a real treat to bite into a sandwich with the freshly smoked sausage (Metwurst). Emma knew to put just the right amount of salt and various spices to enhance the flavor.

Our first winter in Sophienhof passed relatively slowly, but we welcomed the arrival of spring with great enthusiasm. On the way home from school, I heard the first skylark sing and watched her ascend high up in the sky; I rejoiced and started singing spring songs silently. We also learned spring poems by heart, which I recited while skipping and running home from school. I had befriended Elisabeth Diercks, the daughter of the dairy manager. She was with me in the second grade; we liked roaming through the forests.

I enjoyed school. I did well in mathematics, geography, history, and religion. My spelling in German needed improvement to be flawless. Summer arrived, and much excitement grew in school to prepare a special celebration called Popinjay (Vogelschiessen in German). According to the designed size and pattern, the 6th-grade boys got busy cutting a bird out of a wooden board. They attached it to a fifty-foot-high pole, dug a hole outside the school premises, and erected the post with the bird. The 6th-grade girls put twelve bottles of the same kind at a certain distance apart in a marked square. Their competition consisted of throwing metal rings around the bottles. The festivity took place shortly before the summer vacation began. The boys arrived with their bows and arrows with a round lead point. At the command of the teacher, the shooting started. The boys got to shoot the bird, which shattered with each hit, and the pieces came flying down. The boy who shot down the most parts was crowned king for the day. The second-best got first prize, and the third-best also got a prize.

Meanwhile, each girl from 6th grade received approximately ten rings. She had to stand behind a line, a certain distance away from the bottles, then throw each ring over the bottle's neck and hope it would not land next to the bottles on the ground. A score-keeper marked down how many bottles each girl had thrown correctly. The girl who had the highest count became queen, and the runners-up received the first and second prizes. The queen wore a wreath of fresh flowers, symbolizing a crown. The teacher placed a wide ribbon over the king's left shoulder and pinned it on the right side above the hip. A short parade through the village led by the king and queen followed the games. Two tall girls carried a bow decorated with fresh flowers over the king and queen and first and second prize couple.

The parade went from the school to Lill's Gasthaus, where a celebration, honoring the king and queen took place. Adults set up enough tables and chairs to accommodate all students and the teacher. Parents brought homemade cakes for the student. Older sisters of the students served milk with the cake. The teacher introduced the king and queen to all the students. Gerd Schluensen played the piano accordion: the king and queen, and the couples who won first and second prize began to waltz to "Ach du Lieber Augustin" (Oh Dear Augustine).

Then Gerd played a foxtrot and asked all students to dance. My feet started to move under the table at the rhythm of the music. How I wished a boy would ask me to dance with him. I did not even dare to look at the boy, Gottfried Keller, whom I liked. But what a surprise when he stood before me, bowed, and asked me for a dance. I blushed at first but quickly said yes, got up, and followed him to the dance floor. I felt a little awkward and clumsy at first, but soon I followed his lead and enjoyed my first dance with a boy. Even though Gottfried danced with other girls, he asked me several times to dance with him. It made me feel very happy and grown-up, and I took a liking to him. Since he danced more frequently with me than with others, I thought that he also liked me.

Edmund and Richard, who were good dancers, asked the older girls to dance with them. After the children's festivities, a dance for the adults began in the evening, which Emma, Meta with their friends, and my older brother Georg attended. They all danced well to the piano accordion's music, played by Gustav, and Hugo in the evening.

Shortly after the Popinjay event, I received my first report card, and summer vacation began. My marks were all good, and I advanced into third grade. The teacher told me I needed to improve my spelling in German. My mother spoke East Prussian dialect at home, which was quite different from the high literary German (Hochdeutsch). Now and then, I used an incorrect Prussian word or misspelled others.

We spent our summer vacation helping Mother in the garden, picking berries, gathering wood for the winter, or doing whatever chores Mother assigned to us, like picking fresh clover for the rabbits my mother raised. However, we always found time for some ball games, playing hide and seek, or other games.

At the beginning of August, Mrs. Hein announced that she and her family would move into a house called Lehmhaus, where they would have more room. Mother welcomed their move. Now, her family would have more space. Meta moved her bed into the vacated room. Later, she had a bed frame made for me. I no longer had to sleep with my sister, cramped up in a small bed; I stretched out and moved freely. We no longer shared the kitchen. Emma painted the walls white. Using a folded rag, dipped in green paint, she rolled a design over the walls. It looked clean and cheerful. We could eat at the same time each day. Life seemed less chaotic now.

Sometimes, I would run to the meadow, where Emma and Meta milked the cows and waited until I could ride home with them on the milk truck. Ernst Seidel, who came as a wounded soldier to Sophienhof and stayed on the farm after the war ended, liked Meta, and they fell in love while both were milking cows.

He always sat next to her while riding back from the pasture to the farm. Ernst liked talking to her and holding her hand. On his day off, he would help Meta in the garden. They enjoyed working together. Meta asked many questions about Ernst Seidel's family and how he ended up at Sophienhof.

META AND ERNST SEIDEL

Ernst told Meta that his mother, Agnes, died when he was only five years old. He had two sisters, Klara, and Frieda, and one brother, Alfred. His father, Gustav, remarried in 1922, and they had one daughter, Else. After Ernst graduated from grammar school, he worked in a glass factory for several years. In 1937, at the age of twenty-two, he was drafted into Hitler's army and underwent rigorous military training. When World War II began on September 1, 1939, Ernst fought on the battlefields in Czechoslovakia, France, and Poland. When the Russian army invaded and encircled East Prussia, Ernst joined the 64th artillery division under O. Steebler. Ernst took care of the horses of high-ranking officers and commanders, besides also engaging in combat. He told Meta about an air raid's harrowing experience while he and three other comrades escaped death. A bomb fell next to the foxhole, where they jumped in for cover. Fortunately, the bomb did not explode; otherwise, he would have been blown to pieces.

Meta took the hand of Ernst, "Thank God for saving your life. Where were you wounded?"

"When I fought in Russia from 1941 until 1945, at the last battle, a shrapnel piece hit me above the left elbow and injured my arm. My comrades and I tried to get help at the hospital. But the Russians advanced, and the army moved the hospital to an island. My unit and I fought our way through the Russian circle, and we reached the harbor of Pilau. A German ship heading to Norway took other injured soldiers and me aboard. Our ship also carried Russian and Polish prisoners that the German army had taken. British ships patrolled the Baltic Sea and captured the German ships, and the soldiers became prisoners of war. However, the British admiralty allowed the ships to land in Kiel, Schleswig-Holstein. The passengers from our ship consisted mainly of German, Polish, and Russian prisoners; some of them and I were sent to Sophienhof rather than to England, which turned out to be my fortune; otherwise, I would not have met you."

"Yes, I am grateful you were released from the British and landed here. Do you want to go back to your family in Schlesien one day?"

"Unfortunately, Schlesien no longer belongs to Germany; According to the Potsdam Peace Treaty, the four allies gave it to Poland. In case I returned to my hometown in Schlesien, the Polish police would capture me. The Poles would have put me in a coal mine or some factory to work under horrible conditions. Many German soldiers who went looking for their families never came back."

Ernst took Meta's hands, looked into her eyes, and implored, "I will stay here with you if you marry me."

Meta blushed for excitement, then squeezed Ernst's hands firmly and said, "Yes, I will."

They sealed their promise with a kiss.

Meta took Ernst quickly to her mother to share the exciting news.

"Mother, Ernst, and I want to get married. Do we have your permission?"

"But children, where are you going to live? There is neither an apartment nor house vacant here at Sophienhof nor in Pratjau."

"Mother, we can put a wood-burning stove in my bedroom and live there."

"Yes, Mrs. Bonacker, we do not mind living in one room," Ernst interjected.

"It is fine with me if you are satisfied with that arrangement. Have you thought already of a date?"

"Not yet, but perhaps this Christmas would be a good time to have a wedding."

"Christmas is the time to get together with all the relatives, so we would have two reasons to celebrate."

"We have four months to make the necessary preparations, which should be sufficient! Will that be all right with you, Ernst?"

"That is fine with me," Ernst responded.

Meta and Ernst set Christmas day as their wedding date.

Emma and Gustav Kirstein became fond of each other and fell in love during the long, arduous journey, and he visited her frequently at Sophienhof. Gustav asked Emma to marry him. Emma obtained our mother's permission first before they set their wedding date. They discussed the dates and selected Christmas Day, Wednesday, December 25, 1946, as their double wedding day. Emma and Meta announced their upcoming wedding to their brothers and sister, who eagerly welcomed the news.

"Are you also going to have a stag party (Polterabend in German)?"

"We will see, as it would fall on Christmas Eve, which is not a good day for a stag party. We would have to move it up one day," Emma told her sister and us.

"There is still enough time; let us not worry about it now. You should think of getting ready for school now," Meta ended the conversation.

By the middle of August the following year, we returned to school. Mr. Wilhelm Reimers, the new schoolteacher, welcomed us. He also introduced his son, Willie, whom he placed in second grade, and his daughter, Anneliese, in third grade. I was surprised Mr. Reimers asked Hannelore, with whom I shared my desk, to move and put his daughter, Anneliese, next to me. It was quite an honor for me to sit next to the teacher's daughter. We got along well, and as time passed, we became good friends. Being the only teacher, Mr. Reimers had to teach German, mathematics, geography, history, religion, music, art, and some physical exercises to the different grades.

While he lectured to one grade, he instructed the other students to work on a subject quietly. It must have been challenging for the teacher to give instructions in various subjects, but he handled the students well and presented each topic with ease and profound knowledge. He developed a good rapport with students, and they grew fond of him. However, he disciplined the students who misbehaved or did not do their homework by either making them stay one hour later after class doing a particular assignment or getting hit with the ruler on the palm. The worst and most embarrassing punishment was getting hit several times on the butt with a thin stick in front of the class. The boys usually received this type of spanking. Both hurt but taught each student the intended lesson that they would not forget very quickly.

Mr. Reimers arranged for Miss Hoffman to come to the school once a week and teach the girls how to knit, crochet, embroider, mend socks, and other items. In the summertime, we sat outside on a big tree trunk while following the instructions to put different embroidery stitches on a strip of cloth; how I enjoyed learning all the various handworks. Now I could help mother mend socks and linens very neatly.

We did not have any notebooks and used the white back of maps to cut in squares and write exams. We wrote our homework or assignments in the school on our slate board.

Once each month, the teacher dismissed the class and took us for an outing called (Wandertag in German) a day of hiking. He hiked with us to historical sites and told us the story of each place. We walked through meadows and forests on other outings, and he would point out different plants and give us the plants' names. He taught us several songs with a good rhythm for hiking. Mr. Reimers would start a song, and we would all join in singing.

One of my favorite outings was driving in an open wagon to the beach of Schoenberg. The workers had attached boards across the ladder for the students to sit on. Early in the morning, we would tie flowers to the sides between the boards. My oldest brother Georg drove one of the three wagons. We would sing along the way until we arrived at the beach. We unpacked our blankets and swimming suits. Each girl changed into her bathing suit, while another girl would hold a blanket around her. The boys helped each other, too. We ran into the water. At first, it felt cold, but we got adjusted quickly to the cool temperature. The boys would splash the girls with water and vice versa. The boys and girls who knew how to swim would swim out quite far. I could not keep afloat long enough to feel safe in deeper waters, so I walked out until I could no longer feel the bottom under my feet, then I swam back to shore. This way, I could always touch the ground and keep my head above water if I developed leg cramps or experienced an emergency.

At noon, the teacher called us to pause and have lunch. The sandwiches we brought from home tasted so good in the open air; we devoured them quickly to go back to swimming, building sand-castles, or playing catch. At 3:00 p.m., the teacher called us to get ready to go back home. We were exhausted but happy after an exciting day at the beach.

Studying the following day was somewhat troublesome; the thoughts flew back to the beach's outing and the day's exhilarating experience. But in no time, I paid close attention when the teacher read to us the poem "Autumn" by Johann Wolfgang von Goethe. Mr. Reimers explained which word to put the emphasis on and how many feet each verse had. It sounded so melodic the way he read a poem to us. Owning my first poetry book called *Der Bluetenbaum* (The Blooming Tree) gave me a chance to familiarize myself with the different poets and their works. I always admired how the poets could express their thoughts, ideas, observations, and stories so poignantly in a few words. Whenever I had a chance to read a poem, I created an image or saw actual pictures of the characters the poet described. Often, I even dreamed about a story that the author expressed in verses.

August and September passed quickly. The teacher gave us the second report card, which was good enough to pass into third grade. My brother Edmund passed into 6th grade and Richard into 5th grade. At the beginning of October, we received a two-week fall vacation. We helped our mother dig up the potatoes from the garden and picked apples from the trees. We also went to the forest to gather dry branches for kindling wood for the winter. The owner allowed each family to cut down a tree of a certain thickness. Georg and Edmund removed the limbs and cut the trunk into foot-long logs. They waited until the logs dried, then split them and stacked them up into the shed so that we would have enough extra firewood for the winter. The amount of coal that the government allocated to our family was not enough to heat the living room and cook on the hearth all winter long.

The dreary November days gave us a foretaste of winter approaching, and of course, our thoughts centered on the upcoming stag party and the two weddings. Edmund and Richard collected broken metal buckets or any piece of metal they could find to make noise. I instead looked around for broken porcelain plates or pottery, which are supposed to bring good luck to the newlyweds. Emma and Gustav decided to have the stag party one day before Christmas Eve, Monday, December 23. Meta wanted no part of this custom, which she called a pagan event. However, Emma and Gustav did not want to disappoint their brothers, sisters, friends, and neighbors.

Monday, late afternoon, the day before Christmas Eve, all the neighborhood children and the unmarried adults gathered in front of the house, carrying various scrap metal or pieces of broken pottery and porcelain. Heinz Steinbeck, a friend of Emma and Gustav, first put a broken plow and other large metal pieces in front of the door. Then everyone else started throwing their items against the metal, trying to make as much noise as possible. The louder the noise, the more the children laughed. The noisemaking and laughter lasted past dusk. Gustav opened the door. Then he dug his way through the rubble and welcomed the persons. He offered some homemade alcoholic drinks (Schnaps) to the adults, and Emma came behind him with cookies for the children. Everyone pitched in to help the couple to clear all the debris from the door.

As a rule, we celebrated Christmas Eve by attending a traditional church service. This year we would all go to the church for the wedding ceremony on Christmas Day. Mr. Jessen provided his private, elegant stagecoach and horses to drive the two couples to Salzau, where the castle's big hall served as the church. At 8:00 a.m., the beautiful stagecoach stopped in front of the door to pick up Emma and Meta. They both wore black dresses, with a short white veil covering their heads and faces. A myrtle wreath held the veil in place. Mother, Horst, I, and Elsa, the sister of Ernst, got to ride with the brides in the elegant stagecoach. We covered ourselves with blankets to keep from freezing.

Several regular wagons went ahead of the brides and grooms; other relatives, friends, and neighbors followed. Just enough snow had fallen to transform the drab autumn scenery into a picturesque winter scene, fitting for Christmas. When our stagecoach arrived, Edmund and Fritz, Gustav's brothers, who also served as best men, came to take the brides into the church, where the grooms, Gustav and Ernst, awaited the brides and their two bridesmaids, Wanda and Greta. Unfortunately, our father was not present to give away his daughters to be wed. The grooms met the brides in a vestibule and walked in with the bridal party shortly before the church service. They stood in front of the altar, awaiting the pastor. Both families and relatives sat in the front rows. The regular worshippers filled the big hall.

When the pastor entered, he greeted the wedding party with a smile and a bow. Then he addressed the worshippers, "Today, we not only celebrate Christmas, but we celebrate the wedding ceremony of two couples. First, let us rise and sing the Christmas song. "Oh, Thou Joyful, Oh, Thou Blessed Christmas Time."

EMMA AND GUSTAV'S WEDDING

Then the pastor had the wedding party step forward. He gave them a short sermon of a husband's and wife's Christian duties, then he had them exchange vows, put the rings on their fingers, and pronounced them husbands and wives. Then the husbands kissed their wives to confirm their marriage vow. After the bridal party sat down, the pastor gave a vivid sermon on the importance of the birth of Christ, which we commemorated that day. Then he elaborated on how drab the world would be if Christ had not been born. All worshippers sang "Silent Night, Holy Night" before the pastor dismissed all worshipers by saying a benediction and wishing everyone a blessed Christmas.

All the family members went over to the newlywed couples to congratulate them before they left the building. Now, both couples drove back to Sophienhof in the same stagecoach, and Mother, Horst, and I joined the rest of our family on Georg's wagon. Mother, Emma, and Meta had baked fresh bread for lunch with homemade sausage and smoked ham. They offered homemade cake and hickory coffee or herb tea in the living room. After Mother served a modest dinner of roast pork, red cabbage, and boiled potatoes, the men took the tables out of the living room. Our uncle August, my father's youngest brother, came also. He played music for singing and dancing on his piano accordion. He knew how to make others happy with his music and zestful personality. The guests who did not dance used some benches and beds to sit on. My brothers Horst, Richard, Edmund, and I crawled on a bed and watched the adults dancing. We sang along with the songs we knew by heart. I always wondered if only I could dance like my sisters and perhaps get married like them one day. The celebration went on until midnight, but I fell asleep much earlier on top of the bed. Mother had to wake me up after all the guests left to get me ready for bed. The second day of Christmas is also a holiday. Usually, friends and neighbors come for cake and coffee in the afternoon. This time more than usual came to congratulate the newlyweds.

Now Ernst and Meta went milking cows in the barn. Mrs. Jessen needed an extra helper to prepare food for the workers, and she asked Emma to assist her regular maid. Gustav instead was employed by Mr. Jessen as a carpenter and handyman doing all kinds of repair work on wagons, equipment, or anything that needed fixing. Living in a small room was not easy for either couple, but they made the best of it. They were grateful to have shelter and food and enough wood and coal to heat the room. Meta and Ernst chose to ring in 1947 at home; so did my mother and us younger children. Emma and Gustav went to Pratjau to join his family and celebrate with them. Gustav played the piano accordion, and neighbors and friends joined them, and they rang in the New Year with music and dancing.

The winter passed slowly at the farm and in school. Since the British occupied Schleswig-Holstein, they made it mandatory for the children in grammar school to study the English language in fifth and sixth grades. I would complete my fourth grade by the end of next summer and, hopefully, pass and enter 5th grade. I looked forward to studying a new language and learning some customs of England. My brothers did not share my enthusiasm; instead, they preferred to work with their hands, fixing things or making toys for our youngest brother Horst.

On January 2, 1947, I celebrated my tenth birthday. My mother had no ingredients to bake cookies for me. She only baked French bread. My mother churned butter to supplement the small amount the government allocated to us. My mother put a small amount of butter on a piece of white bread and spread some honey over it, substituting a cake. It tasted delicious. We only got this treat on special occasions. Mr. Diercks raised bees and gave us a jar of honey now and then.

The rest of January and February passed uneventfully. By the end of March, the temperatures rose, and the glory of the rising sun filtering through the curtain of clouds painted the sky with many hues of pastel colors. The skylark returned and filled the air with her trills rising high into the sky to sing pianissimo and fortissimo again as she descended. The snowbells already pierced their pointed leaves through the soil and showed off their pretty white bells. Nature awakened, and the first sign of furled leaves appeared on the trees. The brown meadows turned lush green, and the workers drove the cows into the pastures. We all helped our mother prepare the garden for planting, which would begin in April.

When May arrived, nature flourished, and Meta announced that she expected a baby in November. The whole family was happy and looked forward to welcoming a new life into this world. Gustav promised to build a cradle for the baby. Emma searched for some delicate yarn to crochet a baby blanket. In school, I had learned to knit simple things, like a tube sock. I asked Emma for a skein of yarn so that I could knit a simple tube sock. November is already cold, and this way, I wanted to give socks to keep the baby's feet warm. All summer long, we thought of the new arrival. November 8, Ernst and Georg drove in a horse and buggy to Schoenberg to inform Dr. Berman, who had taken care of Meta during her pregnancy, that Meta was already having labor pains. Dr. Berman dismissed his patients in the office, told them to come back tomorrow, and drove with Ernst and Georg to Sophienhof. Mother and Emma stayed with Meta, kept a pot of boiling water on the stove, and prepared the cradle and the baby clothes. Edmund, Richard, Horst, and I waited behind closed doors to hear the baby's first cry. When Ernst, who did not want to see the actual delivery, joined us, we knew the baby would enter this world soon. About ten minutes passed when we heard the first cry of the baby. Emma called out loud, "It is a boy!"

Ernst smiled and was proud that his firstborn baby was a boy. After Emma bathed the baby, put a bandage around the naval, and dressed him, she called us to see the little boy. Ernst went over to Meta and kissed her on the forehead, "I am grateful all went well, and we have a son." Even though Meta was exhausted, she was happy that all went well, and God gave them a son. My brothers and I went over to the cradle and admired the baby boy.

"You know, Hilde, you are an aunt now, and I am an uncle, and he is our little nephew," Edmund told me.

"I thought aunts and uncles are supposed to be much older than we are; I am only ten years old. What about Horst? He is only five years old; is he an uncle also?" I joked.

"Uncle Horst, yes, you are an uncle."

"That sounds funny."

Ernst picked up his son and pressed him gently to his heart, "Welcome, my little son. We will call you Manfred. May you be a blessing to us."

I would have liked to hold him, too, but he looked so tiny and fragile; I did not dare to touch him.

"Come, children, let us leave the parents alone with their newborn son!" Mother took Horst by the hand and left the room with him. We all followed her. We enjoyed so much watching little Manfred growing stronger. When he held his head up, Meta allowed us to hold him for a short time. When December arrived, and the first snow fell, we thought of Christmas, and we got busy making gifts. I asked Emma for some yarn and a crocheting hook. In school, Fraeulein Hoffman taught me how to crochet. She helped me start a small cap for Manfred. I crocheted round and round until I had about a half a foot-long big tube. I gathered one end and closed it. Then I asked my home economics teacher to show me how to make a pom-pom. I fastened it to the top of the cap. It turned out to be quite lovely. I could hardly wait to give it to my sister for Manfred.

In school, we also learned more Christmas songs and another play, this time, the fairy tale of Rumpelstilzchen. We would perform it for our parents before Christmas vacation started on December 21, 1947. Having a baby in the family made Christmas Eve and Christmas Day very special and reminded us of baby Jesus's birth, whose remembrance we celebrated. We exchanged gifts as usual on Christmas Eve. I gave Meta the little cap, "Look, Meta, what I made for Manfred!"

"You made it yourself. That is very nice. Thank you."

"Can you see how it fits?" Meta removed the cap he was wearing and put mine on.

"It is just the right size and looks so nice. We have to put a ribbon on each side, so we can tie it and prevent it from falling off the baby's head."

"I can crochet them and put them on. You can take it off now. I will fix it later."

Emma had knitted a little jacket for him, and my mother knitted a baby blanket. Meta was grateful to have warmer clothes for him for winter. January 1948 started with a snow blizzard, and the wind rattled the windows, and the snow pelted at the glass, creating an eerie sound. The whole month of January was frigid, and it was challenging to keep the rooms comfortably warm, especially at night. The glowing ember stayed hot under a pile of ashes but did not sufficiently warm the entire room. We crawled under the featherbeds to keep warm.

My mother woke up first in the morning, removed the ashes, and put some kindling sticks on the glowing ambers. She waited until the kindling wood caught on fire before she placed thicker logs on top. She went to the kitchen and did the same on the stove to be ready to cook breakfast. Emma and Gustav had no oven or stove in their room. They took each a heated brick to bed to keep their feet warm during the night. Meta and Ernst had only a stove for cooking that they kept burning all day long.

Meta took about a month and a half off from milking cows. When she returned to work, my mother would watch Manfred. I would also help her changing diapers or playing with him after I came back from school. In February, Manfred got sick and started crying. When Meta got back from milking, Manfred was running a high fever and had difficulty breathing. Meta suspected he had pneumonia. No doctor was in the area. Meta immediately asked Ernst to take them to the Children's Clinic in Kiel. He asked the neighbor if he could have a horse and buggy to go to Schoenberg. Georg went with Ernst to take Meta to the train station in Schoenberg. She held Manfred in her arms wrapped in a blanket. After she got on the train, Ernst and Georg returned to the farm because they had to work the following day.

Meta uncovered the head of the baby and touched the forehead; it felt even hotter than before. The breathing was shallow, and after a while, he stopped breathing altogether. Meta let out a cry in desperation, "My God, my God, don't let him die." It was too late. Manfred did not breathe again, and then he closed his eyes, turned pale, and passed away. Devastated, Meta buried her head in the blanket and cried until she arrived in Kiel. The conductor came to Meta and asked her where she wanted to get off. Meta still wanted to go to the Children's hospital and have a doctor look at Manfred. The train conductor helped Meta get off the train, close to the Children's Hospital. She carried her lifeless son into the hospital. After giving all the information to the admitting office, a nurse took them to a room. She unwrapped the baby and placed him on the bed. Then she called a doctor to examine the baby. The doctor checked the lungs and pulse, found no sign of life in them, and pronounced the baby dead. He expressed his condolences and left the grieving and crying mother with the nurse.

"What am I going to do? I cannot take the dead baby back to the farm. There is no place where I could bury him." Those and other questions crossed Meta's mind. The nurse told Meta; she would send for the hospital pastor who would help her. Meta waited for about an hour, which seemed long before the nurse returned with the pastor. The nurse had explained the circumstances to the pastor, who expressed his condolences and then looked at the lifeless pale baby with a compassionate expression.

"I am so sorry you lost your son. We have a church and a cemetery nearby. You can bury your son in our cemetery; however, we have no place to keep the body. You will have to arrange for him to stay at the hospital until the funeral. The nurse will assist you. We could have the funeral Sunday afternoon. Would that be sufficient time to notify your husband, family and relatives?"

"I think that would suffice. My family could be here by 1:00 p.m. and still get back to the ranch before it gets dark. Is that a good time for you, Pastor?"

"Yes, I will see you and your family Sunday, November 14, 1948. May God comfort you." He shook her hand as he said goodbye and departed. Meanwhile, the sun descended, and darkness not only settled over the city but also in Meta's heart as she looked at the lifeless body of her firstborn son. Then she buried her head in the blanket as the tears flowed down her cheeks. The nurse told Meta she would have to take the baby and put him in the morgue. Meta pressed one more kiss on the cold forehead before the nurse took the baby and carried him away. The nurse told Meta she would be back shortly. When the nurse returned, she told Meta she was in no condition to go back to the farm tonight. I will get you a blanket to keep warm, you can stay in the lobby. The nurse took Meta's arm and led her to the lobby.

"Sit down on the sofa. Perhaps, you might even be able to sleep. Can I get you something to eat or drink? You must be hungry."

"I do not feel like eating, but perhaps a cup of tea would help to relax me."

"Good, I'll see that someone brings you a cup of tea."

Meta sat down on the sofa. Someone brought her a cup of tea. She drank it slowly, then covered herself and continued to sob and blow her nose for some time until she collapsed on the sofa and fell asleep. The flow of patients into the hospital awoke Meta. It took her a few minutes to reorientate herself where she was and why she was there. The nurse, who had taken care of Meta, approached her. She told Meta to go back home to plan for the funeral with the family. Meta thanked the nurse for the blanket and said she would be back Sunday morning.

Meta, broken-hearted, strolled to the train station and got a train ticket. When the train arrived, Meta stepped on the platform, entered the train car, sank on the seat, and cried. When the conductor checked the tickets, she told him about her loss and asked him to tell her when the train reached Schoenberg. About an hour later, the conductor came and told Meta the next stop would be Schoenberg. Meta folded the baby blanket she had taken with her and got off the train. Meta had no means of communicating with her husband, so she had to walk back to Sophienhof on the unpaved, bumpy country road. At times, she staggered, stepping into a deep pothole. Her heart overflowed with grief. Then she looked up to heaven and cried out, "God, why did my firstborn son die?" Then she thought for a while. God must have suffered to see his son being hung on the cross to die for our sins, even though He was without sin. She thought, "My baby was also without sin, and You took him from me, which is difficult for me to accept." Then the Bible passage came to her to not let her heart be troubled but to trust God, and in due time He will comfort her. These words calmed her mind, even though the heart remained filled with grief.

By noon, she arrived at Sophienhof. Ernst still worked in the stable. Mother and her four sons and I sat around the table and ate their lunch when Meta entered.

"Manfred died before we could reach the hospital."

Mother got up, embraced Meta, and expressed her sympathy. Both cried before she sat down to eat with us and told us the whole story, which made me cry too. Then Meta went to her room and waited for her husband to return from work. When Ernst entered, Meta got up, embraced him, and started to cry. Ernst knew without Meta uttering a word that their son had died. For a while, nobody was able to speak a word. Then Meta told Ernst the arrangement she had made for Manfred's funeral.

"Yes, it is a good idea to bury him in Kiel, where the funeral home will look after his grave. When we leave Sophienhof, which eventually we will do, the local cemetery would abandon his grave. You made the right decision."

"We can ask Gustav to make a coffin for Manfred. Emma and I will prepare the cushions. I can use his baptism outfit to dress him. We do not have much time; please, go to Gustav right away." Ernst had seen Gustav repairing a wagon wheel. Ernst, who could not believe that he lost his little son, went to Gustav, told him about his son's death, and asked him if he could make a tiny coffin for him about two feet long. We need it by Sunday."

"I am so sorry about your loss. I will look around where I can find nice wooden boards I can use. I will let you know when I have it ready."

We could only communicate with relatives by mail or personal messengers; both ways would take too long to have them arrive on time. Sunday morning, Georg hitched the horses to the wagon and drove Ernst, Meta, Emma, Gustav, Mother, Edmund, and me to the train station in Schoenberg. Richard had to stay home to watch Horst. Ernst carried the coffin in a sack, and Meta took along all the clothes for Manfred. After we arrived in Kiel, we went to the hospital to get Manfred ready in the coffin. Meta looked for the same nurse who had helped her before. The nurse took Meta and Ernst to the morgue. Tears welled up in their eyes as they saw the lifeless little body lying on a small table in the hospital morgue. We waited in the hospital lobby for them. When Ernst came carrying the coffin under his arm, Gustav released him by taking it from him, "You hold on to Meta; she needs your support. Let us go, Meta, you lead the way to church."

The pastor awaited us in the chapel of the cemetery. After Gustav placed the tiny coffin on the table in front of the altar, he opened the cover. Manfred looked like a sleeping angel in his white baptism dress. The pastor expressed his condolences to Ernst and all of us.

"Yes, it is very tough to lose your first child, but he is in heaven now, where there is no suffering, and God will comfort you too."

The pastor preached a short sermon about the seasons of life and how fragile life is. If we have faith, we will join Manfred one day and live eternally. The thought of seeing him in heaven gave us a glimmer of comfort and hope. After the sermon, we went to the coffin to take a last close look and say our final farewell to little Manfred. Meta and Ernst kissed him on the forehead while the tears filled their eyes, and some even dropped on his forehead. The rest of our family touched his ice-cold little hands, crossed on his body. Then Gustav closed the coffin. The pastor said a prayer before Gustav and Ernst carried the coffin to the burial site and lowered it into the dug-out grave. It was bitterly cold, so the pastor spoke only a few passages before putting the first shovel of dirt on the coffin. Meta and Ernst did likewise. The pastor said another prayer, shook their hands and gave them a blessing before saying goodbye to everyone.

We picked up our belongings in the chapel and headed toward the train station, waiting to take Schoenberg's train. When we arrived in Schoenberg, Georg waited for us outside the train station. He had also brought some more blankets to keep us warm. Before we pulled into Sophienhof, the sun had set, and darkness not only covered the landscape but also drenched our hearts. But a glimmer of hope remained, that if we believe in God, He will not only comfort us, but we will see Manfred in heaven again. Emma and her mother prepared some sandwiches for all of us before we went to bed. We were hoping to find rest from a long, emotionally exhausting day. Meta's spirit was grief-stricken tonight; she was not able to fall asleep for a long time. The next day, she was too exhausted and too heartbroken to go to work. She put on a black dress, which was a German custom when a close family member died. The women wore only black dresses for a whole year, and men wore a black ribbon on the jacket's left upper sleeve. Meta and Ernst followed this tradition. The winter passed slowly for us. We barely had enough coal and wood to keep us warm through the winter. We greeted spring with open arms. We were glad to explore the outdoors again, run through the meadows and forests, play ball, and other games with the neighborhood children.

Before we got our summer vacation, two events took place on April 3, 1948; President Truman signed Europe's economic recovery plan. It is also known as the Marshall Plan,[16] named after the secretary of State, George Marshall. The United States allocated billions of dollars and goods to sixteen European countries to restore the economic infrastructure and create political stability in Europe. The United States and Britain thought it necessary to block communism from infiltrating Europe. The Soviet Union did not accept the Marshall plan; they feared it would weaken their satellite states' influence. Only five percent of the money grants were required to be paid back by each country to implement the program. During and after the war, the German economy had collapsed. Prices were fixed, food was rationed, goods were difficult to get, which created an uncontrollable black market and a high inflation rate. Industrial and food production had dropped considerably. The people from the cities had to go to the country to barter for food. President Truman realized Germany needed a currency reform that would eliminate rationing and create a free market.

On June 20, 1948, the currency reform began, which changed people's lives in Germany and ours as well.

The relationship between the American, British, and Russian governments deteriorated after World War II. President Truman and Prime Minister Churchill realized an economically strong Germany and Europe were needed to keep Russia at bay. Both allies came up with the idea to create a new currency for Germany, called Deutsche Mark, which would replace the inflated Reichsmark and Military Mark. President Truman had the Deutsche Mark printed in the United States. Five hundred tons of currency packed in 23,000 boxes, marked doorknobs, were shipped secretly to Bremerhaven. This secret event was called Operation Bird Dog.[17] From Bremerhaven, 800 trucks transported the boxes of currency to Frankfurt. Ludwig Erhard, who politically opposed Hitler and refused to accept a centralized economy under Hitler, was appointed to work out the new currency details. Officials informed factories to withhold delivery of goods until the new currency took effect.

On June 20, 1948, 40.00 DM. (Forty Deutsche Mark) were allocated to each person. My Mother would receive 240.00 DM for her six-person household and 20.00 DM more per person at a later date. Emma went the following day to the village, where she picked up the rationing stamps to get the money for herself and Gustav, and our family. The officials already had all the information on each family, which implemented the program quickly. Suddenly in all of Germany, an abundance of goods and food filled the empty stores and shelves. For the first time, since the beginning of World War II, almost nine years ago, persons could buy without limits whatever their heart desired. A wave of jubilation rushed through the country.

Emma took Edmund, Richard, and me on a shopping trip to Kiel. Many ruins of bombed structures were dismantled, some demolished, and new buildings emerged among downtown's ruins. Businesses reopened. Students started to plant trees in the debris areas. The city administration rebuilt the train station, repaired the train tracks, and the trains ran again. After we got off at the train station, Emma looked around for a fabric store. She bought some fabric for a dress for herself as well as for my mother and me. Emma let me pick the material I liked. Next, we went to a clothing store, where she bought a pair of shorts for Georg, Edmund, Richard, and Horst. Before we headed home, she treated us to an ice cream cone, which we had never eaten before. It tasted so good. We took the train going back to Schoenberg. From Schoenberg, we walked home, carrying our packages to Sophienhof. Even though tired from the day's shopping in the big city, we were thrilled to show our purchases to Mother. We gave her the material we bought for her. We all looked forward to a new dress of our choice.

Mr. Puck and his van, carrying food, also stopped coming. Now he had so much merchandise, which he could no longer fit into his small van. We all walked to his store in Bendfeld. Things started to go forward from then on. With the money from the Marshall Plan and the Deutsche Mark's stable value, Germany rebuilt the infrastructure, cleared the debris, and reconstructed cities and villages. Even though Germany was the most-destroyed country and received the least money per capita, Germans rapidly rebuilt their country. The economic miracle began, also called Wirtschaftswunder. A lot of persons who lived among the ruins found or built apartments or houses. Most importantly, we could buy sufficient food once more.

However, Russia neither accepted aid from the Marshall Plan nor allowed the Deutsche Mark to circulate in Germany's Russian-occupied zone. They feared it would weaken their influence over their satellite states. Even though Berlin, the capital of Germany, was in the Russian-occupied area, the four allies divided Berlin into American, English, French, and Russian sectors. The downside of Russia not allowing the Deutsche Mark to be the currency in their occupied zone divided Germany into East Germany and West Germany. All merchandise and goods from West Germany needed to be transported through the Russian-occupied area by trucks or trains to Berlin, located on the main transportation route one hundred miles from West Germany's border. Four days after Russia refused to accept the Deutsche Mark in the Eastern Zone, they tried to force the three allies out of Berlin. The Russians blocked all roads, train tracks, and waterways coming into Berlin. Russia was trying to starve the two million people of West Berlin, so the Western allies would give in and move out of Berlin. The Berlin Blockade was the first major international crisis, and the first conflict between Russia and her allies escalated into the Cold War.[18] Russia also closed the allied-controlled airbase.

The allies had three options: give up their occupied part of Berlin and let Russia take over, which meant let Russia have its way, and permit them to make more demands in the future or using military force to prevent the blockade, which could cause a third World War, another tragedy. They chose to stand firm and not give in to Russia's demands. General William Turner came up with a plan that would not jeopardize the Americans and their allies' strong stand. He organized what later was called Operation Vittles. General William Turner designed a plan to use 220 C 54 Bomber planes to fly nonstop tons of food, coal, gasoline, and other raw material into Berlin to keep the people from starving. Soon pilots from Great Britain, France, and other countries joined in the operation, and all airplanes landed in the British Zone because the allied-controlled airbase was closed. Day and night, in storms or bad weather, airplanes carried out their mission. Civilians joined, helping unload the goods, so the planes could fly out quickly and make room for the subsequent aircraft to land. Military, as well as private pilots and aircraft, joined Operation Vittles. Among the supplies air-lifted into Berlin, 500,000 Care Packages were delivered.

When Pilot Gail Halverson landed at Tempelhof airport, he encountered raggedy-clothed children standing behind a barbwire fence. When he asked them what they would like to have, they answered, peace. The answer of the children evoked compassion for them. He had only a stick of chewing gum, which he broke in four pieces and gave them to a boy with the wrapper. The boy cut the paper wrapper into pieces and handed them to the children to smell the paper's mint. Pilot Halverson was so impressed by the children's behavior that he wanted to do something for them. He decided to collect candy and drop them off from the plane for the children. He knew he needed permission from the proper authorities, but there was no time to obtain it. The word of his operation spread, and his friends and people from all over sent him candy for the children. He told the children he would wiggle the wings when he approached the airport. This way, they would identify his plane and be ready to go and pick up the candy. He attached the candy to white handkerchiefs, which served as a small parachutes and made it easy to find the candy. Captain Halverson became known as the Candy Bomber and Uncle Wiggly Wings.

During the winter of 1948 and 1949, the operation became temporarily tricky, and some days, no planes could take off due to bad weather. Operation Vittles continued and became the most outstanding airlift achievement in history. Stalin realized that the allies would not leave Berlin at any cost, and he lifted the blockade on May 12, 1949. Before Pilot Halverson and other pilots left Tempelhof Airport, hundreds of children and adults came to Tempelhof airport, some with bouquets, others with notes to thank the pilots for their kindness and humanitarian help in keeping them from starving. The Allies and people from around the world showed so much humanity toward the German citizens in Berlin. Pilots and people working together to save Berlin residents from starving began healing the post-war trauma and wounds.

Even our group of refugees received care packages from the Americans at Sophienhof. Each time the Yellow Mail Coach came, we would run over to watch the mailman unloading the mail. If we saw a care package, we were so happy. We ran home to tell our mother that a package arrived. We could pick up the mail between 1:00 and 2:00 p.m. Mrs. Diercks, who handled the mail service, unpacked the goods, placing all the food on one side of the table and the clothes on the other side. By 1:00 p.m., a group of people and children stood in front of the table, eyeing all those beautiful things displayed. Mrs. Diercks allowed only one person at a time to pick an item. She distributed the food to each mother.

Once I was thrilled to find a skirt with beautiful red and white flowers surrounded by green leaves. It became the prize possession that I wore only on Sundays, going to church. Mother, Emma, and Meta got dresses. The boys sometimes got pants and at other times, sweaters or shirts. How we treasured those items and were so grateful to the American government and people for their generosity. It was said, "Every care package is a personal contribution to the world peace; our nation seeks. It expresses America's concern and friendship in a language all people understand." We surely understood the language of having enough food to eat and receiving something special, which we called luxury clothing. How proud I felt going to school with a new skirt that I received from a care package.

Germany needed to resolve many political problems. After Germany lost World War II, the Third Reich collapsed. Germany had no central government from 1945 until 1949.

The allies divided Germany into four occupation zones controlled by American, British, French, and Russian administrations. The four allies also divided and occupied the city of Berlin, located in the Russian zone. When conflicts arose between the Soviet Union and Germany, the three partners, the United States, Great Britain, and France, decided the outcome and ruled Germany.

On May 23, 1949, the first West German Parliamentary council met and formally declared the establishment of the Federal Republic of Germany.[19] Conrad Adenauer, the council president, announced, "Today, a new Germany arises." People became free to join the party of their choice and vote for a president of their choice. They elected Dr. Theodor Heuss as the first president of Germany's Federal Republic on September 12, 1949.

Konrad Adenauer became a just and humanitarian leader with a Christian upbringing and he was familiar with political ideologies. He developed a good relationship with the three allies of West Germany. His economic minister Ludwig Erhard abolished the rationing program after the currency reform in 1948. The new German government aimed to balance social programs for the workers and civilians and capital investment opportunities for indutrialists, commercial businesses, and entrepreneurs. The miticulously designed plans of Ludwig Erhard succeeded in the economic recovery. It took several years of hard work to benefit Germany and Europe. Later it was called (Wirtschafwunder) economical miracle.

Chancellor Adenauer also met in 1952 with Israeli foreign minister Moshe Sharett and signed a reparation agreement to compansate Holocaust survivers for their sufffering during World War II. This agreement is still in effect today. The Soviet government responded quickly to West Germany's action by forming in October 1949, The German Democratic Republic of East Germany or DDR. These actions made the reunification of the divided Germany remote. It divided Germany and the world, created animosity, and fueled the Cold War between the East, the communist-controlled countries, and the West, the free world.

The economy in East Germany digressed, and life became difficult under the communistic dictatorship of Russia. Many East Germans fled to West Germany. In 1961 the Russian government built a wall, later called the iron curtain, from the Baltic Sea along the entire border visably deviding East and West Germany. A five-mile-wide military zone along the border served to patrol and prevent persons from crossing the border without special permits. Anyone caught escaping would be shot on the spot or taken prisoner to be punished. Only certain checkpoints opened with severe restrictions for travelers from East to West Germany and vice versa.

However, prohibiting free traveling, shortages of goods and other restrictions caused people to rebel and hold rallies. First traveling restrictions eased. On November 9, 1989, thousands of citizens gathered in East Berlin and stormed to the wall with hammers and pickaxes and broke pieces of the wall. The guards could no longer control the angry crowd and let them cross into West Berlin. Later, Russian President Mikhail Gorbachev, who also introduced "the perestroika" openness to the Russian people, permitted the iron curtain's removal and East and West Germany to unite.

At last, with the consent of the United States, France, the United Kingdom, and the Soviet Union, the two Germanys were united and regained their sovereignty. The Two Plus Four Agreement signed in Moscow on September 12, 1990 sealed the re-unification of East and West Germany. The four essential terms were that the allied forces withdraw their troups and return full sovereignty to Germany. A limit of 370, 000 German Armed Forces were allowed. Germany had to vow not to make any future claims to the territory that belonged to Germany before 1945. Unfortunately, one-third of Germany, including my beloved East Prussia, was gone forever after both world wars ended.

Let me go back to my grammar school in 1949. When Mr. Reimers dismissed us for our summer vacation and gave us our report cards, he told the students who finish sixth grade next year could apply to a high school in Schoenberg. It will not be easy to get in. Due to a shortage of teachers and a small teaching facility, only a few students could be accommodated. Students would have to undergo an intensive written and oral exam for two weeks. The high school accepted only the best students. Knowing I would finish sixth grade next year, I immediately thought of going to high school. Would my grades be good enough to pass the exams? But how would I get there? Would my mother allow me to go? A lot of thoughts raced through my mind. I also hoped other girls or boys would be interested in going.

I ran home and told my mother about the possibility of going to high school and asked if she would permit me to attend high school providing I would pass the required tests.

"Let me think about it for a while, how we could make it possible. You would need a bicycle because no public transportation is available to Schoenberg. You will also need more and better clothes. We cannot afford to get all these things for you just now. There might also be tuition to be paid."

"Please, please, Mother, let me go. You can make it possible."

"Just be patient; we will see what we can do."

For now, I had to be satisfied that my mother did not respond with a flat no. Presently, I did not even know how to ride a bicycle very well. I needed more practice. Whenever I saw someone bicycling, I asked if they would let me ride their bike. In the beginning, starting and getting my balance on the bicycle caused me to fall frequently. But soon, I felt more secure and took off without tumbling.

During the summer of 1949, potato beetles infested the young plants. Mr. Jessen decided to employ children to pick the beetles from the plants to save the potato crop. He, in turn, would pay a few pennies per hour to each child. A group of my neighbors and I volunteered so I could earn some money toward buying a bicycle. One of the farmworkers would keep track of how many hours each child would work and pay them at the end of the week. I would bring home my few DMs and give them to my mother.

"Look, Mother, I earned some money this week. We can use it toward buying a bicycle for going to school."

"Yes, Hildke that's how mother called me in the East Prussian dialect I will save it for you."

I was so encouraged by contributing to the bicycle's purchase, which might become a reality if not this year, perhaps next year.

In the fall, my youngest brother, being six years old, began grammar school. I took him to school and introduced him to Mr. Reimers. At first, he was timid, but he became more social once he got to know his classmates. He excelled in sports and enjoyed running and playing soccer games.

After Edmund graduated from grammar school, he went to work for the Groth family in Fargau. Mr. Groth was the mayor of Fargau; he also owned a small ranch. Edmund managed the farm for Mr. Groth, who also bought our two horses. Mr. Jessen, the owner of Sophienhof, no longer wanted to provide fodder for our horses, which forced us to sell them. We all were sad to part from our brave horses, Kastan and Kobel, who saved our lives during the long, treacherous journey from East Prussia to our present place in Schleswig-Holstein.

Mother accepted some changes, but others she did not. She adhered to her Christian values and expected all her children to follow her example. Emma and Meta did this by accepting Jesus Christ as their personal Savior. One day Meta gave me a leaflet of Werner Heuchelbach, describing how to be saved. After reading it with great interest, I knelt and asked Jesus to wash away all my sins and come into my heart. I felt a warm light coming over me, and great joy filled my heart. I ran to Mother and Meta and shared this wonderful experience with them. They rejoiced with me. From then on, I listened carefully to the preacher in the church, for I wanted to learn more about Christ's teachings and how to put the words He taught into action. Being a born-again Christian, my faith in God suddenly became alive and meaningful and was not only a religious ritual. Now I not only obeyed my mother dutifully but because God commands us to honor our mother and father. I got a *Catechisms*, compiled by Martin Luther, a book used in schools to teach us the basic rules of our faith and for us to memorize before confirmation at the age of fourteen. It contained the Ten Commandments, The Lord's Prayer, the confession of faith, the Holy Sacraments' explanations, and some church history. The Lutheran and Catholic catechisms differ in some points because the Lutherans, our family's denomination, do not believe in the pope and his infallibility.

The Sunday before confirmation, the students would be asked random questions from the catechism to answer in front of the congregation and recite Bible verses, religious history, and hymns' lyrics. Whenever I had a spare moment, I would read a page or two and memorize the contents. Emma and Meta, both born-again Christians, answered many of my questions about growing in faith.

Meta was expecting another baby, and on June 1, 1950, she gave birth to a healthy baby girl. Meta and Ernst, and all of us welcomed the additional family member named Agnes with joy. Whenever I had a free moment, I would go into Meta's room to look and touch the baby. This time Meta stayed home from work longer to take care of her little daughter.

My brother Richard graduated from grammar school and began going to trade school in Schoenberg. He was very gifted in making things from metal. He wanted to study the craftsmanship of ironwork, or blacksmith, as it is called in German. Richard attended a year of classes in a trade school before becoming an apprentice in a master blacksmith shop. The trade school happened to be in Schoenberg in the same building as the high school I wanted to attend.

During the summer, I worked on the farm whenever I could to earn a few marks. By the end of the summer, I had accumulated some money, and I asked my mother if it was enough to buy a bicycle.

"Not really, but I will add the balance to get you a bicycle, and you can go to high school."

I ran to my mother, embraced her, and shouted, "Thank you, thank you, that is wonderful. When are we going to buy a bicycle?"

"We will wait until next year during your summer vacation."

"That is fine; I can wait."

I could hardly wait to go back to school and tell my teacher the excellent news. When I got back to school and entered sixth grade, I told the teacher that my mother let me enroll in high school. The teacher responded, "I am glad for you too." Then he asked if there was another student who would like to attend high school? When nobody answered, I knew I would have to go alone. But that did not matter to me. I would go regardless of being the only student from my grammar school class. Fall and winter passed slowly and uneventfully. I was counting the months until summer vacation.

The day before our vacation began, we received our report cards. I did not get mine and was wondering why. Then Mr. Reimers told me to wait in the classroom; he wanted to talk to me. After all, students left, he came over to my desk, showed me my report card with my grades, and said, "You see, Hildegard, knowing that you are going to high school, I lowered your grades on purpose. I'll tell you why, when the teachers in high school see your grades, they will not expect much from you, but you surprise them and give them your best, which will be more than they presume. I know you will do well. You are a good student and eager to learn."

At first, I was perplexed. Then I thought a moment, and I said, "I certainly will do my best."

Then he handed me my report card and a sheet of paper with the high school's name, the address, the date of registering, and the beginning of the two-week testing period.

"Remember, also, mature and remain pure."

"I will remember; thank you so much for all you taught me."

With a handshake and a curtsey, I said goodbye and left. I felt somewhat sad that Mr. Reimers no longer would be my teacher because I learned so much from him in the last four years. He taught his students and me not only subjects but wisdom for life. As I slowly walked home, I pondered his action and comment, and I began to understand his motive. Mr. Reimers tried to teach me a vital lesson, to be or do more than expected. The verse he wrote in my album came to my mind: "True beauty is the light that radiates through your eyes from the spirit within."

When I got home, I told my mother the teacher's reason for lowering my grades. She fully agreed with him. I asked her when we could buy the bicycle. I am certainly going to high school. I gave her the date for registering and when the two-week exams would start.

"Maybe Richard will take you to Schoenberg on his bicycle. I will ask him to find out the price first. He can also take you to register."

As soon as I saw Richard walk in the door, I ran over to him, "Richard, Mother wants you to take me to Schoenberg to buy a bicycle. Will you do it?"

"I will do it if my mother says so. Let me talk to Mother first."

Richard went over to my mother, who was cleaning lettuce.

"Mother, do you want me to buy a bicycle for Hilde?"

"Yes, she decided to go to high school and needs a bicycle. When you go to Schoenberg tomorrow, look around for a bicycle shop and find out how much a lady's bicycle costs."

"You, see, Richard, Mother wants me to have a bicycle, and I want it as soon as possible."

"All right, I will find out the price tomorrow."

"Thank you, Richard."

I also told Horst and Georg the good news about getting a bicycle. Horst finished first grade and began second grade in the fall. Georg was the only brother who could not learn a trade because he had to work on the farm to provide food for our family.

When bedtime came, I was too excited about going to high school and owning a new bike that I could not fall asleep for a long time. When I woke up the following day, Richard had already gone to school. I could not wait until he returned to the ranch; I walked ahead to meet him. As soon as I saw my brother in the distance, I ran to greet him.

"Did you find a bike shop? What are the prices?"

"Yes, I found a very nice bicycle shop in Schoenberg, where you can get a decent lady's bike between 60.00 DM and 100.00 DM."

"That is good. I already earned about 25.00 DM during the summer that I gave to Mother. I am sure she will make up for the rest of the money."

"I think she will."

"Let us go to our mother and tell her the good news."

Richard approached our mother and told her about the price of a lady's bicycle and asked her if he could buy it for me.

"I will give you 100.00 DM, and you can take her along tomorrow to buy a bicycle for Hildke."

I stood nearby and let out a shout of joy, "That is wonderful, thank you, Mother, and thank Thee, God, for making my dream come true."

The next morning, I got up early, put on my best Sunday outfit, and off we went to Schoenberg with me on Richard's handlebar. It was a rough ride for Richard, who had to peddle really hard, carrying my extra weight, and for me, sitting on the hard iron bar for over an hour was also uncomfortable. When we entered the bicycle shop, we forgot about the discomfort of the ride. I looked around then went to every lady's bike to scrutinize it before I made my choice. One bicycle caught my attention, and I went back to it several times and carefully checked it out. It was a 1950 red Victoria bike. It even had a crocheted skirt protector and two springs in the seat. I told Richard that I wanted to buy that specific bike. Richard asked how much it cost, then paid the salesman 75.00 DM, who in turn took it over to me with these words, "You made a good choice, and if you take good care of the bicycle, it will last you a long time."

"Thank you, I sure will take good care of it."

Happy as a lark to own a bicycle, I pushed it out of the shop.

"Would you like me to go to the school with you and wait for you there? The building of the school is at the periphery of town. I can also check where you will have to register for the tests."

"You can come with me to check the place for registration; however, you do not have to wait at the school. I will finish my classes by 2:00 p.m. You can go back to town and look at the shops."

"That is a wonderful idea. I will do that."

"Just make sure you are not too late. Here are 2.00 DM, get yourself something to eat for lunch."

"Thank you. I will not be late. See you at 2:00 p.m."

I put my bike next to Richard's and went into the building to inquire where the high school registration office was. A lady showed me the office. I went in to check which documents I would be needing and when the deadline was. After I obtained the necessary information, I went happily back to town. I stopped at each lady's clothing store and admired beautiful dresses, skirts, and blouses. The shoe stores also attracted me—such dainty leather sandals in different colors for the summer. But every time I desired some item, I looked at my brand-new bicycle and then wished for nothing else. I heard the clocks from the church towers strike twelve times. I knew it was time to get something to eat. When I saw a bakery, I went in and bought a sizeable fresh pretzel. A few tables with chairs let the customers stay and consume their pastries in the bakery. I paused and ate my pretzel before deciding to walk back slowly to the school to meet Richard. By now, I was tired of walking. I found a place, sat down, and waited for Richard. At 2:00 p.m., the main entrance door opened, and out came the students. When I spotted Richard, I picked up my bike and walked toward him.

"Hello, Richard, you see, I am on time."

"Very good, let us get going. I have a lot of homework to do."

Richard picked up his bike, and off we went toward Sophienhof over the bumpy unpaved country road and arrived about an hour later.

I put my bike in front of the entrance and ran into the house to my mother. I took her by the hand and led her to my new bike.

"Look, Mother, isn't it a beautiful bike? Thank you so much."

"Yes, it sure is a nice-looking bike. You made a good choice."

"Thank you! Can I bring it inside? I do not want to leave it outside during the night."

"Put it at the entrance behind the ladder; it will be out of the way." I did as my mother told me.

The next day, I rode around the ranch, showed all the neighbors my new bike, and told them I would apply for high school on Wednesday.

Wednesday morning, I took my report card and my ID card and went with Richard to Schoenberg to register for the entrance exam to attend high school. When I arrived, a long line already stood in the hallway. After waiting, what seemed like a long time, the office door opened, a mother and daughter came out, and a lady asked me to come in.

"Good morning, I curtseyed; I am Hildegard Bonacker; here is my report card and ID."

"Good morning, Miss Bonacker; please have a seat while I check your report card and enter you in the register."

I said, "Thank you," and sat down.

The secretary looked at the ID first, entered my name, birth date, and address into her book. Then she looked over my report card, made notes of my grades, and returned both documents to me. The secretary told me the exams would begin Monday, July 10, at 8:00 a.m. and finish on July 24, 1950.

"Bring some notebooks, a pencil, and a fountain pen. We would notify you one week later if you passed the tests and will be accepted or not. Regular classes will start on August 7, 1950, for the students who have passed the exams."

"Goodbye, Miss Bonacker. We will see you on July 10."

I got up, curtsied, said goodbye, and left the office.

Meanwhile, I did not have enough time to go to town, so I waited outside for Richard. When he finished his classes, we met and rode home together. I told him I registered and would start the tests on July 10, 1950.

Sunday, July 9, the whole family, and several neighbors drove to church at the castle Salzau. After we ate lunch, I immediately began putting my notebook, pencil, and fountain pen, filled with ink, in a bag for Monday's high school tests to ensure I would not forget anything. The following day, I got up really early. Mother fixed breakfast for me. Then she prepared a sandwich with butter and homemade salami to take along for lunch. Off I drove to Schoenberg while the sun had just risen and cast her brilliant rays across the fields, and brightened my day also. I arrived half an hour early and checked into the room designated for the students to be tested.

The principal of the school introduced himself as Professor Foerster. Then he asked each student individually to stand up and state his/her name. There were a few more girls than boys in the room. The teacher, in turn, told us which subjects he will test us in. The teachers taught Math, German, English, History, and Geography lessons for the next two weeks and then tested us in each subject. We learned about all the unusual plants and creatures of Australia. The teacher showed us pictures of a platypus, a koala bear, kangaroos, the aboriginal inhabitants of the deserts, and bottle trees' unique shapes and sizes. These different creatures and plants fascinated me. On the way riding home, I repeated all the names to make sure I would not forget them. One day, Professor Foerster left the school at the same time I pulled out with my bicycle. He invited me to walk with him to his house, which was not too far away from the school. I felt honored and pushed my bike while we walked and talked. He told me how much he liked roses and what varieties he already cultivated. I listened attentively, and now and then, I gave him an answer to a question about where I was born, where I lived, and what flowers I liked. In no time, we arrived at his house, and saw the multi-colored roses in bloom that filled his garden,

"How beautiful your roses are," I said, admiring the variety of the colors. Then he said, "Goodbye, Miss Bonacker." I curtseyed and said with a smile, "Goodbye, Professor Foerster."

Happily, I mounted my bike and rode home quickly to tell my mother and sisters about my walk with the professor—the first week passed without difficulty. We took written tests. In the second week, the teachers of the various subjects gave us oral examinations. The first time I had to get up in front of the class and answer questions in the presence of a group of teachers, my nerves tensed up, and my answers came slowly, but I relaxed more and more with each question asked. The teachers made notes after each student had answered the questions. I hoped I had given correct answers to most questions. When the teacher dismissed us on the last day, he told us we would get the written notice before July 31, and classes would start on August 7 for the students who will be accepted. I rode home, wondering if I did well enough to be admitted or not.

Each time the mail wagon came, I ran immediately to check if a letter arrived for me from the high school in Schoenberg. Three days passed, and no mail came. When the letter had not arrived by the end of July, I began to worry that I did not pass the exams. When by Tuesday, August 1, I received no notice, I was desperate. Did I fail the exams, or did something happen to the mail service? What shall I do? Should I accept that I could not go to high school or go and find out what happened? I spent a restless night and prayed to God to show me what I should do. I could not comprehend having my dream broken and face my grammar schoolteacher's embarrassment and tell all the students that I did not pass the tests. The office in the school would probably be closed for the week before school starts. What can I do? I prayed to God, what must I do to find out what happened?

Then I thought of Professor Foerster. I remembered where he lived. Why don't I go to him and talk to him? Yes, that is what I would do tomorrow, Wednesday, August 2. I got up early but did not leave right away. If I arrive at his house by 10:00 a.m., I thought he would have had breakfast, and perhaps I would find him working in the garden. I waited until 9:00 a.m. before I left. When I arrived at Professor Foerster's house, I found him trimming the dead rose blossoms from the bushes. I stopped at the gate and gave him my name, and before he asked me into the garden, I expressed my apology for coming to his home, but I needed to talk to him urgently.

"What happened, Miss Bonacker? Please come in."

I entered the garden,

"Please, continue with your work, Professor Foerster. Remember me taking all the exams, it is only five days before school starts, and I have received no notification whether I passed the tests and was accepted or not."

With great anticipation, I awaited his answer, "Of course, Miss Bonacker, you passed all the tests well and have been accepted."

"Really?" Half in disbelief but then thrilled, I reached out to Professor Foerster's right hand. We shook hands while I exclaimed, "Thank you, thank you, Professor. You have no idea how happy your answer made me. I will be there Monday morning to begin classes." Then I said goodbye, and off I rode. I thanked God that I inquired personally that I passed the exams and was accepted. My spirit lifted me, and I felt like I flew on eagle's wings back to Sophienhof.

I dashed into the kitchen to tell my mother the good news, which made her happy, too. After lunch, I rode to grammar school to tell my teacher, Mr. Reimers, that I passed the exams and would start high school the following week. He was delighted. "I had no doubt you would be accepted. I wish you well." I thanked him for teaching me the educational curriculum and the wisdom and moral values necessary to develop a noble character. I left with mixed emotions, sad to part from my excellent teacher and classmates, but glad to start high school. On the way home, the five years spent in this one-room school with such a wise and knowledgeable teacher flashed across my mind. I again remembered the verse he wrote in my album, "True beauty is the light that radiates through your eyes from the spirit within." He also taught us, "Nothing in this world is constant, except change." Later in life, I thought of what maturity meant to me, and I wrote the following poem:

What Is Maturity
It is a godly noble goal for sure
To mature and always remain pure.

Maturity is more than gaining knowledge, years,
It's choosing wisely what one thinks, does, and hears.

It's knowing when to listen when to speak.
Respect the strong, the gentle, and the weak.
Forgiving persons who offend anew
And saying I am sorry when it's due.
When I keep my promise and my word,
Trust and honor will be a great reward.
To finish tasks that I began to do
Even though it's sacrificial to pursue.
I wisely utilize my goods, my time
Trust and obey God's word, sublime.
He shows me how to do what's right and best,
So, I and others will be richly blessed.
Loving God, myself, my friends, my brothers
And be inspired to do good for others.

It is a godly, noble goal for sure,
To mature and always remain pure.

I realized my life encountered a change. At first, it filled me with some sadness to leave behind the familiar. Then I welcomed the new opportunity of higher learning with enthusiasm, and joy filled my heart. Only three days remained before I began a new phase of my life. I washed and polished my bike and washed and ironed my best outfit. I filled my fountain pen with ink and sharpened my pencil. I took two notebooks along, one with squares and one with lines. On August 7, I rose at 5:00 a.m., and by 6:30 a.m., I started my ride to school. I wanted to make sure I would arrive at least half an hour before classes began.

Other students began arriving, and soon the yard filled up. One of the teachers lined up each class in a row before entering the building and the designated classroom. Senior students entered first; our row entered last. Another teacher awaited us in the classroom and assigned two students per desk. Two rows of ten desks with boys and two rows with girls. When all students sat in their assigned seats, one student after the other stood up and introduced themselves by name. Inge Dunger and I sat in the first center row. Miss Bond introduced herself and told us that each student had to take "German, mathematics, algebra, geography, history, biology, chemistry, and art. These subjects were mandatory. Since Schleswig Holstein was occupied by the British, English is also mandatory."

"However, we also offer Latin and French classes as volunteer subjects. You can sign up for these classes at the end of this session." Miss Bond handed out the week's schedule and what time a teacher would teach a specific subject. After the war, due to a shortage of teachers, each teacher taught more than one subject. The first week demanded much attention to learn the teachers' names and which subject they taught in which classroom. We also needed to acquaint ourselves with the names of our classmates. After two weeks, we developed a specific routine and felt comfortable and well adjusted.

Professor Foerster taught English, French, and Latin. We learned the new nasal sounds in French and correctly wrote and pronounced the French, Latin, and English words. I thoroughly enjoyed his classes and worked hard not to disappoint Prof. Foerster. Whenever we wrote a test, and I did not make a spelling mistake, he smiled while handing the notebook to me. Once I made a spelling error, and he reprimanded me in front of the whole class, "I expected more from you," he told me and lowered the grade by one point. I felt embarrassed and worked even harder in the three languages so as not to disappoint the professor and avoid humiliation.

Another pleasant surprise came my way; our mathematics teacher, Mr. Sabrow, was the same teacher I had the first year in grammar school in Pratjau. He recognized me and knew I liked math. He called me now and then to the blackboard to explain an algebra formula or a math problem for the students.

Professor Augustine instructed geography and history. He sustained an injury during World War II to his right leg, which caused him to limp and use a cane. However, when he spoke with a gentle but firm voice, you could not help but like him. First, we learned by heart the names of each European country's capital, the important cities, rivers, mountains, flora and fauna and what each country produced.

We began our history lesson with the Roman Empire, followed by the migration of the various tribes to Europe's different parts. Professor Augustine presented history vividly, and we listened attentively to the names of the tribes and where each tribe settled. At the end of each lesson, he would quote a proverb to teach us wisdom. One of his quotes, I still remember: "Whoever lies once will not be believed even after he speaks the truth later."

Miss Bond taught German grammar, spelling, and literature. She acquainted us with the two epic poets, Johann Wolfgang von Goethe and Friedrich Schiller, and many other famous poets and authors of various countries. We also had to learn poems by heart and recite them in front of the class. I enjoyed learning new subjects and riding my bicycle to school each day.

One day, while I rode on a curvy part of the road, a boy in his teens cut the curve and collided with me. I fell and hit my head against the handlebar. The boy helped me up, straightened my handlebar, and continued to drive to his destination in the opposite direction. I proceeded on my way to school even though I developed a splitting headache. When Professor Foerster looked at me, he knew I did not feel right. Before he even started teaching, he asked me what happened. I told him about the accident.

"You are in no condition to stay in school. Do you know who can take you home?"

"My brother Richard is in trade school here."

"Good. I will send someone to Richard's class and ask the teacher's permission to take you home. Don't ride the bike; you might get dizzy and fall again."

"Thank you, Professor Foerster."

Several minutes later, Richard came, and we started pushing our bikes home. My headache intensified. I barely made it back home. When my mother saw my bloody left eye, I told her what happened; she immediately put me to bed. She placed a cold, damp cloth over my left eye. It felt better, and I fell asleep. My growling stomach woke me up in the late afternoon.

"Mother, I am hungry. Can you bring me something to eat?"

My mother came back with a sandwich and a glass of milk. I sat up, took a bite, and when I began to chew, each movement of the jaw was painful.

I handed the sandwich to my mother.

"Sorry, it is too painful to eat the sandwich. I'll have another glass of milk to fill my stomach now."

"I will make you some soup later on."

"Thank you, Mother."

My sisters Emma and Meta were surprised to find me in bed, and so was my brother Horst after he came home from school and Georg after he finished working. They expressed their compassion for me. Mother prepared a light soup with some tiny dumplings, which I swallowed without chewing. I spent a restless night and could only sleep on the right side. The slightest pressure on the left cheek hurt. When I got up the following day and looked in the mirror, blood covered the entire eye and black and blue patches formed on the left upper cheek. After the morning routine and a bowl of light milk soup, I returned to bed again. This time I took my poetry book with me, hoping I might be able to read while I kept my head still. I read the poem, "The Erlking (Der Erlkoenig)." It expresses the emotional pain of a father who takes his sick son on horseback to the doctor, and the son dies along the way. Reading so many poems made me appreciate and admire the poet's ability to paint a vivid mental picture with few words. I thought, if only I would have that ability, that would be wonderful. I also utilized the time to study the Lutheran Catechism and read the Bible. I stayed up longer and longer each day and walked around the ranch to see my friends and neighbors. The pain lessened. After one week, I told my mother I was going back to school. I did not want to miss too many classes.

"I think it is too soon, yet."

"I will ride slowly and be all right."

"I'll feel better if Richard takes you on the first day. If you got dizzy, you could fall; he would be there to help you."

"OK, mother, I will go with Richard."

The following Monday, we rode off to school. I felt a shooting pain in my left cheek each time I hit a pothole on the bumpy unpaved country road. I did not dare mentioning it to Richard for fear he would tell Mother, and she would make me stay home longer. In my English class, Professor Foerster welcomed me back and asked me to come forward so he could take a close look at my eye.

"It looks discolored, but do you feel well?"

"Oh yes, I am fine," I answered quickly, so he would not suspect that I still suffered from pain and discomfort. The discoloring faded each day, and the eye cleared up, but the soreness did not disappear completely. After two weeks, I decided on the way home from school to see Dr. Schmidt in Bendfeld. I told him about the accident; he examined me. When he put pressure on the left cheekbone, I felt a sharp pain, like a knife stabbing me in the cheek.

"I think your cheekbone is fractured," he said; however, there is nothing I can do. It will take some time to heal by itself. Meanwhile, avoid sports and any strenuous exercise like running and jumping. Take some aspirin when the pain gets too severe. Make sure you do not participate in sport activities for the next month or so."

"Thank you, Dr. Schmidt. I will do so."

I went home. I told nobody about the doctor's diagnosis. I did not want to miss school. After a month, the pain subsided, and I felt comfortable participating in sports again.

I especially liked the field trips when Professor Foerster took us to specific historical sights. One day we went by train to Laboe, located on the Baltic Sea. Here we visited the Naval Memorial, which was started in 1927 and completed in 1936. Originally it was built in memory of the royal marines, who died in World War I. Later, in 1945 the names of the killed marines of World War II were added to the monument. From Laboe, we took a boat to Kiel; how exciting to glide over the water's surface and feel the wind caress the cheeks. When we arrived at Kiel's harbor, Professor Foerster told us the sad story about Kiel's massive destruction during World War II. Later, the British and the American Air Force bombarded the industrial area heavily because it was an essential harbor for maritime shipbuilding. Fortunately, many buildings, infrastructure, and factories were rebuilt, and some were still under construction.

Kaiser Wilhelm II had ordered a canal to connect the Kiel Fjord at Holtenau with the North Sea at Brunsbuettel. It was named Kaiser-Wilhelm-Kanal to honor Kaiser Wilhelm I, the father of Kaiser Wilhelm II, who initiated the canal's construction and finished it in 1895. It saved more than 250 nautical miles of distance cruising around the Jutland Peninsula and avoided passing through storm-prone seas. Later, it was renamed Nord-Ostsee-Kanal (North-Baltic-Sea Canal. He informed us about Kiel's old prestigious university, the largest in Schleswig-Holstein, founded in 1665. He also mentioned The Kiel Week (Kieler Woche); this event began with twenty sailing participants in 1882, was closed during World War II, reopened in 1948, and grew into one of the biggest sailing competitions and folk festivals in the world. I stayed close to Professor Foerster; I did not want to miss any of his commentaries. When I had the opportunity, I asked questions, which he always answered politely. The students, and mostly me, developed a great admiration and liking for Professor Foerster. We studied hard not to disappoint him, and the girls competed and tried to outdo the boys, which we frequently accomplished. Come summer or winter, I never was late or missed a day of school because of bad weather. During snowstorms, I had to rise early, and in the dark, I pushed the bicycle over the bumpy, frozen road with the snow and wind blowing in my face.

After all the students got to know each other, some would invite me to stay overnight at their homes. I also found out where distant relatives of mine lived in Schoenberg. They had children my same age. After I visited them and introduced myself, they invited me to spend a weekend here and there with them. I thoroughly enjoyed their company and having only a short bike ride to school the following day was a bonus.

We all studied hard; nobody wanted to be left behind to repeat a year or be expelled after failing the second year. Miss Bond, who taught German, demanded that we memorize poems of famous German poets. My favorite poem, written by Friedrich Schiller, was Das Lied von der Glocke "The Song of The Bell" (The Bell) It is the longest (430 verses) and most well-known poem ever written in German literature. We only needed to learn individual sections by heart. In this poem, Friedrich Schiller describes the making of a bell in poignant verses and how the bell's ringing accompanies a person from birth to death through joy or sorrow. He expresses that all earthly things vanish and change continuously. He hoped the first sound of the new bell would proclaim peace.

All German people longed for lasting peace to rebuild their lives and country. However, did real peace begin after the German generals were forced to surrender unconditionally five years ago, or was it only a truce for ending the combat? What price was Germany forced to pay, and what additional sacrifices were demanded from the German citizens?

President Franklin D. Roosevelt and Prime Minister Winston Churchill had good intentions when they met on August 14, 1941, on the Battleship Prince of Wales and drafted the Atlantic Charter document. They defined the post-war world's goals in eight paragraphs that all the allies and eleven European countries confirmed and accepted at a meeting on September 24, 1941, in St. James Palace in London. They all promised to realize these declarations to the best of their ability. In January 1942, a group of twenty-six Allied nations pledged their support.

1. Their countries seek no aggrandizement, territorial, or others
2. They desire to see no territorial changes that do not accord with the freely expressed wishes of the people concerned.
3. They respect the right of all people to choose the form of government under which they will live, and they wish to see sovereign rights and self-government restored to those who have been forcibly deprived of them.
4. They will endeavor, with due respect for their existing obligations, to further enjoyment by all States, great or small,

victor or vanquished of access, on equal terms, to the trade and to the raw materials of the world which are needed for their economic prosperity.

5. They desire to bring about the fullest collaboration between all nations in the economic field with the object of securing, for all, improved labor standards, economic advancement, and social security.

6. After the final destruction of the Nazi tyranny, they hope to see established a peace that will afford to all nations the means of dwelling in safety within their boundaries. And assure all men in all the lands to live out their lives in freedom from fear and want.

7. Such peace should enable all men to traverse the high seas and oceans without hindrance.

8. They believe that all the nations of the world, for real and spiritual reasons, must abandon the use of force. Since no future peace can be maintained if land, sea, or air armaments continue to be employed by nations which threaten, or may threaten aggression outside of their frontiers, they believe, pending the establishment of a wider and permanent system of general security that the Disarmament of such nations is essential. Likewise, they will aid and encourage all other practicable measures to lighten the crushing burden of armaments for peace-loving people.

Another meeting took place by President Franklin D. Roosevelt, Prime Minister Winston S. Churchill, and Joseph V. Stalin from February 3 to 11, 1945, to discuss Germany's post-World War II fate. At that meeting, they again resolved to uphold the contents of the Atlantic Charter's eight paragraphs and treat the victors and the vanquished with the same dignity and respect.[20]

What happened? Why weren't the promises of the rules written in the eight paragraphs in the proposed declaration of the Atlantic Charter upheld? Why were the German people, against their own will, forced to give up a big part of Eastern Germany, Pomerania, Newmark (Mark Brandenburg), and Silesia (Schlesien) to Poland? Why were southern East Prussia, the Memel Region, and Danzig's city also taken away from the Germans and given to Poland? Why did the three allies and the United Nations permit Joseph Stalin to take the northern part of East Prussia with the harbor and University City, Koenigsberg, now called Kaliningrad? Why were the German people not allowed to govern their own country? After the capitulation of Germany, the German Reich ended. The American, British, French, and Russian governments divided Germany into four zones, occupied them with their troops, and set up their main headquarters in Berlin and satellite headquarters in each zone. For four years, Germany had no government. The four representatives who signed the Berliner Declaration were General Dwight Eisenhower, USA; Marshall Georgi Schukow, Russia; General Bernhard Montgomery, Britain; and General Jean de Lattre de Tassigny, France. The four allies set no limit on the duration of the occupation. They governed Germany from their respective countries. The four partners set up all these regulations without a representative or the approval of the German people.

Why did the allies and United Nation's representatives not enforce their own rules and permit the Russian government to mistreat and use the German women and young people who could not escape in time as slave workers under inhumane conditions? Why were the Russians allowed to strip the German inhabitants of all their goods and property and be driven from their homes or shipped in freight trains like cattle to the Russian-occupied zone of Germany? Why were many German prisoners of war allowed to be taken to Siberia to work under inhumane conditions and treatments? Why did General Dwight Eisenhower remove the prisoner of war status from the captured German soldiers and treated them as disarmed enemy forces (DEF)? This way, the DEFs had no protection under the international law of the Geneva Convention. They were at the mercy of the victor's capriciousness. By failing to comply with international regulations, the allies also committed war crimes.

RHEINWIESENLAGER, PHOTO FROM PUBLIC DOMAIN

Why was Poland allowed to retain prisoners of war as slave workers long after the war was over, making them work under horrible conditions, with little food, beating them, and mutilating their bodies?

My father became a prisoner of war in Poland in 1945. After the war ended on May 8, 1945, with Germany's unconditional surrender, he returned to his home in East Prussia, hoping to find his family there. Unfortunately, the Polish police caught him and put him in prison for eight years. He had to work in stone quarries and coal mines during those eight years. Even after being released from jail, he had to stay an additional four years in the area before receiving permission in November 1957, to join his wife Emilie and youngest son, Horst, in Essingen, Germany.

Why did General Dwight Eisenhower set up and oversee the prison camps along the Rhine River? Why did he put the prisoners behind barbed wire fences in open fields without any shelter so that the prisoners had to dig holes to keep warm?[21] When it rained, the gaps filled up with mud, and they had no facilities for washing their clothes. They had to stand in line for ten hours to get a cup of chlorinated water from the Rhine River to quench their thirst. Why did he give them little food and water and let hundreds and thousands die of malnutrition, typhoid fever, and dysentery diseases? Why did he not let the Red Cross and private food supplies be given to the prisoners when the American army's abundant food supply was available? Why didn't the United Nations step in and stop these atrocities in the Rhine meadow camps?

Why was the population of Germany subjected to physical and psychic trauma unparalleled in history? Why did the German people's suffering and sacrifices, mainly from East Germany, remain unknown to the world?

Why are only the Fuehrer's crimes and his military publicized and often even magnified and twisted, and the allies' crimes passed over as if they did not occur? Why didn't the allies, who condemned war crimes and said the victors and the vanquished should be treated equally, also commit war crimes, some even worse?[22] Why did the press not inform the public of these war crimes? Instead, the American people treated the German prisoners, who had the fortune to go to the United States with respect and helped them. They gave them work for pay and welcomed them as good and responsible workers and persons.

In England, under Norman Cross's management, the British government went to great lengths to treat the prisoners of war humanely and provide the same kind of food for them as the local people had. Heinz Kraemer, a prisoner of war in England, was invited by the British Pastor Small to spend Christmas in their home. The wife of Pastor Small was German, and she wanted to celebrate Christmas with traditional German Christmas songs. My friend was overwhelmed by the emotional experience of celebrating Christmas in a private home while being a prisoner of war in England. However, in some English prison camps, the prisoners had to work in labor camps and were poorly treated.

Instead, the German Wehrmacht, who invaded Paris in June 1940, and captured many French soldiers as prisoners of war, divided the prison camps by ranks, Oflags (Offizierslager) for the officer's camp and Stalags (Stammlager) for the ordinary POW camps. The prisoners lived in barracks, fortresses, asylums, or specially constructed facilities and could work in Germany's fields or factories. The treatment of the prisoners varied according to the commander in charge. However, many cultural events took place within most camps. The prisoners formed clubs, bands, and sports teams, and listened to lectures. Many prisoners did not live in camps; some lived among the civilians and were treated according to the Geneva Convention. They received a small portion of their salary—part of their pay went to the German Wehrmacht Operation. Officers sometimes were exempt from working.

Why, when the four Allies did not set a time limit for the duration of the occupation did the occupants demand students to learn the language of their countries? So many questions remain unanswered.

Since we lived in the British zone, it was mandatory to study English in grammar school's fifth and sixth grades and throughout high school and university.

As months passed, we learned to quote some parts of Caesar in Latin, read some simple French stories, and wrote essays in English. I thoroughly enjoyed, not only foreign languages, but all other subjects too. Since I started high school and had a lot of homework each day, little time remained for playing with my friends from my former grammar school and on the farm.

One day in spring, when I got home from school, my mother announced the great news that the Red Cross notified her that they found her daughter Marta after many years of searching. She lived in Silkerode in Thüringen, was married, and had two children. The Red Cross gave Marta's address to us and our address to Marta. Emma wrote immediately to Marta and asked her to come and visit us. Marta wrote back, saying she and her family would come by train to Schoenberg Saturday May 13, 1951. We were all excited to see our sister Marta after so many years and meet our two nephews. Unfortunately, I could not drive with my brother Georg to the train station; I had to be at school that day. Mother, Emma, and Horst went along in the stagecoach, which Mr. Jessen permitted Georg to use. Mother and all of us were thrilled to see her and her two sons, Erhard and Bernhard. I rushed home from school as fast as possible to embrace my dear sister Marta and meet my two nephews. After she hugged me, she stepped back, took a good look at me, and exclaimed, "My, have you grown since I saw you six years ago! You no longer look like a child; you look like a young lady."

"Thank you; I am going to high school, too," I proudly announced.

"That is good; I wished I could have gone to high school. I was grateful to finish grammar school; afterward, I had to go to work. I would have rather become a seamstress, but the war changed all my plans."

"I am so sorry that you could not pursue your desired career. You always sewed such beautiful clothes for me and my dolls."

"I still sew for my boys and me. I like being a mother and homemaker."

"I am glad you like your role as a homemaker; I like to sew, crochet, and knit, too. Perhaps, one day, I will get married and have a family like you."

"Just wait until you get a good education first before you think of getting married."

"I would like to become a teacher after I graduate from high school."

"Good teachers are always needed."

"Excuse me, I have to do a lot of homework for tomorrow. I like to finish it before dinner."

Mother demanded that we all eat at the same time. We waited until Georg would come home from work at 5:00 p.m. She allowed enough time for him to clean up, and at 6:00 p.m., we all had to be seated at the table. Today, my mother put her best sausages on the table for the special occasion along with her home-baked bread. She even had baked a plain cake, which was a real treat for all of us. After Mother bowed her head and said grace, we began to eat.

"I know we all are eager to hear about Marta's escape and how she ended up in Silkerode," Mother said, "Tonight, she is tired. We will wait until tomorrow to hear her story." We sat quietly and consumed our delicious sausage sandwiches.

I still had classes on Saturday morning, I waited anxiously for the classes to finish, and then I rushed home. After lunch, I asked if I could take Erhard and Bernhard for a walk and show them some farm animals. I warned them not to go beyond the fence into the meadow; there is a mean bull, and he might hurt them. When we returned to the house, both were tired and took a nap while I did my homework. Mother and Emma prepared chicken, red cabbage, and mashed potatoes for dinner. We all enjoyed the treat, especially Edmund, who came home that weekend from Schoenberg, where he worked as an apprentice making barrels. After Mother, my sisters, and I cleared the table and washed the dishes, we all sat around the kitchen table and bombarded Marta with questions about the last six years' events we were separated. Meta and Ernst joined us also.

"Now, children, just be quiet and let Marta tell us her story."

While all eyes looked at her, she began to tell us, "As you know, in 1944, I worked for the teacher Mr. Kessler in Hellrau. I helped his wife raising their three sons and one daughter. The youngest boy just started to walk. I would spend evenings in my room above the school and sewed skirts, knitted gloves, or sweaters for my youngest sister Hilde. Often, after the children went to bed, we would also play some board games. At the end of July 1944, we heard on the radio that the residents of Wizajny had to flee because the Russian front advanced rapidly toward our area. We celebrated the oldest son's birthday on August 1 and left the next day by horse and buggy and joined the long trek of refugees."

"Where did you go?" Mother asked.

"Our trek drove through the Rominter Heide, thinking we would be more protected from bombing attacks among the thick forests. It was not so; every night, we heard the droning of planes above us, the piercing noise of bombs dropping and exploding, not knowing if the next bomb would land on us. It was extremely frightening. The next day we had to drive around the bomb craters. Dead horses, cows, and human bodies lay among broken wagons. Some people hitched cows to their wagons so that they would have fresh milk for their children. Slowly we drove through Angerburg and Loetzen and reached Allenstein. Here, we left our horses and wagon and all our belongings and continued by train to Bunzlau, Schlesien, where Mr. and Mrs. Kessler had some friends. We stayed there until February. We were supposed to continue by bus to Dresden, but the bus never showed up. Mr. Kessler decided to take the train. When we arrived at the train station, we found the train completely packed. Even outside was no more standing room. On a different track stood a few empty wagons. All the people rushed to them and entered the wagons without a locomotive. We were fortunate; the train's conductor took the fully occupied train out of the city, disengaged the locomotive, and returned to the train station to pick up the additional wagons. He changed tracks, then connected the other wagons to the train and took off. We barely left the train station when a bomb hit and blew up the train station. What a horrible sight to see the building's debris flying up into the air, followed by a blast and fire. It was even worse to think; if the conductor had not returned for the additional wagons, we also would have been blown to pieces. We thanked God for saving our lives."

DRESDEN BOMBING OF 1945

Marta's face turned pale and tense while talking and reliving this terrifying experience. I sat next to Marta and trembled. I grabbed her hand and tried to comfort her, "Praise God for saving you and all the people on the train. Did you arrive safely in Dresden?"

"Yes, we did. We decided to stay in Dresden, but bombs destroyed most of the city, and we could hardly get around; Mr. Kessler and his family found a place to stay outside the city. I volunteered to help in a temporary hospital that was set up for wounded soldiers. I met Edith, a nurse who worked there also. We became good friends, and both of us lived in a nearby refugee camp. Edith was engaged to a soldier. When the war ended, and the hospital closed its doors, Edith went to Juetzenbach, where her fiancé lived. On her way, she passed through Silkerode, where she stopped to ask directions. The person who gave her directions happened to be a gardener. After Edith had a long conversation with the gardener, he introduced himself as Karl Spitzer, and he asked if she and her girlfriend Marta could come and work for him. He told her that Juetzenbach, where her fiancé lives, is only ten miles away from Silkerode. Edith told the gardener that she could not work for him, but she would ask Marta. After Edith visited her boyfriend, she returned to the camp in Dresden and told me about the gardener's job offer. I was glad to get out of the camp, accepted the offer, and began working for Mr. Spitzer in September 1945. Slowly I got to know the people from this quaint village. When I met Hermann Volz, we were attracted to each other and enjoyed good conversation and dancing. When his mother died in 1946, he asked me to marry him. I gladly accepted his proposal, and we exchanged vows on April 21, 1946. The following year in August, my son Erhard was born, and a year later, Bernhard joined our family."

Mother got up, embraced Marta; tears of joy welled up as she said, "My dear daughter, I am overjoyed that God protected you, that we found each other, you married a good husband and have two lovely sons."

"So am I," Marta uttered while tears of joy rolled down her cheeks.

"What is your husband's profession?" Mother asked.

"He is a city clerk and works for the mayor of Silkerode."

"That is very good."

Marta continued, "Unfortunately, Herman sustained a head injury during World War II, while supplying hand grenades to the soldiers in Kalinin, Russia. After being in a coma for six weeks, he regained consciousness but lost his left eye. Hermann must wear special glasses to cover the cavity of the missing eye. He suffers from frequent headaches. However, he is very kind to the children and me. We all get along well, and I am grateful to have a loving husband. Now, let me hear how and when you came to Sophienhof?"

Then Mother began to tell her, "In mid-July 1944, Father was drafted. The Russian front advanced quickly on the Eastern border. Before midnight, August 2, a messenger from the mayor of Wizayny came and told us to be ready to leave from the city square by 9:00 a.m." Emma, Meta, my brothers, and I interjected now and then and described graphic scenes, which left horrible impressions on us. We only told her the first part of our escape.

"We will tell you more tomorrow evening. Now it is time for the children to take their baths, a Saturday evening tradition, and go to bed."

We did not go to church on Sunday morning because we wanted to spend much time with Marta and our nephews, but we still wore our best clothes. Mother was all smiles today, knowing that all her eight children were gathered around her. Gustav and Ernst also joined us for lunch.

After lunch, our nephews, Richard, Horst, and I took a walk to the nearby forest called Kaelberholz. In springtime, an abundance of flowers blossomed on the ground under the giant beech trees. Yellow irises stood near the shore of the pond. I could not resist picking a few iris blossoms for my mother. I helped Erhard pick a bouquet of wildflowers for his mother, too. Birds chirped, and others sang while the breeze combed through the branches, adding a soothing background sound to the forest concert. We walked back content, and Erhard and I joyfully presented the flowers to our mothers who thanked us and put one bouquet on the kitchen table and the other in the living room. Erhard and Bernhard laid down on my mother's bed and took a long nap. Mother, Emma, Meta, Marta, and I sat around the living room table, and Marta wanted to know when we left home, which way we traveled, and how and when we arrived at Sophienhof? Mother, Emma, and Meta answered one question after the other until dinner time. Marta, seeing Meta pregnant, asked when she was expecting her baby.

Meta told her in two weeks at the beginning of June.

"I sure hope all goes well, and you deliver a healthy baby,"

"I pray that God will give me a healthy child and that it will stay alive this time. Unfortunately, my first child, Manfred, died from pneumonia when he was only three months old."

They continued their conversation after dinner until it was time to go to bed. Each day we shared our experiences of the last six years. The week spent with Marta and her family passed quickly. The sad day arrived when we had to say goodbye to them. Tears filled mother's and Marta's eyes when they parted. Georg had asked Mr. Jessen if he could use the stagecoach to drive them to Schoenberg's train station. I insisted on going with them. My mother finally gave her consent. I enjoyed sitting in the elegant stagecoach behind the coachman with my two nephews and watching the scenery pass. I did not mind the bumps in the unpaved country road. We arrived early and waited until they boarded the train and took off. I felt sad to see them go. I sat with my brother in front and enjoyed the landscape from the coachman's perspective on the way home.

We all got back into our routine again. on June first, Meta announced that she was having labor pains. Ernst drove rapidly to Schoenberg to call the midwife. The midwife had seen Meta several times before and made sure to be available at her due date. Emma and my mother stayed with Meta. Mother and Emma waited to assist the midwife. My mother checked the cradle and made sure the clothes, diapers, and blankets were there. She let Meta squeeze her hand whenever the pain was too severe. She frequently called for Ernst, who finally arrived with the midwife two hours later. The midwife put her instruments in the pot of boiling water, waited for about fifteen minutes, then put them on a clean towel on the table. She sat down in front of Meta and waited. Ernst went into the other room and remained there. Finally, the water bag broke, and the midwife helped the baby to enter the new world. She cut the umbilical cord, held the baby upside down, and gave her a gentle slap on the buttocks to make her cry. Then she handed the baby to Emma, who bathed, dressed her and put the baby in the cradle. Emma went to the other room announcing to Ernst, "It's a girl."

Ernst rushed to Meta, kissed her on the forehead, "I am glad all went well, and we have a little daughter." Then he walked over to the cradle and looked at his newborn daughter with a big smiley face. Mother was proud to be a grandmother again, and my brothers and sisters enjoyed their new niece. This time, Ernst did not let Meta go back to work. He wanted to prevent losing his little daughter if she got sick during the absence of her mother. After being baptized and strong enough, Meta allowed us to pick up Agnes and play with her. Meta enjoyed her role of being a mother again.

By the middle of July, summer vacation started, which all the students waited for anxiously. On the last day of school, Miss Bond, our German teacher, handed us our first report card. Quickly I opened mine and checked my grades in every subject. When I read (versetzt), I passed from the first to the second grade, making me very happy. Two boys were not so lucky. They had to repeat the same class for another year. One boy even had to leave the school altogether because he had failed the same class for the second time. I felt terrible for him. Tears rolled down his cheeks as he said goodbye to us, knowing he would not return in August. I rushed home and told my mother that my report card was good, and I would begin the second year of high school in late summer. Of course, I had to proudly announce to my grammar school classmates that I did well in high school and would advance to the next grade.

In the summer, I helped my mother pick raspberries, currants, and gooseberries, which grew in the garden. Emma took us to a hedge of a field where blackberries grew. When we had a medium bucket full, we would go home and give them to our mother, who would make marmalade or juice from them and the berries from the garden. Sometimes, my girlfriend, Elisabeth, would join us. We talked about sewing and that I liked sewing. She told me she had a sewing machine and asked me to sew a dress for her.

I thought I could try. Elisabeth brought a large envelope with the design of the dress on the outside and large sheets of thin paper with various lines inside. We had to find out which lines the pattern of her dress had, then trace it with a small wheel with teeth on another piece of paper. We traced all the sections with the same line-markings. After we checked and ensured we had all the dress parts, we cut each form out of the paper. Then put the pattern over the material. The black fabric had white lines and small red flowers between the lines. We placed the fabric so that the lines would all be straight, then I pinned the pattern to the material and cut out the material an inch bigger, allowing for the seam.

First, I sewed the bodice, then attached the skirt to it. I called Elisabeth to try it on. The sides of the bodice needed to be taken in a little; otherwise, it fit her well. Now came the most challenging part: to fit the short sleeves. I struggled until I had pinned it properly, then sewed it by hand first and afterward with the sewing machine. I did not know how to sew the zipper with the machine, so I did it by hand on the upper skirt and lower bodice's left side. When I finished, I went to Elisabeth, handed her the dress, and asked her to try it on. It fit. The style looked lovely on her. We both were pleased. I was encouraged to sew more things on her sewing machine.

We also allowed some time for summer fun, swimming in Lake Selenter with Frieda, Elisabeth, Katie, and other friends. I did not know how to swim very well. I walked out as far as I could, touched the bottom, and then swam back to shore. Once, I went out too far, and suddenly, I hit a hole in the bottom of the lake, and I went down fast. I got scared, and quickly I got my head above water and paddled back to shore. Elisabeth told me later that a bomb landed in the lake, creating a big hole. From then on, I avoided going in that direction.

By the middle of August, summer vacation ended, and school began. Seeing the classmates and sharing our vacation adventures was exciting. Then we began studying the different subjects again and reading more stories of Julius Caesar in Latin. In English, the novel *Daddy-Long-Legs* by Jean Webster and excerpts of Molière's *Le Malade Imaginaire* (The Imaginary Invalid) delighted us. The teacher, Miss Bond, who taught German, acquainted us with the well-known author Thomas Mann, who wrote *The Buddenbrooks* depicting the life of a family of Schleswig-Holstein in Germany and several other authors. We also had to learn by heart several poems by the well-known poets Johann Wolfgang von Goethe, Friedrich Schiller, Theodor Storm, Heinrich Heine, and Herman Hesse. Next to Friedrich Schiller, Johann Wolfgang von Goethe was considered the most significant German poet and author. We were required to learn several of his poems by heart, like the "Apprentice" Wander's Night Song" and "The Erlking." I still remember the first verse of the poem:

"*Wer reitet so spät durch Nacht und Wind?*
Es ist der Vater mit seinem Kind:
Er hat den Knaben wohl in dem Arm,
Er fasst ihn sicher, er hält ihn warm."

Translated
Who rides so late through the night and wind?
It is the father with his child.
He has the boy in his arms
He holds him safely; he keeps him warm.[23]

Franz Schubert composed melodies to many of Johann Wolfgang von Goethe's poems. Ludwig von Beethoven composed music to some of the plays Goethe wrote, like Faust. Ludwig von Beethoven also composed a melody to Friedrich Schiller's poem, "The Ode to Joy," sung by choirs worldwide. I always admired poets who create images with few selective, poignant words. Getting to know different parts of the world and learning about their history and cultures fascinated me, especially Japan's foot-binding. I also liked math and algebra. Remembering all the elements' formulas in chemistry bored me. However, I enjoyed biology and learning more about the environment. Fall arrived. All the trees displayed their colorful leaves before the frost plucked them from the branches. The wind whirled them around and around before dropping them on the ground. Flocks of Canadian geese landed in the mowed fields before migrating south to a warmer climate. Winter followed with bitter cold temperatures and bicycling against the cold wind slowed down my speed. I had to get up way before sunrise to be on time for classes, especially when I had to push the bicycle on the icy road instead of riding it. But regardless of how bad the weather was, I never missed a day of school because of bad weather.

Christmas time came, and we got two weeks of vacation. This Christmas was unique, with baby Agnes delighting the family when we gathered around the Christmas tree. Her eyes sparkled when looking at the lit candles and hearing us singing Christmas songs. Emma had knitted a lovely pink jacket for Agnes. I crocheted a pink cap for her, and my mother gave her a baby blanket that she knitted. We did not know this was going to be the last Christmas we would spend with them. Emma and Gustav announced they would like to immigrate with their family to America. They already had applied for their visas. A year-long procedure followed to complete all the necessary documents, undergo medical examinations, and have their background checked to receive the final immigration permit. In August 1951, they went with their families from Bremerhaven by ship to New York. Then they continued by train to York, Pennsylvania, where they settled down to live.

Mother and all my brothers and I felt sad to see them go. I grew attached to Emma. Due to the thirteen years age difference, I considered her like my second mother. Ernst and Meta told my mother they would like to immigrate to the United States also. Before they applied for their visas, they asked if my mother and the rest of the family would like to go with them. Mother told Meta she wanted to stay in Germany, hoping that our father would return one day. However, my mother received a notice that she could move to southern Germany. The German government tried to relocate the refugees from the crowded regions to the less crowded ones.

Chapter 11
Move to and Life in Essingen

MOTHER REALIZED THERE was no future for her children on a farm. She asked us if we would like to move. Georg, Edmund, and Richard welcomed a change. Instead, I would have preferred finishing high school in Schoenberg.

The winter months passed slowly. In spring, Meta announced she was expecting another baby. On November 26, 1951, a midwife delivered a baby girl. Meta and Ernst named her Ilse, and they were happy that Agnes had a little sister. All along, they were working on securing their immigration papers. By April, they received their visas, and on April 10, 1952, Ernst, Meta, and their two daughters flew from Hamburg to New York. They continued by train to Prairie du Chien and by bus to a family farm in Froehlich, Iowa. Once they arrived at their destination, Meta wrote that Ernst worked on the farm for a small salary of $90.00 per month plus some food for his family. It was a humble beginning. The language barrier added hardship to communicating with the farmer, but they lived in a small house alone, and they were content. We all missed our sisters Emma and Meta and our nieces.

Meanwhile, the mayor of Pratjau handled all the necessary paperwork for our family's move. By June 1952, my mother received a notice that we could move to Landau, Pfalz, in July. I begged my mother to wait until summer vacation began, so I would not miss many days of school, and I would also be able to get my report card from an entire semester. Mother agreed. The following weekend I spent with my distant relatives in Neu Schoenberg. I told Waldi

279

and his younger sister, Greta, this was my last visit because my family was moving. They felt sorry to see me go. I, too, felt sad. We always looked forward to spending a weekend together and playing different games.

When I returned to school, I waited until a week before vacation started to tell Professor Foerster that my family would move to southern Germany by the end of July.

"Hildegard, I am so sorry to see you go."

"Professor Foerster, I regret very much to leave you and your school."

"I will give you my address; you can write to me."

"That is so kind of you. I surely will."

"I like to hear where you will be going and which school you will attend in the town."

Then I told my other classmates the last week of school that my family and I would move to Landau in the region of Palatine. Some were sad, others indifferent to me leaving school. Inge, who sat next to me and became my friend, told me that she and her family also planned to move that summer. Her father rented a house in the well-known beach resort town of Timmendorfer Strand on the Baltic Sea. Inge told me she enjoyed swimming, and she looked forward to life on the beach.

On the last day of school, Professor Foerster called each student by name to go forward and receive their report cards. When he gave me my report card, tears welled up in my eyes and rolled down my cheeks. I could only utter "Danke (Thank you)." I took my report card and sat down at my desk to wipe my tears, which kept flowing. After each student received their report cards, Professor Foerster told the class he felt sad to see two of his favorite students, Inge and Hildegard, leaving school simultaneously. Then he came over to Inge and me. He shook our hands and wished us well for the future.

Many more tears flowed while saying goodbye to Inge and some other dear classmates. Reluctantly, I picked up my bicycle and started my way home. This time I pushed my bike through town, just to take in for the last time all the window displays in the stores and the beautiful gardens. I also stopped at the house of Professor Foerster and looked at the various roses in bloom. Deep gratitude filled my heart for the marvelous learning experience at the high school. Professor Foerster taught me not only French, Latin, and English but also moral principles. He and all other teachers encouraged us always to be and do our best in life regardless of circumstances. On the way home, I rode my bike slowly, and on particular stretches, I pushed my bike to take in for the last time the impressive sights of gardens and fields that had become so familiar and dear to me. That afternoon and evening, I hardly spoke. My heart overflowed with the sadness of having left high school. The following days tears flowed, saying goodbye to many of my playmates and friends from Sophienhof and Pratjau. Georg, Edmund, and Richard had to notify their employers who were dismayed to lose them. All three of my brothers worked hard and did their jobs well. However, Georg welcomed the move. He looked forward to something different than taking care of horses and working in the fields of Mr. Jessen's ranch.

The following week, my mother reminded me to check my clothes, give away the ones that were too small, and wash the rest. We should have everything packed by Sunday, July 20, and be ready to leave Monday, July 21, 1952. Each brother and I could only take one suitcase full of clothes, report cards, books, and personal items. Mother put Horst's clothes and her own in a larger suitcase. She had a big wooden box made for her few household articles and the feather beds. She insisted that each one of us should have our down comforter and pillow, which she, Emma, and Meta stuffed with the goose down feathers we raised at home in East Prussia.

Monday morning, Mother also took the linens, dishes, and silverware and wrapped them into the big box among the feather beds. After Edmund closed the box by nailing the loose boards to the frame, he wrote our destination's address on the trunk of the assigned camp in Queichheim-Landau/Pfalz.

At 8:00 a.m., Rudi, our neighbor, arrived with the stagecoach outside the gate. He helped us load our belongings in the back of the stagecoach. Georg rode with Rudi in front while our mother, Edmund, Richard, Horst, and I sat down in the stagecoach back seats. Usually, I would be excited about riding in Mr. Jessen's prestigious stagecoach, but today my heart was filled with sadness, leaving my high school and friends behind. One phase ended, and an unknown phase began. We all sat quietly, each absorbed in their own thoughts until we reached the train station in Schoenberg. A clerk of the mayor in Pratjau had purchased our train tickets before and brought them to us. Rudi checked from which track our train would leave. Then he helped us to carry all our belongings to that track. We waited for the train to go to Preetz, a small city situated between Lanker and Post Lake. We reached the train station, located in the center of town, about an hour later. From there, we continued to Hamburg, Hanover, via Frankfort, and on to Landau. Seeing the big cities and the landscape of Germany's interior with its hills, valleys, and many forests passing by the windows fascinated us. We arrived at the train station in Landau late at night. A bus driver awaited us there and took us to a Gast Staette (Inn) called Wirtschaft zum Lamm in Queichheim, a Landau suburb. We were hungry and exhausted from the long trip. The innkeeper prepared a sandwich for each of us, which we ate in the restaurant. Then he took us to a big hall, where mattresses placed on the floor served for other families and us as temporary sleeping quarters. With a flashlight, he showed us where the washroom was and which six mattresses we should occupy. We did not want to wake up the other people. We put our suitcases next to us, took off our shoes, laid down on our mattresses, and fell asleep quickly.

The next morning, we woke up relatively late. Most of the people had already gone to the restaurant. We quickly washed our faces, brushed our teeth, and joined the other refugees for breakfast. We sat next to a family with four boys and one daughter. They also had escaped from East Prussia and waited to be assigned to a new place to settle down. We introduced ourselves and befriended the Ehrlich family. Mr. Ehrlich had asthma. After each sentence, he breathed heavily to have enough air for the following sentence. Mrs. Ehrlich was a delicate and refined lady, and the four boys, Wolfgang, Freddie, Juergen, and Dieter, obeyed their parents and were respectful toward other persons and us. I befriended their daughter Inge, who was a few years younger than me. When the boys explored the neighborhood, we would walk and talk about our hobbies and the schools we attended.

My mother would talk about her home in East Prussia, and so did Mrs. Ehrlich. The boys found out that merry-go-rounds and other attractions were in town. One evening, the boys decided to go into the city of Landau. They asked permission from their parents, and we from our mother, and Inge and I went along. Georg, who had some money, treated us to a ride on a merry-go-round. Inge and I decided to sit in one of the round seats while the boys mounted the horses. When everyone was aboard, the music began playing, and our seats started to turn around faster and faster. I felt nauseated, and my poor stomach wanted to throw up its contents. I put a hand in front of my mouth and could hardly wait until the merry-go-round stopped. I wobbled out of my seat and tried to find an inconspicuous spot where to release the content of my stomach. Then I went back to Inge and the boys. I guess the merry-go-rounds and other turning rides did not agree with me. Fortunately, I recovered quickly. After sunset, when the sky darkened, suddenly we heard a big bang and fireworks illuminated the sky. We looked in awe at all the different configurations and colors of the display. It mesmerized us. We had never seen such a spectacle in the sky. After it was over, we went back to the camp and told our parents about the marvelous fireworks we saw.

The next day, a city clerk came and told us that a bus would arrive at 2:00 p.m. and take us to Essingen and the Ehrlich family to Edesheim. We packed all our belongings, and shortly before 2:00 p.m., took them outside to the street where the bus stopped. The Ehrlich family did the same. The bus driver loaded our luggage on the bus and drove us first to Essingen, a small town about five miles northeast of Landau, and then continued to Edesheim, about eight and a half miles due north of Landau. We were sad to part from the Ehrlich family but promised we would see each other soon. Mr. and Mrs. Ehrlich and the boys took note of the appearance and the location of the house we moved into, so they would be able to come and visit us. We thanked the bus driver before he drove off with the Ehrlich family.

Georg and Edmund took the big box up into the apartment. Then they came back and carried the other suitcases into the living room. The brown wood panels of the walls made the room appear dark, but the apartment was clean and had two bedrooms, a kitchen, and a spacious living room. The people from the village provided the essential furniture, a table with six chairs in the kitchen, a sofa, with two side tables and light in the living room, and two twin beds with mattresses in each bedroom. A wooden freestanding clothes closet in each bedroom served to hang our wardrobe and store the linens. We were grateful for the significant improvement over the cramped up one-bedroom apartment we shared with Emma and Meta. Mother unpacked the linens and featherbeds and the household articles first, and then my brothers unpacked their clothes, shoes, and the few personal belongings they had brought. Our mother gave Georg money and asked him to find a grocery store and buy some bread and sausage. Georg left the house and asked the first person he met where a grocery store was. The man pointed down the street where Bender's store sold groceries, sausage, produce, and other foods. In a few days, we got settled.

Two other families lived in the same building, which was called the teacher's house. Mrs. Wistof and her four sons, Edelmut, Freimut, Wismut, and Hartmut, lived on the left side of the entrance, and Mr. and Mrs. Buchert, their young son Willie and a teenage daughter, Carla, occupied the center apartment and we the apartment to the right of them. We had to go to the mayor's office to register our family and our current residence address. Georg asked if someone in town needed a helping hand. Since he did not have a chance to acquire a trade due to the war, he would accept any work. Horst, being only ten years old, needed to finish grammar school. I inquired where the closest high school was. The equivalent school, Neusprachliches Gymnasium (gymnasium for new languages), was in Landau. I took the train to Landau, then asked for direction and found the school building. I inquired when and where I could register before school began Monday, August 11, 1952.

Edmund found a place to continue his carpentry training in Herxheim, a village ten miles south of Essingen. Richard looked around for a blacksmith, where he could finish his apprenticeship and get his master's certification. A blacksmith in Ramstein hired Richard. Ramstein, also an American military base, is located approximately twelve miles west of Kaiserslautern. Georg found work at Mr. Feldman's winery in Essingen. After the summer vacation ended, Horst attended the local grammar school, and I went to the Neusprachliches Gymnasium in Landau. My mother stayed home alone every morning. She shopped at the local grocery store, and the butcher, prepared food for Horst and me, and took care of all the household chores.

On the first day of school, I put on my best Sunday dress, a black skirt with the bodice's pink stripes. I left the house relatively early, walked to the train station in Knoerringen-Essingen, and took the train to Landau. The school was approximately a fifteen-minute walk from the train station. The classes began at 8:00 a.m. When I saw the sign for the fourth-grade classroom, I entered. Slowly, the room filled up. Everyone had a designated seat; since I was new, I stood up and waited for the teacher to assign one for me. Finally, the teacher entered the classroom. All students stood up and greeted the teacher who returned the greeting and asked them to sit down. I remained standing. The teacher turned to me and asked my name and where I lived. Then the teacher introduced himself as Mr. Gritzan and assigned me to sit next to Barbara Bliemel in the second row to his left. He moved the other student, sitting next to her, to the empty desk in the back. We received a schedule for the coming week with the subjects and which classroom they would be taught. It took me a little time to get acquainted with the teachers and the students.

A priest instructed the Catholic doctrine to catholic students, and a pastor taught the evangelical doctrine to protestant students. My French classes presented me with difficulty since I was two years behind. In the French occupied Palatine's state (Pfalz); it was mandatory to start French in the sixth grade of grammar school. Since I came from a British-occupied part of Germany, I was two years ahead in my English class and two years behind in French. I gave up Latin to catch up with my French. I struggled and spent much extra time expanding my French vocabulary and learning new grammar rules. With all the other subjects, I had no problem, and I did well.

I also got acquainted with the persons who went to the railroad station Knoerringen-Essingen every morning. Edelmut Wistof, who lived in the same building, went to trade school, so did Herman

Jaeger, who lived in the house on the village plaza close to the end of town. His sister Heidrun attended a girl's school in Landau. We engaged in vivid conversations during the fifteen-minute walk to the railroad station and the half-hour train ride to Landau. On the way home, I walked with a few students who took the same train I did. Riding the train to Landau and watching the Hardt mountains passing to the right was much more enjoyable and more comfortable than bicycling to school alone on the bumpy country road to Schoenberg. My English teacher, Miss Kleiner, also lived in Essingen. Sometimes we met on the train.

I soon got to know the school director, Mrs. Stelzemueller, and the teachers and their subjects. I liked all the teachers, but Dr. Freitag, who joined the staff later and taught German and History, became my favorite. He was strict and demanded much from the students but presented each historical episode vividly and captivated our attention. At the end of each class, he would tell us an anecdote or a quote from a famous author or philosopher to give us practical advice for life. One quote stuck in my mind. "A constant drop penetrates even a rock" (*Steter Tropfen huellt den Stein*), equivalent to the saying, *persistence pays off*. We had to write an essay on this subject. We also presented a book review or a talk about a real-life experience in front of the class. I choose to talk about our escape from East Prussia. At first, I was nervous about getting up to present my personal and sad real-life encounter in front of the class. The words flowed effortlessly when I saw how the classmates listened attentively and even wiped tears from their eyes. Recalling some episodes, I had to swallow the lump in my throat and wipe tears from my eyes before finishing my review. The teacher, as well as my classmates, were moved by my real, yet tragic, story. A short silence followed before even the teacher uttered a thank you, and I could return to my seat.

When we reached the history of World War II, he also told us how unfair the Allies treated the German people. Wernher von Braun, who developed rocket science, was forced to divulge the top scientists' names. The Americans and Russians took the patents from the rockets, leading scientists, and other significant scientific discoveries in space exploration from Germany. The American government selected Wernher von Braun plus many other scientists, technicians, and equipment to work for the American government. The Russian government did the same. Dr. Freitag told us several times,

"Man learns from history that man does not learn anything from history."

Doing gymnastics in the beautiful gym with Miss Letterle was sometimes strenuous but mostly fun. She demanded that we perform all movements on the horse, bar, or floor correctly.

Mrs. Setlazek gave music lessons and taught us to remember all the names of music notes and their sounds and the different signs. When she taught us a song, she would first play it on the piano and then repeat the words from the music sheet and have us sing the melody. She taught us about the different types of music, the structure of compositions, like a symphony, rondo, sonata opera, operetta, and various other musical pieces. We also learned a lot of folk songs by heart. Landau offered musical performances at the theater called Festhalle. When I heard that the opera *Otello* would be performed at the Festhalle, I decided to get tickets and attend the performance.[24] I knew Mother would not let me go alone in the evening. I asked my brother Edmund if he would accompany me. He agreed, and I got two low-priced tickets. I could hardly wait for the day in September to arrive when I would see my first opera performance. I put on my best dress and Edmund his best suit, and we rode off on his small motorcycle to Landau. I had to hold on to my apparel as well as to my brother.

When we arrived at the Festhalle, Edmund put his motorcycle in a designated area. We entered the theater, showed our tickets to the usher, he pointed to the upper balcony where we went, and sat down. The excitement mounted when the lights went out, and the curtain opened. Thunder rumbled, and lightning splashed as Otello entered the stage. He returned from the battlefield victoriously. He was welcomed by the people as well as by his beautiful wife, Desdemona. They expressed their love in a moving duet and were happy to be reunited. The dramatic arias and music moved me. But my brother fell asleep. Thank goodness he did not snore. I would have been very embarrassed. In the next act, Iago, a soldier, sets up a plot to make Otello believe that his wife was unfaithful to him and his friend Cassio betrayed him. In the last act, Otello accused Desdemona of being unfaithful, threw her on the bed, and killed Desdemona. After his friend Cassio told Otello it was not true, Otello kills himself. Mortally wounded, he walks over to Desdemona, kisses her, and falls lifeless on the floor next to Desdemona. A lump formed in my throat as I watched the opera's tragic ending. The curtain closed. When the artists came in front of the curtain, the applause filled the theater, and Edmund woke up.

"Where are we?" He uttered as he wiped the sleep out of his eyes.

"We are in the theater, and the opera just ended. Come, let us go home now."

We got out of the theater, mounted our motorbike, and rode home. I thought of the dramatic performance on the way home and recalled the scene of love, betrayal, and the tragic ending for many days.

The next day in school, Mrs. Gritzan taught classes in religion for the Evangelical and Lutheran students. A priest taught the Catholic students. We studied the reformation that began when Martin Luther, a Catholic monk, who later became a theology professor, saw that the Catholic Church under Pope Leo

X took advantage of their followers.[25] They sold absolution from sin not only for the living but also for the dead. Professor Martin Luther wrote his "95 Theses," expressing the corrupt practices of the Catholic Church. He nailed his letter at the Wittenberg Castle Church on October 31, 1517. Professor Martin Luther believed that according to the Bible, man is saved by grace alone and not by good works. Pope Leo X read the "95 Theses," called Prof. Martin Luther a heretic, and excommunicated him on January 3, 1521. Pope Leo X gave him a chance to renounce his criticism and accusations of the Catholic church in the presence of Emperor Charles V (Kaiser Karl V), dukes, and bishops in Worms on April 17, 1521. When Prof. Martin Luther refused defiantly to recant his writings and adhered to the Bible's teachings, the emperor declared him a heretic and an outlaw. The elector of Saxony, Frederic III the Wise (Kurfuerst Friedrich III der Weise) gave Prof. Martin Luther protection in his Wartburg castle. He got married to Katharina von Bora and had six children. During his hiding, he translated the Bible, written in Latin, into the German language. It took him ten years of work. Now all the German people could read the Word of God and not just the privileged and educated religious leaders. Prof. Martin Luther wrote several books and a catechism, a condensed book to teach the young people the Ten Commandments, the meaning of the holy Sacraments, and the fundamental Lutheran doctrine. We had to know it by heart before we were confirmed. Prof. Martin Luther died of a stroke on February 18, 1546, at sixty-two, and the city buried him in the Castle Church in Wittenberg.

Since many denominations and religions existed, I often pondered which one was the right one. During one class, I asked Mrs. Gritzan, "Since each denomination and religion teaches a different doctrine and claims to be correct, can you tell me which one is the right one?"

"It is like this, Hildegard," she said, "the Bible, which is the Word of God, contains the answers to all the human needs; if you need comfort, you will find comfort in it. If you need guidance, you will find guidance in it. If you seek salvation, you will find salvation in it. Unfortunately, some religious leaders of various denominations took part of the Bible's contents and made it the law for their church members to obey. God looks at the heart of each individual and not the outer form of worshipping."

"Mrs. Gritzan, thank you so much for your explanation. Now I understand how to apply the Word of God in daily life."

The husband of Mrs. Gritzan taught mathematics and algebra. I enjoyed learning how to solve different mathematical problems and getting acquainted with algebra formulas.

Miss Kist introduced us to the art of calligraphy and watercolor painting. We used special pens and ink to write words in the old English form. She did not give us definite instructions on how to paint a subject. She wanted to stimulate our imagination and let us use our designs and color schemes. My pictures looked very rudimentary in comparison to the ones of other students. I admired the paintings of Heidi Hartung and Hildegard Weigel. However, with each class, the brush strokes flowed more effortlessly, and the color combinations improved, as did the overall composition of each subject. Creating pictures captured my interest, so much so, that I chose painting as my hobby later on in life. The more I learned about the various forms of art and artists, the more I appreciated the great masters' paintings.

Miss Walker taught physics and chemistry. Memorizing all the abbreviations of all the elements and combining various elements to create a new substance did not interest me at first. But Miss Walker knew how to capture our attention, and I did well in both subjects. Geography fascinated me, mainly when Dr. Stumbaum lectured about Africa. We had to memorize the different states, their capitals, what each state produced industrially, and in agriculture. Pictures of elephants, giraffes, lions, and other exotic animals kindled in me a desire to travel and see the world. When Dr. Stumbaum also told us about the missionary work of the German Medical Missionary Albert Schweitzer in Lambarene in French Equatorial Africa and the explorations and the missionary work of David Livingston from Scotland, I even nurtured the idea of going as a missionary helper to Africa. Learning about the different climates, time zones, topography, and vegetation of all the earth's continents fascinated me. I made sure I did all my exams in geography to the satisfaction of Dr. Stumbaum. He rewarded me with the highest grade in geography.

The lowest grade I received was in French. Mr. Euler, our French teacher, knew that I was two years behind in French. No matter how hard I tried and spent extra time reading and writing French, I could not catch up with the students who were two years ahead. At that time, we could not obtain books from the past years either. I tried hard to get a passing grade, which I did. English, taught by Miss Kleiner, was too elementary since I began studying English already in grammar school, I was way ahead of my class. It became rather dull. I liked Miss Kleiner. She also lived in Essingen, and I saw her now and then at special events in the village. I thanked God each night that life improved for all of us after moving to Essingen.

As I grew familiar with the teachers and my classmates, I enjoyed going to school. We got acquainted with boys and girls from other schools while going to the train station, about 1 kilometer from the village. We engaged in meaningful conversations during the train rides and continued discussing historical events and Europe's future.

The year 1952 brought many changes in our lives. Georg enjoyed working for the owner of a vineyard, Mr. Feldman, in Essingen. In spring, he cultivated the vineyards, helped with the harvesting in fall, and kept the enormous oak barrels clean. He also transferred the fermented vine from one barrel to another. Then he got rid of all the sediment from the bottom of the barrels. He checked the fermenting process frequently to ensure the quality of the vine.

Edmund advanced with his training in carpentry. Richard became skillful, learning how to make objects from raw iron and other metals. Horst, the youngest brother, had a few more years to attend grammar school before choosing a profession or trade.

Besides going to the local Evangelical church in Essingen, we had a pastor, Armin Schlender, who visited the Lutheran refugees from Eastern Europe once or twice a year. He would not only preach but also teach the young people before he confirmed them. On Sunday, August 31, 1952, Pastor Armin Schlender confirmed only me in the local church. Usually, each young person had to answer two or three random questions. I had to answer all the questions Pastor Schlender asked me about church history, quoting Bible verses, reciting the Ten Commandments, and so many more for at least twenty minutes to half an hour. At first, I felt intimidated, standing alone in front of the whole congregation. I was afraid of giving the wrong answer to some questions. After providing the proper responses several times, I built up confidence and answered all the questions correctly. Pastor Schlender nodded and said, "Well done, Hildegard." He handed me my confirmation certificate with these words from Psalm 37:5 "Commit everything you do to the Lord. Trust Him, and he will bring it to pass." He shook my hand and congratulated me. Then I went back and sat down with my family while Pastor Schlender sat in the front row for the regular church service held by Pastor Bruenings. After the service, many parishioners congratulated me. We went home. A friend had cooked lunch for us. Pastor Schlender, some relatives, and close friends joined us to celebrate my confirmation's happy event.

Another event worth mentioning was forming a youth group for refugees from East Germany called Deutsche Jugend des Ostens, DJO. Heinz Equart, a children's group leader in Landau, asked me to form a children's group in Essingen. The objective was to keep the history, culture, and music of Eastern Germany alive. Of course, I said no at first, stating that I had no experience organizing and leading a group of children. However, after a long talk, Mr. Equart persuaded me to agree when he volunteered to hold the first meetings, and he would provide the necessary material for the gatherings. I began recruiting children between the age of six and twelve years old. Local children were also welcome. After three local and nine refugees joined the group, I obtained permission to use a community building room. I notified Mr. Equart. He came on a Wednesday afternoon to hold the first meeting, explaining the purpose of our get-togethers, which was to learn and keep alive the history of Germany's lost regions and learn their folk songs and dances. In between, he introduced some games we could play to keep the young people interested in returning.

Mr. Equart brought a wooden flute, on which he would play the melody of a song. Then he would say one line at a time and make us repeat the words a few times before we could sing the whole song. We met each Wednesday at 3:00 p.m. for an hour or more after I got home from school. The children enjoyed learning new songs and games. In the third meeting, Mr. Equart brought Willie, who played the piano accordion, to teach us a folk dance. Since we had five boys and seven girls, one girl had to play a boy's dancing role. Mr. Equart walked with a cane due to an injury he sustained during World War II, so he could not physically demonstrate the dance movements, but he gave precise instructions to the boys and girls. They observed each step and tried to remember them. The children learned quickly and enjoyed hopping and turning to the rhythm of the music. We closed that meeting, singing East Prussia's song: "Land of the dark forests and crystal-clear lakes." It sounded so much nicer, accompanied by Willie's accordion music. I got to know the children better, and in due time, we cultivated lasting friendships.

In October, Mr. Equart brought a play and suggested we practice to perform for our parents and the village inhabitants for Christmas. The play was called "The Lost Doll." Mr. Equart briefly explained the story, "A child lost a doll, and two boys set out to find it." He gave me the script and the assignment to choose the right person for each role, which I did at the following meeting. I decided the youngest six-year-old girl, Gudrun, to be our doll. My brother Horst and Peter were to be the two boys looking for the doll. All the other children got the role of persons the two boys encountered while looking for the lost doll. During the first session, I asked each child to read their part. In the second session, I made them put more feelings into each word they said—the next time; I expected them to know most of their parts by heart. Then we practiced enacting their roles over and over. It took time, patience, and persistence, and repeated practice until it sounded and looked satisfactory. We also played games and sang folk songs after each rehearsal so that the children could have fun also. December arrived. I asked Mr. Equart to watch our play and let us know where we could improve the acting. In general, he liked the way the children interpreted their roles. Only now and then, he stopped and made some corrections. On Sunday, December 14, the children performed in the gym of the village. We went half an hour earlier to put on the children's costumes and be ready at 5:00 p.m. The gym started to fill up with the parents of the children as well as a lot of residents from the village.

The speaker announced the program of starting with several Christmas songs followed by the DJO group's children presenting us with the play, "The Lost Doll," under Miss Hildegard Bonacker's direction. Butterflies fluttered in my stomach, but I could not show the children that I was nervous. When the song "Oh Christmas Tree, Oh Christmas Tree" ended, our play began. Horst and Peter entered the stage timidly but soon gained confidence and played their roles well, so did the found doll and the entire cast. When I heard the audience's enthusiastic applause as we all gathered on the stage at the end of the performance, I breathed a sigh of relief. The speaker thanked all the children for their excellent performance. I was proud of my group and thanked them also.

The following spring, our village of Essingen had a special celebration, and our group performed the play for the occasion. Unfortunately, I came down with measles, and the children had to perform by themselves. The audience enjoyed the play, and I was proud of the children performing without my presence.

I respected the opinions of Heinz Equart and his friend, Heinz Kraemer, whom he introduced to me. Heinz Kraemer led an adult DJO group of Landau. They became my advisers in helping me to choose a career. Both lived on the way from high school to the train station. Frequently I would visit them, especially when I had any subject to discuss with them.

As the time came close to graduating from high school, Heinz Equart asked me, "what profession do you want to choose?"

I told him, "I was thinking of becoming a nurse. I liked the medical profession."

"You would be too much like a prisoner working different shifts in the hospital and studying at the same time. You love life too much to be locked up in the hospital. Why don't you become a doctor's assistant, work in a doctor's office during the week, and have the weekends free? You will be much happier than being a nurse."

"I think that is an excellent idea, but I am sure the tuition is costly. I do not have any money, and my mother doesn't either."

"Since your father did not return from the war, you could apply for financial assistance from the government. I will look in the newspaper to find a medical school."

"Where would I apply for educational funds?"

"There is a government office here in Landau where you can ask for assistance. Come back next week, and I will give you the address."

"Thank you so much, Mr. Equart. I will be back soon."

I shook his hand, said goodbye to him and his wife, and went to the train station. While sitting on the train, the thought of becoming a doctor's assistant appealed to me more and more, and I started to think of how I could make it possible. I would need a new wardrobe also. The few dresses and pairs of shoes I owned would not be adequate. But the thought became ingrained in my mind, and I pondered how I could make it a reality.

The following week I stopped again at Mr. Equart's apartment. Mrs. Equart was always kind and offered me a sandwich if they happened to eat lunch when I arrived. I immediately asked, "Did you get the address of the financial office (Finanzamt)?" Mr. Equart got up from the table, picked up a slip of paper from his desk, and said while handing it to me,

"Here is the name and address of the IRS office," while handing me the sheet of paper.

"I did not find the name of the medical school yet, but I will get it for you."

"Thank you so much. I can't stay long today; I have a lot of homework to do," and with these words, I said goodbye.

I told my mother about my plans. She had no objection but told me she had no means of paying for any further education. I mentioned I might be able to apply for possible aid from the government.

"Go ahead if you can get assistance from the government."

"I am grateful, Mother, that you approve of my plan."

During the next visit to Mr. Equart's, he presented me with a name and address of a medical school in Essen. Dr. Glaeser's school trained students in the business and the medical field to be doctors' assistants. I was very grateful for the information. I immediately wrote to Dr. Glaser's school, asking about the requirements to attend his medical school. I also had to find out how much the tuition would be before applying for government funds. Knowing how slow government agencies operate, I had to think of what to do during the waiting period. I decided to look for a job after I graduate from high school. It would also give me some money to buy new clothes. Every day, I waited anxiously for a letter from the medical school. Finally, it arrived, stating that the tuition was 350.00 DM (Appr. $83.00 US dollars) per month. The following day, I went to the financial institution, presented the letter to the office, and explained my intentions to attend medical school. I asked if I would be eligible to receive some aid from the government. He told me I would have to meet specific requirements to receive government funds. I asked him what documents were necessary to submit with the application. He gave me a form to fill out. He also told me to bring a certificate that my father was still a prisoner of war, and my mother had to raise eight children by herself. I thanked the official and told him I would be back as soon as I had the documents. The next day I went to the mayor of Essingen and obtained the required statement. I filled out the application and took it to the financial institution. The official told me he would process the application and to come back in a month. I went back in one month. The official asked me if I have an older brother who works? I told him I did. Then bring me a letter from his boss about how much he makes per month and return in a month. It dragged on and on, each time asking for different papers and postponing a definite and positive answer.

Meanwhile, I graduated from high school in the late spring of 1954. There was no special celebration neither in school nor at home. Dr. Freitag, our History and German teacher, handed each of us our report card, which served as a diploma, and wished us well. Less than half the classmates continued for another three years to finish the Abitur, equivalent to a college degree. Barbara, who was sitting next to me, also stayed. I was sad to leave all my classmates, not knowing if going to medical school would become a reality. I prayed to God that it would. I knew I could not just stay home and wait indefinitely for an answer from the government, so I looked for work.

First, I went to a fashionable boutique, where they sold elegant ladies' clothes. I presented my high school diploma and a brief resume (Lebenslauf). After the manager glanced over my credentials, she told me she was looking for someone to purchase the boutique's clothes. Since I did not have any experience in the field, they would offer me the opportunity to learn the trade. I told the manager that I looked only for a temporary position while waiting for government assistance to attend medical school. Thank you for your offer, but it would not be fair to train me when I could not fill the position permanently. She thanked me for being honest. Before I left, in turn, I thanked her for offering me a job.

Next, I applied for a job in a light bulb factory located in Landau's outskirts. I went to the director of the plant and asked if he could employ me. I mentioned that I just got out of school and had no experience working in a factory, but I was willing to learn whatever was required to do the job. He sent me to Mr. Becker, the manager of the laboratory, who needed an extra worker. After a short interview, Mr. Becker hired me and offered to train me on the job. Before I left, I asked Mr. Becker when I should start.

"You can start Tuesday, June 1, 1954, at 8:00 a.m."

"Thank you so much, Mr. Becker. I will be here Tuesday."

I departed with a handshake and a heart filled with gratitude, and left happily.

On the way to the train station, I stopped at Mr. Equart's to tell him the good news about being hired by the light bulb factory. I mentioned that I would work there temporarily until I received funds from the government to enroll in medical school.

"I understand it is good for you to work while waiting. By the way, would you contact enough older boys and girls to form another youth group in Essingen?"

"Let me see how many of my friends would be willing to join our group."

After I started work, I had to commute by train. During the walk to the train station, I asked Hermann Jaeger and his sister Heidrun to form a DJO group and to suggest other friends. I also solicited friends from other towns. Within a short period, we had thirteen young adults committed to establishing another group. Mr. Equart worked together with Mr. Kraemer, who led the adult group in Landau. Mr. Kraemer held the first meetings in the local grammar schoolroom. Hermann obtained permission from the principal to use one room. Mr. Kraemer made the meetings enjoyable. However, he asked who would be willing to hold future gatherings and set up programs for the group. Hermann Jaeger volunteered. He was an intelligent young man with high moral values and a musical background, playing the violin. His sisters Heidrun and Helga, who played piano, also joined the group. My brother Richard, two friends of ours, Anneliese and Fritz Gutzler, two brothers Edelmuth and Freimuth Wistof, Barbara and Brigitte Maywald, Inge Hoffman, and Fritz Hunzinger also joined. Only eight young people were refugees from East Germany; the others were native residents of Essingen and surrounding villages.

BOTH DJO YOUTH GROUPS

Mr. Kraemer explained the purpose of the DJO (Deutsche Jugend des Ostens—German Youth of the East), DJO Groups formed all over Germany, and a seminar in Bad Kissingen taught young people how to be good leaders. Hermann attended the workshop. He became our outstanding leader, who led us not only in singing but also in folk dancing. Hermann also shared his historical knowledge of Germany. He acquainted us with the beauty and historical sights of our surroundings. Once a year, groups from all parts of Germany would meet and compete in singing, folk dancing, and sports. Our group usually won first prize in singing. After the competitions were over, the young people sat around a campfire in the evening and sang while watching the stars brighten the dark velvet sky. At other times, Hermann would organize a trip by train to a castle or historical site; we would hike for several hours through the beautiful deciduous forests, observing the flowers covering the ground and listening to the birds sing while we sang too. We began singing from the time we entered the train and sang until the time we got home. We knew many songs by heart. When we stopped in a restaurant for lunch, we would spend extra time, and Hermann invited the customers to sing along with us. They always enjoyed the opportunity to express their joy through music. We developed a meaningful and respectful camaraderie among the boys and girls, and Mr. Kraemer was also pleased with our Essinger group. He planned certain events together with his group from Landau. For New Year's Eve of 1954, both of our groups were to join others in Boppard, a quaint city located on the Rhine River south of Koblenz. Hermann, our youth group leader, several other members, and I met with the Landau group, led by Mr. Kramer. We took the train to Boppard and checked in at a Youth Hostel located on top of a hill overlooking Boppard and the Rhine River. After the groups of other towns checked in on Friday, December 31, 1954, and had supper, we gathered in the big hall around the fireplace.

First, we sang a few songs, then the storyteller, Ursula Winters, told us the fairy tale of "The Golden Goose,"[26] written by the Brothers Grimm.

Ursula Winters, the storyteller, asked for volunteers willing to play the roles of the different characters in the story. After having enough persons, she first requested which part each wanted to play and assigned the remaining to the volunteers. Then she mentioned that each person would have to write and recite their script and make their costumes. The fairy tale performance would take place the next day in front of the fireplace at 6:00 p.m. The actors could gather in the room behind the fireplace before the show would start.

Next, someone recited a poem about New Year's Eve. Then we sang folk songs until shortly before midnight. The innkeeper of the Youth Hostel supplied champagne. Briefly, before midnight, we looked at the clock. When both handles pointed to midnight, we lifted our glasses and shouted, "Prosit Neujahr" (Happy New Year). Then we embraced our close friends and wished them personally a

Happy New Year. After I left the hall to retire for the night, I went outside. I stood on the hill, looking at the illuminated city. I listened to the church bells ringing in the year 1955.

My thoughts went home to my family. Then I looked up to heaven and thanked God that he had given me another year. I prayed for guidance, protection, and His help with my plans for my career. A few snowflakes started to fall gently, like a shower of blessings, as if they were God's messengers saying, "Peace, I leave with you. Do not let your heart be troubled. Do not be afraid. I am with you, always." Such peace descended over me. I stood there mesmerized by the scenic beauty and by the solemnity of the divine moment. Quietly, I returned to the room and placed the New Year into God's loving hands, prayed for my family, and fell asleep.

The next day, the persons who volunteered to act tried to find or make the right costumes fitting their characters and created and recited their roles. Sigrid, from the Landau group, volunteered to be a clown. She asked me if I could lend her my colorful green pajama with red and white flowers. It fit loosely. She tied a ribbon around each wrist and ankle and ruffled up the pajama's sleeves and legs. We doubled a scarf, then put it around her neck and tied the ribbon around it. I pulled it together evenly into ruffles. Now, Sigrid looked like a real clown. Her role was to put on funny facial expressions and perform a few acrobatic stunts to make the princess laugh.

"What about the big shoes?"

"We will have to make them from socks. We can ask Mr. Kramer if he is willing to lend us a pair of his socks."

Sigrid took off her costume and went to ask Mr. Kramer if he could lend her a pair of socks. He did. Promptly we stuffed each sock with fine toilet paper and tied a ribbon around the tip, forming a little ball. The second part was more prominent, and the last one was long enough to look like a shoe's long tip. Sigrid tried them on and tied them to her feet so she would not lose them when walking. We had to adjust the toilet paper's firmness so the tips would not bend when she walked. Sigrid was satisfied with her appearance. Next, she wanted to recite some of her lines in private. Boys and girls busied themselves all day long, making appropriate costumes for their roles and quietly making up the lyrics fitting their characters. Excitement filled the youth hostel, and everyone waited anxiously for the show.

The actors, an elderly father, mother, and three adult sons sat around the fireplace at six o'clock. The father lamented, "Our supply of firewood is almost down to nothing. We need to go to the forest to cut some wood." Addressing the oldest boy, "Son, I want you to go to the forest and cut some wood."

Mother added, "I baked a cake for you, so you will not have to starve while working; I'll also give you a bottle of wine." The son took his bag with the food, wine, saw, and went to the forest. The parents and the two sons moved off the stage. The next scene changed quickly. Two boys carried a branch representing a tree on the stage and erected it between logs. The son began to cut the tree with an improvised saw made from a twig and a string. While he paused to eat, a little old man came and asked him, "I am hungry. Can you give me some of your food?"

"No, I won't!" he replied. After he finished eating, he continued cutting the tree. The saw slipped. He lacerated his leg. Screaming, he threw the saw away and rushed home. The tree disappeared from the stage, and the parents with the other two sons appeared again. The injured son limped into the room, moaning. The mother rushed to him, embraced him, "My son, my dear son, what happened to you?"

"The saw slipped, and cut my leg."

The mother immediately put him on the chair, cleaned the wound, and wrapped a bandage around the leg.

"Just rest until it heals."

Then she addresses the second oldest son, "You go and chop wood, the winter is approaching, and we do not have enough firewood."

"Yes, Mother, I shall go"!

His mother also supplied him with a luscious cake and fine wine. The second son said goodbye and went out to chop wood. The parents and the injured son leave the scene. A boy quickly put a branch in a pile of logs. The second son puts the saw against the stem. A little old man appeared while he moved the saw back and forth, trying to cut down the tree.

"Young man, do you have some food you can share with a hungry old man like me?"

"I do not want to share my food with you, wretched creature; go away, and do not interrupt my work," the boy shouts and tries to push him to the side. At that moment, the saw slipped and cut his left leg. He screamed and cursed the older man and limped home.

The scene changes again to the home of the parents.

"Mother, Mother look what happened to me, I tried to chase a beggar away, and the saw hit my leg."

"My poor son, even you had bad luck. Come, let me take care of your wound."

The father sat by the fireplace. raised his right hand in despair and hit the table with his fist. "What are we going to do now? We sure can't send Simpleton. He doesn't know how to do anything, right?"

"Yes, it is a dilemma," addressing her husband, she continued, "You might have to go yourself."

At that moment, Simpleton entered the room. When he saw that both of his brothers were injured, he offered to go to the forest to cut wood.

At first, the mother rejected his offer, "What makes you think you can do it if your brothers were not able to finish the task?"

"Let me go, Mother. I'll try to do my best."

The mother still doubted his capability to accomplish anything worthwhile.

She only prepared a cake baked in ashes for him and gave him a bottle of sour beer.

"Here, son, take this and go." She did not even embrace him as she did her two older, preferred sons.

The scene changed. The branch, which represented the make-belief tree, appeared again on the stage. Logs surrounded the branch on the bottom. Simpleton whistled while sawing the tree. After some time passed, the little old man limped by.

"I am hungry? Can you spare some of your food?"

"Of course, come and sit down, and we will eat together," Simpleton replies,

Simpleton sat next to the old man, unwrapped his cake, broke it in half, and offered half to the little older man.

"Take this; I don't want you to go hungry."

"Thank you," said the old man and took a bite of the plain cake.

"Here is a drink for you, too."

The older man took a big gulp from the bottle Simpleton handed him. He finished his piece of cake, thanked Simpleton, and left, saying, "Keep cutting; it will bring you good luck."

Simpleton continued cutting the tree. When the tree fell to the ground, he saw a golden goose in the trunk. He picked it up and began pondering what to do next.

"What should I do? I do not feel like going home. My family will only laugh at me. I think I will go to the nearby tavern and have a drink, a good meal, and spend the night at the inn."

Simpleton walked off the stage, whistling a happy tune. Boys removed the tree and wooden logs and quickly set up a tavern scene consisting of a long table and two benches. Boys sat on both benches lifting their glasses and singing a drinking song. Three young waitresses, who were the daughters of the innkeeper, refilled the empty glasses. When Simpleton walked in with the golden goose under his arms, the three sisters were curious. They walked over to him and ask.

"What do you have there?" pointing to the golden goose.

"That is my magic golden goose."

"A goose all made out of pure gold," the youngest sister said. Then she thought, if I could only have one feather, I would be rich and would no longer need to work in the tavern. The two older sisters thought the same.

After a while, the customers left the tavern. The lights dimmed, and Simpleton laid down on the bench and put the goose on the table. Simpleton snored, pretending to sleep. First, the oldest sister tiptoes over to the goose and tries to pluck a feather. When she tried to remove her hand, it stuck to the golden goose. The same thing happened to the other two sisters. They waited until Simpleton woke up and begged him.

"Get us loose! Get us loose!"

"I have no power over the magic of the golden goose. Sorry, you will have to come with me."

Simpleton finished breakfast and left the tavern with the golden goose. The three sisters followed him as the father watched with great anguish his three daughters departing.

"Release my daughters, right now," he demanded, shaking his fist at Simpleton.

"Sorry, I have no power; they will have to come with me," he replied while leaving the tavern.

Two boys cleared the tavern's furniture and changed the stage into a road leading through a field to a village.

A parson came along. When he saw the three girls following a young man, he shouted,

"Shame on you, you naughty girls; why do you run after a young fellow?"

He walked over to them, trying to pull the girls away, "Come, let go," he ordered. But instead of getting them loose, he also got stuck and had to follow wherever Simpleton went.

Then a sexton came along. When he saw the parson following Simpleton and the three girls, he was astonished and called out, "Sir Parson, where are you going? Don't you know we have a christening today?" He ran after the parson and grabbed his coat, trying to separate him. Unfortunately, he, too, got stuck. The same tragedy also happened to two workers who wanted to free the parson. The seven following Simpleton walked off the stage, lamenting and shouting at him angrily.

The stage changed rapidly. The two boys erected two windows made from cardboard, put a turret on each side, resembling a castle. A king and his daughter sat behind the window. The daughter was so serious and never smiled. The king announced,

"Whoever can make my daughter laugh shall have her as his wife."

First came the clown, who made all kinds of funny faces and acrobatic stunts, but the princess did not smile. Many other suiters tried hard but without success, too.

Along came Simpleton with his entourage. When the princess saw them, she started laughing so hard and could not stop.

Simpleton, who knew the king's promise, went to ask the king for his daughter's hand in marriage. The king was angry that a plain woodcutter should marry his daughter. He expected a nobleman as a son-in-law and not a common woodcutter.

The king tried to discourage Simpleton by making three challenging demands that he thought he could not fulfill.

When he fulfilled all three demands, the king could not deny him his daughter as a wife. The king and his daughter came out of the castle on the stage, and the king placed his daughter's hand into the hand of Simpleton. The beauty of the princess mesmerized Simpleton. He still could not believe that she was going to be his wife. The king walked off the stage, followed by the princess holding the hand of Simpleton, and all the people walked behind them. The audience applauded. The actors came to the stage and took a bow. The audience of young people applauded again. Then Ursula Winters, the storyteller, came to the stage.

"Thank you all; you acted out your parts well. The costumes, under the circumstances, were creative. I hope you learned the lesson from the fairytale; God rewards good deeds and punishes bad deeds."

After the play, participants changed and returned to the main meeting room; we sang a few more folk songs before retiring for the night. The following morning, a group of boys gathered below my window and sang the East Prussian song, "Aennchen von Tharau." I looked out the window, and I saw Herman leading the boys serenading me for my birthday. Their thoughtfulness touched me; after singing the German birthday song, "Hail to the birthday child," Hermann congratulated me personally for my eighteenth birthday. When I went down for breakfast, someone had put an arch of flowers around my plate. Heinz Kraemer, the Landau group leader, and Hermann, our group leader, sat next to me. Whenever Hermann looked at me, his eyes expressed affection for me. Whenever our eyes met, they overflowed with an appreciation for each other. Instead of saying a prayer, we sang a song to express our gratitude to God for his blessings and the food. Before we began eating, Heinz Kraemer got up and congratulated me, and the entire group sang the birthday song again. Being honored in such an incredible way for my 18th birthday moved me deeply. I felt I reached a milestone of independence. I thought I could make more of my own decisions now as an adult. After breakfast, our group and the one from Landau left the youth hostel by bus and went to the train station to take the train home. We were all absorbed in our thoughts about the marvelous way we rang in the year 1955. I relived every moment of the extraordinary way I celebrated my 18th birthday.

It took me a few days to get back into the daily routine—working five days a week, leading my children's group each Wednesday, and meeting with the older group once a week on Thursday. We felt rewarded to learn new songs or folk dances under Hermann's direction and enjoyed stimulating conversations about various art forms, literature, and our own country and other country's history.

In February, the first Sunday, Hermann passed by the house and asked me to go tobogganing with him. With my mother's permission, I agreed to join him. We pulled the sled behind us through the fields over the newly fallen snow, transforming the scenery into a magical white dream world. On the outskirts of town, we approached a small hill. Together we pulled the sled uphill. Then Hermann let me sit down in front. He pushed the sled to put it in motion, jumped on the sled, and sat behind me. I held on to the front of the sled with both hands. Hermann held on to the sled with one hand and with the other arm holding me. We rushed downhill, shouting for joy. Sometimes Hermann laid down on the sled and skidded down the slope by himself. I did the same thing, and together we happily tobogganed until dusk.

Meanwhile, the evening tiptoed into the village and wrapped the houses in a dark cloak. The full moon rose and spread a soft light over the entire scenery. We stopped tobogganing and started to go home. The magic and peace of the moment transcended our thoughts. Hermann began to sing, "The Moon Rose" (Der Mond ist aufgegangen). I joined him softly. We sang together until we reached the village, pulling the sled behind us. When we got to our house, I shook his hand, and said, "Thank you, Hermann; good night." He pulled me close to him, embraced me, and declared, "Hilde, I love you very much. I would like you to be my wife." Then he kissed me on my lips. That kiss rested only a moment on my lips but would remain a lifelong memory.

I was perplexed and could not speak a word. I cared for Hermann as a friend, but I had not yet thought about becoming his wife. I freed myself; without uttering a word, I quickly ran into the house, closed the door, and left him speechless outdoors. I am sure he had not expected me to respond to his request in such a negative manner. It took me a long time to fall asleep. The thoughts spun around in my head. One moment I felt happy that he thought so highly of me that he wanted to marry me. The next minute I thought I was too young to be tied down and felt terrible to disappoint Hermann. First, I wanted to get a profession, work for a while, and then think about marriage. The following day, we took the train to Landau; Hermann looked crushed. I felt like consoling him and explaining why I acted the way I did. Neither one of us said a word because many other persons also walked to the train. It took Hermann some time to get over my adverse reaction to his marriage proposal.

Chapter 12
Enrollment in Medical School

PRESENTLY, I HAD to face reality and continue requesting financial aid from the government I had applied for several months ago without getting a positive response. Each time I went to the Internal Revenue Office (Finanzamt), the secretary requested another document rather than giving me a positive answer. It became frustrating! I felt the clerk dragged out the processing of my application, hoping I would get discouraged, give up and forget about my request for educational aid. I was determined to pursue bugging the office until the government would grant me the assistance I was entitled to receive. January and February passed. I made several more trips to the Internal Revenue Office without a commitment on their part to even help me with the tuition for the medical school. April 1, 1955, was the deadline to enroll in Dr. Glaeser's Vocational School for Commercial-Practical Medical Assistants in Essen. On March 1, I still worked in the bulb factory. What should I do? Should I give up going to medical school this year altogether? The idea to continue working for another year in the factory did not appeal to me. I prayed that God would help me to reach the right decision. It appeared clear to me that I should enroll regardless of the government's commitment to grant me financial assistance. I thought I had saved enough money for the first few months of tuition and room and board.

Monday, March 7, I went to the director of the factory. I told him I would like to enroll in a medical school by April 1, and I would have to quit by March 21.

"I am sorry to see you go. You have been a good employee. I understand with your qualifications that you want to acquire a different profession. I wish you well."

I thanked Mr. Becker for the opportunity to have worked for him and the on-the-job training.

During the next two weeks, I went twice to the Internal Revenue Office, hoping to receive a positive commitment. Each time I left the office disappointed. Regardless of not receiving financial aid from the government, I decided to enroll in Dr. Glaeser's Vocational Medical School.

On my last day of work, I went again to the boss to say goodbye and get a reference letter. I was pleased with the letter's content when I read the description of my good conduct and work quality. Parting from my coworkers, with whom I had developed a courteous and trustworthy relationship, was difficult for them and me. It was too painful for me to say goodbye to the boys and girls of my youth group. At the last gathering of the adult youth group, I felt sad saying goodbye to the boys and girls. We had grown fond of each other and had developed an outstanding camaraderie among us. I mostly felt the emotional pain parting from Hermann. I would miss our special friendship and our vivid conversations.

Now I had to concentrate on going to Essen to enroll in the Vocational School for Commercial-Practical Medical Assistants. Dr. Ernst Glaeser was the director of the school. On Wednesday, March 30, I said goodbye to Mother and Emma. Mother and Emma held me a long time in their arms and cried. So did I. I took the earliest train from Essingen to Landau, where I bought a ticket to Essen. I changed trains in several cities. Fortunately, I arrived on time to find the office of the medical school still open. I knocked on the door, a lady, who I assumed was the secretary, asked me to come in. I introduced myself. Then I told her that I would like to enroll in Dr. Glaeser's Medical School.

"You will have to talk to Dr. Glaeser; he will let you know if it is possible this late to add another student.

The secretary introduced me to Dr. Glaeser, "Fraeulein Bonacker would like to know if we can still accept another student for this semester?"

"Good afternoon Dr. Glaeser; I am sorry I did not formally apply sooner, I waited and waited for government assistance, which they did not approve. But I have enough money saved for the first few months' tuition. Could you still accept one more student?"

"Let me look at the list of how many students are already enrolled. I see one student canceled at the last minute. I guess you can take her place."

"Thank you, Dr. Glaeser, that is wonderful!"

"Perhaps you can stay with Mrs. Mohrmann, who offered to give room and board for four students. Due to the last cancelation, she has taken only three so far."

Dr. Glaeser handed me a piece of paper with Mrs. Mohrmann's address,

"Here is her address. Take the train to Essen-Rellinghausen, and from there you can walk; it is not too far to her place. If she does not want to take one more student, come back, and we will find another place for you."

Dr. Glaeser handed me several sheets with the school's program, where the teachers would hold classes, and which subject they would teach.

"Familiarize yourself with the names of the teachers and the classes' locations. Be here in the classroom next door on Friday, April 1, to meet all the students and to get the list of the classes for the coming week."

I took the slip of paper, got up, shook his hand,

"Dr. Glaeser, thank you, thank you so very much. I will be in class on Friday."

I curtseyed and left the office. Only God, whom I thanked immediately, and I will ever know how grateful and glad I was at that moment of being accepted by the medical school. I picked up my suitcase, left the office, and began swinging it back and forth joyfully. I followed the instructions and found Hauptstr. 79, in Rellinghausen, a suburb of Essen. I looked at the entrance of the apartment complex for Mrs. Mohrmann's name. I walked up to the second floor and knocked on the door. A middle-aged lady opened the door, asking,

"What can I help you with?"

"I am Hildegard Bonacker. I just enrolled in Dr. Glaeser's Medical School. Dr. Glaeser told me you might still have room for one more student?"

"Yes, I do."

"Would you consider taking me?" She let her eyes glide over me from tip to toe, then said,

"I guess I can. But you and the other three students are supposed to come tomorrow."

I explained to Mrs. Mohrmannn my circumstances and asked her if I could stay at her place already today. She was understanding and let me enter. First, she introduced me to her elderly mother. Then she showed me the bedroom where I would sleep.

"But you will have to share a bed with another student."

The bed looked spacious enough and had two down covers.

"I do not mind at all; thank you."

She showed me the rest of her apartment.

"You can unpack your things now and join us in an hour for dinner."

"Thank you, that is very kind of you; I will."

I looked at my wristwatch; it indicated 6:00 p.m. I had not eaten all day long. I was starved.

At 7:00 p.m., I went into the dining room where Mrs.
Mohrmann and her mother were waiting for me at a table filled
with bread, cheese, and various cold cuts. What a feast for the eyes
of a hungry person like me. I waited to be seated and to get permission to start helping myself. I picked up a slice of bread, spread
butter on it, put several pieces of Salami on top, and savored every
bite of it. Then I ate another slice of ham and cheese. I could have
eaten three more sandwiches, but I did not want to appear impolite
and create a wrong impression, so I said no, thank you when Mrs.
Mohrmann asked me to help myself again. When Mrs. Mohrmann
and her mother finished their sandwiches, they asked me many
questions about my background. After they got up, I offered to
help clear the table and do the dishes. I finished the dishes, then
I excused myself and went to the bedroom. My heart overflowed
with appreciation that I was accepted into medical school and had
found such a nice place to stay. I knelt and prayed, expressing my
gratitude for God's help, and asked Him to guide me in the future.
All my concerns vanished, and pure joy filled my heart. I slept
sound and well. The next day after breakfast, I went for a walk to
familiarize myself with the surrounding neighborhood. Finding a
forest nearby delighted me. I enjoyed strolling through the woods
and listening to the birds singing. Today, my heart sang a joyful
song with the birds but without words. Nearby I found a church
which I planned to attend on Sundays.

Thursday, March 31, Gertrud, Gerda, and Friedel arrived. After
Mrs. Mohrmann introduced us to each other, she assigned them to
the sleeping quarters. Gertrud and Gerda would share one room
with two beds, and Friedel and I would be roommates and sleep
in the same bed. I did not mind at all. Four young ladies living
together should be fascinating.

During the first dinner, we ate together; we shared our backgrounds and our family stories. All three were the only child in

their families. Only I came from a family of eight children. Gerda was adopted. The following day, we all left early and took a train to Essen's inner city, where the school was. The room next to the office filled up quickly. When Dr. Glaeser entered, all of us rose. After he greeted us, he asked each student, when called by name, to get up, introduce herself, and briefly state where she came from and about her family background. Then he gave a schedule with the teachers' names, and which subjects they would teach for the coming week. Dr. Glaeser dismissed us before noon, and we still got back at Mrs. Mohrmann's on time for lunch.

Saturday, after breakfast, Friedel, my roommate, and I went for a walk in the woods. Today, people did not work, and more persons hiked through the forest than usual. Nevertheless, we enjoyed watching the fresh green leaves on the trees and the spring flowers covering the ground. We talked a little. She, too, enjoyed nature very much. I was glad we had something in common. When she told me that she does not permit anyone to get to know her inner being, I was puzzled and asked myself, "Why?" Then she warned me not even to attempt to explore her thoughts. Instead, I told her I have no secrets; I think and act the same, and everyone can see who I am. I guess she attempted to prevent me from asking her personal questions in the future. I thought, whenever someone wants to hide information, something must not be quite right, but whatever she decided was fine with me.

The following Sunday, I asked all three girls if they wanted to go to the nearby church. Each one found the excuse; they wanted to write to their parents. I thought I should write home also. I preferred to go to church in the morning and wait until the afternoon to write. The pastor preached the sermon about the prodigal son. One son left home and squandered his wealth on the pleasures of the world. Disillusioned and destitute, he returned to his father's house to beg forgiveness and be his father's servant. The father not only forgave his son but dressed him in fine clothes, prepared a feast for him, and restored family ties. The older son felt short-changed and jealous. He had stayed faithfully at home and done his father's will, and he never received such honor. God rejoices when a sinner, who was lost, finds the way to return to God. Then the pastor added, the jealous person only harms himself. But when jealousy turns to admiration and love, both persons feel rewarded with gladness. That was a good lesson for me to remember. When I meet someone, I think she is more intelligent and beautiful than I am; I should not be jealous but express my admiration.

April and May demanded a lot of discipline and concentration to remember all the teachers' names and the subjects they taught. I quickly picked my favorite teacher, Dr. Dreisine, a woman doctor who taught Gynecology. I liked the way Dr. Reiche presented Minor Surgery. Dr. von Grabe instructed General Medicine and Pathology classes in an illustrative manner that demanded 100 percent attention. The doctors not only taught in school but also had private practices. They often brought examples from their inter-actions with their patients to show us how to apply our theory in practice with patients.

The subject I liked least was typing taught by Mrs. Weber. During exams, I missed words when I tried to type fast, or I mis-spelled words. I excelled in Mr. Puersten's stenography class and did satisfactorily in German, instructed by Mr. Dietrich. I did not care much for business correspondence, nor the instructor Mrs. Schmitz Hartmann.

There was still a shortage of buildings, and Dr. Glaeser did not have a school of his own; teachers held classes at different loca-tions for each subject. Sometimes the four of us attended the same courses, sometimes separate ones. Various classes lasted half a day, others a whole day. It was not easy at times for Mrs. Mohrmann to prepare lunch for us. We had to give her the schedule for each day to prepare sandwiches to be taken along when needed. We all ate dinner together. We enjoyed our coffee and cake (Kaffeeklatsch) in the afternoon on the weekends and exchanged memorable week's experiences.

I also wrote a letter to the Internal Revenue Office (Finanzamt). I informed them that I had enrolled in the Vocational School for Commercial Practical Medical Assistants and to send the allocated funds, when granted, to my address at Mrs. Mohrmann's. By the beginning of June, I still had not received a positive answer. The letters I wrote each month remained unanswered. My finances slowly dwindled. I was very concerned about paying for the rest of the tuition, transportation, and room and board if I did not receive any assistance. In desperation, I wrote to my brother Edmund and asked him for money. I had also corresponded with Hermann and explained to him that I appreciated his affection for me. Still, at the moment, I wanted to concentrate on obtaining my profession and perhaps work for a few years before thinking of marriage. Maybe it would be better for both of us to forget each other and not communicate anymore. I waited anxiously for his response to my letter. I waited each day in vain for a message from Hermann as well as from my brother Edmund.

I tried even harder to concentrate on my studies and not think of my grave financial situation. Friedel, Gerda, Gertrude, and I often took along our notebooks when we went for a walk through the forest. Each one looked for a quiet place to study. At a specific time, we would meet at a designated area, ask questions about the subject matter taught in school so we would be prepared to review in class the following day. We could not always study undisturbed. Sometimes we engaged in conversations with people we met along the way.

At times, we joined a Bible study youth group on Wednesday. Each week Mr. Pfeiffer taught us chapters of the Bible and the history of various church architectures. We got acquainted with the attendees of the group. Peter, Karl-Heinz, and Ferdi lived in the neighborhood, and Werner lived in the same apartment building on the lower floor. They always treated us respectfully and courteously. We went for walks in the forest or attended special local events together. During our walks, Peter displayed a different personality each time. One never knew which was acting or which was reality. He also had a sense of humor and made us laugh. In June, after the water of the Baldeney Lake warmed up, we four girls went swimming on weekends. Even though I was not a good swimmer, I enjoyed playing in the cold refreshing water.

By the end of June, heat and humidity made me uncomfortable. Some days I went alone to classes. I did not mind being alone with my thoughts. One day as I got off the train at Stadtwald, I could not believe my eyes. I saw Hermann standing at the train station. I looked, again and again, to see if it was him. I never expected to meet him here. When he saw me, he greeted me with a smile. He probably was just as surprised to meet me at the train station as I was. I had waited for a letter, and now he was here in person. Unbelievable! He told me he only had a few minutes before his train would leave. We exchanged a few words about our well-being. With a quick embrace and saying goodbye, he promised to see me the following Tuesday. He stepped onto the train, which set in motion. He was gone. For a moment, I stood perplexed and in a stupor by the train tracks before I walked back to the apartment, absorbed in my thoughts. After dinner, I could not concentrate on doing any homework. I thought all night about Hermann. What will he tell me when he comes on Tuesday? Will he try to talk me into changing my mind and marry him? Will I be strong enough to resist him if he does? Those and similar thoughts filled my mind. Before I went to bed, I prayed to God to show me His will to guide me in saying the right words and making the right choice.

Saturday, Elisabeth had invited Renate and me for cake and coffee. We enjoyed sharing our Christian faith and talking about various subjects, also about our brothers and marriage. We all had a brother; we were close. Elisabeth felt hurt when her brother got married and completely neglected her. I told them how grateful I was to my brother, who was not married yet but cared for me and helped me. I could never disappoint him. Renate said her brother felt closer to her than to his wife. She asked me what Christ would say? I could not give her an appropriate answer. However, I disagreed with her following statement. She felt that marriage was the death of love. She also did not want to have any children. I thought just the opposite: marriage is the fulfillment of love, and the children are an added blessing.

After we finished savoring the delicious cake and coffee, we took a long walk through the forest and found a place where we sat down. Not uttering a word, we just enjoyed the beauty of the scenery and the reflection of the moonlight on the lake. Distant accordion music interrupted the silence as if playing a lullaby to nature. My thoughts returned to my home in East Prussia where our family had lived happily, and we had left almost eleven years ago. Who inhabited our house now? How did the house and garden look? Would we ever be able to go back? I could have sat there for hours, dreaming about life at home; however, momentarily, I was in a strange town all by myself with my thoughts.

On Monday, June 27, on the way to the train station, I met a big crowd. I had to push my way through to get on the train. Sports enthusiasts welcomed the Essen Soccer team that had won the German Cup. The crowd threw flowers at them and celebrated their victory with boisterous shouts.

The next day, Tuesday, June 28, as promised, Hermann arrived in the early afternoon. I missed my afternoon classes so we could spend the time together. We chose a quiet spot in the nearby forest, where we had a view overlooking the lake. First, he told me that he took a course at the University of South Westphalia in Education and Pedagogy. He briefly described by giving practical examples of the highlights of the subjects. We also talked about different viewpoints of life. I admired his profound knowledge and wisdom of human nature and character analysis. He also told me that I am so different from my brothers and sisters. I must have inherited some character traits from my father.

"I would like to meet him."

"Perhaps, one day when he will come home from Poland, where he was captured as a prisoner of war. Yes, I did inherit his zest for life and his sense of humor."

We both paused for a while, then he turned to me and embraced me, and gave me a lengthy kiss. My blood rushed through my body, and my heart was beating faster. But I did not try to free myself forcefully this time. When he released me, he held both of my hands, looked into my eyes, and expressed his sentiments for me,

"Hildegard, did you think the content of your last letter would stop me from loving you and make me forget you and our relationship completely? No, that is impossible. Your last letter annoyed me."

He pulled the letter out of the jacket pocket. I took it out of his hand, tore it to pieces, and threw it in a nearby bush.

"I am sorry, I am ashamed that I wrote that negative letter."

Then he kissed me again.

"Now, I need you even more. After I come home from work and I sit in the evening alone in my room, I long to be near you."

At that moment, I realized how much his friendship and love meant to me, too, and how much I had learned from him.

"Hermann, I am so happy you came, and you still love me, even after telling you I would not marry you."

Another kiss followed to which I responded. "The kiss does not belong to our friendship any longer."

"Nonsense, then you mean everything was wrong?"

"No, but our thoughts were different before."

"Why should I not be allowed to give a kiss to the person I love? You wrote we should forget about each other and stop all communications with each other," Hermann answered.

"I find it ridiculous to avoid seeing each other. Then love could turn to hate, which is detrimental for both. Just the opposite, I wish we could see each other as often as possible and nurture our friendship. By the way, I wish you a husband who will understand you."

His selfless answer took me by surprise. I appreciated his mature thinking and noble character at that moment even more.

"I wish you only the best for your future and a fine spouse, too," I uttered. Another kiss and embrace followed.

For a moment, I pondered about our unusual yet beautiful friendship. Our paths crossed now and then, and we always realized how much our lives were enriched by sharing those special moments, respecting each other's sentiments and thoughts, and living by the same moral principle: *mature and remain pure.*

The afternoon passed only too fast. The sunset behind the hills on the opposite lakeshore spread a translucent pale orange veil over the smooth surface. It was time to leave. We went back to the apartment. We ate a bowl of soup that Mrs. Mohrmann had saved for us. Then I accompanied Hermann only a short way to the train station. We said goodbye, not knowing when and where we would see each other again. Hermann went to Essingen, and I remained in Essen. I thanked God that we had spent such a delightful, meaningful afternoon together. I was daydreaming and absorbed in thought. I still could not comprehend that such a beautiful mental and spiritual friendship could exist between a young man and a young woman. According to the Greek philosopher Plato, Hermann and I were blessed with a loving friendship, called platonic (spiritual) love, which enriched our lives with virtue, joy, mystery, anguish, and sacrifice.

The next day I woke up and was shocked when I did not see my roommate Friedel in bed. I was worried about what could have happened to her. Then I recalled she had gone for a walk with Werner. I wanted to ask him where she was. I went to Werner's room and knocked on the door. I was even more shocked to find Friedel in Werner's place. She had spent the night with Werner. She said Werner and she had gone for a walk. They came home late, and when she knocked on our door, nobody opened the door for her, so she went down to Werner's room and slept there. Luckily, Mrs. Mohrmann was not home that morning and did not know what had happened. We hoped she would never find out about it. Friedel was nervous and paced the floor; she feared that Mrs. Mohrman would evict her if she discovered her bad behavior. Even though I disapproved of Friedel's conduct, I could not reprimand her. A few days later, the mother of Werner told Mrs. Mohrmann what happened. Mrs. Mohrmann was furious and scolded her terribly. I felt sorry for Friedel. After things quieted down a little, I went to Mrs. Mohrmann and asked her to forgive Friedel and not show her any animosity. Instead, I treated her with kindness and helped her get over this mishap. Mrs. Mohrmann was understanding and agreed to do so. With the help of God, I did the same, and we grew closer to each other than we were before. God showed me how He heals our hurts when we can forgive and treat an offender with love rather than hate. If we let go of negative thoughts about a person and other negative feelings and replace them with compassion and kindness, we grow and mature. I thanked God for showing me His way of acting in this situation.

In the week that followed, Friedel and I frequently went to the forest to study and talk. Often, I thought about our home in East Prussia, about my father when and if he would return from

Poland. I thought of my sister Emma and her three-year-old son, Bernhard, who lived with our mother, after they returned from America. Then I thought about my future. Will the government approve the monetary assistance so I will be able to finish my medical education? Where will I find a position? Who will I one day marry? Could it be Hermann? These and other thoughts crossed my mind. I wished to love a person wholeheartedly and make my future spouse happy. However, now I had to give my full attention to studying and writing the best exams I possibly could. We got an interim report card to present with our job applications. Now and then, Friedel and I, and sometimes Gertrud and Gerda, would join us, and we would see a good movie together. Gerda enjoyed writing stories. Once she wrote a story about the merry widow and the four students. She knew how to exaggerate matters and put a lot of humor into her writing.

Gerda had a fear of animals. When we went for a walk, and a bug would crawl on the ground, or a deer would pass by, she jumped up and down and screamed. We would laugh instead. One day we tried to play a trick on her. Friedel and I went into the garden and caught a frog. We hid it in an umbrella and took it to her room. We wanted to wrap the frog in her nightgown. Just then, she came into the room. When she saw the frog jumping out of her bed, she screamed so loud that the whole neighborhood could hear her. We thought she was going to have a heart attack. Thank goodness Mrs. Mohrmann had gone shopping that afternoon; otherwise, she would have reprimanded us. From henceforth, we would not play such tricks on her. We accepted her animal phobia as part of her personality.

One week passed, and the mailman delivered a letter from Hermann. I opened the envelope quickly and read:

It is 9:15 PM. I am sitting in my office and am listening to the song, The Moon Ascended. It brings back memories of when I was in my room alone. Every evening I opened the window, looked at the moon and the stars, and thought of you and our happiness and future. Today I think of you also but under different circumstances. The passionate love I had for you before dwindled and made room for our initial warm friendship. It is all right, perhaps even better that way.

He was right. I admired his wisdom and understanding. Yet, the content of his letter also brought me emotional pain. I realized I cared for him even more now than before. Perhaps his visit nurtured my love for him? Would it have been better if he had not come? But now I think it is better this way. I answered Hermann's letter the next day; I told him how grateful I was for his friendship and understanding. I did not mention how much I cared for him now. It also hurt me to have disappointed him in not accepting his proposal. But presently, my common sense overruled my emotions, and I thought I had made the right decision. I prayed to God that he would teach me to choose wisely in the future and that my conduct would please Him. Our heavenly Father sends us challenges and difficulties in life, but if, with God's help, we meet them victoriously, even making sacrifices to please Him, He always rewards us with joy, inner peace, and spiritual growth.

Edmund sent me a package with a few things I needed and 150 DM (Deutsche Marks). I could only thank him at the time and hope one day; I could return his kindness and generosity. I also received a letter from my girlfriend Lore. She enclosed a photo of herself. She looked so solemn and somewhat sad. I wished I could be with her to comfort her and cheer her up. She worried a lot about her parents' deteriorating health and felt lonely to be an only child. She wished she had a brother or sister to plan events together or share thoughts. I answered both letters right away. My heart overflowed with gratitude for my four brothers and three sisters, whom I loved dearly. I felt closest to my sister Emma and my brother Edmund. Whenever I thought of the future and marriage, I always wanted to have many children. I wondered why Mrs. Mohrmann had no children. One evening she told me she had two miscarriages. Her husband was then killed during World War II, and she did not want to remarry to start a family. Yes, the instinct and desire of most women are to have children and have a happy marriage. Not every woman attains that goal. However, there is a higher goal: to be saved by the blood of Jesus Christ, serve, and love God first and our neighbors as ourselves, regardless of our providence.

Yes, I often pondered whom I would marry and what my destiny would be. But presently, I had to concentrate on studying and passing the exams taken in all the subjects. I had to discipline myself not to get sidetracked. But my roommate Friedel had a way to pry into my personal life by asking many questions about a subject I felt uncomfortable disclosing. She inquired.

"Does your mother ever write to you?"

"No."

"Why, don't you and your mother not get along?"

"I am ashamed to say that my mother does not know how to write. She grew up close to the Russian border. The Russian officials took her parents away when she was young, and she could not go to school. However, she learned to read the Bible. She was satisfied with that."

"I am sorry to hear that. But do you and your mother have a close relationship?"

"Not very close; my mother seldom expresses her feelings or love to my brothers, sisters, and me. She never asks us how we feel or what we think. She only reprimands us if we do not obey her. If necessary, she uses a belt or a twig to beat us if we do something she thinks is wrong."

"It must be horrible not to feel loved or not be understood by your mother?"

"Yes, at times, it is painful. Sometimes, I ask myself, am I not worthy of being loved by my mother, or does my mother not have the ability to express her love to her children?"

I felt tears welling up. I pulled the pillow up on the side, so Friedel could not see me cry. I told myself to be strong. I said good night to Friedel, so she would stop asking more questions. But my thoughts of my mother continued to occupy my mind until late at night. When I stopped crying, I thought how difficult it must have been for my mother to be separated from her parents during World War I and raise eight children during World War II. Then, she lost her home and everything she ever owned. Father was drafted as a soldier before the war ended. For many years she did not know whether her husband was still alive or not. The war ended eleven years ago, and yet he did not come home. Perhaps all the suffering Mother went through made her taciturn. I felt compassion and gratitude toward my mother for raising all eight of us with Christian and high moral values. I was also grateful she permitted me to go to high school and study to become a doctor's assistant. I felt ashamed what I had said about my mother to Friedel. At home in East Prussia, we were happy as a family, and I longed for home. My mother showed her love for her children by taking care of their needs. Now I felt homeless, wondering who lived on our farm and if we would ever be allowed to return to our birthplace. Should I be discontented with my lot? No, I turned to God in prayer. After I asked to forgive me, I felt His love surrounded me. I thanked God for helping me through all my life's challenges and asked Him to teach me to live in harmony with people and love them unconditionally. I fell into a deep sleep, and the next day I was ready to tackle new challenges.

For the last two days, Mrs. Mohrmann scolded and criticized us. She hurt our feelings. But I sealed my lips and continued being courteous to her. I could not understand how changeable she could be. We tried our best to accommodate her. Whenever the situation at the apartment became unpleasant, we sought refuge in the forest. The fresh air and nature's beauty had a calming effect on us and gave Mrs. Mohrmann a chance to collect her thoughts and change her grumpy attitude.

After we returned from our walk, I found a letter from Hermann.

I opened it quickly and read the content with mixed emotions; the following part impressed me:

Just now, I listen to the sports commentary about the kayak race on Baldeney Lake. The Baldeney See appears again in front of me, and I see you sitting next to me. They are beautiful memories, and they will, even without a photo, video, or description, always remain vivid for us. At this place, we both grew more mature. TO REMAIN PURE AND MATURE IS THE MOST BEAUTIFUL AND ALSO THE MOST DIFFICULT ART OF LIFE. (Rein bleiben und reif werden ist die schoenste und schwerste Lebenskunst) It is a goal to be obtained not only during youth, but throughout our entire life.

How right Hermann was. I answered and told him how delighted I was that we both had high moral values and lived by them. When I passed by the spot where we both spent time together, I thought of him and longed to be with him to enjoy a vivid conversation and absorb the scenery's beauty together. Whenever I heard certain songs, my thoughts traveled to him. I also thanked him for understanding me and respecting my sentiments. Even though my negative response shattered his dream of spending our lives together, he acted so honorably. I thanked him that we decided to be friends and stay in touch with each other. I also mentioned how much I had to study momentarily for the upcoming exams. Each time I wrote a letter to him, I already looked forward to his answer. His two sisters, Helge and Heidrun, also corresponded with me. Heidrun was still in the youth group and informed me about the next meeting of the youth groups from Rhineland-Palatine in Bingen. They were hoping that our group would win another prize in singing and dancing. How much I wished I could be with our group. Helge could not join them either. She studied to be a nurse and simultaneously worked at the hospital for her practical training. I thought of where I would do my on-the-job training one day. After learning all the theories in the various medical subjects, it would be necessary to put them into practice.

After a hard day of exams and Bible study about creation, Friedel and I decided to take a walk in the forest. It was a clear and calm evening. The moon rose and spread a silver ribbon across the lake. The lights of the houses on the opposite lakeshore reflected on the surface of the dark water. We found a quiet spot, and without saying a word, we sat down and absorbed the beauty of the scenery. Suddenly a trumpet sounded and played a song and later was joined by an orchestra. It added so much to the moment's festive mood, mainly when they played the Christian hymn, "Oh the Power of God, All Else Transcending." When the concert ended by playing the German National Anthem, my thoughts ascended to God, and I thanked Him for having guided and protected me so wonderfully up to now. Then my thoughts flew home to the magical world in East Prussia. I felt homesick and had a hard time keeping the unwept tears from overflowing in my eyes. While we both were silent, two young men approached us and wanted to join us. At first, we rejected their request. They introduced themselves as Heinz and Franz. They began to talk about music and that they would like to sing for us. Their courteous manners persuaded us to let them accompany us. Both had pleasant voices and behaved respectfully. Heinz mentioned he played the accordion and offered to entertain us on Saturday. We agreed to meet at the same place and looked forward to a musical interlude.

For the rest of the week, we studied and wrote exams in various subjects. I still made too many typing mistakes and worried I would not get a passing grade on my report card. Dr. Reiche, who taught minor surgery, knew how to present his subject to captivate our attention. Now and then, he would give examples from his practice and interaction with his patients. He appeared strict but just. As a patient, I would trust him completely. He possessed the knowledge and personality to be the ideal surgeon who knew how to treat patients and people.

Saturday after dinner, we went to the Baldeney Lake to listen to the accordion player Heinz and his friend Franz, the singer. They were late, but they came. First, Heinz played songs we wished to hear. Then he picked songs or musical pieces at random. Friedel and I sat at the bench and listened attentively. When he sang the song "Mother Dear, Give me a Colt" (Mamatschi schenk mir ein Pferdchen). This song must have brought back painful memories for him. He choked and stopped singing. Then Heinz told us why this song made him so sad.

"I was only five years old. My mother did not believe in Hitler's regime. One day she voiced her negative opinion about Hitler. Someone reported her to the Gestapo. The next day the Gestapo came to the house, grabbed her, and took my mother away into a concentration camp. I never heard from her, and I never saw her again."

I felt so sorry and expressed my compassion for him.

"How cruel to be separated from your mother at such a young age. Yes, how much suffering was inflicted on countless innocent persons of all ages and nationalities during World War II. Only God knows all the anguish and suffering people endured. I lost my home in East Prussia, and my father still has not returned after being taken as a prisoner of war in Poland."

"I am sorry to hear about your family's tragedy."

Heinz played a few more songs while Franz sang before we started to go back home. Along the way, Heinz told us that he could analyze characters. We asked him to analyze ours. At the next lantern, we stopped. Heinz started with me by positioning my head under the lantern to see my face. He looked me straight in the eyes and began telling me.

"Hildegard, you love art and nature. You do not think much of modern art. You are open and honest but firm. You do not permit anyone to come too close to you. If someone has done you wrong, you cannot forget it easily. You are a very loyal and caring person. However, your high aspirations are not always met. You should demand your right more often and avoid people taking advantage of your kindness. You are not quite healthy. You should see a doctor and have him examine you."

Then Friedel stepped under the light, and Heinz began to tell her.

"Friedel, you are open and honest but not always loyal. You will only be loyal to the person whom you think meets your expectations. You also love nature and art. All your wishes will not be fulfilled for you either. You have the gift of extracting secret information from people without revealing your thoughts or secrets. You are attached to some people but not steadfast; you should be as steadfast as Hildegard."

Then he looked at me and said, "You possess the ability to evaluate human characters, but it takes you a long time. However, both of you are intelligent young ladies." We were both perplexed about the accurate character analysis by a stranger who knew us only for a few hours. We thanked Heinz and Franz for entertaining us before we said goodbye. They left the following day, and we never saw them again.

The next day I received a long letter from my brother. I asked him what I should do if I cannot get a position in a doctor's office right away? He told me to be patient, and I will find a place to practice my newly acquired profession. Then he wrote to me that my brother Georg married a woman who had a problematic character besides being older and handicapped. Edmund told me that Georg would regret having made such a choice without projecting the future consequences. I felt sorry for my brother Georg. He was kind, a hard worker, and always ready to help others. He deserved a good wife and a happy life. Edmund told me he would like to send me some gifts as a reward for passing all the interim exams.

I needed many things, but he had already done so much for me. I would feel guilty to ask for more. I wrote back that he had already done so much for me, and it was unnecessary to send me a special gift now. The same day I received a card from Hermann about the DJO meeting in Bingen. He wrote that our youth group won the first prize in singing and third place in folk dancing. We both should be delighted with their performance. It is partly the result of our work together in the group. We enjoyed working together, setting high standards, and achieving results. I missed our group and especially Hermann.

Each day I waited for a response from the IRS Office. The government still did not notify me if I would get financial aid from them. I was running out of funds. I begged my brother to send me some money. One day I did not even have enough to pay for the train ticket. Friedel lent me 1.00 DM so I could go to class. After some time passed, she noticed that I could not pay it back; she told me she would forgive my debt if I would eat a slice of bread with sardines and marmalade. The sight alone nauseated me. I took one bite and had difficulty swallowing it. It tasted horrible. When

I finished the last morsel, she said, you paid your debt. I excused myself, ran to the bathroom, and released the stomach's content into the toilet bowl. Whenever my roommates bought one Coca-Cola, they got four straws for sharing it, so I would not feel so bad.

At the beginning of August, I received my interim report card to send with each application for a position. I was grateful that I had passing grades in all subjects, even in typing. Doctors looking for assistants sent in their names, addresses, and which type of practice they had. Immediately, I copied eight doctor's names and addresses. I wrote eight letters. I included a resume and my report card, hoping that one doctor would offer me a position. The same evening, when I went to Bible study, Mr. Pfeiffer said he would also check and see if he could recommend a doctor looking for an assistant. I was grateful to him. I prayed to God to help me to find a position and strengthen my faith.

The next day Mr. Pfeiffer gave me the addresses of two doctors.

The same evening, I went to Dr. Kelt. After I waited an hour and a half, he asked me if I had any practical experience. My answer was no. I am still going to school.

"Which school"?

"Dr. Glaeser's school."

"My current assistant is from the same school. My wife and I are going on vacation shortly. Another doctor will take care of my practice during my absence. If she does not meet the approval of my colleague, you might be able to start working for me by November 1, 1955. Contact me by the end of October."

I thanked Dr. Kelt and left his office with a glimmer of hope. He also gave me a bus fare, but I opted to walk back to the apartment and pass by Mr. Pfeiffer. I told him about my interview with Dr. Kelt and that I would go to Dr. Hinterleitner tomorrow. The next day, after Dr. Grabe taught the pathology of the upper respiratory organs, Gertrud and I took the train to Essen-West to look for Dr. Hinterleitner. When we arrived, Dr. Hinterleitner told me that he had already hired someone recently, but he was kind enough to give me the address of a friend, an ophthalmologist. I thanked Dr. Hinterleitner for his recommendation. Disappointed, I left his office.

I took a streetcar to the part of the city where the Ophthalmologist Dr. Baberowski's office was. A young man entered at the next stop and sat down next to me. He told me he was a well-known soccer player. His wife died, and he had two sons. His sons were also soccer players. He was thirty-eight years old, and he was looking for a wife. He handed me his address and asked me to visit him. I refused. I was glad to get off at the next stop. I barely entered Dr. Baberowski's office when heavy rain poured down, pelting against the windows. I waited for a while until Dr. Baberowski called me into his private office. He asked me about my background, my medical experience, and if I knew how to type. Without giving me an answer, he excused himself. He had to see more patients. He asked me to come back after office hours at 5:00 p.m. the following Monday. I liked Dr. Baberowski but not his small, dark, and old-fashioned office, which was located in a run-down section of town. I doubted if I would be satisfied working in his office. The rain stopped. Tired, I arrived at the apartment. Before I fell asleep, I prayed to God to help me find a position with the right doctor.

By the middle of August, I received the first response to my job inquiries from Dr. Jerg in Wendlingen; he already hired an assistant. Saddened, I decided to go back to Dr. Baberowski's interview. After asking more questions, he took the time to test me in filing records and typing. The outdated typewriter gave me trouble, and I did not do so well. He said he would buy a new one. He also checked my handwriting by making me copy a part of an article. I had difficulty writing with his fountain pen, too. When I asked him how much the salary would be if he decided to hire me, he did not give me a definite answer but reassured me he was not miserly. He also talked about a plan for building a new office. He treated me courteously and even took me in his car to the train station. As I sat on the train, I thought I would not use all the medical knowledge I just acquired if I worked for an ophthalmologist. The more I pondered about it, the less I favored accepting the position of Dr. Baberowski. If I could not find a place in family practice, would I consider accepting his offer?

On the way home, I joined my roommates, Gertrud, Gerda, and Friedel, to see the second part of the movie, My Father's Horses. In the first part of the film, a sick boy, while hospitalized, gave up the desire to live. During a visit to the hospital, a girlfriend read the diary of his father to him. He vividly relived the past events that he had with his father. The memory of his father encouraged him to live. His health improved, and he found a purpose for living again. In the second part, the movie producer passed on much wisdom for living a rewarding life. Several quotes impressed me, and I wrote them down.

"Treat both women and horses with love. Life is not always a fair game. Honesty outlasts everything. However, the person who forever remains honest has a challenging but more rewarding life experience. When help is needed, God always provides it at the right time."

I was grateful for the excellent advice passed on to me and am sure others were, also. God often helped me through difficult and life-threatening situations in the past; I trusted Him then and do the same now and will in the future. Life is a continuous battle, and to be victorious in meeting all the challenges, I asked God to give me His guidance, strength, and wisdom to make the right choices now and in the future.

The following day Dr. Glaeser called me to his office; he told me he received a letter from Dr. Mossen, whom I had seen in Landau before attending Dr. Glaeser's Medical School. Dr. Mossen asked for my qualifications; if good, he offered a position as an apprentice for an x-ray technician. He would pay $30.00 DM per month. Dr. Glaeser was outraged about the salary Dr. Mossen proposed to pay for a medical assistant. He said he planned to send him an appropriate reply to his insulting letter. I thanked Dr. Glaeser. I apologized for not having paid August's tuition. I mentioned, "I applied over a year ago for educational assistance. My father had not returned yet from having been captured and held by the Polish government. Being considered a half-orphan, I was entitled to government assistance for education. Nevertheless, I had not received any money. I used up all the money I saved and the money my brother had sent me. Please, Dr. Glaeser, let me finish school. As soon as I find a job, I will pay off my debts."

"Bring me the address from the IRS officer, and I will send him a stiff letter. It is shameful that they did not allocate you the funds before you started school."

"Thank you, Dr. Glaeser, for your understanding and for contacting the IRS officer. I will bring you the address and the name of the office manager."

When I got back to the apartment, I found a letter from my sister Emma. She wrote that my mother had experienced massive uterine hemorrhaging. The gynecologist hospitalized her and scheduled her for a hysterectomy. I prayed to God the operation would go well. I was grateful to my sister Emma that she was with my mother to help her during the postoperative recovery period. She asked me if I had already found a place to work. Unfortunately, I had to answer her that I had not yet. The same day I received two more negative replies, one from a doctor in Muensingen and Giessen. It was very disappointing.

Thursday, August 18, was Gerda's birthday. Gertrud, Friedel, and I bought her a book. Mrs. Mohrmann gave her a beautiful candle and a stuffed baby deer. She was delighted. Mrs. Mohrmann also baked a cake for her and prepared an impressive punch for a celebration. However, when we asked Mrs. Mohrmann to celebrate with us in the afternoon, she gave us a blunt *no* for an answer. She also refused to drink the punch that Gerda offered her. Gerda felt hurt and started crying. I felt sorry for her. I asked Mrs. Mohrmann why she refused to celebrate with us. She answered sarcastically, "I have my reasons." Then I wondered why the sudden mood changes. However, we did not want Mrs. Mohrmann's mood to spoil Gerda's birthday. We had mentioned to the boys from the youth group about Gerda's birthday. They offered to celebrate with us. We packed utensils, cake, and punch in a basket and took it in the evening to the room where the Bible study was held. Peter, Ferdi, Werner, and Karl-Heinz were thoughtful and got her some small presents, which Gerda appreciated. Peter delighted me with a bouquet of roses. We enjoyed the cake and punch and sang several folk songs together. Everyone was happy. I was grateful that Gerda cheered up and enjoyed her special eighteenth birthday celebration.

Mrs. Mohrmann hurt my feelings when she blamed me for not asking her to celebrate with us, which was not true. She unloaded her complaints about us to Gertrud. I also told Mrs. Mohrmann that I did not have the money to pay for the room and board for August. I informed her I waited for my brother Edmund to send me some money and to be patient. However, Mrs. Mohrmann told the other girls that she would send me away if I did not pay shortly. I felt embarrassed and humiliated and deeply hurt. Wasn't it enough to tell me? Did she have to talk behind my back to my roommates about my debt? In desperation, I wrote again to my brother and Mr. Dobereiner at the Internal Revenue Service, urging him to send the assistance I was entitled to, or I could not finish medical school. Yes, it is not easy to deal with indifferent government officials who are neither understanding nor altruistic. It made me realize that my life would be challenging. I would have to face many difficulties in the future. Then I reasoned, it is good, for hardship and suffering make me think. Thinking makes me wise and strong. Wisdom gives joy in life. Even though I suffered emotional pain today, I was grateful to God that He taught me how to live by His rules. God always gives me the proper comfort and strength for each day. Yes, I have so much to learn yet. I asked God to provide me with a receptive mind, a loving heart, and a righteous spirit.

The last Saturday in August, we had no classes. Gertrud and I went to the river Ruhr where many young people camped, kayaked, and swam. Some campers sang folk songs accompanied by a guitar player; Gertrud and I sat down on a bench nearby and sang along. We felt happy singing and continued singing on the way home also. When we got home, we found Peter's mother, Mrs. Haertel, waiting for us. She was in distress and told us that her son was missing since yesterday. He left home without saying goodbye and without taking anything with him. She asked us if he had mentioned to us about leaving home or where he wanted to go? Even though I remembered him talking about becoming a soldier and going to the Foreign Legion, I thought it was only a fantasy. How could I cause more grief to a worried mother by telling her about the Foreign Legion? I opted not to say anything. Gertrud, Gerda, and Friedel gave no definite hint to Mrs. Haertel either.

I remembered Peter acted strangely and distracted lately. Perhaps, he was fabricating the plan for leaving home. Mrs. Haertel left heartbroken and crying. We could not give her clues of where he went.

I pondered what the reason was for his leaving home. He told us that his mother set stringent rules for him to follow and treated him like a child. She forgot that he is a grown adult now and deserves some freedom and respect for his way of thinking. The mother, who lost her husband in World War II, only had one son, Peter. She treated him like a child and held on to him so tight that the son resented her complete control. He left home, hoping to free himself and live like an adult. I certainly hoped he had not joined the French Foreign Legion. Their soldiers were not well treated. I prayed that God, who knew Peter's whereabout and thoughts, would protect him and bring him home safely to his grieving mother to whom he meant everything. I asked God to comfort the mother's bleeding heart and wipe away her tears while she was waiting for her son's return.

My waiting for a positive answer to the many job applications finally rewarded me. Dr. Samietz from Gelnhausen and Dr. Flaecher from Waibstadt asked for more information. The following day, I mailed the requested material with a photo of mine—at last, a glimmer of hope to get a position before school ended. I also received 150.00 DM from my brother Edmund. I went immediately to Mrs. Mohrmann and paid the rent for August. She said, "You know the rent for September is also due."

"Yes, I know. I will pay you as soon as I get some more money. Please, be patient; this is all the money I have at the moment."

I felt sad that she did not understand my dire financial situation; neither did Mr. Doebereiner from the IRS Office. He wrote a letter with another excuse but no money. Even though I felt bad always asking my brother for money, I wrote to him requesting him to send me more whenever he could. I still owed two months of tuition and one month of room and board. When I went to Bible study in the evening, I discussed my financial problem with Mr. Pfeiffer. He was kind enough to offer to write a letter to Mr. Doebereiner begging him to pay at least for the last two months' tuition and room and board. I told him Dr. Glaeser had already written to the IRS office; let us wait until we get a response first. I was emotionally exhausted. Before I fell asleep, I prayed to God, "You know my desperate situation; nothing is impossible for Thee.

I trust You wholeheartedly that You will work out everything for my best. Watch over my mother, give her strength to recover well from surgery. Comfort Peter's heartbroken mother. Keep Peter from making a mistake that he will regret for the rest of his life. Heavenly Father, You know the needs of every person, and You will meet them in your time." After I committed everyone and my life into God's loving care, I fell asleep peacefully.

The last month of school arrived. I welcomed September with mixed emotions. I enjoyed school but felt terrible and embarrassed to continuously ask my brother Edmund for money, mainly when Emma wrote that he did not earn too much lately. Neither did my brothers Georg or Richard. Richard was still an apprentice and earned only 30.00 DM per month, living at the blacksmith's premises. Mother got barely enough to pay rent and buy food for herself and my youngest brother Horst, only twelve years old.

A letter from Hermann brought me delight. He included a beautiful verse in the letter.

> As the stars circle eternally in harmony,
> So, shall our lives also be?
> In the immense and minute appears God.
> All creation moves in rhythm
> Joy is her noble song.
> Only humans do not appreciate her beauty
> And search tiresome for other pleasures.
> Friends seek the meaning in God's wonders
> So that joy will fill your hearts.

Hermann closed with the saying:

> "Look up to the stars and pay attention to your path."

I realized we had so much in common. We both enjoyed nature and God's wonders with the perpetual changes, pleasing our senses. We loved classical and folk music that lifted our spirits and good literature, especially poetry, which spoke to our hearts. We both not only had set high moral standards for our lives but adhered to them regardless of the sacrifice it took. Each letter deepened my respect and admiration for him. The memories of the few times spent together would always be cherished by both of us. I just was not ready yet to commit to marriage. I asked God for guidance so I would make the right decision at the right time.

The time spent in Essen will end in less than a month, and a new phase of my life will begin. Every moment I had free, I went to the lake. I always took my notebooks along and had good intentions to study. However, sometimes pleasant interruptions prevented me from doing so. One Saturday afternoon, I sat on the lakeshore, splashing the water back and forth with my feet. A wind made waves rolling to the shore. I listened to the rhythmic sound and watched the white waves breaking on the sandy beach. I was daydreaming. When I looked up, a sailboat approached the shore, and a voice called,

"Fraeulein, you want to sail with us?" First, I was startled and reluctant. Then I thought I never had a chance to sail before. Why not?

"Yes, gladly," I answered before I realized the two sailors had landed the boat on the beach next to me. One young man got out of the boat and helped me get into it. Afterward, he walked the sailboat until it was in deeper water, then came aboard himself. One sailor handled the sails, the other the rudder. The wind filled the sails, and we took off toward the center of the lake. How exhilarating for me to glide quietly over the surface of the water. I had always wanted to go sailing. Now my wish had come true. I enjoyed the experience which the two sailors presented to me in such an unexpected way. Both sailors were so absorbed in maneuvering the boat that they hardly talked. They only smiled when they looked at me and saw how much I enjoyed sailing with them. The afternoon passed only too quickly. They took me back to the same spot where they picked me up. We introduced ourselves before we parted. No questions asked, no demands made, only enjoying the afternoon sailing together in the beautiful Baldeney Lake. I could not thank them enough for fulfilling one of my dreams.

Another dream came true when I received the first positive response to my many applications. Dr. Samietz from Gelnhausen offered me 200.00 DM per month, a room with central heating, and ten days paid vacation for the first year. I could start on October 10, 1955. I immediately wrote back that I would accept his offer and could begin at the suggested time. He confirmed my acceptance with a courteous letter. I thanked God for allowing me to practice all the knowledge I had acquired in Dr. Glaeser's Medical School. I was also delighted to have nine days to spend at home before I began working. I shared the good news with my roommates. They also were happy for me.

Toward the evening, Gertrud and Gerda came into our room. We all sat on the bed and told funny stories. We laughed loud. Mrs. Mohrmann swung the door open, yelled at us, and reprimanded us for sitting on the bed. I was shocked at the harsh language she used, and my whole body trembled. We did not say a word and waited until she left. Then Gerda and Gertrud went to their room. After I calmed down, I decided to go to Bible class. Mr. Pfeiffer spoke about how to deal with the shortcomings of other people. If there is a conflict between you and other people, check your conscience before accusing the other person; that was just the right message for today. I thought about how to handle the incident with Mrs. Mohrmann. I asked God to forgive me if I did anything wrong. In turn, I would forgive her also and treat her with the same courtesy as before. Gerda created a more unpleasant situation, talked bad about the three of us, then complained about Mrs. Mohrmann. She was angry with us and discourteous. During the last month of school, I felt sad that such discord developed between us when we had to study intensely for the final exams.

One day we had an hour and a half break between classes. Christel, whom I had befriended, and I went to the room where the typewriters were. I practiced typing. Christel recited some quotes. I liked them very much, and I asked her to write them down for me.

1. *Let us not ask for a light burden but a strong back.*
2. *Whoever wants to reach heights has to unload weight.*
3. *Our craving for happiness is so limitless that it can only be satisfied in heaven.*
4. *If you want to know yourself, act, and you will know who you are.*
5. *My heart, I will ask you what love is? Tell me,*
   "Two souls and one thought.
   Two hearts and one beat."

After classes, I went back to the apartment, and Mrs. Mohrmann still reprimanded us during dinner. I felt so bad that our stay should end in such a disharmonious way. I prayed to God that He would show me where I had done anything wrong and that He would forgive me, and I would forgive Mrs. Mohrmann for hurting my feelings. Mrs. Mohrmann also exposed Friedel's negative character traits and made me responsible for not correcting her and being kind to Friedel. She also complained about Gerda and Gertrud for not following every wish of hers. We all felt terrible, apologized to Mrs. Mohrmann, forgave each other, and hoped peace and harmony would be restored.

Each day brought more studying and exams. Thoughts of returning home to my family occupied me more and more as the school's end neared. I looked forward to seeing my mother, Emma, Edmund, Horst, and Bernie, my sister Emma's son. Hermann also wrote that he planned a vacation during October and would spend some time with his family in Essingen. He also mentioned his mother was arranging a family reunion when he would be home, and he was anxious to see me.

One week before school ended, I received a letter from the government with a 690.00 DM check. I was grateful that Mr. Dobereiner, finally, after about a year and a half, responded positively to Dr. Glaeser's letter, which he wrote some time ago. The next day, I went to Dr. Glaeser's office, paid the balance of my tuition, and thanked him for having helped me complete my medical education. I paid the balance for room and board. I thanked Mrs. Mohrmann for being patient, waiting for the money. She was courteous again, which made me content that peace and harmony returned among us. Before I fell asleep, I thanked God, I had enough money to pay my debts, I finished school with good grades, and I had a position secured in a doctor's office. I asked God to give me a loving heart to care for the patients in Dr. Samietz's clinic. My great desire was to serve and honor God with all my heart and soul in the best possible way.

Saying goodbye to our instructors and classmates, for whom I had developed a fondness, filled my heart with mixed emotions. I was sad that I would probably never see them again but glad to have obtained a profession and a job in a doctor's clinic to practice my newly acquired medical and practical skills. I looked forward to seeing my family. I packed my belongings in my wooden suitcase and purchased my railroad ticket two days in advance.

On September 30, 1955, all the students gathered in a big hall, and Dr. Glaeser handed out the final report cards and then wished us well. Each student shook his hand before leaving the classroom. I expressed my deep gratitude to Dr. Glaeser for helping me obtain the government aid and finish the seminar. Looking over my report card, I was satisfied with receiving primarily good grades, one very good in shorthand and one satisfactory in minor surgery. I liked the subject but did not know why I got such a low grade and how I could have improved. Thursday evening, we all went once more through the forest to Baldeney Lake, which we treasured during our stay in Essen. All the time spent at the lake would remain unforgettable memories of our youth and part of our life.

Friday, September 30, Friedel, Gerda, and Gertrud said goodbye to Mrs. Mohrmann and me. They left a day earlier. I was content that Mrs. Mohrmann displayed her best manners and wished them well for the future. I embraced Gerda, Gertrud, and Friedel and expressed my best wishes for their future also. We exchanged addresses just in case we wanted to correspond with each other. I asked their forgiveness if I had hurt their feelings unintentionally. Friedel did the same. We all parted harmoniously. I left the following day, and Mrs. Mohrmann was very kind to me. The temporary bickering had passed, and the air was clear again. I apologized for having unintentionally hurt her feelings. She embraced me and said, "It is all forgotten, and I am not angry with you."

I left feeling relieved and content. I took my suitcase and handbag, walked down the stairs, and went to the train station to catch an early train to Duisburg where I would connect with other trains to Landau/Palatine and Knoeringen/Essingen, my final destination. The train ride took less than twenty minutes to Duisburg, where I had to get off to catch the train to Koblenz. I had only a short time to change to the track where the train would leave for Koblenz.

After I embarked on the train and settled down in the car, only one elderly gentleman entered the same train car. He limped and walked with a cane. He carried a violin case which he placed carefully next to him on the seat. It must have been a valuable instrument that he did not want to have damaged by falling from the overhead bin. We sat on opposite benches quietly and waited for the train to leave the station. We watched the houses pass by faster and faster until we left the city of Duisburg behind. After a while, the gentleman passenger introduced himself as Karl Berger with a handshake. I responded and stated my name.

We began a vivid conversation about music. Mr. Berger told me that he played the violin in the Symphony Orchestra of Essen, and he was going to visit his son Charles in Koblenz. His son was a virtuoso on the piano, and they both enjoyed playing together. He especially liked playing compositions by Mozart, Schubert, and Beethoven. I told him that I appreciated the three composers' music, but I also enjoyed opera performances, especially Giuseppe Verdi's operas. He, in turn, preferred instrumental music. We also talked about literature and history. His joyful disposition changed to sadness when he spoke of World War II. He despised Hitler's cruel actions and regime but did not like how the allies humiliated and mistreated the German people. Even though President Roosevelt and Prime Minister Winston Churchill had promised that victors and vanquished should be treated equally, they agreed to give some of the Eastern regions of our country to Russia and Poland as part of the peace treaty.

I told Mr. Berger that I was born in East Prussia, and now Poland claimed the southern part of East Prussia. I probably will never be able to return to my native place. We paused for a while, reflecting on the dire consequences of World War II, which saddened us. Then Mr. Berger started our conversation about literature and Germany's favorite poets and authors. We were engulfed in a conversation that we paid little attention to passing through Cologne and Bonn, Germany's present capital. When we reached Koblenz, we both disembarked, said goodbye, and wished each other the best for the future.

I had only a few minutes to find the track where the train would depart going to Mainz. The trains in Germany are primarily punctual, but I made it on time. The car filled up with passengers. I was lucky to secure a window seat. This time I wanted to watch the scenery and not get engaged in conversations. I looked out the window and enjoyed the Rhine Valley's beautiful scenery nestled between the Hunsrueck and Taunus Mountain chains. The vineyards were changing to their colorful hues of yellow, orange, red, and rust. Harvesting the grapes had begun early. People gathered in the fields to pick the grapes. My eyes feasted on the brilliant fall colors. It looked as if God had painted an exquisite work of art using giant paintbrushes and every color on the palette. The Germans celebrated Thanksgiving on October 1. Farmers and other persons took some of their home-grown wheat or produce to the church altar, thanking God for an abundant harvest. The poor people in the community received the offerings and the food. Since October 1 fell on Saturday this year, Thanksgiving was celebrated in church Sunday, Oct. 2. I would be home on time to celebrate this special day with my family.

We reached Mainz, located at the confluence of the Rhine and Main rivers. Mainz is the capital of Rhineland-Palatine. It is known as Johannes Gutenberg's birthplace, who invented the first printing press with movable metal letters. In 1454 he printed the first forty-two pages of the Bible and completed printing the entire Bible in 1455. Since each page contained forty-two lines, he called it the forty-two-page Bible. Some pages he had embellished with art designs. Johannes Gutenberg also made his own ink. After he finished printing almost two hundred Bibles, he also printed a Book of Psalms, which revolutionized Europe and the world. For the first time, the public could read printed books. Before, all manuscripts were hand-written by monks and only accessible to the popes, clergy, and intellectuals. When the German publisher brought the first

Bible to the United States in 1847, the custom officers removed their hats in reverence to the Holy Bible, the word of God. 1946, one year after World War II, Mainz built, named, and dedicated a university in honor of Johannes Gutenberg.

I had to change trains in Mainz and then travel via Schifferstadt, Neustadt, and Landau to Knoerringen-Essingen. Traveling along the Vine Road (Weinstrasse), I watched the Hardt mountain's colorful grape fields and forests. An abundance of chestnut trees grew among the beech and oak trees. The late afternoon sun made the fall colors of the woods glow. And memories of the many hikes we used to take with the youth group came alive when picking ripe chestnuts in the forest.

Only one more train change in Landau to Knoerringen-Essingen, and I would be home. Since we had no phones to let my brothers know the time of my arrival, nobody met me at the last train station. I got off the train and carried my suitcase home. When I reached the town, I met a few villagers standing on the street conversing. On Saturdays, everyone swept the street in front of their houses or shops. My steps went quicker and quicker as I approached the place where we lived. I put my suitcase down, swung the door open, and ran to my mother to embrace her first, then my sister Emma, and brothers Edmund, Richard, and Horst, who were home for this weekend. Then I picked up my little nephew Bernie and gave him a big hug.

"My, how you have grown, Bernie!"

"Yes, I am three years old and do not have a wife,"

Bernie answered. I smiled,

"Young man, you can still wait a while until you find a wife."
Everyone welcomed me affectionately. Edmund brought in my suitcase and put it on the bench in the kitchen. I took out the candy and gave a few to Bernie and offered some to my family. Mother and Emma had prepared one of my favorite foods, Sauerbraten,

stuffed potato dumplings, and red cabbage. For dessert, Emma made apple strudel. It sure tasted good. After dinner, I talked about the school and that I would start Monday, October 10, working for Dr. Samietz in Gelnhausen. Edmund and Emma expressed their sentiments by being glad that I had finished school successfully and secured a position in a doctor's office. Mother remained taciturn. However, when she looked at me and smiled, I accepted it as her approval. I would have appreciated her verbal consent even more.

On Sunday, after we heard the church bells ring three times, we all walked to church to celebrate the day of Thanksgiving. The church was a half-block away from the new apartment. After the opening liturgy of the service, the farmers brought fruits of their harvests to the altar. The church choir sang the song "Now Thank Ye All Our God," expressing gratitude to God for a good harvest. The message of the sermon emphasized the blessings of giving and the abundant rewards received in return. After the church service, I met several choir members and Pastor Bruenings, our new neighbor, greeted me.

"I am glad to see you again. Are you back to stay?"

"No, I will leave next Sunday. I got a position in a doctor's office in Gelnhausen."

He added,

"God bless you, and I wish you well."

"Thank you, Pastor Bruenings; I will come back now and then."

On Monday, Edmund and Richard went back to their place of work. They said they would return the following weekend. The next few days, I washed and ironed all my clothes and assorted all my things. Then, on Thursday evening, I went to the meeting of the DJO youth group. They embraced me, and we expressed our delight to see each other again. Hermann, who spent his brief vacation at home, also attended the meeting; his embrace lasted longer. Seeing Hermann again filled my heart with joy, and I recalled all the happy moments of our wonderful friendship. Our eyes frequently met, expressing our admiration and affection. We had developed a fondness for each other, and parting saddened our hearts. But we promised each other to stay in touch in the future. We closed the meeting with the song: "Ade zur guten Nacht jetzt wird der Schluss gemacht, das ich muss scheiden." (Farewell, Good Night, the Time Has Come to Part). A lump formed in my throat when we said goodbye to each person. I tried to put on a smile when Hermann approached me. He invited me to join his family reunion this coming Saturday, October 8, at 3:00 p.m. His Uncle Heiner, who was an artist, would also be there.

"Thank you; I would love to join you. I am looking forward to seeing your uncle and your family."

"I am glad you will join us. See you Saturday at 3:00 p.m."

Thursday, I took a quick bicycle ride to Landau. I visited both youth leaders, Heinz Kraemer, and Heinz Equart, to thank them for having directed and helped me obtain a degree as a medical and practical doctor's assistant. I also told them the difficulty I had to receive government assistance. It was finally granted the last month of school. Both were glad to hear that all went well in the end and that I had secured a position. I also passed by my favorite boutique and bought a white blouse and a black skirt to wear to church on special occasions. It was a chilly but sunny day, and I enjoyed the brisk breeze caressing my cheeks while peddling back to Essingen. I sent prayers of gratitude to God for having led me so wonderfully through all the difficulties. Soon I will have an opportunity to serve Him by helping patients in a medical clinic.

On Saturday afternoon, I walked over to Hermann's house. In the courtyard, Uncle Heiner had set up a collection of paintings. He offered them for sale and had already sold some to the people from the village. I admired his oil paintings as well as his pastel paintings very much. One oil painting with a cross on a hill surrounded by forests at sunset captured my attention. I would have liked to buy the picture, but of course, I did not have any money. This painting awoke in me the desire to paint. I thought,

"If I could only paint like that, I would be so very happy."

After the public showing was over, Mrs. Jaeger invited the family, relatives, and close friends to her big upstairs dining room for cake and coffee. Mrs. Jaeger baked delicious cakes and played the guitar well. Uncle Heiner was a virtuoso on the harp, Helge played the piano, and Hermann the violin. We cleared the tables, and then we gathered around the piano and began singing folk songs accompanied by the piano, guitar, violin, and harp. The joyful music filled the room and my heart as well as the hearts of everyone present. Now and then, Uncle Heiner sang a solo while he played the harp. He reminded me so much of King David singing one of his psalms. He expressed so much sentiment in his songs. His personality radiated love and peace. Just being in his presence made me feel cheerful and serene. He also wrote inspiring poetry. He traveled to various places to paint picturesque scenes. He loved the mountain sceneries of the Alps, which he captured magnificently in his oil paintings. After the music session finished, I said goodbye to Mrs. Jaeger and her brother Uncle Heiner and all the family members and guests. Hermann walked me to the door. I thanked him for letting me spend this special event with his family and relatives. I gave him the address of the place I would work. We promised to stay in touch. He wished me well as we parted with an embrace that expressed our profound friendship, which we promised to maintain. He told me he still had vacation until Wednesday next week. I, unfortunately, had to leave by Sunday and start working Monday.

"I am sorry we can't travel together until Frankfurt. I wonder when we will be able to see each other again?"

"I wished we could; perhaps we will have a chance to meet again during our next vacation." He embraced me once more and kissed me on the forehead,

"Goodbye." I uttered, "Goodbye," and left.

When I walked back to our apartment, Mother, Emma, Bernie, and my four brothers waited for me. We all had dinner together. Emma told us that she and Bernie might return to the United States. Gustav, who stayed in Aalen with his parents and family, wanted her to come along also. Unfortunately, her husband was more attached to his parents and siblings than to his wife and son. He and his family did not treat Emma kindly. She was not comfortable going back with them but did not have much choice. I felt so sorry to hear about her emotional suffering and that she would leave us. But she loved her son, Bernie, and wanted him to grow up with his father also. Gustav, her husband, and his entire family had already applied for the immigration visa for themselves and also for my sister and Bernie. They all waited for their immigration documents to be approved the second time.

On Sunday morning, I was not able to go to church. After I said goodbye to my mother and my brothers, my sister Emma, and Bernie, my brother Edmund took me and my wooden suitcase on his motorcycle to Landau's train station. I chose an early train so that I could arrive in Gelnhausen by the afternoon. I had to change trains in Mannheim and Frankfurt to connect to Gelnhausen. The train traveled along the Main River. I went to the train's dining car, where I indulged in a cup of coffee and a piece of pastry. I watched the beautiful scenery passing. Shortly after I returned to my seat, the train stopped, and I arrived at Gelnhausen.

Chapter 13

First Position in a Medical Clinic

A GENTLEMAN HELPED ME with my suitcase. He asked me where I was going.

I told him, "I am going to Dr. Samietz's clinic."

"I am going in that direction, and I will show you where he lives. What takes you to him on a Sunday?"

"I am a doctor's assistant and will start working for him tomorrow."

"Good luck. Dr. Samietz is a little rough, but he is a good doctor."

"Thank you for telling me about Dr. Samietz being rough; I will have to adjust to his personality."

We chatted for a few minutes, and before I realized, we arrived at Barbarossa Street 6. The gentlemen pointed to the terracotta-colored stone house, "This is where Dr. Samietz lives. He has his clinic in the same building."

I thanked the gentleman for his help. Then I knocked on the big door. Shortly a lady opened the door. We introduced each other.

"I am Fraeulein Bonacker, the doctor's assistant."

"I am Frau Samietz. Come in. We were expecting you."

I picked up my suitcase and entered an immense hallway with a dark brown staircase leading up.

"Follow me; I will take you to the room where you will be staying."

I picked up my suitcase and followed Mrs. Samietz. She opened the door to a small room with a bed, a table with two chairs, a small sofa, and a dresser.

"This is the room for you. I will show you the clinic tomorrow morning before you start working at 8:00 a.m. Now, just get your things unpacked. I will see you tomorrow."

"Thank you, Mrs. Samietz; I meet you downstairs tomorrow morning."

Mrs. Samietz added, "By the way, the toilet and shower are across from this room. You will have to share it with my daughter Ursula."

"Thank you; that is all right."

First, I looked out of the window. I saw part of the city on the left and a hill with a castle's ruins to the right. It pleased me to have a nice view. Then I lifted the suitcase onto the bed and unpacked my belongings. I hung the dresses, blouses, and skirts on the rack and placed the rest in different drawers. I pushed the three pairs of shoes I brought under the bed and my wooden suitcase too. A steam radiator heated the room. A ceramic sink with hot and cold running water stood next to the door. The room was simple, but I was satisfied to have my own place for the first time. I was not sure yet what arrangements I could make for my meals. I ate a few cookies I had brought with me for tonight, and I drank the water from the faucet just to satisfy my thirst. Before I went to bed, I read for a while. I set the alarm I had brought with me for 6:00 a.m. Then I prayed and thanked God that I had a place to stay and work. I asked God to show me His way in the new chapter of my life, working in a medical clinic.

I got up at 6:00 a.m. the following day. I ate some more cookies and drank a glass of hot water from the faucet. I brushed my teeth, washed up, dressed, and went downstairs at 7:45 a.m. The door to the clinic was still locked. I found the door to the kitchen open, where I saw a lady washing dishes. I entered and introduced myself. She told me her name was Lioba, and she worked for Dr. and Mrs. Samietz as a domestic helper and cooked for them. The kitchen was all white, fundamental, without any decorations. We talked for a few minutes. When I heard someone coming down the stairway, I went to the hallway to greet Mrs. Samietz. She said good morning to me and unlocked the door to the clinic.

"This is the examining room, where Dr. Samietz checks and treats the patients. You will be giving injections and doing some tests on the patients here."

In the center of the room stood an examining table. A small table with two chairs was closed to the door set up with the necessary items to give intravenous injections. Mounted cabinets on the wall and others on the floor were on the opposite side. A bed stood against one wall too. Mrs. Samietz opened the door to the consultation room. A desk with a big chair behind for the doctor and two smaller chairs for the patients in front. Mrs. Samietz pointed to a smaller desk with a chair on the opposite side. On the desk stood an old typewriter.

"This is where you will be sitting. The records of the patients are in the drawers. We do not go by appointment. Whenever patients enter the waiting room, you pull out their charts. You call the patients to see the doctor in the sequence they come in. Then you put the chart on the doctor's desk. Before the patient leaves, make sure to enter each procedure or injection given on the chart. Then you file them in alphabetical order."

Next, she opened the door to the big waiting room with chairs placed along all the walls. A low table covered with reading material stood in the center of the room. She unlocked the door leading to the outside, where patients would enter. The first patient was already waiting. Mrs. Samietz greeted her, "Good morning Mrs. Fehl; I want you to meet our new doctor's assistant Miss Hildegard Bonacker." I greeted her also and responded,

"It is nice to meet you, Mrs. Fehl. Please come in and have a seat in the waiting room."

Then Mrs. Samietz showed me another room with a colossal x-ray machine in it, "This is the x-ray room. Do you know how to take x-rays?"

"No, we were not taught how to operate an x-ray machine, but I am willing to learn how to take x-rays."

I heard steps coming down the stairs. Dr. Samietz met us in the hallway after we left the x-ray room. I greeted him, "Good morning Dr. Samietz."

"Good morning, Miss Bonacker. Welcome to our clinic."

"Thank you."

His physical appearance surprised me. He weighed way over three hundred pounds. The weight of his chubby cheeks dropped practically to the chin. We followed Dr. Samietz into the consultation room. He put on his white coat before he sat down behind his desk. His protruded belly rested on the chair. However, his smile was genuine and friendly. Mrs. Samietz pulled out the first patient's chart, Mrs. Fehl, and told me to call her to come in. I placed the patient's chart on Dr. Samietz's desk. I learned that Mrs. Fehl had diabetes and needed to have a prescription refilled. Dr. Samietz wrote the prescription, asked her how she was feeling, and then told her to come back in a month. The waiting room started to fill up. Mrs. Samietz told me each patient's name, then I pulled their charts and lined them up in the sequence they came in. We saw one patient after the other, and before we realized, it was noon; Mrs. Samietz closed the outside door to the waiting room. Dr. and Mrs. Samietz would take a lunch break until 4:00 p.m. I remained in the office until I filed all the charts and I tidied the waiting and examining room. Mrs. Samietz instructed me to start at 3:00 p.m. to familiarize myself with the patient's names and items in the examining room.

By now, my stomach growled. But I stayed the extra hour, filed all the charts, placed all the magazines in order in the waiting room, and checked the cabinets' contents in the examining room. I went to the kitchen, where Lioba was doing dishes, and asked her where the closest grocery store was. Then I climbed up the stairs, took my purse, put on a jacket, and went shopping. I bought six rolls, 100 grams of soft sausage (Metwurst), just enough to spread on the rolls. I also purchased a small jar of marmalade, 100 grams of butter, a carton of milk, and pumpernickel bread for breakfast. I ate two of my rolls and drank part of the milk for lunch. The first month I had to be frugal with the money my brother gave me. Once I received my salary, I would be able to afford more food items and perhaps some fruits, too. But for now, I was glad to have something to put into my growling stomach. At 3:00 p.m., I went downstairs again. My room was on the third floor. Lioba told me that the dining, living, and bedroom of Dr. and Mrs. Samietz were on the second floor; so was a private room of Dr. Samietz where he would keep his medical books and take care of his correspondence and phone calls. Both Dr. and Mrs. Samietz took a nap each day after lunch. The food, prepared by Lioba, would be sent up with a manual dumb waiter from the kitchen to the dining room. The dirty dishes were then sent down to the kitchen again to be washed and stored in the kitchen cabinets.

At 4:00 p.m., Dr. and Mrs. Samietz came downstairs. I had already opened the waiting room shortly before. I pulled out the first patient's chart and placed it on my desk first and on the doctor's desk after he sat down. Most patients came for prescription refills, flu, other minor health problems, and some injections. Mrs. Samietz showed me the sterilized syringes and ampules with the medication the patient received. I observed very carefully and was able to give the third intermuscular injection by myself. Mrs. Samietz gave the patient a choice to have a shot in the arm or the butt. I did the same. Mrs. Samietz demonstrated how to give an intravenous injection of calcium. Mrs. Samietz asked me if I had given any intravenous injections. I told her we did not learn how to give intravenous injections.

"Today, we have a patient coming for a calcium injection. The doctor will show you how to give intravenous injections. We usually let the patient lay down on the bed. If you inject the calcium rapidly, the patient can faint. It comes in a 10 ml ampoule. She broke off the top of the ampoule and filled the syringe with the liquid calcium. She left the needle with the attached syringe in the ampoule. Then she took a cotton ball, soaked it into alcohol, and placed it next to the syringe and the tourniquet.

"Every time you will give an intravenous injection, you have to show the doctor the ampoule with the filled syringe and tell him what the medication is and who will receive the shot. This precaution avoids mistakes."

"Yes, Mrs. Samietz, I shall do so."

"Now, the doctor will show you how to give the intravenous injection. Call the patient and tell the doctor that everything is ready."

"Yes, Mrs. Samietz. I will."

I called in Mr. Krueger and then told Dr. Samietz that everything was ready. After the patient stretched out on the bed, Dr. Samietz sat down on the chair next to him. He placed the tourniquet on the upper arm, tightened it, and started to look for the vein in the elbow's groin. Once he found a vein, he let me feel it, too. Then he sterilized the area with a cotton ball soaked in alcohol, put the needle in the vein and retracted the syringe's plunger until a small amount of blood entered the fluid. Once assured that the needle was in the vein, he released the tourniquet and started to inject the solution slowly.

"Just let me know if you get hot," Dr. Samietz asked the patient. If he said yes, the doctor would stop for a while and then continue.

"As you can see, Miss Bonacker, the calcium injections have to be given very slowly; otherwise, the patient gets very hot and faints."

"Yes, Dr. Samietz, I shall inject the calcium very slowly."

Once the doctor finished, he returned to the consultation room. I called in the following patient for him. Mrs. Samietz remained in the examining room with Mr. Krueger a little longer to ensure he was all right. Then she let him out from the side door through the hallway. She did not want to disturb the doctor and the next patient in the consultation room. By 6:00 p.m., the waiting room was empty. Mrs. Samietz asked me to close the door and file all the charts before going upstairs, which I did. Even though the first day was challenging, I thanked God that all went well. I consumed my two buns with the sausage and read the New Testament for a while. I sank tired but content into my bed and slept well and peacefully.

The next day was almost a repeat of the first day. Things went well again. I had a chance to meet more patients whose names I tried to remember. Wednesday was my day off. After breakfast, I went to familiarize myself with the town and surroundings. I climbed up the hill to explore the ruins of what appeared to have once been a castle. In the courtyard, a teacher explained the history of the castle to her students. I stayed close to her and listened.

"The castle was constructed in the 12th century for Friedrich Barbarossa in the Romanesque architectural style. Gelnhausen is also called the Barbarossa town. Friedrich Barbarossa was crowned king of Germany in Aachen, Germany, Roman emperor in Rome, and king of Italy in Pavia. He reigned from 1155 until 1190. During the thirty-year-long war with France, Spain, Sweden, and Germany from 1618 to 1648, the castle was destroyed by a Swedish ambush. It used to be an independent municipality; once dissolved in the late 19th century, it became part of the city of Gelnhausen. The ruins became a tourist attraction and an inspiration for art-loving scholars. The Emperor also built a place on the Kinzig river island, called Emperor Place (Kaiserplatz)."

The teacher pointed downhill,

"From here, you have a beautiful view of Gelnhausen and the Kinzig River. Let us go further uphill, where we will enter the forest. We will take a short walk through the nearby forest, which also belonged to the castle."

The class left. I stayed behind for a while and observed the city's commanding view of the Kinzig river valley. Then I walked uphill and strolled through the forest. The sun slithered through the beech and oak trees' partly bare branches while some leaves were still falling. The dry leaves rustled as I stepped on them. I looked for beechnuts that I hoped the squirrels had not yet devoured. Here and there, I found one. I enjoyed the flavor of them. At noon, I returned to the town, went to the grocery store, and bought sausage and buns for lunch. After lunch, I took a nap, read my New Testament, wrote a letter home, and one to my girlfriend, Lore, in Niederbexbach. Before I retired for the night, I thanked God for the forest's beauty and a lovely day.

The next few days went well also. Mrs. Samietz stressed the importance of getting an insurance form for every patient seeing the doctor.

"Whenever a patient comes, check if they have an insurance form (Krankenschein) from the government. If not, ask them to bring it next time. We will have to list all the doctor's services and send them to the Health Insurance Office for payment collection by the end of each quarter of the year. The patients will also need a new form every three months."

"Yes, Mrs. Samietz, I will check and make sure the patients have brought their forms."

Friday, a patient came in having difficulty breathing. Dr. Samietz wanted a chest x-ray. Mrs. Samietz took the patient to the x-ray room. I followed her, observed how to set the dials on the x-ray machine, put the film in the cassette, and place it in a holder. Then she positioned the patient in front of the cassette and put both shoulders against the cassette. She instructed the patient to take a deep breath and hold it. Then she pushed a button on the x-ray machine. When she heard the click, she told the patient to breathe again and have a seat while she developed the film. We both went into the darkroom. Mrs. Samietz carefully removed the film, put it on a special hanger, then dipped it into one tank filled with a solution.

"This is the developer. You move the film gently up and down until you see the image of the object you x-rayed appear clearly on the film. Then, wash off the developer in the water tank and place it into the fixer for a few minutes. This solution stops the developing process and retains the image taken. In the end, you dip the film in the water again and let it dry. However, you can show it to the doctor before it is dry."

She took the wet film and showed it to the doctor. He looked at the film, noted something abnormal, and told Mrs. Samietz he would like to do a fluoroscopy of the patient's lungs. Dr. Samietz walked into the x-ray room, put on the lead apron, and sat on the chair. He asked the patient to stand behind the dark movable x-ray screen and positioned the patient behind the screen. The doctor moved the patient and the screen to see the lungs' lobes from different angles to check for abnormalities. This procedure took ten to twenty minutes. When he finished, he told the patient he saw a tumor. Dr. Samietz filled out a particular form (Ueberweisung) to admit the patient to the local hospital for a biopsy and further evaluation and treatment. On Saturday, the office was only open for half a day. Mrs. Samietz informed me that every weekend when the doctor's offices are closed, one of the local doctors is on call for emergencies. On the last weekend of the month, Dr. Mantel will substitute for her husband. You will have to take the phone calls from the patients. I listened carefully. However, I still had two weekends free to get acquainted with more places in and around town.

Lioba had told me about a café called the Little Castle (Das Schloesschen), located on the hill. She mentioned the owner plays the piano, and sometimes people will also sing. Besides, he serves good food and tasty pastries. I thought I might splurge a little on Sunday and check it out for myself. She also informed me which and where the Evangelistic Church was to find out about the services. I planned to go there the following Sunday. Today, I wanted to satisfy my craving for something sweet. The road to the Café led through an apple orchard. By now, the orchard owner had picked the apples, and the leaves had fallen from the branches. Here and there, a shriveled apple hung on the tree. I would have plucked one or two if they were on the lower limbs close to the road. An apple would have tasted good, even somewhat sun-dried. I reached the café late in the afternoon. A waiter seated me by the window at a small table, covered with a white tablecloth and a vase with fresh flowers decorating it. The café looked very inviting, and I felt good sitting by the window with a city view. The waiter brought the menu.

"Would you like your coffee now or with dessert?"

"With dessert, please."

The menu offered a variety of lush pastries. I liked the Black Forest Cake (Schwarzwaelder Kirschtorte), but the price was too high for my current skimpy budget. I settled for the less expensive apple cake (Apfeltorte). The waiter returned,

"Fraeulein, are you ready to order?"

"Yes, I would like the Apfeltorte and a cup of coffee with cream, please."

"Thank you, is that all?"

"Yes, that would be all."

Today, only a few customers visited the café early, but more persons came in after 3:30 p.m. The owner entered, sat down on the bench in front of the piano, and began to play Schubert's "Serenade." Then a couple got up, went over to the piano, and asked the owner if he could accompany them to the aria from *The Gypsy Baron*, "Who Married Us?" (Wer Uns Getraut). The pianist looked through his sheets of music. Then he said, "Here it is; we can start."

The couple held hands, looking into each other's eyes, expressing so much love for each other, and sang the beautiful duet from the Operetta, *The Gypsy Baron*, composed by Johann Strauss. Their voices sounded heavenly. They also sang a few songs by Schubert and duets from other operettas. The music absorbed me completely. I took a bite of my apple torte and a sip of coffee to make it last as long as possible. When they stopped singing, I finished my desert. I paid the waiter and happily wandered down the hill. I watched the sun dipping lower and lower, casting a gray veil over the mountain and town. I got back before the night drenched the city in darkness. I thanked God for the exhilarating music. I stayed awake for some time. I dreamed that I would meet my prince charming one day, be in love like the singers, and experience more wonderful musical events.

The following week, Mrs. Samietz let me work by myself in the clinic. All went well. Wednesday, I did my shopping for the rest of the week. Dr. Samietz informed me that he would be on call this weekend, and Dr. Mantel would substitute for him. My duty was to answer the phone, take the patient's name and address, and the patient's medical emergency. On Saturday by noon, we finished office hours. Dr. Mantel arrived. Dr. Samietz introduced me to her. Then he told me to take the telephone upstairs, connect it to the outlet outside of my door, and place it on the small table.

"Dr. Mantel will be dining with us. She will be spending the night in my private room on the second floor. Anytime you receive an emergency call, knock on the door and give her the patient's information."

"Yes, Dr. Samietz, I will do so," I answered before I retrieved the phone and took it upstairs. I left my door open day and night in order not to miss a phone call. I ate my sandwich. Then I sat down facing the open door, reading a German translation of the book by Anne Murrow Lindbergh, *The Gift from the Sea*. In it, she describes what the sea and individual shells have taught her. She particularly liked the oyster shells. The tireless adaptability and tenacity drew her astonished admiration. The oyster is comfortable in its homeliness and familiarity. I liked her quote about the love of a partner. It prompted me to put it down in its entirety:

"When each partner loves so completely that he has forgotten to ask himself whether or not he is loved in return; when he only knows that he loves and is moving to its music then, and then only are two people able to dance perfectly in tune to the same rhythm."

The other quote impressed me and reminded me of God creating so much beauty in flowers. "Arranging a bowl of flowers in the morning can give a sense of quiet in a crowded day—like writing a poem or saying a prayer."

I always liked a bouquet of fresh wildflowers on my table. I consider them God's smiles.

In spring and summer, I would pick them in the forest or along the walkways. I cut dry grasses, small branches with colored leaves, or whatever I could find that would look pretty in fall. I shared my passion for flowers with Anne Morrow Lindbergh's. As I continued reading her book, the phone rang. I put down the book and dashed to the hallway to answer the phone, "This is Dr. Samietz's assistant; how can I help you?" A worried mother on the phone informed me that her child ran a high fever, and she would like the doctor to see her sick child. I took down all the necessary information and assured the mother, Dr. Mantel will be there as soon as possible. The mother was relieved to hear that the doctor would make a house call shortly. It was late in the afternoon. Dr. Mantel would still be downstairs with Dr. and Mrs. Samietz. I immediately went downstairs and knocked on the door: Mrs. Samietz came to open the door. I apologized for intruding but told her that a mother just called and would like the doctor to see her sick child. I handed the slip of paper with the name and address of the patient to Mrs. Samietz. She thanked me and told me Dr. Mantel would be on the way shortly.

I walked upstairs again to make sure I would not miss a phone call. I picked up my book and began reading. I paused a short time to have a sandwich for supper. I continued reading until late at night. I did not dare to go to bed. At midnight, the phone rang again. A worried daughter informed me that her elderly mother had fallen and was in a lot of pain. Could the doctor come and see her? After I had written down all the information, I went and knocked on the room where Dr. Mantel slept, "Sorry to disturb you, Dr. Mantel, I have another call for you." She came to the door, "What is wrong with the patient that I need to see?"

"An elderly lady fell and is in a lot of pain; here is her name and address."

I handed her the slip of paper and returned to my room. I sat at the table and began reading again. By now, I was tired and had a hard time staying awake. I must have dozed off. When the phone rang again, I jumped up and quickly ran to the phone. A distressed lady told me that her husband was having a gallbladder attack and was in a lot of pain. I assured her that Dr. Mantel would be there as soon as she could. The wife calmed down somewhat, knowing that her husband would get help. When I gave the information to Dr. Mantel, she asked me to get an ampule of morphine and a syringe from downstairs, which I did. Soon, Dr. Mantel was on her way to see the patient. On Monday morning, as tired as I was from hardly sleeping all night, I had to be in the office by 8:00 a.m.. Dr. Mantel came down also to let me know what services she provided to the patients she visited. She gave a penicillin injection to the child with a high fever and wrote a hospital admission form for the lady who fell. Dr. Mantel suspected a fractured hip. She gave an intravenous injection of morphine to the patient who had a gallbladder attack. I had to make a chart for each patient and enter the house call and the injections given. Then I had to call the patients to bring the insurance forms to collect the fee for the services rendered. Before Dr. Mantel left, she thanked me and said she would be back in one month. I liked her courteous manners and looked forward to working with her again. The following month, I got to know more patients, and some of them liked me well enough to invite me for lunch, or cake and coffee on Sunday afternoon, which made me feel appreciated, and I enjoyed their kindness. I learned how to do glucose tolerance tests, check blood sugars, do CBCs, take samples of the stomach fluid, do x-rays, and develop films. I started to build up self-confidence and felt comfortable working with the doctor and especially with the patients. After the morning office hours, Dr. Samietz dictated a letter to me, and I had to write it down in shorthand. He dictated rather quickly. Unfortunately, I missed certain words. But I did not dare to ask him to repeat them. I assumed; I would fill in the proper words when I would type the letter. After Dr. Samietz went for his lunch break, I remained in the office to type on the old typewriter. I had to slowly push each letter on the keyboard; otherwise, two bars would crisscross and get stuck. I had to stop and disengage them, which was a waste of time. Some letters were unclear, like the a and e, because too much ink from the ribbon had built up on them. When I came to the blanks, I filled them in with words that I thought would fit. I spend part of my lunch hour finishing the letter. I placed it on the desk of Dr. Samietz so that he could read it at his convenience.

We were busy in the afternoon, and he did not get to read the letter until all the patients were gone. I held my breath, hoping to have typed it to his satisfaction. After he finished reading, he threw the letter on the desk and screamed at me, "This is not what I dictated, you are stupid, and you will never amount to anything." His words were like a knife stabbing me in my heart. My body trembled, and I turned pale. I choked. Dr. Samietz wrote his words over my substituted ones, threw the letter at me, "Type it again correctly!"

Without uttering a word, I put the letter on my desk. I was still shocked by the doctor's derogatory, rude comments. After he left, I sat down and cried for a while before retyping the letter. I had a hard time concentrating on the content of the letter. I felt like putting the uncorrected letter on his desk with a note, saying, "I do not like to be treated like this. I quit!"

I called on God to show me how to act in this situation that would honor Him. I reasoned that God would not want me to run away from a problem. He would like me to be strong and face the challenge, do whatever I could to resolve it, and trust God to help me find a way to act correctly. Retyping the letter drained me emotionally. But I finished it, read it several times, put it on Dr. Samietz's desk, and went upstairs. It was past dinner time. I temporarily lost my appetite. I flung myself on the bed, and many thoughts raced through my mind.

Quitting and running away from a problem is like being a coward and would haunt me in the future. To return rudeness for rudeness would be unchristian and make me feel bad. What would be the best solution for this problem according to God's will? I would stay and practice shorthand daily until I would become proficient in taking dictations. I avowed, with the help of God, to become the best person I possibly could be. Several times I repeated the sentence, "I will amount to something. I show you; I will amount to something! God help me to turn this human disappointment into a divine appointment." I swore if I ever have employees in the future, I would never be rude to them or degrade them. I would treat them with the utmost respect and courtesy. Before I went to sleep, I regained my inner peace by believing that with the help of God, I had made the right decision. I thanked God for showing me His will and hoped all would work out all right.

Every morning, I got up one hour earlier and practiced short-hand to take dictations faster and faster. Each time Dr. Samietz dictated a letter, I got nervous and was afraid to make a mistake. In due time, I wrote the letters to his satisfaction and avoided his rude remarks and unpleasant confrontations.

The end of October neared. The Lutheran and the Evangelic Protestant churches celebrated each year on October 31, Reformation Day. It is a commemoration of the day in 1517 when Martin Luther, a German monk, nailed the famous ninety-five theses on the castle church's door in Wittenberg. He disagreed strongly with the Catholic Church's teaching that a person can earn salvation through good works. Dr. Luther did not believe in buying and selling indulgences. He regarded that by faith in God and accepting Jesus Christ as Savior, a person obtains salvation as God's gift. Dr. Luther recognized the Bible as the religious authority. This year, we celebrated Reformation Day on Sunday, October 30. I decided to go to the Evangelic Marienkirche.

I walked through the old section of town before I reached the church, built in the later romanesque and early gothic style of two-tone pink sandstone with dark, high towers. I entered through the massive door framed by ornate stone columns—carved statues placed above the door's arch. The interior, especially the altar, impressed me even more with all the tall, exquisite sculptures and paintings—light penetrating the tall arched stained-glass windows casting a soft glow on the altar, and the stone walls. Statues, pictures, and chandeliers decorated the vestibules and all areas. After the church filled up and I sat down, the organist began to play. What a marvelous and inspiring sound filled the entire church. The pastor, dressed in a long, black robe, stepped behind the altar. The congregation rose. After the liturgy, the worshippers sang, "A Mighty Fortress is our God." Then the pastor preached about the meaning of the reformation and Martin Luther's role in beginning the reformation. After the sermon, the congregation sang one more song before the pastor dismissed the parishioners with a benediction.

I went back to my apartment, satisfied with having found a church to attend as often as I could. On November 1, I received my first salary in cash. Even though it was only for three weeks, I appreciated being able to buy a few of what I considered luxury items, like an electric burner, a pot, and a pan to fix myself hot meals for lunch. Up to now I ate only sandwiches for dinner. Since there was no refrigerator in the apartmtnt, I had to go shopping several times a week to buy fresh meat or sausages. I managed to stretch my funds until the next payday.

One night, I heard a knock on my door, "Fraeulein Bonacker, hurry downstairs. Dr. Samietz is in a lot of pain; he is having a gallbladder attack. Get morphine and come and give him a shot."

"Yes, Mrs. Samietz, I will."

I put on my robe quickly, got the syringe and ampule of morphine, the tourniquet, soaked a cotton ball in alcohol, and ran upstairs. I found Dr. Samietz moaning and groaning. He was in severe pain. When he saw me entering the room, he stretched out his left arm, "Quickly, give me the shot; I am in a lot of pain!"

"Yes, Dr. Samietz, I shall."

I drew the morphine into the syringe, then rapidly put the tourniquet on his left arm and asked him to make a fist. When I could feel the vein, I sterilized the area with alcohol and pushed the needle into the vein. Luckily, I did not miss the vein on the first attempt. I was relieved. Then I started to inject the morphine slowly.

Knowing that the morphine would relieve the pain made him relax. I thanked God that I did not miss the vein and cause him to get angry at me. Mrs. Samietz thanked me before I left the room. I took all the things downstairs to the clinic before I went back to bed. The next day was Wednesday, so the doctor could recover from the exhausting, painful night. By Thursday, Dr. Samietz was back in the clinic, seeing patients again. He even told me that I gave good intravenous injections. I was glad to hear him say so. As time progressed, we became comfortable working together. I knew what he expected of me, and I tried to meet his expectations wherever I could.

During my weekly grocery shopping, two or three American soldiers often followed me and wanted to engage in a conversation. I pretended I did not understand English, and I continued walking. When I saw a store, I entered, looked around, and waited until they passed, and I felt safe, not being seen by them. An American garrison occupied Gelnhausen, and many soldiers lived in town. Some of the soldiers contracted gonorrhea. They did not like to go to the medical office at the base for treatment. They would be embarrassed to have it charted in their medical records. They opted to go to local doctors for their penicillin shots. We had soldiers knocking on the main door frequently, requesting penicillin shots. I took them directly to the examining room to give them the penicillin shot in the arm. They paid 20.00 DM per injection, which I gave promptly to the doctor. It was an additional unrecorded income.

One day, Dr. and Mrs. Samietz went out for the day. The maid had left. Only I remained alone in the house. I heard a knock on the door. When I went downstairs to open the door, a very tall colored soldier stood in front of me, saying, "Penicillin Spritze, bitte, (Shot of penicillin, please)." He completely surprised and intimidated me at first. I was unsure if I should close the door, saying the doctor is not here or just let him in and give him the shot. I opted to let him in rather than letting him know that the doctor was not home. I

Gone With the World Wars

prayed for the protection of God while I prepared and gave him the shot in the arm. He handed me the 20.00 DM and left. I thanked God that he did not molest me. The soldiers would return for penicillin injections until their symptoms cleared up. When Dr. and Mrs. Samietz returned, I handed the 20.00 DM bill to the doctor.

On one Sunday, Mrs. Fehl asked me for lunch. She introduced me to her son Hans and daughter-in-law, Helen, and a friend, named Franz, an organist. They all appreciated classical and organ music, as did I. Franz, the organist, told me that he goes to the church to practice now and then. He asked me if I would be interested in joining and listening to him play.

"I would be delighted to hear you play. I could do it on my day off on Wednesday."

"I can meet you on Wednesday at 4:00 p.m."

"Very good; I will see you then in the church."

We spent a pleasant afternoon together. I thanked Mrs. Fehl and her family for the delicious lunch. I also thanked the organist for his invitation to hear him play.

On Wednesday morning, after I practiced shorthand, I cleaned my room, prepared some sauerkraut, sausage, and potato stew for lunch, read until 3:30 p.m., walked over to the church, and sat down on the bench of the last row. The church remained unheated in fall and winter. I was glad I wore a heavy coat and gloves. While I looked around and admired all the exquisite religious decorations again, Franz, the organist, came to greet me,

"Good afternoon Fraeulein Hildegard. It is good to see you here, and you came punctually, too. I will start playing shortly."

"Good afternoon, Mr. Franz. I am anxious to hear you play."

He walked over to the organ, sat down, and began to play. As Franz touched the keys, the sound left the organ pipes and floated through the empty church. When the sacred melodies reached my ears and touched my heart and spirit, they reverberated with great joy. The moving music and the surrounding beauty of the church décor elevated my soul. I sat enraptured in my seat, forgetting about time and everything else. When the music stopped, I felt like I awakened from a pleasant dream. Mr. Franz came over to me. I told him how much I enjoyed listening to the music he played on the organ.

"I am glad you liked the music. Perhaps you can come again?"

"I certainly would like to hear you play again."

I thanked him, and we parted with a handshake. I returned to my room and read until bedtime. I thanked God for this uplifting musical experience.

The dreary days of November, when bare branches mourned the loss of their leaves, passed slowly. The last Sunday, November 27, we celebrated the first day of Advent, a Christian tradition to prepare for the birth of Jesus. The Wednesday before, I went to the forest, broke off some pine branches, crafted a wreath, and secured four candles on it. I placed it on my table, and each Sunday evening, I lit one more candle. I would watch the flickering candlelight, meditate, and read my Bible or some poems from my Bluetenbaum poetry book. I began to think of Christmas. I knew Dr. Samietz would not grant me time off after I only worked two months for him. It meant I would not be able to go home. Dr. and Mrs. Samietz had not invited me once for dinner or any meal; they probably would not ask me for Christmas either. I did not like the idea of spending this memorable holiday by myself in my room. I waited patiently for someone to invite me.

Meanwhile, I wrote my Christmas cards to my mother, my sisters Marta and Meta, my close relatives, my girlfriend Lore, and Hermann. By the middle of December, Lioba asked me to spend Christmas Eve and Christmas Day with her family. I accepted her invitation joyfully and thanked her for being so thoughtful. Having received only two salaries so far did not allow me to buy Christmas presents for Lioba and her parents. I decided to buy some firm sheets of paper and make stars to hang on the Christmas tree, which the whole family could enjoy. Every evening, I cut paper strips and folded them into stars. My sister Emma had taught me how to make stars from paper strips as well as from straw. I sure would miss being home with my family at Christmas. I could not even call them because they did not have a telephone. Close to Christmas, I received a Christmas card and a letter from my brother Edmund. He enclosed 50.00 DM in the card so that I could buy a gift for myself. I was very grateful to him. My brown shoes looked worn out, and I had only a few dresses. I bought myself a pair of brown shoes and a light brown dress that I would wear for Christmas. Some thoughtful patients brought me boxes of candy for Christmas. A letter and card from Hermann were among the cards and letters I received with Merry Christmas wishes. I appreciated being remembered at this festive time and especially by Hermann. His message brought back the precious moments we shared, encouraging each other to live up to our high ideals.

Friday, December 23, we still had office hours. But on Christmas Eve, Christmas, and December 26, Dr. Samietz closed the office. On Christmas Eve, Lioba came early to prepare the meal for Christmas Eve and Christmas Day. By noon she was ready to leave. She commuted by bicycle from Biebergemuend to Gelnhausen. She told me her older brother, Peter, would come by motorcycle to pick me up, which he did. I had packed my overnight bag and waited for him downstairs in the kitchen with Lioba. In December, winter entered with a vengeance. The temperature dropped below zero. I bundled up in my heavy coat, put a scarf on my head, and wrapped it around my face before I mounted the motorcycle. I felt sorry for Lioba riding her bike even in the cold winter weather from Biebergemuend to Gelnhausen, half an hour each way. I wore nylon stockings, and my legs froze during the ride. Fortunately, it was only six miles away. Mr. and Mrs. Krack welcomed me into their modest but tastefully decorated home in Biebergemuend. I also met the younger brother Erhard. We all waited until Lioba arrived. At 3:00 p.m., Mrs. Krack served cake and coffee while we enjoyed chatting.

Christmas Eve, Mrs. Krack served a carp with potato salad, which I enjoyed very much. At 11:00 p.m., we all walked over to the Catholic church, and celebrated the festive midnight mass. However, I had a hard time staying awake that late at night. Lioba was kind enough to sleep on the sofa and let me sleep in her comfortable bed. I slept very well and rather late; we did not need to go to church today. Mrs. Krack served an elaborate lunch of roasted goose, red cabbage, and potato dumplings for lunch. The roasted goose's aroma reminded me of my mother's home cooking; I missed being with my family but was grateful to the Krack family for inviting me to celebrate Christmas with them. After we had cake and coffee in the afternoon, Peter took me back to Gelnhausen. Primarily I thanked God for His great love for us that He sent His only son Jesus Christ, whose birthday we commemorate each year at Christmas. I thought of Christ's journey from the crib to the cross and how He gave his life so that we can have salvation and eternal life. I thanked God also that I did not have to be alone at this special celebration.

On Friday, December 30, 1955, Mrs. Samietz showed me how to fill out the insurance forms for the last quarter of the year. I entered on each patient's insurance form all office visits, injections, and medical services rendered. It took me longer than I expected, and I finished the last entry late Saturday, even though the office was closed that day.

On New Year's Eve, Saturday, December 31, 1955, I opted to stay home. I read my Bible and meditated on all the past year's events and how wonderfully God had brought me through all challenges and trials. I trusted God. He never let me down. God filled my heart with joy and peace. I went to bed relatively early. At midnight, the church bells announced the arrival of the New Year 1956. The ringing of the bells woke me up. I stayed awake for some time, wondering what God had in store for me this coming year. I had a custom of choosing a Bible verse for each year. This year it was Mark 4:39, "And He arose, and rebuked the wind, and said unto the sea, Peace be still. And the wind ceased, and there was a great calm."

I pondered how this would apply to my life. Yes, God and my Savior calmed many storms in my life and helped me through tough times. I trusted He would do the same in the future. I went to church Sunday morning. In the afternoon, I decided to go to the Castle Café early to treat myself to a piece of cake and a cup of coffee. Today, the owner played the piano, but no artist sang to the delight of the customers. I just had received my third monthly salary. I felt like treating myself to a piece of Black Forest cake. It was delicious. I went back early before it got dark.

The next day, on my birthday, I had to work. During my lunch break, I went to the post office to mail the government's insurance forms. I did not do anything special for my birthday. Dr. and Mrs. Samietz did not remember my birthday. I only told Lioba that my 19th birthday was January 2. She brought a piece of cake for me the following day. I was very grateful for her friendship and thoughtfulness and that she came five days a week to Dr. and Mrs. Samietz. If I wanted to talk to her, I would go into the kitchen, where she worked most of the day.

Sometimes seminars were held for farmers or other special groups in Gelnhausen. In January, a young man from one group came to the clinic with an upper respiratory infection. Dr. Samietz ordered a penicillin shot for him. While I gave him the injection in the arm, he engaged me in conversation. He told me he was a refugee from East Prussia. He was attending the dairy seminar and eventually wanted to immigrate to Alberta, Canada. I told him I also was born in East Prussia, and my family escaped from the Russians in 1944. He asked me what my name was and if he could take me out for lunch or dinner one day after becoming well. I introduced myself and told him it would be permissible to call me during office hours and that my free days were Wednesdays and Sundays.

"Perhaps we can meet one Sunday. I do not have any lectures on Sunday."

"Sunday afternoon will be fine with me."

"Very good, Fraeulein Bonacker; I will call you when I am well. Goodbye."

"Goodbye, Mr. Gollnick." We shook hands, and he left.

Two weeks later, Horst Gollnick called and asked me to hike in the Buedinger Forest on Sunday. I told him I could make it in the early afternoon after church services. We agreed to leave at 1:00 p.m. Punctually at 1:00 p.m., he knocked on the door. I walked down the stairs and opened the door. We greeted each other politely and then started walking uphill to the castle, chatting about the events of the past two weeks. When we entered the forest, we stopped talking. We observed the beautiful transformation of the woods by the freshly fallen snow. The eyes feasted, watching the pure white magical winter scenery. We heard the crackling sound under our boots as we walked on the snow. Now and then, a clump of snow fell from a tree and broke the peaceful silence of the forest. My thoughts traveled back in time to East Prussia, where I was born and grew up as a child surrounded by woods. Horst broke the silence by asking where I was born and where we lived after the war. I asked him the same questions since he was also born in East Prussia. We exchanged various events of the war. We both had survived many dangerous situations and were grateful to be still alive. We did not realize how time had passed so quickly.

When we reached a restaurant in the woods, Horst invited me to join him for a bite to eat. After having been out in the cold for some time, something warm to eat sounded good. We sat down in the rustic restaurant and placed our orders for hot split pea soup. I ordered a tea to drink and Horst a cup of coffee. We enjoyed the cozy atmosphere along with our food and drinks before we headed back to town. The late afternoon sun slithered through the bare branches, and the trees' shadows grew longer and longer. We reached the city just before sunset. Somewhat tired but at the same time exhilarated, we said goodbye. Being out in nature had a calming effect on my body and soul.

Before we said goodbye, Horst asked, "May I call you again? I enjoyed your company."

"Yes, you may. I also liked reminiscing about our homes in East Prussia."

With a handshake, we parted. I liked the courteous and respectful manners of Horst.

In the next few weeks, many patients came down with flu and pneumonia. I gave a lot of penicillin injections. Dr. Samietz admitted the patients with severe lung infections to the hospital, where the hospital staff doctors would continue to treat the patients. I enjoyed the weekends when Dr. Mantel came to take the emergency calls for Dr. Samietz. Whatever questions I had, she always answered them without making me feel stupid. She appreciated that I wanted to learn new things in the medical field. We developed a cordial relationship with each other and with the patients. During January, the coldest month of the year, I came down with the flu. I did not dare to take off work. Even though I had a fever, I still worked in the clinic. Dr. Samietz must have noticed that I did not feel right, and the fever blushed my face.

"What is the matter, Fraeulein Bonacker? You do not look well."

"I feel feverish, and my body aches."

"Come, let me check you."

I walked over to the doctor. He put his hand on my forehead and said, "You sure do have a fever. Take some aspirin and go upstairs to rest. I will call my wife to help me in the clinic."

"Thank you, Dr. Samietz; I shall do that."

I excused myself and went upstairs. I made myself a cup of tea, ate a sandwich, and went to bed, even though it was only the early afternoon. I perspired all night. The next day was Wednesday, my day off. I only got up to eat, then spent the rest of the day in bed. By Thursday, I felt better. I went to work for the rest of the week. Sunday, I rested again. It took an additional week to recover from the flu completely.

The following Wednesday afternoon, I heard a knock on the door. After Lioba opened the door, she called to me, "There is a gentleman at the door; he wants to see you."

I rushed down the stairs to be greeted by Horst Gollnick.

"Good afternoon, Fraeulein Bonacker."

"Good afternoon, Mr. Gollnick. What can I do for you?"

"Can I invite you for Sunday to go to Frankfurt with me to see the play *The Hypochondriac* by Moliere?"[27]

"Thank you; I think I can join you. What time?"

"I will pick you up at 10:00 a.m. The train ride does not take more than an hour. We can have lunch before the play starts."

"Very good; I will see you Sunday."

"Goodbye, until Sunday."

"Goodbye!"

Happily, I ran upstairs thinking of seeing a play in Frankfurt.

Sunday came, and so did Mr. Gollnick punctually at 10:00 a.m. After a short greeting, we walked to the train station. Mr. Gollnick bought the roundtrip tickets. However, I preferred to pay for mine. We had only a short wait before the train left. We were fortunate to find a train that did not make any stops. The scenery just flew by. We arrived relatively early at the main Railroad Station and started walking. Mr. Gollnick asked directions to the Willy Brandt Platz, where the Municipal Theatre's Big House was. We walked on Taunus Street to the Willy Brandt Platz. Mr. Gollnick asked for directions to a good restaurant near the theater. The gentleman told him that Restaurant Francais in the Frankfurter Hof Hotel has excellent food. It is located a short distance from here on the Kaiser Platz.

Since we had time to spare before the play began, Mr. Gollnick invited me for lunch. We walked to the Frankfurter Hof Hotel, where we found the luxurious restaurant. An elegantly dressed waiter seated us at a table covered with a white tablecloth. A small bouquet of fresh flowers with two candles stood in the center. It looked inviting. The waiter brought us the menu written in French. Mr. Gollnick and I looked at each other, not knowing what to order. We both were not familiar with the French dishes listed on the menu. I looked at the table next to me and showed the waiter that I wanted that particular dish. Mr. Gollnick looked at a different table and ordered by pointing at the plate. Etiquette and table manners are essential in Germany and Europe. One does not want to be criticized or feel humiliated in society. We watched how the persons ate the food we ordered so we would eat it correctly. Now and then, we looked at each other and smiled. Mr. Gollnick also ordered a bottle of wine. The waiter brought the glasses and filled them with the wine. Mr. Gollnick lifted the glass, "Fraeulein Bonacker, I make a toast and propose we call each other by our first names. Of course, only if it is agreeable with you?"

"Mr. Gollnick, I agree." We lifted our glasses gently, then touched each other's glass, and Horst said, "Prost! (To your health), Hildegard." I responded. "Prost, Horst!"

Then Horst began in a less formal tone telling me about his plans of going to a dairy farm in Alberta, Canada, saying, "I will work there for a while, and perhaps I might acquire a dairy farm of my own one day. "Do you have any plans for the future, Hildegard?" he asked.

"Not yet. I will continue working for Dr. Samietz for a while. This spring, my older brother will come to visit me. I will see what he has in mind."

"Perhaps, one day, you might consider joining me in Canada? I do not expect you to give me an answer now. It is just a thought for the future."

"Thank you for asking me, but I cannot make any commitment now. I prefer we just remain friends without any strings attached."

The waiter brought the food—a spinach souffle for me and an omelet filled with many ingredients Horst had ordered. We looked at each other, smiled, wished each other bon appetit in French, and began to eat. We needed only a fork to eat our dishes and used the knife to spread the butter on the croissants. We felt very proper now, blending in with all the other guests while enjoying our French food. It was too early to go to the theater. We decided to take a walk along the Main River on Mainkai Street. Even though it was still winter, it did not feel too chilly with the sun on the horizon. We reached the theater and got comfortable seats in the center section of the theater. The décor of the theater was not elaborate but pleasing, and the stage was relatively small. By 2:00 p.m., every seat was occupied, and the curtain of the stage rose.

Act I: In the middle of the stage stood a bed with a patient lying in it—a doctor examined the patient with his stethoscope. The second wife, Beline, daughter Angelique, and maid Toinette are also present. He laments that the doctor and the pharmacist, the brother of the doctor, will bankrupt him. Toinette tries hard to convince Aragan, the name of the patient, that he was not sick but is not successful in doing so. However, Beline and the doctor collude to get money from Aragan. For the daughter not to interfere with their plan, they try to convince Aragon to send her to a convent. But Aragan wants to see his daughter married to Thomas, the doctor's son; this way, he will have a family doctor giving him free medical service. Angelique, however, loves someone else by the name of Cleante. She scolds her father for trying to force her, against her will, to marry someone she does not love. While arguing back and forth, the curtain closes on Act I. The audience, content with the excellent acting, applauds. A short pause before the curtain rises again.

In Act II, Toinette sympathizes with Angelique. She tells her friend Cleante that Angelique is supposed to marry Thomas, the son of the doctor. Cleante disguises himself as the friend of Angelique's singing teacher to spend time alone with Angelique. He finds Thomas not very bright. Cleante cannot imagine Angelique being married to Thomas. She pleads with her father to give her time to think it over. The father gives her four days to marry Thomas or to go to the convent. Beralde, the brother of Aragan, appears on the stage and pleads on Angelique's behalf but to no avail. Beralde sends the doctor and the pharmacist away. The curtain closes. Applause follows.

In Act III, Beralde and Toinette design a plan to trick Aragan. Toinette disguises herself as a doctor and tells Aragan that the previous doctor treated him for the wrong sickness. The lungs are sick and not the bowels. She goes on and on while the audience is laughing. Beralde pleads with Aragan not to put Angelique in the convent that it was Beline's idea. Beralde and Toinette have a solution to convince Aragan how little Beline loves him. They tell Aragan to lie down on the couch and pretend that he is dead. Beralde hides behind a screen. When Beline enters the stage, she finds Toinette crying. She tells Beline that Aragan is dead. Beline does not shed a tear. She calls him names and is out for his money. At that moment, Aragan gets up from the couch, and Beline runs off the stage, still cursing him. Toinette tells Aragan to lay down on the couch again and pretend to be dead. Angelique enters the scene. When she finds out that her father died, she breaks down and cries. The love of his daughter moves the father. He gets up from the couch, embraces her, and tells her she can marry Cleante, but he should study to be a doctor.

Geralde has a better idea. He suggests that his brother should become a doctor. He knows a faculty that can make him a doctor overnight. They invite gypsy dancers to the stage. They perform the ceremony and declare Aragan to be a doctor.

The curtain closes. The audience applauds. The actors come in front of the curtain and bow before the audience.

"Horst, that was a delightful play. I enjoyed the acting as well as the comical story. Did you like it?"

"Yes, I liked it also. Moliere gives us a glimpse of how powerful the mind is in creating imaginary sicknesses."

"He also demonstrates how certain circumstances will reveal the true character of a person," I added.

"Yes, Moliere showed that also in his play."

We left the theater and walked to the railroad station to catch the next train to Gelnhausen, where we arrived shortly after sunset. Strolling back to the house of Dr. Samietz, Horst told me, "I will complete the seminar soon. A formal farewell celebration with music and dancing will be given to all the participants at the end. Could you join me?"

"Depending on the date. When will it be?"

"The party will be one week after Easter."

"After Easter, I will be delighted to join you. However, I do not dance during the Lent season. Neither do I listen to music for the forty days of Lent to commemorate the suffering of Christ."

"I am glad the party is not during Lent, and you can attend this special celebration. I will give you the date, time, and place shortly before the event."

"Very good."

"May I call you before?"

"You may."

"Good night, Hildegard. Thank you for spending a delightful day with me."

"Thank you very much. I also enjoyed the trip to Frankfurt and our theater attendance. Good night, Horst."

We shook hands, and he left.

The next day the waiting room was packed. We treated most patients for upper respiratory infections, flu, and colds. Some got injections for anemia or other chronic diseases. We finished the morning office hours relatively late. I did not have time to go shopping for food. A sandwich with butter and salami had to be sufficient for lunch. Fewer patients came in the afternoon. By the evening, I was tired and went to bed early after I consumed another sandwich. Each month that passed, I became more comfortable taking dictations. Practicing shorthand every morning helped. I made fewer mistakes. I was grateful for that.

I enjoyed being invited by patients, meeting them personally, and, of course, sharing their delicious home-cooked meals and cakes. Mrs. Fehl asked me to celebrate with them Easter, which was April 1 this year. The clinic was closed for Good Friday. I decided to boil some eggs and decorate them with colored pencils. I drew daffodils, violets, and tulips on the eggs for Mrs. Fehl, her daughter, and her son-in-law. I decorated three eggs with red poppies, blue cornflower, and pink tulips, which I placed on the table. At home we had a good Friday tradition that we were not allowed to talk. While we were silent, my mother reminded us to think of the pain Christ suffered on the cross. Since I spent the day alone, I followed my mother's instructions faithfully. Easter Sunday arrived with a glorious sunrise. I went to church to celebrate the resurrection of Christ with the worshipers of the Marienkirche. The church choir sang the *Hallelujah Chorus* from Handel's Messiah. Before and after the sermon about Christ rising from the grave, the attendants sang joyful songs of the risen savior. We not only celebrated the resurrection of Christ but the awakening of new life in nature. Joyfully, I walked home.

I waited until shortly before noon. I took my Easter eggs and went to Mrs. Fehl's. After a friendly greeting, I gave each person one of my self-decorated eggs. They thanked me and put them on the table. Then Mrs. Fehl asked me to sit down on a beautifully decorated table with fresh spring flowers and colored Easter eggs. The daughter-in-law served a lamb roast, fresh asparagus, and German potato salad. I had not had such a delicious meal for a long time. At 3:00 p.m., we relished the desert, a Frankfurter Kranz cake filled with buttercream and decorated with colored Easter eggs and a chocolate bunny in the center.

The son-in-law, being a teacher, explained how the Easter bunny and eggs, which are fertility and life symbols, dated back to the 15th century of a German pagan celebration of the Teutonic Goddess Eostre. Rabbits being a sign of fertility and eggs of new life. These symbols were absorbed and became part of our Christian tradition. It also coincides with the Jewish celebration of Passover, a commemoration of the Jews' deliverance from being slaves in Egypt. I was fascinated by learning about other historical backgrounds of Easter.

We passed a delightful afternoon. I thanked Mrs. Fehl and her family for including me in their family celebration. Happily, I returned to my apartment. I thanked God for resurrecting Christ and for allowing me to celebrate this special day with a Christian family and not by myself. I also prayed to my living Lord and Savior to help me live my life in such a way that would reflect His image. Easter Monday was also celebrated, mostly with relatives, friends, or neighbors, and nobody worked. Since I had the day off, I decided to go during the afternoon to the Berg Schloesschen Café. What a delight to stroll through the apple orchard, watching the apple leaves sprouting and preparing the blossoms to burst open shortly. The skylark ascended and twittered a happy tune. It filled my heart with joy, not only listening to the skylark and other birds but also watching the awakening of nature after the long, dreary winter rest. Many people walked up to the café on this beautiful spring day and stopped for a treat. Luckily, I found a small empty table.

Today a fresh bouquet of violets decorated the table. Being a holiday, I ordered a hazelnut torte with a cup of coffee. The waiter also brought a small chocolate egg on a plate for the special occasion. The owner played the interlude from "Cavalleria Rusticana". Later a tenor got up and sang arias from the operetta, "The Student Prince". When he sang the drinking song, the guests joined, lifting their vine glasses or cups and swaying them happily back and forth. When the tenor paused, the owner played some Mozart, Schubert, and Beethoven compositions. I could have stayed all night long and listened to the beautiful music after not hearing any for forty days. The sun started to set, and I had to get back before it was completely swallowed by darkness.

Since the clinic was closed for two days, on Tuesday, the waiting room overflowed with patients suffering from stomach trouble, allergies, arthritis, and various other sicknesses. We finished the morning office hours late. During the next two weeks, I thought of what to wear to the banquet of Horst's graduation party. I did not own a formal or elegant evening gown. My cousin, Emmi, from East Germany, had sent me a beige dress with black flowers. She wanted me to have it dyed emerald green. In East Germany, she could not buy dye, so she asked me to have it dyed. I took it to a place to have it professionally done. It turned out very well. I tried on the dress. It fit me and looked attractive on me. So, I thought she would not mind if I wore it for this special occasion. I could not phone her, but I would explain in a letter that I wore her dress once for a special occasion. I opted not to charge her for the dyeing of the dress as a gesture of gratitude.

On Saturday, April 14, we only worked in the morning. Thank goodness, we did not have any emergency call service for that weekend. I had ample time to get ready for the banquet. Today I put on my high heels and even wore lipstick. I also created a fancier hairstyle.

At 5:00 p.m., Horst arrived. He looked elegant, dressed in a black suit, white shirt, and bowtie.

"Good evening, Hildegard. You look lovely. I also like your new hairstyle."

"Thank you."

"You look very elegant too."

"Thank you. You think you will be comfortable walking in high heels to Kauffmann's Restaurant?"

"I think I can manage."

Horst offered me his arm. I agreed to walk arm in arm to hold on to him in case I would stumble. Twenty minutes later, we arrived at the restaurant and entered a banquet room. The tables were arranged in a horseshoe fashion and beautifully decorated with different bouquets of yellow roses, red tulips, and baby's breath with a candle in the center. Horst walked over to a friend and introduced me. We both sat down at the table next to his friend. A lot of other young men and their companions had already arrived. After the waiters brought wine and appetizers, they served dinner, which consisted of a wiener schnitzel, potato dumplings, and red cabbage. Dessert consisted of a glass of fruit, topped with whipping cream, grated chocolate, and decorated with a fresh mint leaf.

"What a delicious meal."

"Yes, Kaufmann's Restaurant is known for its quality food. I have eaten here a few times already." Horst added.

As soon as the waiters cleared the tables, a small band arrived consisting of an accordion player, a violinist, and a guitarist. They began playing music for dancing.

Horst got up and invited me to dance the waltz to the melody of the happy gypsy life. I had not danced for some time. I felt delighted to be able to twirl and turn to the waltz rhythm of the music. Horst knew how to lead well, and I followed his every move promptly. We both enjoyed the various dances until midnight when the music stopped, and we all got up and sang the song: "Aufwiedersehn, Aufwiedersehn, Bleib Nicht So Lange Fort" (Goodbye, Goodbye, Do Not Stay Away too Long). We said good night to some of the table guests before we left. Above us, the new moon and the stars studded the dark sky, and next to us, the dim streetlights helped us see the way back. By now, my feet ached from walking on the cement road. When we arrived at the doctor's house door, I thanked Horst for the beautiful evening.

"I enjoyed very much dancing with you also. I feel sad that my time in Gelnhausen ends soon, and I will be heading to Alberta, Canada. Can I write to you?"

"Yes, you may. You know my address!"

"Well, Hildegard, I wish you the best for the future. Perhaps, we will see each other again."

"I wish you good luck in Canada. I do not know yet what the future has in store for me. At this time, I can't make any commitments."

He embraced me and kissed me on the forehead,

"Goodbye, Hildegard."

I responded, "Goodbye, Horst. May God bless you in the future."

And thus, we parted, feeling sad, not knowing if we would ever see each other again.

The next day, Sunday, I got up relatively late. I rested my sore feet so that I would be fit for work the following day. On Monday, checking the business mail, I found a letter from my brother Edmund. He wrote that he wanted to visit me Sunday, April 29, and stay until Tuesday, May 1ˢᵗ· I looked forward to seeing him again. But where was he going to sleep? My room had only one small bed and a bathroom shared with Ursula, the doctor's daughter. I would have to find a reasonable hotel room for him. On Wednesday, I walked to some of the hotels in town and checked which were low-priced. For now, I was happy he would come. Today, I went to the Altstadt Hotel near the Marienkirche on Kaiser Platz. Since my brother worked as a carpenter now, I thought he could afford to pay for a small hotel room. I wrote him I was glad he could visit me, and I would make a reservation for him at a hotel in town. I cleaned my room thoroughly, as well as the window. I felt terrible that I did not have an oven to bake a cake for him.

On Sunday morning, I stayed home, not knowing what time Edmund would arrive. I cooked a stew of sauerkraut, pork hocks, and potatoes. I frequently looked through the window to see if I could spot him on the motorcycle. Finally, at noon, he arrived. I ran downstairs to greet him with a big hug,

"Am I glad to see you! I hope you had a good trip?"

"The heavy traffic in Frankfurt slowed me down, but I am glad I made it safely."

"So am I."

"Where can I put my motorcycle?"

"Dr. Samietz suggested to put it behind the garage in the garden. It will be safe there."

After he parked the motorcycle, we walked upstairs.

"Welcome to my room; this is where I live now. It is small, but I am content. The only thing I miss is not having a stove with an oven. I cannot cook complete meals. Please, be seated at the table. I made you a stew of sauerkraut and pork hocks with potatoes."

I turned on my one-coil electric burner to reheat the food. I set the table ahead of time with a lace tablecloth and fresh flowers.

"You must be hungry. Let me fill your plate."

After we said grace, we ate the stew, and for dessert, I had bought a bee sting cake (Bienenstich Kuchen), filled with buttercream and topped with slivered roasted caramel almonds. We enjoyed the food but especially the cake with a cup of instant coffee.

I asked him how our mother, Horst, Emma, and Bernie were doing. He told me that Emma and Bernie are going back to the United States shortly with her husband and his family. Edmund was worried about them and wanted to go also.

"I do not like to leave you behind. Would you consider joining me?"

This question surprised me.

"I am not of age to make my own decision. I would need the permission of my mother. I am not even sure she would be willing to let me go. Meta is already gone. Emma will be leaving shortly, and Marta lives in the demilitarized zone far away from her."

"Leave that matter to me. I will see what I can do."

"If you can get our mother's permission, I can join you for a few years. I want to get to know the United States. However, I would like to return to Germany again and find another place to work."

"When I get back home, I will start applying for my immigration papers. I will talk to our mother and let you know her decision. What future do you have here, living in this small room and working hard for a meager salary?"

"I do not think I would like to stay here for a long time. Perhaps, one day, I will get married and have my own family and maybe even my own house. Hermann would be delighted if I would tell him I changed my mind."

"Please, do not think of marriage now. Think of going to America with me. You might have a better future there."

"Okay, I will come with you if you get mother's permission."

How exciting the plan sounded, but I did not want to raise my hopes too high yet. After I cleared the table and washed the dishes, I asked Edmund if he wanted to take a nap. Traveling through the congested cities must have been tiresome.

"Yes, I think I will take a short nap. It will feel good to stretch my legs."

"Good, I will be quiet and read."

I sat down at the table and opened the Bible. I had a hard time concentrating on the text in front of me. My thoughts meandered in all directions, thinking about a possible voyage to America. How will Dr. Samietz react when I tell him I will be quitting? Where and how would I end up living in America? And many other thoughts crossed my mind. After I prayed and placed this matter into God's care and asked Him to help me make the right decision according to his will, I regained my inner peace.

Edmund had fallen sound asleep. By 4:00 p.m., I woke him up. It was time to go to the hotel and check him in.

"We better go to the Altstadt Hotel now. Do you think you want to leave your motorcycle in the garden? I think it is safe here. The hotel is within walking distance from the house."

"Okay, I will only take my bag along. Let us go."

We walked to the old part of Gelnhausen, passing by the beautiful Marienkirche and the Old Town Bakery, where I shopped for bread and cakes. Before we arrived at the hotel, I told Edmund it was not a fancy but modestly priced hotel and very clean. I thought it would do for one night. When we arrived at the Altstadt Hotel, we entered the lobby. A friendly male receptionist greeted us.

"What can I do for you?"

"I am Miss Bonacker. I made a reservation for my brother Edmund for tonight."

"One moment, please, let me look at the guest register. Yes, I reserved room 305 for Edmund Bonaker. While pointing to the stairway, he instructed us how to get to the room. It is upstairs on the third floor. You can walk up these stairs."

"Do you want me to pay you now?" Edmund asked.

"Whatever you prefer, now or tomorrow, when you check out."

"I prefer to pay now. How much is the room?"

"100.00 DM or 24.00 American Dollars."

"I'll pay in DM. Here is the money."

Edmund handed him two 50.00 DM bills.

"Thank you. Wait, I get you the receipt."

"Here is the receipt and the key."

Edmund took the receipt and the key. We walked upstairs to the room; it was modestly furnished but clean and had a nice view overlooking the city.

"It will be fine for one night," Edmund remarked.

"Would you like to have dinner at my place? I bought sausages and bread, or would you prefer to eat in a restaurant?"

"I think we can eat in a restaurant. Do you know a good one in town?"

"Yes, I ate once at Kaufmann's; their food is excellent."

"Then let us go there," I told Edmund how good the wiener schnitzel tasted, which I ate at Kaufmann's Restaurant. I'd like to have a venison roast that I saw on the menu. We enjoyed the food as well as the prompt service. We enjoyed the unexpected indulgence and were invigorated by the music they played. However, we could not stay too late. Edmund had to go back tomorrow, and he needed a good night's rest before heading home. He walked me back to my place, and he would return tomorrow morning for breakfast. That night, it did not take me too long to fall asleep; I was too tired to think about the future. Since May 1 was a national holiday, German Labor Day, we also did not work. I was glad to have the extra time to spend with my brother. He wanted to leave Monday in order not to be caught in the heavy holiday traffic. I brewed coffee, set the table with all the sausages. As soon as Edmund arrived, we ate a hearty breakfast.

We talked for a while about the immigration plans. Edmund would write to me immediately after he obtained our mother's permission. He mentioned he had already begun the immigration process of getting a visa to go to the United States. Without a doubt, he did not want to leave me behind. I also would not like to be separated from my sister Emma and brother Edmund. The ultimate decision rested on my mother. I prayed that she would be understanding and let me go. The thought that we would be so far away from each other if my mother would not give me her permission made me sad.

On May 1, we celebrated Labor Day. Many persons enjoyed hiking in the forests, welcoming the new awakening of nature. The sun begged me to get out of the house and go for a walk. After lunch, I strolled through the apple orchard, with the trees in full bloom. Bees buzzed from blossom to blossom while the birds twittered happily, flying from tree to tree, catching insects. It made me forget about my immigration concern for the moment. After a two-hour hike in the forest, I went to my favorite café, Berg Schloesschen (Mountain Castle). Since it was a memorable holiday, many persons came and filled the café. However, the waiter and owner knew me as a steady customer; they found a small table by the window. I thought I would order a special dessert, crepes, for the occasion. The waiter brought a plate not only with a crepe but also garnished with fresh strawberries, blueberries, raspberries, and a scoop of ice cream. It certainly looked appetizing, and it tasted heavenly with a cup of coffee. I took a bite of each but finished the ice cream first. I ate slowly, picking a piece of strawberry or another berry to make it last a long time while listening to the piano music. After a while, a lady got up and sang popular songs. The audience sang happily along, and so did I. I went home before sunset, still humming some melodies.

A constant flow of patients in the office kept us busy. As I became more proficient in the clinic, Dr. Samietz treated me more courteously. However, each day that passed, I thought of immigrating with my brother to the United States. Anxiously I awaited mail from my brother. Finally, after one week, a letter arrived from Edmund. I could not wait to open it. However, I could not read it in the presence of the doctor or patients. I excused myself, saying I had to go to the washroom. Quickly, I opened the envelope, and my eyes skimmed over the letter to find the word permission. I saw the sentence in which my mother said yes. That is all I wanted to know for now. The rest of the letter I would read after office hours. I rushed back to the reception room to help take care of the patients. This good news made my heart race. I had a hard time staying calm and concentrating on my duties. After office hours were over, I rushed upstairs. First, I read the letter in its entirety before I fixed lunch.

Had I understood correctly? My mother gave me her consent to join Edmund immigrating to America? Then he also wrote he had an accident with his motorcycle on the way home from Gelnhausen. While he passed a truck, the piston overheated, the bike stopped, and he fell with the bike on the street's shoulder. Luckily, he fell on the soft shoulder ahead of the truck. If he had fallen on the road, the truck would have run over him and killed him. Thank God, that did not happen, and he did not injure himself severely. He waited until the piston cooled off and continued slowly home, not passing any other vehicles. Now I thought of how to apply for the immigration documents. I could not tell anyone yet about my plan. I must handle the whole process in secret. I did not want to jeopardize my job or feel embarrassed if the visa would not be granted.

Immediately I wrote back to Edmund that I would start the process next Wednesday, which I did.

I took an early train to Frankfurt so I would arrive when the American Consulate office would open. The ticket office clerk told me the American Consulate was on 30 Giessener Street and gave me directions on how to get there. A friendly clerk called me in and asked me what he could do for me. I explained to him that I was a refugee from East Prussia and that my two sisters had already immigrated to the United States and that my brother Edmund and I would also like to join them. The clerk explained that America's quota was still open, and I could apply for an immigration visa. Then he handed me a list with all the documents needed and an application for a permanent visa.

"When you have all the required documents, come back; we will start working on your application. If all documents are in order, it takes approximately half a year to get the approval or disapproval notice."

"Thank you; I will get the necessary documents to you as soon as possible. Goodbye."

By the time I left the office, it was noon. I stopped at a small restaurant and had a sandwich of bratwurst with sauerkraut. I strolled by the display windows of the textile stores. For now, I could only dream of owning expensive and elegant clothes. I walked to the train station, boarded the train, and arrived in Gelnhausen late in the afternoon. Immediately I wrote a letter to my brother Edmund. First, I asked him to thank my mother for permitting me to go to America, and I thanked Edmund for obtaining it. Then I listed all the documents that I needed him to send to me. I had only taken my identification card with me. However, I also needed to apply for a German passport. On my day off the following Wednesday, I went to the Citizen Office in Gelnhausen to inquire about which documents I needed to apply for a passport.

They required select photos and my ID card. I asked where the closest photoshop was. I had my pictures taken, then returned to the Citizen Office and gave them the pictures and my ID card. The clerk copied all my information from my ID card and told me it would take four to six weeks to get the passport.

Each day I waited for mail from my brother Edmund. Finally, the package arrived containing my birth certificate, confirmation certificate, report cards from my high school and Dr. Glaeser, and the letter of reference from my first job. The following Wednesday, I took a train to Frankfurt and presented all the required documents to the American Consulate's Immigration Office. After the clerk checked the documents, he informed me that they need to have the originals translated into English and be approved by the Immigration Department director. It would take about a month for the procedure. You can pick them up at your next visit in a month. If all reports are in order, you will have to have a complete medical examination, too.

"Goodbye, Miss Bonacker; come back in one month."

"Goodbye, sir; I will see you in a month."

Thus, I started a lengthy procedure of going back and forth to the American consulate, picking up original documents, taking new ones, and waiting until the office had checked my background. I underwent a complete medical examination, including chest x-rays and an electrocardiogram. Meanwhile, I carried on my work in the clinic without letting Dr. and Mrs. Samietz or patients or friends know my plans to immigrate to America. I only wrote letters to my brother and told him about the progress of my visa application.

As often as I had a free Wednesday, I went hiking in the forest. Listening to the birds singing and the breeze rustling through the branches delighted me. I treated myself to a quarter pound of coconut candy, which I consumed slowly. I made them last for the whole time I hiked. On the way back, I would stop and shop groceries for the next three days, mainly bread, rolls, and sausages, a pork chop or two, and a jar of sauerkraut. I continued visiting the mountain castle for my Sunday treats. Each Sunday, the owner played semi-classical or popular music to the delight of the guests. Now and then, opera divas or some famous singers would get up and entertain the visitors. Some folk singers invited the guests to sing along. Most persons had quite an extensive repertoire of folk songs and were pleased to join the singer or the pianist. I always enjoyed Sunday afternoon at the café and the hike up and down the hill, covered by apple orchards.

Meanwhile, my brother Edmund wrote that my sister Emma, her husband Gustav, and their son Bernard would go to the United States by the middle of July. I felt sad that I could not go home to say goodbye to my sister, Emma, and nephew, Bernie. But I knew Dr. Samietz would not give me time off before I met my vacation requirements. Edmund send me a photo of Bernie dressed in a German blue-and-white navy outfit, including the cap with the two ribbons in the back. He looked adorable in it. When someone asked him how old he was, he would reply, "I am three years old and do not have a wife." His reply would make people chuckle. My sister, her family, and her in-laws flew with a Flying Tigers Charter Company's transport plane. They left from Hamburg and flew to New York, then continued by train to Chicago. They decided to stay in Chicago, where many Germans lived. Finding work in a big city should be easier than in a small town.

Edmund felt sad to see our sister leave home. He hoped to join her soon. He already applied for his immigration documents in Munich, and he waited for his visa. We both remained in anticipation of the final approval. The summer passed, and fall, with all its colorful splendor, arrived in fields and forests. The apple trees in the orchard bore their ripe fruit ready to be harvested. On the way to the mountain castle, I would pick up an apple that had fallen to the ground. When the strong winds combed through the trees' crowns, they detached more apples and threw them on the ground and by the wayside. Then I would gather enough to make fried apples as a treat. However, my joy came to hear from my brother Edmund that he received his visa. During my last trip to Frankfurt, I learned that I met all immigration requirements, and my visa was also approved. Now I was sure we would join my sister Emma and her family soon in Chicago. December 16, 1956 was my designated departure date from Bremerhaven with the American military transport ship called General Harry Tayler.

Edmund instead chose to fly to the United States. His plane was supposed to leave from Hamburg by the beginning of November. I would have preferred to go with my brother by aircraft rather than traveling by ship. The ocean can be rough in winter. For now, I thanked God that we would not be separated and that we both could go to the United States. It did not matter that each one of us left on a different date. We also looked forward to seeing sister Meta and her family, who had already lived in Wisconsin for a few years. I wrote to my sister that I would like to stay with them until I found a medical position. I asked where it would be easiest to come and pick me up.

Now came the difficult question: how and when would I tell Dr. Samietz my plan and give the notice to terminate work with him. How would he react? I prayed that God would give me the right words and show me the right timing. I had to tell Dr. Samietz first and afterward my friends and patients. I waited until I had completed one year working at the clinic. On Saturday, October 13, after seeing all the patients, I went over to Dr. Samietz's desk and said, Dr. Samietz, I would like to tell you that I have received my approval to immigrate to the United States.

"You want to go where? You want to go to America?"

"Yes, my brother Edmund will be leaving in November. My departure by ship is scheduled for December 16."

"How long can you still work?"

"I think I can stay until the end of November. I thought I would give you advance notice, so you have sufficient time to find another assistant."

"I guess, if that is the case, I cannot stop you from leaving. Now that you have learned how to fulfill all work to my satisfaction and the patients like you, I had hoped you would have stayed longer. But I can't hold you here against your will."

"Thank you, Dr. Samietz. Would you also be so kind and write a letter of reference for me? I am sure if I apply for a position in the States, the new employer would like to know how I performed my duties in my previous job."

"I will do that. I know my patients will miss you. They like you."

"I know I will miss them also. I grew fond of many of your patients. But we all have different destinies to follow."

"I guess I have to let you go."

"Thank you, Dr. Samietz, for being so understanding."

I was grateful that all went well, and Dr. Samietz did not reprimand me. He was understanding and very polite. I guess patients who told me that Dr. Samietz appears rough on the outside but is gentle on the inside were right. My respect for him grew. I remained in the office and filed the records of the patients. I finished putting all items back in order in the waiting room and the examining room before going upstairs. I breathed a sigh of relief that Dr. Samietz accepted my resignation rather politely and not angrily. The next day, I told Lioba, their maid, my plans. As time passed, I shared my intention with the patients I had grown fond of. Some were sad, others indifferent to my leaving the clinic.

Before leaving Germany, I wanted to see my sister Marta and her family, who lived in the five-mile-wide military zone in East

Germany. Traveling in and out of their region was restricted, and the East German consulate, under Russian rule, granted few permissions. Persons living in East Germany were not allowed to travel to West Germany either. I was concerned if there would be a possibility of visiting her before I immigrated to America. I went to a local traveling agent and explained my position. Then I asked how to obtain a traveling permit to visit my sister in the military zone of East Germany. The travel agent asked me when I saw my sister last. I told her it was over ten years ago.

"There is a slim chance, the East German consulate might honor your request and let you see her. Do you have your ID and passport with you? When would you like to go, and for how long would you like to stay with your sister?"

"I would like to stay with her for ten days, from Monday, December 4, until Friday, December 14." I handed her my passport and personal ID card. She copied all the necessary information on an application.

"I will send the application to Berlin for approval. It might take about three to four weeks to receive an answer."

"Thank you; I will return in three weeks. Goodbye." I sure hoped and prayed to God that my wish would be granted. My sister and her family would be delighted that I could spend at least a few days with them before departing to another country.

I had only six more weeks left working at the clinic. I wrote to my mother and Edmund that I wanted to visit my sister Marta and her family in East Germany and applied for a traveling permit. However, I did not have the assurance of receiving it. I also let them know that I would be home on December 1. Edmund wrote back that he would fly Tuesday, November 13, from Hamburg to New York and then take a train to Chicago, where our sister Emma and her family lived. He would write to me as soon as he arrived in Chicago. Often, I caught myself distracted, thinking of all the things I still had to prepare before I would leave. Thoughts of excitement about going to another country buzzed like a swarm of bees in my brain. I had to force myself to focus on my work. I prayed to God that I would not make a mistake, like giving a wrong shot or causing a patient unnecessary pain or suffering. I thanked God that so far, not one traumatic incident had occurred. I hoped during the remaining time I worked that none would happen. I also wrote to my aunts and uncles and my girlfriends and Hermann that I would leave in December to go to the United States of America. At this point, I had no idea if it would be a visit for a limited time or a permanent stay. I wondered what Hermann thought of me leaving Germany and if I still would have a chance to see him. I also notified the city administration of Gelnhausen, which required registering when taking residence in the city and the date when leaving the city. Three and a half weeks later, I went to the travel agency. When I entered the traveling bureau, the clerk greeted me with a reassuring smile.

"Fraeulein Bonacker, I have good news for you. I got the traveling permit for you." Then she looked among her correspondence and handed me my visa with these words, "Just make sure you notify the village police station when you arrive in Silkerode and when you leave. Limit traveling to other cities. If you need to go somewhere else, always take your permit and passport with you to avoid unpleasant confrontations."

"Thank you for procuring the visa on time. I will follow your advice closely. Goodbye."

Happily, I returned to my room and wrote a letter to my sister Marta, knowing she and her family would be overjoyed hearing the good news about my visit.

The last Sunday in November, I took my usual walk up to the Mountain Castle Café. It was a gloomy, chilly fall day. The apple branches mourned the loss of their leaves and fruits. I also mourned the departure from my favorite café in town. The owner,

Mr. Krueger, always greeted me friendly as one of his loyal guests. Today he noticed the sadness of my expression and asked me what was troubling me. I told him that this was my last visit, and I plan to immigrate to America next month.

"Sorry to see you go, but I wish you good luck in America. Come, come, now cheer up. I will play some special music for you that I recently composed. I shall dedicate it to you as my goodbye present."

After I sat down at a table, the owner-pianist walked over to the piano and played his composition. Mr. Krueger overwhelmed me by the beauty of the music and his gesture of dedicating his composition to me. I got up and thanked him with a handshake. Then I returned to my table and ordered an apple strudel with hot vanilla sauce, one of the café's specialties, and my usual cup of coffee. The hot sauce tasted so good on this wet and gloomy day. Being chilly, not too many persons showed up this Sunday. But the present ones enjoyed their treats while listening to a variety of music. After I finished eating, I waited until Mr. Krueger finished playing the Schubert "Serenade." Then I walked over to him and said, "Mr. Krueger, I am sorry I have to leave now. I want to thank you for your composition and for all the delight you brought to me with your music and, of course, all your delicious cakes and special desserts. I shall always treasure the memories of my visits here."

"Miss Bonacker, I will also miss seeing you each Sunday. You were such a delightful guest."

He got up, embraced me, and said farewell. Then he told the customers Miss Bonacker is leaving us to go to America; let us all sing "Goodbye" (Aufwiedersehn) to her. While the clients sang a cappella, they moved me to tears. When they finished singing, I wiped my tears quickly, thanked the people and Mr. Krueger, and left. My heart overflowed with mixed emotions of sadness and gladness as I walked down the hill through the apple orchard for the last time.

Two days before I terminated my work, Dr. Samietz gave me a letter of reference with these words, "Here is the letter of recommendation. All in all, you did well, and I wish you good luck in finding the right position in America."

"Thank you, Dr. Samietz; I sure hope I will. Thank you also for teaching me so many medical procedures while working for you."

I could hardly wait to go to my room and read the content of his letter. Here is a translation of what he wrote:

Dr. med. Walther Samietz Gelnhausen, 28. November 1956
Barbarossa Str. 6 Tel 24 56

Report for Miss Bonacker, Hilde, born January 2, 1937

I employed Miss Hilde Bonacker as a commercial and medical assistant from October 10. 1955 until the end of November 1956. During that time, she performed all her required duties in the clinic. She served as my medical assistant and performed all laboratory analyses herself. I could rely on the results of her doing gastric studies, blood counts, glucose, and other laboratory tests, for she was proficient and did the tests well. Miss Bonacker also took x-rays. She managed all the medical records, correspondence, and collecting the doctor's fees from the government. She executed all her assigned work conscientiously and to my great satisfaction.

Miss Bonacker also lived in my house and was a pleasant and courteous tenant. Her manners and comportment were always flawless.

Miss Bonacker terminates her employment with me because she wants to immigrate to America. I regret losing her, but I wish her all the best for the future.

Dr. Walther Samietz

The content of Dr. Samietz's letter astonished me at first. He very seldom showed me that he even appreciated my exceptional work and flawless manners. He proved to me again that under the rough appearance was a gentle heart. I thanked God for that night and Dr. Samietz the following morning for the letter of such high recommendation. He just responded with a big smile, and so did I. All the ill feelings of the past vanished in oblivion.

On Thursday and Friday, I did the last-minute packing and cleaned the room. I wanted to leave everything spotless and in order. After we saw the last patient on Friday, I said goodbye to Dr. Samietz. Mrs. Samietz also came down to the reception room to say goodbye to me. They thanked me for having been such a capable and courteous medical assistant. In turn, I thanked Dr. Samietz for the opportunity to have acquired practical experience working for and with him. They wished me well, and so did I. Lioba, their maid felt very sad that I was leaving. We had grown fond of each other, and I knew I would miss her. Ursula, the daughter of Dr. and Mrs. Samietz, came to say goodbye Friday evening. We both had developed a cordial relationship, and she expressed how much she enjoyed confiding in me and regretted seeing me go.

Saturday morning, I walked with two suitcases to the train station to catch Frankfurt's early train. I stopped once along the way to take one more look at the Marienkirche, the ruins of the castle, the Mountain Castle, and other familiar places I had enjoyed while residing one year in Gelnhausen. I will never forget my Wednesday walks through the forest while slowly consuming my coconut candy and listening to the birds singing. I welcomed the changes in the seasons in the woods, especially the awakening of nature in spring. I watched the snow covering the dry leaves and remnants of fall with multitudes of white flakes, transforming the forest into a peaceful winter wonderland. I always felt close to God and His creation in the woods. After each walk, the beauty, wildlife, and wonders of the forest refreshed my mind and inspired my soul.

Presently my mind returned quickly to my walk to the train station. I arrived just on time to catch the early train to Frankfurt. I had to change Frankfurt's train, going to Mannheim and Neustadt before reaching Landau late in the afternoon. In Landau, I took the local train to Knoerringen-Essingen. From there, it was only a short walk to Essingen, where my mother and brother Horst still lived. Traveling by train and seeing the various sceneries passing by the window appealed to me; so did meeting interesting traveling companions. But today, my thoughts already traveled to my sister Marta in East Germany, and I did not pay full attention to the passing scenery.

Exhausted, I finally reached home. My brother Richard had come home for the weekend; when he saw me through the window, he came to help me carry my suitcases into the house. Seeing him brought back all the childhood memories from East Prussia, and I was glad that he had the weekend off. Mother and Horst were happy to see me again after a year. In the morning, we all went to church. It happened to be the first Sunday of Advent. After we sat down, I remembered when I stood alone in front of the altar the day I was confirmed and answered all the questions correctly which Pastor Armin Schlender asked. Then I looked up at the balcony, where the church choir sat. My brother Georg and I had joined the choir shortly after we arrived in Essingen. Mr. Jaeger, the conductor, taught us many religious hymns, and we always looked forward to the yearly picnic. Many memories flashed across my mind before the pastor welcomed the parishioners, and we began to sing the Advent song, "O come O come Emmanuel."

After we finished the traditional liturgy, the church choir sang, "Daughter of Zion, rejoice, rejoice, see thy king is coming to you." I looked at the balcony. I saw all the familiar singers and silently said goodbye to them. Pastor Bruenings preached the sermon on how to prepare our hearts for the coming of the Savior. After the sermon, the parishioners went to the altar to receive the holy communion. Then we sang the first three verses, "Entrust your way and what grieves your heart to the most faithful care." I sang it with such zealous trust in the unknown path that God would lead me in the future. The pastor said the benediction and dismissed us. I told my mother I wanted to wait and say goodbye to Pastor Bruenings. Mother, Richard, and Horst said they would go home, only half a block away from the church, and get lunch ready. While I waited for the pastor, I talked to neighbors and some church choir members, too. They were glad to see me but sad to see me leave the country. When Pastor Bruenings approached me, I told him that I was going to America soon, but first, I planned to visit my sister Marta in East Germany.

"I am sorry to see you go, but may God go with you and protect you always and wherever you will be."

"Thank you, Pastor Bruenings; I wish you and your family also God's blessings."

"When are you leaving?"

"Tuesday; I will be traveling to my sister Marta in Silkerode, and my ship leaves from Bremerhaven on December 16."

"Goodbye, Hildegard and God bless you. I will tell my daughter Gudrun to see you tomorrow."

"Thank you; say goodbye to Mrs. Bruenings and your family, too. Goodbye, Pastor Bruenings."

We shook hands, and I walked home. When I entered the kitchen, I could smell the duck roasting in the oven. Mother prepared my favorite meal. For dessert, she had baked an apple cake. I savored her cooking; so did my three brothers. Georg, who worked for a local winery of Mr. Feldmann, joined us in the church and for lunch. Being only fourteen years old, my youngest brother Horst seemed very sad that I was leaving Germany soon. My mother was even more sad to see her third and youngest daughter depart to another country. I tried relentlessly to cheer them up by talking with great enthusiasm about America. I also left the possibility open to returning if, for any reason, I would not like living there. They forced themselves to be more cheerful, but it was only by appearance. Sunday evening, Richard had to return to his workplace, and so did Georg, who lived in the winery. Tears flowed as we said goodbye to each other. I thanked Georg for having taken on his father's role during our escape from East Prussia. He fed the horses and helped us survive the seventy-four day long journey by horse and buggy through a bitter cold winter during World War II's horrific conditions and dangers. I will always be indebted to him and the Kirstein brothers Fritz and Gustav, who helped us bravely with repairs of wagons, supplying food for us and fodder for the horses. But mostly, I will always thank God that He protected us and kept us all alive through the dangers and bombings of World War II. Now I asked God to protect me and guide me while I began a new journey to another part of the world.

Sunday afternoon, I visited the Wistof family. Three brothers. Edelmuth, Freimuth, and Hartmuth belonged to our youth group, as did the two sisters, Helge and Heidrun of Hermann Jaeger. I was hoping to see Hermann as well. I briefly passed by to see Gudrun and Norbert Kleinschmidt and Heidi and Ingrid Freytag, who had joined my younger children's group. I was grateful for the time we had spent together and the many beautiful events we attended and sad to leave them all behind. I got back in time for dinner. After dinner, we sat around close to the radiator and reminisced about life in East Prussia. Before I went to sleep, I thanked God that He allowed me to see so many friends and neighbors before leaving. I also thanked God for His guidance and love until now. I trustingly put all my future concerns in His loving hands.

On Monday, I planned to pack two suitcases, one with my clothes for visiting my sister in East Germany, and a bigger wooden one I would send directly to Bremerhaven to the ship, General Harry Taylor. While I busily checked through my books, Mother suggested, "Take a featherbed along, which I stuffed with down feathers of the geese from our farm in East Prussia. It will always keep you warm. It will also bring back memories of how the feather beds saved us in World War II from freezing during the escape from East Prussia."

"How can I fit one into my suitcase?" I thought. But then I pondered the words of my mother, "It will always keep you warm and remind you of home." I decided to take one along.

Mother went to the closet, where she had stored the one from the boys, "Here, take this one and the linens for it, too."

"Mother, I will do that. Thank you!"

Then I looked through all my books, report cards, and notebooks. I had to be very selective with such limited space. I took all my report cards, letters of reference, my book of poetry called *The Blooming Tree* (Der Bluetenbaum), a lexicon, and my Bible. I also took three dessert plates with cups and saucers. Friends had given them to me for my confirmation. They would always remind me of the kindness of my friends and the special celebration. I packed each piece individually in paper and placed it between the down cover to make sure they would not break. I stuffed all other items I had selected to take along and the down blanket before locking the suitcase. I wrote the address of the shipping company on top of the trunk and took it to the post office in the late afternoon. Horst, who had returned from school, came with me and helped me carry the wooden suitcase to the post office. We rushed home. I went through my wardrobe and picked some warm clothes to take along also. I kept all my immigration papers, passport, and ID card in my oversized purse and some D Marks I had saved while working in the clinic.

After dinner, we talked for a while. I expressed my gratitude to my mother for making it possible for me to go to high school and permitting me to immigrate to the United States. I knew it was a great sacrifice for her to let me go, but she did not want to do anything contrary to God's plans and my aspirations. When I went to bed late and physically tired, my mind remained awake for a long time. Thoughts of the past and the future raced back and forth in my head. Past midnight I finally fell asleep for a few hours. At 5:00 a.m., the alarm clock rang. It was time to get up and get ready. My mother also got up to make breakfast. Horst woke up an hour later. He did not have to go to school until 8:00 a.m. I put my suitcase and purse by the door before we sat down and had breakfast. Neither one could put our thoughts and emotions in words; only our facial expressions revealed our hearts' feelings. The time of saying goodbye arrived. We only looked at each other, then embraced each other and let our tears flow. Then I had to let go of my mother. She uttered, "May God go with you and protect you always."

"Thank you, Mother; He will. May God be with you and comfort you."

I grabbed my handbag and Horst the suitcase, and we left. However, one part of my life stayed behind.

The day dawned when Horst and I reached the railroad station. Slowly more persons arrived. The majority went to Landau. Today I had to go in the opposite direction to Neustadt. I said goodbye to Horst when my train arrived. I embraced him and asked him to take care of our mother, saying, "She will need you even more now that all your sisters are far away from home." I held back my tears and embarked rapidly on the train. Luckily, no other person came into the wagon. I sat down, put my suitcase next to me, took out my handkerchief, and wiped my tears. The engineer blew the whistle and started the engine of the locomotive. The wheels began to turn while the steam and smoke escaped through the locomotive's chimney and left a white vapor band behind.

Mixed forests covered the Haardt Mountains and rolled by the window. Today, the deciduous trees without leaves exposed the castles and other landmarks, which I could recognize from a distance. The Palatine Forest was a hiker's paradise, rewarding them with small rivers and ponds to relax and refresh themselves. A rich flora covered the ground in the springtime and created a colorful living carpet of moss and various wildflowers. In the fall, we harvested an abundance of sweet chestnuts. I remember the many invigorating hikes we took in the forest while singing folk songs. In autumn, we would collect the fallen chestnuts and roast them on an open fire while sipping the newly fermented opaque white vine. After our stomachs were content, we would sit around the campfire and sing. In winter, we found a hill for tobogganing or skiing. I remembered when I first put on a pair of skis and went down the mountain. I did not know how to stop. I just fell on one side, got up, walked up the hill, and asked how to stop correctly on the next run. Picking berries and mushrooms in the forest were also one of my favorite pastimes. Now, the past was just a treasured memory. The future was just a mystery and dream. When the conductor came to check the ticket, he brought me back to the present. When he looked at my ticket and saw all the names of the cities where I had to change trains, he remarked,

"Fraeulein, you have a long way ahead of you. Next, you need to change the train in Neustadt going to Mannheim."

"Thank you. I will do that."

The conductor passed through the aisle when we reached Neustadt, calling, "Next stop Neustadt." I got ready to disembark. I carried my suitcase to the ticket office and asked the clerk on which track the train to Mannheim leaves? When the train rolled in, I got on. In Mannheim, I changed the train going to Frankfurt. Since I had traveled through Frankfurt several times, I was familiar with the railroad station there. I had ample time to get a pretzel and a Coca-Cola while waiting for the train going to Hanau. In Hanau, I took the train to Eisenach, which was at the border of East Germany. Even though the train stopped in the big cities along the way, I did not have to change trains until I reached Eisenach. When I embarked on the train in Hanau, I chose a compartment in the middle of the wagon, less noisy and rocky. At the stops, some persons got off the train; others got on. Some people enjoyed conversing with travelers; others read books, newspapers or even took naps. My favorite pastime while traveling by train was going to the dining room wagon, having either a meal or just dessert and a cup of coffee while watching the rapidly changing scenery passing by.

At the next stop in Schuechtern, a distinguished gentleman entered the car and sat down opposite me. After he removed his coat, hat, and gloves and put his briefcase in the upper storage bin, he began a conversation, asking me about my travel destination. I told him that my last goal was New York per ship. Now I am on the way to visit my sister in Silkerode, East Germany.

"But Fraeulein, I hope you do not have all your immigration documents with you?"

"Yes, I do.

"I think it is not safe to take them with you to East Germany. In case one of the guards at the border might be despiteful, he could take them away from you and ruin all your plans."

"I did not think of that possibility. What do you suggest I do?"

"Can't you send them home and then go back to pick them up?"

"I wished I could, but I do not have the time to go home; it is also out of my way. I will be staying with my sister in Silkerode until December 14. Then I have to travel to Bremerhaven to take the ship to New York on December 16."

"Don't you have a relative or a friend on the way to Bremerhaven, where you could send the documents and then pick them up on your return?"

I pondered for a moment. Then I thought, perhaps, I should send the documents to Hermann in Hamburg. I could stop on the way to Bremerhaven to pick them up.

"Yes, sir, I have a friend in Hamburg where I could send them and then pick them up after visiting my sister."

"That is a good idea. The next stop is Fulda. We have about half an hour. You can go to the ticket office and mail the documents from there. My destination is Bad Hersfeld. I can watch your luggage."

"Thank you, sir, that is very kind of you. I will do that. Would you happen to have a blank sheet of paper that you could spare?"

"Yes, I do. Wait, I get it for you." The gentleman reached for his briefcase, opened it, and handed me a sheet of paper. Sorry, I do not have a large envelope; otherwise, I would give it to you."

"Thank you; I have the documents in a large blank envelope. I can use the same for mailing,"

I excused myself while writing a note to Hermann. Then I put the visa and the immigration documents in the envelope and addressed them to Hermann. Since I did not have a residence, I put my mother's return address on the envelope. Then I placed it in my purse.

"Now I can mail the letter in Fulda. I hope it will arrive before I do; otherwise, I literally will miss the boat."

"I think it will. Here the mail service is reliable. May I ask what your reason is to go to America?"

"One of my brothers and two sisters are already in the States. I want to join them. America, Canada, Australia, and South America have a quota to accept only so many refugees. Since I am a refugee from East Prussia and my brother and two sisters are already there, I chose to join them in America."

"When did you leave East Prussia?"

"My mother, with seven children, fled by horse and buggy in August 1944. We traveled in treks for eight months making several stops along the way before we landed in Schleswig Holstein shortly before the war ended."

"Where was your father?"

"My father was drafted in the army two weeks before we left East Prussia. The Polish Army captured my father and held him as a prisoner and later as a forced laborer in a stone quarry and coal mines. To this date, he has not returned."

"I am sorry to hear that; Yes, World War II brought so much destruction and insurmountable suffering to so many families. I was lucky to survive. I saw so many of my comrades wounded and killed. I was fortunate to sustain only minor injuries and recovered completely. In Bad Hersfeld, we had an American prison camp in April and May 1945. Professor Ernst Hermann Ruebsam lived in Bad Hersfeld and was a prisoner in the Haune Meadow Camp himself for twelve days. Even though the war had already ended, the Americans kept him as a prisoner in the camp. Perhaps I should not tell you about his horrible experience since you are going to America? I do not want to paint a negative picture of America to you?"

"My sisters, as well as my brother, have only good things to say how the Americans are treating them. I hope they will treat me respectfully also. You can tell me what took place at the Bad Hersfeld Camp. I am very much interested in the personal stories of soldiers and civilians who survived World War II."

"When Professor Ernst Hermann Ruebsam first stepped into the camp, he could not believe his eyes. Wounded soldiers with amputated limbs wrapped in bloody bandages lay on the bare, muddy ground. No shelter or even a tent protected them from the elements or to keep them warm. They lay behind barbed wire in so-called cages. The hungry, freezing soldiers desperately called for help, but no help came. The wounded must have been brought from a hospital and just dumped into the cages. The soldiers dug holes in the ground with their bare hands, a spoon, or whatever was left with them after being stripped of their personal belongings before the guards chased them like cattle into the cages. This camp was in a swamp by the Haune river, and if the soldiers dug too deep, the groundwater would fill up the hole. Then they got out of the hole and walked around, trying to get warm. Sleeping on the damp cold ground was almost impossible for a longer period. When the side touching the ground turned too cold, the person woke up and turned to the other side or got up and walked. The bright searchlights moving over the camp all night long also prevented the soldiers from sleeping. Each morning they had to stand in line to get half a cup of water. Some even collapsed while waiting in line. At noon, the poor, living, malnourished, weak soldiers had to stand in line again to receive one meal per day. It consisted of two crackers put in one bare hand and four canned plums on the other hand. No running water or regular showers or toilets; only one latrine was dug out for each cage. Many prisoners died from malnutrition, pneumonia, and diarrhea. Soldiers and civilians suspected to be Hitler's SS members or thought guilty of war crimes were executed on the spot without a trial. If they did not run on their own accord to the place of execution, they were beaten. Screams of desperation preceded the sound of bullets, then quiet. The bodies were collected and hauled away in trucks. Nobody notified family members, just none registered nameless corpses. Even after the war had ended, the killing in these cages continued. Kill or let die was the policy of General Eisenhower who was in charge of the American

Rhein-Wiesen Camp. He prohibited any civilian or soldier from bringing food to the prisoners. The punishment for anyone caught in the act of trying to help the starving soldier was death, regardless if it was a child, a woman, or an American guard. The Red Cross had thirteen million packages of food, lots of toiletries, and even material for new uniforms. The guards denied giving the goods to the prisoners in this camp. When the Red Cross tried to expose the truth, it was quickly covered by lies."

I shook my head in disbelief—a lump formed in my throat, hearing this unbelievable report. I tried to hold back my tears of compassion for those poor prisoners. I got my handkerchief out and wiped the tears that escaped. Many tears remained unshed. I wondered which kind of stories my father will have to tell if he ever got out of the Polish prison. Then my thoughts quickly came back to the presence. I noticed that even for the gentleman, it was painful to talk about this subject as his somber facial expression revealed.

I asked, "How could such treatment of the prisoners be allowed? According to the Geneva Convention of 1929, prisoners are supposed to be treated with the same respect as soldiers of the victor's army and released after the war ends?"

"Yes, that is true. But in order not to obey the Geneva Convention, General Eisenhower, with the permission of President Roosevelt and the American government, renamed the prisoners of war to Disarmd Enemy Forces, DEF, which did not grant them the protection of the Geneva Convention."

"That is really cruel and so detrimental for the poor victims of World War II. I hope not in all camps the DEFs were treated this cruelly?"

"No, in some camps, the American soldiers guarding the camps were more compassionate and helped the German soldiers or allowed the Red Cross or the civilians to bring food to the camps. However, that was not the case in Bad Hersfeld. American trucks picked up the camp inhabitants and transported them to the Bad Kreuznach Camp by the middle of May, where conditions were even worse. At first, the prisoners had a glimmer of hope to be taken to the headquarters to be released. But when they landed in Bad Kreuznach, desperation replaced their hope. The millions of prisoners taken after May 8, the day of capitulation, were supposed to be released. But the allies already planned to keep them as forced laborers. They used the argument that the allies never signed a peace treaty with Germany. The German Prisoner of War (POWs) had no rights and protection after changing their status to Disarmed Enemy Force, DEF. Neither were their names registered in the camps. They removed all ranks from officers and generals. The ones who survived these atrocities had no right to claim any compensation. That's why of the three and a half million prisoners, one million could not be accounted for."

I asked the gentleman, "How could such treatment be permitted? Where was the United Nations who had written the Atlantic Charter that victors and vanquished should be treated equally? Why didn't the Press report these unfair practices?"

"It was very tragic after the Third Reich collapsed. Germany had no central government to defend itself. The four allies divided Germany into four parts; Russia occupied East Germany, England the northern part, France the western part, and the United States the central and southern part of Germany. The allies ruled each zone by their military laws. Germany was at their mercy. France also took over eight Rhein Meadow camps. They shipped many prisoners to France.[28] Two thousand of them were in such poor physical condition that they died en route. One-third of them were just living skeletons and too weak to work. It became known that the Division of General Philippe Leclerc doused the German prisoners with gasoline, then watched them burn alive. He also ran with his tanks over the prisoners and crushed them to death. Lieutenant

Gallay drove five hundred prisoners into a barn. Then he threw a hand grenade in the barn and watched after the explosion, limbs and parts of the human body fly up in the air. Guards shot the survivors with machine guns.

"Yes, little is known how inhuman the four allies, United States, Britain, France, and Russia, treated not only the prisoners of war but also the German people. Like you, the refugees from the eastern part of Germany lost their homes and had to escape suffering so much. The families or elderly persons who remained were stripped of their belongings and driven by the Russians and Poles from their homes like animals. They were never allowed to return. The victims were left with broken bodies, bleeding hearts, crushed spirits, and plunged into the night of darkness and oblivion but not forgotten by God and by the persons who love God, family, friends, and people who love the truth. They will seek the truth and find it."

When the gentleman paused, I added, "Only God knows the whole truth. We find bits and pieces while searching for the truth. We try to put the knowledge we gained in the right perspective. We get a different picture than what we were originally told by the propaganda, the press, newspapers or white-washed reports covering the truth with lies."

The gentleman continued, "That is true. Often it takes generations to suffer from the stigma of the unfair propaganda spread by the country that wanted to enter into the war. The propaganda paints a horrible picture of the country against which it chooses as its enemy to justify the entry into the war to fight and conquer the portrayed enemy. However, worldwide propaganda remains in the people's minds; only the survivors know, and the truth seekers will get a clearer picture of reality. James Bacque, a Canadian journalist, visited such camps and described the deplorable conditions he found. However, Professor Ernst Hermann Ruebsam lived from May 9 to May 21, 1945, in the Bad Hersfeld Camp, and he told us the same stories.[29] He said, '*It is the grace of God to have survived these cruelties and grace not to have been affected by them.*' On May 21, An American guard took Prof. Ruebsam to a barrack to discharge him. He had the luxury to take a shower for the first time in twelve days and to sleep one night under cover rather than on the cold bare ground under the open sky. Before he and other comrades were released, the American guard took them outside overlooking their town, saying, '*We did not come to liberate Germany. We did not occupy Germany to liberate the Germans. Germany will be occupied a conquered enemy nation,*' Prof. Ruebsam felt humiliated by these remarks."

"What a humiliating remark. You and I are still considered enemies of America because eleven years have passed since Germany is still occupied by the United States and the three allies. Do you think the time will come when the allies will leave our country, and Germany will regain sovereignty?"

"We sure hope so, but I do not know if or when that might happen. Another tragic exploitation of Germany was *Operation Paperclip.* Even two years before Germany surrendered, United States secretly pursued programs harvesting technical and scientific data and patents. Secret agents collected names of top German scientists. As soon as the war ended, the leading scientists, including Wernher von Braun, an aerospace engineer, and whoever would be useful to further the rocket program, were taken to America. There were also other teams to exploit Germany by confiscating scientific documents, research facilities, and aircrafts. Russia had a similar program called *Ossawakim.*

As soon as the Russians occupied East Germany, their government collected two thousand scientists and specialists to serving them and transported them and their families forcefully to Russia. They also dismantled many factories and shipped the machinery and equipment to Russia.

England had Operation *Epsilon*. Ten German scientists were captured in 1945 and taken to Farm Hall near Cambridge to be interrogated for six months. Farm hall wiretapped the scientists' rooms to listen to the scientists' conversations to determine how advanced Germany was in constructing the atomic bomb. England treated these scientists luxuriously. However, regular German prisoners were also renamed DEF (Disarmed Enemy Forces) and stripped of their rights of the Geneva Convention. The prisoners worked as forced laborers, not receiving enough food; they were malnourished and mistreated by the British government, who also captured civilians they thought to be communists."

"Heinz Kraemer, the leader of the youth group DJO I had joined, told me how respectfully the guard in the English prison treated him. He invited him to celebrate Christmas with his family. His wife was German, and she wanted to hear German Christmas songs again, which he sang for them. He will never forget their act of kindness and thoughtfulness."

"Yes, the people of each country are often different and more compassionate than the government officials or their military commanders. One should never generalize. Good and evil coexists and always will. War will allow the evil person to act out his lust for power and greed and eliminate or torture those in their way. Even in the most tragic circumstances, a good person will act with compassion and kindness, helping fellow humans regardless of faith, race, or nationality. It would be ideal if people worldwide would live by the golden rule, *"Treat others as you wish others to treat you."*

"That certainly would transform the world if every person would live by the golden rule. It would eliminate wars and much human suffering. The world would be a more civil and a safe place to live in. God commanded us to love Him first and our neighbor as ourselves. If we can treat our fellow human beings the way Christ treated the people and love and forgive others, we would coexist and live in peace; yet hate evil."

"I would add, as Christians, we can transcend the golden rule. We can learn to act as Jesus showed us to act by loving unconditionally."

The conductor went through the hallway and announced, "Fulda next stop."

I excused myself and got ready to disembark to mail the letter. I immediately went to the window where tickets were sold and asked how long it would take for a letter to get from Fulda to Hamburg. The clerk at the window assured me it takes approximately a week or less. I handed the envelope with all the documents to the clerk and mailed it. I certainly hoped the letter would arrive in Hamburg before I did. I also had to change my railroad ticket going from Hannover to Hamburg and from Hamburg to Bremerhaven. I was grateful I had enough money to pay for the unexpected, additional postage, and fare. I returned to my wagon and thanked the gentleman for watching my suitcase.

"I sure hope the mail will arrive on time."

"I think so; the postal service is pretty punctual."

After we passed through Huenfeld, the train stopped in Bad Hersfeld, where the gentleman got off.

"Goodbye, Fraeulein, you were a pleasant traveling companion, and I wish you the best in America."

"Thank you, sir. I am glad you cautioned me about not taking my immigration documents with me to East Germany. Thank you for describing the German prisoners' fate in Bad Hersfeld, England, France, and Russia. I wish you the best for the future, also. Goodbye, sir!" We shook hands and parted. I remained in my train compartment, and the thoughts of the German prisoners' tragic destiny settled in my mind, and I could not delete them. I looked out of the window without really being aware of the passing scenery. Bebra was the following stop before I reached Eisenach and the border of East Germany.

In Eisenach, all passengers had to get off the train. The persons who wanted to continue by train into East Germany walked over to a checkpoint of the heavily guarded border. When I reached the guards, they checked my passport, the special permit, and my ID. Then they asked me to open my suitcase. They went through every item not only in the suitcase but also in my purse. When they found everything in order, they asked me where I was going and how long I would stay with my sister. He continued, "Make sure you go to the police station immediately when you arrive in Silkerode and when you leave also. Should you want to go to another village, you must notify the police where you will be going and how long you will be staying there."

"Yes, sir, I will do that."

I pushed my clothes down in the suitcase and closed it. Then I asked the guard where I could get the train to Erfurt. I followed his directions, and after waiting a while, I embarked on the train to Erfurt. I sure was glad that I did not have my immigration documents with me. As thoroughly as the guards checked through everything, they would have found them and could have confiscated them. I thanked God that a strange gentleman advised me to mail them before I entered East Germany.

I noticed such a difference between West Germany and East Germany. The trains in West Germany were well maintained, but in East Germany, hardly anything was done to the trains or the buildings since the war ended. The buildings were gray, some in dire need of repair. Even the facial expressions of the persons here were somber. Hardly anyone talked to each other. I also remained quiet, and my thoughts could not free themselves from the German prisoners of war's ill fate and how the Russian military government controlled each person's life here. The winter scenery looked gray and dreary also. Now and then, the snow-covered mountaintops created a pleasant sight. In Erfurt, I had to change trains to go to Nordhausen. Even the train station in Erfurt looked run down, and the walls were in dire need of painting. I could not believe the difference a government makes to the country and people's lives.

When I arrived in Nordhausen, I found the conditions the same. From Nordhausen, I took the local train to Zwinge and arrived in the late afternoon. From there, I had to walk to Silkerode. Since I had no way of letting my sister know my arrival time, nobody could come to meet me at the train station. I had to walk over two miles from Zwinge to Silkerode. At first, I felt good to move after sitting most of the day on trains or railroad stations. But after a while, my feet ached, and my arms grew tired from carrying the suitcase.

Chapter 14
Visiting Sister Marta

MEANWHILE, THE SUN descended lower and lower. I tried to increase my pace to get to my sister's house before it was completely dark. I felt exhausted but happy that I finally arrived at my sister's home shortly after sunset. My sister Marta, brother-in-law Hermann, nephews Erhard and Bernhard, and my little niece Beate, whom I had not met yet, were thrilled to see me, and so was I. After the heartfelt welcome, Marta asked me to sit down at the dining table, which she had set ahead of time. She served bread and homemade salami, and liver sausage. Being hungry, I savored the homemade sausage and cake. After I helped to clear the table, I excused myself.

SISTER MARTA AND HER FAMILY

Niece Beate

I was tired and looked forward to a good night's sleep. Before Marta took me upstairs to a loft with a bed in a small room, she showed me where the downstairs washroom was. I got ready and went upstairs to the bedroom. Before I undressed in the cold room, I knelt in front of the bed to pray. I thanked God that the train ride went well and that I could visit my sister Marta and her family after many years of separation. I put on my nightgown, and quickly crawled under the feather bed and fell asleep. The next morning, I got up relatively late. By the time I got downstairs, I had found Marta alone in the kitchen. Hermann had gone to work for the village administration in the local town hall. Erhard and Bernhard attended grammar school, and Beate went to kindergarten. Marta cleaned the kitchen and got all the ingredients together to prepare lunch. Lunch is the main meal of the day and is usually eaten at noon or after the children come home from school. Since the village administration office was within walking distance from the house, Hermann would come home for lunch. I peeled potatoes and cleaned and chopped the vegetables she stored in the cellar.

While we worked, we talked. I asked her how life is in the five kilometers border zone.

"At first, it was not so bad; we were able to travel to the surrounding villages, but now the guards are so strict, and we can't cross the border into West Germany. We cannot get permission to visit our family in West Germany unless we are retired. The Russian government is afraid a worker would not return to East Germany. If they catch someone crossing the border illegally, they shoot them on the spot."

"How tragic; I can't believe what a difference there is between East and West Germany. Here everything is run down, while many buildings are reconstructed and already repaired in West Germany."

"Yes, it is difficult to get material, also to have enough money to afford to buy material when it is available. Our house is old and needs a lot of work done, but we can only do a little at a time. I am grateful we have the space to raise two pigs and poultry, so my family has enough to eat. We sell one pig to get extra money to buy other needed items. We also have a big vegetable garden. I preserve in glasses and cans a lot of fruits and some vegetables for the winter that we store in the cellar."

"Do you still have to have stamps for butter, flour, and sugar?"

"Yes, we still do and a few other items, too. I am glad we can get rye bread and rolls without stamps and good quality, too."

"Where do you get all the fodder for your pigs and poultry?"

"We are fortunate to have four acres of land. We till it and sow rye, oats, and wheat. Unfortunately, we do not have any machinery. We do all things by hand. It is hard work. The boys have to help Hermann and me tilling the soil and harvesting the grain as well as the potatoes."

"That is hard work for eight- and nine-year-old boys."

"It is hard work, but every member of the family has to pitch in, even younger boys. I wished they could avoid working so hard at a young age, but it is a matter of survival. Neighbors also help each other when needed."

I did not realize how quickly the morning had passed. It was already noon when Hermann walked in the door, followed by the children. I helped the children remove their heavy winter coats, caps, and scarves and gave each one a big hug. They had already removed their shoes at the entrance and put on slippers to keep the inside of the house clean. Marta prepared a rabbit stew, mashed potatoes, and a red beet salad for lunch that we all enjoyed. Hermann took a short nap before he returned to work. The boys went to feed the rabbits. They also brought some more firewood into the house. Beate, as little as she was, helped to clear the table and with doing the dishes. Erhard and Bernhard did their homework for school. After Marta and I finished the dishes, she sat down by the tiled stove (Kachelofen) in the living room and knitted a pair of socks. I asked Beate if I should tell her a fairytale. She wholeheartedly agreed. I took her on my lap. We sat down next to the tiled stove to keep warm. While the flames were crackling and dancing among the logs, I told her the fairytale of Hansel and Gretel. She listened attentively, and when I mentioned the witch in the story, her eyes grew big, and she feared the witch would throw Hansel and Gretel into the burning oven. But when Hansel pushed the witch into the oven, she took a deep breath and exclaimed, "That is good that the wicked witch died, and Hansel and Gretel found their way home again." I concluded. "and they lived happily ever after."

Before dinner, Marta, Beate, and I set the table to have everything ready for Hermann's return. We had a lively conversation while dining. Erhard and Bernhard told their mother and father what they had learned in school today. Beate expressed her delight that Aunt Hilde told her a fairytale of Hansel, Gretel, and the wicked witch. After dinner, the boys played some board games; then the children went to bed. Marta continued knitting. Hermann was wearing an eye patch. I was curious and asked him how Hermann sustained his eye injury.

"When the army drafted me, I was ordered to build reinforcement walls on the coast of France and Norway. In 1941, when the Russians invaded East Prussia, my battalion was sent to the Eastern Front, and I ended up in Stalingrad. In one of the battles, a bullet entered my skull on the left side. The direction of the shell changed and escaped through the left eye-opening, completely shattering the eye. I was admitted to the hospital in Berlin, where I stayed for a long time. Being declared unfit to fight, the doctor sent me home. I am grateful the Russians did not capture me, but many of my comrades became prisoners of war. Most of them were sent to Siberia as forced laborers and never returned home. The army rewarded me with the iron cross for saving the life of a wounded comrade.

"That is so tragic that you lost your eye! Didn't you get an artificial eye for esthetic reasons?"

"Yes, I had one artificial eye made. It was attached to the eyeglasses. When I go to work, I wear the glasses with the eye. At home, I remove the glasses and just wear an eye patch."

"Do you still have pain or discomfort?"

"Yes, especially when the weather changes. I also get frequent headaches if I work too hard physically. But I learned to live with this problem."

"Yes, many persons will have to learn to live with problems inflicted on them by World War II. I wonder if my father will ever return from Poland. He was captured eleven years ago as a prisoner of war and still is not home."

"Yes, it is a tragedy that the German prisoners of war were not given the protection of the Geneva Convention as they deserved."

"During the train ride, I met a gentleman from Bad Hersfeld, where an American prison camp of German soldiers was located on open fields behind barbwire. He told me how subhuman standards existed in the camps and how cruel the American guards treated the poor captured soldiers. I always thought the American generals were the most humane. However, General Eisenhower was an exception."

"Unfortunately, the war brings out either the best or the worst character traits in persons, especially in high-ranking officials."

"Let us forget about the war now and think of something more pleasant. What are your favorite occupations?"

"I like weaving baskets and making brooms as well as repairing shoes or other items for the neighbors to earn a little extra money. The veteran pension I get and the small salary I receive from the city is not sufficient to raise a family and take care of the buildings."

"That is hard work for you and Marta."

"Yes, the boys help after they come home from school and do their homework. They get fresh greens to feed the rabbits and clean their cages. They are good boys and help a lot. Even Beate, as little as she is, tries to help her mother in the kitchen."

"I am glad you have enough food for your family. A lot of families who live in big cities go hungry."

"Yes, the city dwellers in East Germany have a hard time getting a sufficient supply of anything, especially food. Sometimes they stand in line for hours to get some meat, fruits, or fresh vegetables. We at least have a garden to grow vegetables and can raise poultry and pigs. Marta knows how to can and preserve many things, so we do not go hungry. The four acres of land we have are enough to grow wheat, oats, and rye to feed the cow, pigs, and poultry."

"I am glad to hear that. How do you till your land?"

"We harness the cow before the plow to turn the soil and then before the rake to break up the clumps of dirt."

"What about mowing the fields?"

"I mow with a scythe by hand, and Marta gathers the sheaves. The boys stack up the sheaves in piles for the grain to dry. Then we take them with the cow and a cart in the barn. One of our neighbors has a threshing machine. He comes over to help us to thresh. We also save the straw and mix it in the feed for the animals.

"That sure is a hard and tedious task."

"Yes, that it is, but we do not go hungry. I am grateful for that."

I looked over to Marta, who was busily knitting. She already had one sock completed and the second half done. I asked her.

"Marta, do you also like to crochet? Perhaps you can show me a new pattern for crocheting borders around handkerchiefs?"

"Tomorrow, I will show you some patterns you can choose. I have a few plain handkerchiefs that you can use."

"Thank you, that is nice, then I can be doing something also."

We talked until the flames in the tile oven were buried under the ashes. We went to bed and buried ourselves under our down covers.

The next day the sun brought delight to us, and the surroundings looked brighter. The boys went to school and Beate to kindergarten. I helped Marta tidying up the kitchen and prepare some vegetables to be cooked for lunch. Marta also baked a cake for the weekend, which we would decorate on Saturday.

After lunch, Marta got out the handkerchiefs. She gave me some white and light pink yarn. With the fine crocheting hook, Marta showed me how to crochet a lace-like border around it. When I finished one row, she showed me the next step. When Hermann came home from work, we ate dinner. The children enjoyed spending time with their father before they went to bed. Marta knitted, and I crocheted. Hermann was always ready to help neighbors wherever he could. Tonight, he repaired a pair of shoes for his neighbor. He first cut the patterns of the soles and heels from a piece of thick leather, then used glue and short nails to attach them to the soles and heels of the shoes. Marta enjoyed listening to music. Hermann had bought her a radio. In the evening, she turned to a station broadcasting Operetta melodies. She would happily hum along. I also liked songs from the different composers, operas and operettas; so did Hermann. While our hands toiled, our hearts rejoiced with the music, and the flames crackled and danced in the oven until it was time to go to bed. Since the children had no school on Saturday, they slept later, and so did Beate. Just the three of us had breakfast together. Marta and Hermann asked me what motivated me to go to America. I told them that I decided to join my brother Edmund and my two sisters Emma and Meta. Edmund did not want to leave me behind. He convinced my mother to permit me to go, too. However, since we both applied at different American consulates, Edmund in Munich, I in Frankfurt, we could not go together. He left by plane in November, and I will be departing on December 16 by ship from Bremerhaven.

"Do you already have a place where you will stay or work?"

"No, not yet. I will first go to my sister Meta and her family. Later I might join my sister Emma and brother Edmund in Chicago. I will see how things go."

"Do you want to stay there permanently or return to Germany again?"

"I do not know that, either. I trust God; He will show me His way.

I will write to you and let you know where I will be and what I will be doing."

"I certainly hope you will not be disappointed."

"I hope so, too."

Meanwhile, the children got up and were ready for breakfast. Marta made flour pancakes for them with scrambled eggs and bacon and a cup of hot chocolate. They devoured it gleefully in no time. Then the boys went with their father to feed the cow, the pigs, and poultry, while Beate stayed in the kitchen and cleared the table. Beate did not want to leave the kitchen today. She knew her mother would make the filling for the special bundt cake she baked yesterday. Marta cooked a generous portion of vanilla pudding. She set it aside to cool. She cut the cake into three layers, then spread some cherry jam on two layers. Marta gradually added small butter portions when the pudding was cold enough while beating it with an eggbeater. When the consistency was firm, she put it between the three layers and over the outside of the cake. Then she sprinkled ground hazelnuts over the cake, decorated it with the little stars of whipping cream, and placed canned cherries on each star's top. It looked luscious. Marta left some buttercream in the bowl for Beate to lick. Her eyes would light up every time she put some buttercream in her mouth. Even my mouth was watering, looking at the beautiful cake. But we had to wait one more day.

Saturday evening was the bathing time for the family. After the family took their baths, Marta threw out the bathwater and filled the aluminum bathtub with fresh water. I first knelt and washed my hair with soap, then used a vinegar solution as a conditioner. It felt good to soak in the warm water. Marta warmed up a towel next to the stove to dry my hair and my body. I felt so refreshed and clean. We washed our faces in a bowl of warm water during the week and took what we called a Russian bath, each using a wet washcloth to clean our bodies.

On Sunday morning, we all put on our best clothes. Only Hermann went to church. This was the only Sunday I would spend with my sister, Marta; she wanted to prepare a special Christmas dinner. Marta roasted a goose, butchered two days before. She also made potato dumplings and red cabbage. We all helped Marta peeling and grating potatoes for the dumplings. Beate and I set the table. We used the best tablecloth and china for this special occasion. We put the wreath of pine branches, called an Advent wreath, with the four candles on the table. We lit two candles for the second Sunday of Advent. Hermann said a blessing, and we all got to savor the roasted goose and the delicious side dishes.

What a treat that was for me, and it was not even Christmas yet.

"I am so happy you could come to visit us before you go to America," Marta said.

"So am I."

We waited anxiously for the cake which we enjoyed at 3:00 p.m. Marta tuned in to a radio station with Advent songs that we were able to sing along. It was so festive and reminded me of home. The cake tasted scrumptious. Now I understood why friends and neighbors asked my sister to bake this delicious cake for their special occasions. Thinking of my mother being without her daughters decorating the Christmas tree and preparing dinner, a certain sadness entered my heart. I also wondered how I would spend Christmas this year on the ship. I did not want anyone to notice my sadness. I looked at the happy children and rejoiced with them. I thanked God and my sister and brother-in-law for celebrating this particular day, commemorating our Lord and Savior Jesus Christ's birth, and bringing back many childhood memories.

The next day, when I woke up, I found snow on the loft. I noticed the roof had a hole where the snow blew in. The children welcomed the snow. They could go tobogganing on the hill in their backyard. I told Beate I would pick her up from kindergarten. We waited until the boys got out of school and walked home together. The snow had built up a few inches by now, and Erhard gathered enough snow to press it into a snowball. He threw it at me gently. I told them that it was all right with me if we would get into a snowball fight. Every time a ball hit me, they laughed. I asked Beate to help me fight against the boys. She formed the balls quickly and then hit one of her brothers, shouting, "I got you!"

After lunch, the boys did their homework and chores quickly so they could go tobogganing. Hermann had made a sled for each boy. Beate took turns riding along with her brothers. When the boys finished their homework, they asked me if I wanted to come and watch them toboggan. They climbed up the hill, pulling the sled. Then they sat on the sled and came rushing down the hill. I observed how they turned or slowed down the sled with their feet. After a few runs downhill, they asked me if I wanted to try. I agreed and walked up what seemed a steep hill to me. Then Erhard handed me his sled. "Here, Tante Hilde, sit down on the sled. Hold on to the rope and the side of the sled. When you get down, put down the right foot if you want to turn right and the left foot if you want to go left."

"Yes, I will do that. Bernhard, you wait and come after me. I do not want to collide with you."

I sat on the sled, Erhard gave me a push to start, and I dashed down the hill; I hardly had time to turn and almost ran into the barn on the bottom of the hill.

"Good, Tante Hilde. Wait for me at the bottom of the hill. I will come down to get the sled. Do you want to go once more?"

"No, thank you, I better go inside. It is getting too cold for me."

"Just leave the sled there. I will come down with Bernhard and get it."

"Good, I see you later inside."

I found Marta knitting and Hermann starting to weave a small basket. After I warmed up my hands, I picked up my handkerchief and began crocheting. I was curious about the type of work Hermann was doing.

"Hermann, can I ask you a question without distracting you from your weaving?"

"No, go ahead. What would you like to know?"

"Which type of work do you do for the town?"

"Our village has only a little over four hundred inhabitants, and not everybody has or can afford to buy a radio. I listen to the news each day. I go through the village and announce through a speaker the important news. I keep the people informed. I also do book-keeping. When I see streets or other infrastructures needing repair, I report it to the mayor, and he sends out a crew to do the work. I also make sure the property owners pay their real estate taxes. If a person is delinquent, I go to their houses to collect the taxes or give a warning if they cannot pay right away or arrange for a plan they feel comfortable with."

"I can see you have quite a responsible position in the village administration."

"Yes, I do. However, the most frustrating thing is not getting material for repairing streets or buildings or waiting for a long time for delivery. Unfortunately, when the Russians occupied East Germany, they dismantled most factories and took machinery and equipment to Russia. They are lying piled up in Russia without being used. I do not understand why the Russian government did not continue to manufacture East Germany's goods as they do in West Germany. Things would have been much easier to maintain the roads as well as the buildings."

"Yes, it is such a tragedy that the four allies occupied Germany. It seems that the people in East Germany under the Russian occupation are the worst off. I sure hope that one day all four military occupations will cease, and we can have our own government again."

"We all hope so, especially for our children; now, they and we are like prisoners in our own country, especially where we live, the so-called five-kilometer border zone. In some areas, the border goes through a town and separates families and neighbors. The guards kill many persons who try to escape by hidden mines or by self-shooting guns. We are not even allowed to visit our relatives in West Germany. At least you can travel freely in all three occupied zones. In West Germany, the economy is so much better than here."

"That is true. I wished for your sake that your area would have been in the American zone also rather in the five-kilometer border zone of the Russian occupation."

"We certainly would have been much better off under the American occupation than the Russian. My dream for my children is to have a free Germany again, not ruled by a communist dictator, but by a democratic government ruled by their own people and permitting them to elect their leaders."

"Yes, we all hope and wish that it will happen one day."

"It is strange how Karl Marx's thoughts from his two manifestos about capitalism and socialism caused the 1917 Russian Revolution thirty years after he died. Vladimir Lenin overthrew the three-century tzarist rule and replaced it with a new proletarian government based on the atheist Karl Marx's belief. Karl Marx was born in Trier, Germany, to Jewish parents. He settled in London and became internationally known for his socialistic and communistic ideas."

"Unfortunately, the communist dictators only enslave the people, making them dependent upon the government. You can see the stark difference between East and West Germany. It is easy to be a communist in a free country, but not a free person in a communist country," Hermann added.

"How true that is. We all hope that one day all the troops will leave Germany and it can regain its sovereignty again as a free country ruled by its people."

"It certainly would make you and your family's life so much easier."

Having seen the hardship of my sister's family and the grave condition of East Germany, I prayed that the military occupations of Germany would cease, and the refugees could return to their place of birth. I wished every citizen would be able to travel in their own country and abroad without restrictions. I prayed that the prisoners still held in other countries, like my father, would be released and return to their families.

Soon I had to think about my traveling to Hamburg. Only three days remained. During the day, we did chores and cooked. My niece enjoyed me picking her up daily from kindergarten. At times, I also took walks with the boys after they had done their homework and chores. In the evening, we relaxed doing handwork and recalling memories of life at home in East Prussia. On Thursday, I packed my suitcase, and by Friday morning, I was ready to leave. I felt sad saying goodbye to the children before they went to school. The children did, too. They asked, "When will you come back, Aunt Hilde?"

Sadly, I had to answer, "I do not know."

My brother-in-law took off from work Friday, so he and my sister could accompany me to Zwinge. When we arrived at the railroad station, I said goodbye to Hermann and thanked him for coming along. Then I embraced my sister Marta. Profound sadness filled our hearts, not knowing when or if we would see each other again. Our tears and tight embrace demonstrated more love than words could have expressed. She held me in her arms for some time before she could find words to say goodbye.

"God go with you and protect you. Write to us as soon as you arrive in America. Goodbye, my dear sister, Hilde."

"Goodbye, my dear sister Marta. God protect you and your family always until we will see each other again."

I quickly embraced Hermann before he and my sister Marta left the railroad station. I remained to wait for the train. The train arrived shortly. I put my suitcase on the platform first and then walked up the steps onto the train. I found an empty railcar, where I entered and made myself comfortable. No other passengers came, which was preferable for me. I was still heartbroken from saying goodbye to my sister and her family. The train rocked, riding through the winding mountain valley on the narrow train tracks. Now and then, I looked out of the window, observing the snow-capped Harz mountains and the dark forests reaching up from the valley to the middle of the peaks. Winter transformed the scenery into a magical, peaceful picture. It also calmed my mind before I reached Nordhausen half an hour later.

There I changed the train going to Hannover. When the train reached the border, the East German guards came and checked all the documents again. They also asked which items I had purchased. Fine Meissen porcelain was off-limits from taking out of the country and some other things too. They let me cross the border into the West when they found no prohibited articles in my suitcase and all my IDs and permits in order. However, they made sure all the citizens from East Germany and the conductors remained in East Germany. Only West German passengers could disembark, cross the border, and travel on other trains through West Germany. I thanked God that I did not encounter any problems with the patrol guards and reentered West Germany safely. I could not believe the difference between East and West Germany. It did not look like it was once the same country. I realized how a government could make or break a nation.

The train passed through the beautiful stretch of the Harz Mountains, leaving the highest peak (3743 feet) called Brocken behind. I enjoyed watching the mountain winter scenery that slowly changed into the rolling hills. At times, the train tracks followed the riverbed of the Leine. Branches and rocks formed beautiful ice sculptures on both river's shores while the water still flowed in the center. Almost three hours later, we reached Hannover, where I had to change trains. In October 1943, during World War II, the train station building was heavily bombed and mostly destroyed. Only in June 1945 was the first passenger train service reinstated. In 1948, the reconstruction of the buildings and tracks began. I noticed the drastic difference between the run-down train stations in East Germany and the reconstructed, well-maintained railroad station in Hannover. Here, I took the train going to Hamburg. After I settled in, I asked the conductor who came to check the tickets for the dining car location.

I went there, sat down at a small table, and ordered smoked salmon with all the trimmings on a special bun and a cup of peppermint tea. The warm vapor from the teacup felt so cozy when looking at the cold winter scenery passing by the window. I savored each morsel of the smoked salmon slowly. When I returned to the train car, I felt relaxed and dozed off. Only when I heard the conductor calling, "Next stop Hamburg-Altona!" I woke up. I put on my coat, got my suitcase down, and was ready to disembark the train, and so were many other passengers.

Chapter 15
Time in Hamburg

As the train slowed down and came to a halt in Hamburg, I looked for Hermann. I did not see him. The thought raced through my mind, "What if the letter with the documents did not arrive? What will I do then?" I decided to stay in one place and wait until all the passengers left. I assumed if Hermann were here, he would do the same so that he could spot me. Finally, all the passengers had cleared the tracks, and I saw Hermann standing at the train's beginning. What a relief. Now I knew he received my letter with my immigration documents. First, I waved, so did he. I grabbed my suitcase and rushed toward him and Hermann toward me.

"What a pleasant surprise to see you." I put down my suitcase to say hello to him. He embraced me and expressed his joy in seeing me again.

"You have no idea how glad I am to see you here, Hermann. Now I know my documents arrived."

"Yes, they just arrived yesterday. You sure are lucky." He picked up my suitcase in one hand and took my hand in the other. We walked hand-in-hand joyfully through the railroad station, being completely oblivious of our surroundings. Hermann ordered a taxi and took me to the place where he lived. He had arranged with his landlady where I could spend the night. As soon as we arrived, Hermann introduced me to his landlady, Mrs. Holz. She was very courteous. Since it was late in the afternoon, she offered us cake and coffee. We engaged in a conversation. She asked me many questions about my trip to the United States and what my purpose was.

I asked her about her family and if she lived in Hamburg during World War II.

"Yes, it is a miracle I survived the big attack of July 25, 1943. Sir Arthur, called Bomber Harris, hated the Germans and sent 792 planes one minute after midnight, and dropped 8,000 tons of bombs over Hamburg, destroying most of the inner city. He used long aluminum strips, called windows, picked up by radar instead of the attacker's airplanes. The Royal Air Force attacked Hamburg at night and the American Air Force during the day, destroying factories and public buildings and killing thousands of people, mostly women and children. Some burned alive, and many were disabled for the rest of their lives. The attacks and firestorms continued for ten more days. Those days and the year 1943, I will never forget. When we dug ourselves out of the rubble, the flames and smoke covered most of the halfway-destroyed city. Skeletons of houses and buildings rose like ghosts from the smoldering debris. Bombs partly destroyed my house; my kitchen and living room were usable until I found a way to rebuild the rest of the house. A lot of people had lost everything and had to leave the town or build a temporary shelter for themselves from the rubble."

I could feel her anguish while she recalled the tragic bombing of Hamburg. Having gone through air raids myself, I expressed my sympathy for her.

"I am so sorry you had to go through this horrible experience. Thank goodness it was not during the winter; otherwise, many persons would have frozen to death. I am glad you survived all the carnage, and that the inhabitants rebuilt most of Hamburg again."

Hermann just listened. We finished our conversation and thanked Mrs. Holz for cake and coffee before we went to his quarters.

"Let us forget about the war now and think of more pleasant things. What would you like to do tonight?"

"I have not danced for some time. Could we go to a place where a live band plays?"

"Yes, there is a restaurant called Zwick's in St. Pauli near the Reeperbahn, where a band plays dance music Saturday nights. Would you like to go there?"

"If you think the band is good, that is fine with me."

"They also serve food. We can go soon to get a good table and eat dinner there."

"That sounds enticing. Do I need to change, or is this dress fit for the occasion?"

"You are fine. It is not a fancy place; people dress casually. If you want to freshen up, here is the washroom."

"Thank you; I shall do so." The washroom and his room had the bare necessities, but Hermann kept both clean and neat, which I liked. At 6:30 p.m., we went outside to look for a taxi. When one passed, Hermann waved and made the driver stop. Within a short time, we arrived at Zwick's Restaurant in St. Pauli. Many occupied tables surrounded the large dancing floor. The waiter assigned a small table to us close to the dance platform. Colored lights and musical instruments decorated the walls, windows, and ceilings. The owner also hung many posters of celebrities on the walls. It looked cozy but cluttered. Hermann assured me that the food they served was outstanding. I ordered wiener schnitzel, and Hermann ordered sauerbraten. While we waited for our food, Hermann looked at me, "I still cannot believe that you stopped in Hamburg to see me. I am so delighted to spend memorable moments with you before you leave for America. Who knows when we will have a chance to see each other again?"

"I am also happy that fate gave us a chance to be together, even if it is only for a short time."

"You have to promise me to write and stay in touch. We should continue to nurture our special friendship. I will always treasure the memories of the time we belonged to the youth group, all the hikes we took in the forests with our group while singing on the train, in restaurants, or at competitions."

"Yes, under your leadership, our group always excelled, especially in singing. And how I enjoyed doing folk dances with you and ballroom dancing as well. I am glad you took me dancing tonight. Who knows when I will be able to dance again?"

"I was always fond of dancing with you. I am grateful for having another unexpected chance to dance with you tonight. We always treasure the unexpected so-called serendipities of life."

"We certainly do. Meeting you at the railroad station in Essen was a pleasant surprise. I will never forget all the wonderful concerts at your home; you played the violin, your sister Helge the piano, and your mother played the guitar, and we all sang along."

"Yes, I miss the musical get-togethers with my family and friends while I am here in Hamburg. However, each time I go home, we have a family reunion with music. I will be going home for Christmas. I look forward to being with my family. My uncle Heinrich promised to come, too."

"How I admired your Uncle Heinrich's exquisite paintings in which he expressed so much love for the beauty of nature. When he played the harp and sang, I thought of King David's presence, delighting us, singing psalms of praises. He radiated so much peace and love. Just being in his presence made me happy. My great wish was and still is to learn to paint like your Uncle Heinrich."

"You never can tell as you have an eye for beauty. Maybe, one day you will learn to paint also. I studied music and love music, but I am a great appreciator of fine art."

"Do you like modern art?"

"Not in particular. Some people like abstract designs, but I prefer realistic motives and paintings."

Meanwhile, the waiter brought our food. My wiener schnitzel was cooked to perfection; it was moist and tender inside with the brown and crunchy breading on the outside. The vegetables were also delicious.

"How is your sauerbraten?"

"It is delicious."

We enjoyed our food.

"What about dessert?"

"Thank you, perhaps, later. For now, I am very satisfied."

The band arrived and set up their instruments. We finished consuming our food; the band began to play the waltz, "On the Reeperbahn" (Auf der Reeperbahn). Hermann got up and asked me to dance. He gave me his hand, I got up, and soon we waltzed happily around and around. Then a polka followed. We did not even sit down in between dances. We knew many lyrics of the songs the band played. We happily sang and danced until midnight without pausing.

"Don't you think we should go now?"

"If you think so, we will leave. I enjoyed the evening tremendously. Who knows when I will be able to dance again?"

The band played the tango, "La Paloma." Can we dance this tango and then go?"

"If it makes you happy, we sure can."

My feet should have been tired by now but dancing the tango and listening to the song's lyrics lifted my spirit to cloud nine.

Knowing this was the last dance, I thanked Hermann for taking me to this lively restaurant.

"I hope you enjoyed the evening just as much as I did!"

"I certainly did. You must be tired by now."

We went to pick up our coats.

"You stay inside. I'll go outside and engage a taxi."

After a short time, Hermann returned and took me to the taxi, waiting for us at Zwick's Restaurant.

By the time we reached the apartment, it was past midnight.

"Would you like to retire right away? Then I'll go over to my landlady's living room. She offered to let me sleep on her sofa for tonight.

"I am not too tired yet. If you like, we can stay up for a while and talk."

"That is good."

Hermann asked me who my favorite poets were. I told him, "Wolfgang von Goethe, Friedrich von Schiller, and Heinrich Heine."

"Yes, those poets left a wealth of wisdom for us. Friedrich von Schiller admired the poems of Wolfgang von Goethe. They were friends."

"I like the quote of Goethe, *'If you want to write in a straightforward style, you have to conceive it clearly in your soul first. If someone wants to write magnificently, he has to have a magnificent character.'*[30]

"That is so true; we can only express what we conceive in our mind and soul and feel in our heart. I like the quote of Friedrich von Schiller, *'Be noble-minded! Our own heart, and no other men's opinions of us, forms our true honor.'*

"*The dignity of mankind is in your hands; protect it. It sinks with you; it will ascend with you. The man of courage thinks not of himself. Help the oppressed and put thy trust in God.*"

Hermann added, "I like the quote of Wolfgang von Goethe, "*Man is not only created for himself but also for his country. The easier the path, the less is required of men. The more complex the task of the people is, the higher the people ascend.*"

"Yes, my grammar schoolteacher told me to choose the more challenging way; it will require more of you. I took it to heart. Leaving my family, country, and even you behind and going to a foreign country and facing the unknown is exceptionally sacrificial for me. I trust God, who will work out all things for the best."

"For me, it is equally difficult, or perhaps, even more, to give you up and see you leave me and your native country. That reminds me of a quote from Emanual Kant, the Great East Prussian philosopher of Pure Reason and Morality, '*You are not rich by what you possess but by what you can give up with dignity.*' According to Emanual Kant, we can consider ourselves to be rich by giving each other up in dignity and adhering to our moral values."

"I will try to remember this, and another quote of his, "*As the beautiful is limited, the sublime is limitless, so that the mind in the presence of the sublime attempting to imagine what it cannot, has pain in the failure but pleasure contemplating the immensity of the attempt.*"

Let us contemplate the sublime to enrich our lives."

"That reminds me of another quote of Friedrich von Schiller, "*For one to be committed to truth and freedom in the highest pursuit of beauty, an artist must find a way to balance existing in space and time, but always strive to transcend their secular society's limitations in a constant search for the eternal.*"

"Yes, we have to look up to heaven and the Universe but also watch our path on the earth and appreciate the beauty that surrounds us."

For a moment, I thought about God's creation's definition of beauty. A poem I wrote later fits this subject.

God created out of love
Men the universe the earth.
To share the beauty of his works and arts,
God filled with wisdom human hearts.
He bid us live in peace with one another,
And love God first and then each brother.
If we love unconditionally

We get a glimpse of eternity.
God teaches us to meet each challenge
With faith in Him and worthy courage.
We'll live with zest and try to do our best,
Then leave to God the worries and the rest.
God will bless us beyond measure
And reward us with His treasure.

I put my whole trust in God and enjoy the beauty of His creation, as well as beautiful works of art, music, literature, and architecture."

"I, too, enjoy the creative works of artists and especially music. My favorite composers are Beethoven, Mozart, and Schubert, and so many other German composers of operettas. We have such a wealth of folksongs that I like also."

"In addition to the composers you named, I also like Giuseppe Verdi's operas. They present various solos, duets, choirs, and ballets, capturing the audience's attention throughout the entire performance. I am not too fond of Richard Wagner's operas. I only like some arias and overtures of his."

"Our country contributed so much to the world in art, music, literature, and especially science. How tragic, our people and country had to be humiliated after World War II because of Hitler's atrocities. Do you think the occupation will end one day, and we will regain our sovereignty?"

"I sure hope so. I wished the European countries would unite and form an alliance to protect themselves from being taken over by Russia and communism. We can only hope for the best."

Before we realized the day dawned, it was time to get ready for my train ride to Bremerhaven.

At 7:00 a.m., Hermann told me that the landlady would serve breakfast for us shortly.

"Let us freshen up before we go over. We will have to leave for the railroad station after breakfast."

When we walked into the kitchen, we found the table already set. An assortment of rolls and a variety of sausages, cheeses as well as boiled eggs awaited us.

"Good morning Mrs. Holz. How kind of you to have prepared breakfast for us."

"Good morning, Miss Bonacker. Good morning, Hermann, did you sleep well?"

"We did not sleep at all. We talked all night long after we came back from the restaurant," Hermann responded.

Mrs. Holz asked us to sit down and help ourselves. We enjoyed the warm rolls with cold cuts and marmalade and a soft-boiled egg.

Before we left, we thanked her for her hospitality and the lovely breakfast she prepared for us. She wished me a safe journey and good luck in America before we said goodbye.

Hermann had ordered a taxi for 8:30 a.m. When the cab arrived, Hermann told the driver to take us to the main railroad station. We both got into the car, sat close to each other, and barely uttered a word. Our emotions of parting from each other were too profound to express in words. Hermann took my hand and held it tight as if to say, stay here with me; we will find our destiny together. Now and then, we looked at each other and saw the sadness in our eyes and facial expressions. When we got out of the taxi, Hermann paid the driver and carried my suitcase into the railroad station. We went to the window, and I purchased the ticket to Bremerhaven. Hermann walked with me to the track where the train was departing. After putting the suitcase down, he first shook my hand and wished me a safe journey and good luck in America. Then he embraced me tightly and whispered, "I am sad to let you go, but remember, I will always love you."

"You will always remain my cherished friend. I will always treasure our friendship, and the memorable times we've spent together," I whispered.

"I, too, will remember our wonderful times spent together and admire you for your high moral values and your noble character. It made it easier for me to uphold our high moral standards under all circumstances."

"Thank you. I respect you highly for being honest and honorable in all your actions. We both *matured and remained pure.* God bless you always."

"Goodbye, my dear Hilde. God be with you, too."

I could only say, "Goodbye, Hermann." He released me and walked away. I remained standing and watching him getting further and further away. My heart said, "Give up your plan and follow him," but my head said to continue with my journey. I obeyed my head and got on the train. Today I was glad to find an empty train compartment and not engage in a conversation with strangers. I leaned against the corner next to the window and thanked God that my immigration documents had arrived at Hermann's address and that we had another chance to share our thoughts and ideas. I put my plans and cares in God's hands and dosed off. I woke up about three hours later when I heard the conductor calling. "Bremerhaven, last stop, all disembark."

Chapter 16

Boat Voyage to New York

AFTER I GOT off the train, I engaged a taxi to take me to the harbor, where the American ships departed. The taxi driver stopped at an office in a big barrack complex. I introduced myself to the clerk and told him I was supposed to leave tomorrow with the soldier transport ship General Harry Taylor. He took out the passengers' list and said, "Yes, you are on the list. But the ship is leaving one day later than scheduled."

"I did not know that. Where can I stay the extra day?"

"You can stay in a room of a barrack. Wait here; I'll call someone to take you there. Here is also a schedule for the departure of the ship. Make sure you arrive there two hours ahead of time."

"Thank you, that is kind of you to let me stay here the extra day. I will be at the harbor on time. By the way, I had sent my luggage ahead of time. Did it arrive? Is there a restaurant in the complex?"

"Yes, there is a restaurant in the big building, where breakfast is served at 7:00 a.m., lunch at noon, and dinner at 6:00 p.m. The clerk checked another list and told me that my luggage arrived. Within a few minutes, a young man came, picked up my suitcase, and asked me to follow him. He took me to a nearby barrack, opened the door, and showed me the room I was supposed to stay in for two nights. I thanked the young man before he left. I was more tired than hungry and opted to take a nap. I woke up just in time to have dinner. I took a long walk after I left the restaurant. Then returned to the room, which had the bare necessities but was clean. I unpacked some clothes for the following day. After showering, I took out the small

New Testament that I kept in my purse. I opened it at random and read Matthew 14: 24 -33.

> *Jesus asked the disciples to get into the boat while Jesus went up to the mountain to pray. When the boat was in the middle of the sea, a storm created high waves and tossed the boat. Jesus walked on the sea towards the boat. The disciples did not recognize Jesus and were afraid. Jesus told them, "Be of good cheer. Do not be afraid; it is I," Peter answered him. "Lord, if it is you, command me to walk on water to you." And Jesus said, "Come." Peter did. When he saw the boisterous wind and big waves, he began to sink and cried out, "Lord, save me." Jesus stretched out his hand and saved him, saying, "Oh, you of little faith, why did you doubt? When they got into the boat, the wind ceased. The people in the boat worshiped Jesus, saying, "Truly, you are the son of God."*

I pondered those words and took it to be a personal message for my upcoming sea voyage, "Do not be afraid even if you encounter rough seas; I am with you, and I will always protect you." Before I went to bed, I prayed and thanked God for His comforting message.

On Monday, December 17, 1956, a worker took me to the harbor, where I joined many people in a big hall. On a nearby dock stood the army transport ship called H. M. S. General Harry Taylor, the ship I was assigned to travel on across the Atlantic to New York. It looked more like a grey battleship than a cruise ship. But it did not matter to me, as long as it was seaworthy.

Letzter Gruß aus Bremen vor der Überfahrt ⁄   M. S. General „Harry Taylor"

MS General Harry Taylor Ship 1956

After an immigration clerk checked the documents of each person, we embarked on the ship. A Marine took me to an enormous room and showed me my bunk bed. When all passengers were on board, the boat got ready to leave. A large crowd had gathered on the pier to wish farewell to family or friends. Instead, I went on deck to say goodbye to my native country. As a band played "Goodbye, Goodbye" (Aufwiedersehn, Aufwiedersehn), a sad feeling filled my heart. I stood on deck until the music faded away, and the shoreline vanished in the distance as the ship set out to the open waters of the North Sea. Then I returned to the large, crowded room assigned to me and found my bunk bed. I looked around for the washrooms and the showers. I met a lovely young lady who had the bunk bed next to me. We decided to explore the ship to find out where the dining room and other facilities were. We went to lunch and dinner together in the big mess hall. With so many people in one place and whole families with young children traveling, I could not fall asleep until late at night. The North Sea was relatively calm. After we passed through the English Channel and entered the Atlantic Ocean, the winds whipped up high waves, rocking the boat fiercely, and passengers became seasick. A young man wearing a blue navy uniform approached me and introduced himself as James Chambers.

"We saw on your records that you are a doctor's assistant. Our doctors need interpreters who speak German and English. Would you be willing to help us?"

"Even though I speak English, I do not know the medical terminology in English. I will try to help if the doctor sees me fit."

"Come with me. I will take you to the doctor's office; we will let the doctor decide."

After introducing me to Dr. Strom and having a short conversation, Dr. Strom asked me to be in his office at 2:00 p.m. Mr. Chambers also informed me that I could stay in one of the hospital section's room, close to the doctor's office. He took me there and showed me the room assigned to me. I thanked Mr. Chambers very much and was glad to have a place to myself. After I returned with my luggage, I met another lady in the hospital. We introduced ourselves. Her name was Olga. She was a nurse from Russia, who spoke English, German, and Russian. Dr. Weiss, the second doctor on board the ship, asked Olga to be his interpreter.

We both felt fortunate to have a room of our own and a more comfortable bed and could sleep void of children crying and people lamenting. Each day we joined the doctors during office hours. The first day that I assisted Dr. Strom and his nurse, Dr. Strom treated only a few seasick persons. The doctor prescribed Dramamine for nausea and vomiting, then told the patients to drink lots of fluids to avoid becoming dehydrated. I learned the English words quickly for the most common seasickness symptoms and a few other diseases and what medicine and treatment the doctor prescribed. If I did not know a name, I would use sign language to get the doctor's message to the patient.

The further we traveled in the Atlantic Ocean, the rougher the ocean became. Huge waves pounded against the hull, splashed on deck, rocking the boat fiercely. More and more patients came to the doctor each day, and fewer people showed up in the dining room. I, too, got seasick. Dr. Strom gave me Dramamine, which made me feel better. I opted to continue assisting Dr. Strom. Now and then, I had to excuse myself and go to the washroom to empty the contents of my stomach. Some dehydrated patients had to be hospitalized and given an intravenous or intramuscular injection of Dramamine along with electrolyte fluids to replace the depleted liquid, minerals, sodium, and potassium. Whenever I had free time, I would crochet borders around handkerchiefs to get my mind off seasickness. After one week of battling the rough sea and plowing through the foaming waves, the wind velocity dropped somewhat and calmed down the turbulent waters.

On December 24, we celebrated Christmas Eve. The crew of the ship had put up a Christmas tree in the chapel. At 10:00 p.m., a service for the evangelical passengers was held, and at midnight a mass for the Catholic passengers. I kept track of the German time, which was six hours ahead of New York time. At 6:00 p.m., which would be midnight in Germany, I went out on the deck. I thought of how my family would celebrate Christmas tomorrow and how Hermann and his family sang for me at midnight the song: "Night Divine of the Shining Stars" (Hohe Nacht der Klaren Sterne)[31] and other beautiful Christmas songs accompanied by Hermann playing the violin, Helge the piano, and Mrs. Jaeger the guitar. In my imagination, I sang along and felt I was in the midst of them. It was a beautiful manifestation of Christmas. I pondered about the real reason why we celebrated Christmas, the birth of our Savior Jesus Christ. My thoughts did not remain with my family and friends in Germany only, but my thoughts traveled to Bethlehem. I saw the babe Jesus in the manger with Mary and Joseph watching over

Him. The shepherds were kneeling in front of the manger and worshipping the newborn King and Savior of the world. I adored the newborn King also.

After dinner, Olga and I went to the 10:00 p.m. Christmas service in the chapel. We listened to the Christmas story and sang several Christmas carols. It was past 11:00 p.m. when the chaplain dismissed the worshippers with a benediction. Before I went to bed, I thanked God that even in the middle of the ocean and among strangers, I could celebrate the birth of Christ in a meaningful Christian way. In Christ, we felt united as brothers and sisters and not like strangers.

The next day after breakfast. Mr. Chambers knocked on the door. When I opened it, he announced joyfully, "Merry Christmas, Hildegard, I've got a present for you." Then he handed me a small package. I opened it and found a bracelet in it.

"That is lovely. Thank you. I have a small gift for you also, but I did not have any wrapping paper."

I gave him a handkerchief with a blue border that I had crocheted during the voyage.

"That is very nice. I will keep it as a memory of you. Hildegard do not ever change; remain the way you are. In a few days, you will leave the ship. I do not know if I will see you again. I wish you only the best in my country. I hope you find a new home and happiness in America. I'll give you my address; you can write to me and let me know where you will be and how life will be for you in the States."

"Mr. Chambers, first let me thank you for being so thoughtful and giving me a Christmas present and for your kindness toward me during the voyage. I appreciate both very much. Once I find a place to stay, I will let you know where I will be living and if I have found work."

"Very good. I wish you a Merry Christmas."

"I also wish you a Merry Christmas and a blessed future."

Mr. Chambers left. His kindness and gift made my Christmas at sea very special.

On Christmas Day, the captain spoke through the loudspeaker. He wished the crew and the passengers a Merry Christmas. He also announced that we would arrive in New York tomorrow in the early evening. Later in the afternoon, a civil Christmas celebration followed. Passengers from various countries sang Christmas songs and played music. Olga and I attended the special event. We also had the traditional American Christmas dinner together: stuffed turkey, sweet potatoes, and green beans. Pumpkin and pecan pie finished the delicious meal. Before I retired for the night, I went on deck to look at the star-studded sky. The moon had diminished to a quarter, making the night dark and the stars more brilliant. The engines' droning, and the bow cutting through the waves, broke the silence. I felt close to God, my family, and my friends. I thanked God for a special Christmas celebration at sea and a safe crossing so far, despite the rough ocean. Grateful and joyfully, I retired for the night.

The next day at the clinic, Dr. Strom asked me where I was going and if I already had a place to work. I told him my sponsor lived in Des Moines, Iowa, and I planned to go to my sister in Garnavillo, Iowa.

"I have a friend in Des Moines at the Beaverdale Clinic. I'll give you a letter of recommendation for him. Perhaps he might be able to help you get a position in the clinic."

"Thank you for your kindness. I appreciate you recommending me to your friend and for letting me assist you in the clinic."

The next morning, I packed all my belongings before I went to the doctor's office. As promised, Dr. Strom gave me the letter. After seeing the last patient, I thanked him for letting me work with him and the recommendation letter. He also thanked me for helping him as an interpreter. Before I went to the cabin, I walked up on deck. The skyline of New York appeared in the distance, and in front stood the Statue of Liberty. Her lit torch welcoming us with the famous lines by Lazarus, "Give me your tired, your poor, your huddled masses yearning to breathe free."

As we approached New York, I stood there fascinated, watching the light of the torch shining brighter and brighter and the Statue of Liberty and the skyscrapers becoming taller and taller. Suddenly the ship stopped when we were close to the entrance of the harbor. The captain announced that we could not enter the port today because the longshoremen were on strike. We would have to wait until they got back to work. We spent Wednesday evening and the night, waiting for permission to enter the harbor. Thursday evening, the captain announced we could enter the port Friday morning, December 28. I did not tire of watching New York's skyline by day and was mesmerized at night when the regular and Christmas lights transformed the city into a magical fairytale picture. A lot of passengers walked on deck to catch fresh air and watch the skyline of New York. I also had a chance to say goodbye to persons I became acquainted with during the voyage.

On Friday morning, the crew pulled up the anchor, and the ship started to move. About an hour later, we entered the Harbor of New York. All passengers disembarked and waited for their luggage, which a crane unloaded in a big net. The crew transported the suitcases and boxes to a nearby warehouse where we could claim them. Passengers who needed to continue their journey were picked up by buses and transported to the airport or the train stations. After I got my luggage, someone carried my big wooden suitcase to the bus going to the train station. I got a ticket to go to Chicago and then continue to Prairie Du Chien, Wisconsin. The pastoral landscapes and city structures passed quickly by the window of the train during the day. During the night, I tried to sleep, but the noise of the train kept me awake. The next day, I changed the train in

Chicago, crossed snow-covered agricultural fields, beautiful forests, and passed lakes in Illinois and Iowa before arriving in Prairie Du Chien. I called my sister, and within a short time, my brother-in-law and sister picked me up at the railroad station.

We drove over the mighty Mississippi River, and after a short trip, we arrived at Garnavillo, Iowa, where my brother-in-law worked on a huge farm. My sister took care of their three daughters, Agnes, Ilse, and Christa, and lived in a spacious and comfortable home. What a wonderful surprise: my sister Emma, nephew Bernie, and brother Edmund came from Chicago to welcome me to America. We were so happy to be united again. Meta handed me a letter addressed to me but sent to my sister's address.

I opened it quickly and found a photo of a beautiful family with three young children. I could not be more surprised to read that Dr. and Mrs. Jefferies, who lived in Des Moines, Iowa, asked me if I would like to reside at their home and help them with the children. I thanked God for this opportunity to live with a beautiful American orthodontist's family. I shared the good news immediately with my family. I also mentioned that Dr. Strom from the ship had given me a letter for his doctor's friend who managed a clinic in Des Moines. Perhaps he might be able to hire me. That left me no choice but to go to Des Moines. I felt terrible to disappoint my sister Emma and brother Edmund that I did not go with them to Chicago, as they had hoped I would do.

The new year just passed; we celebrated my 20th birthday on Wednesday, January 2, 1957. Meta prepared a roast goose with all the trimmings and a German chocolate cake for dessert. For me, it was a joy to share their life experiences in America and my events of the past year. On Wednesday, I called Dr. and Mrs. Jefferies and told them that I would accept their offer. I asked if I could see them on January 3, 1957. They agreed to meet me in person on Thursday. Before my brother-in-law Ernst drove me to Des Moines, he took my sister Emma, nephew Bernie, and brother Edmund to the railroad station in Prairie Du Chien. I felt sad not to go with them, but God had other plans for me.

Dr. & Mrs. Jefferies, with Jon Kim & Jill

Kent Jefferies

When I arrived at the residence of Dr. and Mrs. Jefferies, they greeted me warmly. We talked for a while, and Mrs. Jefferies explained what they expected of me. After I agreed, they accepted me to stay with their family. My brother-in-law left, after knowing that I was accepted to stay with the Jefferies family. I also mentioned to Dr. and Mrs. Jefferies that I had worked with Dr. Strom on board the ship as an interpreter. Dr. Strom had given me a letter of recommendation to a doctor's friend at the Beaverdale Clinic. The following Monday, January 7, 1957, Mrs. Jefferies drove me to the Beaverdale Clinic. I presented the letter of Dr. Strom to the manager. After reading it, he offered me a temporary position in the x-ray department and later in the laboratory for half a day. I could not thank God enough for how wonderfully he had provided a special place to stay and work nearby in the same town.

The Jefferies family and I developed a comfortable routine. Dr. Jefferies started his office hours at 8:30 a.m. in downtown Des Moines. I began to work in the clinic at 8:00 a.m. Each morning, Dr. Jefferies fixed a sumptuous breakfast of toast, bacon or sausage and eggs, fruit juice, and coffee. Then he dropped me off at the clinic before he went to his office. Mrs. Jefferies got up later and made breakfast for the children. Jon and Kim went to school, Jill, four years old, to kindergarten, and Kent, eight months old, not shown in the photo, remained at home. At noon, Mrs. Jefferies picked me up at the clinic. She made lunch for all of us. After lunch, Kent and Jill took a nap. When they woke up, I went with Kent in the stroller for a walk and sometimes took Jill along.

I helped to clear the table, clean the house, and do laundry and ironing. They treated me as part of their family. I never had it so good in my life. I thanked God each day for the kindness of the whole family. I also welcomed the opportunity to learn conversational English. Mrs. Jefferies, having been a former stewardess, spoke beautifully literary English. So did Dr. Jefferies. Both were highly intelligent. We always had a German-English dictionary on the kitchen counter. If I did not know a word in English, I would look it up in the dictionary. I also took advanced English classes at the university, where I met young ladies that I befriended.

I felt terrible I could not visit my sister Meta before going to Chicago. Later they bought a ranch in Boscobel, Wisconsin, and had two more daughters, Angelika and Anita.

Chapter 17
Going to Chicago

Everything seemed so perfect, and I was very content with life. However, my brother Edmund and my sister Emma wanted me to come to Chicago. At first, the idea did not appeal to me to give up my wonderful life with the Jefferies family. I prayed for God's guidance. As time passed, it seemed more apparent that I should join my family. One day, when Mrs. Jefferies mentioned how she had met her husband in Chicago, she added, "Hildegard, I will never let you go to Chicago."

"Mrs Jeferies, I am sorry to disappoint you. I just promised my brother and sister I would join them in Chicago."

"But you can't just leave us. Aren't you happy here?"

"I am delighted living with you and your family, and it is hard for me to leave you, but my family needs me in Chicago."

"I guess I have to let you go, even though we will be sad to see you go and we will miss you. When do you want to leave?"

"Perhaps in two weeks. I want to give a two-week notice to the clinic, also. I could leave Monday, July 1."

That evening Mrs. Jefferies broke the news to her family that I was going to leave July 1.

"Why are you leaving us so soon?"

"I am pleased with your family and grateful to all, but my family wants me to join them in Chicago."

"I guess if you already made the promise, we have to let you go." Jon and Kim also expressed their sadness and asked me to stay. I had grown fond of the children, and leaving them made me unhappy, too. The personal at the Beaverdale Clinic felt sad to see me go; so did I. They all treated me very warmly. I enjoyed working with the technicians and nurses.

Monday, July 1, was the last breakfast I had with Dr. Jefferies. We both felt sad, but he wished me the best before driving off alone to his office. Then I helped Mrs. Jefferies get the children off to school before taking me to the train station.

"Hildegard, I feel downhearted to see you go, but please write to us and let us know how you are doing in Chicago."

"I will write to you. Thank you very much for having been so kind as to accept me as part of your family. I will forever be grateful to all of you." Tears were beginning to well up in my eyes as Mrs. Jefferies embraced me, and we said goodbye to each other.

Once I arrived in Chicago, my sister Emma and my brother Edmund welcomed me with open arms. Edmund had rented an apartment on Racine Street close to the German neighborhood. He also introduced me to a church officiated by a German pastor. I got acquainted with many young German parishioners, and we joined the church choir. I found temporary employment at Bankers Life and Casualty Insurance Co. in the claim department. During that time, I learned the medical terms in English of many diseases. However, sitting behind a desk for eight hours every day did not satisfy me completely. I missed the contact with patients.

FATHER RETURNS FROM POLAND, 1957

Another important event took place. In September 1957, after more than twelve years in captivity, my father returned from Poland. I wished I could have rushed back to Germany to welcome him personally, but financially I could not afford to pay the airfare to Germany. I knew I had to look for a better-paying job to travel to Germany to visit my father, whom I had not seen for thirteen years. My brother Horst sent me a written report from my father and his experiences of the last twelve years, which I translated into English:

I, Gustav Bonacker, born September 4, 1902, in Wizajny, Kreis Sudauen, East Prussia, reside in Essingen, Germany, Landauerstr. 184.

I was drafted in July 1944 into the German Army (Wehrmacht). I was sent to the Construction Division in Modlin, Poland. I was with this Division until May 1945. After the war ended, I became an American prisoner of war and was sent to the French camp Chalon where I stayed until I was released in October 1945. Since I assumed that my family was still in East Prussia, I wanted to return to our home in East Prussia. When other soldiers and I arrived by train in Sudauen, the other German soldiers and I were taken prisoners by the Polish police. After several days of interrogation by the Polish police, I was imprisoned close to Sudauen. Here I was kept until October 1946. Then I was sentenced to six more years in the Bialystock prison camp.

Four weeks later, I got transported to jail in Warthenburg, East Prussia. I remained there until July 1947. From there, I was sent to the prison in Rawitch, where I stayed until 1950. After a medical examination, I was sent with other prisoners who could still work, to Gross-Strenlitz. Here we worked in a stone quarry until I was transferred in 1951 or 1952 to the coal mine of Katowich. I worked there until March 17, 1953. My prison term ended, and I was released. Three weeks before, the officer in charge of the prison asked me what I intended to do after my release. When I told him I wanted to join my family in West Germany, he strictly forbade me to go there. I was only allowed to live in the province of Sudauen. I agreed, being glad to get out of the prison. Until April 1956, I worked as a free laborer in the forest. Afterward, I looked for a job in Treuburg, East Prussia, where I worked in the woods until September 1957, when I was allowed to leave Poland.

I feel compelled to mention that until the year 1947, we were treated very brutally. We were beaten frequently and mistreated, resulting in a mutilated ear and a damaged index finger on my right hand. In December 1947, I was beaten so severely that I had to be hospitalized for almost four weeks. My whole body was swollen, and all my joints ached. The nourishment was also very poor. Many comrades died from malnutrition or cruel treatment.

Reading my father's report saddened me considerably. I wanted to rush home as soon as possible to see him. First, I had to find a better-paying job to save enough for the trip. On New Year's Eve, I went to an employment agency in downtown Chicago. The clerk sent me for an interview at the American Hospital. Even though I told the pathologist, Dr. Eisenstadt, who interviewed me, I had never worked in histology, he hired me. He said, "The technician,

Irene, will teach you. We need a laboratory technician in histology for Bethesda Hospital, which will open in February 1958."

I accepted the position. Two weeks later, Irene taught me the histology procedures, and I started working at Bethesda Hospital at the beginning of March. Margaret, the Bethesda Hospital laboratory manager, also taught me how to perform chemistry, serology, hematology, and bacteriology tests. I enjoyed working with the laboratory technicians, and the manager Margaret, and meeting the administrator, Mr. Glass, the nurses, other employees, and some doctors on the Bethesda hospital staff. I thanked God for working in the medical field again, which I enjoyed very much.

In 1958, I flew to Frankfurt, Germany, and then took the train to Landau. My brother Horst and my father came to pick me up at the train station. Even though I still recognized my father, he did not remember me. He had seen me last when I was seven years old. I had changed beyond recognition during the last thirteen years. He exclaimed in disbelief, "You are my little Hildchen. You grew up to be a beautiful young Fraeulein." We connected immediately and enjoyed reminiscing about life at home in East Prussia before the war. He also described the run-down conditions after the Polish people took over our land. We talked about so many family celebrations of the past. He had not lost his sense of humor and his smile despite the tragic years of imprisonment. The two weeks passed only too fast, reminiscing about life at home in East Prussia before and after World War II and telling me some experiences of the last twelve years. Unfortunately, I had to return to Chicago again. However, I was glad to see my father and renew our family bond.

All seemed to go well. However, one year later, my brother Edmund was drafted into the American Army despite not being an American citizen. After boot camp training in Fort Worth, he was sent to Germany. I was left behind. He had recently purchased a car on credit. My salary alone was insufficient to make the monthly payments, so I looked for another part-time job.

Not too far from where I lived, another small hospital had opened recently. After the administrator of Roosevelt Memorial Hospital, Mrs. Jones, interviewed me; she hired me. Birute, the head laboratory technician, worked in the morning, Mr. Chapman, in the afternoon, and I covered the evening hours. Dr. Robert Stein, a brilliant pathologist, came several days a week to describe the macroscopic surgical specimens and microscopically examined and diagnosed the slides I had prepared for him of the previous surgical sections. During the day, he worked at the Research Center of Abbot Laboratory. Besides being the pathologist of Roosevelt Memorial Hospital in Chicago, Dr. Stein also worked some evenings at Mc Henry Hospital in McHenry. He studied forensic pathology and held seminars in that field. I enjoyed preparing the slides for his lectures. He also let me do all the autopsies with him, where I learned how the different diseases affected the human body's organs. Dr. Stein was an excellent teacher and a humble and kind human being, contrasting with Dr. Eisenstadt's demanding, authoritarian personality at Bethesda Hospital. Now and then, Dr. Eisenstadt would check my medical knowledge by asking me specific questions about a blood smear or abnormal lab tests. However, he seemed satisfied with my answers.

One day, after taking blood samples from a patient and walking down the stairs to the laboratory, I met Dr. Bruni. He went upstairs to see his patients. I made it a point to address each doctor by name. I greeted him courteously, "Good morning, Dr. Bruni; how are you today?" Dr. Bruni gave me such a penetrating look that it startled me. I blushed, then froze and almost dropped my tray. From that moment on, it became a mutual attraction that flourished into a vital companionship and love.

Whenever Dr. Bruni visited his patients in the hospital, he stopped in the laboratory to check his patients' blood or other tests and always gave me an affectionate glance. One day, Dr. Bruni asked me if I would be interested in working in his office. He set up an appointment for an interview. After picking me up for the interview, he took me first to a restaurant for dinner, then to dance in the elegant Aragon Ballroom in Chicago, where a big band played that evening. How elegantly Dr. Bruni danced the waltz, the foxtrot, and especially the tango. We both enjoyed ballroom dancing immensely. Dr. Bruni never interviewed me about working for him in his Chicago clinic. Later, he told me he had already found a nurse. Perhaps he had other plans for me?

Working twelve hours a day took a toll on my health. I wrote to my brother Edmund and told him I would have to give up one job. I asked him if we could sell the car to eliminate mortgage payments. With my brother's consent, I sold his car. Since working at Roosevelt Memorial Hospital would cut my traveling time in half, I chose to ask for full employment there. After talking to the hospital administrator, Mrs. Jones, she hired me to cover the afternoon and evening hours. I gave notice to Dr. Eisenstadt at Bethesda Hospital that I would like to quit. I wanted to work full-time at Roosevelt Memorial Hospital. Dr. Eisenstadt was angry that I left so soon after he allowed me to train in histology. However, Dr. Stein welcomed me as a full-time employee at Roosevelt Memorial Hospital. My health improved, and I felt invigorated. I also found an apartment within walking distance of the hospital. I thanked God for the change. Since Dr. Bruni saw me no longer at Bethesda Hospital, he came whenever his schedule allowed him to see me in the morning. He visited his hospitalized patients in the morning and assisted the surgeon during the operations on his patients. His office hours at the clinic began at 1:00 p.m. and ended at 9:00 p.m. with an hour break for dinner between 5:00 p.m. and 6:00 p.m.

With each visit, our attraction for each other grew, and an exciting, romantic courtship began. We started to call each other by first names. Aldo called me Hilda instead of Hildegard. He held no office hours on Wednesday. He took me boating on Lake Michigan, or we went fishing in Lake Shangri-La, Wisconsin. We discovered many beautiful scenic regions of Wisconsin. We enjoyed lectures at the Chicago Planetarium, Museum of Science and Industry, or Art Museums. We shared many interests and enjoyed opera music.

Meanwhile, my brother Edmund fell in love with a beautiful young lady named Karin Mieke while in Germany. They married on August 6, 1960 in the famous Cathedral of Ulm. The following year he returned to Chicago with his lovely bride.

Wedding of Karin and Edmund

My sister and I found an apartment for them next door to where we lived on Wayne Street. We also bought the essential items and furniture for them. They liked living on the second floor with a beautiful front yard filled with colorful flowers. Edmund asked me when I planned to get married. I mentioned that Aldo intended to marry me, but we had not set a date yet.

One evening, while strolling along the shore of Lake Michigan, Aldo stopped, took both of my hands, and said, "I have something important to tell you. I am married and have four children. I am in the middle of divorcing my wife. As soon as I finalize the divorce, I will marry you. Forgive me for not breaking this news sooner to you. I do love you very much, and I did not want to lose you."

Aldo's confession shocked me. A chill ran down my spine. I froze and could not utter a word. Aldo embraced me and whispered, "My dear Hilda, I am so sorry to hurt you. Let me take you home."

I sat speechless on the way home and could only say, "Good night, please give me some time to collect myself and my thoughts."

Aldo took me in his arms and told me how much he loved me, and he hoped not to lose me.

I went up to my apartment. I felt like darkness drenched my heart. I suddenly felt guilty for loving Aldo. The thought that he might divorce his wife and leave his four children because of me disturbed me. I sank into my pillow, cried, and prayed to God to show me what to do. As a few days passed, I understood what God wanted me to do. To clear my conscience of any guilt toward his family, I had to give Aldo time and space to reconsider his decision and reconcile with his family. I wanted to do God's will even though it meant for me to make the most significant sacrifice of my life, giving up Aldo, whom I loved profoundly.

When Aldo came to visit me the next time, I told him my plan. He reassured me that he did not divorce his wife because of me. The divorce settlement took so much longer than expected because her attorney passed away. He told me, "As soon as the new attorney finalizes the divorce, we can get married."

However, I had to find out for myself, even if it cost me to leave or lose Aldo, my family, job, and friends. I wanted to do God's will.

"But where will you go? What will you do?"

"I would like to go to Denver, Colorado. It will take some time to notify Roosevelt Memorial Hospital and the landlady and break the news to my family. Even though I told only my family the real reason for my leaving, I stunned everyone else with a sudden departure. A few months earlier, I had bought a second-hand blue Studebaker station wagon. I loaded my personal belongings into the station wagon. I left the furniture in the apartment. I wanted to drive my loaded station wagon alone, but Aldo insisted on coming with me. After terminating my employment and saying goodbye to my family and friends, we left for Denver. Under normal circumstances, this would have been a delightful trip. However, leaving everyone behind and thinking of giving up Aldo and of Aldo, losing me, made the journey excruciating for both of us.

In Wheatridge, a suburb of Denver, I found an apartment. After unpacking, saying a tearful goodbye to each other, Aldo took a flight back to Chicago. I remained heartbroken behind in Wheatridge. I looked for work and found a position as a laboratory technician at Dr. Meyer's Clinic in downtown Denver. I became a member of the Holy Cross Lutheran Church and joined their choir, where I made some friends. However, often, my thoughts traveled back to Aldo, and I wondered if he had reconciled with his family or if he continued with the divorce procedure. Not wanting to influence his decision, I neither gave Aldo my address nor wrote to him. Each day I wondered how he coped with our separation.

Did he miss me as much as I missed him? Did he return to his family, or did he finalize the divorce? Months passed. I prayed that God would reveal to Aldo and me what He planned for our future. One day I received a letter from Aldo. I could not contain my excitement and curiosity. I opened the envelope quickly. He told me he had gotten my address from my sister and let me know he finalized the divorce. All the time that passed, he missed me terribly and never stopped loving me. We could get married now, and he asked me to become his wife. I prayed to God to show me His way. The following day I felt relieved knowing that Aldo did not get divorced because of me. Now I could marry Aldo without having a guilty conscience. I had never ceased loving him, and neither had he stopped loving me.

I wrote back to him, "Dear Aldo since you did not go back to your family, you convinced me that I was not the reason for your divorce. Now my conscience will no longer bother me. I will gladly marry you."

Chapter 18
Marrying Dr. Aldo Bruni, MD

We set April 2, 1966, as our wedding date. Aldo and I rejoiced not only in being reunited physically but also elated to join in holy matrimony.

Marrying Dr. Aldo Bruni

Pastor Edwards married us at the Holy Cross Lutheran Church in Wheatridge, Colorado. He gave a simple but profound sermon about the duties of husband and wife in a marriage. An elegant reception with newly made friends followed in the evening at the

Brown Palace in Denver, where we spent the night in one of their luxury suites. The following day, we went on a honeymoon trip to Vail, Colorado. I quit my job, dismissed my apartment and packed my personal belongings in the station wagon before driving back to Chicago.

We delighted in watching spring arrive in the Rocky Mountains and cover the prairies with lush grass and wildflowers. With excitement, we planned our future together. We stayed in Chicago for a while in the one-bedroom apartment, where Aldo lived alone during separation from his former wife and family. We opened a second medical office in Island Lake, which I managed. We also bought a new home in Barrington Harbor Estates on a handshake from Mr. Hubschman, the area developer. He lived across the street. Mr. Hubschman became not only a patient of ours but a lifelong friend. When the Island Lake office became too small, Aldo built a medical center in Barrington, only five minutes away from our residence. We employed a medical secretary and a nurse. I managed the Barrington Medical Center and worked part-time in the clinic. We also rented offices to doctors and a dentist.

When Barrington's practice flourished, Aldo sold the medical center and the commercial building on Touhy Avenue in Chicago and practiced only in Barrington. Now we had more time for sailing on Lake Michigan. We enjoyed strolling along Lake Michigan's shores, observing the changes during the different times of the day and the seasons. We frequented theaters and exhibits at various museums and listened to inspiring lectures at the Planetarium and other places. Attending opera performances at the Lyric Opera House in Chicago and listening to favorite artists highlighted our winters. During the summer, we joined opera singers and friends to participate in concerts at the beautiful Ravinia Park in Highland Park. On one of the cruises from Rome, Italy, to New York, Aldo befriended the famous lyric tenor Ferruccio Tagliavini, who was engaged to sing at the Metropolitan Opera in New York. Ferrucio Talglianvini became a friend of Aldo's and the Bruni family. Whenever we listened to opera music, Aldo would sing along with the artists. He knew the lyrics of many famous arias.

Another highlight each winter was the dinner dance of each hospital in a fancy restaurant or club. Exquisite flower arrangements decorated the tables and enhanced the pretty setting. The doctors wore tuxedos, and their wives or companions wore long elegant gowns and luxurious fur coats. Aldo and I enjoyed the delicious food, ballroom dancing, and vivid conversations with his colleagues.

I admired Aldo's bedside manners with his patients. Sometimes, when the specialists gave up hope, Aldo would fight for his patients' lives by encouraging them to get well. I remember the patient, Clara Cernocky, running a high fever and having heart problems besides an extended abdomen. While in the hospital, an x-ray showed a small chicken bone perforated the intestine and caused acute peritonitis. Aldo immediately scheduled her for surgery. She barely survived the surgery, and the surgeon did not think she would recover. The same evening, after we finished office hours at 9:00 p.m., we drove to Holy Family Hospital to see Clara. She lay pale and lifeless, connected to so many IV bottles and monitors. She was even too weak to speak. After Aldo checked the intravenous fluid intake and monitors, he picked up her hand and said, "Clara, you will make it!" She looked up at him and smiled. Aldo kissed her on the forehead. She smiled again as we said goodbye, and from that day on, her recovery improved daily. After two weeks, she left the hospital and lived for many more years. Her husband was so grateful to Aldo for saving his wife's life that he and his wife became good friends of ours.

I enjoyed working with Aldo in the clinic, caring for his patients. By knowing the patients and the office procedures, I helped ease the professional stress. I wanted to be the best wife possible and also create a relaxing atmosphere at home. Wherever I found good advice, I read and copied it. Every three months, we got a small booklet from the A.H. Robins Pharmaceutical Co. called Robins Readers. I copied the five rules of a happy marriage by Reverend J. H. Randolph Ray:[32]

1. *Have a common goal for your marriage.*
2. *Watch every day acts, and let the big occasions take care of themselves.*
3. *Have equal rights financially.*
4. *Mind your manners. Courtesy is the guardian angel of Love.*
5. *Be kind! Kindness is life's blood, the elixir of marriage. This is the Golden Rule of marriage and the secret of making love last through the years.*

I tried to follow these rules to make my husband happy. Life seemed content on the outside, but we both missed having children of our own. Just being a weekend father neither fulfilled the desires of Aldo nor the children's. After several years passed, and I could not conceive, we found that exposure to x-rays without proper protection damaged my ovaries while working in the doctor's office in Germany. We both felt disillusioned. I felt sad not to fulfill Aldo's wish to bear a child or two for him. We even thought of adopting a boy and a girl, but the orphanages we contacted made it too complicated.

Aldo's Children, Gilda, Christine, Joanne, Frank

I prayed for God to show me a way of getting closer to Aldo's four children. At first, they considered me an intruder into their family and resented me, which was understandable. As time passed, I hoped we would develop a spontaneous mutual affection for each other, which we did. With the son Frank and the oldest daughter Joanne, we cultivated a profound love and family bond. I could not have asked for any better children of my own. The younger daughters, Christine and Gilda, respected me as their father's wife but did not become as close to me as Frank and Joanne. I accepted their spontaneous sentiments toward me, even though Aldo and I wished it would have been more amicable. We learned to live in the present and let each day's work absorb our interests, energy, and enthusiasm.

When Joanne and Frank got married and had children, we enjoyed spending time with the grandchildren. Whenever we had a free weekend, we would go to Joanne's house and pick up Patricia and Paul. They had their suitcases ready and were always excited to stay overnight with Grandpa and Omi (grandma in German). Aldo took Paul fishing on the Fox River while Patricia and I baked a cake or prepared meals together. She enjoyed riding on Red, our Irish Setter. We also enjoyed spending time with Frank's children,

Julia, Carla, and Phillip, who had vivid imaginations. We even took Paul with us on a two-week-long trip to Florida and Key West.

We celebrated our tenth wedding anniversary on April 2, 1976. The same year the United States commemorated the 200th anniversary of its founding. I wanted to give Aldo something special. I learned how to write poetry. For one year, I secretly wrote 100 poems about our personal life, nature, faith, and other subjects. To celebrate this special event, we flew to Las Vegas and stayed at the MGM Hotel for one week. Before we went for dinner on our anniversary, Aldo handed me a card, "To my wife on our anniversary," expressing his love and gratitude to me.

The card read:

I love you for being so wonderful Dear,
each day of the week, and each month of the year,
and the more we're together, the more that I know
I will always be happy in loving you so.

Aldo wrote:

And now, my dear, let me express my gratitude for your kindness, patience, sincerity, and all other qualities I have found in you. These are the best gifts you can offer me since these are gifts which cannot be obtained with money and are difficult to find in this perverted corrupted world. Only with these qualities we can be sure of a happy and contemplated future regardless of the past and future obstacles which have and will obstruct our ways. Only armed with these qualities, we can hope for success.

Thank you again, my dear, for every little thing you have done for me, and forgive my blindness if, at times, I have condemned your actions.

May your hopes and dreams be fulfilled because only in the fulfillment of yours I can see mine come true. Your Aldo

Aldo's words filled my heart with an even deeper love for him. I got up, embraced him, and thanked him for his exquisite card and noble thoughts. Then I gave him the book of my 100 hand-written poems. I could hardly wait to see his reaction.

He opened the book and read the first poem. Then he asked me, "Where did you find this poem about our first meeting?"

"I wrote all the poems during the last year."

"You wrote all these poems? When did you write them without me knowing about it?"

"Whenever you were away, or I sneaked out of the room during the night to write. I wanted to surprise you and give you a very personal and unexpected gift to make you happy."

"Thank you, sweetheart. Your thoughtfulness certainly made me happy. Let us go and eat now. I will read more later."

Joyfully we ate dinner in the most elegant dining room of the MGM Hotel-Casino. After we got back to our room, Aldo read some more of my poems aloud. When Aldo told me how much he liked them, I felt encouraged to continue writing more poetry. We enjoyed watching shows, trying our luck on poker machines, and exploring the outskirts of Las Vegas for a week.

Each year, we took a trip to different parts of the United States or a cruise to foreign countries or islands. For our silver anniversary, we booked a South Pacific cruise. We made friends with the captain and his family and had the honor to dine at the captain's table. While cruising close to the Hawaiian Islands, we watched the volcano erupt, spewing molten lava in the air. The glowing lava slid down the mountain, crashed into the ocean, and created a fountain of foam and fire. During one of our trips to Rome, we attended a performance of the opera "Aida" at the famous outdoor Theater of Caracalla in Rome. The big stage permitted even animals to enter the platform. We enjoyed the beautiful aria, "Celeste Aida" (Divine Aida), and the spectacular (Triumphal March). But the aria I will never forget is when Aida, the captured Ethiopian Princess, sang *O patria mia te vedro mai piu* (Oh, my homeland, I will not see you again). A live camel lay next to her, and behind a palm tree, the moon rose and created the perfect setting for the homesick aria of Princess Aida. I shared Aida's feelings, wondering if I would ever see my home again. We will always treasure the excellent performance in the magical setting. The following evening, we watched Cavalleria Rusticana with a live horse on the stage, which excelled also.

At times, life presented us with challenges. Aldo worked hard. Dealing with patients, performing surgery, and visiting patients in the hospital creates a lot of stress. I learned to deal not only with professional stress but also with an explosive Italian temper. I would be quiet or leave the scene until Aldo calmed down and was in a better mood. He did everything with a passion, which I learned to appreciate; suffering and joy, agony, and ecstasy are part of life, and I accepted them as such.

Since I enjoyed art, I took classes at various times in oil painting, watercolor and porcelain painting. I learned to understand seeing things with an artist's eye. I especially liked painting flowers with all their different shapes of colored blossoms. Attending the Academy of Art at downtown Chicago, or classes at Harper College rewarded me with better compositions and works of art. Clementyna Porzak introduced me to the fine art of porcelain painting. I painted a whole set of china for eight with a rose design.

Oil Painting of Flowers

Another new and exciting adventure began when we looked for a place to retire in Oregon. After we found no place that met all our expectations, we drove to Yosemite National Park. On the way, we stopped at Lake Tahoe. The beauty of the crystal-clear lake and the surrounding mountains enchanted both of us. Aldo, being dynamic and ambitious, decided to retire in South Lake Tahoe. Immediately he bought a residential lot with a scenic view of the lake and the mountains. Aldo sketched a floor plan for the house and gave it to an architect. The Tahoe Regional Planning Agency issued only a few building permits each year. We were fortunate to obtain one, and Aldo engaged a contractor to put in the foundation among the giant boulders. The following year, the contractor completed the house.

Aldo surprised everyone when he announced he wanted to retire within a year. Even I thought it was too soon, perhaps in five years sounded more acceptable to me. I felt sad to leave my family, friends, and also the patients we learned to cherish. I did not want to show Aldo how his decision of early retirement upset me. On the way home from church, which I did not want to leave, I found a secluded spot overlooking the pastoral scenery where I parked and cried to release my emotional distress. Once a policeman stopped and asked if he could help. I quickly wiped my tears and told him, "No, thank you, I am just meditating."

Soon I forgot about my feeling sorry for myself and began preparing for the big move to South Lake Tahoe. Aldo found a doctor to whom he introduced his long-time loyal patients. Aldo and I worked for one year with Dr. Leong before he took over our practice. On the closing day of the clinic, we saw many patients and finished late. The last patients were four generations, who had followed Aldo from the time he opened his first medical center in Chicago. Aldo treated the mother, her daughter, and delivered the son Frank, who also had a son. When Aldo told them we would soon move to California and thanked them for their loyalty, Mrs. Gugliani embraced Aldo and started to cry; so did the daughter, Mrs. Mariani. It was a very touching moment for all of us to say goodbye to our loyal patients and leave the medical center.

Slowly with God's help, everything fell into place. Saying goodbye to family and friends saddened both of us. So did leaving our first home, where we enjoyed many splendid parties. At Aldo's last birthday celebration, opera singers and an accordion player entertained our guests. Our family, friends, and doctors had a marvelous time. I treasure the tape I recorded of this special event. Many fond memories flashed across our minds before we locked the empty house and drove away.

Chapter 19
Moving to Lake Tahoe

With the move to South Lake Tahoe and retiring, a new chapter of our life began. The excitement of moving into a new home and decorating each room eased my sadness about leaving Barrington. Aldo created among the massive rocks a platform with various train tracks and illuminated villages. Aldo designed a fairy-land setting around the Jacuzzi. I decorated the upper rooms, which pleased Aldo. The panoramic view of the crystal-clear lake and the rugged mountains enchanted us.

PANORAMIC VIEW FROM HOUSE OF LAKE TAHOE

We went sailing, hiking, fishing in smaller lakes, and got acquainted with Lake Tahoe's natural beauty and wonders. However, the first winter caught us by surprise — it snowed not inches but feet and reached the garage roof. Aldo dug a tunnel to get out of the garage. Driving up and down the steep hill also presented a challenge. Aldo made plans to buy a motorhome and go south the following winter. We spent some time in scenic Palm Springs and continued to the Baha of California. We decided to spend the rest of the winter at the Posada RV Park south of Mulege on the Bay of Conception.We liked the location, leased a lot close to the beach, and built a home the following winter.

OUR FALCON PEDRO

A worker brought an injured falcon to Aldo during construction and asked him to care for the bird. Aldo immobilized the injured wing with a piece of a nylon stocking and put a splint on the damaged leg. The falcon recovered completely. Before we returned to the States, we set the falcon free. He flew to the beach and sat down. Several seagulls attacked him. We could not fathom letting the seagulls kill our falcon, whom we affectionately named Pedro. We decided to take him with us to Lake Tahoe, even though it meant risking paying a high fine or being put in jail. Luckily, we crossed the border without the border patrol discovering Pedro. Once released, Pedro adapted well to the change of climate and new environment. He brought us joy for more than thirty years by returning each year and circling over the house or flying by the patio when we were outside.

During the winter months we relished boating, fishing, clamming and swimming in the Bay of Conception for three years. However, driving the curvy and dangerous road of the Baha twice each season became cumbersome. A neighbor told us to take the ferry from Santa Rosalia to Guaymas. From there, we could take the newly constructed toll road to Nogales and the States, which we did. When we reached Guaymas, we drove around the area and discovered San Carlos. We liked the town and location and looked for a house. Once we found a home to our satisfaction, Aldo made an offer. The owner accepted our offer, so two weeks later, we sold the house on the Baha and started remodeling the San Carlos home. God worked out everything perfectly. I thanked God; we no longer needed to drive the treacherous highway through the Baha to the Posada. Now we could drive to Nogales and take the four lane toll road to San Carlos, Mexico. Thus, San Carlos became our winter residence in 1989.

Chapter 20
Life in San Carlos

OUR HOME IN San Carlos, which we called our winter residence, offered a 360-degree panoramic view with a bridge connecting the house to a tall tower. At each time of the day, the picture changed. Waking up at dawn, we could see the rising sun with all its vivid pastel colors over Honeymoon Island. The sunset displayed brilliant red, orange, and yellow clouds above the Tetakava Mountain. During the night, we watched either with a telescope or binoculars the different constellations of the stars. The climate, where the desert, mountains, and sea meet, agreed with us.

SCENIC VIEW FROM HOUSE IN SAN CARLOS

We enjoyed boating, swimming, and fishing in the picturesque Sea of Cortez. We made many friends, joined the San Carlos Community Church, a Christian Church of many denominations. The pastor followed no religious preferences but preached only the Word of God from the Bible. The church not only supported many missionaries but helped the local people wherever needed.

In the church's small lobby, books displayed on shelves were offered to the parishioners. One day I picked up a book called The Case for Easter by Lee Strobel.[33] Lee Strobel, an investigative journalist for the *Chicago Tribune*, set out to disclaim the resurrection of Jesus Christ. To conclude his task, Mr. Strobel interviewed pathologists, doctors, scientists, physicists, and others. To my amazement, I found Mr. Strobel's first interview to be with Dr. Robert Stein, with whom I worked for five years at Roosevelt Memorial Hospital in Chicago. Dr. Stein's knowledge impressed Mr. Strobel to the point that he called him a walking encyclopedia. I agreed wholeheartedly that Dr. Stein was not only brilliant in his profession of forensic pathology but a kind and humble person and an excellent teacher. Dr. Stein became the medical examiner for Cook County, and the newly constructed facility was named the Dr. Robert Stein Institute. After Lee Strobel finished his interviews and investigations, he came to the following conclusion: "God is the Creator of the universe and of many complex functioning systems."[34]

The human body consists of thousands of complex systems that operate perfectly. It arises with the external influence of intelligence, and the function is interrupted without ongoing guidance. The external intelligence (thought or idea) has first to imagine the objects or systems and then gather all the elements and components to build them. The more complex the system, the more external intelligence is required. Human intelligence can create machines and objects, but God, who created nature with its millions of functioning systems, has far higher intelligence than the human mind.

Mr. Strobel observed that no complex functioning system ever originates without external intelligence's ongoing guidance; there must be an external intelligence that created countless functioning systems in nature. These two realities are profound and undeniable scientific proofs of God. The truth will always remain: Science without a shadow of a doubt proves that God exists, no matter how many oppose the truth with the theory of evolution, an unproven theory. Most people are led to believe faith in God is unscientific, and belief in evolution is scientific. Not all we learn in school and by the media is true. They create the illusion that science makes God superfluous, while the opposite is true. Science is acquiring new knowledge through observing realities and integrating or correcting previous knowledge. A supernatural force supersedes nature. Many doctors witnessed healing through divine intervention in hopeless cases.

The English scientist, Sir Isaac Newton, states:

> *This most beautiful system of the sun planets and comets could only proceed from the counsel and dominion of an intelligent Being. And if the fixed stars are the center of other like systems, these being formed by like wise counsel, must all be subject to the dominion of One. This Being governs all things not as a soul of the world but as a Lord of all.*

The scientist Albert Einstein expresses the existence of God like this:

> *Everyone who is seriously involved in the pursuit of science becomes convinced that a spirit is manifest in the laws of the Universe—a spirit vastly superior to*

that of man and one in the face of which we with our modest powers must feel humble.

Max Karl Planck, Nobel Prize winner in Physics writes:

Both religion and science require a belief in God. For believers, God is in the beginning, and for physicists, God is at the end of all considerations. To the former, He is the foundation, to the latter the crown of the edifice of every generalized world view.

Most of us believe what we want to believe while we are in a free country, but the truth is, we often think the way the media and secular education force upon our minds. The atheist believes you are considered an intelligent human being if you deny the existence of God. If you dare to even think about the possible presence of God, you will be labeled as ignorant, religious, and unscientific.

Lee Strobel's life-changing experience from being an atheist to becoming a Christian evangelist prompted him to write many Christian books and give Christian and other institutions lectures. One of his best-known books is *The Case for Christ*. I read Lee Strobel's first written book, *The Case for Easter*, with great interest not only because of his writing skills but also because he interviewed Dr. Robert Stein, who taught me not only medical knowledge but life's wisdom during the time I worked with him.

My husband continued utilizing his medical skills. Once a month, he donated his medical service to the Jacqui Indians in Baccum. The village children greeted Dr. Bruni with enthusiasm when he distributed dresses, pants, or toys that I collected for them. I thanked God that Aldo continued to use his medical knowledge to help poor people who had no means to see a doctor.

Even after we retired, we continued to take a cruise or a trip to different parts of the world. When we visited New Zealand, Aldo fell in love with its scenic beauty and thought of spending the winters in New Zealand. On impulse, he bought a fifty-acre farm with a view of the ocean in Orewa, close to Auckland. When we returned from our trip, Aldo put the house in San Carlos up for sale. I felt heartbroken; I not only liked our house but mostly the many wonderful friends we made in San Carlos. I prayed to God to show me what to do. I promised Aldo I would only make a move under one condition: we would live on the farm for some time to see if it made him happy.

When we returned to New Zealand, we spent November, December, and part of January on our ranch. Aldo hired a contractor to repair and paint the house. We went to antique stores and garage sales to buy furniture and kitchen utensils. We attractively arranged the furniture, and I sewed curtains for the windows. It began to rain. It rained and rained. The sun brightened only a few days during our stay at the farm. Aldo came down with the flu and a high fever, and I developed shingles over the left eye and on the head. With Christmas approaching, we both thought of the joy-filled celebration in sunny San Carlos and felt homesick. Aldo, in his desperation, shouted, "Let's the hell get out of this country." These words sounded like sweet music to my ears. We immediately leased the property to the lady and her two children who sold us the property and flew back to Mexico. We thanked God the realtor had not sold the house in San Carlos. We sold the Orewa farm after difficulties with the New Zealand tenants not paying the rent on time and running down the property. I thanked God for ending the New Zealand adventure two years later.

Aldo settled down and began writing his memoirs. He had such a clear and poignant way of expressing his thoughts. With the ocean's panoramic view and rugged mountains, the tower became his favorite place to write. He finished writing his memoirs in 2001. I edited his script and had it published in 2002. At the same time, I compiled the poems I had written for my husband, the ones I wrote for the 200th anniversary of the United States, and many others and published them at the same time. I called my collection *"A Song in the Night"* with the subtitle, "The darker the Night the brighter the Starlight."

Unfortunately, a year later, Aldo's health deteriorated. One day he could hardly breathe. Dr. Canale, when called, came to the house immediately and saved his life. I was and still am very grateful to Dr. Canale for his prompt help. He admitted Aldo to CIMA Hospital in Hermosillo, where he got excellent treatment in the intensive care unit for seventeen days. Physically he recovered, but mentally he declined. It was heartbreaking for me to see his brilliant mind fail him gradually. Every day presented new challenges. I was grateful for my kind-hearted maid Rosalba (nicknamed Chava), who helped me care for my sick husband.

My Maid Chava & her sons, Fernando, and Adelyte

She walked with Aldo each day while he could still move. They would sing together and just be jovial. Her sister Sulma also helped us when needed. I also appreciated the kindness of the family and many kind friends. They understood, supported, and stayed with my husband when I went to church, shopping, or to other functions. After almost forty years, God answered my ceaseless prayer when Aldo became a confessing Christian at the onset of his sickness. Aldo became more patient, kind, loving, and never complained. He always smiled and felt secure in my presence. He called me his angel, just like at the beginning of our courtship. Every time I noticed a decline in Aldo's mental capacity, I mourned its loss. God's grace and the profound love for each other helped us meet life's complex challenges and rewarded us with inner peace and joy. Together we tasted the agony and ecstasy of matrimony and life.

In the summer of 2009, his oldest daughter Joanne and her husband, Dr. David Trotter, visited us in Lake Tahoe. Even though they knew it was the last time they would see him, they were grateful their dad still recognized them and could express his love for them and they their love for him. In September, his son, Frank, and daughter-in-law Peggy visited us in Lake Tahoe. Aldo suddenly became very ill and breathed with difficulty. We called the ambulance, which rushed him to Barton Memorial Hospital. The attending physician and nurses shared our grief while saying the last goodbye to my beloved husband and Frank and Peggy to their dad. At 1:00 a.m. the following day, Aldo took his last breath, and his soul ascended into heaven, but his love and the memories of our life together will continue to blossom within my heart and mind. I always will be grateful to Frank and Peggy for being with me during this difficult time of mourning my husband's and their father's loss. I appreciated the compassion and comfort of family and friends, but mainly that Aldo accepted Christ, and he parted peacefully without prolonged suffering. The patients, whom he sincerely cared for, will always remember Dr. Aldo Bruni. His dedication and compassion for his patients brought hope and courage to the most hopeless cases. I will end this chapter with Aldo's words from his book, *My Memoirs*:

> *When ultimately this life, like everything else in this world reaches its final stage, let these brief memories of mine, so simply expressed in my work, be disclosed to my children and all my intimate family members with the hope it will be carried on to the coming generations as a remembrance of the past and to stimulate a better future.*

As the last rose of summer withered, so did the life of my beloved husband Aldo after flourishing eighty-five years.

Chapter 21
Life as a Widow

LOSING A HUSBAND is heart-breaking but changing all the necessary documents is a lengthy and trying process. My attorney, Mr. R. Alling, prepared all the legal documents promptly. It allowed me to go back to San Carlos one month later. I appreciated Mr. Alling's excellent and prompt, professional advice and service. I needed to change legal documents in Mexico, which did not go as smoothly as in the States. It took several years to transfer the trust into my name.

However, all my friends in San Carlos from the San Carlos Community Church comforted me by inviting me to their homes for the holidays or dinners. My most incredible comfort came from God. He gave me new strength for each day to handle all the transitions and adjustments I needed to make as a widow. I continuously thanked God from the bottom of my heart and trusted Him for meeting each need at His perfect timing.

I filled the void of my husband's loss by comforting and helping others. Passing on God's love and the love I had for my husband to make others happy cured my grief. Each challenge I met, I used as a steppingstone to develop a closer and more meaningful relationship with God, family, and friends.

Family members and friends came to visit me. We always spent delightful days together. One time my stepson Frank and Peggy and my friends, Sue and Ed from San Diego, visited me in Lake Tahoe at the same time. They treated me to a river rafting trip on the Truckee River. For me, it was an exhilarating experience to sway back and forth while passing over rapids or rocks. Luckily, I only fell into the rubber boat three times and not out of the boat.

I enjoyed spending time with my stepdaughter Joanne, and her husband, Dr. David Trotter, at their beautiful home in Laguna Beach. We watched the Pageant of the Masters, a spectacular show recreating a painting, a statue, or an event with real people every three minutes. A live orchestra plays appropriate music for each exhibit. "The Last Supper" by Leonardo Da Vinci finishes the magnificent show. Before the show began, we watched the displays of the various types of art and jewelry and enjoyed dinner together in the park's ambiance. Sometimes Frank and Peggy or my friends from San Diego enjoyed the gracious hospitality of Joanne and Dave at the same time I did.

Having more time on my hands, I concentrated on writing my book, I had begun several years ago, not only writing but researching facts about both World Wars I and II. I looked for answers to many questions. I wanted to know the truth and not what the propaganda and the media publicized. Having lived in Germany during World War II and speaking both German and English helped me find various information. At times, the media or the leaders exaggerated facts, white-washed some, took some out of context, or omitted facts to keep a good public appearance. The leaders or people even created lies if they served their cause. Good and evil have existed since the creation of man. Sometimes the criminal will blame the victim for his crimes to cover or minimize his guilt.

Chapter 22
The Holocaust and Other War Crimes

WRITING ABOUT THE Holocaust and the allies' crimes was the most challenging subject for me. When a country's leader commits a crime, I ascribe the crime to the leader and do not call all inhabitants of the country criminals. Documents of some leader's and many well known person's from the late 20th- and early 21st century were made public, and those who speak the truth will not be put to jail or punished for revealing the truth. Only God knows all the truth and intrigues of the background of the historical facts. I read numerous articles in German and English on various subjects and found conflicting information about both wars. I often wondered how and who counted the six million Jews killed in concentration camps? Not only I, but professors, historians, and persons from all walks of life and many countries set out on a fact-finding mission. I came across a website called Beforeitsnews.com, Part 1, "Emperor of all lies." The Holocaust of six million Jews lists ten newspapers mentioning the six million figure first. "The Holocaust is the paragon for Jewish suffering and is treated as being beyond examination."

We will never know all the facts about World War II's atrocities and the crimes against humanity by all countries involved, but we get a glimpse of the truth here and there. Only God knows the whole truth.

According to the article, the six million figure existed long before Adolf Hitler came to power. During World War I, the British government had agreed to support the Belfour Declaration to establish a Palestine homeland for the Jews. In return, they asked to secure a Jewish lobby in America and join them as allies. After the end of World War I, the British government did not make good on its promise. From 1919, appeals published that six million Jews were threatened to be exterminated in Europe unless they got a Palestine homeland. While in office, British Prime Minister Stanley Baldwin spread a lie that six million Jews were gassed in Germany. He later admitted that the gas chambers did not exist at that time; it was only propaganda. He publicly apologized to the German people for his racist slur on them. Still, the damage was done, and the propaganda remained in people's minds, damaging the German people's reputation. This happened fourteen years before Hitler came to full power in 1934.

More recently, after the confiscated Holocaust records of Auschwitz were returned by the Soviet Leader Gorbachev to the German Red Cross, the number of Jews who died there was only 30,000. The rest were internees from all over Europe or political opponents of the Hitler regime. Not one document speaks of an extermination program, mass killing, or gassing. A Jewish lady, Marika Frank, arrived there from Hungary when 25,000 Jews were supposed to have been gassed daily. She saw nothing of what she had been told. After they served their sentences, they were released and could go home. Yehuda Bauer states if it would have been a mass murder camp, as people were made to believe after the war, why would anyone be set free to expose the atrocities that went on? The research chemist William B. Lindsay after careful on-site examination of the "gas chambers" at Auschwitz, Birkenau, and Majdanek, stated, "I have concluded that no one was willfully or purposefully killed with Zyklon B (hydrocyanic acid gas) in this manner. I consider it absolutely impossible."

After meticulous on-site investigation and research, an American Jew, David Cole, found the gas chamber was created in 1947, two years after the war ended. Some walls were removed to create a big room. A hole was opened in the roof to throw the gas on the victims. This so-called "gas chamber" was invented to make the mass gassing story plausible to the public, and still today, to the many tourists who come to visit the facility, now turned into a museum. The director and tour guides of the Auschwitz Museum are instructed on what to say to the visitors to camouflage some of the truth. Thousands of inmates were freed after the war and were interviewed by the Red Cross to see if they witnessed the alleged gassing. They responded negatively. When the new victims arrived at the facility, a small amount of Zyklon B powder was poured through the ceiling's hole to disinfect the people.

Then what was the real purpose and function of the so-called concentration camps? In one of his articles, "The Truth of World War II," John S. Torell states:

> As early as 1870, was a war between Germany and their Allie Japan in the planning against England, France, Soviet Union, and the United States. Albert Pike, the American General, was commissioned by the World Government' to draw a plan of big wars, to create a condition that all nations could be forced to be ruled by one World Leader. As early as 1934, the American Ford Motor Co. and the International Telegraph Co. (ITT) built factories in Germany and Russia where tanks, trucks, and airplanes were man-ufactured for Hitler and Stalin. These war factories' directors had doubts about employing only German

workers, fearing they might lose them when the war broke out. They knew most of the German men would be drafted as soldiers during the war. To solve this problem, they came up with the idea of forced labor and slave camps. Hitler saw the advantage of getting rid of all the people who opposed his regime. Adolf Hitler appointed Heinrich Himmler and Adolf Eichmann, both Jews, to oversee and manage the camps. The communistic party leaders, social democratic party, German pastors, and Christians opposing the Hitler Regime were secretly sentenced and put into these camps. Later came the gypsies, and only in 1938 was the first group of 20,000 Jews. It is not true that these camps were constructed and used to exterminate Jews like the Holocaust propaganda wants everyone to believe. American financiers and German Industrial companies like Krupp and others developed these industrial parks and labor camps that belonged to the World Leader Group to secure products and war machines for WORLD WAR II. Most people who died in the concentration camps were prisoners from Germany or other countries and not Jews only, as the public is made to believe.[35]

According to a recent article by the *Independent News:Dan Plesch, author of* The Human Rights after Hitler, *The Allied Powers were aware of the Jewish Holocaust scale two-and-a-half years earlier than it is generally assumed. Despite this, he commented that the Allied Powers did very little to rescue or provide sanctuary to those in mortal danger.*

In lengthy studies about the Holocaust and the treatment of the German prisoners of war, authors wrote about a lot of facts not known before. Only recently, getting original documents from archives and information available on the internet was such a compilation of data possible. Unfortunately, so many innocent victims suffered, and some villains were celebrated as heroes. A crime is a crime, regardless of who commits it. The criminals should be brought to justice, and not all citizens of the country should be called criminals and be punished for their leader's crimes.

In a summery about the persecution of the Jews from 1933-1945, and the fate of the German prisoners of war and civilians after 1945 manyAuthors compiled recently new information and facts about the concentration camps. The photos of the piled-up corpses that general Eisenhower took were corpses of German prisoners from the American Rhein-Wiesen Prison camp. According to a report, the movie producer Alfred Hitchcock arranged the corpses in such a way that they looked like being all jews. By creating an image of mass murder of Jews, General Eisenhower covered up his own criminal activities of intentionally letting die the German prisoners of war. Even Stalin sent Jews to the Gulags (Forced Labor Camps) and killed over a million, because he found no use for them. Unfortunately, these manipulated photos were also used against the so-called war criminals at the Nuernberg trials. At the end of World War II not only prisoners of war but German citizens and citizens of all the countries involved in the war, suffered physical injuries and illnesses also emotional trauma. Not only millions of Jews died as a consequence of World War II, but millions of innocent children and families from every country where the war raged.

We should never *forget* the Holocaust and persecution of the Jews during World War II.

However, we should also **remember** the suffering of all the innocent people and victims from all countries of both world wars and expose the real criminals of humanity, which covered their crimes by blaming others. No civilians or soldiers were subjected to more inhumane treatment than the Germans through the fire-bombing of the cities and the Japanese being burned alive and mutilated by the atomic bombs. Besides 14,000,000 Germans being robbed of their belongings and driven from their homeland, Germany was forced to permanently give up one-third of their territory.

People who have never been in a war do not know what the soldiers give up and how many injuries and emotional trauma they endure. People who have never lived in a war zone will never know how many atrocities the civilians and prisoners suffered and what sacrifices they were forced to make.

A document by Michael Palomino, published in 2003 and updated in 2015, sums up some unknown facts about the Jews' persecution and some of the allies' atrocities that Hollywood made into movies, being spread worldwide.[36] Nobody talked about the inhumane treatment of the German soldiers killed in the Rhine Meadow Camps or other forced labor camps of the four allies. Only recently, historians, war survivors, and truth seekers write about the 14,000,000 German displaced civilians from East Germany and the one-third of German territories given to Poland and Russia after both world wars. Some residents who could not escape before World War II ended had to work hard for just a little food. The Russians sexually abused women and young girls. Under inhumane conditions, they were stripped of their belongings, driven from their properties, and shipped in crowded train cars to the West. However, the German prisoners of war who worked for private farmers or factories in the United States, France, and England were treated well and respected. The leaders and persons in charge exercised their hate and revenge on particular groups and the allies' governments against the German prisoners of war and civilians. Germany's entire population was held responsible for Hitler's crimes, in this case, condemning mistreating and humiliating them. The generals and soldiers of the allies who hid their crimes from the public were celebrated as heroes by their countries. Instead, most German generals and soldiers who became prisoners of war were treated like disarmed enemy forces and not like prisoners of war by the Geneva Convention rules. Generals and soldiers of all countries who fight or die in the line of duty should be treated respectfully; so should each country's civilians be treated with dignity after the end of a war. The commanders-in-chief of each country start wars, not the civilians. President Roosevelt and Prime Minister Winston Churchill set up rules that victors and vanquished should be treated equally.

"Why didn't they follow their own rules after the end of World War II?"

So many questions are and perhaps will remain unanswered. We only get a glimpse of declassified documents and facts as more declassified information is discovered and publicized on the internet, books, and public media. Only God knows all the truth, and He is in control of the people on earth and His whole magnificent creation of the universe. Even God felt sorry at times that He had created humans when he saw the evil they committed. However, God, in his boundless mercy, saved them again and again from extinction. Knowing how difficult it was to obtain salvation by fulfilling the law, God sacrificed His beloved son Jesus Christ so people can be saved by grace alone and not by good works.

My heart goes out to all the innocent people of all the countries who suffered atrocities in both world wars. I condemn the crime but do not hate the criminals. I pray people from all countries might do the same. I remember many compassionate and honorable things, like the airlift of Berlin and the American Marshall Plan helping rebuild Germany and Europe's countries and economies. Let us hope that we have learned to work together with world countries and settle differences through diplomacy and understanding rather than wars.

Before, during, and after the wars, propaganda and lies were spread to further the world leaders' causes. It takes years of meticulous research and compilation of information to separate fiction from facts, myth from reality, and lies from the truth.

"Only when we know the truth, and we must diligently search the truth — we will be free and more able to interpret the intrigues of historical events. Then, hopefully, we also learn to forgive the criminals of humanity and live peacefully with our global inhabitants.

The question arose once at a dinner party in London, "Who will dominate the future?"

Professor Huxley stated, The Nation who sticks closely to the facts. Gentlemen to all the facts, and the greatest fact of history is God. God is the answer to all our questions. He reveals His answers to all human questions in his Holy Word, the Bible."[37]

Chapter 23

Baltic Cruise and Other Visits

EVER SINCE I learned the history of Catherine the Great in high school, I desired to one day visit Russia and see the influence she left behind for her adopted country, Russia. Her reign as Tzarina of all Russia fascinated me, and I always wanted to see where she ruled. Catherine, the Great was born May 2, 1729, in Stettin, Prussia, as Princess Sophie of Anhalt-Zerbst. She became the ruler of Russia for 34 years after her husband Tzar Peter III died. She attracted many Germans to Russia by giving them some land, promising religious freedom and other privileges. She converted to the Eastern Orthodox Church, governed by Prussian example, and brought European art and culture to Russia. Since the Baltic cruise stopped in St. Petersburg, I decided to join a cruise in August 2011 to visit seven countries on the Baltic Sea. Stopping in St. Petersburg and seeing the influence of Peter the Great and Catherine the Great delighted my eyes and mind. Peter the Great sent artisans, sculptures, and architects worldwide to study designs for palaces, fountains, and statues for St. Petersburg's plans to build a city. Peter the Great, who ruled the Russian Empire from 1682 to 1725, built a fort in May 1703 to protect the city from being invaded by the Swedes. Later, the Swiss architect Tressini continued constructing the city, and thousands of forced laborers died in erecting the town's buildings in a swamp. The gold-plated statues, cascading waterfalls, and landscaping impressed me as well as the other tourists. All fountains worked by water pressure from tanks built at different levels. No electrical-powered motors are needed to operate the many fountains.

When I saw Catherine the Great's summer palace's elegance, I was overwhelmed and also by the restored amber room's splendor. The original amber room décor disappeared during World War II. The amber room restoration began in 1979 and took twenty-four years at the cost of eleven million dollars. Russian President Vladimir Putin and then German Chancellor Gerhard Schroeder dedicated the restored amber room, marking also the 300th anniversary of St. Petersburg. However, the disappearance of the original dismantled amber walls is still a mystery. The son of Friedrich the Great, King of Prussia, gave the original amber room in 1716 as a gift to Peter the Great, Tzar of Russia, who expressed his admiration for the exquisite artwork during one of his visits. It was also commemorated by a treaty between the two rulers against Charles XII of Sweden. Now it is considered the eighth wonder of the world.

Viewing the art and antique collection surrounded by the Hermitage Museum's ambiance and elegance left me speechless. I especially liked the life-size painting of the Return of the Prodigal Son by Rembrandt. Standing in front of Leonardo da Vinci's original artwork, the Madonna Litta, humbled me. The paintings by Titian with such beautifully balanced light and shade effects always fascinated me. An English entrepreneur, James Cox, created the animated Golden Peacock featuring three life-size birds, a peacock, a rooster, and an owl. It is turned on only once a week on Wednesday at 1:00 p.m. One of Catherine the Great's admirers wanted to impress the tzarina with this unique gift. In 1764, Catherine the Great acquired her first art collection in Berlin from Johann Gotzkowski, who had procured the artwork for King Frederick II of Prussia. She wanted to bring culture and prestige to the throne and intended to show it only to her friends and the court's close circle at her winter palace. While Tzar Nicolas II reigned, he opened the museum to the public. During the 1917 Revolution, the museum became public property, and the state operates the most extensive art collection globally, three million artworks, of which only one million are permanently displayed. The reign of Catherine the Great brought prestige to Russia and among the European countries. Attending a Russian ballet performance and watching the graceful ballerinas dancing to the music from Cinderella by Sergei Prokofiev, finished my memorable visit to St. Petersburg.

When the cruise ship stopped in Warnemuende, Germany, I arranged a meeting with the former leader of our DJO Youth Group, Heinz Kraemer, and his son-in-law Michael Glueber. They both lived in Harsefeld, southwest of Hamburg. We had not seen each other for over fifty years. I admired how much he contributed to the youth groups of the refugees. He lost his home in Pomerania, Germany, which was given to Poland after World War II. We reminisced about different events of the past and the many changes in the present. Even though he already reached ninety years, he still wrote reports and poems for special occasions and lectured schools about his World War II experiences. Our vivid conversation and the joy of seeing each other after such a long time will remain unforgettable. We stayed in close contact all the time. Unfortunately, he passed away a few years after we saw each other.

Three years later, I flew to Germany to visit my youngest brother Horst in Offenbach. We attended a confirmation of my great grand-nephew Ramon Martin in Herleshausen. My brother arranged a meeting with several former members of the young and older DJO Youth Group and their spouses. The son of my girlfriend, Bernd Russy, and an accordion player entertained us. We all sang along and exchanged many events of the past and the present. We kept in touch with each other for over fifty years. We stopped along the way to see some more friends from the former DJO Youth Group. I also made a reservation for ten days at the Hilda Stift in Wiesbaden. I thought it to be a spa for tourists. Instead, it turned out to be an older people's home. I looked forward to attending an opera performance. Unfortunately, during that time, no opera or concerts were scheduled. However, my grand-niece, Jana Martin, came to stay with me for a few days. We explored the city and parks and savored the delicious food in Italian restaurants. Also, Hildegard Kleinschmidt, a classmate from high school, and her husband, professor in Pedagogy, Gottfried Kleinschmidt, visited me in Wiesbaden. We spent a memorable day together. I also enjoyed a musical presentation at the Hilda Stift, meeting residents and savoring their good food daily, mainly the tasty pastries served each afternoon.

The following year, I flew to Naples, Florida, visiting my husband's children and celebrating Frank's birthday with his family and friends. Gigi, Christine, and Frank decorated their homes beautifully and lived in a prestigious section of Naples. We enjoyed the delicious food Frank and Peggy prepared, both being excellent cooks. I also enjoyed meeting their kind neighbors and friends, as well as a ride with Frank on his motorcycle through the beautifully landscaped neighborhood. Together, we cruised the Bay of Naples, seeing the magnificent mansions of wealthy politicians and business tycoons.

On the way, I stopped in Hot Springs to celebrate my girlfriend Ilse Stritzke's birthday on March 15. We strolled through Hot Springs, looked at all the exquisite antiques displayed in the windows, and even booked a massage. Ilse was also born in East Prussia. We met in Chicago while attending the same Lutheran Church in Chicago. Her family did not escape before the Russians invaded East Prussia, and they lived for three years with the Russian occupants. Russian soldiers treated the women and girls atrociously. She told me how her baby brother died of malnutrition, and her sister was put in jail for bringing home a potato from the field. She died in prison. We talked about many subjects and experiences and how God helped us through the war and incomprehensible postwar times.

All my life, I desired to see the art collection of the biggest museum in the world, the Louvre, in Paris. In spring 2016, I planned to combine a visit to the Louvre and a Danube River Cruise. I planned to fly to Brussels to visit my girlfriend Elisabeth Bruns, who lived in Oudenaarde, Belgium, and then travel by train to Paris. Elisabeth also booked a visit to the Hieronymus Bosch exhibit in Hertogenbosch. At that time, artwork from all over the world came home. The artist primarily painted religious subjects in oil on large wooden panels. The Garden of Earthly Delight and the Last Judgement panels, which he painted in the 15th century, became famous. We both regretted that I had to cancel the visit to my girlfriend, Elisabeth. My plans changed at the last minute when terrorists attacked the airport in Brussels, destroyed part of the structure, causing it to close. I rebooked my Brussels flight to Frankfurt, Germany, and stayed the extra week with my niece Beate Martin and her husband Gerald in Silkerode. She was delighted, and after I got over my disappointment, I was also. They treated me royally and introduced me to some of her friends. When I mentioned to her about the cancelation of my trip to the Louvre, she said, "No problem, we can watch the art exhibit on the big screen." My niece and her husband enjoyed watching nature films and installed a giant TV screen on the entire wall. We watched the magnificent Renaissance Palace holding the works of art and the world-famous paintings, sculptures, and statues for two evenings.

Of course, seeing the famous Mona Lisa by Leonardo Da Vinci is always impressive. When I looked closely at Mona Lisa, I noticed the artist did not paint eyebrows on her. Leonardo Da

Vinci believed simplicity to be the ultimate sophistication. We saw the original painting, The Lady on the Swing, by Fragonard from 1766, of which we own a copy by an Italian artist. We watched Liberty by Eugene Delacroix 1830 and so many other famous masterpieces in the comfort of their home without battling the crowd. Originally the Louvre palace served as the residence of the French kings. When King Louis XVI decided to reside in Versailles's palace, the king transformed the castle into a museum where over ten million people visit each year.

My niece's girlfriend, Sabine Scheideman, who taught English, Russian, and art in Bischofrode's school, asked me to lecture to her students in English class. Even though I had no time to prepare, the students asked several questions about my past experiences. The students absorbed all my comments attentively and showed interest in my poetry book and writing. At the end of class, a student presented me with a bouquet of tulips as a token of appreciation. When the students graduated and went on a field trip, they wrote a postcard to me, signed by each student. I appreciated their thoughtfulness. I in turn sent to the teacher and each student a book of my poems, called A Song in the Night.

I joined travel agent Melissa Porzak from San Diego and her group on a Danube cruise one week later. First, we all met at the luxurious Aria Hotel in the beautiful city of Prague. Next, we took a bus to Vilshofen, where we embarked on the Ama cruise ship. After Melissa, our tour director, introduced all of us to one another, we became an extended family for the rest of the land excursions and meals. The bus trip through the Southern Bavarian Lake region stopped at Mondsee, Austria, to visit the Collegiate church of St. Michaels. Maria and Georg von Trapp's marriage ceremony in the musical The Sound of Music was filmed in the church. The exquisitely decorated altar displayed in the lower section relics of former Austrian rulers, decorated with precious jewelry. While filming the wedding scene of Julie Andrews and Christopher Plummer for The Sound of Music, the photographer had some of the relics covered. The adjacent medieval historic Mondsee Abbey houses a prominent book collection, including some original music sheets of Ludwig von Beethoven's compositions. I admired the concept of beauty, the artists who created all the ornate gilded statues between columns, not only on the altar but also on both sides of the church. All-day long, the eyes feasted not only on the human-made work of art but on God's creation of such beautiful scenery as well.

Visiting Vienna, Austria's capital, we saw the influence of Empress Maria Theresa (1740-1780) and Emperor Franz Joseph (1848 -1916), who created many monumental buildings in the Baroque style. We visited the emperor's castle and the structure across from it, the stable of the Spanish Riding School's famous Lipizzaner Horses. We only got a glimpse of some horses and, unfortunately, did not see their magnificent performance. Vienna boasts of many cultural and musical events and attracts artists from all over the world. The Vienna Symphony Orchestra, Vienna Philharmonic Orchestra, the Vienna Boys' Choir, and Opera Galas are world-renowned; so are the music festivals at Castle Schoenbrun. Fortunately, we attended a concert at Orchestra Hall. I recall an incident happening to me before the beginning of the performance. On the way to the upstairs washroom, I met a musician with a violin. I asked him, "Do I have enough time to go to the washroom?" He replied politely, "Yes." When I returned, I discovered the musician I spoke to was the conductor of the orchestra. He waited until I took my seat and then began conducting and playing the violin, a Vienna Walz, "The Blue Danube" by Johann Strauss. A tenor and soprano sang opera arias, and two ballerinas, male and female, danced for the audience. We rewarded all performers with thunderous applause. Of course, we could not leave Vienna without seeing the giant Ferris wheel in the Prater Amusement Park and tasting an authentic wiener apple strudel with hot vanilla Sauce.

The next town we floated through was Budapest. Cruising through Budapest at night with the Parliament and all the historical buildings illuminated ended the memorable cruise with a grand finale. A certain sadness filled my heart while parting from my traveling companions who showed me kindness and interest in my book I was writing. They all gave me their email addresses so I could notify them when my book would be published. From Budapest, I flew to London, San Francisco, and back to Reno.

During the summer, I had many visitors; even the teacher Sabine Scheideman came with her husband and daughter from Germany, two nieces, Christa and Ilse with their husbands, Rick and Ron, and friends Sue and Ed Guzek from San Diego. We all enjoyed each other's company and the scenic beauty of Lake Tahoe.

Later that summer, at the routine yearly mammogram, the radiologist discovered a lump in my left breast. The biopsy confirmed a cancerous growth, which the surgeon Dr. Evans removed shortly after the biopsy. During my preparations for surgery, I saw Dr. Evans leaning against the wall with her hands folded. I thought she prayed, and I felt at peace, too. I found out later that Dr. Evans was a Christian surgeon and did pray for her patients before, during, and after surgery. Dr. Alexis Carrel, a Nobel prize winner in 1912 and whose research paved the way for organ transplants, had this to say about prayer:

> Prayer is the only power in the world that seems to overcome the "Laws of Nature." Properly understood, prayer is a mature activity indispensable to the fullest development of personality—the ultimate integration of man's highest faculties. Only in prayer do we achieve that complete and

harmonious assembly of body, mind, and spirit, which gives the frail human reed its unshakable strength.[38]

My girlfriend, Carol Miller, waited for me in the lobby. After I got up without being dizzy from the gurney in the recovery room, Carol took me home. A few hours later, I still had no pain and felt very well, so Carol decided to go home, rather than staying overnight. The plastic spray-on bandage allowed me to shower, and I never suffered discomfort or pain. I thanked God for the surgery results, done by a Christian surgeon, and that the oncologist prescribed no chemotherapy.

Chapter 24
Special Celebrations

SINCE MY HUSBAND, Dr. Aldo Bruni, passed away, September 28, 2009, I wanted to honor him with a special event celebrating his life. Each year, when I thought about preparing for the event, grief overwhelmed me, and tears flowed down my cheeks and stopped my plans. Seven years later, I thought, why not have a double event, celebrate my husband's life at the end of January 2017 and my eightieth birthday at the same time. I talked to my husband's and my family, and they agreed. So I began designing the invitation and the program for the event at the San Carlos Country Club. As a souvenir, I created bookmarks with a rose for the ladies and bachelor buttons for the gentlemen, with a poem I wrote about friends."Friends are like golden sunshine. They brighten our days by showing love and kindness in many different ways." I also printed a brief biography of my husband for each couple or a single guest. I worked diligently for several months; my friends and my maid Chava helped me wherever they could.

The semi-formal event began on Sunday, January 29, at 3:00 p.m.

I had engaged four young boys of the McLean family to take the guests to the tables, set with bouquets of pink roses, small blue flowers, white margaritas, green mums, and baby breaths. During dinner, Valeria, an opera soprano, sang popular songs accompanied by her fiancé, Roberto, on the piano. Also, a priest dressed in an elegantly embroidered suit and matching sombrero sang accompanied by a guitar. My family, Peggy, Frank, Joanne, and Dave delighted me with their presence. My wonderful neighbors Kelly and Ron from South Lake Tahoe, my friend Marcia Bogan from Bakersfield, and Penny from Phoenix. Dr. Benda and Dr. Patterson, Mark and Curt, part of the Medical Team from Bozeman, Montana, celebrated with me, as did Pastor Glenn Driedger and Jeannine and over one hundred guests. After the waiters served an early dinner of filet mignon and coconut shrimp, my master of ceremony, David Long, eloquently welcomed the guests and announced the program's beginning, honoring my late husband, Dr. Aldo R. Bruni.

80ᵀᴴ BIRTHDAY AND MEMORIAL FOR DR. ALDO R. BRUNI

Jenny Navarra translated the biography and speeches into Spanish. Padre Rogelio began the program by singing "Amore Eterno" (Eternal Love) by Juan Gabriel while I stood on the stage in front of my husband's large portrait next to my friend Maria de Los Angeles. Juan Gabriel wrote this emotional song when his mother died in 1984

Then my master of ceremony, David Long, began reading my husband's biography. David put so much emotion into his excellent presentation that he captured the audience's attention fully. During a brief pause, Valeria sang one of my husband's and my favorite arias, "Casta Diva," from the opera "Norma" by Bellini. Monserat sang "You lift me up," and Ricardo "Non ti scordar mai di me" (Never forget about me), one of my husband's favorite popular songs. Next, Joanne and Frank expressed their love for their father, mentioning some important events shared. They also showed their gratitude toward me and how much I contributed to their lives and their father's life. Their speeches moved me; so did the one by Tato, a thirteen-year-old boy whose grandmother and mother were friends of mine. Tato asked me if he could also give a short speech. I agreed without knowing what to expect. His mother, whom he loved dearly, had cancer and other health issues, and sharing her pain, matured him prematurely. Tato expressed his affection for me and that he learned from me to live in the present time, to appreciate each moment's good, and to love unconditionally. We usually acquire this lesson later in life, and he had learned it from me while still a teenager. I felt humbled. After Tato's speech, my maid Chava began reading her notes. She started crying and could not finish expressing her appreciation and admiration for the way we treated her. Then Valeria, Monserat, and Aubrey sang "The Last Rose of Summer." Each young lady gave me a pink rose to symbolize that life goes on, even if a loved one passes away, and we find beauty again along the changed walk of life.

After a brief pause, Nancy Dreiling brought the cake tastefully decorated with the same flowers as the centerpieces and two candles saying 80 on top. Everyone sang "Happy Birthday" in English first and then the Mexican birthday song "Las Mananitas," translated: It's the day it is the morning you get treated like a king because this morning is your birthday and your praises we will sing.

Meanwhile, Obregon's folkloric dancers, dressed in stunning colorful costumes, came on the stage and performed Mexican dances for over an hour. At the end of the performance, the guests stepped outside to release inflated illuminated balloons and watched fireworks that a friend arranged as a gift. Most guests left. However, Marcello, who had brought his accordion, entertained my family and close friends for another hour. He sang Italian songs, and we sang along with him. Six hours later, at 9:00 p.m., we all went home tired but content that all went well. I thanked God for all his guidance and blessings.

Before my family and friends from the States left, I catered a Mexican dinner, and as a surprise, I engaged a Mariachi band to entertain them. Just when everyone finished eating, the door opened, and the performing musicians entered the room. We all went out to the patio and listened to the mariachi music under the star-studded sky. Before everyone left, I thanked my dear family and friends for making the event memorable for all of us.

My brother Edmund and sister-in-law Karin visited me in Lake Tahoe during the summer. We enjoyed reminiscing about our childhood in East Prussia, savoring food that our mother used to cook, and Lake Tahoe's beautiful scenery. Even though East Prussia was gone with both world wars our childhood memories of home will always remain.

Another pleasant event was the Mexican wedding celebration of my friends, Valeria and Roberto, on November 19, 2017, which acquainted me with the Mexican tradition. Valeria asked me if her bridal party could get ready in my apartment. I agreed. Sunday morning, four beauticians arrived first and transformed the place into a beauty parlor. Then the mothers of the bride and groom and the eight bridesmaids came. Each bridesmaid wore a colored satin jacket the bride had given them, indicating the gown's color they would wear for the ceremony on the beach of the San Carlos Plaza Hotel. The beauticians created fancy and different hairstyles for each lady, including me. After they put on their gowns, they all looked stunning. One bridesmaid forgot to bring her formal dress with her; someone had to get it from Guaymas. It delayed the beginning of the ceremony by one hour. Workers set up a wooden platform on the sandy beach with white chairs for the guests behind a decorated altar. The pastor also included the bride and groom's parents in the ceremony when he placed a large rosary over the bride and groom's shoulders while joining them as husband and wife. The parents and the guests congratulated the newlyweds. After the ceremony, the families and guests helped themselves to appetizers, wine, and soft drinks from a beautifully arranged table on the beach. A reception at a banquet hall followed in the evening with Mariachi music entertaining the family members and friends until late at night. As a wedding gift, I let the newlyweds stay at my apartment for one week. Before they left, I invited their families and friends for dinner. Later, I presented the following poem I wrote for them:

"*Love Is a Song*"

Love is a song that never needs to end.
It has the sweetest melody to grant.

The beautiful love of newlyweds only is
A prologue of a stronger loving bliss.
After sharing years of joy and sorrow,
Their love grows deeper; then tomorrow
Will reflect God's endless love divine,
And be selfless, giving, and sublime.
Their hearts will overflow with melodies
Lasting here and through eternities.

Love is a song that never needs to end,
It has the sweetest melody to grant.

Both Valerie and Roberto liked the poem so much that Roberto composed a melody to it. Valeria sang the new song with so much sentiment at our next gathering; it deeply moved me. Everyone enjoyed our musical events, so we decided to have one each year at my house. Valeria, Roberto, and her father Louis brought so much joy to my friends and me; we treasure our friendships.

When I returned to Lake Tahoe the following spring, I had the pleasure to meet my new neighbors Dr. Tatjana, her husband Keith, and their two daughters Erika and Evelina, as well as some of their friends and their neighbors Rayna and Dan Currier. We also got together with my immediate neighbors and friends Kelly and Ron. We all enjoyed each other's company and helped each other whenever necessary. Spending the Fourth of July with Kelly and Ron and their friends, enjoying the delicious food and Kelly's gracious hospitality, and watching the firework display on the Lake from their beautiful home is always a treat. Both are not only caring neighbors but also treasured friends.

The following year, I met a lady doctor, Connie Hahn, who came with the medical team from Bozeman, Montana, to San Carlos, Mexico. While visiting Lake Tahoe, Dr. Hahn introduced me to her doctor's friend Dr. Pattie Francis, who lives in Lake Tahoe. Dr. Francis and Dr. Hahn belong to the Christian organization called Christian Woman Physicians for Christ (CWPC). When fifteen members met at Dr. Francis's house to plan the agenda for the next five years, they also included me in their circle. I admired their mission to donate their time to help needy patients in foreign countries, who do not have the means to pay for medical services.

For the Fourth of July 2019, I invited Dr. Francis and her family. I also had a couple from Idaho visiting me. We all spent a memorable evening watching the fireworks over the lake from the balcony of my house. Hundreds of boats with their red and green lights encircled the barges, from which the fireworks were launched. They add a special effect to the colorful displays close to the water and up in the sky. At the finale, when many fireworks are going up simultaneously, my guests were in awe, and so was I.

Unfortunately, I fell when I tried to put an egg carton in the garbage bin the next day. Thinking it was only a muscle injury of the upper arm, I took some pain pills and hoped it would heal soon.

In August, my friends Sue and Ed from San Diego came to visit me. Dan and Rayna invited my friends Sue, Ed, and me for a day-long boat trip, observing Lake Tahoe's shoreline's beauty with all the magnificent mansions. Dan is an excellent captain who maneuvers the boat well in tight corners, but he also explains the history of Lake Tahoe's unique places, like a professional tour guide. When Sue and Ed drove back to San Diego, I went with them. We stopped in Bakersfield and visited my friend Marcia Bogan, who had recent spine surgery and wore a full-body cast. She and her son Gene met us in the well-known Basque restaurant, the Woolgrowers. Despite being incapacitated, Marcia seemed in good spirits, and we were happy to see each other again. She calls me her sister in Christ. We met in San Carlos many years ago. However, after her husband passed away, she and her son returned to Bakersfield to be close to her mother. We drove directly to Laguna Beach from Bakersfield to see my stepdaughter Joanne and her husband, Dr. Trotter.

Ed had an engagement the following morning, so he returned to San Diego. The next day Mary Ellen, the sister of Sue, joined us to see the Pageant of the Masters. The year's theme was "The Time Machine," combining art and science in the exhibit. In addition, the producer of the pageant included a moon landing recreated with a live astronaut–very impressive. The Finale, Leonardo Da Vinci's "Last Supper" with the live orchestra's appropriate background music is the show's culmination, which we all relished.

When I came back from San Diego, my right shoulder's pain had subsided, but I noticed some limited movements of my right arm. I decided to see an orthopedic surgeon. The MRI of the right shoulder showed a complete tear of the humerus's tendon and arthritic changes. The orthopedic surgeon suggested a total shoulder replacement. I told the doctor I had plans to leave for Mexico the next month and I'll think about surgery. I immediately emailed the report to my stepson-in-law David, an excellent orthopedic surgeon, and asked his opinion. He called me and asked me only one question, "Are you in a lot of pain?" When I surprised him with the answer, "No." He replied, "With the severity of your report, you should be in a lot of pain. Since you have none, I suggest not to have any surgery." I followed his advice and learned to live with the limited function of the right arm. I thanked God that I had no pain and needed no shoulder replacement or specific treatments. One month later, my maid Chava and I drove off happily to Mexico.

Shortly after I arrived in San Carlos, my dear friend Carol Miller's tragic death shocked me and her family and close friends. We all miss her kind, loving, and generous friendship. Her son, James, and his family, who live in Reno, became friends of mine, and they also visited me in Lake Tahoe. The same year I also lost two other dear friends, Betty Barengo and Maria Esther Morales. When we moved to San Carlos, Betty introduced me to Club Recuerdo, and we worked together for many years and donated the money we raised to charities and needy people. Maria Esther also passed away after long-time suffering from cancer and spine problems. Maria Esther's daughter Monserat and sons Tato and Ricardo, three gifted and intelligent children, brought a lot of joy to me by singing or cooking together.

Unfortunately, I also lost my ninety-year-old sister Meta Seidel. She went to meet her Lord whom she served all her life faithfully. Before Mother met her Savior face to face, she taught us by example Christian values and that suffering is necessary in life to develop a noble Christian character. We tried to live by her moral values and to meet her expectations. My father, my older sisters Emma, and Marta as well as my brothers Georg and Richard also passed away. As a result, our family dwindled to my brothers Edmund, Horst, and me.

The Lebanese author, Kahlil Gibran, best known for "The Prophet", quotes: "Sorrow stretches the heart so it can contain more joy." Life's loss brings sorrow, but a newborn baby brings joy to the parents, family, and friends. My friends Katie and Denver Janz welcomed their daughter, Noel and Valeria, and Roberto, their son, Robertito. Valeria delivered her baby by a cesarian section, and her husband played piano in the operating room during the entire delivery. They hope their son will become either a singer or a pianist. When Valeria and her family came to a birthday celebration of three of my lady friends and me in January 2020, Robertito kicked his little feet rhythmically while the mother sang beautiful arias and popular Mexican songs. My friends, Judy Long's and Maggie Snell's, birthdays were January 1, mine January 2, and Sahsha Sturt's December 10. We decided to celebrate with our mutual friends at home. Valeria's father, Luis Quijada, played the guitar and sang solo or with his daughter. We all enjoyed a delightful musical afternoon.

In February, the COVID-19 infection of the coronavirus spread, causing a global pandemic. Immediately social distancing and wearing masks became mandatory. The world leaders restricted international traveling and ordered many businesses, like hotels and restaurants, to close. Performing artists canceled live concerts and public events. To the detriment of sports fans, they could not watch their favorite games in person. Many families could not celebrate their weddings and other gatherings due to the rapidly spreading infections. Universities, schools, and churches closed, creating a completely different social norm for people worldwide. The temporarily reduced production of paper goods and other items began shortages and long lines at supermarkets. Worst of all, many who contracted COVID-19 died, and the families could not even get together for their funerals. My heart went out, and I prayed for unfortunate people who lost loved ones, jobs, and homes in countries where the government did not give them any financial assistance like the American government did.

All summer long, fires raged around the Lake Tahoe Basin, and the dense smoke made the mountains and the lake invisible. Fortunately, I could return to Mexico in the fall again. My friends Kathryn and Harvey Teitzel, who own a condominium in Seattle and San Carlos, Mexico, picked me up on their way to San Carlos. Kathryn drove my car and her husband theirs. We enjoyed vivid conversations about her Russian mission work and my past experiences during World War II. We always thanked God for victoriously helping us through our storms of life and blessing us beyond measure.

When we arrived in San Carlos, my maid, Rosalba (Chava), came to the house on her day off to help me unpack the car. She welcomed me with open arms and put fresh flowers on the tables to my delight. I am grateful for her kindness, thoughtfulness, and loyalty. She always encourages me to write. The day I tell her I wrote a few pages, she claps her hands and gleefully exclaims, "That is good." She has worked for me for fourteen years. In turn, I always kept and still keep my promise I made to God sixty-four years ago to treat employees with respect and never belittle them but praise and help them where indicated.

Social distancing is in effect in San Carlos; It felt strange to watch some of our church services on the internet rather than meeting with the worshippers in the church. We also avoided many social gatherings. However, I stay in touch with all my family and friends by calling and sending email messages. We comfort and encourage each other to remain focused on God, and I have learned from this chaotic time's hardship to become a better person.

Chapter 25

Looking Back with Gratitude

WHILE I WROTE my book, I looked back at my life with gratitude toward God first. Jesus saved me by grace while still a child. He led my family and me victoriously through both world wars. God helped us getting through dangers, sufferings, famine, hardships, grief, disappointments, and sickness while we trusted and obeyed His will. I marvel at how many times He tore us from the claws of death itself during the war and saved our lives. When emotional darkness surrounded us, God brought light and joy into our lives, often in miraculous ways. Life is like a blank canvas. The final work of art depends on whether we engage a divine or secular artist. God will use all our disappointments and sufferings as shadows and the joys and happiness as the painting's highlights. I trusted God with my life. He added His graceful golden strokes to give beauty and radiance to the finished masterpiece, delighting and bringing joy to people.

On the other hand, if I had let the world's influence and evil create a painting, it would look bleak and depressing and displease or even disgust the viewers. As an individual, I had the choice, regardless of circumstances, which life's work I would create. I am grateful that my mother raised my siblings and me with Christian principles. The teachers taught not only their assigned curriculum but also moral values and practical wisdom for life. I treasure the many friends God sent me to share life's experiences. A joy shared multiplies it; a sorrow shared diminishes it. God let me taste the agony and ecstasy of life. I learned that protected ease is not the most favorable condition of life.

On the contrary, hardship, and faith in God create a strong and noble character. I am grateful to God for taking me on arduous and incredible journeys through many stormy seas and dangers and also peaceful mountaintops. Still, He always landed me safely and triumphantly in His loving arms, enriched and blessed beyond measure. God fulfilled all the promises I claimed and especially the one in Romans 8:28: "All things work together for good to them that love God."

Now my goal is to live by the rules of God and replace the golden rule with what I call my platinum rule, thinking and acting the way my Lord and Savior taught me by His example. I know I have shortcomings, but I trust with God's grace, guidance, and help to overcome some. I want to give God all the glory and bring comfort and joy to others.

Even though I know that gone with the world wars are my native East Prussia and home, God has prepared an eternal home in heaven for all His faithful children and me. What an unimaginable and grandiose splendor it will be to see God the Father and His Son Jesus Christ face-to-face and hear the glorious angel's voices singing. I will rejoin all my loved ones, friends, and Christians from all nations of the world who went to heaven before me. God's love healed all wounds, wiped away all tears, and He will replace them with eternal joy. I will worship, praise, and glorify my heavenly Father and my Lord and Savior Jesus Christ forever and ever.

Hildegard Bonacker Bruni

Hildegard was born in East Prussia
Near the King's and Kaiser's hunting ground.
In World War Two she escaped from Prussia.
And in the West a home she found.

She received her former education
As a Doctor's Assistant in Medicine.
Then left behind her German Nation.
And became an American Citizen.

To be an Artist at her best,
This dream she nursed deep in her heart.
She studied intensly without rest
At the Academy of Art.

In Chicago, and in Palatine
At Harper College for many years.
Teachers helped her technique to refine,
And recognized the rare talent of hers.

She designs on porcelain with great care,
And masters watercolor and oil.
With flowers she has quite a flair,
Paints portraits, still lives also well.

Hildegard new challenges loves.
She never fails to give her best.
Whether painting for you, art shows,
Or exhibiting in the Midwest.

Her paintings are not art alone,
Nor merely nature; but the two
Joined in a mystic marriage, and born
Is a lovely work of art for you.

A Professor from the U.C.L.A.
Has this about her paintings to say:
"The richness of color, harmonious display
Her inner joy and beauty portray."

POEM OF ARTIST HILDEGARD BONACKER BRUNI

Links to review for more information

Up-to-date information about gassing Auschwitz for further research information:

Emperor of all lies (Part 1)
waykiwayki.com.

This is information about the Allied war crimes that took place between 1941-1950:

https://www.thetruthseeker.co.uk/?p=242411

For more information about the forming of the First Federal Republic of Germany:

https://www.nationsonline.org/oneworld/History/Federal-Republic-Germany-history.htm

For more information about the terms of the Two by Four Treaty:

https://www.deutschland.de/en/topic/politics/germany-europe/two-plus-four-treaty.

Endnotes

1   Wikipedia, "The Kingdom of Prussia," https://en.wikipedia.org.

2   Ostpreussen.de Geschichte, "Landsmannschaft Ostpreussen," https://ostpreussen.de/Ospreussen/geschichte.htm.

3   Britannica, "World War 1 History Summary," https://Britannica.com/event/world/war.

4   Ansprache zum Ausbruch des 1 Weltkrieges, "Wilhelm II War Speeches," https://wwi.lib.buy.edu>index.php>Wilhelm II's.war.

5   Roger Hummel, "Review of *The Lusitania* by Colin Simpson," *Reason,* 1976.

6   History.com, "Armistice Day: World War I Ends," https://www.history.com>this-day-in-history>world-...

7

8   History.com, "The Versailles Treaty," A&E TV Network, October 29, 2009, https://www.history.com<topics>world-war-I>treaty.

9   History.com, "The Weimar Republic – History," A&E TV Network, December 4, 2017, https://www.history.com/topics/Germany/Weimar-Republic.

10 Adolf Hitler, *Mein Kampf* (Germany, 1925).

11 Britannica, "Third Reich: Facts & History," http://www.britannica.com>...>HistoricalPlaces.

12 Britannica, "World War II Facts and Summary: History, Dates, Combatants, 2 Minutes Summary," September 27, 2021, http://www.britannnica.com>events>World-War-II.

13 Wikipedia, "The Potsdam Conference," http://en.wikipedia.org>Potsdam_Agreement.

14 Kurt Dieckert and Grossman Horst, *Der Kampf um Ostpreußen* (Lindenbaum Verlag, GmbH, 2010).

15 Paul Gerhardt, "Commit whatever Grieves thee," 1867, http://hymnary.org/text/commit_whatever_grieves_the.

16 History.com, "Marshall Plan – History," December 16, 2009, https://www.history.com/topics/world-war-ii/marshall-plan-1...

17 Time, "The Nations: Operation Bird Dog," http://content.time.com>magazine>article.

18 Brian Dorn and Jennifer Llewellyn, "The Berlin Blockade – The Cold War," Alpha History, http://alphahistory.com/coldwar/berlin-blockade.

19 History.com, "Formation of the Federal Republic of Germany," Britannica, November 13, 2009, https://www.history.com>this-day-in-history>federal...

20 Wikipedia, "Content and Analysis: Atlantic Charter," http://en.wikipedia.org/wiki/Atlantic-charter.

21 Richard Stockton, "The Dark Secret of WWII German Death Camp," Allthatinteresting.com, January 13, 2017, https://allthatinteresting.com>Rheinwiesenlager.

22 John Wear, "Did the Allies Outdo the Germans in Crimes and Atrocities," Renegade Tribune, www.renegadetribune.com/allies-outdo-germans-crime-atrocities.

23 Johann Wolfgang von Goethe, "The Erl-King," Britannica, 1782, https://www.britannica.com>Literature>Poetry.

24 Giuseppe Verdi, *Opera Otello*, Teatro Alla Scala Milan, February 5, 1887.

25 Hans Hildebrand, "Martin Luther/Biography/Reformation/Accomplishments/German religious leader," Britannica, http://www.britannica.com>biography>Martin-Luther.

26 Jacob Grimm and Wilhelm Grimm, *The Golden Goose Fairytale* (1812).

27 Jean-Baptiste Moliere, *Hypochondriac or Imaginary Invalid – Three act comedy*, Theatre du Palais-Royal, February 10, 1673.

28 Andreas Noll, "After World War II, German POWs were enlisted to rebuild France," DW, August 5, 2020, https://www.dw.com>a533374941.

29 Prof. Ernst Hermann Rübsam, "POWs in American camps," *Mein Heimatland.*

30 Heinrich Tieck, *Freund so du etwas bist* (Wien, Austria: Scheuerman, 1960).

31 Hans Bauman, "Hohe Nacht der klaren Sterne (High night of the clear stars)," 1936, https://dewikipedia.org>wiki>Hoh...

32 Reverend J.H. Randolph Ray, *Robins Reader No 1, 1972 for Physicians and Patients: How to be Happy Though Married* (New York: Little Church around the Corner, 1972).

33 Lee Strobel, *The Case for Easter* (Zondervan, 2009).

34 Lee Strobel, *Images of Science and God in Bing.com Images* (2012).

35 John Torell, "The Truth about the Second World War," Die Warheit über den Zweiten Weltkreig, http://www.eaec-de.org/Warheit_ueber_den_2.Weltkrieg.

36 Michael Palamino, "Summary about the persecution of the Jews 1933 – 1945," 2003, http://www.hist.com/judentum-aktenlage/hd/6-mio-partition-GB.htm.

37 Mrs. Chas. E. Cowman, *Streams in the Desert, Twenty-first Edition* (Los Angeles: Oriental Missionary Society, 1941).

38 Dr. Alexis Carrel, *Robins Reader Spring 1986 for Physicians and Patients: A Doctor Looks at Prayer.*

BEDLAM LOST

LOST

JACK♜CASTLE

EDGE-Lite

An Imprint of HADES PUBLICATIONS, INC.
CALGARY

BEDLAM LOST

Copyright © 2016 by Chris Tortora

EDGE-Lite

An Imprint of HADES PUBLICATIONS, INC.
P.O. Box 1714, Calgary, Alberta, T2P 2L7, Canada

The EDGE-Lite Team:
Producer: Brian Hades
Editor: Ella Beaumont
Cover Artist: Ben Goode
Book Design: Mark Steele
Publicist: Janice Shoults

ISBN: 978-1-77053-109-3

EDGE Science Fiction and Fantasy Publishing and Hades Publications, Inc. acknowledges the ongoing support of the Alberta Foundation for the Arts and the Canada Council for the Arts for our publishing programme.

Canada Council Conseil des arts
for the Arts du Canada

Library and Archives Canada Cataloguing in Publication
CIP Data on file with the National Library of Canada
ISBN: 978-1-77053-109-3
(e-Book ISBN: 978-1-77053-105-5)

FIRST EDITION
(20161129)
Printed in USA
www.edgewebsite.com

Publisher's Note:

Thank you for purchasing this book. It began as an idea, was shaped by the creativity of its talented author, and was subsequently molded into the book you have before you by a team of editors and designers.

Like all EDGE books, this book is the result of the creative talents of a dedicated team of individuals who all believe that books (whether in print or pixels) have the magical ability to take you on an adventure to new and wondrous places powered by the author's imagination.

As EDGE's publisher, I hope that you enjoy this book. It is a part of our ongoing quest to discover talented authors and to make their creative writing available to you.

We also hope that you will share your discovery and enjoyment of this novel on social media through Facebook, Twitter, Goodreads, Pinterest, etc., and by posting your opinions and/or reviews on Amazon and other review sites and blogs. By doing so, others will be able to share your discovery and passion for this book.

Brian Hades, publisher

Dedications

Dedicated to those who kept the dream alive:
Wife, muse, and soulmate Tracy Tortora
My two best friends Chad Bryant and Greg Wahlman
Mentor Dr. J.P. Waller.
Our Lord and Savior.

I would also like to acknowledge and thank the fine folks
at EDGE Science Fiction and Fantasy Publishing: Editor
Supreme Ella Beaumont, Publicist and Fairy God-Mamma
Janice Shoults, Formatter and Support Man of Awesome
Mark Steele, and of course, the Mad Hatter in charge of it
all, Mr. Brian Hades.

"From thereupon do I this body bring.
To tell you who I am were speech in vain,
Because my name as yet makes no great noise."

"And of that second kingdom will I sing
Wherein the human spirit doth purge itself,
And to ascend to heaven becometh worthy."
—Dante Alighieri, The Divine Comedy

"How seldom we recognize the sound when the
bolt of our fate slides home."
—Thomas Harrison, Miami 2000

Chapter 1

Hank

"PLEASE ... PLEASE DON'T kill me."
The disembodied voice sobbed in the darkness, begging for his life. The hammer of a heavy-duty revolver drew back...

A tiny light in the distance: a pinprick of light at the end of a long tunnel moved rapidly closer. The growing hot white light, accompanied by a roaring sound, increased in severity and relentlessness.

CLANG-CLANG-CLANG-CLANG!

Hank McCarthy bolted awake to the sound of a roaring locomotive heaving straight for the car. He flashed open his eyes, squinting from the light and found himself sitting behind the wheel of a crimson red Ford Explorer. He jerked back, but there was no place to go. Far too late to move, he braced for final impact.

As the deafening train ripped past his SUV a scant few yards away, he realized he was idling *parallel* to the railroad tracks. The intense pain of the train's horn still registered in his ears and his body trembled violently for a few seconds while he emerged from his deep slumber. It took him another moment to realize he still wasn't in danger of becoming track paste.

Where am I?

A light touch on his shoulder revealed creamy white, French-manicured fingers. Their owner lovely: almond-shaped eyes, perfect white teeth, and curly nutmeg hair framing a face that would make even a fairytale princess envious. His wife, Sarah.

"Wow, babe," she laughed nervously. "I knew you were tired but you were really out there." He had been driving for a long time. She gave him a funny look. "You want me to drive the rest of the way?"

Hank's throat was so dry his tongue had swelled two sizes. When he finally managed to talk it was above a hoarse whisper. "Honey, where are we?" He wanted to scream the question at her. The whisper was all he could manage.

"Are we there yet, Daddy?"

A glance in the mirror confirmed what he already knew: five year old Annabelle sat strapped in her car seat by a five-point retention harness originally designed for fighter pilots. Little Annabelle shared her mom's good looks, but had inherited *his* limited patience.

"Almost there sweetheart," Sarah answered for him. "We just have to board the train."

"But I'm so-o hungry," Annabelle complained.

"Have some more Goldfishes, honey," Sarah answered. Without missing a beat the box came over the seat with two quick shakes, and Annabelle beheld the delicious golden baked treats.

Annabelle was placated for now. She stared out the window with her mother's hazel eyes as she absentmindedly devoured the helpless fishes in her hand.

One year old Henry snoozed soundly in his car seat beside her. When it came to the looks department, Henry took more after his pop. Dark wavy hair, firm jaw affixed to a kind face. And dark blue eyes, somehow sweet and fierce at the same time.

Hank took this all in, but none of this answered the question that still burned in his aching head: *Where the hell am I?*

He peered through the SUV's open window. A majestic wilderness with snow-capped mountains, stitched with evergreens, sprawled out around them seemingly endless. The overcast skies and down-creeping snowline suggested winter was closing in. *This looks like the Pacific Northwest?* That didn't make sense.

The train tracks emerged from the forest in the distance, miles behind them, and then came up to a rickety but serviceable train station smack dab in the middle of nowhere. The station sign read HavenPort, Alaska.

Alaska? When the hell did we decide on Alaska? I must be dreaming. We live in the desert. Two thousand miles away.

"Look Mommy, look!" Annabelle yelled wildly from her car seat. "A moose, Mommy, a moose!"

Hank turned his head and groaned at the stabbing pain in his temples. He rubbed at them mightily: If his hand weren't already there, he'd have thought he'd been stabbed on both sides of his head with an ice pick. *Must've slept wrong while I was snoozing behind the wheel.*

"Oh Hank, she's right." Sarah cooed beside him. "There's a moose in the lake over there."

Just beyond Sarah's window he could make out the moose meandering across a shallow lake.

Hank suppressed the huge urge to punch the windshield. *Why will no one answer me? Where are we?*

Sarah turned towards him. "Do you see him?" Before he could answer, she dug frantically through her mommy purse the size of a saddlebag. "Now where's my camera?" She turned back to the kids, "Annabelle, honey, do you know where mommy's camera is?"

This doesn't make sense. We live in Wyoming. I don't even remember deciding to come to Alaska, let alone driving here.

"There it is." Sarah took her camera from the center console compartment. Before she could snap a picture…

WHUMP, WHUMP.

Hank jumped at the sound of a large man pounding the palm of his meaty hand on the hood of the Explorer.

"Hey pretty boy, you're holding up the line," he said in a gruff voice, "We ain't got all day." The big man was dressed in overalls and a baseball cap. His rough, heavily-pockmarked face, oversized bulbous nose, and squinty eyes loomed over Hank. He stepped to the side of the hood and motioned Hank to pull forward. An impatient driver in a rusted Ford-150 behind them laid on his horn.

"C'mon buddy," the driver shouted.

On autopilot, Hank shifted into drive and pulled forward. The SUV drove forward up a dirt incline ramp and onto a flatbed train car. They were one of many; all lined up behind an antique locomotive the color of charcoal. Hank put the car in park and switched off the engine.

"We're on a train!" Annabelle shouted with glee.

As other cars loaded up onto the freight cars, Hank saw something strange on the train depot platform. It was a comely woman wearing horn-rimmed glasses. Unlike the people wearing layers of warm coats and hats around her, she was only wearing a long physician's lab coat. Not so strange in itself, but the white in her coat was so sharp in color, and such a shocking contrast to the drab filtered daylight, it was as though someone wearing bright colors had stepped into an old black-and-white movie. It actually hurt Hank's eyes to stare at it.

The disembarking passengers bustling about didn't seem to notice the strange doctor woman, and she seemed equally disinterested in them. She didn't appear to have anyplace else she needed to be. Instead, she kept staring intently at Hank. She wasn't just looking at the train or at their vehicle, only at him.

What's her problem, why is she staring at me?

He felt his eyes squint and his brow furrow, but before he could ask Sarah if she saw the strange woman, the train jostled into motion. The woman in the lab coat still studied him. Hank looked away, pressed his eyes with the palms of his hands, and then attempted to clear his vision of her by rubbing away the sleep. At this, the doctor, as he thought of her, frowned and wrote notes on her clipboard.

The back of his neck throbbed so bad he stared rigidly forward. The locomotive chugged away, leaving the depot, and the strange doctor lady, behind. The train then negotiated a bend and soon the tracks straightened again. Hank could now see their destination: a dark tunnel opening at the base of an enormous snow-capped mountain. Huge piles of shale flanked the entrance as though they were bones spewed up from those who had dared to enter the gaping mouth before. The impatient driver parked behind them turned up his radio and AC/DC's, 'I'm on the Highway to Hell', blared over his speakers.

"Mommy, where is the train taking us?" Annabelle must have also noticed the foreboding tunnel opening for she added, "It looks scary."

You got that right.

Sarah barely heard her. She was toggling through her shots of the moose on her camera. She answered, absently, "Remember sweety? There are no roads into town. The only way in is to load your car on the train. The three mile long tunnel is the only way in or out."

Hank opened his mouth to speak, but the vortex suddenly gobbled up the locomotive engine clanking down the tracks ahead in one enormous bite. The dozen train cars that immediately followed also vanished one-by-one into darkness.

With great effort Hank worked up the will to speak, "Sarah… I don't want to go in there." Hank shivered uncontrollably. He found both hands clenched on the steering wheel and he could feel his feet pressing into the floorboards. As if that would do any good.

Sarah ignored him. "Look kids, here we go."

Hank glanced at a wooden sign at the tunnel's entrance. The finely crafted sign was supported by two thick tree poles. The sign had seen better days Hank thought, but he could just make out the faded white lettering.

Welcome to HavenPort!
Year Round Population: 492

Before Hank and his family were swallowed by the mouth of the tunnel completely and the darkness closed out the last of the fleeting light, Hank glimpsed a shocking image in the rearview mirror. His children's broken bodies littered the back seat and his blood-spattered wife lay dead in the seat beside him.

Chapter 2

Emma

WHEN EMMA'S EYELIDS fluttered open she found her cheek pressed against the dirty rope of an old wooden swing.

Did I fall asleep?

The swing hung from the solid branch of a very old and monstrous oak tree. As far as she could see, a field of wheat breathed with each pass of billowing wind. The only blemish on the golden landscape was a scarecrow, just like the one in, *The Wizard of Oz*. It hung from its perch a good seven feet in the air. Emma could almost hear the *We're Off To See The Wizard* song in her head and half expected the straw-stuffed mannequin to jump off its perch and start singing and dancing.

A porch door creaked behind her. "Emma!" came an old woman's voice. It was her Mee-Maw. *Wait a minute, Mee-Maw died a few years ago, didn't she?*

"C'mon inside, girl, supper's getting cold."

Emma turned her head to glance over her shoulder. When she did, a piercing pain manifested itself at her temples. It was so bad, she even cried out a little and expected to find open wounds on both sides of her head, but when she rubbed at it furiously with the palm of her hand, the hurt began to fade.

What the heck was that, a brain aneurysm?

Still reeling from the echo of pain she heard a door clanging shut behind her.

The screen door banging in the wind belonged to a quaint farmhouse with a faded red sheet metal roof. It was a cozy two-story farmhouse that sat atop a modest hill surrounded by a few acres of Kentucky blue grass. The house and yard was a small oasis in the endless ocean of the billowing wheat stalks. Emma slid down from the swing. She found herself in a white dress and bare feet; the fresh-cut grass felt good as it scrunched beneath her toes.

The last thing she remembered... *What is the last thing I remember? Wasn't I working in New York? How'd I get back home?*

Before she could give it any further thought, the screen door creaked open once more, only with more force this time. A heavy set, older woman, wearing a moo-moo, was holding a silver pot filled with mashed potatoes in the crook of one arm and stirring its contents madly with a gargantuan wooden spoon. It was a utensil Emma's childhood bottom knew well.

"Emma, everyone is waiting on you," Mee-Maw shouted with irritation.

Emma started across the lawn but some movement caught her eye in the wheat field. For a moment, she spotted nothing but the billowing stalks. She was about to turn away when she saw someone standing out there. He was watching her. He was too far away to make out the features beneath the ridiculous hat he wore. It was then she realized the scarecrow was no longer upon his perch.

What happened to the scarecrow?

Emma stared at the man in the hat. It *was* the scarecrow. He now appeared to be standing in the field ... staring back at her. Her heart started beating faster and her breath became rapid and shallow. She shook her head and said aloud, "No way."

A stiff breeze swept the wheat field and she shuddered from the chill.

That's ridiculous. He probably just fell off his perch in the wind. It only looks like he's standing up because he's propped against the stalks of wheat.

"Mee-Maw," she began to ask, forming a question about the creepy scarecrow in the wheat field.

But Mee-Maw's patience was long gone. "Girl! Get your bottom inside. Don't think you ain't old enough for me to tan your hide with my wooden spoon!"

"Mee-Maw," Emma began again. She wondered why her words were so slow and clumsy. Her tongue felt too large for her mouth.

Her dainty feet carted her across the wooden deck boards of the porch and into the house. As Mee-Maw practically shoved her inside, she could hear her youngest brother shout, "C'mon, Emma, I'm hungry. Everyone's waiting on you so we can say grace."

As the door CLANG-CLANG-CLANGED closed and open three more times, she glimpsed the scarecrow standing in the field one last time.

Was he holding a clipboard?

Chapter 3

The Note

EATING DINNER WOULD only take half the time it took for Uncle John to say grace. He was always the self-righteous one, except on really hot days when you found him throwing up whiskey behind the barn.

Uncle John had come to live with the family ever since Paw had died last year. He was an out-of-work minister who needed a home. Mee-Maw needed a man around the house. The only problem was Uncle John wasn't half the man Paw was.

"Emma, look at me, look at me," cried a sweet, childlike voice shrieking with delight.

Emma's twelve year old sister, Missy, had taken two straws and stuck them up inside her mouth. "I'm a walrus." Like Emma, Missy had hair the color of caramel, light skin, and big, expressive, bright blue eyes. She was pretty when she smiled, but embarrassed by her two front teeth which were slightly crooked. The Smith household couldn't quite afford braces yet. Missy giggled. She was easily the best part about coming home.

"Oh yeah? Well try them up your nose." This came from Thomas who sat beside Missy. Despite their similar looks, he was the opposite of his sister in almost every way.

The siblings snorted and laughed and then unintentionally spat food on the table from doing both. After three years in New York, their laughter was music to Emma's ears.

A thunderclap cut short the happy moment.

Uncle John's fist slammed down so hard on the table it had made the chinaware jump. "You kids cut it out or so help me Lord, I'll knock the crap out of both of you." He took a napkin and dabbed at the sweat collecting on his massive bald cranium.

Everyone at the table immediately grew silent. Emma knew Uncle John would've never talked that way to Thomas and Missy if Paw were still alive. Paw fiercely loved the twins.

"You're not my Paw," Missy shot back. "And who asked you to come live here with us anyway?"

For a tense moment, it appeared as though Uncle John might rise from his chair and go after Missy, but then he seemed to remember Emma was at the table. He grabbed his beer and drowned the rage swelling behind those beady eyes of his.

"Go to your room young lady," Mee-Maw commanded.

"Maw," Missy whined. "I ain't eaten nuthin' since breakfast."

"Well, you should-a-thought of that before you mouthed off to your uncle."

Missy got up from her chair. She flashed Emma a look that was almost pleading, then pushed in her chair and headed for the stairs that led up to her bedroom. As she did so, Emma thought she saw Uncle John watch her walk away through half-slit eyes.

Emma dismissed Uncle John's appreciative glances as her imagination. Besides, she had enough of her own problems. She still hadn't told Mee-Maw what had really happened in New York.

"So, Emma, how long you going to be in town for? Long time I hope?"

"I don't know yet, Mee-Maw." Emma noticed every time Uncle John threw back his beer Thomas swiped another piece of chicken and wrapped it discretely into his shirt. "I'm hoping to visit for at least a little while."

"Well, you're welcome to stay with us as long as you like, child. Thomas already put your luggage in the downstairs guest room and I put fresh flannel sheets on the bed."

Certain he had enough food for his sister, Thomas plotted his escape. "Uncle John, did you take a shower today? You're awl' kinds of smelly."

Uncle John sat there dumbfounded. Before he could lather up into a frenzy Mee-Maw barked, "Thomas Michael Smith, what in the world has gotten into you? Go up to your room right now, young man."

Emma was fairly certain Mee-Maw had seen what Thomas was up to and was merely assisting him with his escape.

"Good riddance," Uncle John said to himself as he chewed another mouthful of food. "Kids ain't got no respect for their elders no more," he muttered between bites.

They finished their meal in silence.

Afterwards, Emma quietly placed her napkin on her plate and said, "You know Mee-Maw, it was a long trip. Would you mind if I got unpacked and took a shower … er, got cleaned up?"

"Not at all, child." She stared at Emma sweetly. "It's just so good to have you back home."

Even though Mee-Maw was only her step mom, Emma loved her as much as any daughter could love a real mother. Emma's birth mother had gone crazy shortly after she was born. No one ever told Emma what happened but she still had the gruesome scar across her back from the incident. On really hot days Emma's scar would itch something fierce, just as it was itching furiously now. And ever since that day Emma's birth mother had lived and died in the state insane asylum. For most of Emma's childhood it was only she and Paw.

Mee-Maw had lived up the road with her folks and had been a close friend of the family ever since Emma was born. Even though they were always close, Paw remarried only after Emma's birth mother had died in the asylum, which was the reason for the twelve years between Emma and the twins. Even though she never really knew her birth mother she liked to think she would have approved of Mee-Maw.

"Sure, sure. Go on," Uncle John said magnanimously, as though it were he who had built the house they were living in with his own two hands and not his brother, "Don't worry about us. Sides, more for me." And with that said, he reached for another helping of Mee-Maw's homemade apple pie.

"Excuse me," Emma replied politely, her chair scraping the floor as she gruffly pushed it back from the table.

As she left the kitchen and entered the guest room down the hall, she heard her Uncle say, "Wha-a-a-t-t-t? Whadda I say?"

—— o ——

Retreating to the guest bedroom, and sure no one was watching, Emma removed a small toiletry kit hidden deep within the confines of her luggage.

God, this is so much harder than I thought.

Even the sound of the bag's zipper opening made her bite down on her lower lip with anticipation and anxiety. Double-checking to see she was still alone and the door was locked she removed the needle within. She put her bare foot up on the bed and carefully placed the needle between her toes. It wouldn't have done for a dancer with the New York City Ballet to have track marks on her legs or arms.

This will be the last time. God, I swear it. Please. I'm begging you.

Emma was convinced it wasn't her fault. After all, she wasn't some drugged-out- prostitute. With a lot of hard work and dedication, she had gotten everything she ever wanted by the age of 23. She had a great job working as a ballet dancer with the New York City Ballet and her own apartment. She even had a great boyfriend, a handsome longshoreman on the docks by day, a tortured artist by night.

But then came the motorcycle crash. Mitchell had dumped his bike at an intersection and Emma got banged up pretty badly in the fall. The doctor had prescribed pain medication for her bruised ribs, broken wrist, and dislocated shoulder. At one-hundred-and-ten pounds, it didn't take much to get hooked. Lord, she had never slept so soundly in her life. When the doctor's prescriptions ran out, a dancer friend, and sub in the show, introduced her to heroin. Before long, she had slept through enough rehearsals to lose her job. It was only afterwards she found out her dancer "friend" didn't even use drugs and took over Emma's now available full-time contract.

Emma still didn't know how she was going to tell Mee-Maw. It would break her heart. She had been so proud. But knowing Mee-Maw, she was probably already well aware. *This will be the last time. I'll get clean, put on a few healthy pounds, then go back out there and start auditioning again.*

As the shiny needle moved between her painted toes, *blue nail polish, what was I thinking*, the harbinger of overflowing joy only a scant inch away... A shocking image appeared.

Instead of a needle she found herself holding a slick-skinned, cold to the touch, black snake! She backed into the dresser behind her — hard. A picture frame and other knick-knacks atop the dresser fell onto the floor. Moving in swift bursts, the snake coiled itself up her arm, its forked tongue stabbing in and out at her. Emma didn't know what kind of snake it was, she didn't know about such things, but she instinctively knew it was poisonous. The black snake with red eyes — *do snakes have red eyes?*—, reared back its head and unsheathed long curved venomous fangs. Before she could stop it, the snake clamped down onto the flesh of her exposed forearm.

Eyes clenched, Emma's body immediately convulsed from the stabbing puncture wounds.

A picture frame crashed to the floor and caused her eyes to open.

The snake was gone. She immediately scanned her forearm: No bite marks. Frantically she lifted each foot, checking the floor and beneath the bed: No snake to be found, anywhere.

That's weird. I've never hallucinated before using ... and never so real.

It took some time but eventually Emma found the dropped syringe on the floor. It had rolled under the night table. Disturbed, but not deterred, she placed her foot back on the bed and moved the needle toward its mark once more. Hesitation. *Last time; I swear it.*

A child screamed. It was Thomas. But Tonka-tough-Thomas never screamed. Emma hid the needle back in her suitcase, bounded through the door and ran for the stairwell. One wouldn't know she was a ballet dancer by the way her feet thudded upon the stairs.

"Sissy's dead. Sissy's dead," Thomas kept shouting at the open doorway to the bathroom. He hadn't called his twin sister Sissy in years.

The light was on in the bathroom and the shower curtain had been pulled back. Emma stood frozen with disbelief. Her little sister was hanging from the shower nozzle by a severed vacuum cord wrapped around her tiny neck.

Uncle John and Mee-Maw arrived and pushed past her. They managed to free Missy from her self-made noose and drag her out of the tub. As they did, Emma heard the sound of Missy's bare skin rubbing on the dry ceramic. It was a sound she would forever associate with the gruesome sight of her little sister hanging in the shower.

"Call 911, call 911!" Uncle John kept yelling, clutching her naked body against his chest.

"Don't you touch her!" Mee-Maw screamed. "This is all your fault." Mee-Maw pounded her fist on Uncle John's back.

"Damn it woman, get out of the way," John roared back.

As Uncle John carried Missy's body out of the bathroom, a crumpled piece of paper fell from her small, lifeless fingers.

It seemed to float to the floor in slow motion. Working in New York, Emma had learned how movie cameras made things appear in slow motion. By filming double the amount of frames in a scene, the characters appeared to be moving in slow motion when played back. This was the same for the human body. The faster the heartbeat, the more snapshots the eyes sent to the brain. Hence, fast heartbeat equates to seeing things in slow motion. But she had never experienced the phenomenon first hand before.

Emma felt the crumpled paper in her hand. She must have picked it up without realizing it. Scribbled writing lay within its edges. What did it say? Would she even want to read it? Would it explain why her sister felt compelled to do such a horrible, horrible thing?

Emma, oh Emma, such a pretty girl
Don't cry for me.
For we will meet again,
In HavenPort Alaska
And live for all of eternity—

Oh, and one more thing...
Kill Uncle John for me.

What a horribly strange thing for Missy to write. *Kill Uncle John?*

Banshees, in the form of police sirens, wailed in the distance. Emma heard the porch door straining open as Uncle John carried Missy outside to greet the paramedics who would cart her little sister away. Downstairs, Mee-Maw continued to wail. She would forever be inconsolable.

Emma heard Tonka-tough-Thomas sobbing in the hall. She finally managed to shuffle out the bathroom and found him sitting with his knees drawn up, and his hands covering his face. Emma slid her back down the wall to sit beside him. She'd sit with him for hours — if that's what it took. When she put an arm around him, he buried his face in her chest, his tears soaking her shirt.

Emma did these things on autopilot, for her brain was occupied with only two thoughts.

The first was HavenPort, Alaska. *Was it even a real place?* She certainly had never heard of it and she didn't recall Missy ever mentioning it.

Her second thought was a much simpler one: *Where did Mee-Maw keep Paw's double-barreled shotgun?*

Chapter 4

Jeb Sutton

"SHERIFF JEB SUTTON," the older man said in response to Hank's greeting, his hand clutching Hank's. "Well, I guess now that you're here, it's just Jeb."

When Hank McCarthy had walked into the HavenPort sheriff's office he'd found the former sheriff sitting in a chair behind his desk even though it was early enough to still be dark outside.

Jeb had the height and build of a former WWF wrestler who had let himself go about a decade ago. He was overweight, sported a bushy walrus mustache and had a grey comb-over that barely covered his baldness. His face and neck were unshaven by several days and when he spoke he revealed a mouth full of crooked, tobacco-stained teeth. This was a man who stopped caring about his job, his life, and personal hygiene a long time ago.

Jeb's office reflected a different cop, however. A well-maintained flag stood in one corner and on the wall was a photo of Jeb as a young Marine sporting an impressive collection of awards. There were also dozens of certifications and commendations in glossy black and white frames. Another frame featured a newspaper clipping with Jeb's photo, describing how he had saved several children who had fallen into the creek after the ice cracked beneath their feet. Comparing the numerous awards with the wreck of the man before him, Hank found himself wondering, *What the hell happened to this guy?*

"You were a cop, right? Down in Wyoming or sumthin'?" Jeb asked, interrupting Hank's thoughts.

"Uh, Deputy Sheriff," Hank answered.

"Why'd you leave? I mean, I hear Wyoming's nice enough."

A glaring blank sheet of paper formed in Hank's head whenever he thought about his last day in Wyoming. He remembered heading out of town with his family but everything after that, right up to their arrival to HavenPort, was one big blank. Hank had decided not to reveal his lack of memory to his wife, Sarah. In some ways, she was as tough as any Pioneer woman back in the day. But Sarah's tenacity depended on him being the proverbial rock in the storm. Besides, whenever he reached for some other bit of information, the memories were there. He perfectly remembered his childhood and growing up on his Uncle's ranch in Wyoming. Same with his eight year stint in the military. His mind swam back to the scene before him and he finally answered, "Wife and I just needed a change of scenery I guess."

Jeb nodded then asked, "You and your family get settled in okay?"

Settled in? That was a big joke. The last five days had been more like a test of survival for he and his family. On the first night the furnace went out and they all had to curl up by an old space heater for warmth. They'd also had to keep all the faucets in the house running to prevent the pipes from freezing. After spending the majority of the second day putting in the new furnace, he discovered a patch of shingles had blown off the roof. Hank knew if he didn't tack down some new ones before winter there'd be some serious structural damage. This was all on top of the movers delivering what seemed like the five thousand boxes Sarah had packed from their old home.

Despite all these hardships, Hank turned away from Jeb's photo and simply answered, "Yeah, we're just fine. Thanks for asking."

Sheriff Sutton seemed to reflect on this for a moment. It was a small town and most likely the friendly, overly talkative clerk at the hardware store had probably shared the McCarthy's household difficulties with everyone. Instead of mentioning this, old Jeb just nodded his head again and reached into his desk. He slowly removed a gold badge and a heavy revolver in a civilian carry holster from one of the drawers and shoved it towards him.

"So I reckon these are yours now."

Hank inspected the firearm. It was a .44 Taurus. He preferred auto pistols but he certainly didn't mind the stopping power of the forty-four. It's one thing to kill a suspect running at you with a knife, as any gun will kill a man eventually, but what's more important is stopping that threat dead in his tracks. Furthermore, the heavy-duty pistol was a lot better protection from a bear. The only con was you had to keep in mind the over penetration factor and be mindful of not hitting innocents in the next room.

Hank expertly hit the ejector with his thumb and a fully loaded cylinder swung out of the frame. The bullets had dust on them. He dipped his pinky in the action and when he pulled it out again his finger was covered in grime.

Jeb must have seen Hank's dirty pinky and disapproving frown because he said with a hint of embarrassment, "Yeah, you might want to clean that."

Hank expertly flipped the cylinder closed, holstered the pistol and clipped both it and the badge to his belt. When he lifted his gaze he noticed a stairwell at the back of the office. A homemade sign over the doorframe read, "Captain's Nest". Hank recalled there was a little apartment over the sheriff's office as part of the incentive package.

Jeb saw him staring at the stairs. "Oh yeah. I uh, didn't expect you to arrive for another week but don't worry, I can be packed up and out of your way by the end of the day."

"You gotta place to stay yet?" Hank asked.

Jeb's face turned sour but the old sheriff put on a brave one and answered, "I got friends with comfortable couches."

"Take your time. As far as I'm concerned, you're still the sheriff until next week. Sarah and I only came in early to beat the first snowfall … and get the house in order."

Where'd that come from? Hank felt as though the thought had been typed into his brain. *Maybe that's how memory comes back when you've lost it.* Jeb didn't seem to hear him. His attention was lost in an old photograph of himself displayed on the wall. It showed a younger version of him in front of the station. "Hard to believe I been sheriff of this here town for close to thirty years." The older man's eyes then lifted and seemed to size Hank up in a glance, "Wasn't much older than you when I came to HavenPort just after my stint in the corps."

"You gonna be all right?" Hank asked with genuine concern. Maybe at one time the old boy was a pretty good cop.

"Heck, son. Don't worry about me." Jeb faltered, then slid open a drawer and pulled out a fireman's helmet with the word "Chief" on it. He slapped the helmet on his head and answered with a big Texas grin, "Hell, I'm still the Fire Chief."

Just then a radio the size of a brick on Jeb's desk crackled. A cheerful woman's voice with a thick Minnesota accent emanated from the tiny speaker. "Sheriff, we got a call from Doc Clemens. He says the Wahlman boys were playing in the Rakewell building when some homeless guy threatened them with a knife."

Jeb frowned. "Ophelia, those boys know better than to play in the Rakewell building."

"That's what I told 'em, there hon. But the doc says the boys think the homeless guy was trying to burn the place down."

Sheriff Jeb rolled his eyes to the ceiling, and then clicked the microphone again. "All right, tell Doc Clemens I'll check it out straight away." After switching the microphone off he asked Hank, "You mind tagging along?"

When Hank nodded he added, "Probably Nuthin' to worry about. Most likely it's some rail bum trying to stay warm."

"Happen a lot?"

"Yeah, but usually not so early in the year." Jeb grabbed his parka from a rack in the corner and strapped on a worn leather gun belt that had seen better days. He then reached across his desk, snatched up the radio, and keyed the microphone one last time. "Ophelia, let the doc know that me and the new sheriff are en route."

Ophelia came back, "Want me to drive the Wahlman boys down there to meet you on site?"

"Naw, if we find the guy, I'd rather the boys I.D. him at the station. Last thing I want is to be searching that damn labyrinth in the dark with those two knuckleheads running about."

"Roger, Sheriff." Ophelia came back. There was a slight pause, "I mean, er, Jeb."

Jeb fastened his radio to his belt and headed for the door. "C'mon son, you might as well meet the local color now rather than later."

Before following Jeb out the door Hank double-checked to see both badge and firearm were clipped firmly to his belt. He was unaccustomed to carrying an untested weapon but this would likely turn out to be nothing more than a simple loitering call. At least the cylinder was fully loaded. Only a dead man carries a weapon without bullets. *That voice again. Who taught him that?* For the life of him, he couldn't remember.

Chapter 5

The Rakewell Building

THE SUN HAD BEGUN to rise over the mountains but lingering shadows still cloaked the town below. Even though the drive from town only took about twenty minutes in Jeb's patrol vehicle, Jeb drove slowly as the winding road up the mountainside was treacherous in the faint lighting.

As the morning rays melted away the ice fog, the steel behemoth known as the Rakewell building appeared out of the mist like a ghost ship. Nine stories tall and the length of a city block, Hank could see the old military fortress was a real monster.

Jeb's SUV slid to a stop on the gravel driveway. They left the truck doors unlocked and the engine running to power the heater. Jeb also left the bar light activated on the roof but removed the ignition keys. That way if anyone tried to drive off with the patrol vehicle, the engine would simply shut off the moment the thief's foot stepped on the brake pedal.

They approached the building on the southeast corner and stood in the driveway of an old motor pool. A security fence had been drawn up around the perimeter with 'WARNING: DO NOT ENTER' signs every ten feet. There was a gate directly in front of them but the chain had been cut to lie like a dead snake beside the skewed section of fence.

Jeb put his fists on his hips, "Doesn't matter how many times we close this thing back up. Almost no point in tryin'." He moved forward to force the gate open and held it for Hank to pass. "The military built this place back in the early forties."

Jeb said as if it were the weather, "Back in those days there were only two things in town, this building and the docks."

Hank squeezed through the gap and turned to hold the gate for Jeb, "Why would the military build a base way out here in the middle of nowhere?"

Jeb slipped past and looked over at him. "You mean you don't know about 'Alaska's Secret Port'?" Hank shook his head, so Jeb explained, "During World War II when the Japanese invaded the Aleutian Islands the government decided there was a need for a secret base in Alaska."

"The Rakewell building?" Hank craned his neck to look up at the looming structure.

"Yep, you got it. In its heyday this place was really something; largest building in the last frontier." Jeb said the last part with pride, as if he had worked on the construction himself. The old sheriff stared at the exterior as though imagining what it must have been like when it was first built. "This is where everybody slept, over six hundred residences in one building. They had their own hospital, school, movie theater, and gun range. Heck, they even had their own bowling alley and indoor swimming pool. Yes sir, this place was really sumthin'."

Hank didn't see any of those things. In a word, the place was dilapidated. Every window was broken. The paint was so faded and covered with filth it was impossible to tell the building's original colors.

They headed toward an opening marked, MOTORPOOL. "Mind your head," Jeb said, ducking under the half-open garage door literally hanging off its hinges. The sound of broken glass crunched underfoot.

"When was the building abandoned?" Hank asked.

"When the war ended, the base of operations moved to Anchorage."

"So why didn't they renovate the building for civilian use?"

"Asbestos, mostly. The stuff is poison and too damn expensive to tear down and ship out."

"Shouldn't we be worried about inhaling this stuff?"

"Naw. We'll be fine. There's no wind. Just try not to breathe too deeply or stir up any dust."

"That's comforting," Hank mumbled under his breath.

As they moved farther into the building and away from the light, Jeb tossed him a heavy aluminum flashlight. Hank clicked the button and swept the light across the ceiling and walls. The beam revealed only glimpses of the interior. Steel girders, cancerous with rust, stuck out of the ceiling. And graffiti was written on every inch of the walls. Most notably were the words, *YOU WILL ALL DIE!* painted in crimson red. Below that proclamation were the words, *Beware the Unfortunates.* On another wall was Matthew 4:10. Hank was raised Catholic and grew up attending Sunday school, but he couldn't recall the verse off the top of his head and made a note to look it up later.

Journeying farther into the dark labyrinth, Hank noted there wasn't any furniture to speak of. Anything of value or combustibility had been taken long ago or dissolved into rubble.

They hadn't taken more than a few steps into the adjoining hallway when Hank noticed the slanted doorways that ran up and down either side. The rooms interiors were so dark you almost needed a new word to describe the absence of light. A line from Milton's Poem, *Paradise Lost*, came to mind, 'No light, rather darkness visible'. Even the light from his flashlight seemed to fear the darkness, barely penetrating the bowels of each room's interior. Anything could be hiding within and they wouldn't see it coming — a bear, a crazy guy with a knife, anything.

Being broad-shouldered and highly trained in tactical procedures, Hank was hardly scared of a couple of homeless vagrants. But every cop knows a domestic call like this one was always the most dangerous because of its unpredictability. His main concern was that Sarah would be so pissed if he got himself killed on his first day of work. Hank was also painfully reminded that he had only a flashlight, his badge, and an untested service revolver badly in need of cleaning. He felt naked without a vest or any intermediary weapons such as a baton or OC spray. *Hell, I don't even have my own radio.*

"Among the homeless, any priors?" he asked, trying to keep the concern out of his voice.

"Nah. For the most part, they're harmless. They probably ran off the moment we pulled up outside. The building's more liable to collapse than any bum attacking you. Hey, that reminds me, did you know there used to be six working elevators in this building?" Not waiting for an answer he continued, "All the elevator doors have fallen off so mind your step when stepping into another room or you might end up taking a nose dive down an elevator shaft."

"Okay, thanks." This little adventure was getting worse by the minute.

"Oh, and watch your step, here," Jeb announced, carefully stepping over a gaping hole in the floor. "If you don't, you'll find yourself in the basement real quick."

Hank cautiously stepped over the hole hoping the entire floor wouldn't collapse completely. It was easy to see why the place was condemned. When he caught up with Jeb, he commented irritably, "I don't see a fire anywhere."

"No, not here. The homeless usually drag empty barrel drums into the center of the building where they can stay the most warm." Jeb stumbled over a fallen chunk of ceiling and cursed. "Usually they don't start this early in the season though. Just the same, we'd better make sure they didn't leave anything burning or they could end up burning down the whole damn town." Jeb shined his light into the next room then vanished once more into the darkness. "C'mon, this way," he called from the pitch blackness.

Hank was about to follow Jeb's bouncing light when the smell hit him. Whatever lay ahead reeked of death.

And then … out of the darkness came the sound of something roaring.

Chapter 6

The Crazy Lady

THE DARKENED HALLWAY ENDED in a large expansive room with windows opposite the space from a natural rock wall. The rising sun was now visible outside through the smashed-out windows spaced every four feet apart. It wasn't much but they now had at least *some* light.

The roaring sound that had raised Hank's hackles was caused by dozens of small waterfalls flooding from multiple holes and cracks in the ceiling. The dark water cascaded into the indoor swimming pool Jeb had mentioned earlier. It must have been fed from a natural source, probably why they'd kept the wall its native rock.

In the amber glow, Hank could just make out the water's surface. He grimaced at the sight of the raw sewage, thick as sludge, floating on the surface.

"Stay away from the edge," Jeb warned. "You do not want to fall in there. Believe you, me."

"Really, no kidding," Hank started to reply sarcastically, but was suddenly overpowered by the heavy odor of urine and excrement.

Jeb chuckled at his discomfort and when Hank flashed him a look of irritation the old sheriff suggested, "Try breathing through your mouth and not your nose."

Hank composed himself and then the old sheriff explained, "This used to be the base swimming pool. Mostly a toilet for the homeless population now."

Hank fought the vile stench permeating his nostrils and the bile creeping up in his throat. "This is... this is..." struggling for words, coming up with only, "...just awful."

Jeb swung his light so it illuminated a stairwell on the back wall. The metallic stairs were little more than a twisted skeleton in the rotting corpse of the building.

"Let's try upstairs," Jeb said, moving towards the stairwell. "Those rail bums are probably on one of the upper levels."

"Right behind you," Hank replied and then gagged again from the smell.

As they clambered up the metal stairs, and away from the light, Hank could hear Jeb wheezing in the darkness above him.

With Jeb still on point, they exited the stairwell and moved in tandem toward the center of the building. The farther in they went the more they had to depend on their flashlights.

On the second floor they passed a bowling alley nearly dissolved into paste. Jeb swung his flashlight over the remnants of a half-dozen lanes.

Past the bowling alley was a large open room with several rows of decayed movie seats. "This used to be the theater. There was both a movie screen and a stage. They had it all back then. Yep, this place was really sumthin'."

Hank finally managed to swallow the last of the bile that had collected in his throat and answered. "Yeah ... something alright."

Hank swung his light inside. He didn't see any evidence of a movie screen but he could just barely make out a stage in the darkness. Despite the giant homeless toilet on the first floor, Hank had to reluctantly agree. With Jeb narrating the tour, it wasn't hard to imagine young servicemen, nurses, and scientists in this mountain retreat.

They climbed five more floors in the darkened stairwell. They reached the seventh floor and immediately apparent was a flickering light from deep in the bowels of the labyrinth.

Jeb must've seen it too for he asked. "You wearing a vest?"

"No," Hank answered matter-of-factly.

"Better stay behind me then."

It was against Hank's nature to let others go before him in harm's way but Jeb was wearing the vest so Hank wasn't going to argue.

Jeb moved toward the fire up ahead, its flickering flames transforming the old sheriff as he went. Hank noted the older man was now walking heel-toe and checking each room before passing in front of the doorframe. *What happened to the old timer? He'd obviously been a really good cop at some point.*

Slowly, methodically, they closed on the room with the flickering light. Stalactites, formed by leaks in the ceiling and dyed rust red, framed the entrance. And inside the room the floor was covered in moss and knee high grass. It was as though they were stepping into a primeval cavern, and not another room belonging to a dilapidated building.

In the room's center, beneath a hole in the ceiling that beamed down morning sunlight, an old woman in her late-fifties sat in a lawn chair next to a burn barrel. All the holes in the barrel made it look like a colander, the fire flickering orange through the holes. The woman was so overweight that Hank guessed if she got up, the chair would have stuck fast to her large behind. She wore a drab scarf over her head and a long coat. One thing that didn't add up though, was that her clothes did not belong to any homeless person Hank had ever seen; they were too clean and appeared relatively new. He couldn't see the woman's face because she was sitting with her back to them. She was facing the wall where an old television set sat on a milk crate. The TV was on; its screen filled with static resembling white snow.

Hank moved to stand shoulder to shoulder with Jeb and asked, "I thought you said this place doesn't have any power?"

"It don't," Jeb grumped back.

Hank followed the cord with a flashlight. It snaked through some patches of grass but the plug wasn't plugged into any outlet. It was just lying there on the floor.

Must be one of those battery-operated jobs.

The television's volume was turned up so loud Jeb had to shout over the static to project his voice to the center of the room. "Ma'am, HavenPort Sheriff's Department."

Nothing.

Hank could feel the heat from the burn barrel. The fire was really hot. Hank was immediately concerned for the woman's safety. If he could feel the heat from where he was standing then she must be roasting alive. Or worse, her clothes would catch fire at any moment.

They moved closer and Hank could see the woman wasn't actually watching the television, but doing something with her hands. And really going at it too. So much so that Hank was surprised she didn't fall over in the rickety lawn chair.

As they closed in Hank noticed the older sheriff was so focused on the old woman he wasn't double-checking the multiple entrances to the room. Hank gave each entrance a quick scan. As vulnerable as he felt he also tried to keep it real. After all, this was obviously just a middle age woman sitting by a burn barrel trying to stay warm.

Jeb signaled with one finger for Hank to circle around to the left so he could come in from the right. Both men had their hands on their pistols but neither of them had drawn. Hank still couldn't see what the older woman was doing in her lap but he could now see her heavily made up face. She wore so much make-up she almost resembled a circus clown. Her eyes stared straight ahead, vacant, and an un-flicked cigarette dangled from her open mouth.

The whole thing was pretty damn creepy.

Hank had circled far enough that he could finally see what she was doing with her hands. The woman had a serrated knife in her right hand and she was madly sawing away on her left wrist. Not just superficial 'pay-attention-to-me' cuts either. Hank vomited in his mouth but immediately swallowed it back down. The bile burned in his throat.

Jeb must've seen the knife at the same time for he yelled, "Knife!"

Both he and Jeb pulled their guns at the same time and drew a bead on her. "Drop the knife! Hands in the air!" they ordered overtop each other.

The woman did not seem to hear them. It was as though she were in a world all her own.

"Wanda?" Jeb asked, his voice tinged with disbelief. "Wanda Parker?" Jeb and Hank exchanged glances. "What are you doing?"

At this, Wanda stopped flaying her wrist. She slowly turned towards Jeb and asked, "Are you going to kill the doctors?"

Jeb blinked away his shock.

"They're not real, you know." She then raised her voice, angry, "Don't you get it? None of this is real." With that said, she dropped her arms to either side of the lawn chair and lowered her head, resembling a puppet with cut strings.

Hank slowly holstered his gun.

"What are you doing, Hank?" Jeb asked in a harsh whisper. "She's still got the knife."

Hank could see the woman was still breathing. He knew the clock was ticking if they had any chance of saving her from her self-inflicted wound. "We can't just let her sit there and bleed out." He began walking towards her with his palms out. To Jeb he asked, "You got her?"

"Yep." Then Jeb raised his voice loud enough for her to hear, "Wanda, please, if you can hear me, don't you move or I will have to shoot."

When Hank got within two feet of her, she began to growl, a deep, animalistic growl, resonating in her chest. At first it was low and rumbling, but as he took another step it rose in pitch. Hank didn't think human vocal cords were capable of making such inhuman sounds.

It was all so macabre.

Hank was only inches from grabbing her by the arm when Wanda sprang to life with impossible speed. She lunged at him with the knife; the chair stuck fast to her bottom as predicted.

Trained in spontaneous knife defense, Hank would have loved to tell his wife later that he had side-stepped the woman, grabbed her by the wrist, snapped the knife out of her hand with a wrist lock, and took her down in a straight-arm-bar-take-down maneuver. The reality was that Wanda moved so fast it scared the crap out of him. With a curse his right leg jerked reflexively into a front kick.

By some miracle he got lucky. The toe of his boot kicked the knife from Wanda's hand.

It didn't stop her from tackling him though.

Hank never believed in possession until that very moment. He outweighed the growling woman by fifty pounds and yet she threw him around like a rodeo bull on crack cocaine. Hank wasn't exactly sure what Jeb was doing but one thing was for certain, he wasn't helping.

After a few moments of getting knocked around, Hank had had enough. He kicked out the back of the woman's knee and sent her sprawling face down to the ground. The chair popped off her butt like a cork and when she tried to get back up, he dropped a knee down on her back.

As she bucked violently under him, he risked a quick glance at Jeb and cried out, "Jeb , throw me your cuffs."

It took Jeb longer than it should have to unsnap his pouch and toss him a pair of handcuffs. The good news was Jeb's cuffs were in serviceable condition and didn't have any spurs on them. The bad news was Hank cuffed one wrist easily enough but when he went to cuff the woman's other wrist he realized only a few strands of uncut tendons connected her left hand to her forearm.

She began bucking underneath him again and Jeb yelled, "What 'er ya waiting for, cuff her already!"

"Cuff her to what?" Hank barked right back, "Her hand's practically fallen off!"

"Just cuff her high on the wrist. I'll call for EMS." Jeb reached for his radio and cued his radio, "Dispatch, dispatch, this is Sheriff Sutton, come-back."

Only static.

"Ophy, it's Jeb. I'm in the Rakewell building, seventh floor. We need the medics ASAP. Repeat, medics, Code 4!"

Still no answer.

Jeb's radio dropped to his side. "Dammit. Concrete's blocking the signal." After thinking for a few moments, he finally added, "Hank, run downstairs and get to my rig outside. Use the truck radio and call for EMS."

As the crazy woman's bucking finally began to subside, Hank removed the scarf from her neck and tied a tourniquet around the bloody stump. As he did so he asked, "Why don't we just carry her down?"

"Six flights of stairs, while she's bleeding out? No way. Best if I stabilize her here until the paramedics arrive." Jeb took his place on Wanda's back and ordered, "Go."

Hank rose to his feet, "Okay, but loosen the tourniquet when it gets too tight." He stopped at the door. Before stepping into the darkness he activated his light and danced it across his palm just to make sure it still worked. "And Jeb, one more thing. Keep checking your six."

"Yeah, why's that?"

"There may be others and this place is creepy as hell."

Chapter 7

Emma's Arrival

UNLIKE MOST MID-OCTOBER mornings in Alaska, the day broke bright and warm.

From the upper observation deck of the ferry Emma could feel the boat's engines vibrating through the soles of her feet. She leaned heavily on the railing, sipping coffee from the Styrofoam cup she cradled in her hands. As she gazed down into the blue-green water churning about the steady moving boat she contemplated the journey ahead.

It was both scary and exciting.

Following her sister's last message scrawled in a suicide note, Emma had been surprised to learn the town of HavenPort did in fact exist. She wondered what she would find in the remote town. And what did her sister mean by, "they would meet again?"

She was clean and sober now. She couldn't recall for how long or when it had happened but she was certain it had been for a while now because she wasn't feeling any of those constant cravings under her skin. She didn't remember checking but she knew there weren't any drugs in her luggage. She took comfort in the fact that the cravings were gone. She couldn't afford the expense anymore. The last of her savings had been spent on her crappy little foreign car safely stored one deck below. In truth, she didn't even remember driving the car on board; she just knew it was below.

Emma noted a flock of sea birds as they suddenly appeared all around the boat. Without any explanation the Captain slowed the ferry to an idle. As she began to wonder what was going on a crowd drew up all around her and started pointing outstretched fingers toward the water.

A trio of sharp-toothed monsters leapt out of the water, their thick bodies arching, a white underbelly with dark gray on the top. One swished near the boat, visible just beneath the water as it turned on its side and peered up at her. Its eyes were black as night, taking her in as if she were the main course. Emma stepped back from the railing.

If demons had fins, this is what they would look like.

"Don't tell me you've never seen a salmon shark before?"

A man a few years younger than her, tan, and with a kind face, wearing rugged clothes, had moved up to stand beside her. He was what Mee-Maw would call a blue-eyed devil in blue jeans.

"Why are they jumping out of the water like that?" she asked.

"They're chasing salmon." He moved back over to the railing and gestured with a nod for her to look over the side.

When she did she saw flashes of pink salmon darting under the hull of the boat seeking refuge. Although scary at first, the sharks splashing about the boat were truly a spectacular sight and a welcome reprieve from the muddle of her thoughts.

"How big do they get?" Emma asked tenuously.

"The sharks or the salmon?"

Emma rolled her head at him, "The sharks."

"About six to eight feet is the norm but my uncle caught one in the Sound when I was a kid that was about twice that."

When all of the excitement generated by the sharks had ebbed, the ferry resumed its course and speed.

"You're not from around here, are you?" The blue-eyed devil asked.

Emma tensed up. She hadn't really considered what she would say until now. How should she answer? *New York. No, then he'll want to know what you did in New York. That will only lead to you being a dancer for the New York City Ballet, which would lead to why you got kicked out.*

"Oh, I'm sorry," the younger man said beside her, interrupting her runaway train of emotions. "I didn't mean to pry."

"No, no. Not at all. I'm from Nebraska," Emma replied; it wasn't entirely untrue.

"Nebraska?" he asked in disbelief. "I would've figured you for more the big city gal."

Wind blew her hair in front of her face and she tucked it behind her ear. She was never good at making small talk and felt the silence growing awkward.

Luckily blue-eyes didn't have that problem. "Name's Horatio."

"Like, as in Hamlet?"

Horatio's face lit up. "A fellow scholar, methinks?" When she didn't grasp his barb right away he added, "In truth, no. Unfortunately dad just really liked the Horatio Hornblower series, more than Shakespeare at least."

Emma couldn't recall who Horatio Hornblower was, an Admiral or something, but she really didn't feel like asking.

"Emma. My name's Emma."

"So, what brings you to the Last Frontier, Emma?"

"Uhmm…" *What do I say? My twelve year old sister hung herself in the shower with a vacuum cord and left me a note to meet her in a town I've never heard of before?*

She must've been silent too long because Horatio said, "Aw geez, there I go being nosy again."

"I'm really not sure why I came here," she practically blurted out.

Horatio thrust his hands in his pocket. "That's cool, that's cool."

The wind picked up a bit and chilled the air. Even wearing layers, Emma was always cold. *The locals always dress in layers.* She read about that in her Alaska guidebook. She might not remember actually getting onto the ferry but she remembered reading the guidebook. Emma was eager about all the activities she could choose from. According to the guidebook she could learn how to kayak, visit a glacier, or go whale watching. And that was just on the water. The town of HavenPort was surrounded by trails that led right up into the surrounding mountains.

The deck shifted under her feet as the Captain slowed the boat and steered them closer towards the mainland.

A few more minutes passed and they were soon chugging past a mountain range with a giant decaying building tumbled across it. The drab concrete building was a stark contrast to the towering peaks, which dripped with startlingly beautiful ice-blue glaciers.

"Horatio, what's that big concrete building called?" she asked, pointing.

"The old military base?" When she nodded, he said, his tone a little less cheerful, "That's the Rakewell building. It used to be a secret supply port back in WWII."

When she craned her neck, Emma thought she saw a flickering blue light through the trees at the base of the building, but then it was gone.

"Anybody live up there?"

"What, in the Rakewell building?" Horatio scoffed. "Heck no. No one's lived there for sixty years."

"Are you sure? I thought I just saw a light up there."

Horatio squinted like someone who needed glasses but wasn't quite ready to admit it yet. "I doubt it. Sometimes squatters will hole up inside for the winter, but the building's been boarded up ever since I was a kid."

Emma was certain she had seen a blue light, like the kind on a police car.

The boat chugged onward past the old military base and as it did so, the sight of the derelict buildings made her pull her jacket tighter around her shoulders.

Chapter 8

Jack-o'-lantern

CLANG-CLANG-CLANG!

Hank's boots pounded on the metal stairs as he zoomed down six flights into the depths of inky blackness. Thankfully, the morning light shining through the bullet shaped holes offered some light, but the descent was still nerve-racking.

Some first day.

He sprinted as fast as he dared past the bowling alley, movie theater, and dormitory rooms. He only slowed his pace when he entered the pool area. The stench overpowered him again, and he gagged.

He knew he had to get back to the south end of the building to reach Jeb's SUV. Hank considered going out one of the broken windows, but if he sliced open his femoral artery on a shard of glass, he wouldn't be of any use to anybody. No. The safest bet was to go back the same route they had come in.

He negotiated the pool, giving the reeking waters a wide berth. The last thing he wanted to do was fall into that toxic tub of human pestilence. About halfway past the pool, Hank skidded to a stop. Someone was standing in the lighted doorway up ahead.

What was immediately apparent was that it wasn't Jeb.

Hank had difficulty making the guy out because the rising sun was directly behind him and shrouded him in brilliant white light. Despite this, Hank could still see the skinny silhouette wasn't the old chubby sheriff he had met this morning.

Hank was about to ask the stranger for help when he noticed the man standing in the doorway wasn't wearing a stitch of clothing. As the naked guy stepped out of the bright light and into the discernible shadows, Hank could see the streaker couldn't have been more than 5'9" and impossibly lean, like a marathon runner. In fact, there wasn't an ounce of body fat on him. An emaciated athlete. Worse, he was covered in excrement; had presumably smeared it all over his face and body.

What the…? Why would someone do that?

The strangest part was the creepy smile on the guy's face. It reminded Hank of jack-o-lanterns he'd carved on Halloween; the same wide, toothy grin with firelight flickering behind the eyes. That was this guy: a skinny, naked jack-o-lantern smeared in filth. And just like the real deal, this jack-o-lantern had a cosmic shine in his eyes that told Hank that he was probably amped up on methamphetamines. This was not the kind of help Hank wanted.

Hank used the flashlight to scan the naked guy for weapons. At first Hank thought he was holding a small pumpkin by the stem — fitting as that would be — because that was about the size of what the naked guy was holding in his left hand.

That isn't a pumpkin…

It was a human head. And he was holding it by its long blond hair.

Hank drew his revolver.

"Don't move!" He commanded, gripping the revolver so hard it made his hand hurt. He could only hope the dirty untested gun would not misfire, or worse, blow up in his hand.

Jack-o'-lantern didn't move. He just kept standing there, with that same wide, toothy grin of his, holding the severed human head as it dripped with blood. And now Hank could hear it, DRIP-DRIP-DRIP.

Hank stood, forehead sweating despite the brisk morning air. Keeping his revolver trained on Jack-o'-lantern he thought about calling out to Jeb for help. Then he realized the naked man was also holding something in his right hand, just out of the sunlight's reach. Hank panned his flashlight slowly down the naked guy's right arm. It was an ax, its steel blade streaked with red. *Oh hell no.*

"Drop the ax. I said, drop the damn ax!" Hank yelled.

But the naked guy didn't move. He just stood there in the light, like an actor in a spotlight on a stage. Jack-o'-lantern slowly lifted the head into the light, so it was only inches from his own face. The victim appeared to be a young woman. Still grinning that creepy mischievous grin, he turned the head in his hand towards himself. He then pantomimed the look of horror on his victim's face.

Only experience kept Hank from freezing up.

The woman upstairs is bleeding out. This lunatic is holding a human head in one hand and an ax in the other. And I've got no backup. Where the hell did we move to, anyway?

Hank was sorely tempted to just shoot the guy. But, despite being armed with the ax, the naked guy hadn't made any threatening moves toward him to justify a shooting — at least, not on paper.

"Buddy," he said evenly, "If you don't drop that damn ax…" Hank cocked back the hammer of his forty-four for emphasis. He was confident if the dirty gun did manage to fire the slug, it would take the naked guy's head clean off at such close range. One problem solved.

This must have occurred to Jack-o'-lantern too because he let the bloody ax slip from his hand and it clattered to the floor.

Before Hank could instruct the suspect further, Jeb's voice rang out from the depths of the labyrinth, "Hank, where are you?"

"Down here!" Hank shouted back.

A painful minute passed then Hank heard the sheriff shout, "Where?" It sounded like the old sheriff was only one floor above him. *Had he come downstairs?*

"Down here, by the pool!"

There was a loud crash and it sounded like ole Jeb cried out in pain. Hank remembered his own words about their being more than one crazy person, further proof of that standing in the doorway before him. "Jeb, you okay?"

No response. At least not from Jeb.

When the naked man spoke it was rhythmic and in a thick southern drawl like a backwoods hick from Alabama trying to recite a clever poem.

"Poor Dumb ole' Sutton,
Doesn't realize, he's been here, Bee-four.
Never ever does he git it right,
Killed all those people with that forty-four
Last chance, Sutton... Last Chance.
Bee-four you are here, -no more."

Poem recited, Jack-o'-lantern tilted his head to one side, studying Hank. "Don't worry, Hank. I've got a poem for you too... but you'll have to wait until we meet again."

Now it took a lot to frighten Hank. He considered himself a rock solid guy in just about every situation. He also had a significant amount of training and experience. Now in his defense, this was his first day on the job and the only thing he'd planned on doing today was meeting up with the old sheriff and signing some paperwork. So, he shouldn't have been ashamed by what happened next. But he was.

"CAW!" A monstrous raven cried out from its perch on an overhead beam.

"Geez!" Hank yelped. It was so loud that he ducked reflexively and nearly dropped his gun. Hank turned. At first he could only see the Raven's red eyes in the darkness. *Did Raven's have red eyes?* The thing was seemingly the size of a pterodactyl, but still just a damn bird. When he switched his gaze back to the naked man blocking the exit, he was gone. Only the severed head remained. It was carefully placed on the floor in the center of the doorway. The naked man had even taken care to place it on an altar of rubble.

Hank immediately went into tactical mode and began scanning all the doorways around him with gun and light. Nearest to him was a set of double-doors off their hinges. Both were lying at his feet like two coffins. The darkness within was beyond the sunlight's reach and the confines only swallowed the flashlight's beam of light.

Screw this. Jeb and I need back up. Hank knew if he could just make it back to the vehicle, he could call for reinforcements and come back with more people and more light.

But before he could take a step for the exit, Jack-o-lantern came lunging out of the darkened interior and barreled into him in a full-on tackle. Hank turned and managed to crank off a round but the shot went high as Jack-o'-Lantern dived under his aim and wrapped his arms around Hank's midsection like a wrestler. Backpedaling, Hank turned his head over his shoulder and glimpsed where they were headed.

Oh God, no. Not there!

Both men stumbled backwards into the pool.

Hank squeezed his eyes shut as he was immediately enveloped by darkness and excrement. Beneath the surface he smacked his head on the bottom of the pool. The sludge penetrated his ears, and nose, and felt vile on his skin.

His gun long gone, he clawed for the surface. What he hoped was the surface. Treading water, he coughed and sputtered, the stench everywhere He swiped a hand across his eyes, risking a look, finding it hard to focus.

The morning light had penetrated more of the pool's water. Hank scanned the surface, frantically searching for his attacker. He was certain they'd both gone into the pool.

Not finding anyone, Hank swam for the shallow end. Putting his feet down, he spit and blew his nose. As nervous as he was about being attacked from behind, he made for the stairs. If there was any justice in the world, Jack-o'-lantern hit his head at the bottom of the pool and would stay there until a hazmat dive team retrieved his dead naked corpse.

Hank's hand was inches from the railing when Jack-O exploded out of the water behind him. A slimy, slippery arm coiled around his throat like a boa constrictor.

I am done fooling around with this guy.

With tremendous force Hank elbowed his attacker in the face. Opponent dazed, Hank was able to slip out of the headlock. Jack-o-lantern fell back beneath the muck.

Hank turned, his fists balled. The next time Jack-o'-lantern surfaced, he would strike to kill.

A minute passed. And then another. No sign of his attacker. He began backing up toward the stairs. When his foot hit the bottom stair he slipped and fell backward onto them. He recovered quickly, checked the surface one last time, turned, and ran.

Wiping the human filth from his eyes with the palms of his shaking hands, he staggered for the exit. He didn't remember seeing the head on the floor through his blurred vision, but he was pretty sure he felt it staring at him as he clumsily negotiated the doorway.

Arriving to Jeb's SUV on shaky legs, he noted the sun had leapt from the mountaintops and into the sky. Shock was beginning to set in and Hank's hand slipped off the door handle of the patrol vehicle on the first try. After getting the door open on the second try he collapsed on his chest and belly onto the front seat and reached for the radio's microphone.

What the hell do I say?

"10-33, 10-33," he stated. Code for an officer needing emergency assistance. Realizing the local dispatcher probably wasn't even aware they even had ten codes, he added, "Officer down, Officer down. Requesting EMS and immediate back up! We're up at the Rakewell building at the uh ... southwest entrance."

Without intending too, Hank slipped off the seat, painfully onto the floorboards, and back out the door.

After everything he had been through, and the shock settling in, his body told him to stay down and wait for reinforcements.

His brain was a different matter.

Got to get back in there and warn Jeb.

Hank doubted the lunatic who tackled him was anywhere other than at the bottom of the pool but he wasn't about to take any chances. Plus, there might be more nutjobs inside. With the way his day was going there would have to be.

Hank knew the revolver was somewhere at the bottom of the pool along with his flashlight. He'd need both gun and light if he was going to go back inside and do Jeb any good.

He crawled back into the patrol car and reached for the standard issue shotgun that would be between the seats. The gun rack was locked and Jeb had the keys. No other firearms were forthcoming.

What about light? They had taken both flashlights. Hank popped the trunk and found a box of flares. *Perfect.* He could not only use the flares for light but he could also leave a trail for the paramedics to follow when they arrived.

He gathered up an armload of flares and headed for the Rakewell behemoth once more.

He didn't get far.

Jeb was standing at the entrance. His grim demeanor told Hank that Wanda had expired.

Scrunching his nose, Jeb asked, "What the hell happened to you?"

Hank braced an arm against the front hood.

As sirens began wailing from down the mountain, Jeb peered inside his vehicle. "Awww, man. You didn't get that crap all over my ride did you?"

Chapter 9

The Harbor

THE TOWN OF HAVENPORT came into view.

As the ferry motored towards the harbor, Emma could see the town was nestled on a flat track of land between the mountains and the bay. As the boat drew closer she saw a pot-bellied fisherman wearing a cap and turtle neck waddling along a boardwalk that ran in front of a delightful variety of shops and charming sea side cafes.

Next, the boat passed a beautiful log home with big windows and a wooden deck overlooking the bay. Two small children, one a handsome little boy with dark wavy hair, the other a cute little girl who had to be about five years old, were standing out on the deck and waving to them energetically. The boat captain must've seen them, too, for he gave the boat horn a long call which delighted the children.

"Hi," Emma shouted, waving back. She doubted the kids could hear her but they surprised her when the little girl yelled hi back.

Turning to Horatio, Emma remarked, "Cute kids. Do you know them?"

"Nope," Horatio said, squinting again. "I heard the new sheriff bought the house, but I haven't met him or his family yet." Horatio stared at his feet then asked, "Do you have a place to stay yet?"

Emma was about to answer no but then a memory flashed inside her head as though it had been typed there.

"The Land's End Bed and Breakfast Hotel," she answered, almost robotically. *That's right.* She had called ahead and had a furnished room waiting for her. *Didn't she?*

Well it doesn't matter, first things first, as soon as we dock; I have to pee.

The ferry docked in the harbor to a few curious onlookers and a class of kayakers paddling out of a nearby cove.

Emma heard herself sigh and said, "Well, I should probably grab my car and be going."

He stood there with his hands in his pockets, smiling at her easily. "I'm sure I'll see you around town."

Emma nodded back and, like everyone else on board, retreated to her vehicle below decks to await departure.

After driving her car down the steel ramps and off the ferry, Emma drove only a short distance before parking in front of a building marked, *HavenPort Harbor Restroom.* The small structure had green sheet metal roofing with a sturdy wood A-frame and faded paint.

As soon as Emma stepped out of her car she immediately felt better. It was good to be off the boat. A cool breeze rolled off the water and she just stood there for a few seconds soaking up the small seaside town.

She took a step towards the bathroom and was suddenly gripped by inexplicable fear. She couldn't put her finger on it but she felt like a deer in a hunter's scope. Emma scanned the parking lot. No one appeared to be around and even the sounds of the happy little town drifted away.

Any port in a storm I suppose. It's either here or on the ground in front of everyone. Hi everyone, my name's Emma. Just rolled into town. Scuse' me while I drop my drawers and take a pee.

She took another step towards the bathroom. *You big baby, what are you afraid of? You're in the middle of downtown main street USA bustling with people. You lived in New York City for years for heaven's sake.*

Honk-honk!

Emma flinched as Horatio drove by in his pickup truck and gave her a little wave. Angry at being startled, she half-heartedly smiled and waved back.

Her bladder abruptly reminded her of the task at hand.
The interior of the restroom was dimly lit with only one light bulb. Old fashioned wooden stalls lined one wall and the door creaked when she opened one. Pleasantly surprised, the stall was clean and there was about a half roll of toilet paper.

Her bladder must've recognized where she was because her urgency meter kicked it up to another level. So much so she barely had time to spin around, unfasten her belt and pants, and drop unceremoniously onto the commode.

She was grateful no unwanted moisture on the seat greeted her buttocks.

Feeling less than graceful she muttered, "Dancer I are."

It took a second for her muscles to finally unclench but when they did she could have doused a small forest fire.

I bet it was all that coffee I drank on the ferry this morning.

CREAK.

Emma froze. Someone had entered the bathroom. She thought it odd that out of the half dozen stalls to choose from they choose the one right next to hers.

Maybe she doesn't realize I'm here, Emma thought, but she doubted it after her thunderous water works.

As Emma was reaching for some toilet paper she heard the woman in the next stall breathing. Now she was certain there wasn't any scientific evidence to support this, but she would swear that the breathing wasn't female.

It was coming from a man. And it was increasing in pitch and intensity.

This is just great.

As Emma reached for one more handful of toilet paper she could see the woman's shoes.

They weren't woman's shoes. They were a man's. Odd looking things too; made out of burlap sacks?

Terrific. I'm not in town ten minutes and some drunk fisherman stumbles mistakenly into the ladies room and is now relieving himself loudly in the stall right next to mine. I'll be sure to mention that in the postcard to Mee-Maw.

As Emma recoiled in disgust she noticed a small circular hole in the wall between them. It was about the size of a silver dollar. Why hadn't she noticed the hole when she had first entered the stall? For a second, she could see light coming through the hole but then it was blocked.

Had the guy blocked up the hole?

Emma wasn't the peeping-Tom sort. Okay, she was a little *snoopy-poopy* at times, but regardless, her curiosity got the better of her, and she leaned forward and peered through the hole.

To her surprise, an eye was staring back at her. And not just any eye. But the same kind of eye she had seen earlier on the salmon shark. Black and soulless.

The drunk fisherman started breathing even faster. *God.* Her seeing him must have excited him in some sick way.

Emma quickly took her handful of toilet paper, crumpled it up into a ball, and after a moment of hesitation, stuffed it inside the hole. It was only there for a second before it was abruptly pulled through from the other side.

The drunk fisherman's breathing became deafening now. IN and OUT, IN and OUT.

Emma didn't cry out but she wanted to. Thankfully, she didn't just freeze up and sit there either. She jumped to her feet, yanked up her drawers, grabbed her purse, and bolted from the stall.

The heavy breathing stopped the instant she exited the stall.

At first, like a slow moving train leaving the station, she shuffled past the drunk fisherman's closed stall, then headed for the door, building up speed.

Emma put her hand on the exit's door handle and made the mistake of glancing back over her shoulder.

The door to the drunk fisherman's stall slammed violently open.

As much as she wanted to close her eyes or at least change the damn channel, she just couldn't drag her eyes away.

And for a moment, nothing happened.

Then the drunk fisherman, if that was what he indeed was, wearing the burlap shoes and sporting black-soulless eyes, launched out of the stall with one mighty leap.

As it turned out, he wasn't a drunk fisherman.

It was the exact same scarecrow she had seen in the wheat fields on Mee-Maw's farm.

The blinding fear a deer must feel when a hunter takes a shot is what danced up and down Emma's spine. And just as a deer might spring into action Emma yanked open the door with all her might and scrambled outside into the blessed sunlight. She didn't stop moving until she reached her car door.

She rifled through her pockets and pulled out her keys. She fumbled for the door key like an idiot girl in those horror movies and of course she had an equal amount of trouble unlocking the door. At last she jumped behind the wheel and slammed the door closed. She noted thankfully that Mr. Scarecrow had not exited the building behind her. Despite this, she slammed the door locks shut with her fist before starting the engine.

Still trembling, she started the car without the cliché problems that plagued horror movie automobiles. *Thank goodness for small mercies?*

The gears ground in reverse and she got the hell out of there.

She glanced in the rearview mirror, half expecting Mr. Scarecrow to be in the back seat. He wasn't. And she was pretty sure she hadn't seen him exit the bathroom.

She turned back to the road and swerved as she realized he was sitting in the seat beside her.

Emma could only scream.

Chapter 10

Latitude 61

WHEN THE VOLUNTEER HAVENPORT firefighters arrived, two men and one woman exited the ambulance and dashed for the building with orange cases and a backboard. Jeb led the way.

"Not you," a fourth paramedic shouted to Hank. It was a middle-aged, short, cherubic woman in a hastily thrown on jacket. The shoulder patch read HavenPort Volunteer Fire Dept. She motioned for Hank to join her at the back of the rescue vehicle.

When she yanked opened the rear of the ambulance Hank saw his reflection in a hard-shelled mirror hanging on the back of the door. His entire body, face and clothes were covered in grunge. An image of the creepy naked guy flashed across his mind, and for a moment he imagined he was standing right behind him with that jack-o-lantern grin of his, but when Hank spun around only the paramedic was there.

"You hurt? Did that crazy lady cut you anywhere?" the paramedic asked as she ineptly slipped on a pair of plastic gloves.

Hank recognized her Michigan accent immediately. "You're the dispatcher on the microphone."

"That's me, dispatcher, gift shop owner, caribou wrangler, and volunteer fire-fighter. Ophelia Pierce but everyone call me Ophy." She wrinkled her small nose at the smell of his clothes. "Forgive me if we don't shake hands."

Hank nodded in complete understanding.

At this, Ophy flashed a broad smile on her wide, rosy-cheeked face.

Hank liked her immediately and said, "I don't think I'm cut anywhere."

"Well, let's get you cleaned up then, sheriff. I must say, you certainly had one hell of a first day."

Ophy was obviously new to the job and the sight of excrement all over his body was making her queasy but Hank had to give her credit; she pushed through it. "You're in luck, Anchorage Fire Department was doing mudflat rescue exercises up the road and they're en route. They should be here in about another ten minutes."

Halfheartedly, Hank replied, "Yeah, aren't I the lucky guy."

—— o ——

Forty-five minutes later, Hank sat on the back of the ambulance in a fresh pair of tight-fitting scrubs and white tennies on loan from one of the volunteer paramedics who happened to be his size.

He wore a towel about his neck and his hair was still wet from the hazmat shower the fire department had set up beside the ambulance. The shower had consisted of a hose over a portable shower ring with a blue curtain. EMS had him strip down to his birthday suit, doused him with cold water, and scrubbed him with cleanser using bristled brushes on the ends of little wooden sticks. *Now I know how elephants feel at the zoo.*

The Rakewell building was now filled with State Troopers, Anchorage Fire Department, and HavenPort volunteer firefighters. Wanda's body had already been carted away to eventually end up at the Anchorage morgue forty-five miles north.

A young and smiling firefighter stepped in front of him wearing a thin hazmat suit over his turnout gear. "G. Wahlman" was stitched on the outside of his jacket. It was one of the firefighters from Anchorage who happened to be training nearby. He was holding a trash bag with Hank's soiled clothes.

"Don't worry, Sheriff. We'll test your clothes for any hazmat and get back to you with the results. In the meantime

I'd recommend you see your doc and get tested for every disease known to man."

Hank nodded and said, "I appreciate you guys coming down."

"Are you kidding?" the young firefighter asked. He took a quick glance over his shoulder at the Rakewell building. Hiking a thumb in its direction he added, "And miss a chance to explore Latitude 61?"

Hank's brow furrowed. "I'm not following you."

The firefighter looked at Ophy for support but clearly she didn't approve of the subject matter. This didn't dissuade the young fireman's enthusiasm in the least. "You never heard of Latitude 61? Why do you think the military built this base in the first place?" Not waiting for a response he answered, "The secret experiments on alien artifacts. Area 51? The chamber beneath the Sphinx? All the alien artifacts ever collected were brought here for testing. Everybody knows it but no one ever talks about it."

"They don't talk about it because it isn't true." Ophy grumped. "The military built the Rakewell building as a supply depot because it's an ice free port and connected to the railroad, and nothing more. They call it Latitude 61 because that's its exact latitude."

"Really? If it's a supply depot, how come they had over nineteen laboratories in there?" Turning back towards Hank, "The entire basement floor was essentially one big test lab."

Hank's interest piqued. "If that were true, why bring all these alien artifacts up to Alaska, out here in the middle of nowhere?"

The firefighter's smiling face immediately turned serious. "In case something went wrong."

Behind the fireman in the distance two men wearing scuba gear exited the building. Jeb Sutton, who was already standing outside, greeted them. One of the divers removed a wet revolver and flashlight from his mesh sack. Hank could just barely make out the diver's words over the sound of the idling trucks. "We didn't find any victims in the pool and we didn't find any severed heads."

Jeb, silent, just kept nodding. Every once in awhile they'd all look over at Hank but he could only hear snippets of their conversation. At one point, he did hear Jeb tell them, "I don't know, he seems like a pretty solid guy to me. He certainly handled himself pretty well in there when Wanda came at him with the knife."

This seemed to satisfy the divers and Hank heard one of them say, "Okay, Jeb. We'll keep searching. Here's his gun." The older diver, the one with a gray mustache and salt-and-pepper crew cut, dropped it into a Ziploc bag.

The younger of the two divers added, "Yeah. He might want to clean it."

No one laughed. The older diver told him, "Get back in the pool, Michael."

After the divers walked back into the building Jeb joined him at the back of the ambulance.

"Well?" Hank asked, his tone more impatient than he intended.

"Well … they didn't find your attacker in the pool. And they didn't find any body parts either."

"What about footprints leading out of the pool?"

Jeb shook his head. "Only yours."

"What about blood in the doorway? The severed head was dripping."

Jeb stared at him, probably searching for a measuring rod to gauge his sanity. "Sorry Hank. Other than poor Wanda. They didn't find anything you described."

Now Hank stood to face him. "Now Jeb, I know what I saw. When I got out I probably sloshed a lot of water on the floor but I remember the head in the doorway. Maybe the guy moved it when he left? Did they check everywhere?"

"Yeah Hank. They did."

"No blood at all? Anywhere? How is that possible?"

Jeb seemed to consider a moment before answering. Then he sighed. "I believe that you believe you saw it." Jeb hooked his thumbs in his belt. "Do you think maybe it's possible you just slipped by the pool, fell in and hit your head or something? I mean, after what happened with Wanda upstairs, and then falling in that mess; I know I'd be freaked out."

Hank stared at him evenly. "I don't exactly freak out that easily."

Jeb sighed a second time and Hank watched goosebumps rise on his arms — he'd abandoned the parka he'd worn as it had been soaked in Wanda's blood, and for all the sun out here, Hank agreed, there was definitely a chill in the air. "Yeah, that's what I figured too." Jeb said softly, "As much as I'd prefer to think you're crazy, the problem is, I do believe you, which means we got ourselves one crazy son-of-a-bitch on the loose."

"What about the woman? She didn't look homeless to me."

"Wanda? She's a bit eccentric, and a recluse sometimes but certainly not homeless. She married a fisherman about twenty years back. The old salt went down on his boat doing what he loves three seasons ago, but his insurance policy left her quite the inheritance." Jeb kicked a rock with the toe of his shoe. "Real shame the ole' girl ended up like that."

Hank watched two State Troopers leave the building and head for their respective patrol vehicles. Clearly the search was winding down and more urgent matters needed tending too.

"What was she talking about, anyway?" Hank struggled to recall. He then snapped his fingers. "Something about little doctors?"

"Yeah, that's what I heard, too," Jeb answered, then noticed the troopers departing. "Closest thing we have to a doctor around here is ole Doc Clemens, but small he ain't."

"Any idea of what she was talking about then?"

Jeb started to say something then stopped. Realizing Hank was still staring, he answered, "Not a one."

"You know one thing you never told me. What happened to the Rakewell building? Why was it abandoned in the first place?"

"Apart from the war being over? Dunno. One day the townsfolk woke up and found the place empty. Everyone had simply left. Near as anyone could figure, they all left during the night. A few days later a cargo ship arrived, packed up everything and shipped it all outta here."

Hank could tell Jeb knew more than that but decided not to press him for now. He made a mental note to follow up on the young fireman's conspiracy theory. *Maybe Wanda wasn't seeing doctors but maybe left over signs of the scientists?* His mind pictured lab coats hanging on long dead coat hooks, or photos of the original staff.

Interrupting his trip down alien conspiracy lane, Jeb asked, "Why don't you have Ophy give you a ride home? If you like, I can pick you up tomorrow morning and you can fill out your report then."

"Sounds good but I think I'll have her drop me off at the station so I can grab my own car. Driving up to the house in an ambulance might not go over so well with Sarah and the kids."

"Yeah, you're right about that."

Before the old timer could turn to walk off, Hank added, "Thanks for backing me up, Jeb."

"Sure thing, Hank. Least I could do for the new sheriff." Jeb smiled sadly then said a few words to Ophy out of earshot before moving back towards the building.

Ophy told him, "Be a few more minutes, hon. You might want to start thinking about what you're gonna tell that pretty wife of yours." And she too was gone.

What the hell am I going to tell Sarah? He wondered exactly how much he should say about his little misadventure. She and the kids loved it here; so serene, and their beautiful home with a deck overlooking the bay. It was perfect. They hadn't even finished unpacking yet.

Really, what did happen to him anyway? Jeb said there were no traces of the naked guy. No severed head or headless corpse. Not even footprints or signs of blood. Maybe it was exactly like Jeb figured; he hit his head on the bottom of the pool and imagined the rest. As for the firefighter's alien conspiracy theories, they were probably exactly that, goofball theories.

Great, I'm either insane or we've got a crazy naked killer on the loose.

As Hank waited for his ride, and debated his sanity, he couldn't see the glowing yellowed eyes studying him intently from the shadows of the treeline. The head was at least two-and-a-half times the size of a normal head, and covered with bristling hair. Its mouth had huge fangs, each easily over three inches in length — and dripping with fresh blood.

Chapter 11

Emma's Hotel Room

THE NIGHTMARE JERKED EMMA awake and she jolted upright. Her head throbbed from the frantic pounding of her heart and fresh memory of the scarecrow man. She found one hand clutched so tightly to her chest it felt like a vice-grip.

This must be what a heart attack feels like.

When her heavy breathing finally began to subside she scanned the room. In the flickering light of a corner lamp, she realized she was no longer in her crappy little foreign car. Instead she was sitting up in a small modest bed with thick wooden corner posts. The room's walls were logs, like a wooden cabin, but she suspected the dwelling was much larger than a simple cabin. Instead of a modern light there was a gas lamp on the wooden nightstand whose flame eerily glowed. In place of a television was a large ceramic water pitcher and matching wash basin perched upon a small table against the wall.

The room did not look familiar.

Where am I?

Emma threw back the moist bed sheets and discovered she wore only a nightgown right from the Victorian age. She was forced to wonder who had dressed her, and where her clothes were. Hopefully, it hadn't been... Her mind shied away from that thought and she decided action was better than thinking about it. She swung her legs over the bed to jump to her feet, but her legs felt as heavy as lead. Taking it more slowly, she was able to stand and could already feel the

blood circulating back into her legs. Her bare feet slid across a plank wood floor.

The wind outside rattled across the glass window and drew Emma's attention. The shade was heavily stained and was accompanied with a stale unpleasant odor.

Gross.

She did not want to touch the stained curtain, but with thumb and forefinger, she carefully peeled it back from the frame. It was dark outside, but a bright orange moon shone in all its glory. She had never seen the moon so bright, almost as bright as the sun. An old-timey clock on the wall showed five-past-midnight.

"Harvest Moon," she muttered, recalling the term from her youth on her parent's farm.

Mesmerized by it, beautiful yet somehow scary and foreboding, she imagined that somewhere there was a wolf baying at the orange disk in the sky. She could see her room was on the second floor of an old wooden structure resembling an old hotel, but beyond that she could only see thick mounds of puffy gray and white snow dotting the tree-line of a coniferous forest.

As she stood there, dark clouds swallowed the moon and soon heavy flakes of snow drifted through the night.

Turning from the window she noticed an antique phone hanging on the wall. It was like the kind she had seen in old western movies. In fact, if she hadn't seen them in the movies, she'd never have known how to operate the antiquated device. Moving over to it, she picked up the receiver at the end of a thin cord and held it to her ear. She spoke hesitantly into the mouthpiece. "Hello, Operator?" There wasn't even a dial tone. She immediately felt foolish. Most likely the contraption was nothing more than a novelty item put in the guest rooms. She decided she was more comfortable with the idea that this was a hotel, a bizarrely themed one admittedly, but this definitely wasn't the secret lair of a creepy scarecrow man.

She was about to hang up when she heard faint breathing.

"Hello?" she said tentatively.

The breathing grew in intensity, going raspy, like sandpaper grinding wood. Emma felt her anger growing and slammed the phone back down hard enough to break it. She was tired of playing games. She headed for the door.

As she approached the door, a chill washed up and down her spine. Instinctively, Emma knew with every fiber of her being she did not want to open this door. She examined the lock. The keyhole was old — the kind that used a cast iron key. She knelt down and put her eye to the hole. Part of her expected to see the same black soulless eye staring back at her as she had in the harbor bathroom, but she saw only an empty hallway.

Emma pressed on the thumb latch, and after giving a few tugs on the door, she found it locked. Anger and perhaps a bit of panic swelling in her chest, she banged the palm of her hand on the door and yelled for help but between knockings there was no answer.

"Damn it."

She turned back to the room. She didn't see anything capable of smashing down the heavy door. Then she realized there was a drawer in the night table that she'd missed on first inspection. For a brief moment she questioned her sanity because she was certain there had been no drawer beneath the flickering oil lamp. Opening the drawer, she found only a solitary item. An iron key. A brief maniacal laugh escaped her lips. The key certainly wasn't one of those fancy new motel card key locks that you swiped — Nope, plain ole' garden variety cast iron.

Her fingers fumbled for the key, and before she lost her courage, she moved back to the door and shoved it in the lock. When she turned the key she was rewarded with the sound of a heavy deadbolt sliding free. Emma froze. Another chill tap dancing on her spine. The door latch had been cold to the touch and she was suddenly aware she could see her own breath.

Before opening the door she detected a faint odor that permeated in the air. It was growing stronger and staler by the second. She caught herself leaning forward and lightly whiffing at the door like a dog sniffing out an intruder on the other side of the wooden barrier. Her mind conjured up foul images of a hospital room gone bad, — blood-stained walls, torn bodies laying about, wheelchairs and gurneys knocked

over, and outdated hospital equipment, particularly an electro-
shock therapy console, still humming, ready for use.

Emma quickly released the handle.

Now where the hell did she get that thought from? Why
did it feel so familiar? Her hand refused to move back towards
the latch.

This is crazy. I can't stand in the room like this forever.

With a nervous laugh, Emma finally stretched out her hand
towards the door once more.

When Emma finally pulled open the squeaky door, she didn't
find a hospital gone wrong, only a quaint and rustic corridor. A
long blood red carpet occupied the middle of a lonely hallway,
and the walls were lined with more gas lamps. She peered to
the left and then to the right. To her left, a staircase, and to
her right, an elevator at the end of the corridor. The elevator
was a welcome sight. It was the first modern convenience she
had seen since awakening. There, she was right; this was just
a themed hotel.

Hotel or not, she still didn't feel safe. No one was supposed
to wake up in a strange room, wearing strange nightclothes, with
no idea how they'd gotten there. Forgoing an elevator she might
find herself trapped in, Emma crept silently in the direction of
the staircase. She trembled as she passed closed doors. Surely
the scarecrow man was behind one of those doors, and at any
moment he'd fling one open and devour her soul.

Traveling down the hall, she noticed several oil paintings
on the walls depicting life in an old frontier mining town;
a rustic train crossing a gorge on a wooden train trestle,
abandoned mining equipment overtaken by brush and growing
rust, a rickety hardware store that would be at home in any
ghost town. All the paintings were similar save one smaller one
near the top of the staircase.

Contrary to the others, this painting depicted a scene of a
mental hospital wing where haughty members of high society
in period gowns were peering at half-naked and miserable
patients on cruel display. A placard below it read:

"The Unfortunates"
Painted by J.P. Clemens, 1735

Again that flash of … what? Fear? Familiarity? Lost memories of what? Visiting her mother in the hospital? She couldn't remember Paw ever taking her.

She forced herself to keep moving.

The staircase followed a curved wall to the ground floor and vanished into the winding blackness. At the moment, Emma would have killed for a flashlight. But as her eyes adjusted to the darkness she saw a flickering light below.

Her knees felt weak, and her body trembled, but she continued with her descent.

At the first landing she paused when she heard a loud CLUMP. Peering into the depths below, she could only make out what appeared to be a dimly lit hotel lobby.

Like at her bedroom door, she knew she could not remain on the landing forever.

She was about to take another step when she spied a shadow upon the curved wall. This brought her to an immediate halt.

The shape was easily recognizable. It was the scarecrow man. Although she couldn't see him, his shadow was easily discernible: frayed straw hat, talon-like hands, impossibly lean form. He was just standing there.

She closed her eyes and took a few quick breaths. A loud CLUMP thrust her eyes back open. Still the thin shape remained, only this time his shadow was one step closer.

Stifling a cry on the back of her hand Emma turned and flew back up the stairs. She ran down the hallway. She ran all the way back to her hotel room. Her door was locked. It must have locked behind her.

Where did I leave the damn key? Of course, in the lock inside the room.

One quick glance back at the stairs. The scarecrow man's shadow neared the top step.

This time Emma bolted for the elevator, dim light bulbs at the end of the hallway flickered on and off as though breathing their last breath.

She pressed the first floor button and wrung her hands before the elevator doors finally parted. Flinging herself inside, she jabbed the button labeled 1. Then tap-tap-tapped the 'close door' button. After a painful moment, the doors finally began to move. As they did, the scarecrow man reached the top of the stairs, and his physical form stepped out of the darkness. He was much taller and leaner than before. So much so he ducked his head just to enter the hallway. His hat scraped the ceiling as he lunged towards her in long, purposeful strides. The gas lamps whiffed out behind him as he passed, his long outstretched arms filling the entire hallway, his claws scratching the walls as he came. As he grew closer and closer she got a look at his disfigured burlap face — his eyes black voids, completely soulless. He opened his jagged mouth and uttered a scream reminiscent of a hog in a slaughterhouse.

Oh God. Oh God... Emma retreated until she felt the elevator wall against her back.

The doors closed. Something slammed into them with a loud THUD causing her to jump. The elevator hummed, and after a slight jolt, began its descent.

As the elevator car reached the first floor, she shrank into the corner, her heart pounding her ribs as she succumbed to the fear that the scarecrow man would be waiting for her when the doors slid open.

As it turned out, what lay beyond the doors was much, much worse.

The elevator did not stop on the first floor but continued its descent to a third choice, "B", for basement. Emma cried no, and tapped the 1 button repeatedly. The "B" above the door flickered on as the elevator slowed to a stop.

Even before the doors parted, brackish water began seeping in through the cracks and began pooling at her feet. *No, no, no...* The four walls seemed closer than before and the seeping water soon closed around her knees.

Emma heard herself gasping for breath. With one hand she reached toward the 1 button. She sobbed and pressed it again.

Please... Oh please.

Heedless of her desire, the elevator dinged and the doors began to open on the basement floor.

As soon as the doors parted, water flooded in and slammed her backwards. As she smacked her head against the back wall she fell beneath the waves. After a moment of panic, she found her footing and came up gasping. The water was now waist high in the elevator and equal to the water level in the flooded basement.

What the hell is this?

She pawed her wet hair out of her eyes. The underground basement seemingly went on forever in an endless chasm of muddy water. Thick wooden posts held up a timbered roof adorned with dingy fluorescent lights.

Using the doorframe on either side as leverage, Emma sloshed her way through the water and stepped out of the elevator. She was about to take another step forward when she saw something swishing back and forth through the water in the distance.

Whatever it was, the majority of it was hidden beneath the surface. She could tell it was fast because of the water displacement as it zigzagged back and forth, moving as though searching for something. Her eyes sought another means of escape, a stairwell, a door, anything. There was nothing, only endless flooded basement.

A fin cut the water.

She had seen the dark color of its skin before. Behind the fin a tail swished the water.

And now the ripples turned and aimed toward her position, unhurried but focused. Salmon sharks.

Horror widened Emma's eyes. *This is ... this can't be...* She covered her mouth with the back of her hand. She sloshed back into the elevator. The shark was nearly upon her. She pressed the number 1 and sparks flew from the water-soaked panel. A second later the elevator lights winked out.

Sobbing, she found a small railing on the elevator walls just above the surface. She scrambled up onto it at the back corner of the elevator car. Emma shrieked when the water erupted with the surge of massive jaws lined by jagged white teeth. The shark's nose slammed into the wall just under her feet.

Again and again, the sea monster lunged out of the water at her legs with gaping jaws. Each time she barely moved from one railing to another just in time. Each time she barely maintained her footing on the slick metal. Emma knew she was going to die here. She had to do something.

With a jump, her hand smacked the ceiling and dislodged a panel. Hope. An access hatch that led to the roof of the elevator. As she reached up and turned the hatch's handle, the shark chomped down on the railing barely a foot away. The creature thrashed, jaws working. There was a rending squeal as the shark managed to tear the metal bar right off its brackets.

Emma would have fallen in had she not jumped for the hatch opening and now struggled to pull herself upwards. She put her feet on the elevator walls to help her shimmy up through the hatch. She was going to make it.

She was wrong.

Her feet had been low enough for the shark to lunge out of the water and clamp down on her legs. Emma's fingers were immediately ripped from the hatch and she fell onto her back, into the water.

Knives cut into her calves as the shark's mouth snapped over both legs. Below the surface she could feel the shark tugging her out of the elevator.

Dragging beneath the water, Emma fought to hang on to either side of the elevator doors. Her mind blanking on white-hot pain. Even submerged she managed to hold on for a few seconds before she was ripped from the elevator completely.

Chapter 12

Check Out

EMMA OPENED HER EYES.

She bolted upright in bed once again and inhaled with the deep gasp of a rescued drowning person. After a time her rapid breathing quieted somewhat, but her heart still pounded in her chest like a ticked off jackhammer.

I don't know how much more of this I can take.

Emma had never experienced a nightmare of such vividness and intensity.

She felt the echoes of pain in her legs. Emma reached down and felt them to make sure both were still there. She even wiggled her toes just to be sure everything still worked.

In addition to her fully functional legs Emma saw that she was no longer wearing the Victorian dress but the same clothes she had worn on the ferry.

Emma scanned her surroundings. Unlike before, bright sunlight emanated from the windows and saturated a modest hotel bedroom. Immediately apparent she was no longer in an old Victorian hotel. Modern day light fixtures had replaced the gas lamps and a television set the size of a horse trough sat on a dresser against the wall.

Spying the window, she slid from the bed and noted the wood floors were now cheap, but clean carpet.

This time when she gazed out the window she saw small town USA about four floors below. The town was back dropped by a happy harbor with snow-capped mountains across the bay in the distance. Were it not for recent events the landscape was serene.

She tugged at the window.

Of course, locked.

When she saw the latches engaged she told herself not to be so quick to panic this time. She undid them and a brisk breeze washed over her. Emma took a deep breath of thankfulness. The air was a combination of the mountains and nearby sea. Listening to the sounds of the beeping cars, boats in the harbor, and normal hustle and bustle of the port town gave her some sense of reality. Either the experience in the flooded basement had been another nightmarish hallucination or some benevolent force had plucked her from the dark place.

This time the hotel room was somehow familiar. She wasn't sure why since she had no recollection of checking in.

She was about to give in to the panic again when she couldn't find her purse but then saw it on a cozy chair by the window. She didn't remember putting it there but it was certainly in a place she would have thrown it.

Suspicious of everything, she checked inside it. The purse appeared to be hers, and not a fake.

I wonder if the key is in the drawer again. This time the night table was drastically different, not old timey. She pulled open the drawer. There was a heavily used Bible inside but no key. She opened the Bible thinking the key might be cleverly hidden inside the pages. Nope. It was a standard, run-of-the-mill hotel Bible.

She felt even more foolish when she noticed a matching pair of hotel card keys on the dresser.

Somebody placed those keys there. Somebody dragged my butt out of my car and brought me here. I am not insane. I am not a drug addict, not anymore. Somebody's playing a sick game.

She glanced out the window again and smelled the salty air. *That's real.*

Leaving her bedroom, she found a modest living room and kitchen area that comprised one space. A bar with two stools separated the kitchen from the living room.

Like her bedroom, the rest of the apartment was sparsely furnished with used but current furnishings. A glass-topped coffee table sat in front of a brownish sofa flanked by end tables.

On one end table was a beige telephone. It too was old and used looking, but far more modern than the antique phone in her nightmare.

Next to the phone was a colorful brochure that read, "Welcome to The Land's End Bed and Breakfast Hotel". Inside were listings of local activities and nearby restaurants.

Emma thought about using the phone for a moment. *Whatever this is, even if it's my insane brain, I'm still going through it.*

She opted not to try the phone and headed for the door. She noticed this time the door was fitted with a modern day fisheye lens. She peeked through it expecting to see a black soulless shark eye, but nope, only an empty hotel hallway.

Emma grabbed the handle, fearful it wouldn't open. She took a breath, turned the latch and found the door unlocked. Heart thumping, she yanked open the door.

One long hall, as before, but this time the doors were more mainstream. Her hotel door number was 407.

Before venturing into the hall, she went back inside to grab her keys and purse. Picking up her purse and tucking it under her arm like nothing happened seemed irrational to her. Like she was playing into 'their' hands, but she still didn't know who 'they' were. But maybe 'they' were spying on her right now.

Staring at her purse, she remembered all those movies where spies would plant tiny microphones and tracking chips in women's purses.

Foiling any attempt to bug or track her, she dumped the contents out onto the dresser and grabbed only the barest essentials: wallet, gum, chapstick, and a pen. *Where is it?* Yes, her Gerber knife that her Mee-Maw had given her when she had first left for New York was still there. She stuffed all but the knife into her jeans pockets. The knife she held opened, at the ready.

Now I'm ready.

Leaving the possibly bugged purse behind and armed with the pocketknife that she kept lowered by her side, Emma now felt a little more in control. She took a breath and opened the door.

There was no spiraling staircase or large oil paintings, only a little arrow sign that pointed to the elevator three doors down.

Emma went over to it, pushed the button, and when it arrived, the doors opened. She was about to enter when she saw a sign that read, "Stairs" near the end of the hall and opted for them instead. An image of the doors parting to reveal an endless flooded basement flashed through her mind.

Leaving the elevator behind, she pushed the crash bar and found a well-lit stairwell.

The stairs led down to the hotel's lobby that was a tad touristy. Several stuffed animals were mounted on pedestals and there was a wall stacked with leafed-through brochures. The only redeeming thing about the lobby was its cozy stone fireplace on the back wall. Several comfy chairs surrounded the hearth, each nestled next to an end table adorned with various magazines.

The bell on the main entrance door rang and announced three fishermen. The three men entered the lobby through the wide, glass-paned front doors. They talked loudly amongst themselves and passed her without so much as a glance. She watched them as they moved over to the elevator and went up to their rooms.

A plump, cheerful-looking woman sat behind the reception desk. She was engrossed in a crossword and gnawed thoughtfully on her pencil.

Emma thought about walking over to her but then wondered what she'd say. Would she make up a story on how she wasn't feeling well and wondered how she got here? If she said anything about her horrific nightmare, people would think she'd gone plumb loco. In the end though, she just didn't care anymore. The more information she had the more empowered she felt.

Okay, I'll tell her I wasn't feeling well and I don't remember anything.

As she approached the very narrow reception desk, the plump woman gazed up from her crossword and said, "Hey there, hon, I thought you were going to sleep the day away."

Emma glanced at the clock on the wall behind the woman. It was past noon. She also saw her name on the cubby mailboxes behind her. She hadn't remembered checking in but her name was printed on a stick-on label beneath one of the mailboxes. She laughed nervously, and managed, "Uh, yeah, I was pretty tired when I came in. Speaking of which, do you remember what time I came in last night."

"I can tell you exactly what time you came in yesterday," she answered as she opened the logbook. Her nametag said Ophelia. "It was exactly ten o'clock. You must've come here straight from the ferry."

"Ten, at night?" Emma asked.

A flash of concern appeared on the woman's cherubic face, "No, hon, ten in the morning. Boy, you must've really been out of it there sweetie."

The woman was certainly pleasant enough. "Uhmm, yeah, thanks ... Ophelia."

"Oh, hon, it ain't nothing. And call me Ophy. I know it ain't exactly the most flattering name but most folks in HavenPort don't know me by anything else."

"Thanks, Ophy," Emma answered, and smiled, if only a little.

"You've had a long journey. Why don't you go back upstairs and rest a bit more? If you're still sleeping I'll wake you around supper time. If you like, we can go over to the diner together for a bite to eat."

Emma did feel exhausted. As likable as Ophy was, she wasn't about to go back upstairs to her room. That's what 'they' would want, keep her contained.

"Thanks just the same but I think I'll stretch my legs a bit and get some fresh air."

"Sounds good, hon. Let me know if you need anything. Now I've got to get back to my crossword. If I don't finish this darn thing by dinner ole' Doc Clemens won't let me hear the end of it."

Clemens... Emma frowned. The name was familiar somehow. She'd heard it, or seen it, before. But then, maybe that was because Uncle John had liked his baseball and she vaguely remembered there being a Clemens who was a famous pitcher.

Exiting the lobby Emma went out the hotel's main entrance and down the steps. The town was bustling with afternoon activity. As much as she didn't want to go back inside, she felt as though she could lie down on the icy sidewalk and go back to sleep.

Before venturing towards Main Street she reran Ophelia's words in her head. Ophy had said she came in on the ferry yesterday morning. After talking to the guy she met, and by the time she got here, it would've been about ten, which meant this is reality, and that hellish acid trip was all just a freaking nightmare.

Maybe I'll go find that cute guy. What was his name? Oh yeah, Horatio.

Emma stepped down off the sidewalk and nearly fell over from exhaustion. She wondered why she was so exhausted if she had been sleeping all night. She realized she couldn't go anywhere in her present condition so opted to go back inside.

Back in the lobby, Ophy was checking in a young couple with an infant in a stroller. Emma decided to rest in one of the recliners by the fireplace rather than go back upstairs to her room.

Avoiding Ophy's gaze, she grabbed a magazine and curled up in one of the chairs facing away from the reception area. *Better Homes and Gardens*. She checked the date on the magazine. It was last month's issue.

No one seemed to notice her, and the fireplace area was safe and warm.

Real or not, after everything that had happened since she stepped off the ferry, she was asleep in seconds.

She didn't even feel the small blanket Ophy draped over her sleeping body.

Chapter 13

Welcome to the Last Frontier!

THE LAST FRONTIER DINER was a dive, and that's the way Hank liked it.

The diner wasn't a far cry from any other small town diner: Bright red plastic cushioned seats on metal framed chairs, shelves stacked with maps, postcards, and other touristy souvenirs in a rack by the door that were for sale, but almost never sold. One wall was covered with dusty photographs of various fishing boats and clearly the smoking ordinance wasn't strictly enforced because even now four fishermen were smoking like chimneys at the counter. The only thing separating the décor from when it was first built in the late 1950's was the flat screen television on the wall. Currently there was a baseball game on that no one was watching.

One unique quality of *The Last Frontier Diner* however was the back wall that featured huge windows with panoramic views of the bay and harbor far below.

Yep. Hank liked everything about the diner except for one thing. On the counter an oversized stuffed otter held up a homemade sign that read: "You Otter behave in HavenPort!" He swore that grinning gremlin was always watching him with that creepy bucktoothed smile of his.

Hank had been living in HavenPort for three weeks now without another serious incident. A couple traffic tickets, a bench warrant, and a few drunk and disorderly fisherman, sure, but certainly nothing like his first day on the job. They never did find any sign of the naked man with the jack-o-Lantern smile that still haunted his dreams.

These days, things were good. The mornings were easily the best part of his workday. Not only was breakfast his favorite meal, but the petty criminals still hadn't woken up yet.

Most mornings he enjoyed the company of town favorite, Doc Clemens. The old boy was quick with a joke and had a story for every occasion. This morning he was running late, so Hank passed the time watching the locals in the diner.

Each morning, around ten, the townies all strolled in for their mid-morning breakfast and exchange of conversation before going about their day.

The usual mid-morning regulars were present. Happy-go-lucky Ophelia, part-time dispatcher, volunteer EMT, hotel operator, and eternal optimist worked the crowd as usual, collecting and giving gossip like a busy little humming bird, picking up little tidbits here and delivering it there in equal portions, but always bringing a warm smile to whomever she happened upon.

Then there were the two white-haired retired fishermen who always sat in one of the back booths against the wall. They avoided him like the plague and when he did have to talk with them, they were always overly nice. Hank suspected this had everything to do with their sizable pot grow hidden in the woods behind the Rakewell building. As long as they limited their pot to personal use and didn't sell to kids, quite frankly, he could care less. Being sheriff was part-time politics, after all.

"Morning Sheriff, your usual?"

Sliding his empty cup closer to his waitress, he answered, "That'd be fine, thanks."

The waitress smiled sweetly, poured his coffee and then darted away at the beckoning of one of the other more beastly servers.

His waitress couldn't have been more than 25. She was pretty enough, milky skin and strawberry-blond hair. The kind of girl you might see working as a barista paying off college debt. But this girl didn't have that warm smile that went along with, "room for cream?" At first glance she had that walking victim look, but if one took the time to look closer, her eyes revealed a steady determination towards life. This twenty-something girl had her whole life ahead of her and was on a mission. By all accounts, she had arrived at HavenPort almost the same time he did. Ophy had told him she used to be a dancer with the New York City Ballet. Hank wondered how someone with that kind of talent ended up here. Alaska wasn't exactly built for timid ballerinas. The answer wasn't hard to figure out. He was a cop after all. Most people who ended up in a small town like this were usually running from something, or someone.

—— o ——

"Hey Cinderella, your order's up."

Emma didn't pay Odessa much mind. She was just a bitter old waitress who Emma had made the mistake of confiding in during her first week. Among other things, she had told the older waitress about her summer gig at Walt Disney World where she'd play the face character of Cinderella. Knowing that the name bothered her, Odessa took great pleasure in calling her that, or variations like Cinder-soot, and Cinder-dulla.

Emma didn't overreact like she might have a few weeks ago prior to her arrival. Life had certainly made a turn for the better over the last few weeks. For one, she had been clean for three weeks (that she was sure of at least) and she'd even managed to put on a few healthy pounds. And she simply loved the town. She made some new friends and best of all; she hadn't had any hallucinations since the day of her arrival.

"Thanks Bob," she said to the fry cook with bottle cap glasses. His thick glasses, combined with his greasy unwashed comb-over and heavily stained shirt, didn't exactly line the girls up at the front door, but Emma knew Bob didn't care. He was good at his job, and on occasion, he was even sweet.

Emma grabbed the order and navigated the busy morning crowd back over to where the sheriff was sitting in his usual spot, a corner booth by the window, his back to the wall. The townsfolk called him the new sheriff and the fat slob who worked with him the old sheriff, but Sheriff Hank McCarthy was the only one Emma had ever known.

For one, he was a creature of habit. No matter what the weather, he always hung up his fur-lined patrol jacket on the long row of peg hooks by the door and wore his long-sleeved work shirt casually rolled up to his elbows. And he always ordered the same breakfast every morning. Coffee, black, two eggs sunny-side up with a side order of sourdough toast and bacon.

"Here you go, Sheriff," she said, laying down his plates of hot food.

Going from dancer to waitress wasn't as hard as most people might have thought. She had applied the discipline she had acquired in dance to every other aspect of her life, even the starting over parts. Probably the hardest thing was when people would find out what she used to be in her former life and then they'd always give her that, 'how'd you end up here?' look.

The sheriff gazed up from his morning paper, another ritual, and said in his deep friendly voice, "Emma, we've been through this, it's just Hank, thanks."

"Sure thing, Sherif— uh, I mean, Hank."

Geez, I'm practically gushing like a school girl.

"You need anything else ... Hank?"

"No thanks, darling. I'm all set."

Emma thought she had detected that Hank was a little embarrassed by the fact that he had slipped and called her darling. She sensed nothing lascivious about his comment, unlike other male customers, he was only being friendly. She liked it and hoped he would call her that again. Emma noted the town of HavenPort was immune from the rest of the world in this regard in that the waitresses still called their customers hon or honey, sweetie-pie or sugar, and the patrons still called their waitresses by, darlin' or Ma'am. Emma sighed happily and headed back towards the kitchen for her next order.

As she entered the kitchen, Odessa was lighting up her fifth cigarette this morning. "Ewww-wee, that sheriff is somethin' else. Why is it all the good-looking ones is always married?"

Before the governor in her brain could kick in, Emma answered, "Yeah, I met his wife and kids in the grocery store the other day and they seem like a really sweet family."

Odessa frowned at this, "Yeah, that's all well and good, but maybe the new sheriff might want a little sumthin'-sumthin' extra on the side." She took another drag on her cigarette and blew the smoke Emma's way.

Bob the fry cook rolled his eyes, but this time Emma remembered to keep her comments to herself. She knew she'd only alienate Odessa further if she said anything about her smoking in the kitchen, coveting married men, or wearing that ridiculous wig she always wore.

Just then, through Bob's window she noticed Horatio had entered the diner. Emma didn't really think of him as her boyfriend. Not yet anyway. He was sweet and kind, and certainly cute enough. Emma shyly smoothed out the front of her uniform and drifted out of the kitchen. She walked over to where Horatio had taken a seat at the counter.

"Morning, Horatio. Oatmeal and orange juice?" she asked. Horatio ate pretty healthy. He was easily the healthiest person in town. And over the last three weeks he had turned out to be a real friend. He helped her sell her car; since she walked everywhere in town there was no reason to keep it. He helped her get this job and he even took her kayaking once. Sometimes they'd go on long walks in the mountains, or around town, and just talk for hours. It had been weeks since the nightmarish incident in the harbor bathroom and the terrifying visions that followed. She hadn't told him about the nightmares, or her previous drug problem, but she did share just about everything else.

"Nope, just making sure we're still on for our hike after lunch," he answered, smiling that sunny grin of his. Checking to see no one was watching, he leaned over and gave her a quick peck on the cheek.

The kiss took Emma by surprise. She quickly glanced over her shoulder to make sure Odessa hadn't seen anything. She could only take so much crap. Fighting blushes, she answered, "Wouldn't miss it."

"Where you two love birds headed?" came a gruff voice, nearby.

It was Jeb. The fat slob everyone called the old sheriff. He had just walked in and was most likely looking for his boss, Hank.

As usual, Horatio was unfazed. 'Water off a duck's back', that was his motto. If anything, he looked downright pleased with himself. "I promised Emma here that I'd take her up to the canyon to see the totem pole."

Emma wasn't sure if Jeb heard Horatio because he was giving Hank a quick wave, but then he answered, "If you kids are hiking up Totem Pole Canyon you best be sure and keep clear of Ole' Barnabus."

Horatio nodded in response, "Sure, Jeb, you bet-chya."

That said, Jeb hiked his pistol belt up around his girth and then ambled back to Hank's corner booth.

—— o ——

When Jeb strode up to his back booth sanctuary, Hank couldn't help but flash Jeb a crooked smile.

"What are you grinning at?" Jeb grumped.

Hank chuckled. "You really want to know?"

Jeb tossed his head around in irritation then shot his hands out to his sides as if to say, 'duh'. Hank had great fun pushing the old boy's buttons.

Hank blew a cooling breath on his coffee before answering calmly, in a low tone, "Your fly's undone."

"What?" Jeb exclaimed, and then he realized not only were his pants unzipped, but his shirt tail was stuck through the zipper making it all the more obvious.

"Why didn't you say sumthin'?" Jeb asked irritably, zipping up his pants then slipping into the seat opposite Hank.

Hank chuckled, "What are you talking about? I just did."

Jeb spoke under his breath. "No, I mean why didn't you say sumthin' when I first walked in?"

Clearly Jeb was bothered. "What did you want me to do, tell you while you were talking to those two kids?" Hank asked, then took another bite of his eggs. Mouth in mid-chew he asked, "By the way, who's Barnabus?"

Jeb signaled for coffee before answering by holding up his empty cup to the young waitress across the diner who was busy serving other customers. When she ignored him he dropped his cup back to the counter with an angry mope. "Oh, just a great big grumpy old bear. The old ladies at the church gave him the name. He likes to break into people's cabins when they're not at home and make a real mess of things." Jeb gazed off into the distance as though seeing ole' Barnabus up close and personal, and added ominously, "A big grumpy ole' bear."

"Dangerous?" Hank asked, wolfing down his food now. He always ate fast. He had picked up the bad habit in the military and as a cop because you never knew when you were going to get that next call that didn't allow you to finish your meal.

"He didn't used to be," Jeb answered. "With all the salmon running up the creeks and patches of berry bushes growing everywhere, bear don't usually bother folks much around here. Hunters have been taking pot shots at ole' Barnabus for years, but nobody's ever managed to take him down."

"With all that lead in his body, he's probably in a lot of pain. No wonder he's grumpy," Hank offered. "I would be."

Jeb signaled for coffee again, this time pointing to the inside of his cup. The waitress pretended not to see him. It seemed Hank wasn't the only one who liked to push Jeb's buttons. "Ain't been right in the head ever since. Some say he don't even hibernate for winter no more, which probably makes him even more dangerous."

Hank nodded. "You gonna order some breakfast?" Hank already knew the answer. Jeb was a one meal, one gigantic meal, a day, and it was never breakfast. Hank secretly hoped Jeb would take off before Doc Clemens arrived so they could have their regular morning 'coffee talk'.

"Naw, I just came by to let you know we got a report that we got more snow headed our way. Most likely we'll be locked in for winter by this weekend."

"Okay, thanks Jeb."

Jeb leaned forward, checked to see if anyone was eavesdropping. "Listen, Hank. During the winter there ain't much to do around here other than drinking, playing cards, and catching up on reading. Folks tend to go a little stir crazy. You'll get your domestic abuse calls, a few fights, but some will start seeing things that ain't really there."

Hank figured Jeb was referring to the Naked Man. They never found any traces of him or his victim. Hank also knew Jeb's heart was in the right place and it was his way of looking out for him. "Thanks, Jeb. I appreciate your watching out for me."

Jeb nodded back with pride. Keeping the old sheriff busy had really turned ole Jeb around. Hank had redone the budget and figured out how to put Jeb on as his fulltime deputy. Since then, Jeb had cut down on the booze, maintained his police equipment better, and even cleaned his guns. Remembering his zipper was another matter. Hank smiled at the thought of his own joke.

Jeb slid his girth back out of the booth and muttered, "All right, I'm headed back to the station. Call me if you need anything."

"We'll do Jeb, thanks."

As Hank lifted the last of his coffee to his lips, a blast of a tug boat horn pulled his attention outside the windows to the harbor below. A large fishing trawler was chugging its way out of the port to deep water.

Hank also noted his reflection in the glass of the window pane. His face was much more relaxed than he remembered in days past and somehow even seemed younger. And why not? HavenPort had certainly been good to him and his family. His daughter loved her school, his wife was taking photography classes and enjoyed photographing the scenery, that is, when she wasn't remodeling the house and taking care of the baby.

Hank was about to look away from his content reflection when he saw a man sitting at one of the tables in the center of the diner almost directly behind him. The man, sixties, white beard, wasn't one of the locals and he certainly wasn't part of the mid-morning group. The man sat perfectly still and was simply staring at Hank. The most terrifying thing about the man was there was a bullet hole in his forehead, and just about the time Hank noticed the open wound, blood began oozing out of it and trickling down the man's face and onto the table.

Before Hank could turn around a disembodied voice whispered in his ear, "Please... please don't kill me."

Hank immediately spun around but the waitress, not his waitress, the large curvy one with the bad wig, blocked his view.

"More coffee, honey?"

Hank leaned way over in his seat to peer around the waitress's double-wide hips, but the man with the gaping hole in his head was gone.

Chapter 14

Totem Pole Canyon

EMMA AND HORATIO had been hiking up the mountain for nearly two hours now. The long, invigorating hike was all up slope, but Emma's dancer legs were grateful for the exercise.

For some reason the bowl of mountains surrounding the town didn't make Emma feel claustrophobic like the town itself did. Main Street, the school, the old grocery store, and Ophy's hotel were all in the same four block area, and encompassed ninety percent of the town's residents. At least the open waterway leading to the ocean offered an escape; that is, to anyone with a boat. Emma had been looking forward to escaping the town with Horatio right up until she spotted the sign that read:

WARNING
GRIZZLY BEAR ALERT

After seeing the photo of an enormous bear munching a three-foot salmon, she didn't feel as adventurous about their hike as she had before. Horatio had convinced her that he had hiked the trail numerous times before and never had a single bear encounter.

At the edge of town the trail started as a narrow path that meandered up the mountain through a thick forest. The woods smelled of pine trees that were pungent, yet pleasant. The trail turned and twisted, sometimes splitting off into other trails. The higher they walked the more the landscape grew rocky; to either side boulders and shade took over with less trees and underbrush. The sound of the babbling brook that ran parallel to the trail was hypnotic and could've easily lulled her to sleep were they not constantly moving. Emma hadn't felt this relaxed, or happy, in a long, long time.

She had not completely forgotten about her sister's suicide, or the note that had brought her here. But this place... It was all so, therapeutic.

And she loved spending time with Horatio. He was a great listener, and she loved their walk-and-talks even more.

Emma found herself smiling. After shouldering her pack higher up on her shoulder, she dug her boots into the slope ahead with renewed vigor.

Occasionally she would stop to look back at Horatio to make sure he was following close behind. As they hiked upwards, they followed a path that ran alongside a set of derelict railroad tracks. The meandering trail took them past several old wooden buildings in various stages of decay and even through an old ghost town. Horatio had explained the relics used to belong to a copper mining camp that once occupied the canyon nearly a hundred years ago. Emma had posed for several pictures with the relics, her favorite being next to a rusted antique truck whose tires had long since withered away.

"Are we almost there?" Emma huffed.

"You tell me," Horatio answered, barely out of breath.

She glanced to the right and saw a curve in the canyon ahead. "Is that where we're supposed to go?"

They rounded the next bend in the canyon, which soon opened into a large clearing with a circular alcove next to the mountain. In the center of the alcove was a twenty-foot tall, monumental totem pole looming out of the mist: a postcard from the distant past.

Flush with excitement, Emma ran over to it. As she gazed upon the totem she realized it was made of stone. "I thought totem poles were made out of wood."

"Most are; usually cedar. The Museum of Anthropology dates regular wood totem poles back to the 1880's, but some anthropologists think this one may have been built when the First People crossed the Beringia Land Bridge."

"What are they for?" Emma asked, gliding her hand over the carved images.

"Normal totem poles depict a story, ancient legends, or clan lineages. The stone's pretty worn down but you can still make out the figures well enough."

Emma could. The totem pole depicted a man at the center being pulled from above and below by two different unnatural figures. The figure below was a beast with a broad smile and fangs protruding up from his lower lip. The demon-like creature was gripping the man's ankle and tugging him downwards. Meanwhile, the carving above was a winged creature reaching down to the man's outstretched hand, but his fingers were just out of reach.

Emma rubbed her arms, but it wasn't from the cold. When Horatio dropped his jacket over her shoulders, she asked, "What do you think the sculptors were trying to convey?"

Horatio pushed his glasses up on the bridge of his nose before answering. "What we do know is that for a thousand years early Alaska Natives called this canyon, Ti-Quan-nah-ha-nah, which is Tlingit for *Place where Heaven meets Hell.*"

Studying the creepy totem, where the good and evil gods battled for the soul between them, Emma thought the name was fairly accurate. She swung her pack to the ground to dig out her camera.

"But according to scholars the stone totem predates the Tlingits and is an early representation of Purgatory."

"I'm sorry. I didn't pay attention in Sunday school when I was a kid. What's Purgatory again?"

Horatio sighed before answering. "Well, it depends on whom you ask. The creation of Purgatory actually predates Catholicism and is actually credited largely to medieval Christians."

"Okay, college boy, but what's it mean?" Emma asked, circling the totem with her digital camera.

"Most people think of Purgatory as a place of post death suffering, torment, and atonement for sin, with eventual soul reconciliation."

"Sounds like hell," Emma said, peeking out from behind the other side of the totem.

"No, that would be *eternal* suffering. Purgatory is more … temporary. I like to think of it as a process of purification, an intermediate state between death and final judgment, if you will."

"So some people go to heaven and others to hell, but if you're on the fence you go to Purgatory so God can figure it out?"

"Something like that. I think to be fair to God, it's more like the fence riders are sent to Purgatory for them to figure it out.

Emma thought about it for a second, and then asked, "So, is Purgatory a bad place?"

"You mean is there pain and fire?"

Emma nodded.

Horatio tilted his head to the side, as he often did when he was trying to recall facts. Emma suspected he had a photographic memory the way he appeared to be reading his recollections out of the corner of his eyes. "In 1206, a peasant in England claimed St. Julian took him on a tour of the place. He said the Saint showed him torture chambers and challenging mazes. And St. Augustine described cleansing fires that were more painful than anything man could ever suffer in life."

"What about that guy, Dante?"

"Hmm-hmm. You're talking about the Italian poet, Dante Alighieri. In the fourteenth century he wrote how Purgatory had seven levels representing the seven deadly sins. Keep in mind, I'm abridging here, but the souls had to pass through the appropriate punishments as they climbed their way to the top of a vast mountain for salvation. If they passed all the tests they were cleansed of all sin and made ready for Heaven."

Emma bit down on her lower lip, and then asked, "So, what do you think?"

Horatio grinned and answered, "Well … I've always known growth to be painful."

Emma threw a snowball and hit him full in the face. Horatio just stood there blinking behind his askew glasses with disbelief. Waiting for her to stop laughing he pointed to the snow still on his face. "You see? You illustrate my point perfectly. Emma does not respond well to sarcasm and the way I learned that was quite painful."

"I'm sssoooo sorry," she said, but couldn't stop laughing. Emma moved over and helped Horatio wipe the snow from his face. "But seriously, what do you think?"

Horatio sat on a rock and started cleaning his glasses with his shirt. His smile faded away and his demeanor became more somber. "I think Purgatory is like a second chance. Basically I think it's God's way of saying, 'I haven't given up on you yet but you've only got one more chance to get it right before I boot your butt downstairs.' We all have choices to make so I guess it's important that we make the right ones."

Silence hung in the air until Emma nudged him with her shoulder, "What are you, my shrink?"

Horatio smiled knowingly. "I like to think of myself more as your spirit guide."

Emma giggled. Though, something about what he'd said made her uncomfortable. She seemed to recall a difficult decision she had made in her recent past. It had been something about her Uncle John, but for the life of her, the outcome eluded her.

Emma cocked an ear to the side. She heard a thundering sound in the distance. "What's that noise?"

Horatio listened for a second. "That? Oh, there's a waterfall at the end of the canyon."

Emma's eyes widened with excitement. "Can we see it?"

Horatio gazed towards the heavens for a moment before answering. "I don't know, it's still a ways up the canyon. Maybe we should head back. Besides, it'll be dark soon."

"Oh, c'mon, you big baby," she said, grabbing his arm and tugging him to his feet. "We've got plenty of daylight left. We can't come up all this way and not see a waterfall. Besides, what's the worst thing that could happen?"

"Emma, wait!" Horatio yelled. He snatched up their packs, and then ran after her.

Chapter 15

The Waterfall

CLEARING A BEND in the canyon a roaring sound exploded up ahead. Emma didn't even slow down. It had to be the waterfall.

It was beautiful. The water launched from a fifty-foot rock face above and cascaded down into an emerald green pool below. In the center of the small lake sat a half-submerged 50's pickup truck. The rusted out red Ford should have marred the scene, but somehow it only enhanced it.

Emma noticed other relics scattered about the grassy area surrounding the lake: An overturned train car, a crumbling shack, and various pieces of rusted mining equipment. At the very back of the canyon Emma noticed a broken train trestle. The old blackened wooden timber beams stood about thirty feet high. At one time the trestle most likely traversed over the canyon they now occupied.

The whole scene seemed familiar somehow, as though ebbing at the distant corners of her memory. A chill ran down her spine as it hit her. The high trestle was one of the paintings she had seen in her nightmares. But how was that possible? It had only been a dream, and she had never been here before.

How can you dream about something you haven't even seen?

"Geez, would you wait up already?"

Horatio ran up beside her. She decided not to tell Horatio about the relics that matched the paintings in her nightmares so vividly. She had told him so much already and didn't want to scare him away.

Horatio stood close enough to let the mist from the waterfall wash over him. As he closed his eyes she found herself gazing at his face. The guy could've been a movie star. She found herself wondering what would happen if she finally gave in to his innocent flirtations.

When Horatio finally opened his eyes and noticed her staring at him his smile dropped and his eyes grew wide. She told herself that if he had crossed over to her right then and took her in his arms, she'd let him.

Before she could find out what would happen, a horrific scream startled them both.

Emma turned her head up to where the broken railroad trestle connected with the mountain. "It came from up there on that ledge."

Horatio thought about it for a second. "Ophelia told me several geologists are camping up on the ridge."

A second horrifying scream reverberated off the canyon walls. Emma's eyes widened at the sound. Whoever it was, they were in excruciating pain. She pounded Horatio on his forearm, "Use your cell phone."

He shook his head. "No cell phones within fifty miles of HavenPort."

Of course Emma knew that. She had found it weird using landlines again. One thing was certain, whoever it was needed help. She spied a ladder that ran up the side of the train trestle near the ridge.

"Where are you going?" Horatio asked as she moved toward it.

"C'mon, someone's in trouble," she yelled back over her shoulder.

Emma arrived at the bottom of the ladder. A closer examination revealed the old timbered scaffolding had to have been built at least a hundred years ago. She wasn't crazy about climbing up a ladder that was well on its way to kindling but clearly there wasn't any other way.

"Emma, you can't go up there. I'm not sure that thing will even hold your weight."

Ignoring him, Emma climbed the first few rungs. They creaked loudly beneath her feet. She stopped her ascent. If the ladder was going to break she'd rather it happen right now while she was only a few feet off the ground, and not thirty feet up in the air. Admittedly, part of her did hope the ladder would break, that way she'd have an excuse for not going up there and finding out the cause of that horrific scream.

But of course the stupid ladder did hold, at least for now anyway, so, playing the part of the reluctant hero, she resumed her ascent.

Horatio shouted after her. "Emma, what are you going to do when you get up there? You don't even have a gun."

She stopped about twelve feet up, and glanced back down at him. "Don't you have one?" When he shook his head, she spat, "Well, why the hell not?"

"I've never needed one before. Climb down and we'll go get the sheriff."

Emma thought it over for a moment then said more to herself than Horatio, "I'll just take a quick look over the ledge and, if it's too dangerous, I'll climb back down." That said, she resumed her climb upward. The footing was treacherous. She almost slipped, and barely caught herself. Several spectators in the form of enormous ravens cawed overhead in laughter. Emma told them to shut up and kept climbing; the wood continued to creak under her weight as she went.

"I'm not sure this is a good idea," Horatio yelled up to her.

Emma was disappointed in him. He seemed to have no concern whatsoever for the screamer.

About twelve feet from the ledge she reached a small landing. Before assaulting the next ladder, she glanced back down over the railing. She was about twenty feet in the air and realized if the platform collapsed out from under her at this height, the fall would probably be fatal. As she moved across the landing the creaking floorboards beneath each step confirmed her worst fears. She considered turning around when she heard a weak voice cry out for help. "I'm coming!" Emma shouted with renewed vigor, and then attacked the next ladder a little less cautiously.

She climbed another ten feet when a man belly flopped onto the ledge above her. He was in his mid-thirties with a light colored scraggily beard and round spectacles. His face was bloody and even from this distance she could see part of his flesh was hanging off his jaw. Whatever had struck him was strong.

His wild eyes eventually found her. "Please, Ma'am," he sobbed, reaching down to her with the desperation of a drowning man, as though her merest touch might pluck him from danger. "Please, help me. I'm not ready to be judged."

Not ready to be judged ... what an odd thing to say.

Emma threw caution to the wind and began climbing faster. Within seconds her fingers were inches of his. There was a deep rumbling growl from somewhere beyond the man and before they could touch, he was violently pulled away, screaming as he vanished from sight.

"Breathe, just breathe," Emma told herself, and was about to finish her climb when the biggest bear Emma had ever seen in her life suddenly thrust his gargantuan head over the ledge. Its skull was massive. His right eye was milky gray, and a hideous scar was visible on his snout from where a bullet must have once grazed his face and eye. This had to be the harbinger of death, Barnabus. The sight of him nearly caused her to fall, and soil her pants. Only clenching muscles prevented both.

Barnabus released a thunderous roar.

She was frozen. The thought of the frightened geologist kept her from climbing down immediately. And after a few long seconds, she realized the bear couldn't reach her. The bear seemed to know this too and gave her a venomous stare with its one good eye. Staring into it, she could see it burned red and made Barnabus seem more like a beast from hell than anything from this world or its past.

Horatio yelled from below, "Holy crap! Emma, get back down here!"

The bear's mighty dome vanished with a WHOOSH and was gone. Still too frightened to move, she could hear him galloping off. As much as she wanted to retreat, she knew there were people up on the ridge that needed help. She wasn't going to be overly heroic to the point of getting herself killed but she also knew she had to try.

As she crept up the last few rungs, she listened intently for any sign of the bear. Hearing none, and summoning every ounce of courage in her body, she peered carefully up over the ledge.

The campsite was little more than a few tents surrounding a smoldering campfire. The single campfire still glowed, and smashed tents, and empty sleeping bags were strewn about like discarded trash. She couldn't see any sign of the bear or anyone else. *At least not from this vantage point.* Emma knew she had to get up on the ridge if she was going to be of any help to anyone.

Too late to turn back now.

Before going onward and upward, Emma focused on her breathing. She wouldn't do anyone any good if she hyperventilated and passed out on the ladder. One advantage she did have as a former ballet dancer was excellent breath control. But, as she took deep controlling breathes, she smelled something pungent and sickening.

Emma reached the top and pulled herself from the ladder, but before leaving it behind and taking another step, she waited. Still no sign of Barnabus. Maybe he was gone. The blood trail that marked where the poor geologist had been dragged away from the ledge, out of the campsite, and into the woods certainly indicated as much.

She decided to check the tents for survivors first. As she ventured toward the campsite, her eyes scanned the ground and searched for a weapon; a rock, a sharp stick, anything. Emma froze when she heard what sounded like a rock striking a coconut. Lifting her gaze from the ground, she squinted through the smoke of the smoldering fire and saw a man on the other side.

Not knowing what else to do, she called out to him. "Hello, are you all right?"

The man didn't answer. He was squatted down on his haunches and using a rock to bang on something lying on the ground. She was about to call out to him again but as she moved closer she realized the man wasn't wearing a stitch of clothes. He was completely naked. Worse still … he wasn't banging on a coconut. It was a human head.

On the last THOCK the naked man cracked the severed head open like an islander splitting open a coconut. He then took two fingers and rooted around inside the decapitated head as though searching for something inside. Not finding whatever he was looking for he sighed heavily, slumped his shoulders, and shook his head in disappointment. He tossed the human head away and then reached for another.

That's when Emma saw the pyramid of severed heads stacked up on the forest floor. The naked man lifted the bloodstained rock high over his head to strike, but then stopped, as though sensing her presence.

Emma's heart sank into her belly. She was rooted to the spot. As harrowing as the bear had been, the scene before her was even more horrific.

Oddly enough her first thought was, 'Why am I not throwing up? I should be throwing up.'

The naked man slowly lifted his gaze. His eyes found her. Emma could never tell anyone why, but somehow his visage scared her far more than the bear. He wasn't a big man, nor dangerous in appearance, but his eyes; they were downright malevolent, and when he saw her, he flashed her a sickening grin akin to a demented child who found a new insect to burn with his magnifying glass.

"Oh God," Emma cried out, and that's when the vomit finally flew from her mouth. She felt with absolute certainty that she would not survive this latest nightmare. Wiping her mouth on the back of her hand she managed feebly, "What are you doing?"

The naked man tilted his head to the side, studying her. "Searching for the truth. Why? What are you doing here?"

Knees buckling, she stammered, "Why did you kill all those people?"

He didn't answer. Instead, he rose with purpose, his intent clear. He was going to kill her. As he passed a tree stump, he grabbed a hatchet buried in its wood without even looking at it.

Emma needed no further urging. She bolted for the ladder.

Arriving to it, she fell on her belly, swung her legs around the way only a dancer could, and was on the ladder in a flash. She climbed down four rungs below the ledge when she felt pain in her scalp and at the nape of her neck. She reached up and felt a bony, but extremely strong hand holding her hair.

The naked, murderous bastard had snagged her. And now she was about to die.

A vision of the hatchet swinging down upon her exposed neck caused her to decide that she'd rather fall to her death than have her skull cracked open like a coconut. So she hooked her toes under the rung beneath her feet and pulled with all of her might. As she fell off the ladder she cried out as a handful of hair ripped from her scalp. Her only hope was that she'd take the murderous sicko with her.

Her flailing hands on the ladder rungs managed to slow some of the descent, but she slammed down onto the landing nearly a dozen feet down and came to rest onto her back.

Air knocked out of her pancaked lungs she spied the naked man laying down on the ledge. He was grinning down at her. It was an unnatural smile, almost ear to ear. Then in the same fashion as the bear, and equally as quick, his head vanished from the ledge.

A hand grasped her shoulder. She tried to scream but couldn't because of the wind vacant from her chest.

Horatio's face loomed over hers. "Oh geez," Horatio cried, concerned. He helped her sit up. "I told you that ladder wouldn't hold."

As breath began to return she stammered, "I saw him." Gulping air she asked, "Did you see him?"

"See who, the bear?"

Emma, in a voice tempered by fear, asked, "Weren't you watching?"

"I saw you climb over the ledge after that bear, so I climbed up after you. The next thing I know you nearly fell down right on top of me."

Emma took another deep breath, realizing that Horatio hadn't seen the horrific images she had.

Gulping air, "We gotta… we gotta go tell the sheriff."

"What about the geologists?"

Emma shivered uncontrollably, took another gulping breath. "They're dead. They are all dead."

Chapter 16

Hunting Barnabus

THE TWO KIDS SITTING outside his office were scared out of their minds.

After all they had been through, plus another two hour scary hike back waiting for another attack; who could blame them.

Hank yanked open the ammo drawer, snatched three cartons of shotgun shells, and shoved them into his vest. If they were going up against ole' Barnabus, he wanted as much firepower as they could carry. It was going to be dark in a couple of hours so he also grabbed an extra flashlight and clipped it to his vest. After what had happened to him in the Rakewell building, he wanted as much light as he could carry too.

The kid, Horatio, had done most of the talking. Hank was hopeful of finding survivors, but he'd read the unspoken truth in Emma's shattered expression. He had been in law enforcement long enough to know she wasn't telling him the whole story, but considering what she'd been through, he decided not to press her for now.

Jeb entered his office with two hunter types trailing behind him. They both wore camouflage pants, stained hunting vests, and heavily worn hiking boots. One was pushing fifty, the other about half that. Judging from their similar builds and facial structures Hank guessed them to be related.

"I knew this would happen. I been saying it for years," Jeb said, as he guided the hunters into his office. "That old bear ain't been right in the brain ever since people started fillin' him with lead. And now those poor geologists had to pay the price."

"Any luck on raising reinforcements?" Hank asked, still loading up his vest.

"Ophelia's put a call to the troopers but the nearest one is at least two hours away, and she said that's only if we're lucky."

Jeb must've seen Hank staring at the two men behind him for he added, "Oh, right. Now Hank, as much as I'd like to take a shot at old Barnabus myself this ole' body a mine isn't up for the trek, but I'm sending you with the two best trappers in HavenPort." He patted the older man on the shoulder. "This here's Yuri and his son Petor."

The older man sneezed loudly into his hand.

"Bless you," Hank said, dryly.

The Russian hunter nodded in thanks as a long oozer dangled from his nose. He wiped the snot on his hand and then offered to shake. "Nice to meet you, Sheriff McCarthy." His Russian accent was thicker than the mucus in his palm.

Hank shook the mucus-ridden hand without hesitation and forced himself not to grimace while doing it. He immediately disliked the two Russians, although he couldn't explain it; Hank never figured himself for a racist. When he glanced over at Petor, he caught the younger man staring appreciatively at the photo of his wife in a picture frame on his desk; staring a little too appreciatively.

"Petor, was it?"

The boy remained silent and merely nodded. Regardless, Hank returned the nod and forced a warm smile.

"There's a lot of bear traps in those woods." Jeb explained. He rolled his eyes to the two trappers. "There's not supposed to be any on the trails, but there are. These fellers will be able to help you steer clear of them seein' how they put most of them up there in the first place."

"I do not know what Jeb is talking about." The elder Russian replied disinterested. Clearly this was an ongoing thing between the two men. "He is crazy person or something."

Jeb snorted, and then continued. "You'll be able to reach the campsite by going in the back way; these boys know the way. The route's a lot longer than the trail, but this way you'll be able to ride in on four-wheelers and get up there a lot faster. Watch out for snow on the ground and the road will be icy in places, but you'll be able to carry out any survivors on the wheelers."

"I'd like to go with you, Sheriff."

It was Emma. The two kids had crept up in the open doorway and must have been eavesdropping. Before he could answer, Horatio, presumably her boyfriend, said to her, "Uh, Emm, maybe that's not such a good idea."

Emma shot him a look that clearly stated he was not her boyfriend and she could do what she wanted. Turning back to Hank she meekly asked, "Excuse me, Sheriff?"

When the two had first arrived, Emma had barely said a word. Turning his full attention towards her, he asked, "What's the matter, Emma?"

"I didn't say anything before…"

Here we go. Now we're getting to the nitty-gritty.

"…but I don't think it was a bear that killed those men."

Jeb scoffed. "What do you mean, girl. What else could have killed those geologists like that?"

"Emma, don't," Horatio interjected, but he was ignored.

"I saw a man."

Hank took a step closer towards her. "Did you see him well enough to get a description?"

"Uh, I think so, but I'm not very good with describing people." The young girl before him looked as though she might come apart at any moment. She was literally trembling. Whatever she'd seen hadn't been pretty. Hank knew he had to slow down or she might clam up completely. "Emma, you're safe now. You know that right? No bear or anyone else can hurt you. Just take your time and tell me what you saw."

Emma nodded solemnly. She took a deep breath that seemed to steady her.

As Hank fished for the small notebook he always kept in his shirt pocket, Jeb blurted out impatiently, "Nationality, height, weight, hair color; that sort of thing."

Emma shot back, "You mean aside from the fact that the guy was naked and trying to kill me with an axe?"

Hank jerked his head up. A chill ran down his spine. "Did you say he was naked?" He remembered full well the first day on the job when he had his own run-in with the naked man in the Rakewell building: the bloody severed head, the smiling jack-o-lantern grin, the ax dripping with blood.

But Jeb still wasn't convinced, "Horatio, did you see this naked guy?"

This time Emma answered for him. "Horatio was busy climbing up the ladder. I'm not crazy. I know what I saw." Her fists clenched at her sides.

Jeb waited for Horatio's answer. Horatio avoided Emma's gaze and sighed before answering. "No, Jeb. I only saw Barnabus when he stuck his head over the ledge."

Emma shot Horatio a look. She seemed a touch heartbroken at his betrayal; then that heartbreak turned to an expression of anger. Horatio finally noticed and added weakly, "But Emma was the only one who set foot on the ridge. Just because I didn't see him, doesn't mean he wasn't there."

Jeb appeared as shocked as he likely was, but Hank felt vindicated. Another eyewitness. It wasn't possible for both of them to be crazy. The jack-o'-lantern guy was real.

The older hunter, Yuri, glanced between them, "Well, if there was naked man up on ridge in these temperatures either bear ate him or damn fool would be frozen to death. Either way, we should go now."

Hank eyed the two untested hunters. They had Jeb's recommendation and their equipment appeared well used though serviceable, but for some reason, he just didn't trust them. If he thought his old "coffee-talk" pal and avid outdoorsman, Doc Clemens, was up for the journey, he would've preferred to take the doc with him instead. Deciding the two hunters would just have to do, he turned to Jeb and said, "Okay, have Ophy call in the doc and tell them both to meet at the trail head with the ambulance. Tell them to be ready for wounded." Turning to the hunters he asked, "You sure you boys are up for this?"

"Da, Sheriff. Back home we seen more than our share of bodies."

That didn't exactly give Hank the warm fuzzies.

Both men headed for the door. Emma filed in behind the two trappers as they made for the well-used four-wheelers parked outside by the curb.

Jeb blocked Emma's path, "Whoa, whoa, where do you think you're going little lady?"

Hank saw the expression on Emma's face; she liked being called little lady about as much as she liked Horatio not backing up her story. Staring at Jeb she said, "Sheriff, would you please tell your deputy to move his arm?"

For a moment, Hank actually considered Emma joining the rescue party. She was young and inexperienced, but she seemed fairly levelheaded, she seemed to be managing her shock well, and he certainly could use an extra pair of hands. If he didn't have the trappers to guide him, and a good location on the victims, he might've taken her. The reality was he didn't have enough manpower to search for survivors and protect her — if it came to that.

Finally he answered, "Thank you Emma, but you've done more than enough. We'll take it from here."

"I wasn't asking for permission, Sheriff," Emma fired back.

Horatio stepped forward, "Emma, let the sheriff do his job."

Emma shot Horatio a venomous glare. That boy was batting a thousand today. Emma was also probably wondering why Horatio wasn't volunteering to go too.

Hank took a less aggressive approach. "Emma, do you even have a four-wheeler?"

Before she could answer, the younger Russian Petor stuck his head back inside and offered a tad bit too enthusiastically, "Girl can ride with me, Sheriff."

Emma looked back at the sheriff with a smug expression and raised eyebrows.

Hank remembered the young man ogling his wife's picture and answered Emma, "Yeah ... I don't think so."

Emma spun around on her toes and headed after the trappers. She stopped only to give Horatio a dismissive glance.

Horatio wore a look of shame but clearly he had no intention of joining them, and then he too filed out the door.

Despite the extra weight, Hank grabbed one more box of ammunition and stuffed it inside his coat pocket. He slammed the drawer closed and moved into his outer office. *Perfect. He should have known these past few weeks were too good to be true. A multiple homicide. The only silver lining of this latest nightmare is at least now someone else had seen the naked man.*

From the reception area he heard Emma call his name and he was surprised to see everyone standing stock still, all staring intently through the front window.

When he switched his gaze from them to the street outside he saw a man strolling down the center of Main Street.

He was naked.

Chapter 17

The Naked Pedestrian

EMMA STARED OUT the front window of the sheriff's office. *Are you kidding me?*

She realized the old sheriff and the trappers had their backs turned. "Uh, Sheriff McCarthy?"

The other men in the room turned and froze as they caught a glimpse of the naked freak strolling down Main Street. *Is that blood?*

"I'm sorry Emma, the answer's still…" Hank began, walking out of his office. Sheriff McCarthy's eyes widened. A pistol appeared in his hand out of nowhere and before anyone else could move, he was sprinting outside. She watched along with everyone else as he drew a bead on the naked man and walked heel-toed towards him. "Stop right there!" she heard him shout in a voice that said he was not going to be messed with.

Once they recovered from the initial shock, everyone filed outside too. When Emma arrived on the sidewalk with everyone else, it was immediately apparent that the naked man's skin was indeed smeared with blood.

Heedless of the sheriff's commands, the naked man continued walking. Hank shouted one more time, "Stop, or I will shoot!" At this, the naked man stopped his forward momentum but he kept walking in place, swinging his arms like one of those speed walkers. His body pointed in the direction he was going for a few more steps, and then he very mechanically marched around in place to face them, still wearing that wide-eyed, pie-eating grin.

Emma shivered. *This guy is so freaky.* As much as she wanted to run away, her legs were rooted to the spot. At least she wasn't alone this time.

"Don't you move!" the sheriff yelled, startling her. If possible, the naked man's smile grew wider, but this time he slowed to a stop.

Stepping up beside the sheriff, Emma heard herself say, "That's the guy, Sheriff, that's the man I saw on the ridge." She suddenly recalled the sheriff's expression when she had first told him about the naked man. Thinking back on the memory there was something about her description that had really rattled him, and Hank sure didn't seem like the kind of guy who was easily rattled. She had seen him take down two burly drunks without breaking a sweat, or losing his temper.

Then the sheriff asked her something weird in a voice loud enough so only she could hear. "So you see him too?" He didn't wait for the answer and stepped forward.

Not crazy…

Emma turned to Horatio, her face flushing, "See, I told you he was real."

Horatio only raised his hands in supplication, his face betraying a sufficient amount of horror and shame.

As the sheriff approached the naked man, Jeb reached up to lower the two Russian hunters' rifles. "Damn it Yuri, lower those things, will ya? You want to hit the sheriff in the behind?"

Jeb then glanced at her, "You sure this is the same guy?"

Emma merely rolled her eyes. "I didn't take a photo, but yeah, I'm pretty sure he's the same guy," she answered dryly.

The sheriff and the naked man faced off in the center of the street about fifty feet apart reminding Emma of the old westerns her Paw liked so much when she was a kid.

Grinning like the madman that he clearly was, naked guy yelled, "Hi Sheriff! I'm still working on that poem for ya!"

"You just keep your hands where I can see them," Sheriff McCarthy ordered evenly.

To Emma's surprise, the naked man raised his hands up, palms facing outward, but as he did so, he began chanting rhythmically, like he was reciting a limerick.

"Boy, that Hank McCarthy sure is sore.

Since his family got dropped down that nasty gorge.
Wife drowned first on her own gore
Kids in the back seat, alive no more.
Better not cross him, or…"
The naked man paused here. He tilted his head to the side, face deep in thought. Emma watched his eyes and mouth smile widen at the same time. "You'll be done for." He bobbed his head in self-satisfaction. Then, as though he forgot he had an audience he gazed back toward them, his eyes dancing with challenge, and said in a terrible John Wayne impersonation, "How um-I-ah doin', Hank? About right?"

Emma had to hand it to the sheriff, he kept his cool. In a commanding voice he answered, "Put your hands on your head, and get down on your knees."

The naked man's face abruptly turned shocked, then quite serious, but Emma couldn't tell if he was faking it or not. "Sure Sheriff, sure," he said raising his hands higher in supplication. "Don't shoot. I know I done wrong. Puh-lease don't shoot."

Without glancing back at him the sheriff called back, "Jeb, you got him?"

Emma saw the old sheriff now had his gun out and was waddling up the street towards the naked man. To Hank he asked in a whisper, "So is this the guy you saw in the pool?"

"Yep." Hank answered evenly, and then slowly holstered his sidearm with his right hand while at the same time he removed his cuffs from his belt with his left. Then to the naked man he said, "Now don't you move."

The naked man shook his head, and stated with mock sadness, "I won't. I is sorry for whut I done."

Hank was a couple of feet away from reaching the naked man with his cuffs when the man sprang to his feet with impossible speed. A shot rang out and everyone ducked reflexively.

Hank spun around, his face angry with shock, and stared hard at Jeb. The old sheriff had panicked and fired off a round into the street only inches from Hank's boot.

Like a missed deer in a clearing, the naked man bolted out of the street and into a nearby alley.

The sheriff cursed and sprinted after him.

Still holding his smoking gun, all Jeb had to say was, "Damn that boy is fast."

Chapter 18

A Not-So-Merry Chase

QUICKLY LEAVING THE OTHERS behind, Hank chased his target into the alley with his revolver drawn.

He ran up to the approaching brick building and flung his back to the cornerstone for cover.

Gripping his pistol, he carefully peered around the alley, ready for attack. Seeing no immediate threat he pressed on, staying close to the wall to make himself less of a target. It was a long alley for the town of Havenport, far longer than any alley he remembered being. As he approached an intersection between his alley and a second he expected to see one of two things, the naked man with his jack-o'-lantern smile, or an empty alley with discarded trash dancing in the wind.

He negotiated the corner—

What he did not expect to see, what he never could have imagined seeing in a million years, was the monstrous shadow that towered over him.

As Hank straightened, he found himself staring at a pair of large eyes, one scorching red, the other a dead and milky white, twelve feet off the ground. The gaping mouth split open wide, revealing a maw of sharp, glistening teeth, and the demon's black, furry mass seemed to absorb any and all light.

Hank's mind went numb.

Nearly paralyzed with fear Hank had enough presence of mind to realize this was not the naked man, but Barnabus, the big ole' grumpy bear.

Barnabus studied him also. Jaws smacking, lips rippling back to reveal all his massive fangs; his growl sounding like a thundering lawnmower. Having left his radio back in his office, Hank had no way to radio for help. Not that help would have changed anything. He was trapped in the alley with a monster.

His breathing grew faster. The alley walls seemed to close in around him.

When Barnabus's growl surged into a roar, Hank's muscles loosened enough that he managed to duck back behind the corner.

The thing is huge! Far too mammoth for the modern day world. Hank wasn't even sure his service pistol would even slow the beast down.

Back to the wall, struggling to control his breathing, he knew he couldn't leave this monster roaming the back alleys. What if some kid wandered by? Any minute now one of the shopkeepers could come out the back door of their business. Summoning his courage he took some quick, calming breaths, or at least tried too, and flung himself back into the alley. He held the barrel of his gun up as steadily as he could muster; his finger taut on the trigger. He knew he was hopelessly outmatched, and prepared to go out firing every last bullet until he was dead.

But Barnabus was gone.

Hank stood his ground, his body shaking. *Where the hell did he go?*

He scanned the alley with his pistol. There wasn't any place for the oversized bear to hide or retreat without Hank seeing him.

Am I hallucinating? Where could he have possibly gone to?

Movement caught his eye at the opposite end of the impossibly long alley, far longer than any alley in HavenPort had any right to be. Hank could just make out the naked man at the opposite opening. Comedic under other circumstances, he was jogging in place again, like a runner ready to start the big race, and he was obviously waiting for Hank to catch up.

Hallucinating Barnabus or not, Hank had a murderer to catch. Hank checked the intersecting alley one more time, then resumed the chase.

As Hank closed in on the naked man still jogging in place, the naked man sneered to him, "I guess you must be the hero in this here tale. How's that saying go? There are young heroes and old soldiers but no old heroes?" He then added with glee, "Catch me if you can!" With that said, the naked man dashed across the street into Ophy's hotel. A young mother on the sidewalk screamed as she ushered her two small children out of harm's way, and a fisherman exiting the hotel's main entrance cursed as he was knocked aside into the bushes.

Hank raced up the stairs after him. Entering the lobby to a bunch of screaming little old ladies that Hank recognized from church. Ophy shouted to him from behind the clerk's desk, "Hank, he went that way, into the elevator!"

As the elevator doors closed, Hank barely glimpsed the naked man waving merrily back at him, still grinning and jogging in place like a madman.

Hank bolted for the stairs and called over his shoulder to Ophy as he ran, "Call Jeb, and let him know where we are."

Chapter 19

A Family Video

HANK EXITED THE STAIRWELL on the fourth floor.

He remembered that after the busy summer season Ophy had decided she was going to paint the exterior of the hotel and do a complete remodel of the top floor. Everything around him was in construction phase, the walls weren't painted, the windows were covered in plastic, and sawhorses stood like grazing cattle. The rooms were open but he couldn't see because plastic vapor barrier hung from the footers forming a labyrinth of construction.

Per his training, Hank had checked each floor on his way up, but he was starting to wonder if maybe he'd missed the naked man on one of the lower floors, and thought about double backing. That's when he heard the loud compression sound, PFTTT... PFTTT... PFTTT.

Four six-inch nails, long enough to pierce his skull, pounded through the drywall inches from his head.

He had the right floor.

A voice emerged from the labyrinth. "Peek-a-boo, Hank, do you see me?"

Hank growled back, "Come out with your hands where I can see them."

No answer.

Walking further into the naked man's inner sanctum, he heard a scream. And not just any scream. It belonged to his wife. Sarah...! A wave of nausea assaulted him. This was a fear far worse than when he'd encountered Barnabus back in the alley. He could hear his wife crying, and then talking, but Hank was too far away to make out any words.

He closed in on the sounds of his wife weeping, every muscle straining to run to her side but training keeping his eyes on every gap in the wall, his long strides measured and sure despite the panic surging in his chest. Gun leading the way, finger tight on the trigger, the sounds led him to an unfinished room. Paint cans were stacked on the floor, discarded tools lay everywhere, and on the back wall sat a television set and old VCR on boards haphazardly strewn across two sawhorses. Hank had entered the room as the video tape finished and went to static. The static roared.

The video reached the end of its reel and the VCR automatically began to rewind. Hank realized it wasn't his wife he had heard but whoever was on the tape. When the VHS got back to the beginning, it began to play again; an endless loop.

Hank took a quick glance around to see if he was being watched but saw only plastic vapor barrier gently blowing in a breeze from a nearby open window.

He turned back to the image shifting to life on the television. The image was of the back end of a yellow oversized Cadillac. The caddy was parked in an open field that seemed somehow familiar to Hank but he couldn't quite place it. The car he knew, the Cadillac's owner was a fisherman normally out to sea a few weeks at a time. The Caddy's trunk had been left open. It was the kind of trunk you could fit a dozen clowns inside. The image was so still Hank figured the camera had to be mounted on a tripod.

The light snow on the ground suggested the video was taken within the last few days, maybe even as recently as this morning.

Oh no...

The naked man's head, the top half anyway since he was too short to appear all the way in the lens, suddenly entered the frame.

"Hi Hank," he said, tapping the lens with a finger. "I made a movie for you." When he walked away from the camera his whole body became visible and Hank could see he was now wearing winter clothes and boots.

Hank's stomach began to twist; Sarah's scream still fresh in his mind. He fought the urge to dash to the nearest phone.

No, no, no...

The naked man disappeared from view for a few seconds and then Hank heard the scream. It was the same one he'd heard earlier. Sarah was violently thrown to the ground within view of the camera. Her wrists were bound in front of her, and her face and arms were severely bruised. Her make-up ran down her face in two rivers that mixed with the blood dripping from a jagged cut on her forehead.

In the film, the naked man, didn't say anything, he just dragged Sarah over to the back of the car. He screamed at her and made her look inside the trunk. But Sarah didn't want to see inside the trunk. So the naked man grabbed her roughly by the back of the head and forced her to gaze within.

Hank fought the bile rising in his throat.

Sarah started crying, words spilling from her mouth,, "No, my babies, no. What did you do?" she moaned, collapsing to her knees and laying her head on the bumper. The naked man grabbed both sides of her head firmly in the palms of his hands.

No... I'm begging you.

Tears clouded Hank's vision. After pawing his eyes, he outstretched his own hand toward the television as though he might be able to pluck her from danger.

With a quick twist of his wrists the naked man broke Sarah's neck.

Hank felt as though a horse kicked him in the heart. He wanted to look away, but he couldn't. The naked man scooped her lifeless body up and laid her into the trunk. He then ceremoniously closed the lid as if he were handling a casket. He then pranced over to the camera and spoke into it, "Now, for my piece-da-resistance!" He ran back over to the car, put it in neutral, and shoved the vehicle until it began to move on its own with the slope of a hill. That's when Hank realized where the car was parked. It was near Angel's Gorge, HavenPort's own version of Lover's Leap.

The naked man ran back to the camera. He removed it from the tripod and followed the car as it drove off the cliff.

"There it goes," he uttered with glee. And then his tone turning to mock seriousness, "Gosh, I hope they were wearing their seatbelts."

Hank felt his legs give out and he dropped to his knees, his hand numb from gripping the revolver so hard.

Before the video went to static, the naked man spun the camera back towards his face and he uttered into its lens, "Ta-Da!"

And that was it. His family was gone in an instant. His beautiful and incredible wife was no more. He would never hear his daughter's infectious laugh again nor would he get to see his little boy grow up into a man. Tears streamed down his face, burning his cheeks. As the sadness twisted into searing rage all Hank could think about was how he was going to kill that grinning bastard. Wrench his fingers back, one by one, until they broke, peel his scalp from his skull and watch him bleed every ounce of blood he had.

And that's when the metal pipe hit him on the head from behind.

Chapter 20

The Fall

EARS RINGING, EYES SEEING only stars, Hank crashed to the floor.

He lay there stunned for a moment, struggling to cling to consciousness. Only pure rage allowed him to rise to all fours. His revolver had gone flying, he didn't see it anywhere, but right now, he didn't care. He didn't care whether he lived or died, just as long as he took that insane, murderous bastard with him.

The naked man, now wearing construction overalls, work boots, and blood-stained gloves, danced around him with the metal pipe in his hand.

"Oh, Hank. You disappoint. I thought you'd be more of a..." he struck Hank in the torso as he was trying to rise to his feet, "...challenge," he finished.

Hank tried to roll away from the incoming strike but the pipe connected with his rib cage.

The naked man, grinning that insane grin of his, twirled his pipe like a cheerleader's baton and circled around him, marching to a nonexistent tune.

"C'mon. Get up! You're missing all the fun. Can't you hear the music?"

Hank coughed and spat blood. "I'll kill you, you son-of-a-bitch!" he growled. Reaching deep, he staggered to his feet. His ribs felt broken. He still had nary a clue where his gun had vanished too.

Blinking past his clouding vision Hank saw his attacker swing on him again. He managed to throw up his left arm and took the brunt of the blow on his shoulder and forearm instead of in the head. A second attack sent him crashing through an unfinished wall.

The naked man had to circle around the wall to enter into the adjoining room giving Hank a precious few seconds to recover.

It was all he needed. When the naked man entered the room, babbling more nonsense, Hank had managed to struggle to his feet. He tackled the smaller man and carried them both through a second unfinished wall. Landing in the third room Hank was the first to regain his feet. As the naked man tried to rise, Hank drove his fist into the man's jaw again, and again, and again. He grabbed the man by his thin upper arms and threw him into a stack of paint cans, then dragged him up by the hair to ram him into the bare studs of a wall under construction. The man's face went through the two-by-four, the wood cracking. The man slumped to the ground, blood and shards of teeth flying from his mouth. They lay like that, his face a bloody pulp, barely recognizable, his breathing sharp and ragged gasps through broken teeth.

Hank could barely stand. He stumbled away and turned to rest with his hands on his knees, waiting a moment for his vision to clear. His thoughts were coming back to him now. He needed to handcuff this guy and get him out of here. He needed to find... *God...* He needed to find that Cadillac.

He didn't see the naked man rising to his feet behind him, but he felt a prickle at the nape of his neck. He glanced back just in time to see the naked man explode with uncanny speed. He barreled into Hank, just like that day at the pool, only this time they both went flying through the fourth story window.

Hank twisted, hands flailing for purchase on the passing window frame. His back slammed into the unfinished balcony beyond, the naked man falling past him over the side where there was no railing. Air knocked out of him, Hank struggled to roll onto his hands and knees. He looked over the side of the balcony and almost jerked back when he found the naked man hanging by one hand from the lip.

"Hi Hank," he said through swollen lips and missing teeth. With a tinge of sadness, he added, "I guess you're pretty mad, huh?"

With every fiber of his being Hank wanted to kill him, or at least let the murdering bastard fall. No one would know, and no one could blame him. But Hank knew in his heart that's not what Sarah would've wanted. She was always the kind one. And he didn't have her anymore, only her memory.

That was when Hank knew, he'd do it for her. This one last act of kindness.

No one was more surprised than Hank when he grabbed his family's murderer by the arm and reached for the man's other hand.

"Give me your hand. I'll pull you up."

"Awww... you're such a good guy, Hank," the naked man jeered. "But you know ... here, death isn't the end of the line. I mean you know that, right? We're just pawns dancing around in their little fish bowl. Since you're such a swell guy. Let me show you." The naked man swung his other hand up to fist in the shoulder of Hank's shirt, and then he twisted his lower body like a gymnast on hanging rings, planted a bare foot on the underside of the balcony, and pushed off. There was no doubt that Hank outweighed the naked man, but somehow the force of his coiled launch pulled Hank over the edge with him.

As he and the naked man fell to their deaths, Hank fought to stay conscious. In the end, whether he wanted to or not, his mind decided to check out, refusing to witness the fatal sudden stop. It was as though he were staring at the screen of an old television set and somebody pulled the plug. The image just shrank down to a little dot of white energy and then even that was gone.

Chapter 21

Visitation

OUTSIDE THE LAND'S END Bed and Breakfast Hotel, Dr. Paula Burnett stood on the icy sidewalk and noted on her clipboard that Emma's heart rate and blood pressure were once again within acceptable norms as she roused from sleep to start her morning routine. Contrary to the brisk weather, Paula still wore a stark-white lab coat, high heels and her hair tied up neatly into a tight bun.

On the sidewalk, a tall, thin shadow appeared and loomed up over her own. Paula spun around and saw that it was only her colleague, Stanley. He was about six inches taller than her and today he wore a ridiculous suit with white gloves, a thin mustache, and a silver bow tie. He also carried an equally ludicrous black cane with a white tip.

"You can choose any form you like and yet you choose that one," he asked derisively. He must have noticed her twitch of disapproval.

"Unlike you, I choose to blend in," she answered dryly.

"Ah, yes, I see… And you blend right in with your glaring white lab coat and clipboard. How many people do you see walking around like that in this dreadful weather?" Stanley breathed in deeply through his pointed nose, "Where's your sense of style? Where's your … imagination."

As much as she hated to admit it, Stanley did have a point. She wasn't exactly dressing in warm functional layers like the locals did. The truth was she found this form the most comforting and writing things down on a clipboard always gave her a sense of organization, even if it was a bit silly given the circumstances. Besides, other than Sheriff Hank McCarthy, who always seemed to have his head on a swivel, most of the residents were so self-absorbed that they were rarely aware of her presence. Usually they went about their business from point A to point B almost as if they had blinders on. Still, she hated to concede to someone as patronizing as Stanley. "Well, you look ridiculous," she snapped back. "And where the hell have you been anyway?"

She must have hurt his feelings because he was pouting now. "May I remind you there are over two dozen candidates...," he said, holding up two fingers on either side of the word candidates, "...in our fair little town of HavenPort." His tone became a more impertinent one. "Your little junkie ballerina isn't the only one. Besides it wouldn't do for you to know everything I'm up to or it wouldn't be a fair test for the candidates, now would it?"

Unfortunately Stanley was right about that too, or at least their superior's would agree with him. Her job was to observe the candidates as they went about their days, taking care to note down all their choices good or bad. Stanley's sole job here was to provide the candidates with the temptation to make the wrong ones. Without him, there was no proof in the pudding, as it were.

"Sorry, it's just that ever since something scared the life out of poor Emma on her first day," she growled, collected herself, and began again. "If I hadn't intervened in time, we would have had another dead candidate on our hands. I still haven't figured out what frightened her so bad in the first place. This project can't afford to have a high mortality rate let alone another loose cannon. Either way it's not going to happen to one of my candidates ever again."

Stanley's tone softened ever so slightly. "Paula. You had nothing to do with the death of that raging psychopath, Simon Privet. Although even I admit, his continued existence in this place is a tad bit ... unnerving. That kind of thing was definitely not part of the design."

Maybe I have Stanley all wrong. Maybe under that snobbish exterior he's really not such a bad guy.

"Curious though," he said, "Seeing as Emma and Hank are your primary responsibilities, weren't *you* watching her on her first day?"

Nope. He's an elitist jerk.

Paula could have told a lie and said she was watching someone else. Unless multiple candidates were in the same place at the same time, even they could only watch one at a time, and even that wasn't 24/7. But she opted to tell the truth. "It was weird, one minute she was in her hotel room and the next, she was gone."

"What do you mean, gone?" Stanley asked, seemingly genuinely concerned, but she couldn't be certain.

"Like vanished. I couldn't find her anywhere."

Stanley scoffed. "That's impossible. You obviously weren't looking hard enough. Did you inform management about this?"

Paula hesitated before answering. She had heard of other candidates vanishing under the radar several times before but she'd never witnessed it firsthand. She was pretty sure this kind of lack of attention was what got her predecessor removed from the project, but then, maybe it hadn't been his fault. "No. Not yet. I wanted to make sure Emma was okay first."

"And ... has your precious little candidate recovered now?"

Did she detect a moment of concern in his voice? Was that even possible? She decided not to set herself up again for disappointment and sighed before answering, "Yes, her regular nightmares seem to be fading and her interactions with the other candidates seems to suggest she's recovered, however we won't know what kind of long term psychological damage has been done until we've completed a full workup."

"Maybe you should turn her over to me. You seem a little to ... attached."

Stanley's smug face caused the anger to swell in her, "You just remember that you've been warned once already. There shouldn't be any more shenanigans like you pulled with Wanda."

Stanley feigned shock, his mouth forming a giant O. "Paula, don't tell me you believe those nasty rumors too. I thought you were above that sort of thing."

"I'm serious, Stanley. If I find out you had anything to do

with that poor woman's death, I'll find a way to make them send you packing."

Stanley's eyes narrowed as he peered down at her. "First of all, I have no idea what you're talking about. Second, as you very well know, I don't answer to you. Third, I am not required to warn you of any tests and I hadn't planned on testing your precious pet project anytime soon in any case." Then he grinned, "Besides, who do you think they could find to replace me, hmmm?"

As much as she hated to admit it, Stanley was right again, as he often was. Changing the subject she asked, "Where's our third? I thought we were all meeting this morning to compare notes?"

Stanley's nostrils flared, "Absent as usual." Making certain the third wasn't indeed present, he added, "I swear, Clemens spends more time in Havenport than even I do."

Trying not to take sides, Paula said, "Maybe Hank chose this morning to wake up and be lucid. Clemens was expecting it might be soon."

"He might have had the decency to reschedule," Stanley muttered.

"Where do you have to be that's so much more important?" He was such an oddball.

"This place doesn't run itself you know. A lot of maintenance goes in to keeping everything just as it should be. What about you? Aren't you on break after this?"

She nodded, "Horatio's taking over for me at the diner."

"Well, enjoy your free time." He smiled and turned to go.

"Stanley … do me a favor. Be careful."

"Awwww … aren't you sweet. And just when I thought we weren't getting along. Fear not Milady, I hold all the cards. I practically built this place. To these people … I am God." That said, Stanley stepped off the curb twirling his ridiculous cane.

Watching him go Paula muttered to herself, "If that's true, then heaven help us all."

Chapter 22

Stanley and the Scarecrow Man

EMMA WAS LATE for work.

For the past week she'd ridden her bicycle from Ophy's hotel to the diner. This morning she had picked up another early shift, figuring she could always use the extra money, but she'd almost forgotten about it until she'd glanced at the time while she was eating breakfast.

As she pedaled hard towards work, her mind skipped back over the past week. It had certainly been a crazy couple of days. First those geologists up on the ridge, and then Sheriff McCarthy's poor wife and kids; it was all just so awful. The media circus had come and gone, and things were finally getting back to normal.

The only really good news was that Sheriff McCarthy was officially on the mend by both Ophy's and Dr. Clemens' admission. She thought about bringing him a pie from the diner after work. Pumpkin was his favorite. In the end she just couldn't summon up enough courage to look someone in the eye who had experienced so much loss. Ever since the incident with the naked man, Emma made it a point to take a route that steered far from the alleyways. She preferred to stay on open streets and was careful not to hit the ice patches on the pavement. The only place on her route that she had to go that wasn't bustling with activity was the short pedestrian tunnel that passed beneath the railroad tracks.

Even though the tunnel was not very long it was still kinda spooky. No matter how tired she was before or after work she would always just power through its shadows until she emerged victorious on the other side.

But today, as she neared the tunnel's entrance a sense of foreboding washed over her. The tunnel seemed more dangerous in the early morning light than it did after her lunch shift. She was about to come to a halt, but she knew if she did that, she'd have a hard time going again.

Just zip on through it, and you'll be at the diner in no time. If you double-back now you'll practically have to peddle halfway across town to get to work.

Besides, she had nothing to worry about, they caught the psychopath responsible for all those murders and as of this morning the guy wasn't even supposed to be in town anymore, not since the State Troopers hauled his butt away.

Emma had learned from Ophy that the naked man's real name was actually Simon Privet.

What an odd name.

—— o ——

At the far end of the tunnel and out of Emma's view, a thin shadow stretched along the tunnel wall.

Scarecrow Man moved into position.

He had been studying her bicycle route for some time and he knew this would be the best place to grab her ... play with her, have fun with her. She was going to be here any minute, and he knew he had to be ready to pounce.

An access ladder midway through the tunnel was the perfect little ambush spot. When Emma rode by on her bike, he was going to jump out and snatch her, and never let her go, not until he was done with her completely this time.

As the scarecrow man waited in his hiding spot, excitement building about the upcoming abduction, the predator didn't realize he had become prey until it was too late.

His first clue was the metal blade growing out of his chest making him look like a macabre version of a unicorn.

It took him another moment to realize someone had walked up behind him and shoved a machete through his back, pushing the three-foot blade out his chest. The scarecrow man didn't know who his attacker was until the man rested his pointy chin delicately on his right shoulder.

"Hi," he said gleefully, smiling an impish grin that spread from ear-to-ear.

Simon Privet, a.k.a. the Naked Man.

The scarecrow man couldn't say anything; he was too stunned to speak.

Wearing a bloodstained Trooper uniform, Simon kept a firm grasp on the handle of the machete. He then reached up with his free hand and grasped the scarecrow man's hat and mask. He yanked it from the scarecrow man's head to expose his true identity.

"Please. Let me go," Stanley Baker managed feebly, then spouted blood from his lips.

"Shhhh…" Simon said soothingly into Stanley's ear. He pulled the incapacitated scarecrow man back into the shadows so Emma wouldn't see either of them as she pedaled by with her head tucked down for speed. Once she was clear of their hiding spot, Simon maneuvered them both back into the light and watched her go with a smile.

"Awww … isn't she just the cutest little thing," Simon said maliciously.

"Simon. How are you even doing this?" Stanley asked, choking. "How could you possibly even exist? I saw you die myself." He then coughed up even more blood.

Angry at the interruption, Simon whispered vehemently into Stanley's ear, "You command this place like it's yours. But it's mine now. Before I kill you, you're going to tell me all of your secrets … and I do mean all of them."

Stanley nodded his head, his eyes wide, "And then you'll let me go?"

Simon considered this for a moment before answering. "No. I'm definitely going to kill you."

Chapter 23

Wake Up Hank

HANK AWOKE IN DARKNESS, certain he was dead.

Suddenly a pinprick of light forced the blackness away. Hank saw a form behind the glowing white light.

God?

"You had quite a fall, Sheriff," said good ole' Doc Clemens, lightly holding open his eyelids, flashing his penlight from eyeball to eyeball. "Next time you decide to jump off Ophy's hotel you might want to consider using a parachute." Clicking off his penlight he then added to himself in a clinical voice, "Pupils look normal, that's good."

Hank lay flat on his back, and not in his bed. "What happened?" he managed, his voice hoarse.

Worry in his eyes, Doc stood bedside, watching Hank. "You fell out of a fourth story window, Hank, that's what happened. The painter's scaffolding below cushioned your fall," he said, his green eyes crinkling beneath his glasses. "Given the tragic circumstances, you might not feel like it, but you're pretty darn lucky to be alive."

"Luck would've been not falling in the first place," Hank grumbled, blinking away the sting of the doc's penlight. "Is my family here?"

Dr. Clemens went silent for a moment before answering. "You don't remember?" he asked in a soothing voice.

Then Hank did remember. It all came flooding back to him now. His worst nightmares were confirmed when the doc spoke again. "Hank, your wife and two children were murdered by that psychopath that killed those geologists up on the ridge." The doc squeezed his shoulder gently, "You have my deepest sympathies."

Hank felt as though his heart were no longer in his chest; only a hallowed out shell of a man was left behind in the HavenPort clinic.

His eyes drifted to the room around him. He was tightly tucked into a hospital bed, in a modest but clean facility. He noted it was dark outside the windows with only a slow glimmer of light rising over the mountains. Early morning.

Rubbing his face, and fighting the urge to scream in anguish, he asked, "How long was I out?"

Doc hesitated just a moment, then answered, "You were in and out of it for about three days, Hank. This isn't the first time you regained consciousness. We talked this through two times before, but I must say this go around you seem more lucid."

Hank's eyes teared up again. He wiped them away to clear them, and then sat up in bed. The room spun as if he were on a carnival ride. He hung on to consciousness until the nausea passed. He was wearing a hospital gown and he felt the catheter still attached.

"Hank, I'd like you to stay here for a few more days," the doctor said.

Hank's voice quavered but he fought to control it. "I'm okay," he said, jaw firm. Desperate to change the subject he asked, "Doc, what about the suspect who fell with me? Did he die in the fall?"

Doc Clemens thought this over for a second before answering. Hank braced himself for what he was certain would be an explanation of how there never was a naked man. How he had imagined the entire thing. Believing he had gone plumb loco was pretty tempting right now. Anything to explain away the nightmare he was now living.

Maybe this is all some stupid dream.

But the doc surprised him when he said, "Considering the fall you two took, he came out even luckier than you. Not a scratch on him. Not sure how he did that one though. Near as I can figure he must have landed on top of you and you cushioned his fall."

Hank felt his eyes widen, taking a breath to control his inner turmoil he asked, "Where is he now?"

"Jeb turned him over to the State Troopers a couple of hours ago. Jeb had to sit with him for three days before the Troopers finally got here. Ophy kept him fed, and I examined him personally. An odd duck that one." The doc shivered slightly from the memory.

Hank threw his legs over the side of the bed and his world tilted a little crazily. He stood still and waited for the dizziness to pass. "Do you know if Jeb ran a background check on him?"

Doc seemed to remember something and pulled a notebook from his pocket. "Jeb passed this along because he knew you would ask. He said to tell you that he sent the guy's fingerprints over to Anchorage FBI and they got a hit. His name is Simon Privet."

This surprised Hank; he honestly didn't expect to get any hits.

Simon Privet. The name of the man who murdered my family, is Simon Privet. He replayed events over and over in his mind. He suspected he would for a very long time. He heard himself ask on sheer autopilot, "Any priors?"

"It says in here they got this guy going into the Army when he was 18 years old, but that was it. No Driver's license, no DD 214." Doc glanced up from the notebook, "I guess that means they don't even know when, or even whether or not, he got out of the army."

"Like he doesn't exist."

Doc nodded. "Yeah, like that."

Hank listened from the edge of the bed. He felt as if he were teetering on a high ledge. What was the point anyway? The video cycled again in his mind, his whole world was collapsing. *Why go on?*

"You really ought to stay in bed."

Against his nature, Hank opted to follow doctor's orders and laid back down on the bed, or at least what was left of him did anyway.

"Dr. Clemens?" came a young female voice from the doorway.

Hank lifted his gaze and saw a young woman enter the room dressed in tight fitting scrubs. The girl had not fully grown into her body and couldn't have been more than nineteen years old. The doc saw Hank staring and, with a slight twinkle in his eyes, mouthed the word, "Intern." Then turning towards her he said in a professional tone, "Yes, Janice, what is it?"

"I'm sorry to bother you but there's an urgent call for the sheriff."

"Well, tell whomever it is that I have not released Sheriff McCarthy from the hospital so they'll just have to…"

"But Doctor, it's Ophy. She's at the diner. She says someone's shooting up the place."

"Who's the shooter?" Hank asked. But in his heart he knew the answer. It had to be the naked man. He'd killed poor Jeb and escaped. Now he was back out on the streets on a murderous rampage. He was sure of it. That was why the intern's answer shocked him.

Her face held a mix of terror and confusion when she answered, "It's Jeb."

Chapter 24

Jeb's Diner

HANK HAD WANTED his friend, and morning coffee-talk buddy, to stay in the car but the doc wouldn't have it.

"I don't want you getting hurt, Doc."

"And if there are wounded, you'll need me to patch them up."

He had a point. "But not before I've got the situation under control."

"Then I'll wait outside the door."

Hank sighed and checked the rounds in his revolver, "Fine." He cycled the cylinder and then slid it home. "Let's go."

As they exited his patrol vehicle, Hank reiterated in his cop voice, "Now Doc, no matter what happens in there, you don't come inside until I give you the all clear. Do you understand?"

As they moved in unison towards the side entrance of the Last Frontier Diner, they heard several shots fired, followed by screams.

Damn.

Hank knew he was the only law enforcement in HavenPort. There was no other police in the small town other than Jeb. And the fact that the aggressor was the only other police officer on the force made the situation all the more dire.

He drew his firearm, made doubly sure that the doc wouldn't follow, and snuck carefully inside.

As soon as Hank slipped through the entrance he could see Jeb holding a shotgun in front of the double doors to the kitchen. It was the shotgun from the gun locker back at the station; a Remington 870, 12-gauge that could hold six rounds, plus one in the chamber. The old sheriff swayed in his stance and appeared even more disheveled than usual, even for him.

Bob the fry cook lay dead in the kitchen doorway. His body propping open the doors and parts of his mutilated corpse painting them red. Three other blood-soaked bodies were lying askew in a corner booth. Hank recognized them as regulars who frequented the diner on most mornings.

At the far end of the diner, Emma and the other waitress, Odessa, were crouched next to an overturned table, covering their ears. Hank could see both women's make-up running down their tear-soaked faces. Odessa was losing her bright pink wig of the day, it lay askew atop her head but she made no attempt to correct it.

Hank's quick assessment ended with the realization that Ophy was cornered in the kitchen, Jeb's gun already leveled against her where she stood in frozen horror beside the phone. From the corner of his eye Jeb must've seen Hank creep in and without averting his gaze from Ophy he said in a loud determined voice, "Hank, if you don't drop that pistol of yours I'm going to blow Ophy's head clean off."

Before Jeb could pull the trigger, Hank said, "Jeb, what are you doing? I need you to drop the shotgun."

"I mean it, Hank!" Jeb roared, his finger tightened on the trigger.

Even if he did have a bead on Jeb, Hank knew he'd never get off a shot in time to save Ophy. "Okay, Jeb, okay. You win. I'm putting my gun on the counter."

Hank gently laid his weapon down, but as he did so, he took a few more steps towards Jeb. If he could close enough distance between them he might have a chance at disarming the old sheriff. To distract Jeb further he asked, "What's going on, Jeb?"

"Hold on a second, Hank, just hold on." Jeb began, slurring his words. "I'm not doing this just for myself ya know, or even for you, but for the safety of the whole damn town."

Through trembling lips Ophy faltered, "Hank, when I was bringing the prisoner some food I saw him whisper something into Jeb's ear through the bars. I don't know what it was but Jeb hasn't been right in the head ever since."

Hank's mind was spinning; he knew he had to keep Jeb talking. As long as he was talking, he wasn't shooting. Keeping his palms open and in front of him, Hank risked a few steps closer. "Jeb, what did Simon say to you?"

"Hank!" Jeb roared and leveled him with a warning glare, "You take one more step and I swear I will blow her head clean off!"

"All right, Jeb, all right. I'm staying right here. What did Simon say to you?"

Jeb sighed heavily, in a manner that suggested he knew he wouldn't be believed. He answered anyway, "He told me that none of this is real. It's not real. And I'm just trying to sort out the real ones, like you and me, from the fake ones, like Bob on the floor over there."

Hank's gaze flashed to the bloody mess that was Bob the fry cook and back to Jeb. "I don't know, Jeb. Bob's corpse looks pretty real to me."

"Don't you think I don't know that?" Jeb yelled. Then in a softer tone and eyeing Hank with a strange look of pity he added, "That's what they want you to think. Don't you see?"

Hank could only shake his head.

Is insanity infectious? If so, it got to Jeb too. If he ever got out of this, Hank promised himself that he would test the water supply, the lead in the paint, anything that might make the townsfolk go nuts.

Risking a quick glance at him and seeing Hank's disappointment, Jeb explained further, "Simon helped me remember, Hank. I remember everything now. He can help you remember too."

"I'd like that, Jeb. I really wish someone would explain to me what the hell is going on around here but look at Ophy, you're scaring her. Put down the gun and we'll talk about it all you want."

"You still don't get it, do you, son. All of this, it ain't real."

"Jeb, what are you talking about?"

"Hold on, and I'll show ya," Before Hank could act, or think of anything to say, Jeb focused his aim on Ophy's face once more. "Ophy, how long have you lived here?"

"My whole life Jeb, you know that," she answered, her body trembling.

A grief-stricken expression came over Jeb's face. For a moment he sagged as though his strings had been cut.

Hank saw the gun go limp in his hands. He took another step towards him, but before he could get any closer Jeb grimaced and said firmly, "Sorry, Ophy, wrong answer." Jeb raised the Remington 870 and ... BOOM!

The projectile was a slug capable of punching a hole through a semi's engine block. At such close range it had nearly vaporized Ophy's head into a pink mist.

Emma screamed.

Hank surged forward, but drew up short when Jeb switched his aim towards him and racked another round. "You see, that's how you know the real ones. Don't chya git it?"

"I don't understand, Jeb!" Hank said, his hands out in front of him, heart thudding in his chest. "You're killing people. God, Look what you did to poor Ophy."

Jeb didn't seem to hear him. Instead, he moved over to the only other two people still alive in the room. "You!" he shouted to Emma, crouching by the overturned table. "How long have you lived here?"

"What?" Emma stammered.

Hank tried to take another step, but Jeb sighted down his shotgun at him, and he froze.

Jeb sighed with deliberate frustration. "How-long-have-you-lived-here?"

She stared at him blankly. "I-I dunno, a couple of months, maybe."

Jeb took a step closer to her. Then put the barrel right up to her head. Hank contemplated just how fast he could recover his weapon on the counter, aim and fire on his best day. Jeb must've read his mind for he said, without looking at him, "Hank, you reach for that pistol back there and I'll kill her for sure. Trust me. This is all for your own good."

"Wait a minute, Jeb. Just try and help me understand. How do we tell 'them' from the real people?"

Jeb sighed. "I already told you, Hank. Real people aint never from here. Long time maybe, but never *from* here."

Thinking fast Hank said, "Okay, how do I explain to someone that real people aren't real?"

Jeb ignored the question and poked Emma in the head with the barrel of the shotgun. "And Emma, take your time here. It's very important you answer the next question very carefully. Are you ready?"

Emma could only nod her head and whimper.

"Geez, Jeb. You're scaring her."

"Shut up, Hank!" Jeb roared. "This is for the good of everyone in town, including hers. I'm trying to save you people."

"How? By killing everyone?"

Jeb finally lifted his eyes from Emma.

That's good, keep his focus off the girl.

"Gosh Hank, is that what you think? You think I'm a murderer?"

Hank raised his eyebrows and held out his hands at the carnage.

Jeb switched back to Emma, his voice becoming more firm. "Okay, Emma. One question and then we're done. How did you get to HavenPort?"

Emma's voice trembled. "Please... please don't kill me."

Emma's plea resonated with Hank as though from some long forgotten nightmare. But the voice in the memory had been a man's voice, not some young girl's, of that he was certain.

"I'm not going to kill you, Emma, not if you answer the damn question. How did you get here?"

"I... I came in on the ferry."

"You see, that's all I wanted to know."

Jeb removed the barrel of the shotgun from Emma's temple, and pressed it against Odessa's. "What about you?"

Odessa didn't glance up. She just kept crying into her forearms.

"Hey, you," Jeb said again, this time Hank detected a slight slur in his speech. "Ugly waitress, how long you been in town?"

At the name calling Odessa picked her head up and spat, "Couple a months, same as Cinder-Soot over here!"

Another few feet and I think I can take him.

Hank swore he would die before he let Jeb kill another person.

"Pretty boy, how about you, how long you lived here?"

Hank was surprised to learn that the boyfriend, Horatio, was cowering behind the overturned table. The kid had been making himself so small, Hank hadn't even see him. *What he should have been doing is shielding Emma's body with his own.*

"Look I can explain everything," Horatio said, rising his hands in supplication.

"How long?" Jeb screamed at him.

"My family grew up here," he answered solemnly.

"Your family grew up here," Jeb repeated mockingly.

Hank could see in Jeb's eyes what he'd seen only moments before he had shot Ophy.

Emma must have seen it too for she quickly offered, "No, that's not true, he came in on the ferry with me."

"Well, which is it?" Jeb asked, his body swaying in place. Hank realized Jeb was drunker than he thought, but not drunk enough to effect his aim.

At that moment, the bell above the front door rang.

Damnit Doc, I told you to wait outside... It wasn't Doc, or at least, he wasn't alone.

Simon Privet entered the diner. He was wearing a blood stained Trooper uniform two sizes too big for him and he was dragging the doc roughly along behind him. The doc's left eye was swollen shut and Simon kept a pistol firmly to his head.

Simon was wearing that same silly grin he always wore, and after gazing around the room at everyone, he finally settled on Hank.

"Hi Hank, remember me?"

Chapter 25

Simon Says

EMMA WASN'T SURE HOW much more she could take.

On her first day of arrival to Havenport she had horrific nightmares about the scarecrow man and salmon sharks in the basement of Ophy's hotel. Then just three days ago she had nearly gotten eaten by a monstrous bear and nearly hacked to pieces by an equally real psychopath. And now today, Jeb had come close to blowing her brains out along with murdering her closest friends.

"Hi Emma, I brought you a present."

The man known as Simon pulled a rolled up brown piece of fabric from his pocket. He unfurled it and plopped it on his head. Emma's blood froze. She recognized the scarecrow man's hat immediately.

"Ta-Da!" Simon said aloud. He removed the hat from his head and with a sense of showmanship flung it spinning through the air where it landed at her feet.

How could he have something that was only in my dream? Am I dreaming now?

"You're the scarecrow man?" Emma asked, both frightened and angry at the same time.

"No my dear, not me," he said, eyeing her with a strange look of sadness, "but rest assured, *He* won't be bothering you anymore."

Horatio took a step towards him. "Simon, listen to me. You don't have to do this."

What shocked Emma most was Horatio didn't sound like a kid anymore. It was as though he had been playing a part in a community theater show but now he was dropping the facade because he was tired of acting. He spoke to Simon the way a schoolteacher might speak to a toddler with a loaded gun: Authoritative, but frightened.

Simon rolled his head towards the young man, and said, "Ah, alas poor Horatio, I knew him well."

Addressing everyone, Horatio said, "Look everybody, this is all just a big misunderstanding."

Sheriff McCarthy asked, "Horatio, what the hell are you talking about?"

Horatio sighed heavily. He seemed to be thinking things over before answering. To no one in particular he said aloud, "I'm not putting up with this crap anymore. This is way above my pay grade."

"Pay grade," Simon snickered. "That's funny."

Emma stood up and put a hand on Horatio's arm. Clearly he was upset, but equally as clear he knew something he wasn't telling, "Horatio, what is it that you know?"

He spun on her, "Didn't you hear me, I am done talking with you people. I want out." He lifted his head, stretched out his hands and spoke to the heavens, "Do you hear me, I said I'm finished."

The sheriff stepped forward and held up a hand, "Maybe you should take it easy, son."

He snorted. "Geez. You guys really don't have a clue where you are. Do you? Well, since *they're* not going to get me out of here, I might as well tell you."

Emma noted that everyone leaned forward, straining to listen, Hank's hand dropping in surprise, Jeb still strangling the shotgun: everyone but one.

"Ah, ah, ah," Simon said, interrupting Horatio, waggling his finger at him. That's quite enough out of you today, Mister... Horatio. We mustn't share secrets. You'll spoil the ending."

Horatio doubled over in pain. And not everyone saw precisely what happened next but Emma sure did. Horatio's mouth vanished. He didn't just shut up, his nose and mouth were completely gone from his face.

Odessa must've seen it too because she screamed, "Je-sus help us ... his face! That boy ain't got no mouth!" She lunged away from him as though face removal was contagious.

Sheer terror in his eyes, Horatio struggled to breathe, one hand clawing at his face. He tried to speak but it came out mumbled beneath his sealed face. He stumbled backwards, crashing into chairs and tables. Then, before he could run out of air completely, he turned and ran across the diner and crashed out the rear windows that overlooked the docks two stories below.

"Oh my Gosh, he done kilt hiself," Odessa cried into the back of her hand. "Horatio done kilt hiself, he kilt his-self."

Emma blinked in shock. *Did I imagine the part about him not having a mouth?*

While everyone was distracted, Emma saw the sheriff yank the shotgun out of Jeb's hands.

"Hey!" When Jeb tried to grab it back, the sheriff struck Jeb in the nose with the butt of the gun. Jeb collapsed in a heap to the floor and lay still. Hank then shot a round that hit the wall near Simon and blew away several bottles on the counter near the door.

Simon stared at the bullet holes and the contents of the bottles leaking out across the counter.

"I missed on purpose," Hank snarled. "This next round is a reserved for your face."

Simon smiled, "I believe you, Hank. That's what I like about you. Always so honest."

Doc, not needing any coaching from Sheriff McCarthy, chose that moment to snatch the pistol out of Simon's hand.

Sheriff McCarthy racked the shotgun's slide several times emptying shells high into the air. Disgusted he threw the empty weapon into the nearest booth.

He then took the pistol from Doc Clemens and in a rage threw Simon up against the wall. Pinning him there the sheriff put the pistol's muzzle under his chin, "Doc, you might want to take a step back; the bullet might ricochet off of the back of his skull and I don't want you to get hurt."

"Awww," Simon cooed. "Even now, still thinking of others. Hank, you're such an honorable guy."

Hank thumb cocked the hammer.

Unfazed Simon narrowed his eyes and taunted, "Hank, you don't know how to kill me."

"I'm going to start by blowing your head off. You think that might work?"

Simon's eyes widened, and his mouth erupted into a smile. "You really should kill me, Hank. I'll just kill again, but then, considering where we are, that'd be a little redundant," he said, singing the last word. Turning his gaze toward Doc Clemens he asked genuinely, "Don't ya think, Doc?"

Doc stepped up beside the sheriff. "Now Hank, you didn't kill him before in the hotel, you don't have to do it now."

"How can you say that, Doc?" Hank began through clenched teeth, "If I had stopped this murdering psychopath three days ago Ophy wouldn't be dead." Hank pressed the barrel more firmly beneath Simon's throat. "No, he has to die."

Simon sighed dramatically. "Okay, fine." Still pinned to the wall by Hank's elbow he turned his eyes to Doc Clemens, "Hey Doc, could you help me out here? I seem to have forgotten my lines again, oh wait, I remember now," he turned back towards Hank, dropping his silly grin, and speaking in a phony faltering voice he said, "Please … please don't kill me."

Hank blinked several times in rapid succession. A look of confusion contorted his face. "Wait a minute, what'd you say?"

Simon sighed again. Like an actor reciting a crummy line he said, "I said, 'Please … please don't kill me.'"

The sheriff stumbled backwards as though struck by a physical blow. He then held both sides of his head as though they were throbbing in pain.

Emma walked over to him, "Sheriff?" she began, then to Simon, "What did you do to him?" As the sheriff wavered as though he might fall, she helped him to sit down over at one of the booths.

Simon stared back at her, "Me? Oh nothing. I just helped him remember is all."

"Sheriff McCarthy… Hank, are you okay?"

He didn't seem to hear her; instead he turned towards Simon, his voice less full of hatred. "That wasn't the way they died, was it?"

Simon shook his head in answer. His demeanor had changed from playful imp to one of sadness. If she didn't know any better it almost seemed as though he genuinely pitied Hank.

Emma grabbed Hank's forearm, "Hank, what's wrong?"

He turned toward her with a strange expression and said softly, "I remember now."

Chapter 26

The Broken Man

NOWHERE, WYOMING

The Russian Wager Saloon

"You're dead ... we ... we killed you!"

Pint-sized Deputy Parnes was only half right, but one could hardly blame the guy for his error. The tall, broken man who staggered through the saloon-style doors was in fact more akin to the walking dead than the usual local living variety.

SCRAPE... SCRAPE... these were the sounds the broken man's work boot made on the floor as he dragged a useless, ruined leg behind him. The pant leg soaked with blood left a crimson trail on the wooden floors behind him. The man's thick flannel shirt was also stained with dark patches of red. He'd have been considered handsome if his left eye weren't swollen shut and his right one filled with blood. How he saw anything at all was anybody's guess. His dark hair was slick with sweat, and blood steadily streamed down the side of a face twisted in anguish. The man's left arm hung loosely at his side like a broken doll's.

The *Russian Wager Saloon*, formerly called the *Buck Shot Saloon* until the Russian mob moved into town and claimed it, resembled the saloons of the old west. The bar did have a few modern conveniences such as a brightly-colored jukebox, digital cash register, and a fancy new mechanical bull in the back room. When the broken man first stumbled through the doors he met the usual cacophony of nightclub sounds: music, laughter and a loud din of conversation. Deputy Aleksandr

Parnes, hardly a good-looking fellow, had been flirting with a black-haired beauty, swaying drunkenly to the tune of Laura Bell Bundy's sultry *"Drop on By"*. Considering Deputy Parnes was most responsible for the broken man's condition, he was understandably the most surprised to see him walk into the bar.

The broken man knew he wasn't long for this world. Only vengeance drove him onwards, if for only a little while longer.

When he spoke, he sounded harsh, his words barely above a whisper. "Deputy Parnes, the next time you murder someone... (cough)," the broken man inhaled and wheezed like a man whose lung had been punctured and was filling with blood, "You might want to make sure he's dead."

At these words Deputy Parnes un-chivalrously shoved jukebox girl aside and reached for his service revolver.

BOOM!

Broken man's gun roared. Normally he kept the .44 Magnum locked in the glove compartment of his wife's SUV. The heavy duty weapon was strictly for camping in the deep woods, so it was loaded with .270 grain bullets. The locals called the heavy duty rounds 'bear killers'. When the small cannon ball roared from the barrel of his gun, the bullet didn't take Parnes' head off, but it came just shy of it. The deputy's left eye was crammed in on itself; the near-headless body thudded to the floor.

But Deputy Parnes wasn't the one the broken-man was really after. Parnes was just one of the hired hands.

Yuri Semyonovich Ivanov, about sixty, had a haggard face and usually wore a disinterested expression. Yuri and his mob had terrorized the town since their arrival from *formerly known as* Russia twelve years ago. Officially Yuri was a local businessman who had somehow acquired the local grocery store, auto shop, and only car dealership in town, all in short order. Unofficially, as most the locals knew, he led the Russian mob. You didn't mess with him, or you'd end up dead.

Presently, Yuri sat at the table with the broken man's soon-to-be-ex boss, Sheriff Larry Landenberg. Sheriff Landenberg sported a typical law enforcement walrus mustache and close-cropped hairdo. The broken man had made the connection between mob boss Yuri and Sheriff Landenberg a little too late. As a result of his dimwittedness his wife and two young children were lying at the bottom of Devil's Gorge.

At the moment, the two dozen people still in the bar stood frozen. Most were armed, but after watching Deputy Parnes' head disintegrate, none reached for their weapon. At least not yet.

"Anybody else who wants to leave best do it now," the broken man mustered. The effort caused him to hack up more blood but his message had come across well enough. All but four men sitting at the table scrambled for the front door. Like the décor, not much had changed from the old west. Not really.

Sitting with Yuri and the sheriff was also a terrified, middle-aged accountant type. When the accountant spoke, his voice quivered like a terrified little boy. "Deputy, I had nothing to do with what happened to your family," he said, slowly rising from the table with his open palms toward the broken man, his briefcase tucked neatly under his armpit. "You know I just do the books. P-p-lease. May I go, too?"

"Abram, you coward," Landenberg growled under his breath.

The broken man tried to reply but only hacked up more blood instead. In answer, he weakly waved the nose of his revolver toward the front door. The accountant scurried for the exit. He nearly tripped as he ran, his pants clearly stained.

"That's enough, Deputy," Sheriff Landenberg said in a commanding voice, "Put that gun down right now!" The sheriff tried to sound authoritative but his voice cracked towards the end. It seemed as though even the seasoned law enforcement officer was a little unsettled by the headless Deputy Parnes.

The broken man leveled his pistol at the sheriff, cocked the hammer, and tightened his finger on the trigger. When the broken man spoke again his voice was more strained. Sheriff Landenberg heard him though because there wasn't a sound in the place, save the bartender crouched behind the bar, urgently whispering into his cell phone to the cops.

"We've been friends for six years, Larry. Our kids went to the same school together. I trusted you." The broken man stifled a sob in the back of his gun hand.

Sheriff Landenberg used the distraction to discreetly slide his hand under the table.

"You know, she didn't die right away ... my wife. Both kids died instantly in the crash but my wife... I listened to her choke on her own blood in the end."

The broken man recalled how Landenberg and Parnes had taken out the tires of his wife's SUV with a well-placed stop-strip on the bridge over Devil's Gorge. After bouncing down the cliff walls their battered vehicle had finally come to rest upside down in the ravine. The creek water trickling in was what first revived him. His children's broken little bodies in the backseat were the first to meet his then focusing eyes.

Sheriff Landenberg raised his one hand still above the table in silent plea. "Now wait a minute. We can still work this out. Just look at yourself. You, you need medical attention. I'm sorry for what happened, I truly am." He pointed at Yuri beside him. "But you've got to know that Yuri made me do it. Please, I've got a wife and kids too." the sheriff said, sniveling now. He thought the broken man wouldn't notice his one hand slowly reaching for his pistol under the table as he begged for his life with the other.

Sheriff Landenberg was wrong, and he did notice.

BOOM!

For a second time that evening the broken man's gun thundered. Sheriff Landenberg, caught in mid-draw, flipped over backward in his chair as though a cannonball had shot him in the face.

The broken man casually cocked an ear towards the exit. He could already hear the State Trooper's sirens screaming for him in the distance. There wasn't much time left.

He turned toward the two remaining men in the bar: Russian mobster Yuri Ivanov and his right hand man, Petrov. Even the bartender who had called the troopers had high-tailed it out the back. Petrov shuddered in his seat, but Yuri was cool as *formerly* Russian snow. "You'd won. We were leaving," the broken man explained, grief-stricken. "You had everything and everyone you could possibly want in this stinking town. Why couldn't you have just let me and my family go?"

Yuri was unafraid. His expression was acceptance. He came from a place much crueler than small town USA. Every day he wasn't gunned down in the street was a surprise to him. When the Russian mobster spoke it was with but the vestige of an accent. Yuri had worked hard to lose it completely over his time in America. "You know that's not the way it works, my boy."

"No," the broken man answered sadly, his vision blurring in his one good eye, breathing for perhaps only a few moments longer. "No, I reckon it ain't."

Yuri and Petrov simultaneously reached for their auto-pistols. The broken man's pistol rang out two more times. Like the corrupt sheriff, Petrov was dead before he hit the floor, but impossibly, Yuri was groaning from the floor a few seconds later.

With his last remaining ounce of strength, the broken man grabbed the table and flipped it over and out of the way.

Yuri's shoulder had been completely blown away but he was still alive. Unlike before, he stared back with a look of fear. "Please … please don't kill me."

The broken-man leveled his pistol at Yuri's face. One bullet left. At this range, he wouldn't miss, even with his vision blurring by the second. He had barely heard the state troopers pulling up outside a few seconds ago. Now they were bursting through the front door, guns drawn, demanding that he drop his weapon. At their range, they wouldn't miss either.

Deputy Sheriff Hank McCarthy's last thoughts were happy ones: his wife and children on last Christmas morn'.

Chapter 27

Memories

HANK STUMBLED TO his feet and steadied himself.

His head ached with one mother of a migraine. The pain soon melted away the recollection, but he knew the memory to be true. He felt pairs of hands on him and realized Emma and the doc were holding him up.

"What happened, Hank?" the doc asked.

Hank checked with both of them before answering, then switched his gaze to Simon. "What did you do to me?"

Simon threw his hands down by his sides and stomped his foot like a spoiled child. "Why does everyone blame me for everything? I don't understand why everyone blames me for everything. I had nothing to do with it. You finally remembered is all. I don't know nuthin'."

Hank wasn't buying it. He moved back over to Simon, put his elbow across his throat and gun to his temple. "If you don't tell me what I want to know…"

"Oh, that's the real commodity these days, isn't it? Information." The human expression vanished and was replaced by his normal madman stare and jack-o'-lantern grin. "Shoot!" he screamed. Before Hank could react he screamed, "Or don't shoot!"

Hank shook his head in disgust.

"Since we both know you're not going to shoot me, it's best if you probably just let me go."

"Why's that?" Hank asked dryly.

"Because if you don't, bad things might happen," he said, practically singing.

"Hank," It was Emma. He glanced at her but she hesitated, her face pale. "Maybe ... maybe we should listen to him."

"Emma, what are you saying? We just let him go? After everything he's done?"

"You didn't see what happened to Horatio before he crashed out the window, did you?"

"What do you mean, Emma?" Doc asked.

"I mean, before he fell out the window, he ... well, Horatio didn't have a mouth."

Odessa, quiet until now perked up at this, "That's right, that's right, I seen it, I seen it. He didn't have no ... mouth."

Ignoring Odessa Hank turned towards Emma, "Are you sure that's what you saw? I mean..."

Emma frowned, and then said in a voice tempered with anger, "I'm as sure as you were of seeing a naked man when no one else did."

Hank nodded. "Point taken."

"Last chance, Hanky-Panky, better let me go," Simon sang again.

"Shut up!" Hank yelled and smacked him over the head with the butt of his pistol, though not enough to knock him out.

"Owww!" Simon complained. "That really hurt."

The first sign of things to come was the drop light over the pool table began swaying back and forth. Simon sighed. "Oh well, too late, too late."

Simon began shaking. No, he wasn't shaking, the ground was shaking. "Uh-oh, you've gone and done it now, Hank."

Hank heard Doc say something weird, "This shouldn't be happening, this shouldn't be happening." And then the whole diner began to shake in earnest. Gently at first, then harder and harder, as though by some enormous hand. A roaring sound assaulted everyone's ears. The windows along the back wall cracked, and eventually blew out. Tables upended and scattered dishes. Every picture frame fell from the wall.

Odessa got down on her knees, put her hands over her head, and started praying. When another good jolt shook the diner her eyes flashed open wide. She glared over at Hank and screamed, "Let him go!"

Hank shook his head.

"You damn fool, he'll kill us all if you don't!" Odessa cursed then crawled unceremoniously under the pool table, or at least tried to; her rump was too large to fit and stuck out.

And then it was over. The shaking subsided as quickly as it had begun.

Hank and Doc still had a firm grip on Simon. The quake hadn't shaken any of them hard enough to send them to the floor. "Everyone okay?" Hank asked.

Emma had fallen onto a seat in one of the booths but nodded. "That wasn't so bad."

Hank flashed Simon a look as if to say, 'Is that it?'

Odessa popped out from underneath the pool table like an ostrich and stumbled to her feet. She ran over to Simon and kneeled before him, hanging on his pant legs like a drowning victim. "Please... I's seen the man with no face, and I's seen your awesome power. Just tell me one thing mister. Tell me ... are we dead?"

Simon appeared extremely pleased with himself. "Now this is more like it."

"Get up off your knees," Hank said, disgusted.

Emma appeared beside her and tried to help Odessa to her feet, "Do you think he really caused that?"

"Get your hands off of me," Odessa shouted. Turning her full anger on Emma she said, "You seen Horatio's face, same as me." She then thudded her chest, and pointed to Simon, "He says let him go or bad things will happen and looky here, we's got ourselves a damn earthquake. So how do you explain that? Huh? How about you, Sheriff?"

In a soothing voice the doc answered, "It's just coincidence, Odessa." But to Hank, the look in the doc's eyes said even he wasn't so sure.

Odessa spun towards him, "Coincidence? I don't think so!" She turned back towards Simon. Still kneeling in front of him she asked in the most pleasant voice she could muster, "Please, mister. Just tell us what we have to do?"

Simon reached down and cupped her cheek. "Oh my dear child, the more important question is what did you do to get sent here in the first place?"

Interrupting everyone's thoughts Doc suddenly blurted, "Wait Hank! Earthquake!"

"What?" Hank asked.

"In 1964, the largest earthquake ever recorded hit Alaska; a 9.2 on the Richter scale. But it wasn't the earthquake tremors that did the real damage; the real damage came when the Tsunami hit the town afterwards."

"Tsunami?" Odessa wondered aloud. Hank stared at Simon who shrugged his shoulders and said quietly, "Surprise."

Hank released Simon roughly. He moved over to the doc who started to appear catatonic. "How long you think we got before we get hit?" Hank asked.

"The speed of a wave travels depends on the depth and displacement of the water." The doc said this more to himself, as though he were thinking aloud. "This shouldn't be happening..."

"Doc... How long?"

"Not knowing the location of the epicenter of the water displacement, it's impossible to know."

Hank glimpsed Simon. He was now sitting up on the counter, swinging his legs joyfully, tapping his watch, and smiling. "Tick-Tock, Tick-Tock."

A loud roaring sound started building in decibels. Simon put his ear to his watch. "Ah, right on time."

Hank ran to the side entrance and opened door. The only good news was that the diner was on high ground and they were on the third floor of the building. Emma, Doc, and Odessa joined him on the balcony overlooking the town. Sucking winds threatened to pull them right over the railing and each of them gripped the railing. Roaring out of the bay was a twenty foot wave racing towards them.

When the massive wave hit the harbor, it smashed aside the boats and swallowed the port whole. As the wave continued onwards down Main Street, it swept cars from the street, engulfed first floor buildings, trees and anyone unlucky enough to be in its path.

The wave raced past them. When it reached the mountains it turned the fuel tanks at the fuel refinery inside out. Fuel slicked the surface of the black water as the wave began to suck back, drawing debris and flotsam with it.

Simon appeared at the railing, he was trying to light a cigarette with a malfunctioning lighter. When Hank saw this, he yanked the unlit cigarette from his mouth and threw it and the lighter to the floor.

"What? It's my smoke break?" Simon complained. "I'm going to talk to HR about this."

"Everyone back inside," Hank commanded. Hank took one last look over his shoulder and realized theirs was the only building in town not underwater.

When they entered the diner something was immediately apparent to Hank. "Wait a minute, where are all the bodies?" "How is that possible?" Emma asked.

There was still blood on the floor and Bob's remains were still splattered across the double doors, but all the bodies had been removed while they were out on the balcony.

Oh no.

Hank scanned the room. "Where's Simon?"

Chapter 28

Is This Purgatory?

AMIDST THE CHAOS the Last Frontier Diner might as well have been an island.

For the past three hours Tsunami waves, smaller with each passing, flooded the streets. All communications were out; they couldn't reach anyone and didn't see any signs of any other survivors on adjoining roof tops or in the water.

Sheriff McCarthy carefully explained that leaving the diner would be suicide. The only thing they could do now was wait for the waters to recede.

They never did find where Simon had disappeared too. He had vanished as if his entire role had been to usher in the apocalypse and exit stage left. Instead, they passed some of the time by scrubbing the blood off the floors and walls and returning the diner somewhat to its former state. At least with the emergency generator in the basement the building still had power, unlike the rest of the town. No one had spoken in the last twenty minutes. Emma had brought out some pumpkin pie she had made earlier that day. So far only Odessa seemed interested in eating any.

Finally, Emma was the first to speak. "Hank, before... What did Simon do to you?"

Emma watched as Hank struggled before answering. Finally, he said, "I don't think Simon Privet killed my wife and kids. I'm not sure who those people on the video were but I don't think they were my family. I think my real wife and kids died back in Wyoming where I was a deputy sheriff."

Doc frowned, "Simon forced you to remember?"

"How'd they die?" Odessa asked, chewing a giant piece of pie.

Hank bit his lower lip. "The Russian mob bought off most of the sheriff's department I worked for. I didn't realize what I was stepping in. I made the connection too late." Gazing out the window he added, "And because I made the connection too late, my wife and kids died."

Emma said, "Oh God, that's awful."

Doc squeezed his shoulder. "Now Hank, you can't blame yourself for all the evil in this world."

"Yeah, but that's not all. When I went to shoot the last mobster, I remember the State Troopers all pointing their guns at me. I was squeezing down on the trigger and the next thing I know, I wake up outside of town."

Emma shuddered, a hand going briefly to her head as a headache had spiked. When she was able she said, "Same thing happened to me."

Emma saw Odessa make a face and roll her eyes, but undeterred she continued, "My step dad did something awful to my sister. I remember wondering where my real Paw kept his shotgun. The next thing you know, I'm on the ferry coming into town."

"And did you get kilt too?" Odessa asked.

"No... I think I remember them walking me out in handcuffs. They said my wrists were so small they had to use children's cuffs. Funny, I hadn't remembered any of that until just now."

"Maybe you kilt yourself, in prison," Odessa offered.

"I doubt that." Emma shot back.

"Really? And just why would you be any different than the rest of us, huh?"

"I know I didn't. I would never do that."

"How do you know?" Odessa pressed.

Emma pulled out a small, modest wooden cross on a leather string about her neck. She rubbed it between thumb and forefinger. "Because if I had I would suffer eternal damnation."

Odessa returned the stare and said, "Well maybe that's exactly what happened."

No one said anything for the next few minutes.

"I was an ice cream man."

Everyone turned and saw Jeb sitting up on the floor. They had made him comfortable with blankets and a pillow. He had spent the last few hours snoozing through the chaos.

With nasal congestion from his broken nose he said, "Sutton's Ice Cream Parlor. It was in my family for three generations. One day a cruise ship company comes to our town. They wanted to build a cruise ship dock in our port. The town immediately voted them down. We liked our privacy and didn't want tourists ruining the natural beauty of the place. But then these sales guys go around telling everybody about all the money we'd make if we'd just vote the cruise ship facility in. They showed me how 2,000 passengers would clamber through my ice cream shop every day making me a rich man. Well I, and the town, fell for it hook, line, and sinker, and we voted the cruise ship port in. I took out a big loan to double the size of my parlor and I took on extra employees to keep up with the summer rush I was promised. Only problem was that passengers boarded their air conditioned motor coaches right on the dock and drove right through town without stopping."

"You kilt yurself too?" Odessa asked.

Jeb shot her a glare. He sniffed loudly and resumed his tale. "Well I lost the business, and as a result, my wife and kids left me. The bank foreclosed on my house, I was left with pretty much nuthin. One day I drank too much. I guess I went a little crazy. I took a shotgun down to the port. I only intended to shoot over their heads, ya know, scare them a little? But like I said, I was drunk." Jeb stared down at his feet. He covered his eyes with one hand. "My first shot ended up hitting a young woman and her baby, killing them instantly. After that, people came running at me, and I just kept firing." When Jeb moved his hand away tears were burning down his cheeks. "I wish I hadn't. I was drunk. I was angry." Fighting back the tears he added, "I never meant to hurt nobody."

Hank and Doc lifted Jeb to his feet, and helped him sit at the table with the rest of them.

Jeb fingered his swollen nose. In attempt to change the mood he joked, "Geez, did you have to hit me so hard, Hank."

Hank spoke, "We all seem to have something in common. We all did something bad, and we all don't remember exactly how we got here."

Odessa countered. "I remember how I got here, I came in on the ferry."

Emma said, "I remember coming in on the ferry too, but do you remember getting on the ferry, cause I don't." The expression on Odessa's face said she didn't.

"Yeah, it was like that for me too," Hank added. "I remember coming in through the tunnel but I don't remember driving from Wyoming to Alaska."

"Maybe we're in Purgatory," Jeb said aloud.

Doc silent up to this point, spoke up, "That would certainly explain a lot. An opportunity to make better choices. Maybe that's why we're here."

"Where do you think we are, Hank?" Emma asked.

"Dunno." Hank got up from the table and grabbed the grease board from the wall. He erased the daily specials with the forearm of his shirt and started writing down all the possibilities.

Hell

Heaven

Government Experiment

Alien Abduction

Latitude 61

Coma

Purgatory

He spun the grease board around to face all of them. "Okay, what does everybody think, anybody want to share any theories?"

When no one said anything Emma figured she had to be the one to get the ball rolling, "I'll go first." Turning to the doc she asked, "Hey Doc, do you know anything about all this Latitude 61 nonsense?"

"Oh, don't worry about that. I know we're not dealing with alien artifacts."

Odessa piped up at this, "Oh yeah, why's that, Doc?"

"The government did do covert experiments in the Rakewell building but it wasn't on any alien technology, they were doing multiple experiments like studying sonar systems on the beluga whales, and other military applications like that."

"How do you know about all that stuff, Doc?" Sheriff McCarthy asked.

"Because before I became the friendly neighborhood Doc Clemens, I was a Lt. Colonel Clemens in the Air Force. Even former rank has its privileges when it comes to getting information."

"Well, I guess we can take that off the list, Sheriff," Emma said.

"Yeah, and you can cross off Heaven, because this here sure ain't my idea of Heaven," Odessa said, finishing the last of her pie and eyeballing the rest.

Hank nodded and drew a line through the two choices.

Emma thought it was good they were now working as a team. She bet the sheriff came up with the idea just for that reason. *Keep us from going crazy and tearing each other's throats out.*

Doc added, "And I think the same goes for Hell, because according to scripture and various sources, Hell is a place of eternal damnation and suffering. I'd imagine it would be far worse than anything we've undergone so far."

"Says you," Odessa grumped.

Emma had enough of the older waitress's negative attitude. "Okay, where do you think we are?"

"I keep telling you, we *is* dead. We all done sumthin' wrong, we all got kilt over it and now we're in Purgatory."

"We all know what *we* did," Emma began, "But what did you do, Odessa? Huh? I imagine it wasn't something pleasant."

Emma braced herself for an assault but Odessa's eyes became vacant, as though she were reliving some awful memory. She then dropped her gazed and muttered, "My business is my own."

Emma recalled the creepy totem pole in the canyon, depicting a man at the center being pulled apart by creatures both angelic and demonic. "When Horatio took me up to Totem Pole Canyon he said the Indians used to call this place," she struggled to remember.

Doc came to her aide, "Ti-Quan-nah-ha-nah, which is Tlingit for *"Place where Heaven meets Hell."*

"Right, thanks Doc," Emma said. "Anyway, he said Purgatory is a place between death and final judgment. And that guy, uh, Dante,"

"The Italian poet, Dante Alighieri," Doc interjected.

"Yeah, that guy, he claimed that in Purgatory souls had to pass through the appropriate punishments for salvation. If they passed all the tests they were cleansed of all sin and made ready for Heaven."

Hank slapped his thighs and stood up. "Okay, that's enough. Nobody's dead. We're not in the afterlife. All of this can be explained. Chances are this is all some elaborate hoax or military experiment." He gazed around the diner. "They're probably watching us on cameras right now, all having a big laugh."

"What about Horatio's mouth?" Emma asked.

"Special effects, have you seen what they're doing on screen lately?"

"What about the missing bodies?"

"Trap doors, I dunno, but I don't think we're dead."

"Hey guys," It was Jeb, he had broken off from the group and was staring out one of the broken out windows. "The water's receded."

Everyone moved back outside to the balcony.

Main Street was a mess. A Jeep Wrangler had crashed into the front of Pete's Hardware Store. Downed power lines swayed and sparks arced overhead.

Emma was the first to speak. "What do you think we should do now, Hank?"

"I know what I'm going to do. Dead or not, Purgatory, Hell, or some secret alien experiment, I'm going to get in my car and get the hell out of this crazy town. You folks are welcome to come with me."

"Wait a minute? Why we listenin' ta him?" Odessa asked, pointing at Hank. "You said so yourself, Doc, he shouldn't have lived. Not after that fall off that building."

"No, I said, he was lucky he didn't die."

Odessa shook her head, "Same difference."

Emma, "You leave Sheriff McCarthy out of this. He's not one of them remember?"

"What about you?" Odessa spat. She held out a steak knife in front of her, "Fars I knows, anyone of youse could be one of them fake people Jeb was babbling about."

"Odessa, put the knife down before you hurt yourself," Sheriff McCarthy ordered, tiredness evident in his voice.

"The only person whose gonna get hurt is the one who messes with me." That said, she backed out of the diner and disappeared through the main entrance. Part of her apron must have got caught in the door because a loud crash was heard from outside. Pink fabric bunched in the door jam and moved a little as Odessa tugged on it with a curse. Finally it pulled free. This was followed by a holler that was cut short when she smacked the pavement with her backside. More cursing ensued and then faded away.

In spite of everything that had happened to them in the last hour, Hank, Emma, Doc, and Jeb shared an uncomfortable laugh.

Chapter 29

The Tunnel

THEY FOUND HANK'S WHITE SUV was still parked in the side alley next to the diner and Hank breathed a sigh of relief for small mercies; it was one of the few remaining operational vehicles in what was probably the whole town.

Hank nosed the vehicle through the flooded murky waters on Main Street and navigated around smashed up cars piled against shattered buildings. Felled trees and scattered debris lay everywhere. Broken and twisted limbs jutted out from every building and a fishing trawler was lying on its side in the middle of the street. "The Unfortunates" was written on its stern in graffiti. A firetruck at the end of the street was sticking through Pete's Hardware Store, bar lights still blazing, and a rusted out tanker, riddled with holes like it had been peppered by a machine gun, lay in the middle of the school like it had been dropped there.

When they finally navigated through the debris field and up onto the tunnel access road, a thick mist was beginning to collect under the trees that lined their path. It wasn't long before the headlights barely cut through the fog.

"How can you see anything?" Emma asked softly, wiping condensation off the inside of the windshield with her sleeve.

Hank glanced over at her, then back at the road. "We're almost to the entrance," he offered reassuringly.

The entrance to the tunnel was at the end of the road; a large opening cut into the mountain, edged with bricks, Hank had a good memory of what it looked like but he couldn't see any of that in this thick soup. He slowed the SUV down to a crawl, his jaw tightening; visibility down to a few feet past the hood.

"I can't see anything, can you?" he asked Emma.

"Want me to walk out in front of the car?" the doc offered from the back seat.

Yeah ... like hell I'm going to let my coffee-talk buddy get taken out by some ghoul in the mist.

Aloud he answered, "No. I think we're okay Doc. I'll just take it nice and easy."

Hank stared through the windshield, watching as the mist danced and swirled over the road. There, white lines passed beneath their wheels; they'd entered the designated waiting zone where cars would line up to be loaded on the train. That would mean the tracks would be somewhere on their left. The tunnel entrance just ahead.

"Are you sure about this?" Doc asked. "We puncture a tire and we're all stuck here."

Hank had never driven a vehicle on train tracks before but he knew the SUV's clearance would be good enough that they could straddle one of the rails with their other wheel in the gravel shoulder. It should work but it would likely be a bumpy ride.

Hank found the level crossing more by luck than anything else and made a sharp turn to put the vehicle on the tracks. He eased up on the speed as the wheels fought for traction between the gravel and the crossties.

All conversation stopped as everyone fought not to swallow their tongues. Hank caught sight of Jeb hastily reaching to buckle his seatbelt.

Darkness swallowed them as they entered the tunnel without warning.

Hank felt Emma tense up in the seat beside him and he was about to tell her not to worry when the headlights caught something unrecognizable in the tunnel ahead.

"There's something in the mist," Emma said, transfixed.

As he brought the SUV to a stop, Hank reflexively reached down and made sure his pistol was still in its holster; he'd let Doc have the shotgun as Jeb still couldn't be trusted. Before he could unsnap his holster, a dark shape cut through the mist and slammed into the hood. Everyone jumped. Whatever had struck the car had fallen down onto tracks in front of the car.

"Did you see what it was?" Jeb asked from the rear seat, peering through the windshield along with the rest of them.

"Wait here in the car while I go check it out," Hank said.

"Like hell you are," Emma said, echoing his own thoughts earlier. "Don't you watch horror movies?"

"Well, yeah of course."

"Then you know that this is the part where you step out of the car and something in the fog snatches you up."

"Yeah, that's true," Hank mused. "But that's not going to happen to me, know why?"

Emma shook her head.

Hank grinned, "Because I'm the wise-cracking hero."

He understood she was scared, they all were, but he also knew he couldn't just roll over whatever had just struck the front of the car. He cracked the door and that's when a howling noise echoed out of the misty tunnel ahead of them.

Emma looked at him with a concerned look on his face and said, "Maybe we should turn around?"

"I don't think this tunnel is wide enough for that," Doc said from the back.

Hank thought about it. "Either way we're not turning around. We're leaving this crazy town behind us." With that said, he closed the door, put the SUV in drive and let the vehicle crawl forward. They went about fifty feet deeper into the tunnel without incident. The mist even clearing a little bit as they traveled further from the entrance. And then, out of the darkness appeared two red pinpricks of light. They flared well above the height of the car, the darkness around them almost thicker somehow.

"Anybody else see that?" Doc asked from the back seat.

"See what?" Jeb asked.

"Oh God, what now?" Emma asked.

Hank gripped the steering wheel a little tighter, his knuckles already white. He peered over the steering wheel into the fog but he didn't stop his forward movement. At first he didn't see what they were talking about, the red glowing lights were just exit signs for service shafts ahead of them, but then he saw the monstrous black shape move as it stretched to fill the width of the tunnel. "Is that a train?"

It puffed steam, whether it was from the mouth of a creature or a train Hank couldn't tell. Hank slammed on the brakes. The thing was coming towards them, whatever it was.

"What the hell is that?"

"It's growling, can't you hear it?" Jeb cried.

"That's crazy," Hank shot back.

"Big and black, glowing red eyes," Jeb said fearfully. "Maybe it's Barnabus?"

"No," Hank began. "Whatever it is, it's a lot bigger than a bear."

Hank felt Emma patting his thigh rapidly, "Back up, back up!" she cried.

He needed no further urging. He threw the SUV in reverse.

"It's moving faster," Doc stated, sounding more amazed than frightened.

As Hank drove backwards out of the tunnel like a stunt car driver, gravel flew from the tires like sea foam in their wake. The creature roared and the tunnel shook, debris raining down from the ceiling to hammer dents in the roof and hood of the Ford Explorer.

"Faster!" Emma cried.

"The tunnel's collapsing," Jeb yelled.

Hank had his arm over the seat and focused only on backing up.

More of the ceiling gave way as the train monster thundered after them, large chunks falling in their path. Hank struggled not to grit his teeth, knowing he couldn't veer while his wheels were straddling the tracks. Their vehicle bounced and bucked over the debris, everyone slamming their heads into the ceiling. More rubble pounded the roof like angry fists.

Finally they reached the entrance, the darkness breaking way to gray afternoon light. Hank guessed his speed at fifty miles an hour when they shot out of the tunnel. He slammed on the brakes even before they reached the level crossing, nearly skidding through it before Hank jerked on the e-brake and skewed the vehicle in an aborted j-turn. The car screamed to a stop, now perpendicular to the tracks. He threw it in drive without missing a beat and they burned rubber as they got back on pavement.

"Keep going, keep going," Emma shouted.

Hank did keep going, but as he did, he risked a glance in his rearview mirror. As the mist shifted, he could see there was no need to hurry. The train monster wasn't following them and the mouth of the tunnel was blocked. With the tunnel sealed, they had no way of getting out of town.

They were trapped.

Chapter 30

The Harbor

"**SOMETHING SANK ALL** the damn boats."

Hank pulled the battered SUV into the harbor parking lot. Emma was right. He turned to where she was pointing out the left side of their SUV. As the mist parted sporadically they all could see the harbor had been reduced to a boat graveyard, and not just from the tsunami. All the hulls were cracked and half-submerged like some leviathan had crushed each of them in angry tentacles.

Hank shut the engine and sighed. Another hope dashed.

But then Jeb said, "Wait, not all of them. Look."

Amidst the broken hulls stood one solitary trawler that appeared relatively unscathed.

"That's Tommy Barton's boat, *The Red Salmon.*"

There's still hope.

"Wait a minute?" Hank had a bad feeling. "Why that one? All the other boats are smashed, why isn't that one?"

"Who cares? Cause I sure as hell ain't going back thru that tunnel," Jeb said impatiently, cracking his door and getting out. Hank was worried about the car's bell dinging making too much noise so he took the keys out of the ignition and put them on the center console.

"No one is, Jeb, I don't know if you noticed but the tunnel's collapsed," Doc said dryly.

Jeb frowned.

Hank was about to get out too when he noticed that Emma had gone white. Something had frightened her, and he didn't think it was the train creature back at the tunnel. No, this was something new. "Emma, what's wrong?"

She was staring at the water. "In the water," she said in a catatonic state.

It took him a moment, but soon Hank saw the shark fins cutting the water as they swam in and out of the wrecked boats, searching hungrily for their next meal.

"I'm not going on the water." Emma shivered and rubbed her shoulders for warmth. Staring at the black fins cutting the water she said, "You guys can go on without me, but I'm not leaving town by going out there, boat or not."

"What, and face that thing in the tunnel?" Jeb asked incredulously. "I'm not going near the water. Leave me the keys and go on without me."

Hank got out and circled around to her side of the car. He gently opened her door and said softly, "Emma, this might be our only chance; this might be our only way out of here."

Doc leaned forward, his chin resting on the seat back, "Emma, we'll be right by your side every step of the way. Okay?"

Hank could tell she wasn't happy about the idea, but Emma allowed him to lead her out of the car. When he went to let go she clasped his hand even tighter.

They started walking across the parking lot towards the docked trawler. They soon reached the gate that lead down one arm of the dock, which in turn would lead to the boat.

Hank took out his master key ring and fiddled with the lock. As he did so he heard Jeb say behind him, "Hank, we got a problem."

Hank turned to see about twenty longshoremen filing out of the port facility and lining up in front of the entrance.

"You think they're friendlies?"

"One way to find out... Hey you guys all right?" Jeb hollered over to them. "You guys made it too, huh?"

But Hank could see they were not all right. Each of them had black soulless eyes. Stranger still, as the horde moved closer, Hank could see strange zipper tracks on their faces, like someone had unzipped their skins, rooted around inside their bodies, and zipped them back up again. He also noted some of them were carrying machetes, another held a tire iron, and a really big guy wearing overalls brandished a fireman's ax.

"C'mon, let's get back to the car," Hank said urgently.

Jeb clearly had set his sights on the boat because he said, "I ain't going back to the car. We've got guns, I say we just blast our way through."

"First of all, those are human beings," Hank said harshly. "Just in case you need the reminder, we can't just go around killing people. Second of all, even if we do need to start shooting, I don't think we have enough ammo to take them all on anyway."

"Anything's better than that thing in the tunnel. And I sure as hell ain't going back to that damn diner."

While he'd been arguing with Jeb, Hank noted the longshoreman horde had managed to fan out into a line.

Emma glanced at him. Fear in her eyes. "Here they come," she warned. Hank pulled her back behind him.

Jeb chambered a round in his shotgun. "Then they better get the hell out of my way."

"Oh, Jeb, violence, violence, violence. That's your answer to everything." Everyone turned and saw Simon sitting on top of a nearby cargo container with that same stupid grin. "I see you haven't learned nuthin' since your days as a jolly old ice cream man."

Gesturing toward the longshoremen Hank asked Simon, "What did you do to them?"

Simon smiled. "They're all Unfortunates now. And the Unfortunates belong unto me. Didn't you read my signs," he held up his hands for dramatic effect, "'Beware the Unfortunates?'" Simon frowned. "Geez, I do all this signage and nobody appreciates it."

"Well I say, bring 'em on," Jeb growled.

In answer, a rock sailed out of the horde, flew high overhead, and landed with a loud THOCK. Hank realized the sound had been the Unfortunate's rock connecting with the top of Jeb's skull. The old sheriff teetered for a moment, blood trickling down from his forehead, and then he fell over on the tarmac, his gun clattering to the ground beside him.

"Emma, give me a hand with Jeb," Hank shouted, but she was already there. It took both of them to hoist a dazed Jeb to his feet.

"What hit me?" he asked drunkenly.

"Help him back to the car." Hank noted the doc had recovered the shotgun. Nodding to the doc he said, "The doc and I will cover your retreat."

"Odessa!" Emma shouted. "I see Odessa."

Hank saw the grumpy waitress's head bobbing up and down behind the crowd of Unfortunates. Even at a distance Hank could tell something was wrong with the way her head kept bouncing up and down like that. Then she vanished in the crowd.

"Just go, Emma. The doc and I will get her," he commanded, knowing full well they wouldn't be able to save their own skins let alone Odessa's. The expression on Doc's face said he knew it too.

"But Odessa's over there," Emma said. She was really losing it now.

"Emma," Hank said soothingly, "I need you to take Jeb to the car, can you do that for me?"

Emma nodded, "Sure, Hank." With Jeb's meaty arm over her slender shoulders, she shuffled towards the car.

"You go too, Doc," Hank said, holding out his hand, "Just leave me the shotgun and I'll buy you guys some time."

In an incredulous tone the doc roared back, "Like hell you will!"

Hank nodded his thanks and drew his pistol. He would wait to the last possible moment to take human life but he was beginning to think that was an eventuality in this situation.

On shotgun, the doc had no such reservations. He spun, leveled the shotgun at the first of the Unfortunates to arrive, and fired. The Unfortunate swinging a pipe wrench wildly overhead was immediately catapulted backwards.

Hank shot the next Unfortunate in the face and what was left of him collapsed to pavement. The combination of his revolver and Doc's shotgun was devastating. They stood back to back and emptied their weapons into the horde of Unfortunates closing in on them. Their gunshots melded into a symphony of chaos. Hank darted out of the way of more machete wielding unfortunates, firing constantly, blowing them apart. He scampered back to Doc, reloading just in time to keep an Unfortunate from driving a heavy screwdriver into his chest.

Three more Longshoremen came at Hank, each of them wielding heavy machetes. *Must have been a sale.* Hank nailed two of them but missed the third one ... who managed to get close enough to slice his jacket open. Doc blasted the Unfortunate with buckshot.

"Thanks!"

Hank noticed Emma and Jeb had nearly made it to the car. At least they were going to make it. He also saw an Unfortunate break away from the pack, a fast one with a butcher's clever, making a beeline for them. It was a long shot but Hank tracked the attacker with the revolver's iron sights. Before he could squeeze the trigger another Unfortunate stepped up and swung a machete at his head. Hank ducked reflexively. Spotting Emma, he could see the clever-wielding Unfortunate was almost at her back. Taking only a split second to control his breathing and line up his shot once more he tracked the target and pulled the trigger.

BOOM!

"Damn, that was a good shot, Hank!" Simon cheered from somewhere nearby.

Hank didn't have time to take a bow; he dodged another swipe from the machete's blade and shot its wielder in the throat. He cracked opened the pistol's cylinder and let the empty shells fall. They tinkled when they hit the ground. He slammed home his last speed loader, flipped the cylinder closed, and shot down four more Unfortunates.

His estimation had been right; far more Unfortunates than they had bullets. Echoing this, the doc yelled beside him. "I'm out of ammo!" In a fit of rage the doc hurled his empty shotgun at one of them and punched another before an arrow suddenly struck him in the shoulder. He cried out in pain.

Hank scanned the trajectory and shot the Unfortunate with the crossbow twice in the chest right as he was loading another bolt. "Doc, you're hurt. Can you make it to the car?"

The doc waivered and Hank stepped up to cushion his fall.

"Hank, you've got to listen to me." He gripped Hank by the back of the neck, his words almost pleading, "You're not where you think you are."

"What are you talking about, Doc?" Hank asked and lowered his injured friend to the ground.

Doc pulled him closer. "Simon ... don't listen to anything he says." Any moment Hank expected to feel a blade pierce his skin. Instead two burly longshoremen ripped Hank from the doc's side and held him up between them.

"Let me go you bastards!" Hank struggled with his attackers but could only watch as the crowd parted to reveal the same man Hank had seen on his first day of arrival. It was the scary guy who pounded on the hood of his car with his meaty hand and told him to hurry up and board the train. Wielding a red fireman's ax he strode forward and buried the blade deep into the doc's chest.

"Nooooo!!" shouted Hank, cursing and swearing vengeance, but he knew it was an idle threat. The Unfortunates holding him were strong and forced him down to his knees. A third man, who was actually a woman, grabbed him by his hair and held his face up so he could see what came next.

The ax wielder braced his foot against the doc's chest and wrenched the ax free. Its blade dripped with the doc's blood. He carried the ax slowly towards Hank, his intent clear.

At least Emma and Jeb got away.

The longshoreman lifted the ax again, and was about to swing down with all his strength into the center of Hank's head when a loud whistle pierced the last wisps of fog.

The horde of Unfortunates still held Hank, but the crowd parted and allowed Simon to enter.

"Hank, Hank, Hank ... what are we going to do with you?"

Hank saw Doc's lifeless body on the pavement. "I'll kill you, you son-of-a-bitch!"

"Awww, Hank. I hate to see you like this. Did you lose your friend? That's okay, I've got someone else you can play with." Simon clapped his hands and held them out, waiting to catch something. It was Odessa's severed head. Simon had mounted it on one end of a broomstick. He rhythmically paraded it up and down, her mouth permanently frozen open in a scream. "Did you know Mrs. Odessa here was a strung out junkie; addicted to crack since birth? Doctors said poor little thing never had a chance. When she was hooking on the streets she became pregnant, ended up throwing her baby in a dumpster. She did that three times in her life by the way." Simon turned towards Odessa's head, "Isn't that right, Odessa?" He grabbed her bottom lip with his free hand and in a bad ventriloquist impression said, "That's right, Mr. Simon," and shrieked, "I was a bad ... wittle girl."

Hank was nauseated…

Simon switched his gaze back to Hank. "Don't worry, Hank, I've got a broomstick for you, too." He nodded to the Unfortunate with the ax indicating he had permission to continue his grisly work.

Exhausted, Hank hung defeated between the two Unfortunates. His journey was over. He took comfort in the fact that Emma and Jeb escaped and he would be seeing his wife and kids again soon.

HONK!!!

The sound of a blaring horn shook Hank out of his despair.

The SUV slammed into the horde of Unfortunates like a giant bowling ball knocking over human-sized pins.

Using the distraction, Hank shook off the Unfortunates holding him and bolted for the car. He glimpsed Emma behind the wheel waving to him to get in.

Hank almost tore off the handle on the driver's side door as he hurried to get inside. Emma jumped in the passenger seat and Hank took her spot behind the wheel.

In the back Jeb was struggling to remove his pistol from its holster around his girth.

The Unfortunates converged on the car.

"Hank, let's go," Emma shouted beside him.

"I see 'em," he answered as he put the car in drive. He took one last sorrowful glance at Doc's body in the rearview mirror, and then punched the accelerator. Tires squealing on the slick road, the SUV sideswiped a cargo container, spitting up sparks as it tore out away from the docks.

Several Unfortunates auditioned for the role of hood ornament.

Chapter 31

The Airport

FOR THE MOMENT they were safe.

As they sped down the road Emma finally was able to control her breathing long enough to ask, "Where to now?"

Hank shook his head. He was out of ideas. He wasn't even sure where he was driving, other than back across town.

"Hey Hank, do you know how to fly a plane?" This was Jeb from the backseat. He was holding a dirty cloth to his bleeding head.

"Fly, yes. Take off, sure. Land, not so much. Why?"

Jeb patted him on the shoulder and pointed out the left window. Hank slowed. A small runway, not much more than a wide dirt road, swathed through the rugged wilderness of the mountainside beyond the edge of town. The clear-cut airfield glowed in the settling light of evening. It was high enough up the hillside the planes should've been unscathed by the tsunamis.

"Don't bother, all the planes will probably be smashed," Emma grumbled.

By the time they reached the airstrip, dusk had turned to night, and they could see Emma's prediction held true as the pale light of the moon glinted off scattered metal parts. Just like the harbor, all the planes had been sabotaged. But not just to the extent of flat tires, or broken wings, the small planes appeared as though King Kong had used them for kickball practice.

"Wait a minute, not all of them," Jeb said.

A solitary plane sat beneath a single working light. Most of the other lights were heavily damaged or were throwing sparks. Beneath the single spotlight, sat a small single engine 250 super cub; it was the plane of choice that Bush pilots used to fly supplies out to rural communities.

Wow, deja vu, this is just like the boats, Hank thought. Before he could mention it, he heard one of the rear passenger doors unlatch. It was Jeb again. "What are we waiting for, let's go."

"Hey Jeb, did you not learn anything at the harbor?"

"What?" Jeb asked, almost whining. "Can you fly or not?"

Hank had been taking flying lessons in Wyoming, and he was just short of his solo flight, but that's not what was bothering him. "I can get us in the air and chart a course but I've never soloed and I'm not sure I could even land us safely. Plus, don't you think it's weird whatever it was wiped out every single plane except one?"

"Who cares, we were overdue for a little luck. If you can get us airborne and the hell out of here, I'm game. Crash us anywhere you like just so long as it's not here in HavenPort."

Emma glanced over at him, "Hank, you're thinking it's a trap, like at the harbor?"

"That's exactly what I'm thinking."

Jeb wasn't satisfied. "All I'm saying is let's just see if the plane's operable, and got gas. If not, then at least we know it's not an option."

As they thought it over Jeb began walking across the airfield.

"Jeb, wait," Hank called after him.

The solitary light bulb above the plane blew out. As fast as his legs could carry him, Jeb was diving back into the car. "Okay, so the airport's out."

Hank didn't wait around for whatever ate the light to venture out onto the road and they sped off.

As they turned back for town, it became quickly apparent that every building in HavenPort that had survived the tsunami was without power, save one.

The diner; the bright yellowish interior lights blazed like a lighthouse to lost souls.

Chapter 32

A Little Remodeling

HANK LED THE WAY into the diner with only two bullets left in his gun.

The shotgun had gotten left behind in the harbor, and after a careful search of the SUV the only remaining ammo they could find was two dropped cartridges under the seat. They had tried driving by the office for more weapons and ammunition, but the buildings had collapsed on both sides of the street and were little more than large piles of rubble, making the way impassable.

They parked in the parking lot. They could hear music playing on the jukebox. The song sounded like an Eagles tune, "Hotel California".

When Hank first opened the door he'd expected to see the diner as they had left it. Instead, he was surprised to find a completely different establishment. Off the cuff, it reminded him of a 50's diner. Bright red swivel stools lined up against a long shiny counter with a golden handrail running the length of the countertop. On the counter Hank saw an old-fashioned malt machine behind an equally antiquated cash register. Paddle-fans gently stirred the air overhead and there was even a frosty ice cream cooler filled with assorted flavors. The diner's normal dingy tables and chairs were gone, replaced with plastic booths. The only thing reminiscent of the old restaurant was that creepy buck toothed stuffed otter and his stupid sign, *'Otter Behave.'* A colorful jukebox continued playing "Hotel California" in the corner. The music grew louder for a moment.

Any minute Hank expected Fonzi from Happy Days to come strolling out of the kitchen double-doors in his leather jacket and say, "Aaaaaaa...," with two thumbs hooked in the air.

"Hi folks, can I get you something?" came a light and cheery voice.

Hank lifted his heavy gaze from the jukebox and saw Simon standing behind the counter. He was cleaned up, wearing a 50's white soda jerk costume, complete with white paper fry hat. At the moment he was furiously shining up the counter with a rag. The countertop was so shiny Hank was certain he'd be able to see his reflection in it.

"What the hell?" Jeb asked, as he entered behind Hank. Jeb and Emma appeared equally shocked by the décor as he was. Emma ran to the windows, which caused Hank to check the outside too. They were still in HavenPort; they could see the harbor below, and the ruined town around them.

"Why don't you folks come on in and have a seat?" Simon said cheerfully, like nothing had happened; like Doc's mutilated corpse wasn't laying back at the harbor parking lot, like Odessa's severed head hadn't been mounted on a broomstick, like he hadn't tried to kill them at every opportunity.

But Hank was exhausted. He was beaten, his ribs hurt like hell, and he'd never fully recovered from the fall. Holding the gun anywhere other than by his side wasn't even an option. He was so tired.

Defeated, he shook his head in disgust. They couldn't get out the tunnel, it was collapsed. They couldn't get out the harbor, all the boats were cracked, and the solitary plane at the airport was obviously a trap. With nothing else to try, he shuffled over to the counter and plopped down on one of the stools.

Simon put his elbow on the counter opposite Hank and dropped his chin into his hand. His voice was gentle and condescending when he said, "Hi, Hank."

Hank hung his head low, and answered with a simple, "Hi, Simon."

"Cup of coffee?" Simon asked sweetly.

"Sure," Hank answered back, the exhaustion in his voice.

"Cream?"

"Black," Hank replied.

"Pie, maybe?" he offered.

"Yeah, okay, Simon."

"It's pumpkin, right?"

Hank exploded from his stool, grabbed Simon by his shirt and dragged him across the counter.

"You murdered my friends," he said through clenched teeth.

"Golly gee sir, I can't say I know what you're talking about, but, but," he said stuttering, "we-we, just got a brand new flavor in", he switched his gaze to Emma and said evenly, "salmon shark delight, it's to die for. Isn't that right, Emma?"

Tears streamed down Emma's cheeks. "I'm not afraid of you." As Hank held him by the collar, she raised her face at him in defiance. "I just want to know one thing, Simon. Are we dead?"

"Yes," Simon answered.

"Where are we?" Emma asked, fighting sobs.

"You said only one question." Simon replied. Seeing she wasn't going to play his little game he added, "Awww, sweety, you haven't figured that out yet?"

Emma shook her head.

"Even after Horatio showed you the totem pole, and everything?" he asked, feigning shock.

"Purgatory?" she asked meekly.

Simon smiled softly, "Just prisoners here."

The music raised again and Simon spoke over the lyrics, "Oh, this is my favorite part, here." He hummed along until the last line and then he sang, "You can check out any time you like, but you can never ever leave."

As the guitar riff played on, Simon flashed his eyes back to Hank. "You really ought to let me go, Hank. My friends won't like it."

Hank quickly surveyed the room; there was no one else in the room. "What friends are those Simon?"

The lights dimmed to complete darkness, for only one single second. When they came back on the room was filled wall to wall with Unfortunates. A loud THHWANGGG, and

Jeb's body crumpled to the floor, a four inch gash on his head. Bob the fry cook, holding a heavy cast iron frying pan, stood over Jeb's lifeless body.

"Jeb!" Hank dropped Simon and took two half steps towards the old sheriff before Emma's cry of surprise drew him up short.

Emma, who was barely holding together cried, "Ophy!." She was so happy to see a familiar face, but as she moved closer, she realized Ophelia had the same black soulless salmon shark eyes as the others.

The Unfortunate who wore Ophelia like a second skin rolled her head at Emma and flashed her a sickly sweet smile. Oversized Frankenstein stitches circled her neckline.

Emma took a step backwards and noticed other townsfolk were there too; Bob the fry cook, Ophelia, and even Horatio, all with the same eyes and zipper-scarred faces.

Emma felt a hand on her shoulder as Hank yanked her behind him, backing them up along the bar.

Simon got up off the floor, brushing himself off, "Geez, Hank. Scare a guy why don't ya? Ya trying to break my arm?"

Simon and his small horde of Unfortunates, pressed in on them until they'd backed them up all the way into the main dining area by the big windows overlooking the bay.

Keeping her behind him, Hank raised his gun and pointed it at Simon's face.

Simon, if anything, appeared amused, and said calmly, "Hank, you've only got two bullets. One … two. We've got you outnumbered by…" Simon gazed around and then used his finger and started counting heads. Frustrated when he lost count he asked the Unfortunate standing silently beside him, "Hey, Horatio, how many people do you think we've got on our side."

The Unfortunate who was once Horatio, and still missing his mouth and nose, merely stared straight ahead, unresponsive.

Simon sighed, and shook his head and said to himself, "Not exactly the conversationalist." Tapping his finger with his chin he wondered aloud, "Now where was I?" His face brightened, "Oh, that's right," changing his voice to fit the dramatic mood, he said in a deep voice, "Now, Hank, we've got ya outnumbered fifty to one." His voice changed back to its original countenance once more, "Did you like that? Did you like the way I lowered my voice like that?"

Hank was too tired for games. Without anymore hesitation he squeezed the trigger and shot him two times in the chest.

The gunshots jerked Simon back for an instant. The Unfortunates behind him stopped their forward advance.

Simon stood back up. Brushing the bullet holes off him like they were bread crumbs. "Ouch. You know, Hank, that might've worked when we first met, but," he moved his eyes over to Emma, "your friend, the scarecrow man? He taught me a few things before he died a most horrible and gruesome death." Simon shivered uncontrollably at the thought of it. Hank suspected his revulsion an act. "Anyway, I'm a god now, so you probably should be nice to me." He hooked his thumb back behind him to the crowd of Unfortunates and added, "That is of course, unless you'd prefer to end up like them."

There was nowhere to run. Hank flipped his empty gun around in his hand and held it like a club. He'd go down fighting right to the end.

Behind him, Emma's gaze lingered over Jeb's seemingly lifeless body. She knew they wouldn't be far behind.

When she lifted her tired gaze, she spotted the large windows on the back wall overlooking the bay and could see boiling storm clouds rolling over choppy water. The clouds thickened, darkening the entire town.

Then, CLANG-CLANG-CLANG! The loud noise echoed through the diner without source.

Emma and Hank flinched. Simon gripped his head in pain, "Owww. What is that infernal noise!"

Simon doubled over, stumbling around in pain; the Unfortunates seemed frozen solid in his distraction.

A television flashed on overhead. The static cleared for a moment and Emma saw a woman with horn-rimmed glasses wearing a white lab coat. She gazed through the television as though she were peering into the room through a periscope. When she saw Emma and Hank staring back, she raised a finger to her lips shushing them.

The clanging noise died out, its ringing still echoing off the walls.

A moment of stillness and heavy breathing, and then the storm clouds unleashed their fury and hailstones began pelting the diner. It sounded like someone was throwing rocks against the windows. Dust fell loose from the ceiling fans as the roof rattled under the onslaught.

Hank saw fear in Simon's eyes and he asked him, "You're not doing this, are you?"

In answer Simon flinched when the building shook and moaned in the grip of battering winds. Windows suddenly popped out in the front entrance.

Jeb groaned, and Hank and Emma helped him to his feet. When Jeb became fully aware of his surroundings, the Unfortunates looming over them, he broke from their grasp in a panic and bolted for the door. The door handle wouldn't budge. Jeb gave it another yank, but instead of opening, the whole wall tore outwards and was swallowed by the storm.

"Jeb!" Hank shouted, but it was too late, the old sheriff was sucked out through the gaping hole like a torpedo. Emma screamed and Hank dragged her into a crouch as the pressure tugged at them.

One by one the Unfortunates were suctioned from their spots and into the swirling winds.

Hank stared out the open wall. It was pitch-black outside, he couldn't see a blasted thing. He heard a rumble, like an oncoming freight train, joined by multiple flashes of thick lightning. In those brief flashes of light he watched as the wind lifted their white SUV and tossed it almost the length of Main Street, and then, as though the car had realized it had left without them, it hung in the air and then bore back down on the diner.

"Get down!" Hank screamed. He dove on Emma and drove her to the ground as the flying SUV crashed over them and took the roof of the diner with it.

Still holding Emma, Hank clutched the counter's golden railing. Debris flew around the room, slicing into Hank's back as he shielded Emma's body with his own. Emma clung to his arm, holding on for her life as the building began crumbling away around them. She knew if she didn't hold on to him, she'd go away with the storm like Jeb did. Shards of sheetrock razored across Hank's face and wallboard and parts of the ceiling bounced off his shoulders. The pressure of the storm pushed down on their bodies, relentless in its power.

Simon had latched on to the railing beside them, hanging on beside Hank. "There's no place like home, there's no place like home," he chanted wildly at the top of his lungs. He moved closer to Hank and tried to pry Hank's fingers from the railing.

"Are you crazy?" Hank yelled back, but he already knew that answer.

Simon stopped for a moment, stared at him directly in the eye and said, "C'mon, Hank. Let's go together. It will be fun!" Then with that same ludicrous grin and wild-eyed stare, he abruptly let go of the railing, shot his arms straight out from his body and was sucked outside into the maelstrom.

"Top of the world, Ma!" he cried as he went.

The diner walls began to disintegrate around them. Hank and Emma heard the splintering of wood and popping of metal as everything but the floor disappeared. Hank glimpsed the mile wide funnel cloud as it raked overhead.

Both he and Emma's legs lifted from the floor.

"Hank, I can't hang on!"

Emma's fingers slipped from the railing.

"I've got you," Hank said, holding her with one hand, while the other held onto the railing with Herculean effort. If only he could hold on for a few seconds longer. If only...

Hank yelled, willing strength into his grip, but in the end it wasn't enough. It was never, ever enough.

Chapter 33

Welcome to Mt. Olympus

TIME MOVED SLOWLY, like ketchup pouring from a brand new bottle.

Hank McCarthy felt a strange bed beneath him. He tried forcing his eyes open, but his lids were far too heavy. He convulsed on the sheets as feeling returned to his limbs. With sheer willpower, he pried open his eyes.

"Hank, where are you?" his dead wife pleaded. "Please don't leave me."

His wife Sara melted away and was replaced with a familiar pain, in his temples.

The sound of whirring motors filled his ears.

Hank couldn't see the needles retracting from either side of his temples but he sure felt them.

"Hank. Wake up."

"Where am I?" he asked groggily, unsure if he wanted to know the answer.

"You're on Mt. Olympus."

Bleary eyed, he could see an angelic face hovering over him. He had thought it would have been called Heaven but judging by the angel's last statement, it seemed the Greeks had it right after all.

His vision finally cleared. The woman who hovered over him, although attractive, was far from a goddess.

She smiled down at him. "Hank, I'm Doctor Paula Burnett. Welcome back to the real world."

"I saw you in a dream," Hank said, his mouth swollen, temples throbbing, "You were on the train platform, just outside the town of HavenPort."

Her tone clinical, she answered, "That was no dream, Hank."

Struggling to order the questions framing in his mind, he took in the room around him; a modern looking hospital room. A technician who resembled Horatio, only far less attractive than the one he had known in HavenPort, was standing beside Dr. Burnett. In addition to being nerdier, and less fit, his body language seemed anxious about something. "He's been under for so long I doubt he'll be able to move."

Dr. Burnett turned her head over her shoulder and talked to Horatio as though Hank wasn't even there, "These hibernation beds are the new 112's, designed for long term coma patients and deep space flight. Besides keeping blood flowing, they exercise the muscle tissue to keep them from atrophying. He could be asleep in one for a year and still get up and walk out of here like he'd only been asleep eight hours."

Hank's body trembled uncontrollably. His mind was sluggish. He thought he heard them say something about people hibernating? Tired of being ignored he said, "I'm freezing."

Burnett didn't waver. "Don't worry, your core body temperature will return momentarily."

"I feel like crap."

Horatio scoffed. "You're lucky; the original procedure required cutting off the top of the skull and attaching dime-sized electrodes to the brain."

Well, that sounds unpleasant.

Burnett must've seen his discomfort for she explained further, "Don't let him scare you, Mr. McCarthy. We haven't used that prototype for years. The Halo nets are much less invasive."

Rubbing his temples he asked, "Then what were those needles?"

"Delivery system," this from Horatio. "We insert nanobots into your blood stream that are able to stimulate all cordial functions."

"I don't understand, where am I?"

"You're on Mt. Olympus," Dr. Burnett answered and attempted a warm smile; a cyborg probably would've had more success.

"Where?" he asked.

Dr. Burnett's tone sounded as though she had better things to do, but she explained to him anyway. "You were part of a trillion-dollar experimental program. Inserted into a computer generated artificial society where your mind was in a controlled and carefully monitored dreamlike state while your body was kept alive here, in cryonic suspension."

"Why," he groped for the words, "Why would you people do this?"

"It's a rehabilitation process for the criminally insane," Paula answered.

Hank scoffed. "I am not criminally insane. I am a cop for Pete's sake."

Horatio made a face. "Hank, you went on a shooting rampage in Wyoming and murdered five people. I think you qualify."

Surprisingly, it was the cold and collected Dr. Burnett who came to his aid and retorted, "After Russian mobsters and members of a corrupt sheriff's department murdered his family."

So that part was real; my family really is dead. And I shot those responsible. But that still doesn't explain how I got here.

Hank's memory of what happened in the simulated reality of HavenPort came flooding back to him. "Emma, Jeb, the doc, are they okay? Were they even real?"

"I'm just fine, Hank. Thanks for asking."

Hank lifted his gaze as Doc Clemens walked into the room. Unlike Horatio, who had appeared more like a supermodel in the artificial environment, the doc pretty much resembled his old, coffee-talk-buddy self.

"And yes, I'm real," he picked up a chart at the foot of Hank's bed and examined it. Satisfied with the results he handed it to Horatio who clipped it back to the bed for him. "Although many of the inhabitants you met in HavenPort were virtual people, others were patients like yourself, like Emma,

Jeb, and Odessa. Additionally, clinical psychologists, like Dr. Paula Burnett here, and Horatio, were also inserted into the Grid to offer you guidance, when needed."

The doc moved over to stand next to his bed and said, "But please remember that, while inside the grid, you were allowed to make your own choices."

"I still don't understand," Hank rasped, thrown by the doc's explanation.

"How much do you remember?" the doc asked.

"Not much, it's all a blur. I'm having trouble separating my real life from what happened in HavenPort."

"What's the last thing you remember before coming to HavenPort?"

Hank told them about the shootout at the Russian Wager Saloon.

"Hank, after that shootout you were incarcerated for ten years for killing the people responsible for murdering your family. Because of your exceptional circumstances, you were a perfect candidate for our experimental program. Someone we could prove was no longer a danger to society. You volunteered to have your memory wiped and be rehabilitated on the grid. You were constantly observed. If you performed well, and deemed no longer a threat to society, you would be released. And you did it. After treatment, when given the chance to make the same choice again, you made a different choice, the right choice. You are living proof that the system works."

"You're saying it was all an artificial dream. But how is that possible? I felt pain."

Horatio answered, "That's the mind and the memory. You burned yourself on the stove as a child. Your mind remembers that."

Paula explained further, "Just like in a nightmare there isn't a complete disconnect between the body and mind. When the terror is imagined in the brain, the heart races just as if the threat were real. In this manner the body is equally affected. This works on many levels."

As Hank struggled to take it all in, he recalled all those who had died. "Can you die in the grid?"

Hank watched as the three of doctors exchanged worried glances. "Originally no. But ever since the nano probe stage was introduced something's changed. We had several fatalities."

Horatio piped in, "And just last month we started having blackouts in the system."

Both the doc and Paula gave the younger man a hard stare. "Blackouts?" Hank asked.

"Everything patients do on the grid is recorded," Horatio explained. He seemed to be the guy with all the technical answers.

Burnett bobbed her head. "Then people started dying. One woman actually woke up, somehow snapped the needles off in the side of her head, found a scalpel, and sawed her hand off before we could stop her. We think she was sleep walking, but we can't really be sure. Another victim simply died in her sleep."

Hank remembered the crazy lady in the abandoned building he had met on his first day on the job.

"What happened?" he asked, and then added, "...to the system I mean."

The doc just kept studying him, Horatio was the first to answer. "To be honest, we just don't know. The original program was never meant to be so violent. HavenPort was meant to be a peaceful, isolated community."

Paula must've decided it was time to redirect because she quickly said, "Of course, as soon as we detected the malfunction, we decided to pull you and the other patients out of the grid."

Horatio, oblivious to Paula's frustration with him was eager to share, "Yeah, but there was a problem. For some reason we were unable to separate you all from the grid. After several failed attempts to literally scare you guys awake we finally just pulled you out. The tornado was my idea. What did you think?"

Forcing down his anger Hank asked, "Wouldn't it have been easier to just dunk us in a tub of water or something?"

Horatio's face went utterly serious. "The shock would've killed you."

Ignoring Horatio, Paula interjected, "Considering this was our first time out, and we had a thirty percent success rate, the board is still classifying the problems only as a minor glitch."

Dr. Clemens made a face that told Hank he suspected it was more than a technical glitch that was responsible, and Hank had a pretty good idea of what, or more specifically who, that glitch might be.

Fearing for her safety, Hank asked, "Emma? Is she out?"

"Yes, Hank. She's fine, and so are Odessa, Jeb, and all the other patients."

"Can I see them?" he asked.

"They're still in the recovery stages, and probably will be for the next twenty-four hours. Quite frankly, we're surprised you woke up so quickly."

Hank forced a nervous laugh, "I've always been a light sleeper." A sense of dread came over him when he realized no one had mentioned one particular person in the grid. He wasn't sure he wanted to know the answer but he asked anyway. "Was Simon real?"

Clearly, the question put them all at unease.

Finally, the doc turned towards Paula and Horatio and simply said, "Give us the room."

Paula took a breath. Biting back her words, and, after exchanging worried glances, the two younger doctors departed the room. The hierarchy was becoming pretty apparent to Hank.

Doc Clemens pulled a chair over and sat down beside Hank's bedside. "Hank, we chose each patient carefully to gain a wide range of the criminally insane. Emma killed her step father when she found out he had raped her stepsister to the point of suicide, Jeb went on a drunken shooting spree at a port, Odessa was addicted to cocaine from birth and shot an off duty police officer in a drug store robbery, and you murdered the ones responsible for killing your wife and children. We wanted to prove to the world each of you could be reintroduced to society. We wanted to give each of you your lives back."

Hank seriously doubted that the welfare of their patients was their honest intent. He decided to let it go for now, instead he asked, "Was Simon real?"

"Yes. The military made us put him in the program. I think they wanted to see if we could undo whatever they did to scramble him up in the first place." He said the next part as though more to himself. "What I don't think those idiot bureaucrats understand is that boy was long scrambled before even they got a hold of him."

The doc stared off into space as though reliving some horrible memory. Maybe it was when the Unfortunate under Simon's control buried an ax in his chest. Realizing Hank was watching him he said, "Perhaps we should pick this up at another time. You've had a pretty big day to say the least and this is all a lot to take in."

"Tell me," Hank said more forcefully than he intended.

The doc studied him carefully before continuing. "At one time, Simon Privet was a real man. Now I know all of this is a lot to take in but Simon died nearly four weeks ago. The man you encountered doesn't exist. In fact, we still can't explain his presence on the grid."

"Then what was he?" Hank asked. "Some kind of virus, an untethered consciousness still stuck in that place…?" *A demon*, Hank added in his mind but didn't dare say aloud for fear of the answer.

Doc shook his head. "Truth is, we don't rightly know." Deciding to change the subject for the better, he quickly patted him on the arm. "But the good news is that all of your suffering hasn't been for naught. I've already spoken to the review board. And, I shouldn't be telling you this, but they're recommending you for a full release. You're going to get your life back."

Memories of his long incarceration began to return in small waves. So much time, so much bitterness, emptiness. Could he really move on? Sarah and the kids were everything to him. According to what the doc was telling him that was over ten years ago.

The doc's knees cracked as he rose to his feet. "Get some rest, Hank. I'll be back in the morning and we can go over what comes next." And with a twinkle in his eye he added, "Maybe even have that talk over a morning cup of coffee."

As Hank watched the doc head for the door and put a hand on the light switch, he asked the one question that couldn't wait until morning. The one question that, if left unanswered, wouldn't let him get any sleep.

"Hey, Doc. What about Simon, where is his body now?"

"Don't worry, Hank. Simon Privet has been in a coma for over a month now. He is completely brain-dead. In fact, we just got the authorization from the military to pull him off life support and a military transport will come and pick up his remains tomorrow morning."

The doc was about to turn and leave but then added, "Not soon enough if you ask me."

Chapter 34

Wakey, Wakey, Rise and Shine

A SMALL HAND CLAMPED over Hank's mouth muffling his scream of surprise.

A harsh whisper, "Be quiet, or he might hear you."

Dr. Burnett's worried face combined with the flashing yellow lights in the darkened corridor outside his room was an immediate indicator that something was terribly wrong. The red hue of emergency lighting also told him someone, or something, had shut the power, and the emergency generators had kicked on.

"Hank, we're in trouble." Dr. Paula Burnett glanced down at him, and then across to Horatio, who was hovering nervously on the other side of the bed.

"We don't have time for this, he could be here any second," Horatio hissed.

"Everyone else is dead; you've got a better idea?" Paula shot back. "You saw what he did to Dr. Clemens."

Hank's heart sank. Just when he thought this nightmare was finally over.

"Emma and Jeb?" Hank asked, as Paula threw the sheets off him and tried to help him sit up.

"Both fine, but for how long, we don't know." That said, she grabbed a syringe, flicked it with a forefinger to remove any errant air bubbles and gave him a quick painful injection. "None of that matters right now because there's a psychopath on the loose in the facility. He's sealed us in with him. Everyone else is dead."

"Don't you people have security?" Hank asked incredulous. *Is this really happening all over again?*

"They're dead." Horatio exclaimed in a shrill voice.

Instinctively Hank knew who the perpetrator was, but he asked anyway. "Simon Privet?"

They stared at him as if surprised that he'd already known somehow.

"I thought you said he was dead?" Hank growled.

Horatio bobbed his head up and down. "He should have been. His brain was dead. But then the moment we pulled him off life support he woke up."

Hank cursed. Why was he surprised? He knew this was going to happen. Thinking quickly he asked, "Who is this guy, I mean really?"

"We think he was former CIA."

"You don't know?" Hank asked.

Horatio fielded his question by answering, "The military wasn't exactly forthcoming when it came to his job description. But I'm pretty sure he didn't work in administration."

Paula added, "Hank, we can't read your minds, or enter your dreams, it's not like that. We can only observe your actions on the mainframe."

Hank tried to get out of bed. He swung his legs over the side, felt them shake violently as he tried standing on them, and then dropped to the floor. The pain was excruciating. It felt as though every single muscle was cramped up into a charley horse.

When he cried out in anguish, Horatio exclaimed in a nervous whisper, "Quiet, quiet. He'll hear you."

Paula knelt next to him and rested a hand on his shoulder. "Your muscles will come back in a moment. I've given you a stimulant to speed up the process. Just sit back and wait for the drugs to take effect." She removed a 9mm pistol from her lab coat pocket. "I took this off one of the dead security guards," she explained, pressing it into his weakened palm.

When he flashed her a look of confusion Paula explained, "I've never even held a gun before today."

Summoning what little strength he had, Hank checked the pistol for ammo and confirmed that it had a round in the chamber. As he did so, he detected a burnt smell from the barrel, indicating the pistol had recently been fired. The pistol was only missing a few rounds so he slammed the clip home.

Horatio, after checking the corridor for the thirteenth time, said to Paula in frightened hushed tones, "I told you this was a waste of time. We should've just left when we had the chance."

"Simon is former CIA. He's obviously a highly trained assassin. When was the last time you ever even fired a gun?"

"Hey, I shot one on the range, once," Horatio protested.

"Really?" Burnett interjected firmly. "At a target five yards away that wasn't moving?"

Horatio's face sank, and he stared at Hank blankly before turning away.

"Thought so," Burnett said. "No. We need to fight fire with fire. No way am I ending up like Dr. Clemens. Hank here's our best chance of getting us out of here."

"And you think a sheriff of some podunk town is going to be much better?"

"As usual, you didn't read the patient's entire file. Before he went into law enforcement Sheriff McCarthy was a U.S. Marine. If anyone can take on that psychopath Privet and get us out of here alive, it's him."

"Ummm, I'm just a podunk sheriff from Wyoming," he began, staring accusingly at Horatio. "So you might want to dumb it down for me, but you want me to kill Simon, when killing is what got me sent here in the first place?"

The irony was not lost on him.

Horatio didn't seem to hear him, instead he was staring at Hank's partially naked form. "Maybe we should get him some clothes."

Paula rolled her eyes, "I concur," she said and handed Hank a pair of scrubs she stole from a nearby drawer.

Hank slipped into the clothes slowly, barely able to move. Everything hurt so much. He could only hope Simon was having equal difficulty moving or they were all finished.

The amber emergency lights flickered, went out, and came back on red. Now the room and hallway outside was even darker than before.

Horatio glanced through the window to check the hallway again. "C'mon. We should go," Horatio whispered as he stepped into the hallway. "I'm not big on the idea of having my head being mounted on a broomstick."

"Horatio, wait, don't be in such a hurry," Hank said, but it was too late.

Showing no initial signs of being unbalanced whatsoever, Simon suddenly jumped from the shadows to land behind Horatio and bashed the young doctor over the head with something heavy. Hank winced from the sound, and before his sluggish body could react, Simon dashed away, sliding back into the darkness.

Grabbing the pistol from the bed and holding it towards the door, Hank pulled Dr. Burnett behind him. He then grabbed Horatio by his outstretched leg and dragged him back into the room.

Dr. Burnett bent down over Horatio and checked his pulse. He was still breathing but his skull was bashed pretty bad.

A voice from the darkness. It was singing. "Hanky-Hankey, wakey-wakey."

Wobbly, Hank could barely carry himself toward the doorway a second time. Before he could pass through it, Simon stepped from the shadows.

Simon was covered in blood. But now he appeared unbalanced enough that he had to lean against the doorframe. His eyelids were shut as he spoke and his head lolled forward as his hands came up to rub his temples. He was breathing heavily and appeared to be doing his best not to throw up. Hank also noted the pinprick holes that leaked blood on either side of his head.

Seeing the blood stained scalpel clenched in Simon's hand Hank raised the handgun with forced vigor and held it aimed squarely at Simon's face. "You know I won't miss at this range."

When Simon opened his eyes at him they were half-dead, drowning in a mass of pain and confusion. "I wouldn't want you to, Hank," he muttered in a tone drowning in defeat. "But then that pesky conscience of yours always gets in the way."

"You wanna bet on that this time?"

"Oh I wouldn't worry yourself, Hank." Simon said, grinning now, the expression worn and haggard where it once beamed. He raised a tired arm and pulled Emma out of the darkened hallway and over to his side. "Because I brought a date."

Of course it was Emma. She appeared even more sluggish than Simon and had the same bloody pinpricks at her temples; her scrubs were soaked crimson.

"What did you do to her?" Hank growled when he saw the blood, but even as he said it he realized it wasn't her blood. It was Simon's. He had slit his own wrists and was rapidly bleeding out.

"Simon, what the hell is wrong with you?"

Simon flinched at his words. "You really don't have any idea of what's going on, do you, Hanky-Pankey?" He pointed his scalpel at Paula. "You still think they're the ones pulling the strings?" His voice rose in anger, "They're not even real, Hank!" then more to himself he added, "I swear, you can be so dense sometimes."

Hank considered Simon's words for a moment. Could all of this be an illusion too? How could he possibly know?

A small whimper escaped Emma's lips and brought him back to the task at hand. "Let her go, Simon. I mean it."

"Nuh-uh, you'll just have to kill me." Simon shook his head and kept raising his scalpel to Emma's throat. "Are you really going to make me kill her, Hank?" He managed a small, knowing, apologetic tilt of his head. "Oh well." He began to draw the blade across her neck.

Hank squeezed the trigger.

The shot hit Simon in his exposed shoulder. He spun in the air, Emma tumbling out of his arms before he thudded to the floor in the hallway.

Emma crumpled to her knees but managed to slow her own descent by using the doorframe.

Still covering Simon with his gun, Hank knelt beside her. "Emma, you okay?"

Emma concentrated hard. She studied him curiously, her eyes pleading. She swallowed hard and then asked, "Where are we?"

Hank managed a quick smile. "That's going to take a lot of serious explaining."

"Hank," a weak tired voice said from the shadows.

Simon lay in a heap, his head canted at an odd angle as his body landed crammed up against the wall. Hank pitied him. He no longer thought of Simon as the man who murdered his family and friends, but a pawn, like him, in the psychologists twisted and experimental nightmare.

As Simon lay there dying he waved him closer with a weak hand.

"Don't go near him, Hank." Dr. Burnett warned from behind him.

Hank frowned back at her.

Spying Simon's dropped scalpel, he kicked it down the hall for good measure. He then moved over to Simon and knelt down beside him. Simon could barely speak, and with a feeble hand, waved Hank even closer.

Hank leaned his ear close to Simon's mouth.

With his dying breath Simon whispered, "What amazes me the most, Hank, is you still think this is all real."

And then Simon Privet died.

Hank tucked the gun in his waistband and then helped Emma up. As feeling returned to her limbs she began to straighten. He slung her arm over his shoulders and half carried her toward the exit.

Paula shouted after him. "Hank, stop. Where are you going?"

Hank felt an upwell of anger inside him. "I'm getting us the hell out of here. We're done being your lab rats."

He opened the door and was blinded by a brilliant white light.

Chapter 35

Dead Reckoning

"**WELCOME ABOARD THE HMS** Explorer World Cruise!"

The resounding pain of the cruise ship's horn still lingered in Hank's ears. His body trembled violently for a few seconds while he emerged from his deep slumber. It took him another moment to realize where he was, standing on a gangplank boarding a ... a cruiseship?

Where am I?

A light touch on his shoulder revealed creamy white, French-manicured fingers. Their owner lovely: Almond-shaped eyes, perfect white teeth, and curly nutmeg hair framing a face that would make even a fairytale princess envious. His wife, Sarah. She was shuffling up the gangplank behind him.

"Wow, babe," she laughed nervously. "I knew you were tired but you were really out of it there."

Hank's throat was so dry his tongue had swelled two sizes. When he finally managed to talk it was barely above a hoarse whisper. "Honey, where are we?" He wanted to scream the question at her. The whisper was all he could manage.

"Hurry up, Daddy, hurry up?" He lowered his gaze and saw his daughter, sweet Annabelle tugging on his hand.

"Patience sweetheart," Sarah answered for him. "We have to wait in line like everyone else."

"But I'm so-o hungry," Annabelle complained.

"Have some more Goldfishes, honey," Sarah answered. Without missing a beat the box came out of her purse, and with two quick shakes Annabelle beheld the delicious golden baked treats in her small hands.

His son was still snoozing soundly in the kid carrier upon his back.

Hank took this all in, but none of it answered the question that still burned in his aching head: *Where the hell am I?*

He peered at the people in the port around him. The port was a bustle of activity as a thousand passengers waited in line to board the majestic cruise ship at the dock.

When did we decide to take a cruise? This didn't make a lick of sense.

"Look Mommy, look!" Annabelle yelled wildly beside him. "A seal, Mommy, a seal!"

Hank turned his head and groaned at the stabbing pain in his temples. He rubbed at them: If his hand wasn't already there, he'd have thought he'd been stabbed on both sides of his head with an ice pick.

Must've slept wrong.

"Oh Hank, she's right." Sarah cooed beside him. "There's a seal in the water over there."

Just beyond the end of the dock he could make out a seal frolicking in the bay.

The line started moving again and Hank suppressed the urge to throw the overweight passenger plodding in front of him over the railing. The guy had the height and build of a former WWF wrestler who had let himself go about a decade ago. And if he was moving any slower he'd be moving backwards. When the rollers of his equally oversized luggage got stuck in-between the floorboards of the gangplank, Hank instinctively lent a hand and lifted the errant wheels out of the cracks for him.

The guy turned around to see who had grabbed his luggage. He sported a bushy walrus mustache and a grey comb-over that barely covered his baldness. His face and neck were unshaven by at least several days. When he muttered a word of thanks, Hank could see a mouth full of crooked, tobacco-stained teeth. This was a man who stopped caring about his job, his life, and personal hygiene a long time ago.

Sarah tapped him on his shoulder. "Do you see him?" Before he could answer, she dug frantically through her mommy purse the size of a saddlebag. "Now where's my camera?" To their daughter she said, "Annabelle, honey, do you know where mommy's camera is?"

This doesn't make sense. We live in Wyoming. I don't even remember deciding to take a cruise, let alone driving to the port.

A cheery voice at a podium located at the top of the gangway suddenly announced, "Okay, whose next?"

The cruise director at the podium was a short, middle-aged, cherubic woman, plump as she was cheerful. Hank thought he detected a Canadian accent. He could just make out her nametag.

Ophy, what an odd name.

And the young woman she was talking to had the lithe form of a dancer. The way she was gazing around at her surroundings with uncertainty, she appeared as dazed and confused as he was.

Spotting the girl, the cruise director said, "Ah, you must be Emma Hudson. It's not often we get a New York City Ballet dancer on board. I'm sure you're going to enjoy working with the entertainment department."

"Oh, bag boy!" the cruise ship director called, practically yelling. A luggage handler appeared as she commanded, "Please help Mrs. Hudson carry her bags to her room."

The luggage handler was an oversized man dressed in overalls and a baseball cap, with big meaty hands. Baggage handler and ballet dancer entered into the dark corridor behind the podium and vanished into bowels of the ship. Although he couldn't explain it, Hank was fairly certain he didn't want to follow them.

A second luggage handler appeared and stretched out his scrawny arm towards him. "Allow me sir," the handler said.

Hank studied the porter. Although he couldn't place him, there was something oddly familiar about the guy.

The man was hardly threatening, little more than 5'9" and impossibly lean, like a marathon runner. In fact, there wasn't an ounce of body fat on him. An emaciated athlete would have been a good way to describe him. But that wasn't the strangest thing about the lean porter. The strangest thing about him was the creepy smile upon the guy's face. It reminded Hank of the jack-o'-lanterns he had carved on Halloween; the same wide, toothy grin with firelight flickering behind the eyes.

"Thanks," was all Hank could manage, handing over his bags, his mind in a fog.

Before letting go of his luggage completely however; Hank asked him. "Hey buddy. Do I know you?"

The luggage handler thought seriously about this for a moment before answering, "Why, I don't think so, sir."

Hank stood there, forehead sweating despite the brisk morning air. He finally let go of the bags. "Thanks," he said a second time.

The luggage handler flashed him another creepy mischievous grin and replied, "You are most welcome sir." He was about to turn away and lead them into the ship, but he stopped in his tracks and said back to Hank. "You know, I think you, and your family, are going to absolutely love it here."

—— <> ——

Afterword

I FIRST VISITED the little seaside town of Whittier when the only way in or out of the town was to drive your car up a dirt ramp and onto flatbed train cars. The train would then take you through an awesome three-mile tunnel through solid rock and into the town.

Much like the town in the novel, the town is cut off from the rest of the world by a crown of impassable mountains. And other than the tunnel, the only way in or out is by port or small plane airport.

The former military base and much of the town actually exists to this day and is still worth a visit. You can't go inside the old WWII military base because it is off limits and boarded up. As illustrated in the novel, it is also extremely unsafe. As you might've guessed from my detailed descriptions of the building's interiors, I may have peeked inside a time or two.

The funny thing about using this town for a setting was I actually composed a letter to one of my favorite authors, Stephen King, telling him about this creepy little town that might make the perfect setting for one of his future books. Needless to say, I'm glad I never sent it (mainly because I thought he'd never read it). Although I am certain I would've thoroughly enjoyed the novel if he had written it instead.

As for the title, I blame my mentor, Dr. J.P. Waller for that one. He once introduced me to the painting mentioned in the book: William Hogarth's 18th century painting of London's celebrated mental hospital, The Bethlehem Royal Hospital, more derisively known as Bedlam. The literal definition of Bedlam is "uproar and confusion." Hogarth's masterful Bedlam painting depicts mentally ill patients on cruel display for the upper class's sheer amusement.

As for the ending of Bedlam. Well, you might be interested to know that I actually wrote three endings. I let my Beta-readers make the final decision. Ironically, the two Beta-readers who can never agree on anything, (Charlsie and Ryan, you know who you are) actually picked the same ending and were extremely vocal about it.

As for a sequel, that really depends on you, my dear readers. If you liked Bedlam, be sure and drop me a line either on Facebook (Author Jack Castle), or on my website (JackCastleBooks.com).

As always, I hope you enjoyed reading these stories as much as I did writing them.

Until next time...

— *Jack Castle*

If you enjoyed this read

Please leave a review on Amazon, Facebook, Good Reads or Instagram.

It takes less than five minutes and it really does make a difference.

If you're not sure how to leave a review on Amazon:

1. *Go to amazon.com.*

2. *Type in Bedlam Lost by Jack Castle and when you see it, click on it.*

3. *Scroll down to Customer Reviews, nearby you'll see a box labeled Write a Review. Click it.*

4. *Now, if you've never written a review before on Amazon, they might ask you to create a name for yourself.*

5. *Reviews can be as simple as, "Loved the book! Can't wait for the Next!" (Please don't give the story away.)*

And that's it!

Brian Hades, publisher

Books by Jack Castle

Europa Journal

Bedlam Lost

White Death

*Here's a sneak peek at other novels by
real life adventurer Jack Castle*

White Death
Prologue
"Iditarod Dad"

Unless you're the lead dog, the view never changes. *Har-har-har.*

These were the thoughts of Tom Holden as he stared at the rumps of his dog sled team. He was running the Iditarod Trail Sled Dog Race in Alaska, traveling through 1,149 miles of the most rugged and cruel landscape of the Last Frontier … and he was in last place.

Holden had never had any illusions about winning. In fact, it surprised him he had made it this far over the harsh tundra, through the jagged mountain passes, and across deadly rivers of ice. He wasn't a professional musher, not by a long shot. In fact, the only reason he was running this ridiculous test of endurance was the locket hanging around his neck. Inside was a picture of his beautiful nineteen-year-old daughter, Shannon. The picture had been taken before the spinal meningitis did its job and she wasted away before his eyes. These were Shannon's dogs, not his. Shannon had raised them from pups and trained them. Her dying wish had been that he run her dogs in the Iditarod race. She told him he didn't have to win or anything. "Just run 'em, dad, run 'em for me." Now, he wasn't a musher, but he had helped Shannon train her dogs enough to know what he was doing, and he was damned if he was going to let his little girl down, even if it killed him.

Like every year, print and television journalists, along with crowds of spectators, attended the various checkpoints along the trail. Somehow, word had gotten out about why he was running the race, and the reporters swelled in number at each checkpoint. At the Skwentna checkpoint, it had been the worst. Three-time Iditarod champions were rudely ignored when he had finally sledded into town. It seemed the world couldn't get enough of a father trying to fulfill his daughter's dying wish. At least the press had put a nice photo of Shannon in the paper. That had made Shannon's mother happy, which she hadn't been for some time.

The trail from the ceremonial start in Anchorage had started out easy enough, sledding over low flat lowlands, and well marked by flags and reflectors. But from there the trail had gotten pretty tough, so much so that mushers started dropping out of the race at a rate of about one every seventy-five miles.

The race had started with forty-two mushers, each with approximately sixteen dogs, but one musher broke her hand right outside of Willow, and another had three of his dogs trampled by a charging moose in "Moose Alley." Another nine teams had dropped out in a fierce blizzard that had struck them in McGrath. That storm had caused whiteout conditions and sub-zero temperatures. Plus, the gale force winds had erased all the trail markers, making the path hard to follow, but Shannon had programed his GPS, and he had weathered the storm just fine. Shannon had also made sure her dad had all the right gear: food, spare dog booties, headlamps, tools, sled parts for repairs, and spare batteries for his night headlamp, and even a satellite phone. They had made the final preparations for his trip in her hospital room, spreading out maps on the foot of her bed. Shannon had made him study the route as carefully as he had scrutinized maps on missions in Afghanistan as a younger man over twenty years before. The trip planning had become a welcome relief from the constant reminder of her imminent departure.

Holden took small comfort in the fact that he was past the worst stretch of the trail, the Dalzell Gorge, a divide that drops one thousand feet in elevation in five miles. Holden had had to ride the brake most of the way down and sometimes use his snow hook for traction. At the bottom of the gorge, one musher had fallen through an ice bridge and had to be airlifted out, bringing the total mushers left in the race to just thirty. But all of them were more experienced than Holden, so if by some miracle Holden did finish, he knew he was a shoe in for the Red Lantern award.

The banks of the trail were lined with snow-covered alders; quarter-sized snowflakes fell from the sky. For most, the wilderness was inspiring, but Holden felt this portion of the trail was long miles of vast emptiness, and his tired muscles ached for a couple of hours of bunking down at the next checkpoint.

After what seemed like an eternity, the narrow corridor through the woods finally began to widen. As the trees became sparser, Holden could make out a huge bonfire in the town up ahead. He knew from Shannon's meticulous tutorial that the next checkpoint would be the ghost town of Takotna, a real commercial hub during Alaska's gold rush days but now, with the exception of Iditarod week, practically a ghost town.

Already he was dreading the host of reporters that would be there to greet him. All he wanted to do was feed his dogs and lie down for some rest, but he'd talk to the reporters for Shannon's sake, and for her mother's.

The bonfire seemed bigger than the others, but as the trail broadened into an open field before him, Holden realized … it wasn't a bonfire that was burning.

It was the town. ⸺ <> ⸺

Holden pulled on the reins, kicked the brake, and brought his team to a stop. He dropped his snow hook for good measure and dismounted the sled in disbelief.

He yanked off his snow mitts and dropped them on the sled, a decision he would come to regret later. As he raised his goggles onto his forehead, he noted that not all the buildings were on fire. The big buildings on the corners were ablaze, but thus far the remainder of the abandoned town was still unscathed. And thanks to the wet snow, the fires were steadily dying out on their own with minimal risk of spreading.

Where the hell is everybody?

The place should've been swarming with reporters, mushers, and invaluable support personnel. Now, there wasn't a soul to be found. Before venturing deeper into the old town, he noted the dogs were sniffing the air as though their noses were detecting something unfamiliar. Normally, they would be barking with excitement and pulling at their tethers to be free. It was these kinds of observations that had kept him and his squad alive overseas.

Holden began searching the old buildings and saw dropped belongings: backpacks, cameras, clothes, all lying in the middle of the street, where the reporters and spectators must have dropped them. Passing the burning buildings, he approached the tiny Main Street located between two rows of dilapidated buildings. Immediately apparent was a large orange Buick in the middle of the street. The left blinker was flashing and the door was wide open. He could hear the engine still chugging and see vapor puffing out the tailpipe. Whatever had happened here, it couldn't have been more than a couple of hours ago.

As he rounded the Buick's trunk, he glanced down and noticed red stains on the snow. The streaks of blood originated from the open car door. They scratched across the powdery snow in the direction of one of the dilapidated buildings, a rickety wooden structure labeled HARDWARE STORE, only most of the letters were partially illegible from neglect. The funny thing was that the blood trails didn't go inside the slanted broken doorway but up the sides of the wallboards and up onto the tin roof. Holden had hiked through the woods enough to know bears were more than capable of climbing trees, but could they climb up the side of walls?

It was common for mushers to suffer from sleep deprivation and to experience hallucinations, but Holden had survived Ranger school, one of the toughest combat courses in the world. Even though that had been twenty years ago, and the Iditarod had been grueling, he didn't think he was seeing things now.

Although rare, it wasn't unheard of for a hibernating bear to wake up hungry during winter because it hadn't stored up enough fat in the fall, but what kind of bear could drag a human being up the side of a building? Holden decided he didn't want to find out. He suddenly became painfully aware that he had left his satellite phone and his own little addition to the expedition, a Taurus Model 44, back on the dogsled.

Damn, rookie mistake. Former Ranger, my butt.

He spun on his heel to trek back to his sled to retrieve both weapon and phone when he heard a woman cry out, "Please help me!" The voice was followed by a desperate shriek that came from inside the hardware store.

Staggering out of the darkness of the slanted doorway was a young woman who couldn't have been much older than Shannon. Half the woman's clothes had been torn away, and she was missing one boot. Her hand was outstretched towards him while the other held onto her stomach. Holden had seen enough combat wounds to recognize the squishy blue tentacles leaking out of her abdomen. Something had eviscerated this poor girl and left her to die.

"Oh, thank God, please help me!" she cried, taking two steps towards him.

Every fiber in his being told him to run for the phone and gun, but he also knew he could never leave this young girl behind to die.

Hesitating only seconds, he started towards her. She managed another step before falling to her knees and then collapsing onto her face.

When he reached her, Holden dropped down onto his knees beside her. "Don't worry. I've got you. You're going to be okay." It was a lie, but he had to say something.

The young woman lost consciousness. Realizing that time was a luxury he did not have, he quickly began removing the small first aid kit he kept on his belt. But in the few seconds it took him to turn away to unzip the kit, something in the hardware store reached out of the shadows, grabbed the young woman by her ankles, and dragged her back inside with such tremendous force that Holden fell backwards.

"Holy crap!" He hadn't seen what had snatched the young woman. It had happened in seconds. He contemplated going into the darkened interior after her, but then he heard a loud rumble emanating deep within the chest of something very large and very pissed off.

The girl must've woken up because Holden heard a loud scream within. This was cut off almost immediately by a menacing growl and sickening powerful CRUNCH. Experience had taught Holden that the silence that followed such horrific sounds was a sure sign he needed to get the hell out of there.

Holden ran. He passed the Buick with the blinking tail light, skidded around the now smoldering buildings, and bolted for his dog sled.

The dogs were going nuts. They weren't barking; they were whining. The majority pulled sharply against the snow hook, but some were trying to bite right through the tethers.

Holden was only a few feet from the dog sled when he saw his dropped anchor wiggling loose from the ice. The dogs pulled in unison, and with the next pull they would be free. Not only were the phone and gun in the sled, but he'd be stranded here with whatever had killed the girl and destroyed the town.

Holden increased what little speed he could and dove for the sled. Desperate, he flung himself forward and slid the remainder of the distance across the ice and managed to grab the anchor's rope. At that exact moment, the dogs pulled the anchor free and bolted for the trail. The rope burned quickly through his hands, and he cried out as the anchor split open his palm.

Gripping his bloody hand, Holden managed to stumble to his feet. He could only watch as his dog team, along with his gun and phone, vanished quickly down the trail.

WHUMP.

Something the size of a small car landed in the snow behind him. Holden had never been the type to freeze in combat, but he wasn't entirely sure he wanted to see what had snatched the poor young girl at the hardware store.

He heard a loud crunch of snow underfoot as whatever it was took a step behind him. Instinctively he knew that if he ran, he wouldn't get more than a few feet.

Summoning his courage, he spun around swiftly.

Holden didn't see the animal in its entirety. He only glimpsed the clawed hand that struck him so hard that his upper torso snapped around to face the woods behind him, splitting his spinal cord in half in an instant.

Tom Holden's broken body crumpled to the snow. He felt the cold of ice under his ruined face, and tasted the acrid blood in his mouth.

His last thoughts were of his daughter and how soon he would be seeing her again.

—— <> ——

For more on White Death visit:
tinyurl.com/edge6015

Europa Journal
Chapter 1
Final Descent

Twinkling stars pinpricked the stark lavender sky and watched like spectators as one of their own arced gracefully across the darkening hemisphere and fell from the heavens.

The U.C.P. deep space transport plummeted from the upper atmosphere on its own decaying path; it slowly and delicately began to glow, its color changing from off-white to rich gold. The glorious blaze expanded into a burning sphere that resembled a shooting star.

Flames and sparks trailed from every engine and wing. Heat-shielding plates flew off the underbelly by the dozens as the space transport began breaking up, a thousand-mile-long jet stream of clouds and debris in its wake. The nosecone began to crumple under the onslaught of the burning winds. Unbelievably, the occupants in the cockpit still fought for their survival.

—— o ——

"MWAAP … MWAAP … MWAAP … Crashing! Crashing! Switch to manual!" the crash program's computer voice announced. After a moment's pause, it repeated the warning, as if the shuddering cockpit, bleating Klaxon, and flames shooting past the forward windshield weren't enough.

"Really, no kidding," Mission Commander MacKenzie O'Bryant, 'Mac' for short, replied to no one in particular. Behind the navigation console, she struggled to keep the quivering *Explorer II* from nosing over and pinning her crew beneath the flaming wreckage.

Out of the corner of her eye, Mac saw the young pilot on her right examining the gauges that screamed for his attention. 'Lt. L. Dalton' was stencilled over the right breast pocket of his uniform, a Canadian flag patch sewn onto the left shoulder. His expression betrayed his growing disgust as highly unacceptable readings came back on the console before him. "Vertical descent — one hundred and twenty-five thousand. No, wait: one hundred and sixty-five thousand — no, twenty-four thousand."

"Which is it, Leo? Twenty or sixty?" Mac asked. *It was a pretty big difference.* Mac wore an American flag on the shoulder of her jumpsuit, as if her Southern accent itself wasn't indicative of her roots.

While she waited for Leo's reply, the few seconds seeming like hours, Mac cast a quick glance at the monitor displaying their three payload passengers who were located one deck below.

Not surprisingly, the three battle-hardened commandos' stolid faces were the epitome of calm. Sure, as their bodies were crushed by g-force, their fists clenched to their seats, and their eyes fluttered and rolled back in their heads, but if they had any idea how bad the situation was, as she suspected they did, they should have been screaming. These men were professionals, the best of the best; they knew that they could do nothing to help, so they resigned themselves to their fate and placed their lives in her hands.

Mac wasn't about to let them down.

"I don't know. It keeps jumping back and forth between the two; I can't get a proper altitude reading. First it's in the twenties and then the sixties," Leo replied, banging on the side of the console. "Wait a minute. There it goes: one hundred and twenty thousand."

But Mac didn't need an altitude reading to know that the ground was coming up much too fast. Passing through the atmosphere the ship had been engulfed in flames, blocking their view, but now that they had finished dropping through a thin layer of clouds, she saw a landmass, one that looked like a big island or a small continent. It came into view a mere 100,000 feet below them.

Mac frowned at her monitor, touched a button, and pulled back on the control column with even more fervor. If she didn't get the nose up, the ship would go into a spin, and if that happened at this speed, they would be finished.

Displayed on the monitor was the image of a Korean man sitting at the flight engineer's station. He announced, "Number two and four anti-gravity generators are still off line." To Leo, he added, "I told you. I told you not to touch it, but you wouldn't listen." Mocking Leo's voice, he said, "Why? What's the worst that could happen?" Nearly hysterical, he replied in his own voice, "Well, we found out didn't we?"

Mac wasn't quite sure what had led up to this latest predicament, but it was pretty clear that her flight engineer felt Leo was somehow responsible.

"Hey," Leo shot back, "I didn't see you doing anything to help."

"Give me an EC pressure reading," Mac shouted to the flight engineer, cutting their argument short.

"EC's in the pike, five-by-five," Tae called forward. It was the first good news she'd heard in the last six minutes.

Of course, Commander O'Bryant had trained for landing a ship after engines failed following shuttle launch. She had even trained to land a malfunctioning transport in Jupiter's infamous gravity well. But no training simulation in the known galaxy could have prepared her for landing a crippled space shuttle on a planet that had never been seen before by human eyes. Deep space travel was a breeze; it was atmospheric landings that caused the majority of shuttle pilot fatalities. As if the situation weren't bad enough, the *Explorer II* hadn't been designed to land under Earth-type gravity conditions.

Still miles above the planet, Mac saw a panorama of mountains coming into view below them. The range of white, snowy peaks was cast in pitch-black shadows and graced by a glint of the departing sun. In a way, it was kind of pretty. *A nice little spot for their final resting place.* No, she couldn't think like that. She had to remain focused, stay positive.

"I have a visual line of sight," Leo announced.

"I can see that," Mac spat back, her tone tense. She didn't dare look away from the landmass filling the cockpit windows, as if her will to keep the vessel aloft might waver the moment she looked away.

"Correct course ten degrees up, four minutes right," Leo offered, monitoring the gauges.

Mac complied with his directions and was rewarded with a reduction in the maelstrom of bouncing winds and heavily quivering bulkhead. The ship, her ship, was finally beginning to ease.

"There, that's a bit better. Try and hold it there if you can," Leo added.

Impossibly, she and her flight crew were pulling it off. She felt her descending ship finally leveling out. There was actually a chance they were going to make it. Barring an extraterrestrial downdraft or some other unpredictable off-world catastrophe. If there was an Order to the Universe, by God, they were going to make it.

But just then, the opposite balance of the universe, the part that some call Chaos, dealt his nasty hand. A panel of circuitry in the molded helm console before Mac sparked several times in quick succession and exploded, enveloping her hands and face in a blazing inferno.

—— o ——

"Oh, geez!" Lt. Leo Dalton didn't miss a beat and grasped his own set of controls the moment the panel erupted in his mission commander's face. He risked a glimpse at her. She was slumped in her harness, burn marks on her cheeks and hands. He was unsure whether she was dead or unconscious, but one thing was for sure: it was up to him to land the spacecraft and up to him alone. *Oh yeah, and Tae.*

The ship suddenly jumped upward, as though in a reverse air pocket, and then resumed its hair-raising descent.

"Did a thruster just fall off?" Leo asked incredulously.

"Yup," Tae replied matter-of-factly. "That's okay. That one wasn't working anyway."

"I'm losing hydraulics," Leo yelled back over his shoulder. He saw a yellow tongue of flame burst from the avionics bay and light up the nosecone like the end of a sparkler on Canada Day.

"That's because everything is on fire," Tae shouted up to him. "That last explosion knocked out another one of the anti-gravity generators."

"Well, put the fires out," Leo ordered through clenched teeth.

Tae flicked a switch and the WHOOSH of the interior cabin fire extinguishers, which were embedded in the fuselage, doused everything and everyone in thick chemical foam.

"Fires' out," Tae said dryly.

No hydraulic system meant no flaps and no brakes, but Leo doubted the ship would hold together long enough to reach the surface, let alone land in a manner that required brakes. *One problem at a time, Leo, one problem at a time.*

"Aw, geez. Terrain's crap," Leo said, but then he spotted a flat, open area just beyond a wide range of mountains. He maneuvered the crippled ship with what little controls he still had and aimed for the large plateau. "I'm going to try and spiral us in toward that mesa as best I can."

The ship entered its final approach and Leo guided the *Explorer II* through a crest of mountains, fighting crosswinds and protesting gusts the entire way. Only a miracle prevented a rock wall from ending their glide path in an abrupt and squishy stop.

Sixty seconds before impact, Leo and Tae could just make out trees peppering the snow-coated peaks.

Ten seconds before impact, the trees and mountains parted like the Red Sea before Moses and revealed the large, flat mesa that Leo had seen from over a mile away.

"Flat land, five degrees right!" Tae shouted.

"I see it; I see it," Leo replied grimly. He was so focused on coaxing the helm controls and maneuvering the falling ship in a do-or-die, wheels-up approach that his voice was nearly inaudible.

The last of the trees vanished, and the snow-covered mesa rose quickly up in greeting. "Wheels unresponsive. I'm going to have to put her down on her belly."

"Six hundred feet and dropping," Tae announced as he focused on the altimeter. "Five, four, three, two, here we go!" The hull vibrated and there was a deafening crash as the ship's metal frame and the planet's unyielding, jagged surface clapped together in unison: one, two, three times. The windows shattered on impact and blasted the exposed skin of the cockpit's occupants with frigid air and thousands of tiny shards of glass.

The ship settled down in a heavy power slide through the snow. "Deploy chutes!" Leo shouted.

"Deploying emergency drag chutes," Tae replied. The deployment of the quadruple chutes threw both men forward in their harnesses.

Leo strangled the flight controls, feeling helpless as the ship slid for what seemed like an eternity. In actuality, it was little more than a half mile until the *Explorer II* finally came to a clumsy, unceremonious stop.

Aside from the sound of Tae purging the last of the fire extinguishers onto the numerous sparking and burning consoles, the only audible sound was the arctic wind rushing through the broken cockpit windshield. *At least we're on the surface.*

Leo was the first to say anything, and as it was, he meant it only for himself. "I did it." It was all his trembling lips could manage.

He stared blank-faced out the windshield. A pile of snow was gathering around the windows and spilling inside, but he no longer saw mountains or trees, only open sky. *That's strange,* Leo thought. *The ship feels level, so I should see something besides open air.* Before he could investigate further, a slight groan from Commander O'Bryant drew his attention. He leaned over in his chair and felt the mission commander's pulse. It was good and strong. She was a little beat up and had some first-degree burns on her face and hands, but it wasn't anything that bandages and burn cream couldn't fix.

Despite everything they had just been through, Leo's thoughts gave way to fancy. Maybe, just maybe, after the commander found out what a spectacular job he did landing this wounded bird and after they got rescued, maybe, just maybe, she'd finally give him the chance he wanted above all else …

But that was as far as Leo's fantasy went, for Chaos still had an ace up his sleeve, and he decided to play it. Leo's heart rose to his throat as he felt the ship tilt. He watched helplessly as the ruined nosecone of the shuttle slowly teetered forward. The view was both breathtaking and horrific.

It was now clear to Leo that the *Explorer II* had not landed on an entirely stable area. The view of open-air nothingness was slowly replaced by a view of a vast ocean far below: the *Explorer II* was balanced on a cliff that had to be at least ten thousand feet high.

That's why we couldn't get a proper reading coming in, Leo thought. *We were reading this plateau and the ocean's surface below it.*

Leo heard the sounds of rock giving way beneath the busted cockpit as the view tipped back to sky. The young lieutenant knew that they didn't have much time. The thrusters and anti-gravity generators were totally stalled. If the ship were to fall now, they'd never survive. From this height, the watery surface might just as well have been concrete.

"Tae, you back there?" Leo whispered into the intercom while holding perfectly still, as if his mere one-hundred-and-eighty-pound frame might keep the enormous transport ship from slipping the rest of the way over the ledge.

"Yeah, but why are you whispering?" Tae's voice came back over the cockpit speakers. Leo could hear the commandos in the payload area speaking amongst themselves near the engineer, congratulating themselves on being alive.

"Tae, listen to me. I need you to get the anti-gravity generators back on line. Do you hear me? I need everything you can give me in as little amount of time as possible."

"Why? What's going on?" Tae asked. The revelry in his voice turned to concern.

"Just do it, Tae," Leo said harshly. The nosecone teetered once more toward the ocean.

"Are we moving? Maybe we should abandon ship."

"Trust me; there's no time." Leo shook his head, biting his lip. With as much calm as he could muster, he said, "Tae, listen to me. If you don't get those A.G. generators back on line, we … are going … to die."

"Okay, okay, just give me about ten seconds."

But they didn't have ten seconds. With Leo shouting, "no, no, no," the shuttle teetered on the edge, and then, gaining momentum, slipped from the rock face and plunged into the gaping void.

—— <> ——

For more on Europa Journal visit:
tinyurl.com/edge6001

For more Science Fiction, Fantasy, and Speculative Fiction titles from EDGE and EDGE-Lite visit us at:

www.edgewebsite.com

——<<<>>>——

Don't forget to sign-up for our Special Offers

——<<<>>>——

JACK♖CASTLE

About the Author:

Jack Castle loves adventure. He has traveled the globe as a professional stuntman for stage, film, and television. While working for Universal Studios, he met Cinderella at Walt Disney World and they were soon married. After moving to Alaska, he worked as a tour guide, police officer, Criminal Justice professor, and certified weapons instructor. He has been stationed on a remote island in the Aleutians as a Response Team Commander and his last job in the Arctic Circle was protecting engineers from ravenous polar bears. He has had several Alaska adventure stories published along with articles in international security periodicals and he has written three novels: Europa Journal, Bedlam Lost, and White Death.

For more real life adventures with Jack Castle
or information on his upcoming books
check out his web page at:

http://www.jackcastlebooks.com/

Made in the USA
Middletown, DE
16 July 2024

57348151R00126